M.F.K. FISHER

A LIFE IN LETTERS

BOOKS BY M. F. K. FISHER

An Alphabet for Gourmets

Among Friends

The Art of Eating

As They Were

The Boss Dog

Consider the Oyster

The Cooking of Provincial France
(*Julia Child and Michael Field, consulting editors*)

A Cordiall Water: A Garland of Odd and Old Receipts
to Assuage the Ills of Man and Beast

Dubious Honors

The Gastronomical Me

Here Let Us Feast: A Book of Banquets

How to Cook a Wolf

Last House: Reflections, Dreams, and Observations 1943–1991

Long Ago in France

Not Now but *Now*

The Physiology of Taste, or Meditations on Transcendental Gastronomy
(*translation and annotation*)

Serve It Forth

Sister Age

Stay Me, Oh Comfort Me: Journals and Stories 1933–1941

The Story of Wine in California

Two Towns in Provence

To Begin Again: Stories and Memoirs 1908–1929

With Bold Knife and Fork

M. F. K. FISHER

A Life in Letters

Correspondence 1929–1991

SELECTED AND COMPILED BY

Norah K. Barr, Marsha Moran, Patrick Moran

Foreword by Anne Lamott

COUNTERPOINT

WASHINGTON, D.C.

Library of Congress Cataloging-in-Publication Data

Fisher, M. F. K. (Mary Frances Kennedy), 1908–1992.
M. F. K. Fisher, a life in letters: correspondence, 1929–1991 / selected and compiled
by Norah K. Barr, Marsha Moran, Patrick Moran.
Includes index.
1. Fisher, M. F. K. (Mary Frances Kennedy), 1908–1992.—Correspondence.
2. Women authors, American—20th century—Correspondence.   3. Food writers—
United States—Correspondence.   4. Gastronomy.   I. Barr, Norah K.
II. Moran, Marsha.   III. Moran, Patrick.   IV. Title.
PS3511.I7428Z48   1997
641′.092—dc21
[B]   97-37116

ISBN 1–887178–46–5 (alk. paper)

Design by David Bullen
Typesetting by Wilsted & Taylor Publishing Services

Printed in the United States of America on acid-free paper that meets
the American National Standards Institute z39–48 Standard.

COUNTERPOINT
P.O. Box 65793
Washington, D.C. 20035-5793

1 3 5 7 9 8 6 4 2

FIRST PRINTING

This book of letters is dedicated to
Lawrence Clark Powell,
an unfailing friend and colleague of M. F. K. Fisher
from 1929 until her death in 1992. He has continued
to offer his warm friendship and invaluable help to
her younger sister.

Contents

Acknowledgments

....

We are indebted to the foresight of Edith Holbrook
Kennedy, Lawrence Clark Powell, Eleanor Kask Friede,
and Arnold Gingrich in saving M. F. K. Fisher's letters,
and to the help of dedicated librarians at the University of
California at Los Angeles and the Schlesinger Library
at Radcliffe College, which house the collected letters.
This book would not have been possible
without their contributions.

Tiny Presents

....

Anne Lamott

I knew Mary Frances Fisher as a friend for the last ten years of her life, but I knew of her as a writer from as early as I can remember. When I was a child, our house was filled with her books; my parents and their friends quoted from them, cooked from them. They found in her work a great and original mind, fastening on the kind of things we don't necessarily think of in the context of originality: food, atmosphere, comfort. They loved the elegance of her writing, that there were no wasted moves, no missing details. They loved the ease at which she put the reader, the way she wrote as if she also spoke that way (which she didn't), the way she drew you in; she was one of the world's wonderful hosts. They loved how tough and funny she could be, that marvelous sense of humor and soul, her bravery with those two little children in France. And they loved how she brought the joys of France to Sonoma without the cultural bitchiness and chilliness. They felt fed by her.

I grew up watching people curled up in armchairs, in pleasure and a certain kind of relief, reading Mary Frances's books. People read out loud from her books to me. And then I came to fall in love with her myself, first in print and then in person. She wrote many books, and there are so many words written about her, that I'm not sure what I can add. But I thought on the occasion of the publication of these letters you might like to see, figuratively, a little of the hand that held the pen, the chairs and ways in which she sat, the mouth that whispered the words when she was too old to scribble anymore.

She was so physical, so catlike! I remember her high cheekbones, and the way she sank into chairs and photos with boneless care. Her nostrils were wonderfully alive. They reminded me of the way a horse tests the air. She seemed so aware of where she was; of where the comfortable, good-smelling places were. And her extraordinary eyes paid wonderful attention to you—caring, amused, maternal. There was also a sense that swirling through her vision were echoes of old memories. She often had a faraway look as if there were more people in the room than the rest of us were seeing: her children when they were younger, her men when they'd been alive.

The house on the Bouverie Ranch in Glen Ellen always smelled at first cool, and then you noticed food cooking out on the stove—soup, probably, or luscious peasant beans with which to feed the people who came to visit. Maybe she ate a little, too, although by the time I met her, she didn't ever seem to eat. We were never allowed to leave without eating something, though, nor could we ever leave empty handed.

The beauty of Sonoma filled her living room, shone in through the big windows that led to the porch. On the porch she had a rattan throne where she sat with a wonderful primness and ease. Her softly lit house, so full of books and beautiful smells, was perfect. I think she had a sense of both exile and settledness at the Bouverie Ranch, a sense of loss and grateful amazement. This became the only house you could imagine her in—quiet, welcoming, and healing—exactly what she needed in the last chapters of her life. She seemed to *wear* her house—it was classic and simple as the perfect dress.

I always loved that she was such an iconoclast—she broke the food world wide open and she had affairs and she crossed her powerful father right and left—and she was also such a lady. I can see her smile a smile of private amusement. I can see that flaming, delirious spirit, hear the laugh that rises up from her toes like candlelight. It was a rare laugh, strong and birdseedy. Sometimes it was so powerful you thought it could erupt into crying, as those mirthful eyes sometimes seemed on the brink of tears. She was so earthy and sensuous. One minute she could look as fancy and posed as a movie star, and the next, as witchy as a gypsy crone taking some mysterious and mischievous pleasure in her surroundings.

Hers was a face anyone would naturally want in the kitchen, a combination of fresh peach and aged potato. You could see the weight and warmth and softness of her cheeks—that tender part a mother would cup in her hands—now grown so old. I love that she loved fats too much, and cheeses; I love that she would not let you eschew either. She was just about the last of the food people who did not get caught up in any modern madness, insisting instead on staying in the luxuriousness of taste and texture and communion.

She looked like the Empress from *The Mikado* in the last few years of her life. Her skull became more prominent, and there was a certain starkness to her face, a guarded attention. In one picture, taken in her living room a year before she died, her mouth and hands are drawn inward, but her eyes are directed very outward, as if once again she is not quite seeing just what is there but also the past and the future. It was the look of someone seeing the end of her life enter the room, pull up a chair, and help itself to whatever marvelous food was simmering on the stove.

She just loved my son, Sam, who came along late in her life. She loved small things in general—she was, after all, a kind of miniaturist. She always sent us away with the smallest presents: books no bigger than playing cards, tiny woven baskets. When she was still fairly well, she had always put her face on—she sprang from a time when women always put their faces on—and sometimes she had put on a great deal of blue fandango eye shadow, which Sam seemed to love. Toward the end she entertained him from the hospital bed in her quiet bedroom, the spot from which she worked until the very last possible moment, whispering her manuscripts into a tape recorder in that tiny, trembly voice. She would always slowly, painstakingly, slide over to make room for him beside her and give him the controls of the hospital bed so he could send them both up and down, up and down.

In Sam's room is a photo of him at two years old, in a navy blue European sailor suit, lying happily beside her in the hospital bed. She can't weigh more than eighty pounds. Egyptian blue eyeshadow fans up over her eyes and she is smiling a big, pleased smile. It's a photo of true joy. I am waiting for him to be old enough to read her books. Some of them are the copies my parents had forty years ago, some are newer ones she inscribed to us. In the meantime, he reads the kids' books she gave him when he was small and fills the little baskets with his treasures.

MF: A Reminiscence

....

Lawrence Clark Powell

She was one of the few who called me Goose to the end of her life—Richman (Ward Ritchie) was another, and Fay, when the matter was serious. MF spelled it Ghuce, from a spurious footnote in my thesis (p. 115) added when the Fishers dared me to include my alias, she giving it the Italian spelling pronounced "Goochey."

We met only once during her year at Occidental [1929], when she had called at the downtown hotel to fetch her sister Anne, Fay's roommate. Everyone but Fay thought I was seeking to seduce her. More than a decade was to pass before Fay and I entered a long marriage that ended only with her death in 1990.

MF and I did not meet again until the fall of 1930 when I was led to Dijon by a letter from her in answer to my query about the university. She and Al accepted me as a fellow boarder at the Pension Rigoulot. To her I was a kind of older brother, whereas to Al I was someone who needed mentoring. That I surely did, and because of what he taught me about organizing my material and adopting regular work habits, I followed him at the University of Dijon a year later with my doctoral dissertation on Robinson Jeffers.

We were a congenial trio, reading aloud our work in progress nightly in the Fisher rooms when all was quiet. Al was writing what became *The Ghost in the Underblows,* and I a novel of my college years called *Jazz Band.* What I had was large desire and small talent. Fisher was right when he said that my work had only the sound of echo. His poem came to an end when in the summer of 1931 MF went home on a visit.

What did she write during those months when everything was new and wonderful? All I know was that she went on knitting and biding her time. I had no perception of what she was to become, one of the best writers of our time.

I was not perceptive of life around me, certainly not that her marriage was beginning to come apart. After Al had finished at Dijon and taken part of a year at Strasbourg, the Fishers went to the fishing village of Cros de Cagnes, where I joined them before they returned to California. Al passed most of his time with the *copains* of the village, not wanting to join me on walks in the hills.

I don't know what MF did. Years later she told me she had advanced their return home by freighter from Marseille when she found herself wanting to join me on those walks. With all of us back in California in 1933, their marriage came apart.

MF welcomed my reunion with Fay, and it was MF's mother, Edith, who greeted us with huge bagsful of groceries. When MF learned that *Westways* was paying for reviews, she submitted her piece called "Coast Village." When she was paid (I recall that *Westways* paid her $25) we celebrated with food and drink.

I admit to having been puzzled by MF's leaving Al for Dillwyn Parrish, one of the homeliest men on earth. I was too dumb to realize that in Timmy she found her life's true love. Fay and I were often together with them during the last year of Tim's life. I was able to arrange for the hanging at UCLA of the final burst of his exalted painting.

Although I did not realize it then, some of us were drawing together in what Jake Zeitlin was to call a "small Renaissance, southern California style." It happened at Jake's tiny bookshop, the calm eye at the heart of the whirlwind. Jake was publisher and Ritchie the printer. When sculptor Gordon Newell perceived MF's latent talent for woodcarving, she took a block of walnut from a Kennedy four-poster and carved me a version of D. H. Lawrence's Phoenix.

The show of Parrish's valedictory work was one of the highest points of those early years during which MF and I were maturing along parallel tracks. Through it all she never stopped believing in me as a creative person, in spite of my labors as librarian, teacher, and administrator. Our relationship was of giving, not taking. No demands were made; everything was freely given. We were spared the destructive emotions that often trouble relationships as close as ours.

MF's letters tell it both linear and interlinear. No citations are needed. We recognized that we had crossed the divide between youth and middle age and we were in the land of downslope, with no hard climbing ahead. We had been half a lifetime reaching that time of recognition.

In the months following our discovery of the whole persons we were, I came as often as I could to the Kennedy Ranch to dine with MF and her father Rex. We met sometimes on Sunday mornings in the Clark Library. I was writing the issues of "Mercurious Redivivus," while she was proofreading her translation of Brillat-Savarin. Alone in that sanctuary, the silence broken only by the creaking and cracking of the oak-paneled walls, we were in a time warp of our own.

After my sabbatical year in England I returned to new burdens, and we were unable to resume the intimacy so briefly shared. Mary Frances moved north, and I seldom saw her. "Come when you can," she said, "whenever you are in San Francisco or Sacramento, steal a few hours for us." Once I broke away from a conference and stayed the night at St. Helena. After dinner we had table talk by daughter Kennedy of her high school life and loves. MF and I listened in silent amusement, all our needs long since met.

After MF moved to Last House I saw her a few more times. Our last meeting was between planes in and out of San Francisco. MF made lunch for the two of us—hearts of romaine, green beans, and rare ground sirloin. I had been reluctant to seek her company in the final years, so thronged was she by her admirers.

It was the first and last time that I saw all of Last House, the two big rooms, one for cooking, eating, and talking, the other for writing and sleep. In the latter were hung three of Timmy's oils—his only portrait of her and those of the twin angels of life and death.

There was one other picture, a plain framed print I had given her after a night in the fall of 1949. It was of a Greek sculpture in marble by an unknown artist, called the Venus of Cyrene. When I came out to say good-bye and thanked her for what I had seen, she smiled and said, "Venus surely did rise from the sea for us!"

1929–1932

....

Dijon, France

Lawrence Clark Powell and M. F. K. Fisher in Dijon in 1931

ONE MONTH after her twenty-first birthday, Mary Frances Kennedy married Alfred Young Fisher and escaped with him to France and the vibrant beginnings of her adult life. The early letters Mary Frances wrote to her family and her friend Lawrence Clark Powell invoke a time and place that have long since disappeared; they reveal a young woman ardently alive and unabashedly enthusiastic about the one place on earth that would become the lodestar of her imagination and writings for the remainder of her life.

Mary Frances's letters from Dijon, where Al studied for a *doctorat ès lettres* and she attended art school, illuminate the passions, the sharp eye, and the sensuousness that underscore the simple yet elegant prose later found in all her published and unpublished works. They were also the raw material for *The Gastronomical Me,* first published in 1943.

Edith Holbrook Kennedy enjoyed her daughter's letters home during this period and managed to save them for her. Several of these letters have been included in this section, along with the first letter Mary Frances wrote to Lawrence Clark Powell, who would later become the librarian at the University of California, Los Angeles, and a noted author. For over sixty years, Powell saved all of Mary Frances's letters to him; the inclusion of many of them here forms a thread that weaves through all the letters, from 1930 to 1991. In Powell's recent reminiscence of M. F. K. Fisher, he hints at the range and depth of their long friendship.

Letters to Lawrence Clark Powell, her family, and later friends, lovers, and fans continued throughout Mary Frances's life. These letters offer a wide view of Mary Frances's deep capacity for affection and empathy, while they also exhibit her clear, occasionally malicious, but always diverting eye for character and eccentricity. Shining through them all are her engaging, sometimes conspiratorial sense of humor and the pure satisfaction she gained from writing and receiving letters.

To: David Kennedy[1]

Dearest Dave—I can't tell you how glad Al and I were to get your letter. It was the second one we've had from home—you see, all our mail goes to Paris first, then comes to Dijon, and we have to go to the post office for it—and the whole process takes quite a long time.

I do wish you could see this town. I never did believe those illustrations in books like Grimm's fairy tales and so on, but I do now. We're all out of films, but we're going to get some postal cards soon, and I'll send them to you and None.[2] All the houses are built right up to the edge of the sidewalks and are from two to five stories tall, and thin—perhaps only 2 rooms wide and a room thick. They are of stone and plaster, and in this town date from 1400 A.D. Al and I spent two days looking for pensions, so we saw the insides of about ten. Of course they belonged to middle-class or rather poor people for the most part. They were very dark, with narrow halls and steep, twisted staircases—solid old furniture—and many peculiar smells. Thousands of smells— some not so bad and some simply foul. We found only one house with a bathtub (the one we're in!) and toilets are absolutely unheard of—they have these silly little john- nies decorated with handpainted roses and landscapes—with washbowls, soapdishes, and pitchers to match. It's a good thing Al and I aren't terribly modest!

Across the street from us is a school for little boys, run by the Catholic priests. They go to school until six o'clock at night, and have long lessons to study at home. Each boy, from Don's size up to yours, carries a leather satchel full of books, and is dressed in shorts under a black smock that buttons down the back, and a beret.

Everyone wears a beanie over here—from the cradle to the grave, almost. You see fat old men with long white whiskers and meerschaum pipes, gawky students, little chil- dren in panties—all in beanies. It's awfully funny sometimes.

The streets are for the most part narrow and very crooked—and terribly hard to locate, because instead of having one name from the beginning to the end, like Greenleaf or Painter, the name changes with every block. The one we're on is la rue du Petit-Potet, but in the next block one way it's la rue Buffon, and the other la rue du Chevalier Saint-Bénique.

It's raining hard today, so we can't go for a ride, as we'd planned. Instead of taxis they use carriages called fiacres here—like this but that's a terrible drawing—darn— you know the kind—like the one the Rat and Marco Loristan rode down the boule- vard in. Well, we were going to rent one for the afternoon ($1.50), and take a ride into the country. This is in the province of Burgundy, where so much of the wine comes from, and right now you can see the peasants picking grapes, and once in a while stamping out the juice with their feet.

The wines are wonderful here. For meals you drink ordinary red wine and water— but if you go to a good restaurant you order a fine wine, and have it served in a little

1. MF's younger brother, age ten in 1929
2. MF's younger sister Norah (also called Noni), age twelve here

wicker cradle—because it has been lying on its side for years and years, and mustn't be disturbed. Drawing the cork is a great ceremony—waiters cluster around the wine-master, and the man who has ordered it listens anxiously to see if the pop sounds right. Then the cork is waved under his nose, and he sniffs it loudly. Finally the wine is poured, still in the cradle, into his glass, and he sips it slowly and with the most amazing noises. The waiters and the wine-master watch his face to see if he likes it, and finally go away. Of course Al and I don't know anything about such persnickety-ness—probably never will. We know five or six kinds now that we like—very common ones.

I must stop now. Please write us another long letter soon, boy—and tell us about school, and everything. I'll answer every letter I get.

Much love to you and Noni—and the family—

···

Dijon, France   *22.X.29*
To: Anne Kennedy

Dearest Sis—The scheme is simply marvelous, and Al and I both hope you can do it.[1] It will be perfect for all of us.

And now I'll spend an hour or so being disagreeable, and telling you all the things I can think of against coming, or things you won't like.

In the first place (this isn't original but I've found it to be true) you simply can't say "Well, I never have to do or eat or see this at home"—everything is so completely different that you can't make any comparisons, or you'll be sunk. For instance, French people eat the most intricate entrails of everything from the horse to the snail; they have perfectly awful table manners, mop up their plates after each course with a piece of bread, change napkins once a week, and have little supports on which you put your knife and fork after a course; the men go casually into any of the fifty thousand open-air johnnies that seem to line the streets, and then spend half a block nonchalantly buttoning up their trousers; dogs, of which there are twenty to a block, all runty, seem to suffer from a permanent summer-complaint; all public water-closets are awful; you don't dare catch the eye of any man, because he'll either follow you or shout if you do—and so on.

Another thing—you might think it rather lonesome over here. There's absolutely no dating, as I told Mam—the only women who are out in public places with men are either well-rounded hausfraus or obvious prostitutes—of which there are plenty, all obviously and frankly what they are. Once in a while you see a scared-looking young girl and boy out with a chaperon—very rarely. Young girls are in convents or at home, and if they do go to universities, they go for the main and simple purpose of studying. There's absolutely no co-ed atmosphere in school.

That's partly because of the clothes, I think. It's the absolute truth that the only women in Dijon who dress as you and I do at home—carefully, swankily, with an eye

1. The "scheme" was for MF's younger sister Anne, age 19 in 1929, to come stay with the Fishers in Dijon in 1930.

for color and so on—are the harlots. People simply don't do it, that's all. Most of the women wear black, and *all* dress very very practically —if I described the costume of a woman in Mother's position, you wouldn't believe me. The men and the babies are the only ones that dress up.

There was a rather nice girl at Aunt B's pension in Paris who had come over for a year as day-pupil in a very swanky school there. She brought the crepe dresses and so on that she'd worn in Washington—and said that she never had been so embarrassed in her life as she was the first day. She was the only girl in silk stockings and silk dress— a dark blue crepe de chine! Mme. de Sena took her in hand and bought cotton and wool stockings and heavy work dresses for her, all dark.

Another thing (you'll probably either forget or laugh at all this, but believe me, it's true), listen to the words of a woman who for six weeks has been hobbling and tripping and stumbling over cobbles (half the time there aren't sidewalks, and the other half there isn't any room on them), and bring *lots* of oxfords—and I mean *oxfords*, with flat soles and little or no heel. Those Mandel and I. Miller street shoes are alright for dress, and then you'll need perhaps a couple of pairs of real pumps—but you simply can't get along in anything but flat shoes. Then in the house you wear cute little black velvet pumps with moderate heels, which cost about $1.50. I'm going to get some soon.

Another thing—you really do need bloomers that have elastic around the knee, of some warm cloth like baby-flannel or challis, *and* woolen stockings, *and* woolen pyjamas. Then you wear gloves all the time, big thick ones—but if I were you, Sis, I'd only bring underwear and shoes and a few things like toothpaste that I tell you next May or so. And a couple of heavy coats with woolen interlining. At Illinois, for instance, you would dress warmly for out-doors, and then wear lighter things in the warm houses, but here you have to wear very warm things in the house, and then double them when you go out. People look like tubs, but nobody cares. Mme. Ollagnier,[2] for example, is a typical middle-class woman I think—and when she gets cold she simply adds another garment, so that by supper time she often has on three dresses, two sweaters, and a couple of woolen mufflers, one on top of another. Where we'd put on another shovelful of coal, they put on another coat—because people simply don't spend money here the way they do at home. They save and scrape and scrimp—it's simply taken for granted. And I can see why they think even poor Americans are millionaires, because we spend what we have more lavishly.

Another thing—it takes simply days to have anything done. For instance, we learned from Mme. O. that we had to have cards of identity, so we went to the police. They said "you must have six passport photographs *immediately*" so we hotfooted it to the photographer's. He said "8 days, no less" (the kind we had done on Main, that day—you know?). In 8 days we got them, and went trampling to the police. They said "Come back tomorrow." We did, and sat for an hour while the man chatted with several friends and had a violent and continuous dispute with a farmer, and filled out our blanks in between. Finally he finished—then said "Take these to the post office, pay

2. The Ollagniers were the Fishers' first landlords in Dijon.

M.F.K. Fisher: A Life in Letters

20 francs each, get a blank and return tomorrow." We did and it took ³/₄ of an hour, while the woman discussed ham in Jerusalem with all her friends, and jotted down little things on our cards once in a while. Well, the next day we took the blanks back to the police. They filled out a few more cards, and gave us each a slip—then said, "In a month or forty days you will receive a card. Bring it to the station and you will get your card of identity." And there you are!

We took 3 shirts and some socks to a laundress, who told us to come back in a week. We did, and she said the clothes weren't dry yet, to come back in three days. We did, and found her sick. Two days later we got the shirts, but the socks weren't dry. Three days and two trips later we got them.

But, darling, you'll love it. It's thrilling, fascinating, marvelous—and it grows better and better. Lamplighters are men who sing little songs to sell the candy they carry in trays on their heads, and hot chestnuts on the streetcorners, and wonderful doorways and cathedral windows, and funny movies and revues and opera for almost nothing, and famous restaurants and perfectly marvelous wines and liqueurs, and hundreds of cafés where you either sit on the pavement and watch the people or go inside and listen to the music—and watch the people—you'll *love* it.

Of course we may not be in Paris—we might be here, or in Strasbourg, or in Lyon—nobody knows—but Paris is the most likely.

And Sis, *do* study French. Get a tutor once a week, or enter a class as listener until Feb. and then start—do *something,* because every word or verb you know will pop up when you need it.

How about that dinner-bet? Have you cut your hair yet? I had a rotten shampoo and a perfect wave today for 48 cents—and 2 tips of 8 cents each.

I've changed my course at Beaux Arts so that I have 3 hours of drawing each morning, two from life, one from casts. Then I'll get into a modelling class later, where I'll learn how the human toe bends or something. It's just what I want to do.

Well, my li'l lambkins—I hope I haven't discouraged you. All I've said is absolutely true, no exaggeratings—especially that part about how wonderful it is. Please write often. (Remember me to Fay and Helen Betts and to Bob,[3] of course).

....

Dijon, France   *9.xii.29*
To: Rex Kennedy

Dearest Rex...

I don't know whether this letter will reach you before Christmas or not, but I hope so, because it is written principally to wish you and all the Family a very merry one... and of course a fine New Year, too, with good crops, lots of advertising, and a hole-in-one for you, and whatever they want for themselves. If that all comes out all right for you, I'll have a good new year too.

3. Fay Shoemaker, Anne's friend, was Larry Powell's girlfriend and, later, his wife; Bob Freeman was an Occidental College student then in love with Anne.

Two weeks from today Al and I will be in Avignon, looking at the Roman theatre. We'll go the next day to a little town named Arles, which is in the heart of the provinces, and that night (Christmas Eve) will take a carriage to a village named Bau or something like that, where the midnight Mass is said to be unforgettable... hundreds of chanting peasants and candles and so on. In France no one goes to bed on Christmas Eve. Everybody waits for the Mass, and afterwards there are great suppers and various other convivial gatherings. It sounds fun, but I should think it would make Christmas Day one big yawn.

Al and I will go down to Marseille, yawns or not, the next day, and from there on out to Cassis without stopping for more than a meal. M. Ollagnier has not only written to the Hotel for us and made out a complete railroad schedule... he's made another list of all the good restaurants and their most famous dishes, so that our progress from here to Cassis and back sounds more like a gastronomic pilgrimage than anything else. That's very French.... These people can tell you about the oyster pie in the tiniest village in France. That isn't all, though. They can discuss the old churches, Roman ruins, latest plays and books, and the Young Plan[1] with equal gusto and knowledge... something that leaves Al and me open-mouthed with wonder and feeling very one-track-ish mentally.

Yesterday we went for a walk in no special direction... just wandered in one part of the suburbs until we found the mud too deep, and then did the same thing in another. We saw lots of queer-looking people... peasants with very baggy corduroy trousers and blue handkerchiefs around their necks, and lots of children who like all French youngsters were either very very pallid and puny or simply bulging with blood and brawn. It's still a wonder to me that any of them pull through the first six years... the poorer ones, I mean. They are sent from their mothers' arms to the gutters of the nearest alley, which is unspeakably filthy, usually.

So many people were wiped out during the war that it is a serious government business now to increase the birthrate... prizes are given to the villages that produce the most babies in one year, and so on. After seeing some of the material from which children are produced, I should think another war would be better for humanity in general.

Of course Dijon is one of the cleanest and most modern cities in France, so according to Lieutenant Mousset and little John Bull Porter we haven't seen anything yet. I'm gradually becoming acclimated, though. I very seldom notice odors that at first made me almost physically sick, and I've learned to pick my steps without realizing it... two very great accomplishments. Of course we pretend that it's the ten thousand dogs who make the sidewalks such precarious footing, but after three months' observation of the personal habits of the Dijonnais that's an old wives' tale that gives us a good chance to leer with skepticism.

But I don't know that the toilet problem is especially interesting to you. There's no reason why it should be. I just happened to talk about it because I saw the butler across

1. A plan for the settlement of reparations after World War I

the street sprinkling lime around his door, which happens to be a favorite rendez-vous of the neighborhood dogs, or something like that. I wonder what our little Anne will do, though, sometimes.

To speak of more genteel things… this afternoon one of my three damsels is coming to talk with me… she in funny English, and I in foul French. Al calls them the Bean, the Tomato and the Spud… and today it's the Bean… a thin freckled girl with rather pretty legs (a most unusual feature in France… they're usually more like those of a piano) and a rather whiny voice. The third… the Spud… I haven't talked to yet, but she seems more what I want… older and very serious looking.

It's very funny how much our perspective about money has changed. When we first came we were simply thrilled at being able to buy a pound of candy for twenty-five cents, or a book for fifty… but now we're worse than the French, I think. Five francs seems outrageous for chocolate creams, and we think for weeks before we spend eighty cents on a dinner.

A while ago Al saw a book he wanted a lot, but it cost forty francs… so he told me he'd like it for Christmas. I went down and looked at it, and almost decided that I couldn't afford it, when I suddenly realized that it cost $1.36 in our money. Of course I bought it… but it still seems a lot to pay… in francs, that is.

As long as I'm talking about money, I'll mention the financial situation. I have $350 in checks, and two francs and a half in my purse. The rent is paid until January, when we'll get perhaps ten dollars back for the meals we miss. I plan to draw out about fifty dollars for the vacation, because I want to buy Al a cane for a present, and I also may see something I'll want to buy, in the South. That'll leave me about $300 to start the year with, and I am positive that after Christmas it won't be as expensive as it was before… because you remember I started out with $650… and at the rate of $100 a month, it's rather costly and rather extravagant. However, I know a lot more now, and don't have to be so expensive. I've had a fine time, though. I seem to have inherited spend-thrift tendencies from someone.

We're really very much excited about the vacation… the plans sound so nice, and everyone is so nice to us, too. Of course it may storm the whole time we're there… but I won't care much. We'll be on the beach, and then it's so much fun to go places together that weather seems to have no effect on me. Cassis is a village of about a thousand… fishermen, mostly… so we're going to wear rough clothes… and that will eliminate a lot of bothersome luggage. Then we'll take down some of the books that I think Mother and Sis have sent for Christmas… the packages look like books, anyway… and Al will study a little, and I'll practice drawing the people and the houses… and that will be the Vacation, probably. It sounds perfect to me… but of course I'm a little bit prejudiced.

It's growing quite dark, so I'll stop this rather pointless letter. We both send very much love, and hope again that you have a wonderful Christmas and New Year. I'll be anxious to hear what you do, and everything.

(As Al would say:)

Yr dvtd srvnt

To: Norah Kennedy

Dearest None-Pone:

From what you and Dave and Mother write to us, your life seems to be a giddy whirl of theatres, new dresses, and an increasing number of inches, all to the tune of your Victrola. Keep it up... you'll be old and hum-drum soon enough, my child.

Thanks a lot for your last letter. Christmas at home sounds as if it was one of the best we've had, and I only wish Al and I could have been there too. As you know by this time, though, we had a perfect time, too... although I must confess that it wasn't exactly Christmas-y.

You ask me to send you some prints, and I'd love to, old dear, but I don't know what kind you mean... the post-cards of imaginary ladies, the old fashion prints, or the picture of the schoolteacher? The last would be impossible, as it's very rare... but I can buy any number of the first... and of course of the second, although they are more expensive, because they're genuine. Please tell me, and I'll stick them in a newspaper and send them to the school. And by the way... if you or Dave ever receive a newspaper from France, ferevvens sake open it carefully and look in every page... because it will mean that Al and I are up to our old trick of cheating the government out of a few cents' duty on some prints or something like that.

Al and I have been having our usual simple and nice time. I honestly couldn't tell you what we do to be so busy all the time. Of course he's at the university all day, and then at night we either read to each other and talk, or else go to a movie. Once a week we go out to dinner, unless we're feeling rather hard up.

Last night we took the nineteen-year-old son of Monsieur Ollagnier to the Three Pheasants for a party. We like him very much. He's tall and well-built and rather young-looking, but like all the French boys I've met, he has a great deal of poise and is much more mature than an American boy of the same age. He knows a great deal about almost anything you care to talk about, but he doesn't try to show off at all... he's simply interested in comparing his ideas—and he has plenty of them—with yours—if you have any at all. Of course the French people have a much better idea of conversation than we have. We think that if we make a few remarks about the weather and the next election, and then devote the evening to talking about golf and the best way to cook ham, we're conversing. On the other hand, the French make it an art. It's as interesting as a good play, to listen to them talk. Of course, after a fine dinner and a good wine, it is more natural, I think, to sit around the table with a cigarette and a glass of coffee and talk about books and plays and politics and fashions in dress and speech than it is to jump up and play bridge. But that may be because I don't like bridge. The fact remains, though, that what we at home would call conversation the French would call an insult to their intelligence... and the result is that boys the age of Ronald[1] and

1. Ronald Kennedy, MF's cousin

Bob are able to talk with interest and some authority about things that are thought to be the conversation of statesmen, diplomats, and professors, at home. They aren't doddering, the French, I mean, though... quite the opposite. After a tea or dinner with French people you feel so excited and wide-awake that it's a matter of hours to quiet down to your usual state of stupidity.

When I think, though, that in a few years I'll have to start going to faculty teas and so on, I could simply howl and scream. Last Sunday Al and I had to go to a tea given for the English and American students here by Monsieur Connes,[2] the head of the English department... and I swear on the Koran that it was the most boring thing I've lived through since I came to France. I got stuck with the Bostonian wife of the American lecturer here at the university and after we'd exhausted the subject of the past, present and future weather in Dijon, Boston, and California we started on her daughter, who is a most remarkable child, it seems. By that time I had a horrible grin frozen on my face and was muttering yes and no automatically... so Al leaped to his feet and said, "Mon dieu... we'll be late for church!" Or some such obvious lie, and dragged me out just as my hands were creeping slowly and relentlessly toward the woman's scrawny throat. And that was the American tea.

French teas are funny, and hard on the ears. So far we've gone away feeling as if we'd been lost for two hours or so in a boiler factory, but people assure us that we'll gradually become used to the noise. Everyone, from the youngest debutante to the oldest dowager, screams at the top of her screamiest voice, and laughs and runs around as if she were nine years old and at a picnic. They play games, too... the kind of cardgame, for instance, in which someone yells a number and then everyone else whoops and pounces on it. It is very funny to see them... extremely dignified old countesses with their Queen Mary hats all on one side, dapper little men with their eyes gleaming wildly above their waxed moustaches, solemn lawyers knocking down the table trying to get at the cards first... and all laughing as if they were mad. When it's over they are themselves again... or perhaps the secret of it is that they are themselves all the time. They kiss your hand with gravity, bow courteously, and say goodbye as if they are taking leave of the king and queen. Tonight Al and I are going to a movie... one of the first things Greta Garbo was ever in, in Sweden, or wherever she came from. And we may go to tea this afternoon... I lost a bet that some man wrote a book, who didn't at all... so I have to take me husband to tea. It's not a hard job.

I hear you're more or less enthralled by the *Smart Set*. Don't take it too seriously, because as we both agreed one time, it's really a lot of awful tripe. What else are you reading, if anything? I've been reading all the books my family sent me for Christmas, and then a couple of books in French... one about witchcraft and voodooism among the negroes of Haiti, and the other a novel about the love affairs of two parrots... believe it or not, very amusing. I must stop. I wish you'd write to me about all these new clothes I hears rumors of... and tell me what you're doing.

Very much love from us both, and an enormous hug with my long arms

2. Georges Connes supervised Al's doctorate and became MF's lifelong friend.

To: Anne Kennedy

Dearest Sis... unless I'm very much mistaken, it's been ten days since I've written to you, and in the meantime I've had a very nice letter from you. Thanks, and please excuse me.

I've been terribly busy, for a change, because as you probably know, I've started to school in earnest (again), and have a course that leaves me about ten minutes a day for letter-writing and such luxuries. I have about thirty hours a week of lessons... three mornings at Beaux Arts, seven hours of French and English with the Spud, Inc., and the rest at the university. That isn't as bad as it sounds, though, because I don't have much "home-work"... only about four hours a week of translating and explanations of various verbs, and so on.

This morning Al and I were so comfortable, listening to the rain and planning the trip to Algeria which I think we'll never take, that we got up too late for me to make the Beaux Arts, much to my disgust. Instead I went around to see a young woman who paints very good things. She has an exhibit on now at one of the local galleries, and was recommended to me by Monsieur Ollagnier, who is secretary of the Art League in Dijon. Mademoiselle Richter was very nice, but she's awfully busy and so am I, so I don't know if we can make connections anywhere. . . .

I found I was on the same street that Miss de Valadares lives on, so I stopped in to see her for a few minutes... and wondered for the thousandth time why I don't do things like that oftener. She was very much touched and pleased, and when I left kissed me on both cheeks. That always gives me a funny feeling... clean old ladies always feel like cold velvet with rice powder sprinkled on it. She's quite batty.

Thanks a lot for the pictures of you and your swain. In the one with him you look about thirty, and in the other two a rather lanky thirteen... a kind of *Alice in Wonderland* illustration for the "hello little feet down there" part. I'll be glad to see Bob again... that is, if I will, this summer. I like him very much. Is he planning to cross paths any time except on the way Home? I imagine so, from what I know of him. I hope so too, though not too often.

Your letter got me down a little, because I'd been tearing around for a week, looking for apartments that had room for you.[1] I found one or two darling ones... high up with no elevators, but with views and wide balconies and so on. However, Al and I couldn't afford one alone, and so we're just going to try to stay on here. The thought of moving all our books and knick-knacks and gew-gaws, not to mention clothes, nauseates me, and there may be a chance that the new proprietor will keep us all year. We don't want to be pensionnaires during the summer, though, because we're planning to take you and Mam to dinner as well as bum dinners from you.

1. Anne's plans had changed; instead of staying in Dijon, she and Edith Kennedy would visit the Fishers in Dijon and then travel with MF to England in the summer of 1930.

If you do decide to stay and I hope you do, for a while at any rate, I think you can get a room here at the Ollagniers'. It's the one Maritza Sakovna[2] had. I guess I didn't tell you that she left Mardi-Gras for Vienna (… amid sighs of relief), and is very nice. Of course it doesn't have running water or anything like that… but then no place does.

In another minute or two I expect the arrival of one of my Girls. It's the tall one that's preparing to enter a convent, and I think that I bore her almost as much as she Bores me. (I don't know why I start so many words with capitals… must be a complex of some kind.)

Al and I are quite elated, because the other day Connes, who prides himself on his English accent (head of English Department), came tiptoeing up to Al in the library and said that he had some "leetle morsels of noowis" for him. The noowis turned out to be good noowis, because for one thing Al doesn't have to write his thesis in French. That would have been a hell of a job, because written French is much harder than spoken French, and Al probably would have had to study much more, and in the end hire a translator. Of course he'll have to defend his in French, before a thesis jury of French Shakespeare scholars (including Stelter's pet Legouis,[3] I think), but that won't be so hard, especially after a year more of theatres and buying candy and bottles of beer. The second piece of good news is that Connes wants Al to take the job of English instructor here next year. Of course Al said yes, because it's only two hours a week on some English novel, it will help him a lot with his French, and it brings in another hundred dollars (that is to say, two months' living expenses, not to be sniffed at). The best thing is that when we get back home, the extra phrase tacked on after the various letters B.A., and so on, won't look at all badly, especially if you don't speak French… "lecteur en Anglais à l'université de Dijon." Al's quite glad that the suggestion came from Connes, too. He didn't ask for the job, and of course didn't ask to write his thesis in English, because until the last director's meeting it was a stiff rule of the college that all theses be written in either French or Latin. It seems too good to be true, and Al's already sniffing around to find the catch in it. Hope there isn't one… but we may be jobless yet.

Have ten more minutes before I have to go to a class in Dictation at the University. It's after lunch now, and my two lessons with the Bean and the Tomato are over for two days, thank God. They weren't so bad today… I got the first started on the lives of the saints, and the last on Modern Literature, and all went well. I read a book yesterday by Pierre Benoit, called *L'Atlantide*, which I think has been translated… if you can find it you ought to read it… a thrilling hair-raiser about the Sahara and lost Atlantis and its queen and various noble and ignoble French officers. A little *Beau Geste*–ish, but darned good reading. I read in French all the time now, but lose more ground than I gain by speaking English with Al, naturally. I can't go stuttering around with him about the latest mended sock and how much I love him and such trivialities.

2. Fellow Ollagnier tenant mentioned in *The Gastronomical Me*
3. Robert Stelter was an English professor at Occidental College; Jean Legouis, Georges Connes's father-in-law, wrote a famous French textbook on English literature.

I'll blow my last air-mail stamp on this, and stick it in the box on my way to school. Not much news, as you can see....... except that I'm having my black and white chiffon, which will be my best for this summer, lengthened, and a little black velvet jacket made for it. The whole thing... work and cloth and everything, only costs eight dollars... not bad. That is, I hope it isn't... it may be a mess.

Love to Fay and Bob... and thanks again for the pictures....

....

Dijon, France   *25.iv.1930*
To: Rex Kennedy
Dear Rex...

Last night Al and I decided that we wouldn't repeat waiting around for his friends from Oxford, who had written rather indefinitely about being here then on their way back from Italy, so we dressed up a little and got ready for an "8-months-1-week" anniversary dinner. We composed a little note, got a pin, and were out in the street looking for a convenient worm-hole in the door in which to stick it, when up behind us slipped a long red car, like a movie-star's, but covered with mud... a Lancia. We didn't pay any attention to it until two young men leaped out and called Al....... and there were his friends, of course: Tom Jeffry and Franklin Gary of his class at Princeton, and a young Englishman called Lorman-Smith. They'd been driving all day in a rain storm, so Al got into the car with them to take them to a hotel, and I went up to the room to wait for them, rather disappointed that our party had exploded and wondering if we'd have enough money to take the three of them to Racouchot's.

They all came back in a few minutes, and Al came running up the stairs for me ahead of them, to whisper with a broad grin that they insisted on taking *us* to dinner, so we'd be able to go out twice this week. Then I went down and crawled into the car, which is one that seems built about three inches off the ground when you get in and out, and not even touching it when you're riding. It was my first... and maybe last... experience with such an exotic name. We went to Racouchot, because Spackman,[1] whom we took there at Christmas time, has been talking about it ever since... especially about a wine we had that night called Chambertin. It's thought by some to be the best wine in the world, and by almost all to be the best in Burgundy, and is accordingly expensive. Al and I blew his Prohibition parents' Christmas present for that bottle. We got back our bread-on-the-waters in double measure last night, though, because when Tom Jeffry saw the Fifth-quart in the bottom of each enormous crystal glass (the biggest glasses I ever saw in my life) he said, "Wouldn't it be nice to see these glasses just a little bit fuller?"... and ordered another bottle!

It was one of the most amusing evenings I ever spent in my life, I think. For one thing, I was surrounded by four very attentive, quite good-looking, and very intelligent young men... three of them in English tweed suits, which always puts me in a good frame of mind. Secondly, I was eating a delicious dinner and drinking good

1. Al met William Spackman at Princeton, and they became lifelong friends.

wine… and thirdly, which is pretty closely connected with the other two, I was in the right mood to be amused.

Franklin Gary is the most amazing brunette reproduction of Bob Freeman that I ever thought of, with the same mouth and round little chin, and the same way of laughing quickly and impetuously at things… especially at his own remarks. I think he's a little more intelligent than Bob… or perhaps only more mature.

He was head of the theatre at Princeton, taught school for a year, finishes Oxford this summer, and will be an instructor at Princeton next year. He has a lot of money……. and I wish like hell that Sis would fall in love with what there is of Bob in him plus Franklin Gary. I found him the most attractive man I've met, outside of Al and you and one or two impossibles like Tom Bailey.[2]

The Englishman didn't talk very much, but sat on his side of the table looking very Tweedish-and-Dunhill-pipe-ish. He seemed very nice, and darned good-looking.

Tom Jeffry, who has the car (as well as three Packards scattered here and there over Europe in case he gets tired of trains at odd moments), is a sickly little fellow with lots of blond hair, tiny hands and feet, and an immense knowledge of Italian art, bullfights, and automobile races. He talks a lot and is very interesting, because he combines a good vocabulary and a sharp tongue with intelligence.

We sat in the Three Pheasants until ten-thirty, drinking coffee and liqueurs and talking, and then drove up to the Miroir and more coffee and liqueurs until after midnight, when they brought us home, and left for the hotel and an early start for Paris this morning. A pleasant evening.

It seemed queer when I realized that last night was the second time I'd been in a car in almost eight months. I hope I won't forget how to drive.

The Ollagniers have finally moved, and all that's left now is a litter of straw and old boxes in the courtyard, and a rather empty feeling in the house. We'll go over there for lunch this noon… not far away.

I'll stop and send this off on our way over… and hope that I'll get a letter from you soon.…

Much love to you and Mother…

Please tell Mother that I can meet her in Southampton any day at 6:15 P.M., and please to tell me right away what day. My ticket (train to Paris, plane to London, train to Southampton-West) will cost about $33.

....

Dijon, France   *11.v.30*
To: Lawrence Clark Powell

Dear Larry… Al and I were very much interested in your letter and are more than glad to tell you anything we can about the why-and-how of our present headquarters.

2. Older relative

It'll be easiest to do, I think, by answering your questions and telling you anything else that might be useful to you.

We came to Dijon in this way. Al was advised by the head of a French publishing house to come to Dijon for at least two months of summer classes in French, before going to Strasbourg, where he'd heard the Shakespeare work was very good. We came here in October, then, planning to leave for Strasbourg the first of November. Everyone to whom we talked told us we were foolish to go on to the other university, because the accent in Alsace is so ghastly. There is a great deal of tension between the German and French elements, and it is necessary to know both languages without ever having a good accent in either. Another thing against Strasbourg is its hellish climate... cold and wet, which neither of us likes. Third, and most important reason... although there are one or two famous men at Strasbourg, the university of Dijon is rated now among the first of the provincial universities, and is coming up fast. The English department, under which Al has to work, is headed by a man who is something of an authority on Shakespeare (and son-in-law of Stelter's near-god, Legouis). And to finish it up... Al and I were more and more enthusiastic about the whole town, and hated to leave... and after eight months, we're completely sunk about it. The people are charming, the climate is not bad (quite a little rain after home, but not much snow), the food and wines are the best in France, the town itself is one of the most interesting and beautiful from an historical and architectural point of view, the theatres are pretty good, the libraries (university and municipal) are fairly good.... In other words, we like it here and are more than glad that we didn't go to Strasbourg.

When you say, "Is all of your work, reading, in French?" I think you mean Al, who is working for the same thing you would be, probably. No, his isn't. His thesis is to be a study of the comedies of Shakespeare, as comedies, tracing the basic principles of the genre, and so on, and consequently he is working with the plays themselves. He reads other theses and books on the subject occasionally, which are for the most part in French, and seems to do it very well. When he came to France he knew absolutely *nothing* about the language... had never studied it in school, couldn't say Bonjour correctly, knew no rules of grammar. He went one month to summer school here, and then started right in on his thesis, so he really hasn't studied it much at all... but even without that, he can carry on long conversations with anyone who is willing to help him fish for words once in a while, and able to listen to a rather bad accent (which is still much better than two-thirds of the foreign ones you hear at the university). The reason for this prodigious prowess is quite simple: you simply can't stay in a place for eight, or even four or three months, without absorbing some of the language. Al's made almost no effort to learn French... but when all the signs are in it, and all the waiters and conductors and plain humans speak it all the time, it's impossible to keep away from it. You think you know nothing... someone tries to give you five francs' change instead of ten... and you hear a string of fairly good French emerging from your rather astonished lips. It's quite easy.

I was a little better off than Al, because I'd had one year of French... less than Fay.

M.F.K. Fisher: A Life in Letters

I've been going to classes for several months (the foreigners have a very good department at the university... about 150 Germans, Roumanians, Arabs, Chinese, English, Swedish and so on), and of course am stronger than Al in grammar and perhaps pronunciation. His is just as effective, though. You'd be very well off, I think, and find that reading a critical treatise is remarkably easy within a very short time.

To enter the university, you come to Dijon, go to the office of the Faculty of Letters (I take it for granted you're not going in for law or biology), and inscribe for a lower degree or matriculate for a post-graduate degree. Al's matriculated, and I'm inscribed. The first costs about fifteen dollars a year, the second a little more. Examinations cost four dollars, not each, but for all that you take. If you're planning to study for a doctorate, you must present your diploma, go at least two semesters to the university (two years is about the least time possible but it has been done in less), present the subject of your thesis and have it accepted, do personal work under the direction of a professor on a thesis which must be at least a hundred printed pages in length, present the university with eighty copies of it after it has been accepted (costs about two hundred dollars to have it printed), and pass two so-called examinations in which you must defend your thesis against the attacks of a group of scholars. You emerge bloody but decorated with a hood and the title of Doctorat ès Lettres de l'Université de Dijon, which is, in France, a Ph.D. At home it isn't, but it's a good degree, and would probably help with a Ph.D.

If you came over here for only one year you could get a certificate of French or English, which would of course be a big help in getting a position as Professor of the language at home but has no degree.

If possible, it is a good idea to follow the summer courses, which go from June 15 to the first of November. They cost $9 for one month, $18 for the whole term, and give you about six hours a day of pronunciation, grammar, literature, history, and so on. They're very good.

The only thing we know about English universities is that they cost more than American ones. You can't go to Oxford for instance for less than $2500 a year. The provincial universities like Birmingham are less, but still pretty expensive. The cost of living is sky-high.

I don't know anything about Marburg, or any other German universities, except that it costs more to live in that country than here.

Your next question is about the advanced degrees at Dijon... and all French universities. Well... first comes the doctorate ès lettres de l'Université, which I've explained a little. After that comes the same doctorat, but de l'État, for which you have to pay the former. After that comes the agrégé, which is a contest between the doctors of the state, from which one is chosen. The first is of course the only one to try for, and unless you have a draft of your thesis, many research notes, and a special permit from the University, is impossible to get in less than two years. Of course you have to defend your thesis in good French... no mean job in itself. As I said, it is a French Ph.D., but not an American one.

The next question... Can two live cheaper than one?... rather amuses me. Are you trying to make me believe that you're naïf, Larry? No, two can't, and never could....... but here in France two can live for about what one would take at home. It's plain, then, that one can live here for much less than he could in America. The scale is about one-fourth to one-half as dear here. In comparison with Paris, Dijon is cheap; of course it costs more here than in a smaller town. I'll give you some figures, as they're easiest, using the present exchange of 25 francs to a dollar:

Average pension, room, linen, three meals a day... from $26 to $32 dollars a month. (Al and I pay $30 each for two adjoining rooms, and a cabinet with running water, gas and electricity and central heating, with good food and a pleasant family. We're within a block of the University.)

Books cost from 25 cents to a dollar.

Theatre tickets range from 18 cents to 60 cents, movie or legit. The best dinner in town at a very famous restaurant costs $1.20, with wines from 20 cents to $2.50 a litre, and champagne starting at 40 cents. A very good dinner of five courses costs 60 cents. At the Students' Union dinner is 20 cents, and usually pretty bad. Beer costs 3 cents a small glass, 5 cents a large, and aperitifs average 10 cents.

The 10% tipping system is standard, thank God.

Dijon is the center of the richest and most interesting province of France... Burgundy... and in an hour or less you can go to famous vineyards, Roman amphitheaters, Spanish cities... anything you like. Trains cost little, bicycles less... and believe it or not, people bike from the cradle to the grave here. Al and I went on a four-day bicycle trip to Vézelay and Autun this vacation, and had the wildest time I've ever spent... slept in old inns, ate with the peasants... so on. There's not much social life, as far as dances and that sort of thing go... one bal des étudiants, one grand bal given by the mayor... a few tea-dances. It's really a rather simple existence... but I continue to enjoy it more than anything I've ever done in my life.

Courses at the Dijon branch of the national Beaux Arts cost nothing, and you learn quite a lot.

If you want to go out at night, but not to the theatre, you go to one of the two big cafés which have pretty good orchestras, and listen to the music, play cards or chess, talk, and drink. They're rather like German beer-gardens... social centers for the whole town, at which you see the lowest beggars, the town council, and all the in-betweens.

Next... Is raw milk obtainable? I suppose so, but nobody drinks it. Instead you drink hot chocolate or café au lait... the latter really hot milk with about a teaspoonful of coffee in it. It seems awful at first... and now I drink it at least once a day, besides a huge bowl of cocoa in the morning. You'd get enough milk, I think. You get a lot of salad (herbs and lettuce) and vegetables, and fruit all the year around. You always have fruit at the end of a meal... and there are lots of fruit stores if you want more.

The food in general is awfully good. Of course you might get into a bad pension, but it's easy to change to a good one. At times food approaches the divine... at the

Three Pheasants, for example, which modestly calls itself, without any correction, "The Temple of Burgundian Gourmets."

You say... Is a background of classical languages required? Al says he doesn't think so. When he went to register, the office simply took his diploma from Princeton and said it would have to look up and see if that university was on its list. It was, his diploma was given back, and that was all. However, that may be a snag for you, because Occidental may not be on the list, as it's rather small. Al will find out and send word to you. If it is, and you have your A.B., you're all right, I think.

That concludes your questions, and I hope very much that I've answered them so they'll be of some use to you. Please ask us anything more you think of... I know we'd have given our souls, if we'd had any, for a few prosaic but necessary remarks about things in general. As it is, we've had marvelous luck, and are very very happy. We've made enough friends to keep us pleasantly bored, and are leading exactly the kind of life we've always wanted to. I don't know you very well, but I think it's more or less the kind you'd like, too.

Naturally, your discreetly worded question about the price of living for two interested me. I'll be just as cautious, and say nothing except that I hope you get married if you want to, and hope you'll be as happy as Al and I are, afterwards. Then I'll throw caution to any wind that wants it, and say that Fay is one of the two girls at Occidental that holds my interest for more than five minutes. Don't know whether there's any connection or not. Anyway, I like Fay.

Another thing, you didn't say anything about it, and probably know more than I do, but Al and I found travelling the most expensive thing about coming to Europe. Of course the trains at home are horribly dear... but we crossed in what is called student third, which is a combination of glorified steerage and degenerated second. It really was surprisingly good, and we were very comfortable. We came on the *Berengaria,* but I think smaller boats are just as good and cost a little less. The whole trick is to get an outside cabin.

Anne writes that Fay is coming over this summer. Hope we see her. And we're looking forward to seeing you, and your wife if you have one.

Please let us know if you think of any more questions, and give our best regards to Fay....

Sincerely, from Al and me...

We're living a life of comparative prodigality for $50 a month each—$30 board and room, $20 amusement, laundry, drinks, occasional trips—

....

London, England   *20.vii.30*
To: Norah Kennedy

This is a letter, None dear, that I should have written to you at least six weeks ago— just as I should have done with Father and Dave. I hope you'll excuse my tardiness, and keep on sending mail to me. You can guess how important letters are to me, when I'm living so far away from you and the family.

This afternoon Mother had an appointment and Sis something else to do, so I went along to the National Galleries—and as so often happens, enjoyed immensely being all by myself. I think that pictures more than anything else should be seen with only two eyes. If there are friends (or amicable enemies), you are jarred and jostled and thoroughly unnerved by a hundred well-meaning noises: O, look at that beautiful blue—my dear, what clearness of color—O, don't you *love* seascapes?—and so on. Of course, each person has a little list of picture-companions, just as each one has an ever-changing but large list of people who ought to be strangled or slowly tortured. My list of humans who, singly or in pairs, would add to my enjoyment of almost any picture, includes several very different people. Al, a girl I used to know, a boy I met once at a dance and never saw again—a few others—and you. Surprised?

Today I thought rather a lot about you, None. I hope I can go back some day with you. I'll take you to some pictures I like very much—and then we can find some more, together. If you want to, that is.

Tonight we aren't at a theatre, for a change, but in our pyjamas around a fire in Mother's room. Today was quite chilly—first sign of Autumn, people say—which must sound awfully silly to you, if the reports of hot weather at home are at all true. . . .

I saw a copy of the poem you had in the last school paper. Don't know that you want criticism of it, favorable or unfavorable—but I suppose you might as well get used to it: that's about all you'll get, if you're going to write poetry. (So Al says, at least—and he's been doing it since he was seven.)

Of course, what I shall, or would, or shall not say about anything you write won't be the criticism of an older sister (for a change, some one snarls in the distance), but rather the candid ideas of a young person who once tried to write poems, and now only reads them. I can tell you this, None, because I think you know what I mean—when I was about your age, I saw beautiful things, I tried to make them into words, as you're beginning to do. And when I showed them to people, they were either smiled at kindly, or ignored—and I was either flattered by my teachers and relatives, or tolerantly endured. Finally I stopped showing anything to anyone. I hated the talk—rather enjoyed the flattery. And then I stopped doing anything, almost. And the trouble was, and still is, that *no* one helped me. Nobody told me *one damned thing* about poetry, about lines and meters and feet and rhythms and word sounds. Sometimes I think of that and scream inside with bitter disappointment with myself and with the world. If some person had only taken my little lines, those gasping, thirsty lines that seem so rotten now and *still* had something decent in them—if someone had truly shown me what a little thought and a little knowledge could have done to them, I might be making better ones now. What I needed more than anything else was some idea of structure, some bony skeleton to shape my words around like skin and muscle. *Now* I know what I didn't then—that there are a thousand beautiful forms, called sonnets and lyrics and triolets and epics and blank verses and couplets and stanzas and quatrains and on and on—and that I could have used them. Of course it takes a vocabulary, and deep and delicate feeling for words—and a lot of good hard sweaty work. And it's a queer fact that most of the people who have written good free verse (the sort of thing you tried) are men and women who have worked for years and years with all the other forms—worked until they know every twist to the language, every covered meaning of the words in the language. What Robert Louis Stevenson did (and how many hundred more?) to make a beautiful style of his own was to write imitations of other poets and authors. Little by little Stevenson and his wonderful way of putting words together crept out of all his laborious copies of Balzac and Goldsmith and Shakespeare and the Bible.

Try it, Noni—write no matter how horrible a copy of "Hiawatha" or of "The Ancient Mariner" or of "Humpty Dumpty"—and if you want to, send it to me. I trust you, because tonight I've told you the sad truth about myself that to some would sound silly, to others just conceited, to you, I hope, nothing but the sad truth—and you can trust me with your poems, if you want to.

If you would be interested (and, needless to say, very secret), I'd like to send you some things I've written this year. I'd like your criticism of them—your honest thoughts, not the polite reply of a dutiful schoolgirl. Tell me you dislike the rhyming-scheme, you don't think the words "clouds swim" make a good combination of sounds, you find my ideas very vague and incoherent—rip the things to pieces, Noni, and you'll be helping both of us, you and me.

All this may bore you. Perhaps you think me slightly mad, and perhaps I am. However, the rest is up to you. If you want to continue this faint beginning of what may be a rather interesting friendship between two girls who see mice in the sky and grey lace 'round the moon, please answer my letter sometime. Or chuck it away, out of your mind and into the fire. Don't talk about it to anyone else, that's all—because I've showed you part of a private me.

Give my love to Nancy Jane and Bobby[1] and the others—and more to Father and Dave, of course. I hope you're having a marvelous time, wherever you are: Albion, Duck Lake, the Grand Canyon. Please tell me about it.

Mam and Anne send their love and say they'll see you soon (before this letter, maybe)—

....

Dijon, France   *28.x.31*
To: Edith Holbrook Kennedy

Dearest Mam—I told you I wouldn't write until after the orgy on Sunday—and for a few minutes Sunday night I thought I'd never write again—nightmare from too much champagne. You see, we had three quarts of it (good Piper Heidsick) and vin ordinaire, and a bottle of Chambertin with the chicken. Then afterwards Papazi[1] brought out a bottle of cognac given him by an old friend—as it was dated 1789 we

1. Kennedy cousins
1. The father of the Fishers' new landlords (the Rigoulots); most others mentioned in this letter are part of the Rigoulot family.

could understand why he hadn't served any of it for 24 years! Sunday was the 21st birthday of André, as well as the 24th wedding anniversary and two other peoples' birthdays—quite a day. It wasn't as bad as I thought it would be—but, as I say, I had a nightmare.

Sunday morning Jo came over to say that Madame Bitsch's[2] funeral would be at two that afternoon—first we'd heard of it. We got tips on French funeral behavior from our favorite waiters and fruit-sellers, and then set out. It wasn't bad, though. First we ordered a big flat bouquet of chrysanthemums. Then we went to the house and shook hands with M. Ollagnier, who was very dramatically black and reserved. To our joy Madame didn't appear. We went into the studio (I don't think you saw it), and there was a tiny little coffin, black and shiny, with scarlet flowers laid on it and twelve enormous white candles burning round it. The curtains were pulled, and white veils were over all the pictures and mirrors. At the foot of the coffin was a bowl of holy water to sprinkle, but Al and I didn't do it, and a silver gong to strike—which we didn't.

Well, that was quickly over. I felt rather awed by the candles and the flowers, rather sad—but mostly I was glad the nice old lady was dead. She suffered a lot. Anyway, she'd lived 82 years—she must have been glad to get out of it all.

Al and I fortified ourselves at the Café de Paris, and then went back to the formal hand shaking: first a dark room lined with the male relatives, all very stiff and temporarily lugubrious; then the darkened studio, with Madame looking strangely shrunken in her weeds. People filed slowly through, shaking hands silently, sprinkling holy water on the little black coffin piled with brilliant flowers, sounding the muted gong, and speaking softly to Madame. She, poor woman, was touched that Al and I had come, and burst into tears on my shoulder. It was quite sad. Outside people waited for the procession to start, and the bell of Saint-Pierre tolled heavily. Well, she's buried now. I hope that the next one will be Miss Lyse. This is her last winter of good health, I'm afraid. I hate to think of her in her little attic. As Al says, she's an out-and-out sponger, brazen as hell—but how else can she live? Today I puffed up the stairs to ask her to tea this Friday, and found her jittering because she had to wait for some wood, or something, and couldn't get anything to eat. First thing I knew, I was shopping for her—buying 8 francs' worth of stuff with four francs she gave me. Of course I told her I'd only spent 3.50f, and gave her back the change!

Tonight Larry and a little Swedish girl and Al and I are staying here in our rooms and talking—accompanied by two bottles of Mousseux (Larry) and some cakes (us). Luckily the girl speaks very good English—more Scandinavians do, it seems to me.

Yesterday I pulled myself together and made a lot of sachets with the powder from London and some old silk stockings. They look rather like biscuits in baby-ribbon, and smell very nice, although they were pretty strong at first. Al thought a mouse had died, when he came into the room last night.

Am I crazy, or have you stopped writing very much? It seems to me I don't get many letters any more—but it's probably my fault.

2. Mme. Ollagnier's mother

You make me ashamed when you say our cable on your anniversary was thoughtful—it was only natural, and I'm furious that I couldn't send anything. I was all ready to send off a brass bucket (another one!) when I learned that that might cause trouble with duty. Then I found something else—but as they were more elaborate than necessary, I decided to send them for Christmas, as a combination present from Al and me. I think Sis may give part of them—she'll tell you. Anyway, if a package comes—if *any* packages come from us—don't open. Wait till Christmas. . . .

What is Dave's new blue trench coat?—wine dyed?

The weather here is foul—dark and dripping. Nevertheless, the fair starts Saturday.

Please give my love to Mrs. Thayer and Aunt Petie.[3] What do you hear from Uncle Evans and Uncle Park[4]—and what about the Gilmans?

I'm going to knit a white blouse—with very large needles, of course. I can remember how to "cast on" but not how to finish. I'll call in Mamazi, if the worst [*sic*] comes to the worst.

Love to all the family—

....

Cros de Cagnes, France[1]　　　　　　　　　　　　　　　　　　　　　*3.iii.32*
To: Edith Holbrook Kennedy

Dearest Mam... I have just finished writing to the Libera office in Marseille. I can do everything indirectly here in Nice. But thought it would be a good idea to do the other. We read that all transatlantic lines were cutting prices—and I have asked if the Libera people are too. If they aren't, it may pay us to go up to Le Havre after all. And I asked about the family reduction too. I think we may be able to save 10% because there are three of us. We might call Noni our child!

I'll try to remember to get your mittens, and maybe some for myself too.

Today Larry and Al and I were planning to go on a picnic, because yesterday was beautiful!... but it rained. Noni has the curse, so she hasn't been down. I have been starting to do things all day. Sundays still have a boarding-school shadow over them for me. I hope I'll outgrow it soon... I waste a lot of time.

Friday Noni and I went to Nice and suddenly found ourselves on a boat. We had a lot of fun... went to a concert and bought some music... Bach's chorale for Mrs. Fisher and she a book of Nice folksongs... and had beer... and so on. The concert was very good... a pianist gone satirist who makes hideous fun of all the things held sacred by bourgeois music-lovers... opera, Debussy... and so on some more. We laughed... and I was glad to see that Noni understood his rather fast French down to the minutest pun. She doesn't talk much. Lets anyone else work if there's the slightest chance of avoiding it herself. She's one of the most docile people... up to a certain point... that I have ever

3. Whittier neighbors
4. Edith Holbrook Kennedy's older brothers
1. The Fishers and Norah left icy Strasbourg in March to spend the following months with Lawrence Clark Powell at Cros de Cagnes.

seen in my life. If you treat her a certain way she never seems to be disturbed or annoyed or even terribly pleased. Just placidly existent. I suppose she'll be different as soon as she catches up to herself.

The sweater for Al is coming along bulgily. I have almost finished the front of it, with only one real mistake. It will be very nice, if I live a long time. . . .

Two months of pension food have made me anxious to be where I can eat all the lettuce I want. I'll be glad to get back to California again. Other reasons too.

Larry came Friday, and lives across the hall from us. He had a letter from his mother in London, saying that his brother is much better, so he feels quite cheerful. He is sad that Al and I won't be here for his soutenance, and we are too. Nothing to do about it, of course. He will stay here until June, and then go up to Dijon until after it is over. Then he and his mother plan to come down here someplace. It's cheaper than at home. I sometimes think we are foolish to spend almost half of our money on the trip home, when we could live over here for a year on it. But of course we will be nearer any possible jobs. And near you all. Our main idea in going home this year was to start a family, if possible. But I don't know whether we ought to have a child unless we can at least pay the doctor bill. What do you think?

Will you please draw me a picture of Rex's foot, without shoe, and I'll get him some espadrilles. Al is completely sold on them, and threatens never to wear anything else. They're cheap enough... 40 cents here, for strong handmade ones. I'll get Dave some too, if he'll send me his foot. But don't wait too long.

I must stop and go up to see Noni. Today the clocks changed to summer time. I like it. I wish we had that in California, it's so nice to have the day last an hour longer.

We don't know yet when we'll leave. It depends on several things... but I'll tell you within a week or so. Anyway, we'll get Noni home before August first. We wonder if you would let Dave meet us in Panama and come up home with us. He could probably make good connections, so he wouldn't be alone down there more than a day or so... and I imagine you could put him under the wing of a friend of a friend or something. He could go down second or third class, and get 10% off his return ticket. It may be a silly scheme... but I think it would be a lot of fun. Give him that instead of a fountain pen, for graduation!

Will write soon again. . . .

....

Cros de Cagnes, France   *19.iv.32.*
To: Edith Holbrook Kennedy

Darling Mam... after I wrote to you on Sunday Al and I decided to tear up the cable we had composed and send you another one instead! By this time you have received it. And by the time you get this, we'll know what you did about it. So there's not much use talking. I know that you must have been thrown in a high Twitch by it. But there was not much else we could do. We talked over our state of mind and money, and decided that if you and Rex could get that thousand to us by this weekend we really ought to catch the *Collins* home, sailing from Marseille May 1. We hate to leave. Everything is so peaceful here. But we might not have much fun if our last five weeks were one long economy. I hate to feel that I'm spending money I shouldn't.

Of course we'll have just that much longer to spend money on at home. But I think that we can manage something. Al will go up to see his family for a week or so. Then he'll try to get some kind of job... anything will do, for a little money. I thought that if you were expecting a lot of relatives we could do as you suggested and take Dave and Noni and any cousins down to Laguna. By doing that Al and I can take care of them and get our food free, or some such thing. I am going to see if I can tutor some dumb student in French... maybe find one through the Pomona laboratories. It's all rather feeble sounding. But I don't know what to do about it, except go home and see what happens. Anyway, we'll all be together for a while at least... and don't worry that we'll be on your hands either. We can help you this summer, and support ourselves a little at the same time. Al has had Depression-answers to all his letters. I don't care. I'd hate to have to go to Texas or Washington for some measly sub-instructor's salary that would be spent on railroads and freight before we even got there. Well, if you get the thousand to us on time, we'll arrive in San Pedro about June 6. If not, we'll manage to keep fit and sun burned and get home about July 8. What's Sis coming home early for... no money, baby? I'm still holding my own on the second point, at least. . . . I was surprised to see contraceptives advertised in the magazines you sent. How shocking. . . .

Ned's wedding sounds very nice... just the way it would be, with pastel colors and so on. But why in God's name doesn't somebody tell Brownson to stop saying Chapeaux. I hate Ned Lewis, anyway. He's so earnest and dull. Where was John, that day? He and Hopey are the only ones who seem to have much more than a cretin's spark of life.[1]

Yesterday morning Al and I went to Nice to send the cable and get the fifty dollars cashed, and in the afternoon Noni and I took a bus to Cannes. We had a good time... wandered around the port looking at the beautiful yachts, and then sat under the new-leaved trees on the quai and listened to a gypsy orchestra and drank café-crème. We both grew very mournful for a while, and then decided that you and Rex should retire soon and come over here for a year or so. You'd be happy, I think. Everybody speaks English in Cannes, and there are good golf-courses and so on. And it isn't true that it is terribly expensive. Of course the big hotels are. But Life... food, rents, and so on... is just like any other place.

Here in the Cros, for instance, you can get a darling three-room furnished villa right on the edge of the sea, and about a stone's throw from the very good golf-course, for about a hundred dollars a year. At Nice there are thousands of much bigger places for rent at any price, and the same at Antibes and Cannes, in fact it's a very cheap place to live in... but of course there's the passage over. Well... maybe some day we'll all be squatting on the edge of the Mediterranean. Hope so. I love California the best, or just

1. Ned, Hope, and John Lewis were the children of the minister Edwin Lewis in Whittier. Mrs. Brownson was the society editor for the Whittier *News*.

as well at least… but I hate with a hideous hatred all these Sunday crowds, bill boards, hot-dog stands, bathing-suit restrictions, cheap stucco apartment houses, and other tumors that have made even Laguna pleasant mostly for what it used to be. We are all very well. Noni is very good looking in an amazonic way. Al's tan is becoming. I think I'm getting rather queer-looking. I see people peering at me with amazement, timidly. I should take it for granted that it's because I'm so beautiful. But there's a mirror in our room and once in a while Al takes a picture of me that shocks even my own ideas of myself. I think I may turn out to be one of these stringy women you read about. I have a heart of gold, though, of course. Eda's[2] working for the London *Times*… in Berlin. I'm so anxious to see you all again. I see thousands of things I want to bring you… but will probably land with nothing but a mitten for your bath.

2. Eda Lord, whom MF met in boarding school, became a writer and lifelong friend.

1935–1949

....

Le Pâquis, Switzerland, and Bareacres, California

Le Pâquis

Elsa's cottage at Bareacres
(MF's nephew Sean Kelly in foreground)

THE THREE happy student years the Fishers spent in France were followed by three years of coping with the Great Depression, living for the most part at the Kennedy's summer house in Laguna Beach. Here Mary Frances and Al met Dillwyn and Gigi Parrish. The journals published in *Stay Me, Oh Comfort Me* recount Mary Frances's gradual and painful realization that her marriage was over, as well as the discovery that she could indeed become a writer.

Al Fisher was offered an instructorship at Occidental College in 1935, a time Mary Frances spent at the Los Angeles Public Library doing research for *Serve It Forth*. Gigi Parrish ended her marriage to Dillwyn, and he asked Mary Frances to accompany him and his mother to Europe. The following year the Fishers and Dillwyn Parrish moved to Vevey, Switzerland, to study and write. But Al soon left, accepting a professorship at Smith College, where he taught until his retirement in the 1960s.

Serve It Forth was published in 1937, the one happy, productive year that Mary Frances and Dillwyn had together at Le Pâquis, the home they built above Lac Léman, near Vevey. During a trip to Bern with Norah and David Kennedy and his sister, Anne Parrish, Dillwyn was stricken with an embolism. The amputation of his leg was the beginning of years of pain and fruitless search for medical relief, which ended with his suicide in 1941. The struggle with Dillwyn's unremitting pain may have given him the power he expressed in his paintings; it gave Mary Frances the strength to write her finest books.

After months of medical treatment on the East coast, the Parrishes found in Southern California a property they called Bareacres. This ranch nurtured Dillwyn's painting and Mary Frances's writing, and was her home base even after his death. *Consider the Oyster* was written there to amuse Dillwyn, but was published too late for him to see.

Mary Frances worked briefly as a screenwriter in 1942. She was able to complete *The Gastronomical Me* during those months, as well as *How to Cook a Wolf*. Her daughter Anna was born in August 1943; although Mary Frances ardently welcomed the birth, she decided to pretend it was an adoption.

Eighteen months after Anna's birth, Mary Frances met Donald Friede in New York and married him three weeks later. Donald was a sophisticated and knowledgeable publisher who had begun his career as partner of Pascal Covici in the 1920s. He was eager to write and to direct Mary Frances's future. Both decided to work at Bareacres, where Donald wrote his memoir, *The Mechanical Angel*. During this period Mary Frances wrote not only her translation of Brillat-Savarin's *The Physiology of Taste,* but also *An Alphabet for Gourmets* and a novel, *Not Now but* Now, in addition to the monthly magazine articles that provided the family's principal source of income. Kennedy Friede, their daughter, was born in March 1946.

Dillwyn's death by suicide was followed in 1942 by that of David Kennedy. When her mother, Edith, died in 1949 after nine years as an invalid, Mary Frances knew that Rex needed her help, at a time she needed an escape from her debt-plagued marriage.

An unfailing source of comfort during this time was Lawrence Powell, whose career as writer and librarian was beginning to flourish at the nearby University of California at Los Angeles.

Le Pâquis, Switzerland   *12.viii.37*
To: Lawrence Clark Powell

Dearest Larry—I have so many things to thank you for—the two grand letters, the clippings, the card, the good list of cookery books. Please forgive me for waiting so long.

—And now here it is two weeks later, and the cat has chewed the paper, and I'm a lot older too—but I'll go on, because I do want to write to you, probably because I want you to write to me. I am furious at having let it go so long.

This has been a wonderful summer, but not the kind that has left much time for pleasant things like letters. I never even read anything, except Books in *Time* and maybe the jokes in the *New Yorker*!

My parents were here for almost a month. We had a grand time indeed. I was a week in Paris with them. Then Rex and Al and Timmy went to Milano. Then when they came back we went many places around here—drank much wine, ate many trout and cheeses and millions of strawberries, laughed and sang a lot. It was fun—Father's first sight of Europe went to his head like champagne, and we all caught his excitement. . . .

The flowers are beautiful too. This year I was too rushed to plant much—I have zinnias, asters, nasturtiums, and yellow and white daisies, with pinks and chrysanthemums in the ground—but the meadow is a mass of poppies, harebells, campion, mourning-brides, on and on—and today, sure sign of winter, I found seven autumn crocuses. I planted Heavenly Blue morning-glories too (they always remind me of Fay, who gave me some in a little white bowl once but they had nary a flower, only great green leaves—altitude, I suppose).

Thanks for the picture, which I return (I hope—I'm always afraid I'll forget to put things in envelopes). Fay looks fine, and so do both the children and Gordon.[1] I wish you were in it—do you have a moustache or a beard now? And did I thank you for the nice little picture you sent a few months ago? It was moustached, I think. You looked very sober in it. I await one of Fay, Weston or no Weston. (It was fine he got the Guggenheim. I tried this year—I think it's quite futile, as I'm already in the Happy Hunting Ground, supposedly, and never heard of a fellowship being granted to go *back* to America. However—it was good experience for filling out blanks.). . . .

A letter from Iona Mouron said you refused to lend her your copy of *Serve It Forth*, because of sales. You are a darling. I wish other people were as thoughtful of me. I know very little of the book, but after reams of good reviews, and enthusiastic letters from relatives who had been trying to get it for two weeks at Macy's or who had been told that Robinson's sold out three times, I was surprised *and* disappointed to get a letter from Harper's (the first since last April!) quoting sales 22 copies one week, 34 another, and so on. *Someone* must have read the damned book—or is it what is called a succès d'estime? I want some money, that's what I want—and to hell with esteem at the moment. Page Mr. Hearst. But I'm glad you like it, even if the public doesn't. . . .

1. Gordon Newell is a sculptor and lifelong friend of Lawrence Powell.

Thank you for the PW[2] notices—they are nice—and the very nice note from Hanna.[3] Will you please tell him that I appreciated it very much indeed? *And* thank you, my dear Larry, for all you've done to get people interested in the book. I hope that someday I can help you in some way. . . .

If I can raise the money, I want to come home this winter, for about two months' work in libraries. I'm trying to write a novel, God help me, and I need more information than I can get here, mainly about Southern California social and political conditions in the 1880s.[4] If you run across any 2nd-hand books that might be useful, and have enough money, please grab them for me. Nothing rare—I'll use libraries for that.

This year promises a fine vintage of what they call "quality" wine. Our vigneron comes as near as he can to cracking a joke when he says that he can hear champagne bubbles in every grape. (*Important:* what U.S. Magazine could handle an article on Swiss vignerons, with wonderful photographs? Let me know, if you can, fairly soon. Would it be *National Geographic*, for instance?)

I must stop. We think often of you. Good luck on your job, whatever it turns out to be. Connes may be here in two weeks. When are you coming? Please forgive my long silence, and Al's longer one, and write to us. Our love to you all—

....

Le Pâquis, Switzerland   5.*x*.37
To: Lawrence Clark Powell

Dearest Larry, thank you for your grand letter, and thank you Dearest Fay for yours. I was so pleased to get them. This will be a note, because I find myself in something of a dither. I'll see you in about six weeks! I planned to be home for New Year's, but we decided to come a month (or less) earlier. I want to see Al, and do some work.[1]

I can see how our unexplained actions might puzzle people, and I'm really terribly sorry if they've caused you any embarrassment with conversations and so on. As you know, I'm not much given to discussing either my own or other people's business, and there must be much that's puzzling. I care *very* much what you and a few others think of me, but for the general run of curiosity-seekers-and-mongers I'd suggest you pay little attention to them. Then they won't perturb you!

Yes, Al is teaching at Smith, a very cushy job with plenty of time for his own work. He decided suddenly to take the bid. It was a rather difficult decision, but I suppose it's for the best.

I'm staying on here at Le Pâquis, working hard on my book, and in the garden. I

2. *Publisher's Weekly*
3. Phil Townsend Hanna, editor of *Westways*, which published MF's first short story, "Pacific Village" (about Laguna)
4. This novel about Southern California was never published and was probably destroyed, along with other manuscripts and journals, in the late 1940s.
1. MF and Al Fisher had separated.

leave in about three weeks, for New York and California and some even harder work. (Damn it!)

About that play by Noël Coward—we're writing our own lives. At present I know only my own, and those poorly, but they are mine. I'm living alone—and liking it.

I can hardly follow your reasoning that Al hasn't written you and is therefore unhappy. As I recall, Al seldom writes to *anyone*. His last letter reports a cold in the head. Otherwise I would say that he is as happy or unhappy as most.

I love your report of the Stelter-Powell tiff. Good for you! I'll get details in a few weeks, when I see you.

I do hope you're still at the L.A.P.L.[2] when I'm home. I'll need some help. But I hope your job goes through, too, whatever it is.

Please give Normie and Wilkie a buss from me. I was so surprised, and amused too, that Hal[3] liked my book. I thought he'd hate it. I considered dedicating it to him, as an ironic gesture.

I'll borrow Prokosch from you. No, I haven't the 3 van Goghs, damn it. They belonged to Gigi Parrish.[4]

Connes is coming any day. I'll give him your love. Matruchot[5] sent the Traven bit, which I'll bring with me. I thought it was good—and interesting too. Much love to you both. Do write Al when you have time. He'll be lonesome for a while.

....

Le Pâquis, Switzerland   *8.iv.38*
To: Lawrence Clark and Fay Powell

Dearest Larry and Fay—I was so glad to get your letter, and to hear about the job, and everything.

The review of the Lawrence catalog is good, but no better than it deserves. It's the best—and best-looking thing of its kind that I have ever seen.

Thank you for the review of the bread-and-destiny book. I don't think I want the book—the review tells me enough—but, as you know, I want anything you see that has a gastronomic angle. (I'm also keen for data on old age—physical, moral, etc.— phenomena, and for anything that comes your way about taking baths.)

And thank you especially, dear Larry, for the Los Angeles books. I had looked at *La Reina* when I was home, but it is much better to have it. The others are good, too. I have the Morrow Mayo book, and can well believe Harry Chandler's horror of it. It's really a beautiful job, except for the Hollywood chapter which is bad. I'd like to meet Morrow Mayo some day. Is "Eine blume aus der goldenen lande oder L.A." the Louis Salvator book *Los Angeles in South California*? It's the McAllister-Zeitlin edition of 1929, in

2. Los Angeles Public Library
3. Henry (Hal) Bieler was MF's and Lawrence Powell's physician, as well as a lifelong friend. He wrote *Food Is Your Best Medicine*.
4. Dillwyn Parrish's first wife
5. Jean Matruchot was a professor at the University of Dijon.

English, that I'd like to have. But not at any fancy price. I don't want Bell's *Reminiscences*—but I would like to have *60 Years in Southern California* by Harris Newmark. I think Houghton-Mifflin brought out an edition in 1930, not too expensive. I've heard of a book by Herman Frank—don't know what it is. You might look at it sometime. What I need is the personal side of Southern California life and politics—gossip, feuds, scandals. And, *important*, some kind of fashion magazine—a *Godey's* or *Harper's Bazaar* or less well-known one, of any time between 1881 and 1886.

Don't bother much about these, Larry. I'm taking it easy on the book. I think it is too good to rush through, and the longer I wait the more I'll know—maybe! I'm working along slowly on it, and am writing a bit of fluff in the meantime.[1] (I'll send some money in a few days.)

And speaking of money—missed out on the Guggenheim. Another thing we have in common. I'm sorry because of the financial angle. But as far as the work goes—and no sour grapes either—I'm relieved. This Quaker book has turned into too big a thing for a one-year project. At least it seems so—I may be crazy.

Your house sounds wonderful. I am so glad you're there, after being in that pressed-in place in Eagle Rock. I wish I could see it.

I'm glad you turned down the Galesburg job—especially for the children. And you're wise not to get tied in with the movies, I think.

Sorry about the rheumatic flu. It must have been painful. I do hope you're all all right now. Was it an epidemic?

I've often fished around for the shortwave broadcasts from America, but never found much until after midnight, when it's mostly jazz. I've been getting some good Lenten music lately, although the anschluss mussed things up a bit. Vienna used to be one of the best stations, for chamber music and good jazz-recordings especially—but now it's just like all the German stations, nothing but jerky loud marches and roaring speeches filled with *Heil Hitlers*. I find that my prejudice against racial prejudice grows stronger with age. I'm in a nauseated sweat over what's happening in Austria and Rumania now. It doesn't help any, of course, to sweat.

I do hope Al remembers to send on the good old typewriter story. I haven't heard from him much lately—a good sign, probably. I know he's working hard, but I can't tell whether he likes it at Smith. Al is convinced that he hates being a professor, but it really is his vocation, I think. It is encouraging that he's working on "Mark Bealer" again, and that he says he'll give you *The Ghost*[2] if he does nothing himself within a few months. Don't you think so?

To quote you, "I can't tell you how badly I feel, and puzzled," myself. You don't suppose I'm enjoying all this, do you? It didn't help any, either, to find you "pretty peeved" at me because I am no longer the "simple girl" I once was. Of course I'm not. It may be unfortunate that I've changed, but if I hadn't it would be pretty much a case of arrested

---

1. *Touch and Go*, a novel written by Dillwyn Parrish and MFKF under the pen name Victoria Berne
2. "Mark Bealer" was a long story by Al Fisher that was never published; *The Ghost* was Fisher's poem written in Dijon and published by L. C. Powell and Ward Ritchie in 1938.

development. To quote Jean Matruchot, tout passe, tout lasse, tout casse (lots of quoting going on here!). And as far as that goes, ou sont les neiges d'antan? François Villon—ah-hah! You're not the same boy I saw cracking his knuckles on a couch at Orr Hall, waiting for Fay to come downstairs in her little cherry-colored coat. Would you want to be?

I got these two new brownies a few weeks ago, when I was in Berne—and I'll send more of the old ones soon. I don't know about posters. They're awful. I may send some, though, just to prove it to you! Much love to you all—

My best to the Newells. Tell Gordon I wish he'd send me the poem he wrote about Clara Fisher.[3] He said he would. She's a strange and fascinating woman, and I am interested to see what a sensitive person feels about her.

....

Le Pâquis, Switzerland   *30.vii.38*
To: Lawrence Clark and Fay Powell

Dearest Powells—I owe letters to both of you, and piles of money for the things you've sent me. I'll get either a bill or an international order, and send it off with this tomorrow.

I can't write much—I'm so busy, in a pleasant but time-consuming way, that all I can do at the end of each day is be grateful for a few hours' sleep. I have a man who does the cleaning, but cooking for 5 to 10 people every day, plus shopping and walks and trips and so on, keeps me hopping. Anne[1] and Dillwyn Parrish and a friend Mary Powers (water-colorist, odd, cranky, perhaps all right) are here all the time—and Dave and Noni and their friends, plus almost constant people who drop in for tea and stay ten days, make the house full to overflowing. I'll be sorry when it ends, and everyone goes home—but it will be fun to have a little time. I haven't even read underneath the drawings in a *New Yorker* for over two months!. . . .

Please tell me if you see Al—how he is, and so on. He says he can't see how I can be interested, and has asked me please not to write to him—but I am and always will be deeply attached to him, by claims that neither of us can ignore with truth. The difference between men and women, I suppose. So please tell me what you hear of him.

I like the clipping about best-sellers. Did you read *Young Man with a Horn*? Dorothy Baker is the first person I ever heard swing a song. I used to ride in the rumble-seat with her, just to hear her sing into the wind. She hated me, because she was terribly in love with Eda.

God but I'm glad to read the fire in your letters. It does seem as if you know now which way to go. I feel rather that way too. Is it turning 30 that does it? I remember Al almost cut his throat then, with disappointment or some kind of spiritual despair. I feel quite the opposite. I feel free of a lot that I never thought I'd want to be free from.

3. Al Fisher's mother, a musician
1. Dillwyn's sister, Anne Parrish, a novelist

It's surprising, and a great relief—the way the Hollywood Bowl might feel when all the people had gone, after a concert. It's made me stop talking, though—except occasionally to you, or in a story. I'm afraid of talking, really, afraid of ever being close to anyone again.

Please send the thing on MacIntyre.[2] I don't know that there'd be much point in giving him my address—we have nothing to say to each other. I know him only through you—and twice at parties when I felt impatient with him for acting so boring when he was really a person.

Anne P. is very anxious to see his Rilke translations. She has a few, done by Charlotte Wilder (Thornton's sister), but she isn't satisfied with them. Tell me when they're published—I'd like to give her a copy.

Give my love to Bieler when you see him. Did you like the bas-relief he did of me? He said he'd give you a copy if you did.

A man I know at Taos writes that Una Jeffers did a fairly good job of trying to kill herself over Mabel Luhan. Is that gossip?

I agree that you're much too good for Oxy's library, but probably you get a kind of perverted pleasure from it. I hope so.

The kids are at Grenoble, doing a lot of drinking and eating. I don't know about any studying—but I think they're learning plenty after school. They come over here quite often. I'm enthusiastic about them, fortunately.

My plans are cloud-cuckoo, and me with them. This place is sold,[3] after October first. I want to go to Arles or some such place, and work hard. Then I think I'll come home in the Spring. I've got to find some kind of income, no matter how small. Maybe I can do a monthly food-paper or some such thing. Don't know. I don't even know where I want to live—if anyplace. This summer has cut at least 5 months out of my working time—and to add to the picture, I think I've got a ruinous agent. Ho Hum, as my old Irish mother often remarks. In the meantime—write to me when you have time. Tell me news, tell me gossip, tell me you're both of you, all four of you, well and happy.

Timmy and Anne together illustrated *Knee-High to a Grasshopper*, *Floating Island*, and *The Dream Coach*. That's all I know about, Fay. He still keeps getting offers of jobs, but I doubt if he ever does another. His painting is getting bigger all the time.

....

Berne, Switzerland   *15.x.38*
To: Lawrence Clark and Fay Powell

Dearest Larry and Fay—I have an awful lot to tell you, and not much time. In the first place, forgive me for not answering your good letters before this. You may have

2. C. F. MacIntyre, poet and English professor at Occidental College, was one of Powell's mentors.
3. Dillwyn Parrish sold Le Pâquis before he fell ill; it was resold at the beginning of World War II to Arnold Gingrich, who raised his family there.

seen Edith and learned a little from her, or you may simply think that I've forgotten you. I'll try to tell you, in a sentence or two, why I haven't had time to do anything but think often of you both.

You probably know that Anne Parrish, a wretched old bag of a woman who came with her, Dave, Noni, Timmy and I were at le Pâquis this summer. To wind things up, we decided to come over to Berne for a party before they all left. We got here in the morning, 7 weeks ago, and at 7 that night T. thought he had a cramp in his leg. Within 15 minutes he was out of his head with pain. The night was dreadful. I got a doctor and nurse right away—fortunately a fine doctor. At three he said there was no chance— an embolism travelling toward the heart and already in the abdomen. But at 7 in the morning T. was still alive—after a fashion. . . . They operated for 3 hours—and the next morning for 2¹/₂—removed the most formidable embolisms either specialist had ever seen. Then there was fear of thrombosis, and of course of pneumonia. And 12 days later the whole left leg was removed. (I'm writing a case history, because this is so rare in people T's age—to send to Hal.) Things are going to the doctor's contentment, and T. can already get around a bit on crutches. He is in constant pain, with really horrible bouts at least twice a day—so far he hasn't lost his nerve.

As you can know, I hated having the children see all this sadness and agony, but there was nothing to do. They were fine, so quiet and generous. Noni was going to stay here until Christmas, and Dave until Spring studying German and French and so on. And Anne, who was here at the hospital all the time, was going up to Adelboden with us when Tim could move and stay until Spring. (We sent the old bag home weeks ago.)

Then the Czech business came and we decided they'd be much less worrisome and more help to us in America. By pulling various and surprising wires I got them the last three berths on a Canadian ship—we'd already had the consular warning to leave pronto—and solely by stepping on about 300 Englishmen who needed the tickets as much as we, permits to go from Berne to London the day before general mobilization. Feathers flew, I can tell you. In a strange tight grey way it was exciting. They were allowed one bag apiece, and were supposed to have cold food enough for 2 days. (Now I've got all the bother of sending on their other luggage!)

They travelled 28 hours—found the French calm and quiet, and the English fleeing back to Albion an hysterical mob of jittery rude people. In London the anti-aircraft guns were almost as thick as telephone poles, and every corner was piled with sand for incendiary bombs, and the parks were messes of what seem to me pretty ineffectual trenches. They went right down to Liverpool, to escape gas-masks and so on—and that afternoon Chamberlain sold the Czechs down the river, and the Munich "Peace" was declared. But I asked them please to go on home—Anne's mother is ill, Rex is none too well, and having them here is a great responsibility.

In Switzerland things were very quiet and tense. There was one night of complete darkness—not a light showing, supposedly, in the whole country, except little blue flash-lights in the trains. You can't imagine how complete darkness changes a big city into the galleries of a deserted mine. The cafés stay lighted but behind cast-iron shutters and layers of black cloth and paper. Here at the hospital we had black over all the openings, even key-holes, and one tiny blue lamp in each room.

The only thing that really sickened me, during the 10 days of pre-Peace, was when I dashed to Vevey to pull wires to get the children and Anne out. I hadn't *liked* things, certainly—the steady tide of mobilization; the hysterical English tourists who pushed me out of the way in telegraph offices, and laughed crazily when they upset ink on my (not their) clothes, with no apology; the black street, the night of the obscurissement; and the way all the people almost stopped talking, for so many days. What really filled me with a sense of hopelessness and revolt was the twenty air-raid sirens that screamed all the three hours I was in Vevey. They were practicing warning the citizens—repeated do-re-do-re-do-re until the planes had gone, and then one long intolerable note. It was awful. That jolly little town of fountains and bright flowers was as empty as if cholera had struck, with a few women scuttling, grey-faced, from one store to another, their arms filled with canned food, and the air one frantic, almost palpable shriek, that vibrated in your ears and your brain and your stomach.

No, I don't like it. I don't seem to feel frightened—none of these civilians do. But I am repulsed by the foulness of it, the noises, the shadows. I *resent* it. That's it, I think—a great mass of *resentment*. Well—

And that, with a few ramifications, is what has been happening—except that in the midst of all this I had to empty Le Pâquis, which was sold, thank God, a little while ago. (It helps, financially.) Dave and Noni helped, and put what furniture I couldn't or wouldn't sell into a small apartment in Vevey. It was a madhouse, but we got everything fairly straight. But I misplaced the *New Masses* article, so I can't send it to Georges Connes. I'm terribly sorry, Larry—I hope you'll understand. If I have a chance to go to Vevey and look for it, of course I will—but it'll be a question of months—I haven't yet been able to see if Steinbeck is in any European library, but will try to do it this week. The Steinbeck pamphlet, which is God knows where at the apartment with the *New Masses*, I'll send on to Dijon as soon as I can. You're right—it is upsetting, to make an understatement. And the worst part of all that, as What's-his-name the Russian says in his introduction to *Yarna the Pit*, is that it is common that nobody thinks it's anything but natural. . . .

—Oh, Larry, I feel so badly about having misplaced all the things you sent me! I do hope you won't stop. These last two months or so have been the wildest of my life, and it will take time to find papers and other things that I can't even remember now. I have the paper on Mac, and will send it as soon as I get a big envelope. It is interesting—as you say, a little bit unrestrained, maybe—certainly worth keeping for future work. I can find only one of the Rilke translations. Oddly enough, it is the only one I really liked. The others I find trite in their phraseology—they'd been said before and in the same dead hackneyed way. I know that will annoy you—both because you are enthusiastic about Mac's work and because you know damn well that I am *nothing* as a judge of poetry. But that's what I think about these. *Autumn Day* is a beautiful one. The others are not anything, to me. The Everson[1] book I liked, especially three or four I marked. That too is somewhere in Vevey. I wanted to ask you more about them—when I find the book, I will.

I was glad you felt less bitter about Al. It's true that he is a strange complicated person, hard to understand, but I've always felt that he loved you, even if not in the way you would like. Since his visit to California, I've been learning some surprising things about myself and my behavior, from various friends who talked with him—surprising chiefly because Al has always seemed to make almost a fetish of silence about his personal life. Apparently he has changed. The only things I can say in answer to the various accusations and so on that the summer has brought me from old friends is that if I had left Al because of Dillwyn—or any other man—it would have been some six years ago. I really don't understand some of the things Al is reported to have said—for instance that I had refused to write to him, and that my letters were too painful for him to read, and so on. Oh well—there's no use getting this way or that, especially at this distance. I hope that some day, before too long, Al and I can meet and talk without any fancy-business, as *people,* not as examples of high-minded sententious platitude-builders. I wonder, though.

About Le Pâquis—you say you were surprised that I had left it. I was too—although it turns out to have been a fortunate thing, as you can see. I thought I would end my days there. I wanted to. And for the first time in my life I gave myself completely to a thing, a place, an idea. It was the last time, too. I can never do that again. It's like suffering—you reach a certain point, and then you know that never again, no matter what happens, can you ever be that way in your whole life. Of course I'll probably live in other places—I'd like to live in the inland in California sometime—but I'll never give my whole spirit. It's just as well, probably.

In a week or ten days I am going up to Adelboden, a high quiet village, with Dillwyn and the nurse. It will be good to get away from the city—although I love Berne. I want to write a novel, just for fun, and do some work on my book on old age. I may learn to skate, too.

As soon as Tim can move, I want to go back to the States, at least temporarily. I'm worried about Rex and Edith—and I have to do some work in a library or two. I want to see Al, too—if he'll agree.

And I want very much to see you two.

When I was home last Christmas-time I was too unhappy, like glass with a flaw in it, to dare talk, or even see you.

How are our finances? The books you've sent are fine—exactly what I wanted. And thank you, dear Larry, for the presents. I think you'd better not send any more Californiana—I'll be there soon. But if you see anything good, hold it for me.

Please let me know, if you can, anything about Al. He asks me not to write, and won't write to me, but as you know, I'm not made of such superhuman stuff, and will *never* be able to kill my interest in everything he is and does. I suppose one answer to

1. William Everson, a.k.a. Brother Antonius, poet

that is that it's no longer any of my business. That's true only technically. As long as either of us is alive, my feelings for him will be warm and alive too. So tell me if you hear of his news. . . .

Please forgive me for falling down so with the papers and so on—and write soon. Love—

....

Berne, Switzerland   6.xi.38
To: Lawrence Clark Powell
Dearest Larry . . .

It's a fine blue day, with snow melting and chuckling in the gutters, and across the little valley a hunter cracking the air for foxes.

Timmy seems out of danger again, but it is doubtful now if he'll ever walk.

I brought the Marconi up here—I'm listening to a Ravel-hour from Beromunster.

Al writes that "someone" is interested in printing privately *The Ghost*. Is it you?

Much love to you all—

I still feel *awful* about misplacing the *New Masses* and the Steinbeck pamphlet.

....

Hotel Huldi   2.xii.38
Adelboden, Switzerland
To: Lawrence Clark Powell
Dearest Larry—Before I forget it, this check is for a copy of *The Ghost* for me. Will you please keep it until I come? And if there's anything left of the check, I want you and Fay to have a little party or something you want—if you're not on the wagon, drink to me, and if you are you can do it just as well in water. It's my last cut off the royalty from *Serve It Forth,* I think. (I was hoping that book would have a small steady Christmas sale, but apparently Harper's has already stopped issuing it—several people have written to ask where they could get copies, but of course I have none. O well—)

I can't tell you how glad I am that *The Ghost* is finally to see light—and especially that you three are going to do it. I think you're doing it exactly the right way, too. Of course Al is convinced that he has no interest in the project, but you mustn't take that too literally. Unless he is an *entirely* different person now, he is really pleased and excited by it. I don't need to tell you how strange it makes me feel, to have something so intimately a part of my life now going on as it should, with me no longer having anything to do with it—except to stand helplessly on the sidelines and ask to buy a copy. That's a bad sentence, but you know what I mean. Anyway—I'm sad but I'm not jealous, and I'm glad you're doing it.

Thank you for writing me such an interesting and good letter. (Dillwyn thanks you too, and says he knows he's lucky to have me here, as you said. I hope you're both right!) I was truly fascinated by what you told me of Al's visit with you, and the things you had heard about him. (Incidentally, it was a fine piece of direct narrative writing—wrong of me to notice in a description of Al's conduct, probably, but I couldn't help being moved and impressed.)

I should like very much, some time, to know "the whole story, from Al's viewpoint." As I told you, such astounding tid-bits have come back to me, from various sources, that the only decent thing I can believe is that Al, a born romancer, must occasionally have got carried away. Certainly he is reported to have told things about us, and especially me—in strictest confidence, of course!—that no person who had ever met me could possibly believe. Probably if he heard them, he'd never believe that he himself had said them. If he did. Of course, Al has always been thoroughly convinced that he is the most secretive and noncommunicative of souls, where as a matter of fact he is a friendly and almost garrulous person, willing to talk intimately to practically anyone. That is one reason why he's an almost inspired lecturer, especially to young people.

I'm sorry, in a way, that he knows I told you of his sexual impotence toward me. It's not a thing that any man likes to have told, and although only you, my father, and Tim knew about it, Al must wonder how many others there are.

Of course nobody saw more clearly than I how difficult it would be for Al and me to go to Switzerland with Tim, and in letters and in countless conversations I did all I could to convince him. But he loathed Occidental and his profession—or thought he did—and he remembered how happy he'd been in Dijon, young, in love, free. Tim and I, too, felt that it was terrible for a man as fine as Al to be so miserable as he felt he was, at Occidental. So— We all went to Switzerland, and before we'd been there five hours Al knew that even my exaggerated tales of how different it would be were not wild enough. He was stuck in a prim, stuffy little commercial town, no longer young, no longer passionate, isolated from any erudite colleagues. You know Al really believes that he is the lonely philosopher, who needs only his pipe, his books, and an occasional evening of Bach, or a solitary roam over the hills. But have you ever known him to do much more than talk about such an existence? He is an extremely social, gregarious person—he *loves* people, and life, and movement—parties, gossip. I don't say this at all bitterly—but I do regret terribly that I didn't realize it before. You remember the constant movie-going we did in Dijon? We were *never* settled down—it was always with some good excuse: our accents, or something—but we were always restless. And then in Laguna, I really think Al almost went crazy with boredom. We had absolutely no money, so we couldn't entertain—but he'd roam off down to the public beach, or visit people—preferably alone—and every spare nickel we got went for movies. By that time I knew his real need for more variety and movement than I could provide (especially on the $32.50 a month that we managed to live on), so I was glad when Stelter gave him a job.

You know how Al protested, constantly and bitterly, his loathing for that job, and indeed for teaching in general. I wonder if he always will? I really believe he loves it—he loves the attention of adoring students, the intrigue and conniving among the faculty—even the occasional weighty research and the occasional publication of an erudite little book on some obscure Greek epigrammatist. But I doubt if he'll ever admit that. He is one of the most thoroughly self-fooled people I've ever known.

You ask if I really thought I could live in the house with two men who were in love with me. (I seem to be going in for Confessional—don't let it bore you, and please realize that it's not my general habit.) It probably seems as strange to you as it does to me, now. But for so long I had throttled all my sexual needs (It took me a long time to get used to living side by side with a man whom I still loved passionately and who was almost actively sickened at the thought of being with me) that I was pretty sure they were well in control. And I had proved that I could be with Tim without setting off any bonfires. So, as far as that part of life went, I truly hadn't a qualm. It was the certainty that Al would be bored that worried me—but when I talked about it, he would always assure me that the only thing he really wanted in the world was complete solitude, time to *think*.

As for my leaving Al for Tim, it is quite untrue. I have told Al that, and I think he knows it, but no man likes to admit that a woman has left him for any other reason than another man. If I had been going to leave him, though, for Tim or any other man, it would have been some six years ago. It is true that I am with Tim now, and will be as long as he lives or wants me—but I would never have left Al for him. I am sorry that Al won't admit that.

Yes, I've gone ahead with the divorce. It will be granted some time in January, probably. It is very unpleasant to me to be the theoretical wife of a man who has not even seen me for over a year—it's distasteful and dishonest to me at least, and I should think would be to Al too. I can't understand his wanting things to stay that way—except that perhaps being legally married is a kind of protection to him. And that leads me to what you tell me of all Al's talk of needing a large measure of ripe flesh. It is rather difficult to talk about. I wish I could tell you how deeply I wish that Al really would *take* some ripe flesh. He *does* need it, and *want* it. But I am fairly sure that he has little of it. Of course he pinches and pokes and leers and strokes—and above all he *talks*. Al is a master of implication. He can (and does) imply the thousand affairs of a rather pedagogic Don Juan. But what are they? They are wish-dreams, almost all of them. Al was 26 or 27 when he married me, and still a virgin. He was, and still is, frightened and repelled by the actual physical act of love. Even at his freest, and happiest, he had to condone it and make it acceptable by quoting what Plato, and Bertrand Russell, and Marie Stopes said about it. And it was disappointing—partly because he was inexperienced—and frightened by years of churchly training from Y.M.C.A. leaders and a father who after 35 years of parochial life could still talk solemnly and resonantly of "the sweet mystery of love and life"—that is to say, sexual intercourse. Al

M.F.K. Fisher: A Life in Letters

was, and still is, horribly frightened by the thought of venereal diseases, which has made him take out his urges in the more or less safe forms of pinching and writing school-boy notes. God—I hate to admit all this, even to myself. I'm proud of Al, and want him to be a full, happy *man*. Of course it was hard on my female pride, for a while, to realize that I had failed to make him one. Then I hoped desperately that his getting away from me would help him. But I don't think it has. Teaching in a girls' school, always having to be circumspect and cautious, certainly doesn't help. But there *are* men who can do that and still live vigorously and wholly. And now I hear, not only from you, that this damnable half-life of flirting and giggling and tickling is still going on, stronger than ever. I am sad.

You are right about Al's letters—they are not the best side of him, inclined to be sententious and humorless. That's not a new development, although I think it is exaggerated at this time by what you rightly call the "spiritual chip on his shoulder." I hope, and very very much, that some day he will allow himself to be loose and easy and free with me. I rather doubt it, though—it will take the warmth and completeness of a life with a real woman to bring that about, and Al is stubborn and self-torturing enough to prevent himself from ever really enjoying life. He is capable of living forever now on pinching-and-telling, and the idealized vision of his life with me. (Even before he left, he was almost sleeping with a picture of me when I was 16 which he'd found at the Ranch. He so hated actuality that he had made a dream of what I was then, some five years before he even met me! It was a kinder, sweeter, weaker child-bride he loved—one he'd never owned.)

Well, dearest Larry—I remember the first time I ever met you, at a dance at Orr Hall, I said that you had something of the father-confessor in you. Certainly I've proved it today—and for the first time, as far as all this goes. I was too unhappy and sad to talk to *anyone*, when I was home. And of course I am quite alone with Dillwyn, who knows most of this from having been so close to both Al and me. Let it stay in the confessional, and think no ill of any of us.

I'm so glad about the Newell boy. Please tell them.

Jean Matruchot could never say that what I'm writing now is "charmant, delicieux."[1] It is so terrible that I reread one chapter and was almost sick. I doubt if I ever try to publish it—no point in rubbing people's noses in their own filth. It's good for me, though, and hard work—different from anything I've ever tried. If I ever finish it, I'll probably ask you to read it.

The change to high altitude that was supposed to help Timmy recuperate almost killed him, and for about 3 weeks it looked bad. Fortunately I had a good nurse. I am convinced that he should be at a lower level, and as soon as he can be moved I want to go down to Vevey, for a few weeks at least. Then he must get used to walking again, and then we'll probably go back to America. He is almost recovered from the phlebitis that occurred when he came up here, but the theoretical foot and leg cause him such agony

1. Probably refers to the unpublished novel about Southern California

that he has to be kept doped most of the time. It's no life for a man, and at times he's hard put to it not to despair. So am I. But we'll see what going down does. Of course it may be even worse than staying here, but we're willing to risk it—*something* must be done, and we've tried almost everything (including injections of cobra-venom! They almost sent him off his head, among other reactions. It's terrible to be so trapped. I *know* what blundering dolts most doctors are, and yet when one suggests something that may help this agony I see before me, I can only say Yes, Yes, anything!).

Please write, and to 30 rue du Château, La Tour-de-Peitz, Vaud, Switzerland. If I don't write before Christmas, this sends you and Fay and the beasties my loving good wishes for then and all the New Year. Tim too. I hope we'll see you before the year ends. Please don't be afraid at my sudden burst of confidence— Love—

My best to Newells and Ritchies, and to your Mother. Love to Hal.

....

Hotel Darling   *28.ii.39*
Wilmington, Delaware
To: Lawrence Clark and Fay Powell

Dearest Fay and Larry—I owe you both nice letters, and this will be only a note. We've been here a month—packed and left in a few hours—left the apartment in La Tour in the doubtful care of a dreamy grave-digger. We evidently got here all right, although now I don't know how, and Tim went right to the hospital. Various ghastly things were done to him to try to find what was wrong, and finally, a week ago, he had another amputation.[1] He's still very ill, but this may straighten things out.

We got married, mainly because Al and I are divorced and there was no longer any reason for continuing to hurt and embarrass Edith. She's very fond of Tim, and feels much happier now—and of course it doesn't matter to us anyway.

I am really sorry about your brother's death, Larry. Edith sent me the write-up in the *Citrograph*. I was startled at your resemblance to him.

I can't give you *any* names for the *Ghost* list. The older I get, the fewer people I know, and the few who might want such a book are so poor I wouldn't dare suggest it. Not much help, and I'm sorry. Everson's remarks were interesting, in spite of his style. (He may grow up, however.)

You're so right about Al, to be patient. He's a fine person, but all askew. I hoped I could help him, but sometimes now I'm afraid I did more harm. Maybe later he'll benefit from our life. I know I have—but I'm a lot simpler, of course.

I wish I could see your da Vinci and Sinclair shows. If Tim pulls through this, we hope to drive west. We'll see you both, and your house, and the beasties, before summer. It will be fine.

1. On the same leg as before

Our book[2] comes out in May—awful trash, but entertaining for hammock-trade
—we hope it will make piles of dough.

Much love to you both—

....

General Delivery,   *2.v.39*
Palm Springs, California
To: Lawrence Clark and Fay Powell

Dearest Larry and Fay—This is a note (I *think*) to tell you that we are at least within
shouting distance of you. We're glad.

We gave up the idea of driving out, and as soon as Tim could travel we hopped a
train, and with a stop-over to see Hal, came right out here. The "season's" over, so we
were able to get a nice little adobe house for not much, and we're growing more and
more enthusiastic about life on the Desert. We're living on a very strict diet, which Hal
thinks will help reduce Tim's suffering, and as soon as he's a little better we'll be seeing
you. I'll let you know. We hope to be able to stay out here several more weeks—the dry
heat and lack of altitude are a big help to T—but summer temperatures of 125 to 140
may change our plans.

I'll write a decent letter soon. Do please write—I hear Al's getting married. That's
fine.

Our book's out—futile but entertaining—*Touch and Go* by Victoria Berne. Don't
waste 2 dollars on it. If I ever get a free copy I'll send it to you. I think ours went to Switzerland! Much love,

....

Moreno, California   *8.xi.39*
To: Lawrence Clark Powell

Dearest Larry—Here are the two typescripts Al speaks of. In spite of his avowal of
complete disinterest in them, I think he cares passionately to safeguard every work he
has ever written, so perhaps you should send them to him when you are through with
them. (Although I have known him to destroy many such things as diaries kept during
his adolescence, which would be invaluable to his biographer but which he hates because they did not show him in too admirable a light.)

At this moment I am feeling hurt and puzzled, so probably I should not allow myself to write. I've just received a note from Al—one of the 8 or 10 received in the last
$2^1/_2$ years—which is even more cruel and coldly insulting than the others. Where is
his opinion about magnanimity? In his own slow complex way he does everything in
his power to keep alive, by occasional letters, a feeling of bitterness and hurt in me.
It shames me that he can succeed at all. In between his notes I forget that he expects

2. *Touch and Go,* by "Victoria Berne"

that from me, and I feel warm and tender and regretful about him and truly full of sympathy. Then I get another letter, usually in answer to one from me, and invariably it is scornful, harsh and invariably like a blow. Hell, I say. Why must he do that? He is happy. I am. We are mature and intelligent. I want to say, Al, *why* do you do that? But that would be too blunt and direct a question, too simple for his complexity.

Well—enough of my grumping. You (and Tim) are the victims, not too often, I hope, because you know about it.

Enough of my grumping except that I thought the longer of the two letters you sent was infernally gracious and patronizing. It made me cross. Temporarily.

How are you? Forgive this mumbling letter of self-pity, and write soon. If Tim is well enough we plan to drive slowly north at the new year, and stay a month in San Francisco—go to the School of Fine Arts. Tim, that is—I'll go to a language school and review Spanish. It will be fun, but we hate the thought of leaving here. . . .

Love to you both—

....

Moreno, California   *5.ii.40*
To: Lawrence Clark and Fay Powell

Dearest Powells... Thank you for your good letters, and for the Powelliana. That article about rare books is fine. It's clear and sensible.

It's a damn shame you have had a cold and so on. Perhaps this rotten drippy weather had something to do with it. Today is clear, for the first time in longer than I can remember, and I am glad. This house is cold as a tomb, and after a few days of rain begins to smell like a mushroom cellar.

The Evanses[1] were down here this weekend. We were terribly disappointed that it rained, but we had fun anyway. Now it's hard to get back to work again. I'm doing a series of food articles again, which may turn into another book.[2]

Yes, I have the ms. of *The Ghost*. You can have it whenever you want.

No, please don't send us the Lawrence books. I want to read them, but not now. I'll get them later. Also *Tropic of Cancer*. I have practically stopped reading, for a while... find that I don't work as long as I have any excuse like a good book around. . . .

I sent you my ms. some time ago.[3] Haven't you got it yet? I sent it express, which may explain the delay.

The stamps were a nice surprise, Fay, but not necessary. Thank you anyway, for being such a rare guest as to think of them.

We're landed gentry again, God help us. We've put our last penny into 90 acres of rocks and rattlesnakes over near Hemet, on the hills by the Ramona Bowl. There's

1. Close friends Jane and Bill Evans from Los Angeles
2. They became *How to Cook a Wolf*.
3. One of the manuscripts that was later destroyed

a very shack-y wooden house, which we'll have to live in "as is" for a while, and there are several springs. We got the whole business, plus a lot of headaches and a great feeling of excitement and happiness, for $2750! We can't move until April or May.

We have a dog, too... the funniest most irritating nicest one I've ever met, named Butch. You'll laugh when you see him. He's a Peke, but not a Toy kind.

I must whip myself through a little work. Write soon again. Our love to you all.

....

Moreno, California   *15.ii.40*
To: Lawrence Clark and Fay Powell
  Dearest Larry and Fay...

Your letters about my book were as manna to me, since only the day before they came I learned that it will really be impossible to publish the thing, and furthermore that I had wrought irrevocable damage to one of the few friendships I care about. I was shocked and terribly surprised. But Tim has always said that I am basically naive, and I suppose that was a proof that he's correct. Anyway... it did me good to learn that you both thought the book had its good points. I'll put it away, and start soon on another one.

And thank you very much more than I can say for reading this one. I must warn you that I'll send the next one to you, too, since you are two people who can criticize with intelligence in spite of your fondness for me as a friend.

It's cold as billybedamned out here now, although there is some sun, and Tim and I have decided that even if we can't afford it, and we can't, we're going to buy an oil-heater for the Squaw-man's House next Fall.

We own the place now, signed and sealed. God help us, and we're terribly happy about it, although it's pretty much of a mess and will stay so for several years or until we write a best-seller and have a couple of one-man shows. There's no heat, light, garage... on and on... and worst of all, no work-room for Tim. But we have time, if nothing else.

We're both working hard. Tim does an average of ten canvases a week, not to mention several pencil and charcoal things. It's a mad pace, but it helps him to get along without too many shots, and he feels that he has to make up for starting so late in life. His work is developing too fast to realize, almost, and I seem to have married myself to another genius.

Speaking of that, how is Al? Has his wife brought forth yet? . . . Tell all.

I'm in my February spate of work (never knew it to fail) and have done several articles which are wowing my agent but so far have produced no fat checks from editors. Will let you know.

Much love to you both and all from us... and as soon as it warms up a bit how about coming out here again? And thank you, more than I can say, for being so swell about my ill-fated brain-child. It warms my heart to know that at least you and Tim believe it's good....

Hotel Muehlebach   *31.vii.40*
Kansas City, Mo.
To: Edith Holbrook Kennedy
   Dearest Edie:
   I got my nice airmail equipment out, and then decided to treat you to a sheet of
Muehlebach's best stationery.
   The hotel is odd, to say practically nothing—1923 elegance plus 1903 cracked lava-
tories plus 1939 cocktail bars. We had a very nice Martini in The Rendezvous, but decided it was too full of schoolgirls and went to The Grill, which was even fuller of
women trying to be schoolgirls. There was a very loud band in powder-blue suits—
somebody or other and his Sugar Blues Boys. We ate cold roast beef and drank Muehlebach brau (which is much better than the hotel), and although we had a lot of fun we
felt as if we were escaping from the inside of a large and very sweet cream-puff when
we "hopped out," as Shaun[1] says.
   The trip was easy and fun, in spite of what the altitudes did to poor Tim. We stayed
in our room most of the time. And when I say room I mean *room*. If you ever go east
again, try to get a Double Bedroom. They cost about between a compartment and a
drawingroom—and I've never seen such a spacious set-up. We had a very nice porter—the whole train was nice, in fact. There were a few Hollywood people and a couple of loud-mouthed politicians going back to D. C. to tell the boys what to do. I took
you and Sis at your words, and wore my blue silk slacks to lunch, and felt rather queer
and extremely comfortable. Broiled mushrooms and bacon on toast made me feel
even more so.
   We came to the hotel at 7:30, and after baths and whatnot I went to sleep for three
hours! I was surprised too.
   I'll write tomorrow from You Know Where. If we have too uncomfortable a night
we may do as we did today, and take baths and so on, and then take a gander at Cousin
Kate's line of 500 people in the afternoon and go back the next morning. I imagine it
will be mostly schoolteachers with colitis at the moment.
   Give my love to Noni, Rex, Sis, and Wee Edie—Tim's too—

Mayo Clinic   *3.viii.40*
Rochester, Minnesota
To: Rex Kennedy Family
   Dearest family—
   The first two days I spent in the waiting-rooms I was interested in the people, but
now suddenly I have looked at them all I want to—or perhaps more than that. The

1. Anne Kennedy Kelly's son

thing that impresses me most about them is a rather pessimistic feeling of their lack of dignity. Most of them are middle-aged or old, and look as if they should have lived and suffered long enough to acquire that clear outline, that repose—that whatever it is that is supposed to show The Dignity of Man. Of course many of them do look nice, or kindly, or funny, or something. But that isn't what I mean. They are *not* clear, but smudged in their outlines, like a bad photograph which could show their spirits as well as their bodies. They are incoherent, bewildered, petty—and make me wonder what use there is in spending a life without really learning anything. Well—

Of course practically every person here is completely absorbed within himself— and that is understandable, because it is hard not to be if you have a gut-ache or any pain. All your thoughts and actions focus on it—and here that is true of everyone you see, except an occasional companion like me who is equally preoccupied by the pain of another person. The only way you can make any contact with others is to ask them about their experiences with suffering, either real or imagined, and since we are not interested in anyone's but D's, and don't care to discuss it, we live in a kind of vacuum.

The waiting-rooms are impressive marble rooms, very cool and spacious. There are rows of comfortable chairs, and a soft buzz of exchanged weights, temperatures, and other more clinical confidences fills the air as people wait for their names or numbers to be called from one of the two desks. Then they hobble or mince or waddle or bound or totter into one of the rows of little consultation rooms, where young and solemn doctors talk to them. Many of them are ill-at-ease as they go out of the big room and grin and blush and pull at their clothes, and look more like self-conscious children than people going to learn about their lives and deaths.

Last night there was a mighty thunderstorm as violent as the ones in Switzerland, but much longer. It made the air better.

There is a carillon on top of the clinic, which is silent at night but rings out a pretty off-key bar or two of a hymn every hour during the day. But yesterday about five o'clock it suddenly broke loose with several Schubert songs, Rachmaninov's Prelude in-whatever-key-it-is, "Flow Gently, Sweet Afton" played like a Bach fugue, part of Dvořák's *New World Symphony*, and a few other such things—and it was actually beautiful, in key and with chords of many bells at once, and as many modulations as a fine organ. I looked out the window, and people down in the streets were stopped, puzzled and excited. I think it must have been some famous carillonneur, maybe from Belgium, who is here to get his gizzard fixed and simply broke loose for a while. Whatever it was, it was certainly swinging those bells around. It is the only time that I have wished you were here.

Our drive yesterday was pleasant. We went up to Winona, across The River, and back—had lunch at a fairly nice little place called Ye Hot Fish Shop, where we ate wall-eyed pike fixed in butter, and drank a watery local beer called Bub's. The country seems like a park, with many woods and neat irregular fields of wheat, corn, barley, and pink clover, and the cows and horses are very handsome. The farmhouses are not beautiful like the ones in Pennsylvania, but the silos and the red barns with curved roofs are very handsome, and look Russian.

Our driver was a pleasant young man who talked occasionally and drove very well. "From here on it's nothing but bluffs, bluffs, bluffs," he said. "All they eat in Wye-nona is fish, fish, fish." "Most of my work is emergency calls, emergency calls, emergency calls." He was not especially bright.

There are a few children here. They all yell when they get stuck for blood-tests, because everybody babies them so.

The hardest thing for most people about the routine tests is having to go without breakfast until eleven or so. In a way it's good, because it diverts their minds, so that even people who are obviously in great trouble can think of nothing but how hungry they are, and for once can discuss that first cup of coffee instead of their metabolism.

Last night it was too hot to sleep, before the storm, so we got dressed and walked around the town. Looking into the sitting-rooms and lobbies of all the lodging-places was horrible, but we couldn't help it. Apparently the men go to bed, but the women stay up, and collect in little circles and talk, talk, talk, as our driver would say.

The shopping district of Rochester looks like that of a much smaller town (it's about 2,800)—mostly candy-stores, cafés, flower shops, and uniform-shops. There are a couple of movies, and a few very dingy-looking bars, which we seem to have no interest in, although the Kahler serves only beer, and that with compressed lips.

Later:

After four hours of consultations I brought what was left of Timmy back to the hotel (he tried to escape once to the toilet for a cigarette, and got called before he had even lit it), and then we had lunch and went looking for a possible place for me to stay. (Meals have sunk to a mean average of liverwurst-on-rye and beer, but don't think we're starving.) I looked at several hotels, and will probably spend two dollars more and stay right here.

Tim goes to St. Mary's (Catholic) Hospital at ten tomorrow, for experiments on his spine. The biggest man in the clinic (for nerves, etc.) said that he could guarantee absolutely nothing, and that nobody knows why men with "good" amputations keep on suffering, one time out of a thousand, when they aren't supposed to. There are two things to do—open the whole leg and trace every nerve for nodules, etc., or block the leg-nerves from the spine. They'll do the latter first, and just with Novocaine. If that works they'll cut the nerve, which will mean complete paralysis of that leg and no more chance of an artificial one. It may also do no good, because all the trouble may be coming from some trouble between the spine (or along the spine) and the brain, caused by shock, disease, what-have-you. In that case they say there is absolutely nothing to do but live partially doped until you die.

Tim is in pretty good shape, mentally and otherwise, and is more than willing to gamble on getting some help.

I'll write tomorrow, probably. Love from us both—

M.F.K. Fisher: A Life in Letters

Mayo Clinic   *6.viii.40*
Rochester, Minnesota
To: Rex Kennedy Family

Dearest family—

Tim left the hospital at eight this morning, much against the nurses' and my better judgment—but in Rochester it's kill or win, and Tim says he can see how many a man comes in on roller skates and goes out on a stretcher or whatever the phrase is backwards. He could hardly walk, but we waited for an hour in the clinic and then had a $2^1/_2$-hour consultation with five doctors—this with no breakfast but castor-oil, to prepare for an intravenous urological examination at 1:30, after no lunch. That lasted for $1^1/_2$ more hours, which he passed strapped to a steel table on his back, which is black and blue from yesterday. So you can imagine that he is somewhat shattered, as Mary Powers would say.

I don't feel very chatty, but I suppose I might as well tell you, and then we can close the subject permanently, that all the discoveries are very bad, and that Tim is in great danger of losing his other leg or, if he is lucky, of dying relatively quickly. He may also get much better and live to a ripe old age, which according to the doctors would be miraculous. By living in a kind of Venetian-glass box he might evade another thrombosis—no cigarettes, no excitement, no movement, no painting. Or he could live as normally as possible, as we've been doing at Bareacres, and take the quicker chance. I think I know which way he'll choose.

He has one more consultation tomorrow—the men are trying to find some substitutes for Analgeticum[1]—and then we'll flee, if Tim is well enough. Our one idea is to escape.

Anyway, I'm getting to the end of my airmail stamps! Love—

Bareacres   *24.xi.40*
Hemet, California
To: Lawrence Clark and Fay Powell

Dearest Powells:

Thank you for your good letter.

Mother asks me to thank you too for the plant. She isn't able to write yet, but is much better, and just as you thought she enjoys mightily having things like the water-orchid to watch.

Our plans have changed again, and Timmy who has been having a very hard time lately, has decided that he should go back to Delaware and see his mother while he is able to… so we start on December 3rd, for about 6 weeks or two months. It seems crazy, when we could do it in a few days by train… but it keeps Timmy occupied and there is

1. Painkiller available only in Europe at that time

so little anyone can do for him that this is nothing. We'll drive back slowly by the southern route, missing most of the bad weather, and will spend about two weeks in the east. I feel very badly, to tell you the truth, about leaving this place for even such a short time... but it will be fun to see new lands... and in spite of the grim reason for our trip, we plan to have a pleasant and perhaps wonderful time.

But... we were so very pleased that you both liked the pictures, and are really excited at the idea of having a show at the library some time soon. Will you please find out as soon as possible, if the thing is at all feasible, about how many pictures would be wanted? Then if there were only ten or so, we would collect a few of the eight or nine in the east, since they are among the best, and bring them back with us. Tim has a possible twenty or more, I would say, to exhibit... but can choose any number.

Please write to me if you can before we leave on the 3rd, not only about pictures but about your selves... and we will be at:

Christmas chez

Mrs. T. C. Parrish

Claymont, Delaware . . .

I am really rather upset about leaving. But Tim feels it is the only thing to do. Love...

....

The Roosevelt   *10.i.41*
New Orleans, Louisiana
To: Rex Kennedy Family

Dearest family:

We got in at dark yesterday. It was grand to find Edie's letter about New Year's and the family. I suppose it will be the last one we get—but we plan to be home in some ten days, if all goes well. We'll be at the Hotel Hilton, El Paso, for at least one night, about the 15th, in case you have time to dash off another letter or so. We're coming a little faster than we left, but are still slouches compared to most tourists. We want to stay overnight at least in San Antonio, which to our surprise is one of the loveliest cities we've found—and we count on a couple of days in El Paso, or really Juarez, where D plans to do some quick drawings for pictures.

Last night, after baths, and such, we went to Galatoire's, where we had a Martini and then ruminated with pleasant messiness over a platter of unshelled river-shrimps. When we'd liquidated them we washed and dried ourselves and had crab newburg, some light beer, and the first good salad since we left New Orleans a month ago. Then we drank coffee—also the first really good since then—and had some kirsch. It was a nice selfish evening which we enjoyed immensely, along with the usual New Orleans crowd of drunks, visiting politicians also pretty drunk, upper-class prostitutes, and more or less serious gastronomers, mostly Jewish.

This hotel, which has a lobby like one of the more intimate corners of the Grand Central Station during an American Legion convention, filled with neon arrows pointing to everything from chiropodists through several kinds of bars to private detective bureaus and playgrounds on the roof, is more comfortable and somewhat cleaner than the Monteleone.[1] It is the same price. Of course, the older I get the more of a complex I get about clean bathrooms, and since Tim feels the same way and has lived even longer, we have left practically every tub, basin and toilet of this trip much cleaner than we found it. There was plenty of room for improvement here, both times—and of course I hid the spittoons—but now we're settled we're more than comfortable. Fortunately the weather isn't heavy and gray as it was last time, and Tim is staying in bed until after lunch and then we'll go to the Picasso exhibit, which is the one he has wanted to see more than any in his life and which happens, miraculously, to be "playing" New Orleans at this moment. Tonight we'll probably go to Antoine's and not eat oysters Rockefeller, and maybe get a guide in the morning and start west again after lunch, since we want to hit San Antonio for a night and the distances in Texas between decent beds are rather irregular. You can't plan to stop whenever darkness finds you, as in the East.

We're both glad we're getting farther West all the time. I'd hate to live anywhere else, I know now more than ever. I'm terribly glad I saw Charleston and Mount Vernon and a little of New England and so on, and of course I'd love to live in one of the old houses you see everywhere—but the West is better. . . .

I told you about Tim's show, didn't I? I'm not quite sure—though it's one of the most important things in our lives. Thanks mainly to Larry Powell's enthusiasm and promoter-instincts, he's to have quite a large one-man show at the gallery at UCLA from April 2 (?) to May 9—anyway, two weeks. No sales, of course, but critics and so on. It's a wonderful break for him, and thanks to that and good weather and a kind of relief at having seen his family, he's in better shape than I've seen him for months, and keen to get home and do some more work before the show. So we'll be there well before the end of the month. We're anxious to see you all— Much much love — . . .

....

Bareacres   *1.vii.41*
Hemet, California
To: Lawrence Clark Powell

Dear Larry:

It's good to know you're back on the Coast again, and that you had a good trip. Please thank Fay for the cards… it was fun to know now and then where you were.

How nice of you to send your hosts my book! (And now I'll get at least $.25 royalty this year… nice too.)

We're really excited about Harvard and your various plans for this fall. Please keep us posted. We don't see much of you two, but even so your going would make things empty for us… and yet we both want you to go east if you can. It would be fine for all of you, in many ways.

1. Another New Orleans hotel

I hate like hell to put off our seeing you, but at this moment the September 1st weekend seems impossible. Timmy has grown much worse in the last few weeks, and it's out of the question to have anyone here. He is increasingly weak, so that he can't walk at all unless I hold him... and his pain is terrible to think of. Most of the time his morale is good, and he manages to work a little almost every day. I'll let you know how things go.

I never leave him any more, so my contacts with the world consist of an occasional good morning with the Grocer-boy and the Indian who comes once a week to help me. And of course Mrs. Purdy[1] comes three times a week. We're well cared for, and lack nothing.

I should be getting a lot of work done but I find it distasteful to me. My mind is distraught. I did a series of articles on gilt-edged gluttony (Diamond Jim et al) which is now sleeping through the summer in Connecticut with my exhausted agent, and I'm writing a long short story about a ghost now. And I plan soon to start on a very disagreeable novel, more to please Tim than myself.

. . . How I wish we could see you both and hear about all the trip and get Joe Goose to play again.[2]... Maybe things will be better soon. In the meantime write when you can....

Our love to you and Fay and the chicks.

....

Note: Exhausted by pain and without hope for relief, Dillwyn Parrish committed suicide at Bareacres in August 1941. Mary Frances then traveled to Mexico to be with her sister Norah and brother David.

....

Bareacres   *10.ix.41*
Hemet, California
To: Lawrence Clark and Fay Powell

Dear Larry and Fay...

This is to both of you, as all my letters are of course. I owe you both answers to your two good ones to me.

I'm so sorry you can't come down on the 26th. Name the nearest one you can and I'll tell you if it's not right for me. I don't know when I go to NY if at all... I don't want to, and am tempted to try to get some sort of part-time work here on the Coast... but get work I must, and if necessary I can borrow money to get East.

Don't let Hal's scientific fervor get the best of his practicality, so that he makes testicles of your ear-lobes or some such trick. I hope whatever he does to you won't hurt. Give him my love.

1. Elsa Purdy was a friend, neighbor, and household helper who later became nanny to MF's daughter Anne.
2. "Joe Goose" is Lawrence Clark Powell, whose first choice of career was as a pianist.

Thanks for the *Time* review... it is nice.[1] Fadiman and luscious Lucius Beebe have both done well by me in NY, and otherwise I know nothing. I wish the book would sell like peanuts.

Poor Larry, oysterless. We must remedy that. Yes, the publishers and the agent too howled like panthers at my being Parrish, which I would have liked. Mainly because Tim wanted it, of course[2]... but still I like the name. But no chance. It doesn't really matter.

I have some of Tim's books which of course you can borrow... not a complete list. *Hung for a Song* is not the best... he tried to pare down the English language too thin, so it's a series of understatements. . . .

My parents are somewhat disturbed just now at David's marriage next week to a pretty little blonde he's known but for two years, in Guadalajara. It's too bad in many ways, but there's something to the theory of gathering rosebuds while you may, especially these days.

I do hope I see you both soon. Did I tell you I'm helping build a little house across the Arroyo? The Purdys will live there. Fine for me. Lots of work.

....

Bareacres   *14.x.41*
Hemet, California
To: Norah Kennedy

My darling Noni:

I have the stories[1] all ready to stick in an already-addressed already-stamped (airmail!) envelope to Mary Pritchett,[2] but before I stick them in I want to tell you the order or at least the vauge (and who would guess that word started out to be vague?) vague order. I put the hat-story first, because it is the most *New Yorker*ish and so is Pritchett and alas I know no other agent at the moment. Then I put "To Bury a Baby," which will kick her in the pants if anything ever did. Then "Trip to Halawa," which leaves a terrible bleakness in my mind after many hours, and then "To Eat to Live," which will be comparatively light (oh joysome word!), and then "Luau for Lepers" which is *very* good but maybe too much like a story they ran lately about a recruit being shown a good time by some suburbanites but I'll take this one any day, and then "Haupa-Hauli Party" which is the quietest and perhaps the most terrible of them all. And God Speed.

I don't know at all what my own situation is anent agents. (That's the first time I ever wrote *Anent*... and perhaps the last.) I am being high-pressured to drop Pritchett... she is too refined, too Junior-League, and so and so. I agree to it all... but it hardly seems kosher to quit without warning just as people are beginning to buzz a bit. Al-

1. Review of *Consider the Oyster*, which appeared in print just after Dillwyn's death
2. MF had already established herself as MFK Fisher.
1. Written by Norah
2. MF's agent

though I agree that she had little to do with the cause of the buzz, and is coasting agreeably now on my impetus. Oh well... we'll see what happens with these things.

And now my dear girl you must write and write and write. I mean that. You have a terrible eye: you see with the pitiless ironic eye of Atget's camera or of Zola. But you are crossed with a bit of K. Mansfield... as who is not and God help us all, I say. And you must write it out of you, and get beyond it, and get beyond Woolf and get beyond X and Y and F until you are terribly alone, because you can be a good writer if you have to be. These things were easy for you, compared to what you may have to write later. I think writing grows harder and harder, probably. But if you have to write you do it, the way a diabetic keeps on urinating and urinating, until it is finally pure exquisite crystals that torture him but creep out of him without his yea or nay. You are now at the point where you can Stop it if you will. A shot of marriage or politics or children or some such thing could stop you. For a time or always, you can go on. If you do go on you must write until you hate it, I would say. (I would also say Who am I to say what I would say?)

Of course I am wondering how you and the jeune ménage and the belle-mère and all that sont (Just to complete my ghastly breach of good taste in using other tongues... or tongue. I had dinner with an ex-pal who spent twelve years in France, and got contaminated to the point of Babelism. She is a consummate hostess, though, who works her guests into a frenzy with voluptuous descriptions of the rare and wonderful ratatouille she will serve at dinner until they never realize that it is nothing but stuffed green peppers. A very beautiful woman, too, which helps the deception... the only one I ever met could wear great swashes of mascara *underneath* her eyes and get away with it.).

All my love to you all...

....

Hollywood, California   *17.iii.42*
To: Lawrence Clark Powell

Dearest Doctor Ghuce...

I meant to answer your good letter before this, but was the victim of hospital routine for three weeks too long, so that my morale has softened alarmingly. It was nice to have it waiting for me at Hal's. . . .

Hal is more than enthusiastic about *Quartet*,[1] and i hope very much that you will let me read it. I suppose one of the four was Eda? I too am working on something... I don't know whether it is a story or not... about her. Perhaps we should compare notes. I hear she is in these parts again, but think I'll wisely let sleeping dogs lie (to coin a phrase).

I go out to Bareacres tomorrow, thank God. It is my real home... I know that now, more strongly than I have ever known it of any place... and I need to be back there.

I refuse to believe that I am to be cut off from all my five or six true friends for the Duration. I'll start investigating bus- and train-routes shortly, so that there will be some line of travel between Bareacres and North Beverly Glen at least. It is such a

1. *Quartet* was the original version of Powell's *Blue Train*, a novel published many years later.

beautiful peaceful place that I think an occasional long weekend there would almost be worth a few hours of bus-trip. I hope you'll feel the same....

I plan to read myself sick, for the next two weeks... *War and Peace* again, *Kristin Lavransdatter* again, all of Proust again, several new books... Rebecca West's, V Woolf's last, Scott Fitzgerald's last, and so on, until I'm really bilious. Then I'll stop for another year or so, and do some of my own work. I don't know what that will be yet... I'm mulling over a novel and maybe another one, and of course always making notes for my magnum opus on old age....

Maybe I'll write a thriller, for fun, and sell it for a fancy sum and come to see you with a thick steak under my arm.... Love...

....

Paramount Studios   *18.i.43*
Hollywood, California
To: Lawrence Clark Powell

Dear Larry:

I've wanted before this to answer your Christmas note... it was good to hear from you after too long a silence. Do you find letters less pleasant to write, or do you simply have less to say than in the past?

As you can see, I'm back at the old abattoir, and not liking it at all. At the moment I'm sitting waiting on the whims of an unpleasant "producer." I have finally reconciled my ethics with my profession, and am working on my own stuff on company time... currently editing and annotating a book of Idwal Jones's.[1] It is gastronomical, and I hope thus to please Sam Sloan who was peeved at me for writing *Peter Cartwright*[2] when I could have been coasting along with "another" *Wolf.* I want to see *Peter* in print, for several reasons, and maybe this present job will be a sort of sop to Cerberus.

Do me a favor, dear Ghuce, and never refer to me again as Lady Bountiful. That brings to mind a sanctimonious, pompous, complete bitch of a woman who gives without generosity, scatters largesse with much noise and no humanity. I know my idea is not yours, or you'd never have called me that... but spare me the hideous feeling the phrase gives me.

I'm sorry I missed your Christmas call... my loss.

I want very much to see you all again, and don't know when it will be. My gas supply is of course limited, and all my trips are toward Whittier: Mother is far from well, and I go out there at least once weekly. I'll call Fay if ever I can head West.

I am so anxious to read your book, and really complimented that you want me to. Could you mail it, or would you rather not?

It's exciting to think that you may land a good job here in town. That would be so much easier, especially during the war, than moving kit and kinder to some other part of the country. Please let me know how it goes. Is it library work?

1. Jones was a southern California writer and friend.
2. Peter Cartright was an evangelical circuit rider in the 1800s; MF edited his autobiography.

The radio-work is temporarily on the shelf. I am here for another two months at least, and then may go East on a government job... very nebulous at the moment, but promising. I really hate what I'm doing now, and think it's a hell of a way to spend some of the most energetic years of my life.

Friends in England write that they have revived letters, for lack of gasoline. Do likewise, cher ami, and write to me....

....

Paramount Studios   *22.ii.43*
Hollywood, California
To: Lawrence Clark Powell
    Dear L...

I return herewith the manuscript,[1] although I'd like to keep it a little longer for another reading... my plans are so chaotic that I feel it wiser not to delay on important things.

I think you've done a fine job. I hope you have the feeling of satisfaction and fulfillment you deserve to have.

The mounting strength and knowledge and growth in the book is truly beautiful. It shows not only in the plot itself, if that word can be used for such a musical line, but in the prose, which increases page by page in intensity, until at the last the first part seems almost a monotone, stilted and thwarted and timid like the section itself.

I must confess to you that I simply cannot understand the apparent reluctance Fay feels about the whole thing. She should feel proud of your craftsmanship, if nothing else... and in this particular case I think she ought to understand the completely dispassionate and analytical nature of the book. I don't know whether I could ever talk to her about it... women either do or do not reach a state of detachment about things they love.

Thank you, dear Ghuce, for letting me see it.

I am sitting close to a volcano, which may suddenly send me on foreign service and a very hush-hush publicity job for the government. I hope for the best, and must keep mum about it all. I'll let you know as much as I can, if anything breaks.[2]

I hope to see you all before long. In the meantime, my love to you... and all my thanks...

....

To: Lawrence Clark Powell   *16.vii.43*
    Dearest L...

Your letters warmed my heart. I couldn't let myself answer right away, as I wanted... I couldn't let myself even look at a newspaper until I finished the book.[1] I

1. First draft of Powell's *Blue Train*
2. MF was pregnant with Anne at this time; this story was probably part of her efforts to keep this a secret.
1. *The Gastronomical Me*

mailed it this morning, by air, to New York. Never worked so hard in my life, because it was conceived and written and typed in ten weeks while I kept on with regular work of interviewing and writing... and of course lately so many people have quit this branch of work because of the troubles in Washington that I've done enough for three or four normally agile brains.

It's over now, at least my private war with it, and I can celebrate by writing to you. (The typing will be even worse than usual, probably... after effects, maybe.)

The book was longer than I thought... 298 small-margined pages. It's an odd thing, and may bore the boys in NY. It's autobiographical all right... but neither True Confessions nor Leaves From My Kitchen Lovebook. I shudder to think what may happen to it. Oh well... I think it's a good job, and there are some stories in it I know you'll like. Then there are sections about Dijon, the Rigoulots, Miss Lyse, Jean Matruchot... all that... that will interest you too. So it won't be time wasted.

I think I'll be home sometime in August. My rather vague agreement expects me to stick around until September, but I've forgone a couple of short vacations, with the understanding I could leave earlier. I am really consumed with a need to be at Bareacres. I've never been away so long, since Tim died... and I'm sure now that I can handle living there alone. Of course I'll have to earn money, but I think I can put it off until the New Year if I'm careful. And maybe by then I'll find myself with one of the two children I am trying to adopt. It's a hell of a discouraging business... can't be done in California at all because legally I'm a spinster! Expensive too.

Here I am talking of myself when it's you I think of. Thank you for sending me the letter from Miller.[2] No wonder you were set up by it. It's really fine. And I like it because he says a lot of things I'd have liked to say too. I hope I meet him, sooner or later... although I feel very shy about people whose creative work I admire. It is sometimes a kind of psychic chore for me to co-relate their physical presences to what I have already assimilated of their work. You know what I mean....

Hal sent me the little folder of war poems by Everson. I liked two of them... can't tell you which ones now but think they were the last two... and found the rest labored and sterile. (But that may be because my own mind has been so labored lately... not sterile, I pray....)

About the bus-driving; it sounds to me like a very good idea indeed, and I hope it or something like it will soon happen for you. I haven't had the chance nor the right, really, to tell you how I've felt about your work at the University... but it has worried me. You've been turned gradually into a slave, drained willynilly of some of the juice that makes you what you are. Some men subject to it and never know it... like Fisher really. Some men never had any juice to begin with... like Clelland.[3] But some men, like you, are too fine, and there is in them a constant fight, which embitters them if through circumstances they must submit too long. I really long to see you out of Academia, Larry... even if you go back later. It will keep you whole. And driving a great bus across the country would be a wonderful antidote at first...

2. Henry Miller
3. George Clelland was an English professor at Occidental College.

all the air and the space and the speed of it. (Even in the small way I did it, leaving Hollywood and going everywhere in this fairly new part of the country for a few weeks, gave me a kind of reborn feeling....) Please tell me what you decide to do. God, I wish I had a lot of money, to get you away from the financial grind for a year or so. But even that way, I think you ought to do something, even for a month or two, like the bus-driving, to limber your spirit after the library. (Forgive me for sounding off this way... but you know that I feel very strongly against the slow-rot of pedagogy.) . . .

I'm so glad you sent off *Quintet*[4]... and I needn't tell you how anxious I am to see the new book. Do you call it anything yet?

Thank you for talking to me about Fay. This situation has puzzled and upset me... her feeling about your work, I mean... but now I am more content about it, although still not really understanding it. At least you have struck a good balance as a man and a female, and that is fine. It is enviable. I don't know whether I'd be able to divorce my creative life, or my lover's, from our physical one... and that of course complicates things. With Al for instance, it made an inner war for him: he was vain enough to want his wife to appear very intelligent, and yet he could not reconcile that wish with his basic desire to keep her on a purely physical relationship with him. With Dillwyn there was no war, perhaps because he had gone all through it with his first wife: we met on an unquestioning and equal basis sexually and creatively and as humans. That was mainly because he was the most matured person I've ever met, the best coordinated. They are rare.

I hope you do write about marriage some day. The subject interests me profoundly. Maybe we could collaborate... and what a stink *that* would raise in the Halls of Western Learning! . . .

I haven't read much since I took this job... strange things like *David Copperfield*, and *American Short Stories*. It has the best editorials in America, I think. My "social consciousness" is gradually developing into something fairly powerful, I think. I don't know what form it will take... but before many more years something is going to bust in my little bosom. I can only hope it won't take a Dorothy Thompson turn!

My feelings are so violent, so increasingly violent, just now that I don't trust myself to talk about them. God knows what I'll do when I get to Whittier and have to hold my tongue whether or no! Something has to be done... and soon... but so far I don't feel powerful enough by myself. Maybe I'll have to get a job on a crusading newspaper... but how do that with 2 children? And how do that and still keep my own more tranquil side alive? Ho hum, to quote my mother.

I wish we could see each other... not a polite little evening of social chitchat.

. . . I hope August is a fine month for you and Fay both. I'll see you before long—
Love—

Love to Hal when you see him

4. A draft of Powell's *Blue Train*

M. F. K. Fisher: A Life in Letters

Bareacres   *3.xi.43*
Hemet, California
To: Lawrence Clark Powell
Home to California...

Dearest Ghuce... I shall ask Hal to give you this letter when next he sees you. I don't like the appearance of secrecy, but now and then I can write more freely to you alone. You understand.

You know how happy I am about the Job.[1] You will do exciting things there, I know.

It's a cool clear night, with a young moon. I've brought my typewriter in by the fire, partly because it's nicer that way and partly to be near Anne[2] while she drinks her supper. The studio is her room now, and I know Tim would like it this way. The pictures are all there, and on the walls now are the *Angels of Birth and of Tranquillity*, and the picture of me which I don't believe we showed... an impression, a bottle of wine, some apples, and a white flower. It was the only thing Tim ever did of me, or about me, that he liked.

Anne is right in every way. She is a healthy, impish little being with merry dark eyes. And now my life seems full and warm and rich again. I was out in the cold for a long time.

Thank you for the little card of Picasso's *Gourmet*. How good it seemed to be getting such a thing again from you! And how good to hear the old voice again, in your letter from Chicago. I was far from there, and doing a job I'll tell you about when the time is ripe, and it is hard to tell you how reassuring and exciting your letter was. I knew that some good things still lived in the world.

The arctic sleeping bag factory sounds like a strange and perhaps entertaining pause in your life. I'd like to do something like that... very hard routine work. (Of course I am working hard with the baby, but I mean something mechanical and dull.) I think you'd be a very good inspector to work under.

The book is on its way to me now. The publishers are apparently delighted with it, and I hope it sells like peanuts, so I won't have to go back to Hollywood... at least for a few more months.

I think it would be almost impossible to find a decent apartment and a nurse and earn enough to pay for both and break at all even, so I shall simply plead Act of God or something if I'm accused of not following my contract. The idea has been to work for two or three months and earn enough cash to live here the rest of the year, but I don't think it's possible in war-time. And the thought of leaving this place and not being with the baby all day is almost unbearable.

I want very much to see you. I'll probably be in town, or rather at the Ranch, between Christmas and the New Year. Perhaps then? Of course I can't leave the baby at night with Mother.... Well, it will work out some way....

In the meantime here's my love....

1. Powell's new position at the UCLA library
2. MF's daughter, Anne Kennedy Parrish, was born on August 15, 1943.

Bareacres   *25.i.44*
Hemet, California
To: Lawrence Clark Powell

Dear Ghuce...

This is, perhaps, the Broadside you've been waiting for. No, not really... but at least it will be more than a note on onion-skin. I hope you can decipher it: my typing doesn't seem to ripen with age....

First, will you please forgive me for not thanking you for Everson's poems and for the Huxley catalog? I am pleased indeed to have both. I must confess that the latter interests me a little more. In the last months I have read so many poetical displays by young, coherent, sensitive G.I.s that I'm a little callous. One or two of the poems I liked, although I don't consider any of them true elegies. If Al lives through the war, he'll either be an insufferable poetical prig, or good. As for the Huxley, you really put on a good show... including the booklet. I wish I'd seen it, in a way. . . .

I'm happier than I can say that you like the new job. It sounds good. I'm anxious to see you, and your new setting. I may be in Los Angeles on Valentine's day... for some sort of Cresta Blanca business and a lot of dentistry... and I'll call you if I can. The trips are hectic... I try to do three months' business in a few hours, and am in chaos. But it's almost impossible to find anyone who can stay more than overnight with the baby. I spend most of my time on the road...

Which leads up to: when can you and Fay come out? How about the weekend of Feb. 25–26–27? I hate to sound so popular, but it's literally true that the one bed (You'll like me now, because I have a big bed for you instead of those wretched bunks)... the one bed is spoken for far in advance. I have no illusions about my own charms... people want to see the baby, and sit by the fire, and have me cook for them! But I am VERY ANXIOUS to see you and Fay... and out here. Do you realize it's been well over two years since the last time? It's the same lovely, peaceful place... a few more ghosts have been laid, and we've changed surely, but it hasn't. I'll write to Fay today, to see *when*. . . .

I wish you'd re-read the book, as you threaten... AND write to me again, about what you think. The first letter was good. It made me think. Some things I couldn't agree with, but the fact that you felt them, even temporarily, was important to me. . . .

My dear, I'll *never* worry about your juices drying up. You'll always know when it's time to thumb your nose at Academia and all the other desiccators... and how to suck their sweet honeys from them. . . .

The story about Eda is, as far as I can find out, completely lost. Perhaps it is just as well... it was a painful piece of writing, but one I had to do, willynilly. I am very glad it was not printed. If the copy that went to New York turns up I'll send it on, and you can burn it for me after you've read it.

... And here I've deleted two and a half full pages of discussion of things you said, mainly about Fisher. I knew when I was writing them I'd better not... and then I had to bathe Anneli and make some telephone calls, and when back here I was sure I'd been right in the first place. Sometime I can *say* them to you.... It is enough that I may be able to see Al and talk to him and have him talk to me as if we were both of us straightforward mature people, stripped of all the ugly, twisting claims of religions and otherwise. He is, and always will be, one of the best things in my life.

No, you never read about Jacques before, I'm sure. I only wrote about him last summer... and not all, of course. I hope he is dead now, or in Africa.[1]

Yes, I think skullduggery has two elles, but the publishers said no. And, re publishers, *Serve It Forth* is out again, in a new format, and, as far as I can tell, just about as stillborn as the other. Why in hell do publishers publish? In this case, I believe it was a question of copyrights and such.... Too bad. And it makes me feel like Zane Grey, to have another edition!

Yes, I'm all for another exhibit of Tim's stuff. Let's lay plans. It should be smaller than the last.

Larry, I'm so very anxious to see you... soon, too. I don't think you need to worry about staying honest... and I don't either, really... but a lot of people are putting pressure on me to write cheap stuff and make piles of dough. I don't *want* piles of dough... just enough to feed myself and a couple of children... and I *won't* turn out snide words. Well... this is better saved until we meet.

Love—

....

San Francisco, California[1]   *30.iii.44*
To: Lawrence Clark Powell

Dear L:

I've wanted to answer your letters ever since they came. I've been both busy and lazy, leading a strange life of motherdom and giddy debauchery which has taken all my energy. I'm gradually coming into focus again... thank God, because I simply must tap out some more gastronomical nonsense to fill up a large hole in my bank book.

How good you are about the story! You give me great encouragement. I myself feel it's a real piece of work, but like you I'm very glad it wasn't printed in the last book. What you say about it helps a lot in my self-fearful plan to write a novel. I didn't put off sending it to you for any reason that I can think of... certainly not for fear you wouldn't like things I said in it.

I always wondered about Al and Eda. I think he was afraid of her, and also very much bewildered in a rather timid way about what she was in my life. Al had read so many books... and he knew so little! I hoped very much that she would seduce him in

1. Jacques appears in *The Gastronomical Me.*
1. MF's friend, San Francisco attorney Harold Price, suggested that she rent a house there for six months, which she did.

Dijon: I felt so sad about his not seeming to want to keep me there, and I felt that perhaps she could teach him something, open up new paths for him so that when I came back he would tread them with me. Perhaps that's a strange attitude for a young wife... but it's the one I had. . . .

Eda's aunt wrote to me that she had heard through the Red Cross that Eda and her friend were finally released from the camp (They were arrested in the north of France somewhere, where the Irish girl had bought a château and was renovating it), and were living in comparative freedom in Aix-en-Provence. Margaret said she wasn't allowed to send anything to Eda... meaning money, I suppose. I think that if E survived the camp without alcohol and without drugs, she may be strong enough to survive the rest of life and make it better than it looked to me in Paris. She really has great strength in her mind... badly flawed. (Have you read *Man Against Himself?* You should, if not.) . . .

This house is wonderful, with a garden full of cherry-trees, and a big room on the third floor that looks west into the Presidio and another park. There are tall pine trees. Ever since I came the sun has shone! Natives shake their heads in wonder. All the windows are open now, and I hear children playing in the park, and occasionally the sentry walks along the Presidio wall with his trained dog. San Francisco is a completely military town, high-pitched with emotion... one last drink, one last kiss, before the convoys pull all these men out like a stream of blood through the Golden Gate. I feel it very strongly.

I'm leading a giddy life, thanks to Price, some of his friends, and the Wine Institute. The latter puts a Packard (WITH GAS!) at my disposal, and I've already made trips to two fine small vineyards. Next week I go farther north, into Napa and Sonoma. I've tasted some of the best wines of my life, in the past two weeks. I'll never have a really fine palate, but I'm slowly learning a little.

I haven't written a thing. But I've thought a lot.

I don't think I can or should go back alone to Bareacres if I must leave SF on (Page Two... so you see I'm really writing a LETTER this time, as you instructed...) April 30. It was hard for me to leave, for many reasons, and now that I'm here I should stay for a time, but it's literally impossible to find a place to stay, and the owner of this really pleasant house insists that she wants to come back. Nobody can see why... she is a widow with two children overseas. I am trying thought-treatment on her, and if necessary will make a small wax image and stick pins in it.

Anneli thrives like a true twig of the green bay tree... not at all pretty, but with such a strong and exciting personality. I don't know how I got along without her.

Give my best to Gordon when next you see him. I hope I'll meet him again... but when I consider the insidious ways of wives, both great and small, it sometimes seems doubtful.

I am the cat who walks alone, huh?

It's the next day now, and the first cold grey one. And the furnace has gone out. Ho hum, as my mother loves to put at least once in each letter. (I'm still glad I'm here.)

Love—

Bareacres   *23.ix.44*
Hemet, California
To: Lawrence Clark and Fay Powell

Dearest Fay and Larry...

Thank you, Fay, for the encouraging note. It came at the rightest moment. I wish more people would be so generous of themselves as you were when you wrote it.

I am in a quandary, to put it mildly, and need your advice. Some time ago, as a member of the Writer's War Board, I volunteered my services for war-bond rallies for a period of "3 or 4 days." I find now, summoned perfunctorily by the treasury department, that I'm expected to leave about October 1st for at least two weeks and about December 1st for at least the same length of time. You can imagine what this has done to my well-laid plans for a peaceful autumn. And worse, what about the show[1] scheduled for Dec. 1? Should we put it off? Should I get everything organized and leave it in the hands of people who would meet your requirements, Larry? What shall we do? I hate to add this to the multiple problems of both of you, but really need your advice. I don't feel I can get out of the WWB. For a person who hates crowds and planes and speeches and noise as much as I, it is a strange form of patriotism to have thrust upon me... but I feel it is the only thing I *can* do. I am in a kind of coma of fear at the thought of it. Probably by December I'll be calloused. I hope so. But in the meantime the show is brewing, and in a way it is as important as war. Anne Parrish sent pictures, which for some reason I've not had the courage to uncrate. I know they are good. There's a fine little collection waiting. Should we put it off until Spring? I am bushed, buggered, bulloxed, bitched, and bewildered. Help!

I leave Oct. 28, so write or telephone collect or wire collect. If you telephone make it person-to-person in case I am marketing or tending a neurotic friend in the Valley or some such thing.

The baby gets more exciting by the minute, and I could howl aloud at the thought of leaving her even for ten hours, much less ten days. She walks everywhere, has six teeth, and sings to the new moon.

Much love to you all...

Bareacres   *16.iv.45*
Hemet, California
To: Lawrence Clark Powell

Dear Larry... thanks for letting me see your interesting Letter. You sound very paternal in it!

A note from Connes says he has written you fully of his "petites aventures" and that you'll no doubt pass it on to me. I'd appreciate seeing it when you have time.

1. Second show of Dillwyn Parrish's paintings mounted by L. C. Powell and exhibited at UCLA

I've been ill for about six weeks, and am pulling up stakes for a time... taking the baby and Elsa[1] to New York until perhaps October. The past 6½ years have done more to me than I realized. Hal thinks my escape is wise, which reassures me. We leave as soon as I can wangle the reservations, probably within a week. I shan't see you before I go, but I hope you'll write to me... 165 East 49th Street. I've turned my back on MFKF for months at least, and plan to sleep and read and walk, and look at pictures, and go to the out-door concerts and ride on river-boats. (I have some very nice elderly people to live here and comfort Butch.)

My best to you all, always.

....

WESTERN UNION TELEGRAM   NEW YORK NY MAY 21 1945
L C POWELL—THE LIBRARY,
UCLA—

TERRIBLY SORRY ABOUT DELAYING CONNES LETTER BUT AM IN
DAZE OF AMUSEMENT EXCITEMENT HAPPINESS BECAUSE I
ACCIDENTALLY GOT MARRIED SATURDAY TO DONALD FRIEDE BLESS ME GHUCE
FAY AND GOSLINGS MUCH LOVE—

....

New York, New York   *28.v.45*
To: Lawrence Clark Powell

Dearest L....

Your letter made me feel even finer. I am increasingly rich and full of well-being, and feel that I have once more proved my incredible luck and found a good man. This one I hope to grow old with. Yes, it's Friede, once the other half of Covici... now the NY story editor for A and S Lyons... a very subtle complex man who is a great challenge to me. I want you to meet, which of course will happen.

What wonderful news about your land, and about the house in the meantime! I envy you. We have the apartment of some friends (the MacKinlay Kantors) for three months, and then, up to now, a shallow cave in Central Park. But I can't worry... not even about Bareacres and the pictures....[1]

I'm sorry about keeping the letter so long. And I'm sorry that this is such a meager note. I am swamped with baby at the moment... Elsa has gone away for a few days. What an odd "honeymoon"... Donald trotting back and forth to his hotel, catching fleeting sights of me between the strung-up diapers and empty milk-bottles! But it doesn't seem to matter at all.

He has much the *same* power Tim had, of making life very real for everyone. And he is fun. He's half German and half Russian, and has several marriages and an overfull life behind him. But so have I. We approve of this marriage and this life....

My love to you all... and I hope we meet soon....

1. Elsa Purdy, neighbor, friend, now nanny to Anne
1. Dillwyn's paintings

         M.F.K. Fisher: A Life in Letters

Bareacres   *30.i.46*
Hemet, California
To: Lawrence Clark Powell

Dearest Ghuce...

I never feel distant and you shouldn't either. We both know too much for that....

I hope that what you hint at is good. Certainly a full heart is, even with pain.

I grow more tub-like and placid daily, but even so am working fast on the novel, and it is so easy and fun after that damned anthology that I feel almost guilty about it.[1]

I have no illusions about its place, if any, in what is still somewhat laughingly called Literature... but is that bad?

When will we meet? There is still no plumbing... and as for me, I move cautiously from bed to kitchen to desk, and go to bed at 7:30 exhausted.... It might be dull for you. We'll see. I'll tell you how it is if and when we ever can flush a toilet proudly for you. Certainly it would be for nobody if not you....

Love...

Bareacres   *26.xi.46*
Hemet, California
To: Lawrence Clark Powell

Dearest Ghuce...

I'd hoped before now to send you a copy of *Here Let Us Feast*, but there seem to be shipping complications. So this note brings you, at least, all my thanks for your unfailing help and generosity.... I rooted that Golden Cockerel collection out of the rare-book room in NY, and gleaned some fine little things from it, thanks to you. I hope you'll like the book. I have no feeling about it, except a profound relief that it's done with. It was, for many unavoidable reasons, a tiring and even unpleasant task.

The old wives' tales about what reproduction does to the female brain are true, in my case, and I've been a zero ever since Kennedy sprang forth. I'm finally coming out of my dream, thank God, and if all goes well I'll have the novel ready to type before Christmas. I hope you'll like it. I can't possibly tell whether it's good... but at worst it will serve to convince people that I'm right about not being ready to do a good one yet!

The translation is in limbo until I finish the novel.[1] Then I'll really have to steam at it, to get it done and the introduction too, by July. I feel increasingly inadequate about ever getting anywhere near Brillat-Savarin's French with my English... but at least I haven't much competition!

. . . Are you having a few free days at Thanksgiving? We head for Whittier tomorrow, that fills me with confusion, but it will be fun once we get there, complete with such familial necessities as pureed zucchini and bottles and such....

1. MF's and Donald's daughter Mary Kennedy Friede was born on March 12, 1946. The novel MF was working on was *Not Now but* Now; the anthology was *Here Let Us Feast*.
1. MF's translation of Brillat-Savarin's *Physiology of Taste*

Please send me your home address when you remember.... Love... and the book will be sent as soon as it comes....

....

Bareacres   *8.ii.47*
Hemet, California
To: Lawrence Clark Powell

Dear Ghuce...

Thank you so very much for the handsome little book... it is a good addition to my collection but that isn't the main reason I like it, as you know....

Yes, Richerand was a sawbones all right, but I wish I could find more than what's in B-S about him. It still astonishes me that all those gossipers of the period were so close-mouthed about B-S and his intimates. Of course he was pretty small potatoes... until a few months before his death, anyway. What I've done so far on the intro is turning into a series of speculations... why didn't he marry, & & &?

I'm getting really steamed up about the period, damn it, and may find myself caught in some sort of book about it. . . .

We await *Quintet* eagerly. Donald may not read it until he finishes his book,[1] which will be in a month... he's afraid of being discouraged or something! Houghton Mifflin has shied away like a startled Boston nag from the first half of the book, much too nasty, succès de scandale, & & &, all of which has for various reasons amused D highly and released him from a lot of restrictions and in a real sense put new life into him, so he's charging ahead and turning out a fast and extremely interesting book... maybe not a true novel, but a first-hand picture of sex in the 20s and what it did to people.... You'll be interested in it. When next we meet we'll talk about the reactions of people to any thoughts or discussion of those days, which most of them seem to prefer to think of in terms of raccoon coats, harmless hi-jinks, all that. The one section of my book that has worried everybody is laid in 1927, and it shocks, outrages, upsets them.

NASTY, they fear... MYMYMY

I just finished, and I mean *finished*, whatever revising I'm going to do. It will be out in the Fall. Of course I'll send a typescript to you as soon as I get one back.

Love... and thank you for the book...

....

Bareacres   *22.ii.47*
Hemet, California
To: Lawrence Clark Powell

Dear Larry:

We had lunch with George Macy[1] in La Quinta yesterday. I had already swung around to his idea about a kind of marginal-gloss type of running comment, much as

1. *The Mechanical Angel*
1. George Macy was editor and publisher of the limited-print edition of *The Physiology of Taste*.

I was opposed to it at first: I am increasingly aware that except for the aficionados, much of B-S is pretty tedious stuff. As Macy says, of the 30,000 basic sales to his subscribers, perhaps 3,000 have even heard of the dear old boy. So... we talked some about the typography, which Meynell will do, and a lot about the illustrations, which to everyone's relief, Picasso can't do because of other commitments. Macy is flirting with the idea of Covarrubias, which I can't see at all.

And when we got home, here was the 1852 illustrated edition, which I do thank you for sending. It is *exactly* what I want... either actual copies of its etchings, or modern imitations of them in the same lusty style by a good man. I called Macy last night (He's terribly impressed at my knowing anyone who can get books from the L of C for me! And so am I!!), and have committed myself to doing something which I know is an imposition on your confidence and god knows what else, and I hope you'll forgive me and I promise never to abuse your kindness again: I am sending the book to Macy at the Ambassador Hotel in Los Angeles, where he arrives tonight. It will go by special delivery. He promises that he will return it to you on or before February 27. He says to tell you that he accepts full responsibility in every way. All of which does not alter the fact that I may have done something inexcusable. The more I think of it the scareder I get....

Meanwhile all my thanks for sending it to me. I can't tell you how relieved I am to have something tangible to back up my pleas for exactly the kind of illustrations that are in it. I simply can't see the book done in flashy Artzybssheff, for instance....

The work goes plodplodplod. Love...

....

Bareacres   *26.iii.47*
Hemet, California
To: Lawrence Clark Powell

Dear Ghuce...Good to get your note, as always.

Don't worry about the present slough... put the whole thing away for a time, I'd say. It's done. Gradually you will begin to twitch to work on it again, and with a new clear focus. I'll wager on that....

We'll send the ms. in a few days, as you direct. D will write you about it. I read it after I'd plowed dutifully through Steinbeck's latest stinker, and it seemed so honest, so straightforward, so *good* and reassuring as writing after Clay-foot John's book, that I felt jubilant. Of course it raises strong ghosts to haunt me... the way you write about places I've known is so clear, too clear at times. As a *novel* there are weaknesses in it, as you know. I could wish for the "feeling" of it that you stayed in France, or perhaps put the London episode in the middle... it jars a little, that change of locale and therefore of feeling, pace, whatever.... But it's good, and I'm really proud of it and you. And terribly excited about what you've done now... because you'll be even better. You're wonderful with Women, Ghuce....

Donald has been really laid low... stayed in Pasadena for a week to be near Hal.

He's still wobbly and at times in pain... something like gravel in his kidney... but is much better and is planning to get back to work soon. His novel is in NY... of course Houghton Mifflin is violently against it, and we wait to see other reactions. Meanwhile D is lining up a series of articles, which will be very good for him.

My book comes out this fall... is now at the printers'. It's called *Not Now But* Now, in spite of antagonism from the sales dept. A section of it, pretty well butchered, will be in the June *Town and Country*.

I have sent a scant half of B-S to the typist to be forwarded to Macy. Donald's trouble has put off the deadline a good month, but there's no use worrying about it. It's a brutal job, and one that keeps me on the verge of jitters. Never again, even for bread-and-butter...

Greetings, all that, and thank you for letting me see the ms. again.

Love—

Will start returning books to Library soon

....

Bareacres   *15.vii.47*
Hemet, California
To: Lawrence Clark Powell

Dearest L...

I have read the book, and it will be returned to you as you direct, as soon as Donald, who is away now, has seen it, which he is anxious to do.

It is impossible for me to read it dispassionately, of course. I must do it both as an intimate friend and as a fellow-craftsman, and at the risk of sounding noncommittal I'll say only the uppermost thoughts I have about it in each category.

It is good. It reminds me of an early Cellini, in that the design is *all there*, even though you know that in a later Cellini that design will be more heavily worked, more deeply accented. It is complete, and the intricacies of the development are so subtle that they are almost invisible until the whole story has been read. I like that and admire it.

The one criticism I am making is that there seems a contradiction in the way you have pictured Julie as a woman of great dignity and poise and even depth, a woman of obvious sensitivity, after some fifteen to twenty years of living with a man who, in spite of your charitable attempts to make him attractive by calling him "merry-faced," is almost a joke-paper caricature of a boorish, stupid, crass, brutal oaf. Of course it is understandable that there may be some idealization of the woman, and endless loathing of the man... but a novelist must not be the prey of his own dreams. If this is fiction, and apparently it is since you have invented names and so on, it cannot be good if you cheat on such a basic thing as your personal feelings toward your characters. And I do not feel that any woman, no matter how basically fine, can live for fifteen years or even fifteen days with a brute and emerge finer instead of marred by that intimacy.

All this brings me to what is not a criticism but a comment. I have always wondered why, in these secret books of yours, you feel you must invent names and all that? Does it give you a feeling, no matter how false, of invisibility, of security? Have you ever tried writing a *whole* story in something like the "journal" you often refer to? Why must you assume a false name, and give one to each of the characters, and make "Fruhling" a widower in Beverly Hills and so on? Since the books, you insist, are hidden books, would they not have a force and a rhythm about them which they now lack, if *nothing* were lied about? As I say, I simply wonder about this, as one writer considering another... I don't mean in any way that your system is wrong.

I'm so proud, Larry, that you think I did anything to encourage you to work. You are a good writer... and the intensity, as well as the technical skill, which you show here is so infinitely greater than in the last book, that I am *excited*. God knows I wish I could feel the same about myself....

Thank you for letting me feel myself a part of *your* progress, at least. Keep on. Renoir had nothing on you, in his basic method at least!...

I enclose another letter, to you and Fay.... Love—

....

Bareacres   *15.vii.47*
Hemet, California
To: Lawrence Clark Powell
Dear L...

Thanks for your good note. Your jaunt north sounds fun, but exhausting, from the reports we've had from our local librarian. I wish I'd had my wits more about me... my good friend Jessica McLachlin of the Wine Institute wrote about the trip up to the vineyards, and in case you or Fay went on it I'd have liked you to give her my love. Maybe you met anyway. She's a good girl... married to a fine doctor, too.

My book is out on the 15th. I expect the copies today. I shiver.

Here's what is happening chez Friede, but it is top-drawer confidential until after August 4, for various political reasons which I needn't go into: Donald has got out of his contract with Lyons, and as of this date will be head of a new story-department for a new small very rich agency in Hollywood. It is an exciting job for him, since he has to have one at all, and promises a year or two of hectic activity with a lot of literary prima-donnas, which is right up his alley after some 25 years of little else. He leaves for NY on July 31, to line up his stable... all very secret until he arrives there of course.

And I, loyal wife-and-mother, go up to Hollywood while he is away and try to find a house big enough for the four of us, Butch, all the manuscripts Donald will have to read and the authors he will have to entertain... and MFKFisher! What a rat-race! We dread it like the pox... but since we must do it we are determined to have as much fun as possible at it, with the weekends our very own for fun alone with the children, and the rest of the time full to the top with our various professional lives. I am sure we can manage it.

We plan to keep Bareacres open and functioning.... It is imperative that the children feel that this is their home, right now.

Anne will be able to go to some sort of pre-school, which will be a very good thing.

And best of all we'll be able to see a very few people like you-all, and Hal, from whom we're pretty well cut off, out here.

I am working like mad, trying pretty futilely to finish the translation by the end of the month. And Donald, goaded into a lather of delight by a very enthusiastic letter from Knopf, has written some 40,000 words in the last ten days, on his book of personal experiences during the 20s and 30s. It is extremely amusing and intelligent and lively stuff. I just finished proofing the first third of the book. He hopes to have the whole first draft to take back with him. You will like it, I know. The two novels have been shelved, needless to say... reactions ranged from outraged horror to well-intentioned doubt, and D said to hell with them.

All of which pointed up the inescapable fact that we can no longer live on "nothing a month." My own income is far from stable since I turned my back on steady hacking, at Donald's insistence, and anyway it wasn't good for Donald to know that what bills got paid were being paid by The Little Woman.

So the move. So we'll see you soon! If life is a circus, our act could certainly be billed as The Four Fantastic Flying Friedes!

It will be good to see the boys again. I can't quite believe that Normie has a motor-bike! I think it's fine, and managed to put a spike in Anne Kelly's mistaken refusal to let her boy learn to drive, by telling her about it....

Your garden sounds wonderful. That's another thing that will be nice about living near the Coast... I can exercise my green thumb a bit, unless it's far too late after the years out here with no water.

The only thing that nags me a bit, in all these chaotic plans, is what will happen to Fisher. I have at least ten more weeks of hard work on the Brillat-Savarin, which was due in NY on July 11. And then I am keen to start a book which I haven't dared even mention to Viking, since it can't be published for an indefinite number of years! And they are very much excited about my old-age book! Well... sufficient unto the day...

Love to you all. Donald will get in touch with you soon about the material he has from the Library....

<hr />

Bareacres   *10.viii.47*
Hemet, California
To: Lawrence Clark Powell

Dearest Ghuce... Thank you for the Western *Books.* I am glad to have it, and know D will be too.

The call to Fay was spontaneous.

D got your letter and felt fine about it. He called this morning... everything is even better than he, the incurable optimist hoped for... he has Knopf, Viking, Dial, Scribner's, Houghton Mifflin, on and on, solidly behind him, and they all seem to be saying Thank God DF is back and he can both read and write. To add to it Knopf is crazy about his book, which is scheduled for Spring, and *Esquire* has bought a lot more of it... cautious Smart....

Forgive this jumpy portable, plus my bad typing...

Your letter did me much good. As *Always*. . . .

I don't reveal myself in this book[1] any more than... as much as... I do in an article for *Harper's Bazaar*. Or in a page of translating Brillat-Savarin. And you can say that is completely. Or not at all. But whatever it is, it is naked.

I was deeply interested in what Fay said on the telephone. I'll tell you.

I'm glad you as un vrai amateur appreciated my occasional "betrayals" of my sex. Wait. Ghuce... some day I'll write better, and you'll like it better.

As for KA Porter and VW[2]... they can and have and will and ad eternitas (or is it *am?*) write rings around and around me. You know that. I want to be good, but I also want children and love and stress and panic and in the end I am too tired to write with the nun-like ascetic self-denial and concentration it takes. If I live to be fifty... ah, that is my song... if I live to fifty I'll know how to write a good book.

The book: No the time-fantasy as you call it was my own idea and worried hell out of my publishers. But I had to do this book this way. The next will be better.

Just wait.

I love your letter. It gives me courage. Forgive this hacky writing... I'm about to get Anneli and the fifteen-year-old Hazel into the car and go to Hollywood... we need a nearer roof over us! Oh What dreadful smudgy elegance we could rent for three times what we make! Oh I love you for cocking your snoot at me and keeping on looking up at the birds in the sky.

....

Los Angeles, California   *27.i.48*
To: Lawrence Clark Powell

Dear Ghuce...

Here is a carbon of my foreword and afterword to the translation, which I think you might like to see. Will you please return it?

Sorry about Fay's father... such things are tough, no matter how circumstances have seemingly prepared us not to find them so....

We are in turmoil, which I'll tell you about soon... are trying to figure *how* we can escape from this place to Bareacres, and still keep ourselves and the children even meagerly fed. We hate this town, most of the people in it, what it does to the few good ones including ourselves, what the climate does to our bodies, what the life does to *our* life... all very destructive, and since we are no longer chicks we want to drain as much joy as we can from the fast fleeting... So... Turmoil. One thing: Donald is definitely

1. *Not Now but* Now
2. Katherine Anne Porter and Virginia Woolf

out of the agency business, thanks to fantastic things which you'll also hear from us, and we are hoping to avoid unpleasant legal stuff while we try to line up enough hack-work to keep us fed. One thing about Life With Friede, there's never a dull moment!

All very exciting... I thrive on it.

I hope I see you very soon.... Call me if and when....

Love—

<hr>

Bareacres   *11.v.48*
Hemet, California
To: Lawrence Clark Powell

Dear Ghuce... That's a good thing about the wine-valley. I like it very much. It's moving too.

I owe you such a good letter too, from April 4! And my thanks as well for your heart-warming notes to Donald.

Well, this is the way it was: we came out on the 1st of March, leaving Georges[1] at the station on our last trip in the loaded wagon. We really fled. It was wonderful to be back again, and we felt powerful and freed. I blandly agreed to do a year's work for *Gourmet* in the next eight weeks or so. Then the Hearnsbergers[2] announced they were leaving for Arkansas! So I worked like a beaver until the middle of the month, to pile up a little backlog of material. And just about then Donald began to fall to pieces... half the re-sult of the bad studio-commissary lunches and such, and half the psychological wear and tear of l'affaire Blum.[3] It was very rough... he was a sick pup, but trying to stay ver-tical because I was doing all the cooking, laundry, babies, all that. But Hal gave one look at him, about the first of April, and tossed him in the back of his car and put him in the hospital. He was there for three weeks. I felt too tired and too jittery about being so far away from him with no human company but the two children, so I simply closed things up here (no mean feat, what with tropical fish, cats, dogs, and so on to be cared for), and went to Whittier. That was not easy either... Mother has a nurse there all the time now, and a very erratic cook, and so on and so on. Well, we all lived through it somehow, but I didn't even write to you because I was in no mood for friendship... you understand. Now we've been home again for two weeks, and it is pure heaven. Donald was discouragingly weak at first, and still takes a long rest in the middle of the day... but he looks and feels better every minute, and is full of force again. He had a very tough time... bad pain, all that. He is the better for it, in many ways... purged of Blum among other poisons.... We are living in complete simplicity. It's fine to be alone, with-out the so-called "help" of anyone. We have a good schedule worked out: I come over here[4] and work from 8 to twelve, and D makes beds and watches the children and so on. Then he rests until 2 and comes over here and works until about 6, while I am

1. Georges Connes
2. Caretakers for Bareacres
3. She's referring to French politics.
4. They had built a separate garage with a studio over it, called Lulu's Place; each used it as a workroom.

cooking, puttering, all that. It gives us more time with each other, in some mysterious way, and much more time with the children... and we are getting a lot done and living just the way we want to. D is on a pretty limited diet, of course, which I enjoy. I have had two of three expected families of kittens, and one of pups... my fish thrive... I have even caught up on my mag deadlines! As for D, he just sold another story to *Esquire*... stinky market, but good pay... and although we are horribly in debt we feel as calm as crickets about it. And that is the story of us for the past two months, and of why I haven't written. All is well once more.

You ask about B-S... it's been announced very flossily in the new Limited Editions brochure... must be for late this year or early next. Sauvage[5] did finish the new illustrations before he died. *Gourmet* wants to publish six long excerpts from it, beginning in November, I think, and using my glosses. I hate the idea. I have always felt uncomfortable about those damned glosses. But I've been paid. So what can I say? . . .

Don't plan to come out this month... put it off until fall. We've waited this long and a few more months won't matter. It's mainly a question of energy... Donald still needs a lot of help to get through the days properly... rests, little bolsterings, all that... and I'm simply not geared, to be frank, to coping with any other people than him and the babies. By autumn things will be better organized, in every way. . . .

I hope to finish this *Gourmet* job before the end of the summer... can do about four articles a week when I am in good form... have contracted to do 26, one for each letter of the alphabet... am now ready for H. It's a banal idea, but inimitably Fisher, natch! Then... god only knows. I'm not at a very creative period... give too much of that élan vital to my immediate life, the children and Donald and puppies and kittens, all that. I don't worry... I have a good ten years to go, I think, and may write that book yet!

Love from me, and from us all. Write when you can.

....

Bareacres   *17.viii.48*
Hemet, California
To: *Lawrence Clark Powell*

Dear Ghuce... It's been too long since I last heard from you. Are you all right? . . .

I've been sweating like a slave, and my enlarged ms.[1] is at the Typist's... goes to Simon and Schuster on the 25th, and I hope they snap it. If not there are other good possibilities... although few publishers want a one-shot, which this has to be because of my Viking contract.

Pat Covici turned up unexpectedly last weekend... flew out to work with Gene Fowler on the Jimmy Walker ms. As I feared and expected, he whipped me into great enthusiasm about "the next book"... I simply balked at a novel... there are too many unimportant ones pouring out as it is, and I'm not mature enough yet to be anything *but* unimportant. So... and here you come in again... I am going to write my own pecu-

5. Sylvain Sauvage illustrated the George Macy edition of *The Physiology of Taste*.
1. *An Alphabet for Gourmets*

liar version of Madame Récamier! No American woman has ever done it, as far as I know... and that proud beauty was such a sexual and intellectual enigma that I'd love to put my own questions up to her... Did she or *didn't* she, with everyone from Napoleon to... to... to..? If not, why and how not? And so on. It means a hideous lot of research... all those witty refugees wrote letters like mad... Madame de Staël and so on. Well, Ghuce, do I pay enough state taxes to have one of your henchmen make me up available material in your stacks? I'm going to have to wear blinkers from the very beginning... sort out only the stuff that adds to my own picture of the *woman* as a product of her time, and let most of the fantastically rich *time* stay in the hands of all the historians who have already worked on it. But I want to read letters, memoirs, preferably in French... and Éd. Herriot's monument to Récamier in either Eng. or Fr.... that sort of thing. I know you have two books by Récamier's niece, in English. I have all the Brillat-Savarin stuff, of course... her cousin. I may find myself going back to Rousseau, for the refugee-mentality that shaped this next generation. I'll need memoirs and such, if any, of the painters etc.... Oh Lord... it frightens me. But if you or Mr. Vosper[2] have any suggestions, good or bad, about how to find out *what* is available, shoot them on to me.

I can come up in September, I think... we have People now, a very pretty sweet-spoken girl and her machinist-husband... they yearn for a large family, so I'll probably be midwife to something besides kittens and puppies, a pleasant change. (Donald calls this Fertility Hill, so Mary Janet has come to the right spot!)

What's going on?

Love—

....

Bareacres   *3.ix.48*
Hemet, California
To: Lawrence Clark Powell

Dear Larry...

It's a deal: you say I am a great creative force in Modn Litrechure. I say you are a great executive force in Modn Liebries et al.

Thank you... seriously.

I hope I get the thing,[1] because I am a little weary of holding back the budget with a flood of hack-stuff.

Meanwhile I am all set to stamp on Juliette Récamier's fair white body... for a price. Either S&S or Viking has taken the last magnum opus... I don't know which, and care only insofar as S&S pays the fatter advance....

I'm to be right up there with the prize prune jam and the blue-ribbon milch-goats at the LA County Fair, as of the 11th for 3 days... so if we can stagger the distance between Pomona and you, we'll come to see you... with fair warning of course.... The

2. Librarian at UCLA

1. A Guggenheim scholarship for which MF had applied with help from L. C. Powell. (She did not get it.)

M.F.K. Fisher: A Life in Letters

county pays the reasonable bills, so D and I plan to rent a motel cabin somewhere near the fair. It sounds fun in a rather confused way. (Oh... I'm on the wine-jury....)

Love to you all. I hope you're above or beyond the smog in this slight case of heat... I am sitting in a *pool* of myself....

....

Bareacres   *18.ii.49*
Hemet, California
To: Lawrence Clark Powell

Dear Ghuce... Thanks for your card. I've meant to make some sort of like gesture in your direction, but what a time! I think we're past it now... one of those periods of chaos that seem to hit families now and then. Can't go into it... but it involved our moving in toto to Whittier, Edith in hospital 5 weeks, Rex gravely threatened with pneumonia... interviewing nurses, some 47 horrible sadistic drunken old bags... ho hum. But now we're home again. Peace, it's wonderful! And the Great Freeze seems over, at last... we've had to lay more than 500 feet of new pipes and so on... but now the air is quivering, le sacre du printemps for fair... birds busting with song, cats making kittens, seeds sprouting... it's hard to stick to the typewriter....

I'm far behind on the Récamier, needless to say. I'm doing a re-write on an article for—*House Beautiful*. I spent two days in a new kind of sanatorium for borderline insanity cases in young women... as soon as it swings into focus I have a very important story there.

We're in wonderful shape. The kids are beauties, in every sense of the word.

Edith is home again, complete with nurse and oxygen tent. What a grim slow way! Rex will recuperate here as soon as he can make the trip. He was laid low, and is in a kind of cosmic rage... does not admit or even *know* that he is 72, if still of solid oak. . . .

We're trying to swing things to give us several months now and then in SF. D has turned down a really fat Hollywood job... nothing is worth what it entails. He may go down in history as The Man Who Wouldn't Go Back to H*******! A dubious fame...

Let's count on meeting, before too much longer. Here all depends on Rex's stay, and his general health, and so on. I'll let you know....

Love—

....

Edith Holbrook Kennedy died on May 9, 1949.

....

Whittier, California   *30.v.49*
To: Lawrence Clark Powell

Dear Ghuce... thanks for your letter. It said all anyone could say about Edith... I've saved it for Rex to read when he's wanting to. So far he hasn't. He's in good shape, thanks to the briefing E gave him for just this period....

Donald has been desperately ill... had a big surgical job a few days ago and may be all right now... is making a good recovery. I hope we'll be home again in a week or ten days.

I'm tired, but all right.

Your life sounds very full and exciting. Good!

Love to you all...

Anxious to read your Zeitlin[1] thing—

....

Bareacres   *28.vi.49*

Hemet, California

To: Lawrence Clark Powell

Dear Ghuce . . .

Those galleys were for *An Alphabet for Gourmets*, which Viking will publish this autumn. It is the 27 articles I did for *Gourmet* Magazine, blown up, annotated, given a good shot in the arm. I don't know what Viking will do with it... it's a hot potato for them and they only took it in order to get my Récamier book, which I have not yet written and which I cannot deliver by the August deadline, thanks to a great many accidents-in-time which I need not go into.

I wish we could meet. I miss you and need to talk with you now and then.

Hal took care of me for a few days... I got too tired and wire-thin emotionally... I'm all right again but am in suspension, trying to get good people to live here with me... I am horribly late on deadlines and am typing "all hours"... I have cut myself loose from Donald for a time... talk to Hal if you wish, about it... D has been in a mental hospital for some weeks... is pulling out of it gallantly... this is between thee and me... I think he will go to New York. He is now at the Ranch in Whittier, and is working hard. He has had a hellish time.

Write when you can.

Love to you all.

....

Bareacres   *19.vii.49*

Hemet, California

To: Lawrence Clark Powell

Yes, I need a transfusion. Meanwhile I care for myself as if I were a rare uncooked egg, everything very gentle-like. And your letter did me much good... perhaps like a coat of wax on the shell.

I am truly happy for you, Ghuce. You have gone over the unavoidable hump of life, which can send you either up or down and for you it is UP. I shall see to it that it is for me too. . . .

1. L. C. Powell wrote a piece about Jake Zeitlin, a bookseller and bookstore owner and lifelong friend of Powell's and MF's.

I hope you do something about Ll. Powys.[1] Here is a bit from a letter of his, which I keep on my bulletin board. You probably know it:

"Writing to be worth anything must have the thumb-mark of life upon it, heavy and spatulate... mock not the cobbler by his black thumb! It must smell of sweat and be uplifted by what Shakespeare named so ruefully 'the brutish sting.' Really good writing has nothing to do with lamps. It uses a grey goose's feather for its mechanical expression but its true inspiration is derived from the bed, the ladle, the crib, and the coffin... part and parcel of a man's spiritual skin... life on the green earth under the golden sun."

I plan to live here as quietly as possible. Then maybe later, when the air is cooler (November is the best month of the year), you can come down?

Love . . .

....

Bareacres   *8.xi.49*
Hemet, California
To: Lawrence Clark Powell

Dearest Ghuce...

Venus Anadyomene has risen again. I do thank you. It is soul-warming....

I'm in an understandable swivet, with ten dozen things to do IMMEDIATELY.

I plan to make my first trek westward on Thursday, with the kids and their books and such-like.[1] If I can, I'll come back a day or two later for some more stuff... tropical fish, potted plants! My god...

Tell me... I have one useless Motorola player to hook into a radio and one desiccated table-model Victor (very fine tone, no changer)... do I have a tinker's chance of any kind of exchange on a very simple very inexpensive very practical player, principally for the kids, who love to listen to every record ever pressed, from Spike Jones to Toscanini? Something I could put upstairs at the Ranch...

It's ominous and beautiful here today, and I feel suspended amongst a thousand wheeling worlds.

twerk twerk...

Love...

....

Whittier, California   *18.xi.49*
To: Lawrence Clark Powell

I started in to be very tender and loving, and now I can't adjust the damned margin-spacing in this goddamned machine and I am mad and full of cuss words and ire and all that.

1. English author Llewelyn Powys
1. MF was moving back to the Ranch to care for Rex.

Oh darling and dearest Friend, do please come out if you can on the 30th. I told Rex about it and he said he'd like to see you, and so you know it will be very much en famille and that thought to me at this point is almost intolerable but by then maybe it will be all right.

I'm gradually getting things to rights. I haven't a cook, and I find it a tough full-time job to care for four people and a ten-room house, but it is rewardingly exhausting, as I know you understand. At night I go to bed almost too tired to be troubled.

Still I am troubled.

Yes, I know what you say when you wonder what may come next. So do I. Let us not be alarmed.

Ghuce, you must write hard. I can't, right now. I am passive, worn a little too thin by my daily tasks of love... with the children, the father, the duties of life. You too are worn thin, but in a different way. And you can withdraw in a way impossible to a woman, especially one as loving as I... and as in love.

Let me be "hale" and "sisterly," as well as what you now know. All is good....

God but that month would be good. Let us consider it done. Let us say we have had it. We both need it. But how can it happen except within us, thus apart, thus remotely together? We must make it, from the whole cloth. I would give much, and when I use that word I mean it, to have the month happen, a strange symbolical word MONTH, a kind of completion, a full swing of the planets. But I do not see it, in actuality.

You know (I'm re-reading your letter, a dubious pleasure I seldom indulge in, because of the aftermath of anguish)... you know the 30th will be fine. You'll have a plethora of my taciturn and sardonic father, my two bouncing virgins... I'll give you food you like and a warm fire and as much of myself as possible....

Yes, you could heal much and hurt none. I must let the knowledge that you *could*, and would, do the work. Can I do as much for you?

Kennedy Ranch, Whittier, California

Kennedy with John and David Barr and Anna at the ranch (1950 or 1951)

MARY FRANCES's move back to the Kennedy ranch in late 1949 left her responsible not only for her two daughters but also for her father, Rex—then a frail, brave, stubborn man dying of fibrosis of the lungs— and for the ranch itself, a decaying place threatened with extinction by the postwar building boom. She continued to write about food for two magazines and worked on a novella, which was published by a women's magazine. She helped Rex write his daily political column and took on as many editorial tasks as she could at the Whittier *News* in order to relieve him. These years devoted to the love and care of her family took their toll on her professional writing life, and she struggled throughout this period with depression and acute anxiety. The greatest contribution to her professional growth of this return to the ranch was in her growing understanding of old age.

Whittier, California   *17.ii.50*
To: Lawrence Clark Powell

Dearest Ghuce...

Howdedo . . .

Things go well here, and the new cook, a quiet firm motherly farm-woman, promises to be just about what we need (... although I am still shuddering at one of our opening remarks, when I told her we all like to eat lots of fresh vegetables and she said, "Oh,
ja... t'ings like potato pancakes and sauerkraut...").

Today there is a heavy grey cold fog... I can't even see the front hedge from my desk
and almost got lost, taking Kennedy to school. She'll stay all day and Rex won't be
home and I'll work like a beaver, typing a pretty good article I wrote yesterday and
perhaps tossing off some other bit of Deathless Prose... good for my amour propre as
well as my pocket book!

Donald returns to SF next week, and will come down for a weekend soon after... he
should see the children, and I hope to be able to talk amicably with him. People are
counseling me (unsolicited advice, I must add...) to "try it again" with him now that
he is temporarily well-monied.[1] I, on the other hand, feel that now I can and *must* come
to a definite arrangement of separation and/or divorce. I would like to live in SF for a
year or so, when I feel that I can decently leave Rex to his own devices again, and there
is no reason in the world why that city would not hold both Donald and me, and perhaps even pleasurably!

I have no reason, and certainly no wish, to keep him from enjoying the children as
much as possible, and I too would like to be able to dine with him, go to concerts with
him... but NOT run his house and all his very unstable emotions 24 hours a day! Perhaps I am being too sanguine?

I had a long and sadly troubled letter from Georges. Do you want to see it? I'll send
it on if you do.

We all say, come out soon again, Herr Doktor... and I think I can promise to be less
addled and raddled... domestic flurries had me on the run when last we met, as I need
not tell you! Would you like me to come in to lunch with you on one of your Clark[2]
days? We could meet in mid-passage, as it were....

Love...

Forgive this typescript, my elbow is better every minute but still creaks when I write
with a pen....[3]

....

Whittier, California   *6.iv.50*
To: Lawrence Clark Powell

Cher ami...

Your letter drove me slightly crazy... it was a great compliment to me and at the

1. Donald's mother had just died.
2. The Clark was a small research library in the UCLA system where MF and Larry would meet.
3. MF had broken her elbow.

same time it mocked me, and unjustly too. My only comment, right now, is that you are hardly the man to whom I can say, as I must postpone an appointment, "How about tomorrow?" You too are hard-to get.......

Damn, Ghuce... time fleets. Soon you will be gone, but London is no farther than Westwood, it seems to me.

Perhaps things are more in balance for me. I now have a "couple," which I've been fighting for ever since I came up here.... Rex loves it because he can deputize dull jobs like bringing in kindling. I don't know about the house, yet.... But I hope that before too long I can go away now and then. I even dream of flying to NY, along in early June... stay with the Covicis, buy a new frock, talk to somebody besides Rex (deaf and 73) and the kids (keen but under 7) and the current cook (dumb, if not actively nympho-klepto-schizo-alcoholic...).

Are you available? Please notify....

Well, Norah has another son, and is happy if haggard. Anne Kelly is unhappy but resolutely haggard. Rex is recovering noisily from a rhume d'hiver. My two kids are in fine shape. I myself am well. I have a couple of small jobs, one for the *SF Chronicle* and then that thing for Joe Jackson.[1] The gastro-literary column hangs fire or perhaps I should say ashes. I feel on the verge of a new lap in the race. Donald has finally cooled off after a voluble counter-attack against divorce, and will probably be down on April 19/, and 20 for the "settlement," which at this point he refuses to consider in any form of trust fund for the kids, which is all that interests me in any way. Ho hum, to quote Edith.

My new cook, an Ozark woman, belches. All the time. But she makes beaten-biscuits.

Love...

You know I can't write the way I want to. Perhaps when I get past this present hurdle I can. Meanwhile be patient with me.

If you feel like it, please call me on Monday. I have to go into Bev Hills to see Frumkes,[2] but will be home before 4. Perhaps I can come in to do a little work at the Clark, that week....

....

Whittier, California   *6. vi .50*
To: Dr. George Frumkes

Dear Dr. Frumkes:

Coming home today I continued my part of our conversation, of course, and managed to state a few things very clearly, at least to myself.

As a result of the hints you gave me today I can now say:

Dillwyn was life, for me. Life is sex, and sex life. Now Dillwyn is dead. Therefore sex, which is also life, is dead or at least means death.

1. Joseph Henry Jackson was the book editor for the *Chronicle*.
2. Dr. George Frumkes, the psychiatrist MF saw during this period

I want Dillwyn, but I cannot have him. I want sex, since I am still alive. But if sex means death to me, at times I want death.

However, I have a very strong sense of personal responsibility, especially toward people I love. I love my two children, and I most earnestly do not want to die as long as I can in any way help them grow. (Perhaps I am mistaken, but I honestly believe that if I could not deliberately create some such tie with life as they are, I would welcome death without a single regret. As it is, I shun it... as long as I remain in control of my impulses.)

Well... what do I do now? Obviously I cannot be alive with a ghost. But I must be alive, for my children and a few other people I love less fully but well. How do I stay alive most neatly, and with the least menace from these dreadful moments of flight? What do I do to get rid of them, to reconcile myself with life every minute of the day and not just $23^{1}/_{4}$ hours of the 24? Passing affairs are not the medicine, both because of my nature and of my circumstances: mature years, three past marriages, two small children, isolation in small town, professional duties... on and on. Do I marry MFK Fisher and retire with her-him-it to an ivory tower and turn out yearly masterpieces of unimportant prose? Do I study Yoga? Chinese? The making of Bombay curries?

Or just myself?

All I want now, in the world and my whole life, is to be able to get rid of such hells as assaulted me yesterday morning in San Francisco, and five days ago while I was taking the children to school. Unless I can, sometime one will hit me that will make my whole life meaningless and wasted, and I don't want that.

1:20 Friday.
Sincerely,

....

Whittier, California   *24.vii.50*
To: Lawrence Clark Powell

Dearest Ghuce...

I know you hate typewritten letters. I do too. But they are better than none at all, or so I do believe, and I want to thank you for sending me the extremely hideous (binding) but welcome June Bulletin. . . .

I am in a really strange period... winding up my rewrite of an old book, whipping out two emergency things for editors who have been patient with *me* in the past (just said yes to a desperate wire from Morton of the *Atlantic*...)... thank god I am increasingly tranquil or at least stable.... Rex almost died of pneumonia for a while... got home from the hospital three days ago and is incredibly weak but equally determined, and today got up and dictated some letters to Norah, who is his current manensis as I used to think it was spelled and pronounced.... He needs a lot of small attentions but it is so much easier than coping with a bored nurse (plus a grim cook & & &).... Norah has been wonderful.... I work, and *sleep*, like a healthy horse... I have neither time nor energy for moping.... I could easily mope a bit, for Bareacres is apparently condemned... *all* the springs are dry and I could neither rent nor sell but instead must probably strip the place, take out what fire-and-theft insurance I can, and abandon the place until the rain-gods forgive us our sins... eight years of drought!... at least I have a place to flee to... but my beloved valley is a tinder-box and I'm best out of it with two children.... As I say, I *could* weep.... Well, Donald was here for four days, fortunately just as Rex collapsed... he was a great help, but I counted the minutes until I could be alone again... the worst part is that he cannot and will not recognize that I distill the same subtle poison for him that he does for me... what a wasteful business! (I say that and then think of little Mary,[1] so sane and sweet, and know I'm wrong....)

I talked of you today, with Norah, with great tenderness and comprehension.

Love,

....

Whittier, California   *30.vii.50*
To: Lawrence Clark Powell

Dearest Ghuce... other phrases come to my mind, even my fingers, but I'll let that suffice... a quick answer to your more than welcome letter... you are and have always been a part of my life, and lately I have missed you keenly. Have no fear. As long as we both shall live... and as for that, as long as *either* of us lives.......

Yes, you go ahead, into the full '50s. I'll sit and watch, and wish I were with you, and know that in my own silent way I *am* with you.

The Rare Book thing seems to have come off very well. You know you have my congratulations.

I am glad you are in pain, really suffering, about pulling up all the roots. You should, if you are a real man, which you are. You must suffer. It is indeed the end of a rich part of your life, the family part with boys floundering about. I hope you and F can go on to be a strong interesting unit... she has done and is doing a fine job, and so are you. You are extraordinary people, and good together, and I need not tell you how much I hope that you will emerge from this present period of spiritual searching with a new strength together. Else, why fight so hard, why battle so many extraneous hungers and win out? I would have liked to be by the side of a familiar man, one scarred with my own wounds, one worn and even somewhat weary of *me*, but loyal. Al and I failed each other, I think... too young and ignorant. Then Death got Dillwyn, my mate. Now, indeed within a few days, I deliberately and stubbornly go through with the divorce from Donald. If we were fifteen years younger and alone I could perhaps cope with his tremendous spiritual demands, but tired as I am and with two tender babes to raise, I find it impossible... he sucks me empty without knowing he does so. So... here I am alone. I've always said that if I lived to be 50 I'd be all right, and now I think that since I've survived the past year, my 41st, I can survive *anything*.

I would like to be with you. The week on a beach in Baja California, the month in Greece, the year in London... the decades... Ho hum...

1. Kennedy was called Mary during her childhood and adolescence.

If it seems right, call and then come out... I'll tell you if things are not propitious here. But don't have it on your mind. It would be one more tiring duty, I'm afraid. Remember me. Write to me when you can. Dream of me, but not regretfully. Give my love to Connes. Ghuce already has it.

....

Whittier, California   *10.xii.50*
To: Donald Friede

Dearest D...

You've been gone but a few hours, and I think it wisest to write a note to you in the heat of combat, as it were, instead of more measuredly from Operation Numb.

Thank you for all the thoughtful and generous things you brought, and the ones you had sent, and the ones you have sent for the future.

Very soon after you left, Rex made his first remark, personal or otherwise, and said that I had been both tactless and heartless last night to discuss even tentatively the Christmas plans with you in the room and not included in them. I tried to explain that you and I were agreed upon such a course, but it was futile and I soon left off. Later, after a generous douse of rum, he said it was a pity for us to be apart, since the children so needed the two of us. That concludes any spoken comment.

I shall repeat, once and for all (How easily such phrases crop up in such emergencies as this!), two things. One: I am relieved for you, and happy, and I want this to be what you have so long looked for.[1] Two: I shall always regret that it was not meant for you to wait, for the children's lives if not ours, until you could be as I repeatedly hoped it would be... well for a year and able to provide for our living (That is, feed and clothe and lodge us from your earnings). Plainly that was not to be. All right. Go in good health.

I shall continue to live as honestly as possible. You know the present situation. And from what you may have learned of me in the past years you also know that when this is done with I'll go on with my whole heart for what I believe is best for the children. Without any bathos or self-dramatization I feel that they are much more important than I, except as I exist for them. You said that very well, a day or two ago. I have had an unusually full fine life, thanks in great part to you. I have deep wells to draw on.

Love.

....

Whittier, California   *23.iii.51*
To: Norah Kennedy Barr

Dearest N

... I have decided that at this stage of my life I am as obviously a letter-writer as other people may be alcoholics or benzedrine-boys. The need to use words and direct them toward a chosen person is almost physically urgent to me, especially in the

1. Refers to his meeting and courting Eleanor Kask

                                             M. F. K. Fisher: A Life in Letters

mornings. I have always liked it. When I was very young, eight or nine, I wrote every Sunday to Uncle Park. I can remember writing postcards and such-like to you and Dave, from boarding-school and boats and France. I wrote to Al as I thought he most liked to have me write. Then to Dillwyn I wrote without restraints. Increasingly I wrote chatty letters to Edith, trying deliberately to please and amuse her. When she died I got a note from Weare Holbrook,[1] with a cryptic message to me which I did not understand then, that when his own mother died he realized that there was not a god-damned soul left who cared whether he wrote a letter or not, and that it was a bitter empty realization. I had got into the habit of a daily note to Edith, but because of Donald's illnesses and absences could keep up a kind of imitation of my habit: he is fun to write to, for we share the same tricks of vocabulary, as do you and I. But now *that* avenue is blocked. I have an occasional hysterically rushed and plainly duty-bound letter from him, suave and smooth and hopeless as the throbbings of a skilled whore. I want for both our sakes to relieve him of that obligation, and can only do it by making my own letters less. That leaves you. I find myself wondering what my wordy brain will do with itself if and when you too withdraw from the field! My wonderings are not morbid, but are of course conditioned by this general atmosphere of restless change. In the mornings I can use up some of this strange energy by attending to the accounts, things like that. At night I go on furiously writing, sometimes very well and wittily indeed, as I take a bath or rub Rex's long cold stinking feet or move quietly from Anne's bed to Mary's and to my own again. The phrases and sentences and paragraphs and even chapters are as fluid and fleeting, as impossible to fix, as postcards of My Trip To Rome 1883 on a magic-lantern screen. And that is all right too.

I look up at this lengthy mumble and doubt very much that I send it to you.

Joe,[2] wheezing and pallid from the flu, totters noisily around the fireplace, scattering dust for Mrs. Brooks to brush up. At noon Marvin Lamont, still panting for some sort of TV show, comes to lunch. (Rex will be at Rotary.) The children are very happy in the sunshine, making an enormous paskha of mud and Chinese lilies (equal parts; mash and stir well). I'll make a salad of avocado and crab legs, and have a bottle of Gamay Rosé. Wow. Also ho hum. I was supposed to take the children to the Farmers Market to lunch with John Gostovich today but backed out... there are many reasons why, but I think the main was/is that I didn't want to go: I could hear myself being amusing and gay, tossing quips with Fred Beck,[3] exchanging reminiscences of Dear-Old-Oxy with Gostovich who was a freshman when I was a sophomore and I think has me firmly confused with Sis since he is gaily bitter about how he never joined a fraternity and Freeman[4] was a PhiGam. Murder. Also ho hum again.

I treated myself, unexpectedly... phone rang on that word... unexpectedly to a rather rough night at Bareacres, the first since I settled the atom-bomb problem, once and for all I like to think, the night Mary was with you at Sunset Beach. My trouble

1. MF's cousin
2. Joe Abegg, caretaker for the Ranch
3. Fred Beck was the editor of a culinary journal.
4. Bob Freeman, Anne Kennedy's college sweetheart

was pretty obviously made up of equal parts of fatigue, cramps, and an unconquerable wave of ou-sont-les-neiges-d'antan. It is basically depressing to realize that every time I go to Bareacres it is less mine, less of me, less of what I have made it and kept it for so long. Each time I leave, I take a car-full of the small thousands of possessions that made it mine and not simply a dust-filled mountain cabin. This time I brought back more records, the player, some music-books, a couple of cookbooks, some scarves, an old belt. And so it goes. And as always I found ugly signs of other people's unconsciously destructive tenancy: fewer glasses and sheets, greasy skillets, emptied bottles, filthy smudged wash-bowls. I did almost nothing to try to make the place look more the way I want it to be. For I know how futile and foolish that is.

We stopped at Elsa's for lunch. I took along the picnic and thought the kids and I would eat in a park or woods. Elsa had a gay little Easter-table out in the front yard, and her neighbor sneaked in and put pink eggs under the bushes. It was so pleasant.... Greta Bader[5] came in with a beautiful cake, much disturbed because the Blood Bank turned her down... high blood pressure. I enjoy her. She is a short thick woman of great poise, with beautiful teeth. We klatsched a little, she left, and the children and I seated ourselves at the pretty table in the sunshine. It was nice. I found myself growing annoyed at Elsa's prying into exactly what hour I had left Whittier, where I had gone, when, why, what for, with whom... when I got to Bareacres and what I did... what I heard from "New York and the newly-weds."[6] I chitchatted, recognizing my irritation and my weariness (a nuit blanche plus getting all Donald's pictures together for shipping plus plus plus...). I started to tell E about the proposed lunch today with John Gostovich. "What's his name?" she asked, her mouth full of hard-boiled egg. "John Gosto-vich," I said. "I wish he'd change it," she muttered in an astonishingly cross small voice, her eyes downcast. "Why?" I asked. I felt my face turn hot and red. She shrugged, still not looking at me but quickly at the two silent children. Her shoulders seemed narrower than I had ever seen them, very sloping and weakly and mean. Her mouth was full. "Jewish, isn't it? It's a Jew name, isn't it?" I thought well I must escape, not now but in the next months, and get away clear away for it is very bad for me very dangerous very wasteful to be as angry as sick-angry as I feel right now and I honestly don't know whether I can continue to speak nicely and sit here and not make a show of myself before the children but what I feel like doing is stamping out although I can't slam any doors which I have never done anyway for the simple reason that there are only trees and bushes and shadows to slam but god damn what made this happen? You know the way it goes, None. I was affronted by my own anger. In one way I felt it was justified, but reason told me that if I had not been tired I could have turned it into a silly gaffe, to be ignored or at least unappreciated. Instead, there I was simply pulsating with a cumulative rage which was using Elsa's stupidity as an excuse. I answered shortly for a few minutes. I am sure Elsa noticed it but I honestly don't think she has the faintest idea why. She probably felt herself very forgiving of my weariness and bad

5. Hemet neighbor
6. Donald and Eleanor Friede

M.F.K. Fisher: A Life in Letters

temper. Well, we left in a half-hour or so. I have thought some of writing to tell her why I was curt, for the few minutes I was. But I'll not do so.

....

Whittier, California   *27.iii.51*
To: Norah Kennedy Barr

Dearest N... A short run-over of the old game of Best-laid-plans-of-mice-and-men: it may interest you and if you can't read Compton-Burnett sired by Dreiser out of either Balzac or Tolstoy or Gide *every* day of the week, you can at least read me. (I have a review which I hope I remember to include, by the way....) (It reminds me for some reason of one Herbert Harris wrote of Dorothy Baker's *Trio* for the *News....*)

Rex is fretting, nicely and to me poignantly, about not having seen Walter[1] since his arrival in Pasadena ten days ago. So I'd arranged, and quite a bit of arranging it took, since Mrs. Brooks is moving this week, to have her take Mary home and then to Broadoaks at one today, and Rex and I would go to Pasadena for lunch and then to see W for a few minutes. Rex got quite a gallant gay gleam in his eye about taking me to the Stufft Shirt (It *is* spelled that way...), and said last night, in his usual ambiguous way, "Well, at least we'll get a good *lunch* out of it...." This morning Nan[2] sounded more dismal than usual, and it seems that Walter finally admitted, or perhaps confessed is a more appropriate word, that his bowels had not moved for some two weeks. Of course the two or three doctors who have attended him had not bothered to check on such a basic problem of feverish aged frightened patients (Chapter XXXIC in my unwritten diatribe!). Various violent purges were tried, with no results beyond exaggerating W's exhaustion. Last night Chuck gave him an enema. The picture haunts me: the dry sensitive little man, the groaning irrigated hulk on the bed, the fear of inevitable ugliness and stench. Nothing happened beyond that. So today Walter will either go to a hospital and be purged or a professional will come to the house. I urged Nan to do the first, if necessary and perhaps advisedly by ambulance. I told her again of Rex's admitted relaxation and quiet when he once got into a hospital bed and no longer fretted about disturbing people and subjecting them and himself to physical duties so easily taken care of by people he PAID to do it. I also urged her to let him stay there at least 24 hours, to rest. I did not tell her what I was thinking, that a man as enfeebled as Walter might easily have a very quick and dangerous reaction to something as drastic as a high colonic job. Well, now Rex will come somewhat jauntily home at noon, to toot off in the Minx (at his request) in one more proof of his durability... and I'll have to kill it. Ho hum. And here I am in my City Clothes... even a garter-belt yet!

Sis called yesterday, to say she had one of those sparkling gay good weekends... Sean is "happy" and was *very* attentive... Sis apparently saw a lot of Van and then took S to a giddy champagne luncheon somewhere and, due entirely to the fact that she was

1. Walter Kennedy, Rex Kennedy's older brother
2. MF's cousin and Walter's daughter, Nancy Newton

riding one of those ghastly cheap planes, which she will never never take again, she missed her plane and had to buy a completely new ticket on another and of course First Class plane. She didn't have time to wire Randy,[3] so he met her at one airport when she was landing at another, and although she had him paged by loud-speaker at *both* airports and also at the Biltmore, where she was finally forced to go in the regular bus, she discovered that he had simply gone on home! It must have been a happy meeting. I undoubtedly added a glandular fillip to her second homecoming, last night, by telling her that I had been what might be called lacking in Southern hospitality (I did not so phrase it) when Randy wove into my room the night before. I decided that I might as well present my version of the incident while it was still what might be called fresh. I have not yet heard from her today, and look forward either to complete silence or storms with equal passivity.

It is odd to tap out this silent klatsch to you, while Mary and a beat-up doll she has unearthed do what she calls acrobatters at my feet. . . .

Oh... I meant to tell you... Sis took one look at Chinatown but it was simply lousy with tourists... a luxury cruise-ship was docked, and there must have been at least two hundred obvious *tourists*.... They were all over everything....

We still have no wood. Rex has almost convinced himself that it is too late in the year to bother to order more, and last night went through the house flinging open doors, saying, "*We* don't need a fire!" How wrong he is! As of tomorrow morning a cord is to be delivered by an unknown Mexican, probably distantly related to Frank Martinez.[4]

I have not heard from Donald for about two weeks... had one dutiful letter after his marriage, to which I did not reply, for it was so agent-like in the main that I'd have found myself putting my address and social-security number after my signature. I am a little amused to find myself hoping that a letter will be in the next mail. It is not that I want to hear from *Donald*, really, but simply that I like other human beings to send up flares now and then. The prospect that I may have a letter from you is actively exciting, as promised in our talk yesterday. I do hope you got to the post office, over the drifts of sand and last week's high school contraceptives and candy-bar wrappers.

....

Whittier, California 8.vi.51
To: Rex Kennedy

Dear Rex... It is now 3:15. I have just picked up apple sauce, graham crackers, and celery from the rug. I have baby-sat for Norah's three kids while she spent some time in Whittier. I have cooked Squash and cut up carrots, green peppers, and celery for the children, and put out apple juice and milk, and made several relays of both brown bread and raisin bread sandwiches. I have made a salad for Norah and myself. I have made a drink for us. I have been, or so I honestly believe, kind and loving with all the

3. Both Van and Randy were Anne Kelly's boyfriends.
4. An old friend of Rex's and a member of the Hispanic community in Whittier

children. Once when John was hitting both Dave and Mary I said, "John, please don't do that again here at the Ranch," and he said, "Who do you think you are, the boss of the whole world?" And so on and so on. It has been a difficult day, in part dictated by the fact that Norah's husband has called twice. I will say truly to you that I think I was patient and hospitable. I may be greatly mistaken, but I have been raised to recognize certain standards and I think I met them. But Norah, who was gone for quite some time and had to eat her lunch at about 2:30, left in an obvious huff, and when I said "What on earth is wrong with you?" she said what's wrong with *you*? She drove off angrily. (She had also said, "What's wrong, don't you feel well?" in a very angry voice, and I can only say that I do feel well, that I have trusted Norah, and that I think her reaction is a fairly normal one after the divorce proceedings of last week.)

However, Rex, I am very tired of being used as the family punching-bag-rest-home-mid-wife-baby-sitter-etc.-etc. I have spent one year and a half cooking and washing dishes and making beds for Norah, her husband, her two or three children, and Anne Kelly and her friend Randy and her son Sean. I have been, at will, family punching bag, rest home, mid-wife, baby sitter, and general maid-of-all-work.

The end result is that everyone seems to feel it quite all right to storm out, slam doors (leaving the dishes undone and the beds unmade), and generally create a minor chaos which I gradually clean up, *alone*. I am the culprit... and how convenient!

Well, I am fed up. I do not want to hurt you or desert you, but by god why don't you get someone else to be the whipping-girl for a change? I have run a short-order restaurant here for too long. I have fed a great many people, and have saved you money on the deal. I am god-damned sick of being pushed around by Sis and Noni just because they think they are having a tough time and "the world owes them a living" (or you owe them a square meal). (When you owe them the meal, I cook it....)

I too have had tough times, and they have been good to me, in their own ways. But I am not used to being pushed around by moody women, and in spite of some practice I do not care to learn now.

I honestly feel that I have kept this house open and welcoming at all times to everybody, since I came here. I have cooked and cared for the Barrs and one or both of the Kellys, from one night to a week to a month. I have received letters, mainly from Norah after I asked, at your request, that the Barrs help with the budget when they were here before the birth of Matthew, which cut me to my heart. To hell with them I have said. I have since talked in confidence with her and have not felt myself too much presuming. Now I do. With this letter I am through. I will do what I can to help you, for you have given me your trust, to help you live nicely. But I am fed up with this thing and by god I refuse to stick around here and be used at will by anyone who cares to drop in for anything from lunch to a weekend to a week to a month, with or without children, and assorted friends.

This letter, according to when and to whom you show it, will be ascribed to mood, fatigue, pettishness, and so on and so on. Dotey is lonely; Dotey is almost 43; Dotey is tired; Dotey doesn't like children who leave graham crackers around; Dotey this and this.... Also... good old Dote... stay over there... the food is good and there are plenty of beds and after all it's our home as much as hers... good old Dote... maybe she'll straighten things out... let's go over for dinner and get a few good drinks... I'll just dash up to the bank and leave the kids with Dote... Dote, I think I'm in labor... Dote, I just got hit by a car... may we come over for lunch on Sunday?... I'll just leave that pile of stuff in the cook-house and you do whatever you want with it... SLAM....

Well, Rex, today I have had enough. And I hasten to add that an overnight trip to Glen Ivy, complete with smorgasbord, will not help. I am just damn well through with this. I think you had better get another girl. You can say I had a nervous breakdown or something. But I refuse, one more time in my whole life, to sit passively by and let my sister, helped by her children (tended by me most of the time), kick me in my already false teeth. It's too expensive, especially when after they have been kicked the kicker rears back and asks affrontedly "Why weren't they stronger so I could kick harder?" (Norah slamming doors and then saying with a blank adolescent stare, "Well, what's wrong with *you?*")

I am sorry about this. I said I would come up to keep house for you and I have. But how about letting one of the other girls take over for a time? I am tired, not of keeping house but of keeping home for *them* and then having them make it so plain that I have "moved in here," that I am "boss," and so on and so on. To hell with it, Rex. I think I had better get away from them for a time. Anne is in San Francisco. Norah is in Sunset Beach. Let one of them take over the job they both manage to infer I have been so poor at.

(Here I collapsed—bitter tears, the first for many months—said nothing to RFK of course, but wrote many invisible letters to Norah—)

....

Whittier, California   3.*vii.51*
To: Norah Kennedy Barr

Dearest N... the first letter of my 44th year! I do not exactly feel young, but rather as if I had not yet grown old, as if I were just beginning. The chilling realization that I am not only *not* beginning, but am at this point quite possibly *ending* a great many things I have always taken for granted, things like conjugal love, slimness, things like that: it does not depress me, but it fills me with a kind of astonishment. I imagine I would feel the same detachment, the same sense of unreality, if I were told that I was gradually turning green, or that all my life I just *thought* I could hear but had really been stone deaf, or that in exactly four hours I would fall down dead.

I thank you again for the Landowska. I played it last night after I went to bed. It was not soothing, of course, for instinctively I kept my mind undrowzy [*sic*], and then there I was, an hour later, very clear and awake. I was glad, for although I resolved nothing, I was able to contemplate several problems without any subterfuge.

This morning is dark and cool. Mary is chatting beside me in her new yellow nightie. Mrs. Brooks has come, bringing me a present which I'll not open until sleepy Anne comes down.......Now I have come back from a lengthy marketing, complete with six sparklers for the girls' Fourth, and so on and so on. Mrs. Brooks gave me a cherry-red satin glove box, very nice indeed. Addie, I judge from Joe's mysterious cacklings with the children, is making me a cake. I have bought myself the Carson McCullers anthology (Have already read the short stories, which are more than disappointing, but I do admire her novels and am glad to have them in one book... have firsts of all of them, I believe, at Bareacres...). I have bought *Kon-Tiki* for Rex... it is really thrilling. I have play-books for the kids. I have four little American flags to stick in our ice cream tonight, and a steak for the family. Mymymy.

I expect an icy few minutes with Rex this noon, for I have done my summer act of removing all the brass around the fireplace and putting plants on the hearth. He hates it, for it limits him to the large bucket for matches and paper and so on. I do it for looks, for fire prevention, and mostly because I have reached a point where I honestly feel that I CAN NOT STAND it if Rex spits once more into the fireplace. I am ashamed of myself, and I keep saying that I can stand anything and that I am a comparatively young and very happy and very healthy human being. But today, perhaps because there is a strong feeling of "the new year" in me, I find myself actually fearing what will happen if Rex spits while I am in the room, or blasts out a long goatish belch in my face, or hawks into the nearest empty envelope. I am afraid I will say something ugly to him, or run from the room in ugly loud tears, or vomit.

After you left, yesterday (R was disappointed to find you gone, and I felt lonely, but you were probably wise...), I was thinking too clearly of What To Do... thanks to our rambling talk and the wine. Mainly I keep my mind pretty well off the subject, for I always come back to the occasionally very dismal conviction that I am honor-bound to care for R as long as he wants me or until I either find or fabricate a job which will enforce my leaving here. So there I was, grinding out another apparently distasteful meal, feeling lonely and *lasse*. And at table R's lack of manners was especially strong, or so it seemed: he gobbled grimly, and before the children had hardly started on the plates of hacked-up smeary stuff he had shoved at them he pushed back his chair and until we cleared the table and brought in dessert he hawked and belched steadily, cleaned his nails, and picked at his nostrils, inspecting his findings. Dessert was the same. Then in came the Doldes[1] (and stayed and stayed and stayed), and although he did spit into his handkerchief a few times, he restrained himself courteously from belching. When they finally left, though, he relaxed, drank a third highball, and really let fly at both ends, with a bland and slightly tiddly smirk on his face. He wanted to sit and talk, so I did. I was beginning to feel actively depressed, and like a dope I fell off my quite comfortable little wagon and drank a bourbon and water, which tasted good, for bourbon and water. Finally he was ready for bed and a rub, which he got. Then I listened to Landowska and was able to look at myself less emotionally. This morning,

1. Whittier friends of Rex and Edith

though, I felt depressed again, and in spite of being stern I have gone on mulling over the thing.

(You must be very tired of this. Apparently it seems quite simple to other people, Sis for instance: walk out, get a good Chinese houseboy, put up or shut up. I think I may have a warped sense of responsibility, the way some people have hare-lips or club-feet. Certainly I derive absolutely no feeling of nobility from it....)

I honestly don't know how to go about finding a part-time job. If I am going to make such a move, I certainly don't want to establish myself even on the fringes of Hollywood again. That leaves SF or NY. For obvious reasons I think it would be a great mistake to be in NY with the children.... Time and Distance are working well for me, and I think I know Donald well enough to believe that his pained wish to stay important to the children will soon be shifted into more comfortable and immediate interests. And of course I don't like the thought of scrimping along with a large slice of my monthly income going for heat and heavy coats and all that. As for SF, I still want very much to live there for a few years with the children. But right now I feel unwilling, indeed rather *ungracious*, about it. I don't want to be Good Old Dote up there. As you say, that would be largely up to me, how much of it I was. But not altogether.

Much later. Rex came home, asked what had happened to the fire-stuff, and when I told him I'd taken it out because of fire hazard he (1) said "good idea" and (2) spat with great show and shakings into a crumpled envelope in the big bucket and (3) tossed me a cheap card of "Indian Jewelry" bracelets, which he said would take the place of the checks he had given you and Sis. (This was the first mention of my birthday.) I saw a happy mischievous gleam in his off eye, so we both played it to the hilt... I called in the kids, and we each put on a bracelet... as a matter of fact they are quite pretty... and he told me he got them at the Whittier CutRate Bazaar... and then of course he tossed me a nice fat check, and got very tearful, to my horror, for I was sitting here mulling over How To Leave when he came in. He said, You're a sweet girl, and I couldn't get along without you... I said, Oh yes you could. He said No, maybe for a few days now and then, but I'm old, Dote... I looked at myself in store windows today... I'm old and lonely. I said, You look old when you slouch, but when you stand up you look wonderful. He said, I look older when I slouch, all right, but what I'm saying is that I need you, Dote, and I can't get along without you. He looked bitter, to have to say such a thing, and shaken, and frightened. I sat there smiling and twisting the little bracelets and fluttering the yellow check, and inside I was saying Oh HELL. And that is it. What strange instinct tells him? He knows so well when to trim my wings....

It is now late afternoon, of a good day. I know I feel much younger than I did a year ago... and in spite of a kind of weariness I felt this morning, perhaps due in part to the unaccustomed bourbon last night, I am strong inside. There is much that I would change, and at times the sense of waste is almost too clear to me. It is not healthy to have to force myself to accept, but surely I am a good enough person to withstand the unhealthiness? Surely I myself am sturdy enough to see to it that my children glean more good than evil from this strange life? It is up to me. Waste is wrong. I refuse to believe that *everything* is wasted: I am doing my best, almost all of the time, to make a good life for Rex and the girls and myself, and I refuse to believe that I am failing, in spite of periods of deep boredom, exasperation, frustration....

So here is another letter you will not receive, N.... It is part of a record, and if I were to read it ten or fifty years from now I honestly do not know what my opinions of the 43-year-old me would be! Am I pusillanimous? or am I merely wordy?

Meanwhile thank you again for the Landowska. I played the record again this afternoon, and almost went to sleep in the seventh fugue... it was suddenly peaceful for me.

Addie brought me a fat cake heavy with pink icing, with DOTY and a lot of periods and commas on it in bright yellow! She is an odd woman.

A letter from Sis... she is not sending me any present, she warns me, because she simply hasn't seen anything I'd *like*. "Jewelry is silly," she says, "because I can't match any of yours (Doggone it, here I was eating my heart out for her to send me another pearl and diamond necklace!)—eau de cologne you have—you need nothing for the house"—and so on.

She reports that "Nardo" Bercovici[2] was in town... "very subdued and nicer than I have ever seen him." Isn't it *funny* what suicide will do to some of the survivors? She says Van has settled into his old routine of two dates and three calls weekly, and that she needs "a new interest." She has also bought a new Studebaker... simply couldn't afford to keep up the old one. She also continues her whimsical and amused scoffing at the crackpots to whom I wrote her letters of introduction: she sees most of them often, and lunches and drinks with them, but they are apparently a bunch of pretentious and/or drunken peasants. Mymymy... She ends by telling me how relieved she is that I no longer plan to bring the children north. "They are very sweet," she says, "but after all I knew you before they did." Mymymy again. (All this sounds sour, but is not. My conversation is so limited to a few shouts at Rex, all pre-destined to at least three repetitions, and some 14 hours of Please pick up those Crayons... Now let's set the table... Don't put your finger in your mouth... with an occasional wild intellectual sortie with *Black Beauty* or *Beautiful Joe*... that I find myself practically mumbling aloud about anything that goes out of the one-syllable class....)

It is time to build myself a little birthday party... I'll start by making a red-white-and-blue centre-piece.... Then we'll eat some caviar! You forgot yours. I'll keep it for you. Then we'll have a steak, sliced tomatoes, fresh corn, ice cream, cake... my god.

I planted a little seed, fertile I think, about Rex's buying a home-size deep freezer... I could save some money on food and a lot of time with one. But what would he do with the money I saved? What would I do with the extra time? (He pays fifteen a month to keep two tough old pheasants and three hens frozen, six to ten months of the year....)

Au revoir... with love.

2. A friend of Sean Kelly

Whittier, California   *6.iv.52*
To: Norah Kennedy Barr

Dearest N... I'm right in the middle of a boring three-way correspondence, trying to settle this business about the wine book.[1] But my mind is buzzing so fast about something else that I'll simply ignore all the duplicate pages, cross-questions, this and that... and write to you.

It is cool grey day... the weatherman fouled us up again and we stayed home from Bareacres because heat was predicted. Of course we did have two very hot days, but yesterday afternoon the weather changed. Oh well, it would have been a real chore for Rex... he feels urgently that he wants to go down before the hot weather... but I know he dreads it. We talk now of spending Easter there. I wish I could dash down one day... but I simply can't make it without leaving work for one morning, and even then it is pretty futile. Rex is going to HATE being cooped into my little house, after the wide porches of the other one and Lulu's. Ho hum . . .

Well, this is what was buzzing in my mind: Last night we had an astonishing offensive in Operation Deep Freeze, over the coffee of course... that seems to be the only time anything much is ever said. Rex opened it and kept in the lead the whole time... I just *sat*, reeling gently. (It was after I went to bed that I had the long talks, silent of course....)

"How are you getting along?" he asked, and I rose to the bait and said "Fine... what about?" "That ice-box," he said impatiently, "haven't you ordered it yet?" (First reel, hopefully disguised...)

"Gods, I told you to go ahead days ago! I thought you had decided you *needed* one." Well, I said yes I certainly could use one and gee whiz I'd get right to work and thank you thank you... and I sat back waiting, for in my suspicious and mistrustful way I suspected a Foul Plot. I had something there: he talked very "openly" and "frankly" and so on, this is what he said.... Dote, I think it's about time you made up your mind and came to a clear-cut decision to settle here in Whittier, raise your children here, make yourself an honest part of the community.

I didn't argue or fight. I said a few things very simply, and asked a few questions. He had an answer for every one of them... he had evidently got this well in order in his mind. I said I was too old to learn all about running a daily... don't even know make-up... couldn't possibly handle a city editor's desk.... Oh dear, I'd better start over... I have answered the phone twice, started Rex's breakfast, and carried on a patter of chitchat with the children.

I said I didn't have the know-how to be editor of a paper like the *News*. I said I was too old. He grinned at me and said I was not as old as he and I gave the familiar riposte,

1. For University of California Press, MF wrote the text for *The Story of Wine in California*, a book of photographs of the wine country by Max Yavno; the book would take ten years to produce.

that he'd been at it since he was nine. He said, "Well, stick Mel[2] in... he's a good man and I've trained him the whole way. He's a Whittier man. He's loyal...." You know... the works. I agreed. I said, Well, if you put Mel on your desk who goes onto his? Howard is too young.... He said, "Hire somebody. You girls can hire and fire at will, as long as you keep your stock." I said Yes but *who*? No answer... except that he told me he'd had a letter lately from Garret Graham asking if CG could buy in. "Gods, you can sell the paper in days if you want to," he said. "But I think it's worth more to you girls than money, and will stay that way for a long time." Well, what would I be, I asked... a kind of snooper for the family interests, president of the board, "publisher," *what*? "You'd be whatever you had the will to make yourself," he said in his inimitable way of goading us. "You were raised here in Whittier. People know you.(?) You seem to get along...." I said Yes but a woman editor here, Rex... can't belong to fraternal lodges or service clubs... all that... and anyway I'm ignorant of things like city management and political procedures in the county and so on... and I'm not a joiner at all and furthermore I am not a good churchwoman.... "You could be," he said coldly, and I didn't say that I did not *want* to be. Toward the end of this rather startling conversation (it was so *direct*... I felt helpless, pinned to the wall...) I said in what sounded a very feeble voice to me, "If I settled here I would want to be *in* Whittier... raise my girls in the *Whittier* schools, not in a dozen of these new ones on the outskirts filled with a fleeting mass... I'd want them to get a feeling of being part of *Whittier*...." He said, "Well, buy some property in town... you like that old house of Ralph Thynses's... buy something like that when I'm gone... fix it up... that would get your girls into Whittier proper." An answer for everything.

Well, that was about the main line... I can't remember much more, except that I thought it was funny, or odd, or something, that I had, this past week, deliberately registered for voting at that old house on South Pickering, where I first saw Aunt Gwen[3] when I was barely four, and that since then I had been thinking almost constantly of it. What a trick!

But of course I talked it all over, after R had long since gone to bed. I sat in the livingroom until the fire went out, and then I went to bed with a highball (lowball... delicious) and talked a lot more... slept peacefully and awoke early to pick up the conversation. Two questions are the strongest: What do I do with MFKFisher, and what do I do with my *self*, or what I still like to think is left of it....

Re Fisher... the old girl is weak and gasping already, a genteel hasbeen now and then asked to speak ten minutes at an arty tea, pretty well given up as hopeless by publishers-agents-editors. Should I quietly hold a private funeral? Should I give the coup de grâce to some 25 years spent developing a minor talent? Should I stop kidding myself that sometime "when this is over" I can write something good? Should I keep on kidding myself that along with running a business and raising two pretty dynamic

2. Mel Rich, managing editor of the Whittier *News*
3. Gwen Shaw, a Whittier neighbor who was like a second mother to MF and her siblings

females I can occasionally write something in any way satisfying? If I killed off Fisher, professionally at least, how would it affect me emotionally? Could I create enough other ways to satisfy my basically fertile nature, without her and past child-bearing and without any sexual outlets? Could I, here in Whittier?

That brings me to Question 2... what happens to what is left of *me*, after the business and maternal sides are taken care of? Do I continue to force myself to be polite, cordial, and even hospitable to people I dislike and occasionally loathe, like Harold Lutz and the Döldes and their banking snobbish completely pusillanimous gang? Do I decide to attach myself, the aging divorcee, to a group of hard-drinking whoring sneaks who pretend to live in Whittier but spend most of their time in Palm Springs and Acapulco and in other people's staterooms on the *Lurline*? Do I begin, tired of being the "extra woman" in a society made up of solid married couples, to accept the covert pats and terrified assignations of people like Ralph T and Harold R? Or in horror at this do I try to teach myself to believe that I can become a good club-woman, churchwoman? Do I doggedly set about becoming a member of the band of local female yearners, people like Mabel George, Dr. Rice of Broadoaks, that Lesbian musician up at the College, that equally mannish psychiatrist at Nelles School? Do we get into passionate little cliques over Schoenberg vs. Milhaud? Or, to continue this strange series of questions to myself, do I try to keep on being the wanderer temporarily come to rest in a small town, the writer temporarily not writing, the attractive young widow temporarily aging rapidly....

I can talk about the other side, of course. Sometimes I feel a kind of revulsion at the prospect of *drifting*, after I leave here... no real roots, nothing really solid to offer the children... a villa here, a winter there, schools for them.... I ask myself if I am trying to recapture for them and myself something I damn well know is forever gone, the carefree excitement (rewarding too) of learning other tongues, living in other ways than the one *built into me* by my upbringing and childhood. Do I want to be that way, drifting? What will it give the children, except a gloss of worldly poise? And a few good accents...

Of course I want them to have all that too. And can I manage it if I settle here and try to run the business for myself and you two sisters? Can I arrange it so that, for the children and myself, we can go away now and then and still lead a good honest life as Whittier People?

I can think of worse places to identify myself with. I know more about it now than I ever did, and I feel that it is good-and-American, and unusual in this part of the country for its solid Quaker background... nothing fly-by-night. The core of the town will last a long time, no matter how the fringes flutter in this boom. Maybe it would be better for me to stop thinking that I could live alone in a great city and raise the girls... I am rather old to feel ambitious about jobs and all that and if I went to Chicago or-or-or I would have to find work. (Of course there is the thing that NY is out, for I don't want the children to know too much of Donald... SF is pretty well out... Paris would be only for a year or so for I want the girls to grow up as Americans....)

I want to keep Bareacres, and here I would be near it. I want to keep the very few people I feel are my dear friends, and except for you, now away, and Aunt Grace in Chicago and Eda in Wales, they are in Southern California: Gloria, Jane, June, Larry.[4] It is true that I see very little of them. But when I am no longer on this strange kind of 24-hour duty I can move about and spend weekends with them and so on… impossible now, even for one night. And I am not ashamed to repeat the truism that it is increasingly more difficult to make good friends as one grows older. It is quite possible that I might be able to establish good solid confidence in someone, here in Whittier or almost anywhere… but that is a gamble…. It is more probable that I would make *acquaintances* wherever I went, and would forever miss the few I love now. A lonely prospect, even with two daughters (who grow farther from me every day…).

But now I have made a beautiful soufflé for Rex, his Sunday fare… taken in the tray, the paper, this-and-that… he looks very handsome in his red velvet jacket… the kids are still playing like crazy… Mary does all the doubling for The Wolf, FeeFiFoFum, Nasty Old Witch… Anne plays the Fairy Princess through thick and thin…. It's time to start thinking of the next meal. . . .

Tuesday the gals and I have lunch in Riverside with Elsa. Wednesday Miss Guthrie comes and we buy some Easter posies for Mrs. Thayer[5] and so on. Thursday we have lunch with June. Friday we have lunch with Gloria. Saturday we go to Bareacres maybe. What a giddy vacation!

I have a silly little box for you. Hope I get it off tomorrow. I'll send it to Paso Robles, that will be easiest for you. Please let me. . . .

Here comes the sun. The walnut leaves are simply bursting out of the tired old twigs…. I have one yellow daisy on my new plants… quite a lot of pinks… a few petunias.

I made a wonderful pizza last night. Ate some for breakfast… nobody touched it but me. Tonight we'll have a steak, baked potatoes, apple pie. That ought to teach them! Tomorrow I plan to invent something, just to worry the Newtons. Nan told me once that I completely upset their whole way of thinking, gastronomically, by admitting that the delicious peas they had just eaten (They gobble here) were frozen. They firmly believed that nothing frozen was fit to swallow. They still do, except here: says she "just can't cook them."… Well, tomorrow I plan to use frozen raw shrimps, frozen oysters, frozen this and that.

Full circle: it suddenly occurs to me that it will be fun to have that deep freeze. I have a good book, and according to the salesman I will have as much cooperation as I want from a very intelligent woman who comes around on call, advising and so on. When I was younger I would despise such a suggestion. Now… Open Arms Department! I must figure out whether I can pry up and off the table and bench… get a good plain bureau to hold the dishtowels and so on… put it where the rickety old bread-table is now… sounds fine…

4. MF's close friends Gloria Stuart, Jane Evans, June Eddy, Larry Powell
5. Miss Guthrie was a dance teacher and physical therapist; Mrs. Thayer, a neighbor.

But what a bribe! That sly old fox...

Noni dear, thank you for continuing to make me feel that I may write this kind of epistle to you. It is indeed a saga... and I'm incapable of writing it to myself, which is of course the main reason why I am not this minute writing a novel instead of this sort of thing: I simply have to have someone I love to write to (and for...).

Love.

....

Whittier, California   *2.v.52*
To: Eda Lord

Dear Eda, it would be inane of me to say I was glad when your letter came. I've been writing to you, or rather talking with you, ever since then. Now that I am actually doing so, I feel clumsy and mute.

Thank you for writing. I'm thankful the 1943 message finally reached you. I think I wrote twice to your Aunt Margaret, once after I'd heard indirectly that you'd been in a camp and then released. I never heard from her, and concluded, sadly, that she felt I was an intruder. I did not give up, for I've always known word would come from you, or about you. Meanwhile I continued to dream occasionally of you, very clear and for the most part good dreams which left me with a feeling of reassurance and even happiness.

I wrote a story[1] about you and Joan B after we met in Paris... will show it to you someday if you wish me to. It is good. (Needless to say, I wrote it for my*self*.)

Yes, I remember Tania, although I never met her except in some pictures taken in Spain. It is kind of her to say that she knows people who like what I've written.

Anne (my sister) lives in Sausalito and has met the Churchills now and then at parties. Will you please give Joan[2] my greetings if you wish? I remember her clearly... very beautiful woman....

I don't know what she sent you that I'd written about Colette... maybe a review from the *Los Angeles Daily News*. That was an odd situation: of course I have considered myself the appointed (anointed?!) translator ever since 1929, even to the place where last year I invested a hundred or so of my almost non-existent dollars on the *Oeuvres Complètes*. The word got around. So Dial Press wrote asking me to "do" the current collection of six novels. When I told Joel, the publisher, exactly how and why I would do it, and my reasons for refusing to touch any existing translations with a ten-foot pole, he backed away in real terror, and got Glenway Westcott to throw together something. Westcott did the best he could, I feel sure... a thankless job of editing. The Flanner tr. is the best in the collection... damning it with the faintest praise indeed! The book sold pretty well, I hear... pretty bad reviews, and deservedly. Thank god I got out of it early. Well, I was asked to review it several times, but knew anything I said would upset Westcott, Joel, et al, so I stayed mum except for one ambiguous thing in the *Daily News*... it

1. "Stay Me, Oh Comfort Me," published in the book of the same title in 1993
2. Eda's friend Joan was related to the Winston Churchills.

may have been re-printed... I don't know. Meanwhile I go right on thinking of myself as THE translator, although I have not yet set a word on paper!

This looks as if it will be a long letter. I hope you don't mind. It's impossible to catch up... so I chatter about Colette....

I've never been in Wales. I stayed often near Penzance with Dillwyn.[3] Did Wales bring you back to your own size and mind? There are many things I want to ask you, when the time comes.

I'll see if I can tell you, *not* chattily, something of what has happened to me. Dillwyn died... maybe you know that... suicide after three years of horror which were still the best in my life, perhaps. I worked in Hollywood... very sterile period it would seem, and yet knew better all the time for

And now it is 10.v.52, which may give you some idea of how much time I find for anything but the immediacies. And I am at the Ranch instead of up at the *News* office where I began this "condensation of a saga."...

Well, Yes, I was not sterile even if the studio job was, for in 1943 I had a daughter... rather complicated feat, as you can imagine, which I brought off to my own complete satisfaction. My daughter Anne is now almost 9, a tall dark introvert, fated to be very beautiful I am afraid... she will probably be a dancer... shows great promise.

About two years after she was born I married Donald Friede, to our mutual damage. We had another daughter, Mary, a premature baby who confounded all the doctors by developing rapidly into a rock of a human being, probably the most straightforward and loving one I have ever known. She is everything good in DF, before he got twisted. I hope to keep her untwisted.

Edith Kennedy died with great difficulty in 1949, and soon after that I started to get a divorce... it's a long job in California. I was in a very bad way... extreme emotional and physical fatigue... Donald could not help whipping me into bigger jobs, bigger royalties, and there I was having babies, helping people die, watching him go into a real psychic collapse... ho hum, what a time. I went to a good doctor, at least the right one for me... worked with him for over two years but did not (could not) go into analysis. Everything seems pretty solid again, and I see him every six months or so, if I want to, which I usually do because he is one of the very few contacts I have right now with The Spoken Word. Everybody I've been able to talk with has either died or disappeared! I keep on talking to myself, of course, awake and asleep. This wordy letter is an indication of my ceaseless conversation....

Let me see... Edith died. I have a beautiful place in the mountains near Hemet, which Dillwyn evolved for me before he died. I am hanging on to it, sometimes desperately and always doggedly, for I believe deeply that it is the place for me to go when I am alone again. And it will do the children good to know that it is there and that I am there. (Their future will need any such reassurance and solidity I can give it....) I came up here to put some order in the place, six months after Edith died... it was going to pieces fast. I planned to stay about two weeks. That was almost three years ago.

3. MF traveled to England with Dillwyn and his mother in 1935.

For a time I rebelled, consciously and other ways, against the turn my life was taking. By now I accept it, with a detached interest in whatever happens. The only thing I could do about it, walk out, is impossible for my nature. So...

I am very busy, or rather I should say occupied. I do the cooking, for a regular family of four and many guests. (Rex is not well enough to go out, and likes people here. And so do I.) I have a charwoman, quite a poor one, most mornings a week. The children are both in a country day-school about six miles from here... trips at 8 and at 5 each day. And for the past few months, since Rex was very ill, I have worked six mornings a week at the *News*. I handle the mail, about 300 letters a morning to edit and direct as I see fit, Rex's personal books (bills, such-like, I mean), his correspondence... I do one column a week and one or two features (Anon.), and pinch-hit on society and re-writes. Somewhere along in there knock off reviews for the Los Angeles paper and a "thing" now and then to keep a faint breath of life in MFKFisher... and of course keep books on the Kennedy Ranches,[4] my Hemet place (90 acres), and the estates of my two girls (I am their legal guardian!). My. I used to think I was busy when to me now it seems I was an orchid. I wonder what the now will seem like in ten years....

I am indeed chattering. I hope it does not bore or irk you.

Rex is very ill. He is dying of pulmonary fibrosis. He is a handsome egocentric man, past 75, whose dignified will-to-exist-with-dignity astounds me. He has taught me a great deal about how to live as well as die (and here I thought I knew something of both!). Edith did too. By the time I am too old to do anything about it, I should know quite a lot.

Perhaps you would like to read of the rest of the family?

My brother David committed suicide a year after Dillwyn's death. A daughter was born two weeks later to his wife. She, the wife, has remarried and reproduced. They all live in up-state NY and I am thankful not to see them.

Anne lives in Sausalito, as I think I said (I don't dare re-read this: I want to be in touch with you and I'd throw it away and not be able to start again...). She has not re-married. Her son, past 19, is in the Air Force. She is slim and chic and I do not envy her.

Norah, who enlisted during the last war as a psychiatric Red Cross worker, married another psychiatrist... they had three sons... they divorced, and after a year of recuperation Norah is now with USO–Travelers Aid at one of the big jump-offs for Korea. She is very beautiful, and has fine children and is keen. I don't know what will happen with her.... She'll probably become Regional Director in Utah or some such place, and marry another beat-up but fertile colleague. She is a wonderful breeder... should be subsidized. I would do it if I could... subsidize her, I mean!

Me, I am not at all the way I vaguely thought of myself as being. For a while I did not like it at all. Now I am, as I said, amused and interested in a rather remote way. I am not at all remote about my children: I find them pretty much my raison d'être, but am fairly sure I'll not let that damage them too much. Physically I have hit a new and

4. Rex had another ranch (Walnuts) down the road.

to me unexpected stride... I am a big woman but not ungainly, with graying hair and a smooth baby-face and tired green eyes... I have great energy for what is necessary, but slump like a felled ox when I have performed my duties each day. Socially I meet almost none except professional and business associates of Rex. Sexually I am in the deep-freeze, a deliberate and costly accomplishment! Morally, I am developing, to make an understatement. Dillwyn always said I might be quite a person if I lived to fifty... I still have six-plus years to go, and some hopes....

Yes, I did say this might be long. It does not embarrass me, and if it's bored you it will have been discarded before you read, again, my thanks for writing. I hope you'll write again. I hope we'll meet again. I plan to come to Lancashire with the children within the next few years, and to live at Le Pâquis again while they learn French and German probably at l'École Pré-Alpin. I'll see you then. Or before.

Love

....

Whittier, California   *23.viii.52*
To: Arnold Gingrich[1]

Dear Arnold:

I'm ashamed of myself for not writing at once to congratulate you and thank you for sending me the wedding announcement, and to thank you for your practically illegible but very welcome letter of some six months ago. I hope you'll forgive me. I was working my head off at the *News*, and when I realized three weeks ago that I was one step ahead of prime number-one shakes and fired myself, I took off for San Francisco with my girls and then got back just in time for Anne's ninth-birthday weekend... quel whirl!

Well, you know I'm so cut off from news and so on that I did not know that you were divorced! You may tell your wife that I've long carried a quietly burning torch for you myself, and that it's a good thing for me that I was kept in the dark... I couldn't possibly have afforded a futile trip to NY.... I do send you my heartfelt wishes for a fine life together, and I hope to see you both before too long.

Now I'll tackle that letter you wrote with the disintegrating French pen. I figure that if you had the courage to fight through two sheets of paper I should reply in kind. You kept your finger on the ruptured gut... I must keep mine on my family's pulse, rather active this morning thanks to the first smog-less morning (Mary is weaving bamboo mats under my window) and the arrival of the September issue of *Jack and Jill* (Anne is lying at my feet reading me corny jokes and riddles)... Salvador is mowing the lawn... Alice Marie is vacuuming... quel brouhaha!

Thank you for saying that I'm not one to whom you'd write a short note. I hope you'll continue to feel that way, at least now and then.

1. Arnold Gingrich owned Le Pâquis during the war years and was the editor of *Esquire* and the smaller *Coronet*.

That slum apartment sounds fine, with the pictures. I hope to see the water color of Le Pâquis. Dillwyn did a lot of architectural sketches and of course portraits of our flowers and cabbages, but never a "picture."

It does sound strange that by now you're probably a grandfather. I too continue to feel unprepared for such progressions, and the fact that yesterday Anne passed her first-year exams in Cecchetti ballet technique dazes me. I've been saying so blandly that I hoped to get her into school in London "by the time she is twelve"... and now she damn near is, and here I sit, rolling to the punches! It's rather like my saying I'd quite probably write a good book by the time I was fifty... I'd jolly well better get busy, or else raise the deadline another ten years. . . .

Are you still an advertising man? (I'm *really* out of "the swing."...) Did that publishing deal ever materialize? In other words, what are you doing and if so do you like it?

I don't know what kind of letter I sent you, to make you brood. That embarrasses me. But at least I sent it to a good person, and I suppose you can accept that compliment, that I did send it to you. Still: please excuse me.

I don't know what script I ever sent you... I mean anything but *Coronet* stuff. It's good of you to think it might be worth exhuming. I don't know if you saw a long short story published, in all things, in the *Ladies' Home Journal* some months ago... April I think. It is the only thing I've sold for more than a year, but that doesn't discourage me at all. Henry Volkening feels pleased to see me writing fiction when I write at all, and I have two more things on the tip of my mind.

Oh, I see you ask who's my agent. HV, of Russell and Volkening. No, Pat[2] didn't get him into the act. Donald did. Donald rowed constantly and most disturbingly with poor Mary Pritchett and I simply had to bow to it at that time... it still embarrasses me and MLP does not speak to me, even so long since. But I like HV very much as a person and admire him for putting up with me, for I am probably his most unproductive patient right now. No, don't talk to anybody about me, for I am currently "fallow," as Pat so nicely puts it... not a good investment. Turned down a fantastic job with *House Beautiful* and feel fine about it. I am managing to keep my place in Hemet going, and my two girls educated, thanks to my native wit and energy and my father's acceptance of us here (glorified housekeeper-cook-chauffeur-bookkeeper-bottle-opener) and a kind of annuity Donald established for the girls when we were divorced. Sooner or later I'll write something and it won't be for money and as almost always with me I'll be paid very well for it!

Not much to report from here. I went to work supposedly as my father's assistant when he was very ill last February... was caught, and had to fight a lot of inner resentment and so on... of course found myself more and more absorbed by the job, for newspaper work is as natural as breathing to me, whether I want it to be or not... first thing I knew I was doing two regular columns a week, a lot of the local features, the weekly Home-Garden-Building sections, plenty of "public relations" stuff... plus my regular work of keeping this decrepit establishment functioning... plus all my father's books

2. Pascal (Pat) Covici, publisher

AND the household books AND the children's books (legal involvements re divorce) AND what was left of MFK Fisher's books. And I was quite literally seeing dark spots in front of my eyes. So I eliminated the only possible job, the editorial one. I also eliminated a very welcome weekly check, and haven't given it a thought! I still do a lot of work at the *News*, and am apparently "appointed" to succeed my father... but, I don't have that daily ordeal of being amusing-considerate-understanding as the Boss's Daughter (synonym in my case: Prize Patsy). I have slept a lot and, as I think I said, taken the girls for their introduction to San Francisco, and I'm about ready to get to work on the story of how I happened to need the 102 sides of Jelly Roll Morton. It ought to be interesting, at least to my family and/or psychiatrist. (Don't have the latter any more... glad I did when I did... could have saved a lot of money if I'd been a good Catholic...)

I'm sorry it took the death of your uncle to needle you into your last letter. I do have a couple of completely impossible ball-point pens, if that would help any. That is to say, I hope you'll write again when you have the time and feel like it, and meanwhile, Arnold, here are Heart's Greetings to you and your wife.

....

Whittier, California   *9.x.52*
To: Norah Kennedy

Dearest N... It is another beautiful sparkly morning, and I would like to be in Hemet, where this is the most beautiful time of the year. Or Atascadero?

I would not like to be here, and I'm glad you're not. Most of the trees were pulled yesterday, and although there is a lull right now, the strange machine is out there catching its breath, panting and snapping. It started with a dreadful sound, a kind of scream as it lunged up over the curbing from the road, at exactly 5:30 yesterday morning, and the children and I shot out of bed as if we'd been hit by a bomb. It worked until almost seven last night. In other words, the day was not a good one, and was perhaps made even worse by my having to take Anne in to town, where she spent over two hours having fillings and x-rays and band-work and Novocaine. It was a real blessing to find a package here from Donald, a wonderful plastic-block set, quite grown-up... the children were absorbed for hours. Halfway through the afternoon I surprised myself by indulging in a few quiet wet sobs. I thought I couldn't stand the noise, I suppose. But I could. Or perhaps it was because of Rex: he is really in a bad state over what's happening, and I can only guess at the confusion and bitter regrets behind his sour old face. He has tottered out several times to *watch*, and to fret about why they are doing this and why they are not doing that and whether he should complain about something else. I've reassured him all I could... but this morning I saw him disappear again into the dust and noise of the back orchard. Ho hum. Last night with coffee he said something very sad... I can't remember it, but something about helping trees to live for forty or fifty years and then kicking them out of the ground (That is literally what the new puller does: long push from the front end and then a violent kick from the rear end and the tree is completely uprooted and on its side...). He looked so tired and miserable that I could have wept, and I thought, O why not talk straight to him, so I told him I wished we could all go away for a week or so, until the dust had settled. Well, it was a most unpleasant little scene, ending with the usual bitter helpless taunt, "You can leave any time you want, you and the girls. I don't need you around here. You can go away and stay away..." and so on. This time there was the added statement that *he* was not running away, but that I was acting according to my usual pattern and simply hadn't the guts to face anything. And so on. It wasn't at all what I'd expected, I can tell you. I honestly thought he might welcome an excuse to drive slowly up or down the Coast and sit in this heavenly sun for a couple of days. But I see now that he can't bear to leave. He must rub and rub that salty wound of being old and disintegrating. Needless to say, I did not reply at all to his sad jibes, except once when he asked me scornfully where I planned to *run* to and I answered that Bareacres would be nice now. Well, having relieved his spleen by hoping to have hurt me in place of Fate or whatever it is that has brought the Ranch to this sorry state, he practically hurled himself into the livingroom, and I sat looking at my coffee and thinking hard and facing the pretty sure fact that I would not make any kind of issue out of this noise from now on and would go right along in as much of the usual pattern as possible. I took a bath and came down and sat and sat and sat, waiting for him to look up from *Ellery Queen*. Finally I simply couldn't stay vertical any longer, so after speaking to him four or five times and at last jiggling his knee, I said "Father, I think I'll fold now" and without even looking up he said "I heard you the first time. Good night." "Good night," I said. To continue his behavior pattern, this morning he did not say Good morning when I took in his tray, ignored the children's greetings when he got the paper from the table, and slammed his door shut. I had everything in order (lunches packed and so on) so that I could take dictation early, for on Thursdays he likes to leave about 8:30 to go to the barber for a rub... but at about 10 to 8 he stalked out of the house. I ran after to say I was all ready to type for him, for we had outlined today's column yesterday and I knew he'd planned to get it done here, but without looking at me he said, "I can take care of my own work thanks. I have things to do." And I saw him go out toward the orchard. I know he is suffering, poor old devil. In a way I think it might be wise for me to take a long weekend with the children, and have the Abeggs[1] here... but really I know it is better to weather this right here, for he is so upset that he really should not have to add the misery of physical loneliness to all the rest of it, and at least we do keep the place more or less livable and alive. If he were younger and stronger I'd be off, and to hell with missing a few days of school, for this noise is plainly destructive no matter how I succeed in putting it out of my immediate mind... and not only for myself but for the children. And it will be the cement-boys next, and then the carpenters, and then the paving machines, all within fifty feet of here. Ho hum. I think I'll go right ahead and put in a couple or three quick-growing trees. I asked Rex a couple of days ago if it might not be a

1. Caretakers of the Ranch

M.F.K. Fisher: A Life in Letters

good idea to start looking at fences, and he said irritably, "You don't need to bother... I've decided to have wire fence put in all 'round." I'm sorry about that, for I'd asked him especially to have a wooden fence put up... wire is so mean-looking, and it takes a good three years to get it covered with ivy or whatever. But what in hell does it matter?

June[2] thinks that for my own good and the children's I should simply tell Rex that I must move on, and that I hope he'll make his home with us. I wonder if she is right? It means selling the *News*, or at least resigning as editor, for Rex. I wish he would. It is increasingly plain that he can no longer carry his weight, and there is a great deal of rather unpleasant unrest at the office now... confusion about authority and so on. And it is very possible that if he got really far from Whittier and established new contacts with Elks and Masons and so on, so that he'd have plenty of people making quite a fuss over him, he'd feel much better. This is really quite grim by now... I mean, his trying to keep up the bluff of still being **RBK** the long-time figure in Whittier....

Well, I must dash off a note of thanks to Donald, and go up and have my elbow rolled around. I'm so damned mad I let it go as long as I did... it's responding beautifully and is better than for at least a year. I was living in real pain, and didn't quite accept the fact until I couldn't stand it much longer. It's shocking to think that many people are as stupid as I. . . .

We're fine—physically I mean—and I'm in good shape otherwise.

....

Whittier, California   *23.xi.52*
To: Lawrence Clark Powell

Dearest Ghuce... triple threats and triple promises seem to have no effect on anything but my spirits, which they cheer!: This coming week two sisters, one complete with small sons, and my cousin, complete with small son and small husband, gather for the so-called "family holiday." I think that as our parents dwindle and decline we feel a need for closeness and warmth... don't know. Anyway I run a damned luxurious pension. I'm just too good a cook? Whatever it is, without this somewhat matriarchal brouhaha with which I manage to surround myself I might be quite bored, currently. And I am very conscious of how little there is left of it for all of us....

Warmth, that is, Not Boredom.

As a matter of fact, I am never bored, I am impatient at times, not to be doing what I'd prefer to this hectic period of self-induced servitude. But I'm pretty sure that it is enriching me in some way... I'll be a better writer for learning to put myself aside.

Sunday is a good day... I love having the children here, and not going to the *News*, I play a lot of records, and stand dreamily in the kitchen where my player is, making cookies and puttering. I have Jelly Roll pretty well in mind now and can pick and choose (102 sides!)... and I have been listening a lot to Flamenco guitars. . . .

Love. And thank you.

2. June Eddy, a longtime friend of MF's

Dearest None... it was wonderful to hear your voice this morning, even with the sorry news that poor John is down with pneumonia. Ho hum indeed. You have had quite a siege, and I hope your enforced leave-of-absence has at least given you a chance for a few naps. Bareacres was in a way quite a workout too, with all three of us with flu and Mary's arm making me stay half-awake... but even so I had some heavenly snoozes and breathed such free air.... May you do the same.

This won't be the letter I meant, for Rex is due home any minute and I have nothing ready for lunch. Mornings are really hectic, and I wonder more and more about schools and so on. Both children have been half-sick for two weeks now, with fleeting fevers and so on, and I swear I think it is partly their complete lack of incentive at school. Anne looks like a bored little ghost. Mary is just bored.

I have rounded up about ten little girls for a noon party on Sat.... outdoors I HOPE... 12 to 2, with the excuse that all ten of them have had flu lately and need to rest(!). I think I'll have Mr. Schroth make a big lizard instead of a cake. I bought Mary quite a nice zither, to give her tomorrow. That is absolutely all I have. Donald sent $50, and I would like to use it on some sort of trip. (I'm not re-reading my letter to you but probably told you of this.) As I reconsider it, it seems more pathetic and more feeble. "Since you have wilfully robbed me of my children, I find it emotionally impossible to be bothered by things like birthdays"... more or less like that! Wow. How far can we run?

Friday noon Larry Powell is coming for lunch, and that night, beside Christy Ann here for the night, I have asked Jim Harker and the Cherrys. For dinner, I mean. I find it much easier to function properly with a lot of people. Last night Rex and I were alone for the first time since I got back from Bareacres and I simply FLOPPED into bed at 9, and slept like a baby until 6 this morning... a few waking moments but not troubled at all. Sis solved the problem while she was here by going out quite a lot... with him, that is... she was really fine about the whole unexpected task.

The thing is that he is so weary. And when he doesn't have to pretend otherwise he simply doesn't. So he sags at every bone, which is just as dull for him as for the by-stander. He is having trouble with both eyes, and reads very little... it looks like a tumorous growth, not cataracts. I'll let you know. . . .

Well, I have missed the mail, apparently, and haven't answered a single one of your many questions and suggestions. Since you know you are going to get this letter, maybe I'd better go right ahead, and you can take it in chapters....

About propositioning the gardener: Isn't it something? I have had such a fine full life in that respect that the actual sexual loneliness no longer makes much of a problem for me, except probably subconsciously. What I miss is intelligent companionship, preferably male. It seems to me as I look back on it that Dillwyn and I not only made love but *Talked* almost steadily for almost the ten years we knew each other... and actually, with one exception, the talking has come ahead of the lovemaking in any relationships since then. . . .

Well... much later... things are so chopped up... people ask me why I don't write a book "as I go along"... but even letters seem increasingly difficult to finish.... Both children are finally home and I have stoked their furnaces... they are famishing at this time and then don't want supper... it is almost time to start that.

Noni, it seems pretty impossible for me to discuss with any continuity the many things I would indeed like to discuss with you. Let us hope that before too much longer we can meet and... well, MEET. Then much will seem clearer, for us both.

Meanwhile I can say that I took the Utah job in a rather daring mood, to use as a kind of wedge for my withdrawal from here.[1] By now I think I was plain silly, but I'll not back out of it. I have absolutely no idea of what I'll do with either the children or Rex, for 8 or 9 days. But both Pat Covici and Henry are simply delighted, and assure me I was very wise, professionally. It will do me good, or so I tell myself, to sharpen my somewhat dull wits a bit. I'll alternate with Malcolm Cowley on the non-fiction. Katherine Anne Porter and Vardis Fisher will do the fiction, and Stephen Spender and somebody else the poetry... awflyawfly, but at least a slight change from the present scene... and conversation. I suppose I'll fly back. Right now I feel sturdy as a rock, perhaps thanks to two weeks of medication, and I can only hope that I'll be sturdy then.

I finally got up nerve enough, and found the rightest moment in between Uncle Walter (He comes and goes, depending on Nan's moods, and while he is here R is either exhausted or hung over...) to "have a talk" with Father. I said, "Rex, I have quite a lot to ask you about, and discuss with you, mostly about the children, and I wonder if this is the right time. I mean, do you feel like talking now?" He took off his glasses, rubbed his eyes, sighed, and said encouragingly, "One time is as good as another. It doesn't matter to me what you say, anyway." So, thus stirred to action, in I plunged.

Hell, I can't go into it, except to say that I told him I'd had no idea I would be raising the children in such a rapidly changing neighborhood (about 180,000 now, and growing daily... very overcrowded and hectic schools... absolutely no feeling of permanence... and so on and so on...), and that I had come to the conclusion that I must re-establish myself in a more settled community. Of course I had a lot of good arguments. Very rapidly they were obliterated, and Rex had assured me, over and above and past anything I could say, that the children are better off here than anywhere. Then I tried to discuss the fact that $3^{1}/_{2}$ years ago I had had no idea that I was to stay, and that I felt it was time for me to move on. He said "You got fooled on that one... came up here just to fire Helen and save my reputation, didn't you?" I said "No, I came up to borrow $3000 so that I could go to a doctor for a year, but I could only borrow $1000 and you suggested I stay here for awhile, until I got things settled." (All this was very amicable... except that I was shouted down and talked over, vocally... only a few needlings,

1. MF agreed to participate in a writers' conference in Salt Lake City in the summer of 1953.

which I ignored.) Well, I managed to present my two plans: Either I must pull out, preferably to the Napa Valley, for a year or so and preferably with him on a leave-of-absence to rest and make new connections and literally take a new lease on life (I think he would, too), or I could move into Whittier where I could either buy or rent property and thus get the children into solider schooling and get a cook and go to work for him as "executive assistant" or something like that... no more cub-reporter stuff, but represent him at conventions and be in his confidence and do his editorial dirty-work, at a decent salary of course and for at least 3 to 5 years. I said that I am almost 45 and that I must stop drifting along, as an unpaid housekeeper-cook, and either mend fences as MFK Fisher or pay my own way in some other job. He said, "Let's go to bed."

The next noon he told me that he had decided I would be "dissatisfied" here in Whittier. I said of course I would... that a woman my age living alone is dissatisfied anyway... but that if I had something tangible to head toward I would be better off than I am now simply living from one day to the next wondering how to pay the bills. He said, "Well, the trouble with you is that you have never stuck with anything in your life... you give it up in four or five months... you're flighty."

I mentioned that I had stuck with this present job for more than three years, and that I had not only produced two children but some ten books in the past 12 years or so, and that I was managing to stick with Bareacres. And so on. He said, "Well, if you'll excuse me, I think I'll take a nap." And that was that, except that I think he and Walter did a lot of talking about trust funds and so on and so on.

It comes down to the fact that I would like to do one of those two things: leave here and have Rex come along, or go to work in a respectable position at the *News*. I'll finish out the school year here, and then, d.v.,[2] go to Utah, and then...

There are many things against my living alone with the children, and I would like Rex to come along. But of course he would be living with a daughter instead of having her live with him... very serious difference.

There is another factor in my wishing to move, either clear away or up into Whittier (This letter is horribly interrupted by phone-calls and people...): the place is increasingly ugly, and expensive in ratio. Right now we are having a fence put up at the end of the little den... a couple of hundred more dollars, and for what? Having the livingroom and diningroom painted and papered, with accompanying jobs, like washing the rugs and buying new rug-pads and so on, cost about a thousand. And already the cracks have opened up again.... Ho hum indeed. Rex's rooms look very shabby... were painted in 1940 or so... and paint is peeling off in great chunks in the guest house and upstairs. What is most oppressive is looking out the windows, as you will see when you are next here... little shoddy houses everywhere, a great clatter and din, telephones ringing, lights blinking in all night. I don't mean that I believe I can flee this for Elysia. But by God I do believe there are quieter more solid places where I can breathe more deeply, and my children too.

I'll not go into the many things I have thought since your suggestion that you come

2. *Deo volente,* God willing

here for a year. But I do feel very strongly that you should come down here for two or three days at least, sometime this Spring, and consider the idea ON THE PREMISES. I honestly don't believe that you would want to have the boys here. I honestly don't believe you would want simply to SIT here. And if you took over some sort of job like the one I suggested, at the *News*, you'd have to hire plenty of help (I spend about $250 a month and do all the cooking and marketing), and I think that would be *very difficult*. For one thing, there is no cook-house I'd put a dog in. For another, since I got the deep-freeze there is no space for rest and eating in the kitchen. You could put Matt in pre-school. But then there are the absolutely unpredictable hours of the local schools, for the two older boys. Above all, there is the abysmally ugly neighborhood. My god, you'll be shocked when you see it.

Or so I think. And I do wish you could get down here for a couple of nights, sometime before the end of school... have some time with Rex, and look things over.

Man proposes, God disposes. Or something like that.

I must put some ham and yams in the oven. The children are watching *Flyboy*, or maybe *Beanie*. I am interested to see what good taste they have in the programs they turn on.

I'll not re-read this. Thank you again for telephoning. Please consider the possibilities of coming down. I can most always come in to meet a plane or train. It would not exactly be a vacation, but do think seriously that you should be here again before you consider seriously uprooting the boys and renting your house and identifying yourself once more with Whittier. It would also be good for us to meet again.

I plan to give Mary a special treat tomorrow by taking her to the Grand Opening of the Shopping Bag... Free Rides for the Kiddies... Whee. Imagine celebrating your birthday that way....

....

Whittier, California   5.v.53
To: Ted Kennedy[1]

Dear Ted... a very quick one to tell you that at Rex's insistence he was brought home yesterday and he has reacted very well so far... is quite gay and triumphant and has eaten and slept better than for a long time. My my... what a feat, what a real man! Let's face it... he is on oxygen the whole time and has three nurses. He either does not know or does not care to admit that things have changed a bit since he bounced back from several cases of lobar pneumonia.

But today he had me raise (salary-wise) Mel Rich to Managing Editor, a very good step... so he knows he'll not be back at the *News* for a time. I have really been put in my place (cook)... Rex simply told me that he could hire people to work for him but he liked my cooking! Well, that should be praise enough. Meanwhile I do nothing but cook... no MFK Fisher... have YOU ever handled the kitchen for an elderly man on a low-sodium diet, three hungry nurses, and two starved Growing Girls? (I do not men-

1. Rex's brother

tion myself... I find that I snatch bites when everybody is asleep or invisible... an occupational hazard which is of course temporary....)

I do hope all is well there with you. Here we thrive, or at least feel happier... Rex to be here and the children and I to have him here.

Love—

....

To: Pat Covici

Dear Pat... It was truly good of you to write so quickly in answer to my basically bothersome questions. I agree with you that it would be much better for all of us if I would or could stop worrying....

I heard from DF today, a very tense letter enclosing Eleanor's press-release about his new job.[1] Naturally I wish him everything that is good.

He continues to ask me to refrain from adding to emotional and physical strain in any way... so I do, insofar as letters are concerned... so then he writes to ask why he has had no news, and so on. My goodness.

Don't worry about me, Pat... it is true I have a great deal on my hands right now, but before much longer I am going to sit under a grapevine and contemplate a navel... mine, the earth's....

I would like to go up into the Napa Valley for a year or so. I love the vineyards and the people who work them, and it would do me much good spiritually. It would be fine for the girls, too.

They are wonderfully well... developing fast, very quick and alive, basically well-adjusted. (Right now they think the three nurses are delightful adventures, and know that Rex is dying... everything seems *natural* to them....)

About the Writers' Conference: to put it most bluntly, if my father dies between now and the 18th of June I shall go as scheduled. If he should die on the 16th or 17th I'd simply have to be late and try to make it up to Brewster. I've not said any of this to B, of course... no use getting him upset. It seems impossible to me that Rex can last much longer, but... I plan to fly both ways, and have already arranged to leave the children with friends. I have also bought some very handsome new clothes, for the first time in $2^1/_2$ years... good for my morale.

Of course I honestly believe that everything I know about the writing of non-fiction (or writing) could be engraved on the head of a pin with a garden hoe... but I'll try to give the poor devils their money's worth, and also keep a journal for Pascal Covici....

Love from us, as always... fine news about the new family.

....

Rex Kennedy died on June 2, 1953; Mary Frances did go to Utah.

....

1. At World Publishing, where Eleanor Friede already worked

M.F.K. Fisher: A Life in Letters

1954–1970

....

St. Helena, California, and Aix-en-Provence, France

CLOCKWISE FROM UPPER LEFT: *MF's Victorian house on Oak Avenue in St. Helena;*
Kennedy, MF, and Anna on the Cours Mirabeau, Aix, 1954; Anna and Kennedy
at Le Tholonet, 1955; Fountain of the Four Dolphins, Rue Cardinale, Aix, 1960.

AFTER HER father, Rex, died in 1953, Mary Frances with her two sisters made the difficult decision to sell the Whittier *News*. The ranch was given to the city for a much-needed park. Mary Frances chose to move to St. Helena, in the Napa Valley wine country, seeking a small friendly town in which to raise her daughters. Equally important to the two girls was Mary Frances's conviction that immersion in other languages and cultures should be part of their upbringing. After a year in the Red Cottage, set idyllicly in the vineyards, she accepted a commission from *Holiday* magazine to write about Dijon's gastronomic fair, and began her long love affair with Aix-en-Provence. She and the girls discovered Le Tholonet, near Aix, when they moved into the château stables, which she described later in *Map of Another Town*, and *A Cordiall Water*. After a second long stay in Lugano, Switzerland, and in Aix in 1959–61, MF bought a Victorian house near the center of St. Helena.

During this period Donald Friede and his wife, Eleanor, both editors at World Publishing, brought out *The Art of Eating*, which brings together the five books written up till 1954 and is still her most widely read volume. Eleanor stayed with the family in Lugano, which deepened a lifelong friendship with MF.

Fisher's long association with *The New Yorker* began with the series of culinary essays published in the magazine as "Gastronomy Recalled." These became chapters in *With Bold Knife and Fork*. Rachel McKenzie, her *New Yorker* editor, encouraged Mary Frances to write the short stories later published in *As They Were* and *Sister Age*.

A commission to write *The Cooking of Provincial France* for the Time-Life Corporation introduced her to Paul and Julia Child, who dearly loved a fine, amusing letter. Through them she met fellow food writer James Beard, whom she labeled "fat Jim" to distinguish him from her old friend "skinny Jim" Beard, a printer in St. Helena. An ardent love affair in 1965 with Arnold Gingrich, editor of *Esquire* and former owner of Le Pâquis, was doomed, as were most of her loves, by family crises. Gingrich, amateur violinist, fly-fisherman, and according to Mary Frances a true eccentric, sometimes wrote her two or three letters a day. Their correspondence ended only with his death in 1976.

Early in the 1960s, Mary Frances was attacked by arthritis and required hospitalization and frequent stays in Berkeley for medical treatment. She spent a winter on Long Island in search of a peaceful place to write *Among Friends*.

Anne Kelly, MF's sister, married William Erskine and moved to

Genoa, Nevada, where Mary Frances joined her for the winter of 1964. She loved the wild mountain country, but returned only to see Anne through her final illness in 1965. *Map of Another Town* was written in Nevada.

In response to the civil rights movement, in 1965 Mary Frances plunged into teaching at an all-black school in Mississippi. This experience, fascinating and enlightening, was devastating to her health; she never fully recovered from the arthritis and a chronic recurring cough.

Every trip to France was an opportunity to visit bookstores in search of treasures for the Napa Valley Wine Library. Mary Frances served on its board of directors, but derived most pleasure from purchasing for the library. Her friends Jim and Yolande Beard, Elsine and Tony ten Broeck, and Marietta Voorhees shared this obsession with her.

A new friend in a neighboring valley, David Pleydell-Bouverie, offered in 1970 to build her a small house on his ranch near Glen Ellen. This was Mary Frances's final home and her resting place, Last House.

To: Dr. Frumkes

Dear Dr. Frumkes:

Thank you for your note of a few weeks ago. I have wanted to write to you for a long time, and of course have written endlessly in my head. It gave me real pleasure to hear from you.

Yes, I think that you did not answer a long letter I sent perhaps six months ago. But that does not matter. I did not expect you to, nor do I now, but I am glad that you manage to let me know that I can still write to you.

I no longer consider myself "on sabbatical" with you, of course, and anything I may write to you is really a professional imposition. But by now I have fairly well sorted out my feelings about you and I so thoroughly think of you as a valued and respected friend that I am not at all hesitant about thus imposing on you, even though I cannot and do not pay you a doctor's fee for reading what I write!

I have been told that most women who work with a psychiatrist fall in love with him. I did not fall in love with you, although it was plain that I was very much attracted to you physically. Perhaps if I had been younger and less weary I would have confused this with love. As it was, and as it now is, I developed a feeling which is stronger as I live with it, that you are somebody I would like to know for a long time. I myself would be glad if I could hear from you whenever you wished, and if I could write to you, and if, were you ever in SF, I might even see you... as an old friend, not as a patient.

The day before my girls and I left for the North I called you, to see if you could lunch with us. But I couldn't get anyone. You were probably on vacation.

I'll be as brief as I can about how things are with us, although I have been saving this letter to you as a kind of treat for myself, a reward for being very good about business affairs, paying bills and so on, and I may be rather wordy.

Rex died on June 2, after some 6½ weeks of illness, partly at the local hospital and, the last half, at home... 3 nurses and oxygen and so on. It was a kind of slowing-down... no real pain except in his mind. He had two or three (?) periods of coma, from which he'd awake in a state of euphoria, with increasing confusion. He became openly hateful of me and afraid of me and was in a state of horror and/or terror some of the time. This was very hard on me but I had one very wise understanding nurse and also a doctor, toward the last when the regular doctor was away, who helped me very much... a Quaker, quite old, who also was with me when my mother died.

There was of course what Rex had predicted, a kind of Roman Holiday. I ran a kind of combination bar and weeping-wall... as of course I had done for many weeks or months. Everyone from the governor to the *News* janitor dropped in for a bit of comfort.

I had accepted a job in Salt Lake City, giving a series of lectures and so on at an annual Writers' Conference... end of June. I went ahead with it... left my girls with Norah in Atascadero. I flew back alone... the first time I had felt well enough for many years to be by myself in a plane (or train or bus ororororor...). Everything was all right, and the stay of 8 days or so was very good for me, because I had to live with people who were much keener and brighter than I, and talk with them, and whet my dull wits a bit. On the way back I discovered that I no longer minded flying. I had once loved it, but had developed a real dislike for it.

I plunged into estate business in Whittier, and also worked at the *News*. It was a rough session, but I got along very well. I am co-executrix with a local banker for Rex's estate, which consists mostly of his controlling interest in the newspaper. My two sisters share equally with me in this inheritance, which cannot be settled for several more months but which we have fairly well decided to sell in one bloc, since none of us wants to live in Whittier and manage the thing properly.

It has been quite a thing for me to decide, for I love newspapers. If I did not have the children I quite possibly would become a hard-faced cold lonely "woman-editor"... and try to run things to suit myself (and my sisters). But I refuse to raise my girls down there... I would have to give at least $3/4$ of myself to the paper, with very little left over for the two refugees in the smog. No.

My sisters and I have given the Ranch, or rather the 2-plus acres left after a sale last year, to the City, for a park for children... it will save the beautiful old trees, and will be a nice way to have his spirit live. Kennedy Park...

I have wanted to be in the Napa Valley since I saw it many years ago, and came up here and within ten minutes had seen the house I wanted to live in. It is old and comfortable, with vineyards on 3 sides and a rising forest of nut-trees and then redwoods and pines on the other. I moved by the end of August, turning the old place in Whittier over to the City. I brought up everything I own, from my place in Hemet, and have spent the past two months putting up temporary bookcases and so on. It is fun to have my own home again, with my own things about me... rather cluttery but cosy, and I feel that it is good for the children too.

They are very well, physically and I think otherwise. For a time after Rex died they were apprehensive about whether I could make a true family by myself, and they wanted me to marry at once, *anybody*, the service-station boy or the 76-year-old gardener. But we moved up here and everything is so peaceful and warm that no further mention has been made of my needing a helper!

They go to the public school, and are Scout and Brownie and also have their own club, and so on... the town is very small, mostly 4th and 5th generation Swiss and Italian vineyard workers of one kind and another. People live very simply up here, whether they are rich or not, and my girls are happy to be in smaller groups and with less nervous and hurried teachers than last year's overcrowded schooling could give them.

My younger sister Norah, who came to your office the first time I saw you, is living in the next vineyard for a few months. It is fine for me, for we are mostly congenial, and her boys and my girls are very good together. She is or rather was exhausted, and this fallow period is very good for her. She seems to dread resuming her life as a psychiatric case-worker, but is in demand and can earn a good salary whenever she wants to.

M.F.K. Fisher: A Life in Letters

I don't like to see her go from one small community to another with her little pack of children... she is shunning any exposure to attractive males, partly because she knows she is vulnerable: she is very handsome, and is only 36... too bad to isolate herself this way, and get any possible stimulation from occasional contact, through me, with safely impossible visitors....

The death of my father was quite important to my sister Anne, who is two years younger than I (Norah is nine younger...), and for a time she clung to me as the last bulwark of family solidity and strength. That honeymoon is almost over, and I expect trouble before long, purportedly over the sale of our stock in the *News*, but actually a revolt, once more, from my position as eldest, best known, most married, and so on and so on. I am not scared, but I must admit I am not happy either... resigned is perhaps the best word?

This letter is too wordy, as they always are when I write to you after a long silence. I feel that you know exactly what I am saying, even in the face of my knowledge that you have a hundred more immediately demanding "cases" between thee and me.

Since I came up here at the end of August I have gone three times to Whittier, to attend to the monthly Board meeting and so on. The first time I went alone, and was gone for four days. It was wasted effort, for I could only act as a kind of 24-hour blotter, and absorb all the woes of the confused and mutually suspicious staff. It marked a real advance for me privately, however, for I spent two nights by myself on the train, I did not actually believe I could do it without climbing out a window! And in spite of the steady emotional as well as physical pressure I was under for all the time in Whittier, I had only one period of trouble (panic, apprehension, shakes), the last day after a most unpleasant scene with the business manager. I took two Danotals, for the first time in many weeks, and although I did not notice any effect from them I got through the next few hours all right and have been untroubled since then.

I have had a lot of company since I got here, mostly congenial... people I did not or could not see according to my own wishes during the four-plus years in Whittier. I enjoy being in my own house again, and cooking as I wish to, and so on. I also think it is good for the children to meet people who are my friends instead of Rex's... his were always very nice to Anne and Mary but not particularly *interested* in them.

My agent was here from NY for four days, the first time I'd seen him in almost nine years. He is of course slightly desperate about my lack of real interest in getting back to work, and kept muttering at me in his own agreeable way. I have announced loudly, having turned down a very fat offer to do my much-planned book on old age, that I am doing it anyway, as *I* wish, and *NOT* for any beautiful monthly advance. It was a rather tough decision, for I am really scratching for money until Rex's estate is settled, but I do not regret it at all.

World Publishing plans to bring out a very plush "omnibus" of five of my gastronomical books, late next year, and I am supposed to write an introduction.[1] I feel like a fool, introducing myself, and wish somebody else would do it.

1. *The Art of Eating*

This deal was engineered by Donald Friede, who is now an editor for World, where his wife also works. It is he who offered me so much money... trying to get me away from Viking and his one other true friend, Pascal Covici. It is not a good situation and I am glad my instincts played me true. My next book, which at this point I have less than no interest in writing, will go, as it should legally and morally, to Viking, which has been a patient and forgiving publisher for many lean years. Donald is very bitter about my decision, and refuses even to speak to his friend of 30 years, Pat C. Ho hum. I think he will overstep himself again, before long, and be out of a job, and then it may well be *my fault*, and *Pat's*... a familiar pattern.

My sister Norah, who is a good judge, hopes that the publication of the omnibus will put a clear-cut end to that gastronomical phase in my life. I think my agent does too... he remains impressed by the story I wrote about adolescent girls, published in a woman's magazine about 18 months ago, and wants me to work hard with fiction.

I can't work hard with anything right now. I am really hibernating or something like that... I have spent two months (!) getting boxes of books unpacked and so on... making curtains... hanging pictures... I have a year's lease on this place but simply can't contemplate moving for at least another ten....

My subconscious or unconscious or whatever it would be, however, is working overtime, and increasingly I write all night while I sleep. Pretty soon I'll get to work.......

I seem to have hit another level of behavior or existence. I have learned a lot about myself, thanks largely to you I believe. Physically I have changed a lot too: I am plainly in the middle years, and walk-sit-eat-sleep-breathe differently, with a different rhythm and necessity. I continue to be very *nice*, and my "God Damned poise" is still there, but I waste a lot less time on a great many things which used to bother me. My relations with the children are good for the most part... I occasionally feel completely bored with them, and am rather short-spoken. I am also unfairly "mature" with Anne, the older, who reminds me too much of many of my own worst sides when I was young... I grow sarcastic and carping with her, for she seems much more than ten years old. But in the main I think both girls are very balanced and keen about life. Mary asks now and then about Donald, but Anne does not. She would like to go to NY to a professional children's school, but not because Donald is there, apparently.

I suppose I can't keep up this dual role forever, but right now it is no burden to be mother-father.

It is very beautiful here. Have you ever been in a wine country?

I am thinking about what I have just written about my writing. Once I told you that writing for me was (is?) a form of making love. I have nobody to make love to, for my children are too young for me to gear my vocabulary (spiritual as well as actual) to their unknown ways of thinking, and otherwise I know only my sisters, my Uncle Walter who is now dying and past my reaching him, and one or two women-friends. Perhaps I should invent a lover, as some children do an imaginary playmate!

My theory may be quite mistaken. But it is certainly plain that right now I am absolutely (except for my unconscious night-work) incapable of anything but a *pretense* at writing. Hard on my pocketbook and my agent!

I don't fret about it, I simply recognize it.

All of which may show that I am gradually maturing.

Thank you again for your note. I hope this has not been any kind of chore or bore for you to read. Just as sincerely I hope you did not bother to read it at all, unless you wanted to.

I wish I could see you again, perhaps not to work with you. But I am in Los Angeles only one Saturday a month. It would be foolish.... The children and I are coming South for dental work and so on in either December or January. Perhaps we could meet then for a howdedo.... Anyway it must be plain to you that I think of you often, and with great warmth. I don't know if this is the correct attitude for a former patient to have toward her doctor?! My best, as always.

....

St. Helena, California   *15.ii.54*
To: Lawrence Clark Powell

Dearest Ghuce... I'm so glad you wrote. I was worrying... afraid you were in trouble. I know from the picture that you aren't. You are just *alive*... and as we both know, that is both heaven and hell and something few people ever achieve. I am happy for you, about it.

The picture is fine. Thanks for letting me see it.

Be together all you can.

I suffer for Fay too, of course. But it exasperates me to hear that she feels you "deserted" her and the boys to take your present assignment. Pooh.

Yes, it is strange and painful to re-learn about being alone. But it is a strengthening experience. Frightening too.

Now about me: I am in a way very peaceful and contented. I love it here. Many things about myself bore me, and I am gnawed by dissatisfaction with much of what I am, and yet too lazy to do much but fret, spiritually. It is an inevitable reaction to the past four years, I know. I don't worry... just force myself to bow. I know it won't last much longer. Meanwhile I sleep more peacefully than for many years, and eat and drink pretty much to my own tastes, and *wait*. I'm not doing any intelligent work... have two stories about one-third done and am still scribbling notes for the book on old age. World is planning a "production" of the Fisher omnibus, and Fadiman[1] will do the introduction. I feel quite plainly repelled by the whole thing, and wish I had never agreed to it... warming a cold corpse, as far as I'm concerned, for the woman who wrote those books has been dead for years.

This place is beautiful, and I hope very much you'll see it... in the vineyards, but with redwoods and olives and madrones at the door. I stand dreaming at the windows. The vineyards are waist-high with wild mustard now. We walk along the little roads, humming and listening to the birds, with mimosa in our topknots.

The children are happy... they like school enough to pass their tests, and have nice friends. Anne is in love with a boy called Eusabio... she inherits my proclivity for wor-

1. Clifton Fadiman, author and friend

shipping the renegades… he is the worst boy in school. She is a Scout and Mary is a Brownie and they even go to Church School, mainly to earn their little gold crosses….

I am going very slowly here… don't see many people… I plan to come here to live, though! (Can change my mind, of course…) I like the way of life, and the people. They are very quiet intense ones, mostly born here. There are a few outlanders, like me but very well known, who live here without a breath of fame… nobody cares if they are authors or neurologists or or or… here they keep quiet like everyone else.

I am thinking of trying to buy the weekly *Star,* in the next few years. It is still a reputable paper, but is in bad shape… laziness. Norah and I might run it. She wants to get into a paper again too. It is quite an exciting idea….

We sold the *News* all right. I am still in a state of shock about it, and probably will be as long as I live. I still feel we did what Rex would have advised. I still know I would cut off my leg if it had failed me….

Next year I hope to live in SF, if I can keep this place for our real home… all the books and pictures… horrible to move them again! I'd get a very small plain flat for the girls and me… they'd go to parochial day-school and Anne to a professional training school, and I'd work. We'd come up here every weekend, and every vacation. It is a dream, but may come true. Then the next year should be France, if I can manage it. I want the girls to get there once before they are adolescent….

By the time we get taxes paid and lawyers and so on, we'll each (my two sisters and I) have a fairly nice sum to be paid over the next five years. We plan to establish trusts, for our kids. I also plan to invest whatever I think advisable in fun… I figure I can do a few things with and for the children which will be much more valuable to them than money they may inherit from me. The first fling will be 9 days in SF for the Easter Vac, at a good apartment-hotel… we'll do everything we never have time for on the monthly trips to the orthodontist. We already have a tentative list of 34 ESSENTIAL things. Murder. And fun. The Mint, the Musée Mécanique, on and on. Norah and her three boys (They live in Berkeley now) will be in on most of it, and of course Anne Kelly, who lives in Sausalito… and assorted cronies.

Do you hear from Hal? I must get busy. Write when you can, my dear old GHUCE… ALL MY LOVE…

I have a new Hermes—keep hitting wrong keys—caps all right though!

When do you come West? Come this way! Can pick you up in SF or Sacramento.

....

St. Helena, California   *8.iii.54*
To: Lawrence Clark Powell

Dearest Ghuce… Thank you for writing. I enclose the letters from Jeanne and Georges.[1] I shall always wish that the former did not continue to set my teeth a little on edge with her inescapable air of meechamy cadging. I like her, I even love much about

1. Georges Connes

her. And then she turns servile and whining and begging. I haven't answered a letter about three years old, in which she asked me for any cast-off rags in order to cover her grandchildren. I can't believe that France and her husband, both practicing doctors, cannot clothe their children properly. Jeanne simply cannot help placing herself in a subservient and boot-licking position.... My own kids are simply but adequately clad, largely with clothes handed down from a cousin and two godchildren, and when the clothes are out-grown they go on to Norah's boys when possible, and to a still younger goddaughter. And so it is, in any large family... and I have nothing left to send to un-known and presumably deserving children in France. End of grouse. Except I wish to hell I didn't feel this way, *always*, when I hear from the tender sweet woman.

An interesting thing to me is that I have a much closer friend, of somewhat the same type, who is suddenly doing exactly what JB does in this letter... they both refer to themselves in the 3rd person! I want to ask a doctor about it. Is it a sign of with-drawal from life, in the 60s? Is it, the other way around, an unconscious attempt to be-come legendary, mysterious, *fictional*? Have you ever noticed it in letters from older women...? I myself have tried it in a journal... referring to myself as "she... her...." (It didn't work!)

So you are working with Haydn... that sounds right.

It's wonderful that you feel as you do about teaching. There may lie your great-ness, Ghuce.

Yes, this place is idyllic... perhaps too much so. I begin to chafe and fret... too damned comfortable. I look forward to a leaner stricter life next year, and meanwhile I lean against the open window and listen to the tractor discing the vineyards, with the bruised mustard, waist-high yesterday, sending out bitter-honey smells.

There is much in the works. I am apparently to do a text for the much discussed Univ. of Calif. book about wines in July and August or before. Frugé, Littell, and Yavno[2] were here three times last week, leaving material. I refused politely to touch it with a 12-foot pole... incomplete, inadequate, feeble stuff. The book has been kicked around too long. As for the omnibus World will bring out in the Fall, it seems to be all right. I feel a great distaste for it. The woman who wrote the stuff died long ago, and the newly-birthed is still in swaddlings. . . .

Your life sounds like the right one for now. Did Fay go back? Do you go to any plays, concerts? Are you well?

Love

....

St. Helena, California   *20.iii.54*
To: Remson Bird, president of Occidental College

Dear Rem... It was wonderful to hear from you again. Thank you for writing.

Your letter has been much in my mind, even though I'm so slow about answering it (... or perhaps because...?). . . .

2. All from the University of California Press

I wish we could talk about your letter... which as always was very stimulating and provocative.

I must tell you bluntly, Rem, that I don't see the scheme in your light. I don't feel that for commercial and touristic reasons you could arbitrarily change the eating habits of a nation... and if you did set up a chain of decent tourist-kitchens, for instance, it would be an arbitrary impingement of your wishes upon the so-called culture of a country, and would very rightly be resented.

I myself would never think of telling the British how to cook... no matter how artfully I might be aided in doing so by wiser people than myself.

What is more, I think people like André Simon and all his able disciples, henchmen, and devotees have pretty well set up a rather fabulous hierarchy of gastronomical perfectionists from upper Scotland to Land's End. It is true that most of them, in desperation, have turned their back on the native cuisine and nurtured the best possible of French and Swiss and and and transplantations. But Simon's *Wine and Food Quarterly* does try honorably to stress the basic goodness that CAN be produced in British kitchens. And he is not the only one....

As we all know, the average style of eating-dining-feeding in England has been brutally lowered by the long years of rationing and scarcities. Tastes have been twisted and changed, willynilly. It is all part of the world-wide progress of what I can only think of as mediocritization... a hideous word... but for me it means the gradual way we *all* of us are led to accept less and less high standards: by now in this country we actually accept, faute de mieux, margarine instead of fresh sweet butter, and so on, just as English children who have never eaten fresh lemons or bananas think powdered chemically treated dried fruits are delicious. It goes on everywhere all the time... and because of the past years the British are several steps lower, or higher, than we are in their mediocritization, gastronomical as well as otherwise.

And so... when we go over there and are appalled at the bad bread instead of the old country-loaves, and the Australian bacon loaded with MSG and fake taste of smoke, and so on and so on, we are unfair. Give us a few pinched years, and we may be eating worse fare and thinking it quite normal! Now we have everything, mediocre though it may be....

Of course there is something in the Anglo-Saxon nature too... in a tiny way it is the same thing that made the Germans accept Hitler... we "accept." The French didn't... they still grow green peas in the springtime, and churn butter when they can. But we Saxons! We are pusillanimous? For reasons we do not bother to question, we are told on the air and in the slick magazines that Mrs. Vanderbilt and Gloria Swanson always serve margarine, although they can afford "much better" (meaning butter...)... and so gradually butter almost disappears and we all think margarine is delicious stuff.

Ah well. Also Ho hum. The subject is too big for me.

Your approach to getting some decent meals in England fascinates me, and I hope that I learn more about it. And please know, my dear friend Rem, that I am not as teasing as I sound: I know very well how much deeper it goes with you than worrying about having to eat overboiled brussels sprouts from London to Glasgow... I'm not as flippant as I may sound. (But I don't need to tell you that.)

Two days and one typewriter later: I don't dare re-read this, but will send it off to you for what very little it is worth. At least it will tell you again how happy I was to hear from you. I wish you would write... let me know how "light and airy" your touch remains, as you go from town to town telling people that unless they improve their fare they'll lose touch with their American Cousins... tell me how you are, in Carmel and everywhere... tell me if there is any chance of my seeing you both again, when next you are in San Francisco. Is there a chance that you'd be up this far? It would be wonderful to see you *here*... the Valley is beautiful, as of course you know, and I have a nice little house (telephone St. Helena 756)....

My very best to you and Helen, as always. Affectionately,

....

St. Helena, California   *10.v.54*
To: Donald Friede

Dearest D... I've been meaning for at least a week to write to you, and have thought every day that I'd know more to tell you about fairly solid plans for next year.

You know I've wanted to take the children to France and Suisse for a year, and when I started them with the SF orthodontist I told him to gear the work toward a year's absence, as of Autumn 1955. Then at Easter when the children went in for their regular work, he told me casually that this Fall would be much better than next! I was completely taken aback: I'd planned to put them in school in SF and live in a very small apartment and keep this place for the weekends and so on.

Well, it seems almost a fait accompli. All I have to do is see about the transportation costs, when I take them to SF on the 19th for teeth and *Brigadoon* (It's Johnnie Barr's 8th birthday... big party at Solari's and then the play... wow...). I'll get round-trip tickets (!)... probably go in the *Champlain*.

We'll sail either late in August, hitting the empty traffic going over, or early in October. It depends a lot on whether I can land a couple of magazine assignments... I'd like to "cover" la Foire Gastronomique de Dijon, for instance, but so many of the Bhoys have already done it... I'll keep you posted, naturally.

Once there we'll see a few people in Paris. But there are too many people there I *don't* want to see (ex-Hollywood... I'd like to see Man and Julie.[1] But of course with two kindern I'm simply not available for any trotting around, which is all right with me. Michel LeGouis[2] is there, and also his little sister Anne, who is just our Anne's age).

We'll head for a small and preferably warm provincial town, maybe something like Arles or even Avignon... question partly of clothes (!), and I'll put the children into separate small pensionnats for the first rough tough plunge into "l'encre sur la table de ma

1. Juliet and Man Ray
2. Michel LeGouis, nephew of Henriette and Georges Connes

belle-mère." They are very keen about learning French and are already pricking up their ears to simple phrases and so on.

About three months of that ought to see them fairly well launched, and of course I'll be nearby, taking lessons myself and feeling very lonely except on weekends with them. I ought to get some real work done. Then we'll go to a small un-chic mountain resort, either in France or Suisse, where the children can get the basics of skiing and skating, along with some more verbs. I myself yearn to do a good figure-8 before I'm doddering....

Paris in the Spring, naturally... I may be able to borrow or rent a small car and show the girls a few donjons at least... they are very much in the *Ivanhoe–Prince Valiant* &&& period, and we can go back later for Chartres and stained glass. I'd like to let them spend some time in Aigues-Mortes, and up north in the basilica at Vézelay, and so on. Then... most astonishing of all perhaps... Norah plans to come over for a year with her three boys! (We'll have to come back in August, for orthodontia and my yearly accounting to the court and so on...)

We talk dreamily of a summer à la Heidi (all the children have seen the new Swiss movie and think that's the life for them...). We'd rent a chalet in a really remote Alpine village, and walk-talk-write, and take lessons from the pastor, and the kids could learn to milk goats and yodel. It sounds idyllic but more than faintly possible.

Then the girls and I would come home.

And so it is. What do you think? (I hate to bother you with all this, for I can guess how completely busy you both are... but I'd like to have you and Eleanor tell me your opinions in every way. I mean, on every thing.)

I am not yet clear about the finances. I'll know the general fees for the round-trip tickets (We'll probably fly to NY...) this Tuesday, as I said. Once I get there, I'll live for somewhat less than I spend here, since perforce I'll be doing it quietly and un-stylishly. And I think this is absolutely the right moment to subject the children to their first inoculation of another language and another culture. They are developing very fast, and in another year Anne will really be in adolescence, with a whole new set of troubles. Now she is on the verge, but is still enough of a child... she is the Lady Rowena one minute and Tom Sawyer the next. Mary is still... guess what... *Mary*. I may have to ask the court's permission to use some of the children's monies... I consider this almost as important as orthodontia (The doctor is doing a beautiful job and they are going to be pretty as pictures...), and I'm sure there'll be no question. Of course I'll let you know.

Do write if you have time, for I am anxious to have your opinions. I do want to do it, and I think it wise to do it *now*, in every possible way. I have good friends in Paris, Dijon, Biarritz, Montreux, and Cavigliano still, thank God, the kind I not only want to see again but would not hesitate to call upon. And we are very well and healthy, all three.

(Oh, Anne took a header off her bike and smashed her thumb, but it is coming along very well... bruised cartilage or however you spell it... a nuisance with the metal splint, but of course she loves the drama of it....)

Love from us to you both...

M.F.K. Fisher: A Life in Letters

St. Helena, California   *19.v.54*
To: Henry Volkening

Dear Henry... three messages from you this morning... the letter of May 10 took a long time... ponies not running on schedule or something....

Of COURSE it is all right about sending back the story. Your doing so simply adds to my respect for you, which sounds rather roundabout but I know you know what I mean. I'll keep right on, as you also know.

You and Natalie are fine friends, to ask us to stay with you. I'd like to accept right this minute, but must tell you and ask you a few things first.

We will sail, d.v., at noon on the 25th of August, on the *Liberté*[1].... I decided second-class on a big ship would be more fun than first on a smaller one, for the children. We plan to take a TWA day-flight from here and arrive in Chicago at night and then go on to NY the next night, arriving at 9:55 I believe.

The prospect of being trotted around to editors dismays me, to put it nicely. I know, I know... my so-called career is not in good shape, and you are trying to look out for it, and so on. But, Henry, could it be done in perhaps just one or two, and I do mean one or two little talks with people like Mr. Fischer? For many reasons I think it unwise for me to be more than about two days in NY, at the most: this whole thing is something of a wild-eyed scheme, to quote my father, and I want to start off in really solid shape (inwardly), and will be subjected to quite a lot of emotional pressure, which is bad for me. (Donald and Pat C are not speaking, for instance, and I am devoted to the Covicis, and of course will have to observe as many as possible of the ex-marital amenities with DF, and so on... I don't want to start off with two troubled over-excited children and treat myself to a fat case of the shakes in mid-Atlantic. And it is a possibility. Except for seeing you, non-professionally, I wish I could go through the Canal and bypass NY....)

Of course you and N may be in Vermont or someplace.

Meanwhile, I'll keep you or her posted about the actual dates, and I do thank you both for your heartwarming invitation.

Don't worry, I know "assignments" are very loose. I meant that if somebody really *wanted* me to write about the Foire Gastronomique I'd see to it that I got to France in time for it. As it is, I'll be there anyway, and may or may not go down to the fair.... I've seen them before, and it depends on whether Georges Connes is in Dijon or in his vineyards in the south....

As for money, I am not counting on earning anything at all to support us. I'll write as it seems best, and maybe something will come of it. If by chance somebody asks me to do something while I am there, so much the better, but I am not counting on it at all. I am going to use all I need of what comes to me from the *News* sale... I figure it is a much better investment in the children's possible "futures" than to hang onto it and leave it to them when I die. They may be in a slave-labor camp by then.... Bankers and lawyers find this attitude deplorable. I do not worry about it... or them! . . .

1. They ended up sailing on the *Diemerdyk*, earlier than planned.

Your reply to DF's letter is a masterpiece. I myself have not heard from him (Business before pleasure or something like that?), but I can tell you right now, unless you convince me to the contrary, that there is absolutely nothing for me to discuss with Donald, as you suggest in your note to him.

His letter appalls me, except that I realize that it should not, since it is a natural part of his nature to be able to conceive of writing it!

Has he forgotten that I am under contract to Viking?

Henry, I realize that I should quite probably be pleased that any publisher wants me to write for him, and that I may be cutting my throat and perhaps even taking a little nick out your already bloody neck, but *I do not want to become any more involved than I already am with World,* and it is that simple, and there are reasons which I need not even mention to you, for you already know *all* of them. I regret with what amounts to a rather unhealthy physical regret that I ever consented to this ominous publication... I think it is *disgusting* to warm up those ashes in public. It is too late now. But I have no right, moral or otherwise, to consider *in any way* such a suggestion as Donald has made.

I loathe involving you in my personal affairs, but I must tell you that I am very unwilling to antagonize DF in any way, and I fear it because his professional and personal natures are so intertwined. My attitude toward him can even be called placative, *up to a certain point,* for I am completely and perhaps at times a little desperately anxious to have the children grow up with me instead of with him. And I don't want to do anything that his very complex and twisted nature will be able to use against my doing so... professionally or otherwise, it does not really matter. I feel that you understand this.

It is indeed a two-edged weapon! Ho hum. And Ah well.

And that is that... except that *if* you are going to be in NY right before August 25 and *if* you want us to, we'd like very much to stop with you. Pat Covici is the children's godfather and I know we should see as much as possible of him and Dorothy if they are there... and of course I should have the children see as much of Donald as he can spare them. But quite frankly, I must repeat, my main interest is getting M. F. K. Fisher off on the *Liberté* in one good stable calm unharried unperturbed chunk. I don't want to start for a year in Europe with little girls and a case of the emotional and professional jitters....

Best to you both, as always...

....

Diemerdyk, Iceland   *23.viii.54*
To: Norah Kennedy Barr

Dearest N... I found a couple of things in Raymond Chandler's essay, "The Simple Art of Murder," which sum up a couple of other and/or the same things I've been saying to myself... not in a defeatist way, I must add, probably unnecessarily to *you.*

He is talking about professional magazine writers, the good ones as opposed to the careless hacks... "Everything a writer learns about the art or craft of fiction takes just a little away from his need or desire to write at all. In the end he knows all the tricks and has nothing to say." This is very true of two or three *good* magazine writers I have known, who, according to Chandler and themselves, keep on trying to "exceed the limits of a formula without destroying it." Witness Harlan Ware, who is a sensitive man of inherent literary taste, and who in his inevitable ennui as a successful and therefore formulized *Satevepost* writer has finally found himself wordless. He can still dish out thousands of dollars' worth of words for radio, but he is in a complete desert, now, as far as writing what the mag-editors want from him. I think this proves his basic goodness. But of course it does not satisfy his very money-and-prestige-conscious wife....

Well... I've lost a couple of other things I meant to throw at you from Chandler. It's a good little piece. It appeared in *Harper's*, I think, quite a time ago. There is a good comparison of English and American styles of mystery writing... he says he prefers the former (except for his own, no doubt!), and sums it up rather nicely: "The English may not always be the best writers in the world, but they are incomparably the best dull writers."

Now about myself: I have no illusions about the scope or depth or whatever it may be of my talents, nor of how I have handled them. They are very limited and small, but not weak or puny... and doubtless I have wasted both time and my ability to use them to mutual advantage. But at the same time I think I have been fortunate, to be offered and to accept contracts when I did, when I was younger and fairly ignorant and self-confident. I always did the best I could... which of course was the reason for the best of all breaks, being fired from Paramount! And I earned money when I had to, in a way that was much more enriching than a straight newspaper or factory or store job would have been.

By now I think I am lucky to have some money outside of what I could still make by contract-writing, for I've reached a point rather like the one Chandler mentions, as far as following a successful formula may go. I could quite easily go on indefinitely with jobs for *House Beautiful* and so forth. But it would be sure slow poison to the good writer in me, which by now is still healthy and with excellent muscles and so on. The way things are, I can, and I believe I will, use whatever I've learned in writing some things which will give me great satisfaction. They may or may not make any money for us. I may very well, and within a couple of years, have to take another contract. But I'll be the better for this period of creative independence.

Or so *I* believe. There are good arguments against it. One is that I work well under moral as well as physical pressure and that I may drift without it. Or it could be said to me that the best work I've yet done is the Brillat-Savarin which was ground out under circumstances which nobody would believe possible. (I wonder if I should write about that sometime?) Well...

....

Aix-en-Provence, France   *le 22!.x.54*
To: Lawrence Clark Powell

Dear Ghuce—I was so glad to get your letter—thanks for it and for the *Hoja V,* which I would say was fairly well monopolized, inadvertently of *course,* by LCP. Your book hasn't come yet, but I thank you in advance. More or less tit-for-tat I have asked World to send you a review copy of the omnibus but *meanwhile* did you never receive one I sent you (*non*-review!)? It had a very noncommittal but still loving "inscription" in it. Ah well. I'll try again! And it may still turn up— . . . When and where did you start having troubles with sinus? No fun. Too much starch... Which reminds me: what of Hal? I wonder how he likes life on the cliff? Tell me any news.... It is of course good news that in their various ways your various wives are "rich-productive-happy..."! Ghuce, you are monstrous and marvelous! (And you may quote me....) Will start sending postcards, mainly of fountains . . . Not an hour ago I put Georges on a bus for Marseille, on his way from Aveyron by way of Aix(!). In spite of having yesterday helped bury his old friend the village priest, he looked well, strong, ironic as ever... dressed in rough corduroys which became him, and heavy mountain boots and a beret. We walked slowly all over this lovely place, where he taught at the Lycée for two years before marrying and going to Dijon in the '20s. (He told me he kept two establishments, one here and one in Marseille for when he got fed up here! Good old Connes!) (This is a completely dull town for young people....) It was Thursday, so my girls came along too... we ate in the bright sunshine at a good Brasserie across from the Palais de Justice, where the kids are in love with the exhausted young waiter and the 5-o'clock hot chocolate equally... it is near their school where I meet them in the afternoons. I ate couscous, quite mild and good. Georges took us to the fashionable café for coffee. We walked and talked. A very nice gentle friendly day... and it did me much good, for I have been in a rather unsettled state of mind lately, and I know that it is partly because I have absolutely nobody to talk with. I'm not at all a chatty person, but there have been a few people with whom I could talk just about as unthinkingly and unreservedly as I breathe or swallow—Eda Lord, Dillwyn, You, occasionally Donald, Norah. And now?... This reminds me of something Anne said the other day at a meal we were eating (devouring really—we'd walked 10 miles for it!) in a little café—she spoke around a large mouthful of cold chicken... "the word *frustrating* is very hard to say, isn't it? Especially if you're frustrated!"

My girls are really very interesting... and I was pleased to have Georges tell me that they seem wonderfully well adjusted or attuned or whatever the word would be to this latest upheaval of country-language-food-etc. God knows that is what I aim at: to make them able to live *any*where, in a prison or on caviar.

I must get to work. Write when you can, my dear over-busy fellow. Love to Hal when you see him... to Pat if she would.

Your faithful slave...

Oh... the children are in Catholic school, as day-girls, and living in a state of increasingly dirty necks and richer vocabularies with the very nice Wytenhoves. I am still, and I hope I can stand it for several more months, with Mme. Lanes—incredibly fusty and "correcte" but there are very few families in Aix who take pensionnaires and they

M. F. K. Fisher: A Life in Letters

are all of the same "poor-but-proud" aristocracy. I often think I will *absolutely die* of a kind of exasperated boredom. But there is no alternative except to live in a hotel, not good for my recognized traits of neurasthenia!!

....

Aix-en-Provence, France   *14.i.55*
To: Lawrence Clark Powell

Dear Ghuce... thank you for sending me the Powelliana... very good stuff and you are indeed piling up an impressive list of it. I sent your thing on Western writers to an old friend, one of the few remaining Rough Riders, who knows quite a lot about the West. In return, dear fellow, is a good thing on Cézanne. I had a catalog for you of the retrospective Dufy show in Marseille, but somebody has borrowed it... it's a very good show, which we saw on Christmas Day... I believe it is to go to Los Angeles and I hope you see it... very gay and pure, like Mozart. There is a show here in town which is good too, and whose catalog someone has "borrowed" from me, of a young Haitian named Turrennes des Près (?)... that reminds me, that the Pré aux Clercs, where you and your mother invited Al and Noni and me before we left for Strasbourg, is now the best restaurant in Dijon, ahead of the Trois Faisans even though that is better since Henri Racouchot died last Autumn and his chef Tournebise took over. Tournebise did the dinner at the Clos Vougeot the night I was made a Chevalière du Tastevin[1] (You may kiss the tip of my nose for twenty cents the next time we meet...), and he handled almost 500 people with impressive skill. He is really a good man, in the modern sense of being able to cope with publicity and all that stuff....

Last night I took Madame Lanes[2] to hear Cortot. It was painful, especially at first, for he is almost zombie-ish, plainly ill and alone, at least for me who am painfully attune with old age. At first he played in a rather mushy dead way, but then he grew warmer until he was at times even masterly... nothing but Chopin and Schumann, but very demanding for such an old man. There is still plenty of feeling against him for his "bad conduct" during the Occupation, but he got a standing ovation at the end and was almost overcome. It was a dream-like experience for me, a kind of summing up of much I have been trying to put into words lately, about age... especially in the Municipal Theatre here, which is one of the few left in France with the early 18 C. décor, like the inside of a very dusty mothy beautiful jewel-box, all hung with faded velvet and edged on three sides right to the painted ceiling with little gilded tufted loges which cry out for fans in gloved hands and so on and instead are stuffed with bobby-soxers chewing American gum and *still* liking the music....

We had a fantastic Christmas. Sean[3] flew up from Casa [Blanca] for five days, and his Mother suddenly flew over instead of going to Costa Rica, and we all went to Mar-

1. This award is traditionally given to only a few connoisseurs of wine and food. MF may have been the first woman to receive it.
2. MF's landlord in Aix; originally the girls lived with the Wytenhoves, where they spoke nothing but French, before joining MF in her lodgings.
3. Sean Kelly, MF's nephew

seille for three days... too much to start telling you about... brilliant cold weather, everything very clear-cut and intense.

There is an interesting bookseller here who is becoming a friend. He has a complete run or whatever you call it of Les Pléiades, from 1946... that makes 13 copies. The first copy, which starts out with Gide of course, ran 3000 and he can sell it for 375 francs or about a dollar, numbered of course. The rest of the copies which run only 200 cost from 600 to 1200 francs. I do not permit myself, a long-standing policy, to start buying this type of item, but I told him I'd tell you, for the Library. Certainly it is something any library interested in avant-guerre French writing should have, for along with the old boys like Gide there are all the new ones, plus fine typography and so on. Have one of your gals give me a yes or no, will you? (Neither of us has any personal interest in this, needless to say... he makes his living, and tries to lure me now and then... for instance Picasso is his friend and often stays here with him and leaves drawings everywhere to say thank-you, with the understanding that Brondino can sell them if he wants to....) (And since Brondino has a large hungry family he sometimes does....) (So far I have remained adamant... I believe that is the word....)

Everything is fine with us, especially since we are living together in the lovely old house I first came to... the girls have a big sunny room where I work. I'm getting a lot done, but am stalling shamefully on the story for *Holiday*,[4] which I obviously hate. I hope to turn out something which will please Viking, at least, this Spring. Then the children and I will come back to SF by way of Stockholm, where we have good Swedish friends... leave here by plane in June, and Gotheburg in July on a Johnson Line freighter. It sounds rather wild but exciting and I think it will be a lot less of an anticlimax than to leave on a French boat from Marseille. I plan to stay here in Aix until we leave, with perhaps one jaunt to Aigues-Mortes or even, if I can sell another story, by plane to Corsica where we have made some good friends. Meanwhile the children are growing in every way both innard and outtard, and we are fine together.

How about you and yours, dear Ghuce? Write when you have half a minute.

....

Aix-en-Provence, France   *15.iv.55*
To: Anne Kelly and Norah Kennedy Barr

Dear Sisters, dear girls, dear Sis and None... Please forgive this joint letter. I loathe them too. But it is just to you, in answer to two fairly alike ones I got from you both in today's mail... and I find myself slightly shaken at the knowledge that I have a possible five more days to get un-organized and out to the country: what to take, what to store, what to have dry-cleaned. Murder.

You both wrote about my plan to bring Monique Wytenhove back with us... Noni somewhat more tersely, but both with the same astonishment-dismay-hurt—and probably much more.

4. About the Foire Gastronomique, commissioned before she left for France

M. F. K. Fisher: A Life in Letters

I'm truly sorry to have thrown any kind of cold water in *any* direction. And I don't think I have, or I wouldn't have done it. Noni, you say that you have felt "dismayed at the prospect of sharing this boat trip with an outsider." But, although you and Monique do not know one another and may even not like one another, she is not an "outsider" to my girls and me, and therefore she is not really one to you.

The word is one I often talked-rowed-argued-suffered over with our parents, and especially Edith, who honestly believed that *any* amount of boredom or bad manners or stinginess were acceptable IF the offender were not an Outsider but One*of*Us... meaning preferably a Holbrook but by marriage a Kennedy. She was not wrong. For her. But I am not wrong, for me, and I honestly believe that our own inner strength and security and happiness and amusement and everything else we have together is intensified and made even moreso by what Edith, and now you, call Outsiders. It is that simple! Most probably we do not agree. But it is a long-standing belief of mine, and as far as I know has never endangered our unity as a Family.

As to "sharing this boat trip," there will be other people than the Barrs and the Friedes[1] on board! I myself do not like the idea of being FOUR in a stuffy cabin... we will of course take the one you'd have had if you had brought Matt along. . . . But I am more philosophical about such things than I used to be... or or or...

Both of you wonder if Monique will not be "equally bored by young and old," to quote N. No, I don't think so. She is one of the most unbored people I've met. Not at all in a cloying *enthusiastic* way. That is to say, she is not as Sis describes Sylvia S and her young man....

I'm sorry the Wytenhoves were in Nice at Christmas. It would have been good to introduce them to you, Sis. (I think you both know that this letter is not in any sense an attempt to *justify* my hope to bring Monique back with us, but is one to explain to you why I think it is a good idea....) If you had met the family, you would know how mistaken it is to say "The girl would be neither servant nor friend, and unless she is retarded mentally, could hardly be considered a companion for your girls."

There is no question of Monique's being a servant, any more than my own children are servants, or I myself. I expect her to help with beds-dishes-marketing and normal responsibilities, and eventually driving (escorted of course), just as I expect my own girls to. There is also no question of her being a friend. She is. She has been an intimate of the children for several months, and I have seen a lot of her, beknownst and otherwise. She is a complicated basically well-balanced female, much older than the average of her age in the States, and much ahead of the French girls of her social class because she lived until she was 11 in Spain, and then a time in Italy, and has gone through a revolution, a war, and a couple of forced emigrations, not to mention the death of her father by cancer. She remains a merry sane person... and I have seen her bleary and feverish, as well as pretty and gay. As for her being mentally retarded in any way, she is not. I know her grades and records at the Lycée (which is a very tough one),

1. MF was still using her married name.

and they are good. She hated school and has gone on only because she thinks it is a good idea. She has no idea of becoming a teacher, which is why most girls in France who will have to earn their living finish their education. She will pass her finals in June... the equivalent of our Junior College... with a slightly-above-average grade according to the head of the Lycée. But she is not at all an "intellectual"... has a good classical background but loves movies and jazz and "les sodas d'ice cream."

As to "keeping up the girls' French"... it's not exactly a beautiful dream, as you say, Sis, but it's a hope. They are now at the point where if they had six more months here the French would be a permanent thing in their thought and life. Monique speaks an excellent well-bred French which when she becomes upset or excited has a slight Spanish accent... unfortunate to a purist like Madame Lanes but merely "normal" to the mixed people here in Provence. Her English is timid and clipped, after several years of school and one summer in England. I hope to be able to work out some sort of quasi-schedule with, say, two French days and five American ones, as far as meals and so on go....

About her being a companion, she is a very good one. She has good manners, which both girls think are WONDERFUL. She is dainty personally, and uses make-up well for a beginner, which Anne thinks is WONDERFUL too. And so on. She also loves younger children with a completely uncomplicated simplicity... finds them interesting, amusing, and never dull... if they are bad-mannered she freezes them (mine at least...).

My expenses will certainly be heavier, but not "doubled" exactly, Sis. A minimum of two baths sounds pretty fancy, for I have seldom enjoyed such a state, and if I ever did, I would immediately seize one for myself ALONE, and let the assorted adolescents scream for the other. There will undoubtedly be boring moments (or hours) in whatever place I finally find, but all four of us have pretty well-groomed bathroom manners and I don't think it will be too difficult to struggle along with one tub and/or shower, a toilet that actually flushes, and a washbasin with water, preferably hot AND cold. (At this point it sounds like heaven....)

There is no *minimum of four bedrooms*, for if I was planning to get two, which I was, I will now hope to find three. I myself prefer, and have always planned, to sleep in a large room which I hope will also serve as living-dining-work room... it is not impossible, and I find I work much better if I can drift about at night, once the young are bedded. I would like very much, this next year, to be able to give each girl a room of her own, no matter how small; but if it is impossible, we can manage otherwise.

I can imagine Noni's experience with the little Utah musician, but I honestly don't think the case is the same. I think Monique will miss her family very much indeed at times, but she is quite experienced in the Art of Separation, thanks to the above mentioned wars and revolution and so on, and is very realistic about the emotional perils of a year away from her mother and sisters and brother.

About schooling: Monique's visa will permit her any kind of education except a "regular" course at a university, and she wants to go to a business-school for typing at least... I want her to learn to drive properly (NOT from me...)... she loves to dance and I'll do what I can about that, probably through her confessor to begin with. Which leads into what you call "the religious angle," Sis.... It doesn't bother me at all. She is a very "normal" well-educated Catholic, and her routine and sincere going about her duties cannot possibly do anything but make the girls and me a little more respectful. That is my honest feeling, and it is not the first time I have bowed to something respectable in the seemingly automatic behavior of people of other faith.

I am not at all worried about her being "a homesick-bewildered girl." She will be both, in her own way, but not in a way to destroy the rest of it. She's simply not the type. And if I am abysmally mistaken and she *is*, I shall know what to do about it.

There will of course be a few changes in our family arrangements... about coming to Sausalito for overnight sometime and so on, as you point out, Sis. Naturally we cannot arrive four instead of three! But you are mistaken to say that "she could hardly be a part of the family." She is of course not a part of the Kennedy Family. But she is a part of my immediate family or I would not in any way consider accepting her for one minute as such, here or in San Francisco. If she proves unacceptable, which I also doubt but which is a possibility, I shall of course get her back to her mother as quickly as possible... and I need not assure you that all this has been arranged.

It is hard for me to believe that you will find it impossible to see Monique as anything but an Outsider. In fact, I *don't*. Maybe that is one more proof of my basic naïveté (Dillwyn's nice word for stupidity!).

Oh... legal responsibility in the event of illness: exactly the same as for my own children, and I shall attend to a covering insurance. Marriage? It has been discussed with her mother... it is unlikely, given her somewhat more stable ideas of marriage than the American ones, and her stronger religious training. But it has *been discussed*. As for her health, which you didn't mention, it is good. I have her complete medical history.

No, I have not "cleared it" with my attorney. I never thought I should, frankly. I have at the request of the Consul General requested (one week or so ago and not yet received) a letter from my banker stating that I have sufficient funds to guarantee her decent maintenance for a year. Naturally I feel that I have, or I would not have undertaken it.

Oh now SIS... actually there are not words in my vocabulary strong enough to express my horror and unbelief that you would seriously suggest such an undertaking... BUT I AM *SHOCKED!!!*

If you still feel so strongly, I'm truly sorry. But I imagine that by now you are feeling more philosophical... perhaps remembering this time last year, when you were *SHOCKED* at my casual Easter Vac remark that I thought I'd take the girls to France for a year.... Here we are. And here you too have been. And I think we are all of us the better for it! I'm not smug or self-satisfied, and I know as well as any of us the moments of being alone or frightened or bored-as-hell, but in the same way as my deciding to come here I have decided that this is a strange and exciting chance to widen my own and my children's experience... and I honestly cannot believe that it will hurt *US, The Family*....

I think we'll all manage to have quite a bit of fun, actually!

We can hardly wait to get home.

Read this letter with your ears open, dear girls, not saying "My God was Dote FURIOUS"...or..."sounding off..." or or or. For I'm not. I feel fine. But I realize it has been startling, and obviously unpleasant to you both, to have me *announce* such a violent change in my household computations! Try to understand me and even forgive me... and don't ever worry about my selling The Family down the river. I feel Monique is quite worthy of us, and can only hope that time will prove me right, in spite of more than one misjudgment you are too kind to remind me of.

Love,

....

Château du Tholonet, Le Tholonet,   *27.iv.55*
par Aix-en-Provence, France
To: *Lawrence Clark Powell*

Dear Ghuce—. . . How I wish you were here this minute, my dear! We are staying for a strange simple 9 days in the small stone house of the Léo Marschutzes[1] (go to our own bare apartment above the stables of the château on May 2, for 2 months,) while they paint in Italy. We get water from a deep well where Cézanne always stopped to rest. We have a fine privy roofed with Provençal tile. I am sitting under a chestnut tree in full flower, and all around me bees hum in the sage-gorse-heather-broom, and the pines turn and sing a little, and the white pigeons bathe in a little pond the children fill from the well. There are cats and kittens. One cat has only 3 paws, so all the others limp as she does. Her lover is plaintive, so at night she carries her new kitten in and puts it on my bed, saying "Enough is Enough," like Rex. We walk down to Tholonet for bread, cheese, the mail (20 minutes) and back up the hill-paths (50!), and grudgingly go into the hectic metropolis which Aix has suddenly become for us, to stock up on things like butter and oranges—about 6 km and a cab comes for us once a week and once in Aix I wonder how I can exist away from it— Have you ever written (here is a column for you!) about the almost furtive pleasure of being alone in someone else's library? Here I am looking-tasting-sniffing in the Marschutzes', re-reading *Tropique du Cancer*, Gauguin's *Private Journal*, Pissarro's *Lettres à son Fils*—I have them at home and have not opened them for years—is it that you borrow the eyes of your absent host? Tuesday (we'll be at the château by then) is the village saint's day—high mass at 10, and then local contest of Boules in the beautiful plantain alleys of the Château beside the long formal pond, and at 5 a *bal* outdoors. We'll be there.

1. Barbara and Léo Marschutz owned the Châteaunoir; Leo was an artist and German Jewish refugee who became head of an art school in Aix.

I feel as if I am *here* with an intensity that almost awes me. It is ridiculous to feel that I can breathe twice and save half of the air for a more stifling day!

I'm building up a psychological protest against going back to California—it's so obvious, so infantile, so unavoidable! Ho hum as Edith would say. I shall probably develop strong physical symptoms, all of them scornfully recognized as such by *ME*, my own victim, as the time approaches—!

My main problem about life-in-general, and in terms of raising my children as best I can, is my sister Anne. She is monstrous. She is something I must guard them against. This probably makes all of us, including her, stronger people. The conflict between my recognition of her as evil, and my complete loyalty, devotion, love to and for her, is an interesting conflict—something for a book, eh?

Have you moved to the beach by now? I do hope you'll be happy there. But for you personally I doubt that it matters *where*!

Love,

....

Le Tholonet   *16 or 17.v.55*

To: Norah Kennedy Barr

Dearest N... As usual we hope today's mail will bring a letter from you. It is chronic. Right now I remind the children occasionally that you could not POSSIBLY have received our letters yet about letting the Boys come here....

I have just finished reading a very good story I wrote! I am bursting with words, sentences... I still think it is foolish for me to try to construct a novel just because people think I should... I can do it, just as almost anybody else can, but I would never feel good about it. I permitted myself to re-read the long story I wrote (for you) about the old dead woman in Brussels, when I was packing to move from Madame Lanes's and it is very good, very true and swift.[1] But Henry despairs of selling it, which is of course his function: the editors find it somber. Somber is in quotes. I don't have a very good idea of how much money I have left, nor how I should best spread it out for the next years, but I suspect that I should try to set up some sort of magazine contract again when I get home... it makes a heavenly difference to have a regular check come every month, even for a slight pound of flesh spiritually. *Gourmet* suggests a kind of "news-letter." But I don't plan to roam for a few years now... Ah well. This stone building with tile floors and so on is cold, and I am wearing wool slacks and a heavy knitted pullover, but outside (where there is too much gusty breeze for me to control paper and so on), it is warm and mostly bright, and the field-flowers are in what would be mid-summer colors at Le Pâquis, the way they were when you were there. There are at least ten different kinds in the posy the children picked yesterday for me... all those pink and purple vetches and dark blue lupines Dillwyn loved, and of course scarlet poppies and cherry-pink lilies and many yellow blooms. And white daisies and clover. It gives me a

1. "The Weather Within," later published in *Sister Age*

strange feeling, to have my *children* bring in what I last saw there with all of us... you the only one left for me, with David and Dillwyn on the Death side, Anne Parrish and Mary Powers[2] accounting ironically enough for the Taxes.... Where do you and I fit in, Girl?

The farmer has the most beautiful pair of plough-horses I have ever seen, mother and daughter. They do everything he whispers or murmurs or sings out to them, like circus stars. Today they are cutting down the flowery hay with an antiquated kind of side-scythe, and this afternoon they will drag a kind of rake over it.

....

Le Tholonet   *20.v.55*
To: Norah Kennedy Barr

Dearest N... here are some things that may amuse you in a moment of complete exhaustion, between two suitcases or something. There are a couple of notes for the boys. The rest throw away.

I am sitting drinking Nescafé, trying to decide whether to go to Aix before lunch and have a gay expensive meal at the Glacier or stay here and finish some ham sandwiches we didn't eat yesterday, whether to go in after lunch and let the girls see a movie while I trot around until six, or whether to get along until next Thursday without a few vital things like a can-opener and some typing paper. Hell, I'll wait until the girls wake up and let them decide.

They sleep along like puppies. They look simply wonderful, and are very sweet and happy. They looked rather peakedy when we came... both had a kind of epidemic quinsy, and were oppressed by the neurasthenic atmosphere chez Lanes. . . .

Yesterday was Ascension Day. I got up early and worked... I'm in a real flurry, but CANNOT even think in terms of long stories or a novel. The girls snoozed along, and then we or rather they had breakfast of big bowls of decaffeinized Nescafé, a passing rage, and brown sugar, and bread and honey. Then they went down to the store for the Thursday bread and some oranges and three caramels, for little Rosie was along (She's 4 1/2 and a nice shadow for them...). Then we flicked a duster around... these bare tile floors are wonderful and I hope to have a house with them someday, with, maybe one LITTLE rug for my typing-feet, a sop to my years.... Lunch: baby artichokes and thin slices of cold steak left from the day before, which is meat-day because the butcher comes on Wednesdays... he had cut an artery and three veins and was quite pale this time, with his pretty wife to help him... we all clustered around and clucked at him.... After lunch lots of people came: we had made a joke-sandwich three feet long of the fresh loaf of bread and a lot of ham and sweet butter and mustard, and were going to cut it after Jacques and Louis Bulidon and the girls came back from a climb up the Colline, as planned. But when they did arrive they brought a rich fancy moulded ice-cream thing for everybody, and it was so nice of them that we said nothing about the sandwich and then Anne and Marie and I went to bed and ate pieces of it later, but we

2. All visitors to Le Pâquis in the summer of 1938

still have about a foot and a half of it. Well, first came Madame Tailleux with her little girl about 9 and her little boy three, to ask us to come to lunch Saturday... come early and let the children get into the water-tank if it's warm enough. We accepted, and she wandered off eventually with the boy, leaving SaSa here to play. She is one of the most beautiful women I have ever seen, gaunt and wild-looking, like Katharine Hepburn if KH were more female. I can see that women are passionately attracted to her... I have observed Barbara Marschutz and Madame Pouillon and my own girls and of course myself... but so are men, which is not the case with KH. She has a vague almost trancelike way of talking and walking, with her grey hair tousled and an old army coat hanging on her frame... drives an ancient enormous US army truck which was abandoned here... always has stray dogs yapping around her. She is an Englishwoman. Tailleux is French, of course, I suppose the most famous of the artists who live around here, after Masson and along with Marschutz. I haven't met him yet.

While Madame T was still here, in came Marjorie and Jan Raven and M's mother, a nice hen-like little woman from Canada, to ask us to go to dinner with them and a couple of Americans tonight down in Palette. We accepted. They stayed for quite a while. M and I drank some vin rosé and Jan talked about killing things: he loves to kill flies-dogs-and I suspect people if he could only keep his job.... He's quite a famous engineer. I am writing about his fly-killing, and may go on to bigger victims before I leave.

As they left, in came the Bulidons. They run a wine-store in Aix. They interest me very much... typical of the self-pitying defeatist French, and also typical of the courageous undying French... ho hum. It sounds as if I am using them for clinical purposes: not at all. They are nice to us, and my girls have worked quite a while now in their private campaign to make Jacques and Louis laugh.... Well, various walks and so on took place, for somewhere along here fourteen of the 34 nephews and nieces of the Bovis family arrived from Marseille for lunch and so on at the Château, and since most of them are about 8 to 12, my girls and SaSa simply joined the pack. They are rough handsome healthy children, very open and friendly, and it is too bad that we must leave just as all of them arrive for the summer. Finally I managed to separate eight of us and get us upstairs, where we divided the elaborate mold or is that mould of ice cream and sat on the stairs and ate it. It was very good... one of those things French pâtissiers run wild on, with layers of this and that flavored here with Grand Marnier and there with coffee and so on. Glug. Finally the Bulidons left. By now my face felt too smiley and my brains were buzzing a little, trying to sort out the influence of Louis's confessor on his schoolwork and the past subjunctive from the past-definite in my inner grammar and so on. Then Madame Tailleux appeared like a strange beautiful ghost up the dark avenue of trees, along the black waters of the ponds... wow. She stayed and stayed, picking fat ticks off one of her stray dogs and squashing them vaguely but very efficiently as she talked about the disappearance of her latest *bonne*. Her little boy presented me with some deep red roses and, at her gentle command, one dazzling smile. Usually his face looks very much like Beethoven's death mask, and I am interested in meeting his father tomorrow. There is also a big hearty English girl there, named Bridget Lady Cartwell or something like that, who came to polish her accent a little and "help with the kiddies," but who to Madame Tailleux's apparent delight does nothing but play Bach and Vivaldi with great perfection, all day long.

Well, bed felt fine, even with no decent reading-lights, and we felt quite dashing to retire to our three little rooms with large sandwiches, two albums of Spirou, and a thriller called *Ball on Black Mountain.* By 9:30, OUT.

The big field of poppies is being plowed under, and a little green field has been reaped, but we know something will be up again before you come.

We are to go Friday June 3 to Marseille to be vaccinated and then to the Consulate to swear Monique in or whatever the ceremony is... everything is in order now except her mother, who is having heat-flashes which I do not mention to the children... they remain, like me, completely sure that Monique should and must come. Ah well.

This house is like the one in Chapala,[1] empty and echoing, so that music sounds wonderful in it... we sing a lot, and suddenly I hear Dave's guitar... last night Mary said, "Isn't it wonderful to whisper and know Dote will hear in the next room?" I long for a record-player. (Schedule, once on land: start on apartment-hunt, get car in St. Helena, get record-player!)

It's crazy to start another page, but I don't want to get to work: I have THREE things to copy, such a dull job. I wrote what I think is a really good short story.... Then I must make up my mind about going in to Aix. If I could wait until tomorrow we could catch the Saturday bus in the village. This way I'll have to telephone, oh murder, for a cab, from the Château. But I do need a can-opener and some more paper.... On the way home we'll go by Fouque, the santonnier... I have ordered cigales for you and Sis and us and even the clubhouse of The Lucky Six, and some little water-whistles the children play on here, very Roman... and a few more santons.[2] I am beginning to suffer, extraneously or sub-cutaneously or or or, from a kind of tightening, or gritting of the teeth.... This thing of leaving! Murder.

Ah well, eh?

Also ho hum.

Much love. (I continue to say *nothing.* But the suspense is great here, about the boys.)

....

Le Tholonet   5.vi.55
To: June Eddy[1]

Dearest June... consider yourself deeply bussed for your birthday. We still speak with reverence and humble pride of the fact that you actually passed That Milestone

1. Mexico, where MF traveled to be with Norah and David Kennedy after Dillwyn died
2. Provençal nativity figurines. Fouque also made good-luck crickets (cigales) and water whistles.
1. Longtime family friend

last year with *us*.... Perhaps unfortunately, it will be a very short time until you pass another one, and right now we wish to put in our bid for your presence, dear girl!

Everything is fine here. I am beginning to feel oddly numb-dizzy about leaving, of course.

This morning Mary went off with the shepherd... up to the colline and then most probably down in three hours or so past the village pub, since it is Sunday and he has a Pernod there once a week while Mary goes quietly crazy directing the three dogs and 250 sheep in the meadow across the road.... She's quite a character. She went off this morning in blue shorts, a green T-shirt, a big floppy straw hat, and some bread and cheese tied in a hankie. "Should have some chewing-tobacco, to be like Batiste," she said solemnly. "But he's a real man and it looks as if I'm a real girl." Then she cackled happily and dashed up to the barns.... Anne is still in bed, reading and sneezing. She is going through the fits-and-spurts stage, with many hours of apparent sleep-walking when she LOOKS awake but is off on Cloud 12. She is now writing and illustrating a collection of short stories about fish, which she feels she *understands*... some atavism about having been a mermaid, I believe.

The Barrs arrive in eight days. WHAM. I still don't know when, where, or how many, but am not disturbed. One of the boys will sleep on a camping-bed, and one of the girls will sleep with me, and if Norah decides to stay a couple of nights I have dibs on a room at the village inn (which has three bedrooms, mostly for famous old senators and their blondes...). Norah seems quite vague, as usual, but apparently does plan to go to Germany to take another look at her young man. She believes she loves him, poor girl. He is FIFTEEN years younger, and I find it ominous that he reminds her very much of David (brother). Ho hum indeed. I am of course absolutely mum. But I pray for them both.

The girls have mapped out a schedule of picnics and ABSOLUTE ESSENTIALS for at least two months, to be followed during the two weeks the boys will be here. My only problem is to keep them all fed, and by now I am quite hep to when and how I can buy a piece of meat or a loaf of bread.... It's really fun.

This week I hired a cab, and went with the children and Monique to Marseille... spent several hours at the military hospital thanking god I was not a pregnant soldier-wife with five small children flying to Rabat that night.... The boring and expensive analyses I had managed to get made here in Le Tholonet–Aix proved useless, since nobody had told me that they must be made within 24 hours of the yellow-fever shots, so we spent a lot of time trotting to and from the hospital lab, drinking lemon pop and beer-beer-beer. Then we had to go to the American Consulate to get Monique through the final permission business, which was complicated by a most odious woman to interview her. THANK GOD she was French, for it would have killed any dreams the poor girl has about Beautiful America. By then it was after one, and I was shattered and bruised and the three kids looked like pest-victims, so I said to hell with the budget and we went to the girls' favorite little pub, which is the most expensive and nicest in Marseille if not the whole world, with waiters who think we are very nice funny people. THEN we went to the travel-agent, who blandly informed me that the boat would probably be five days to a week late in sailing (which adds about $50 a day MINIMUM expenses in hotels etc...) and that we might have to leave from Genoa, since a new law has been passed by the ministry of Marine that a ship of that tonnage must not have more than 12 passengers on leaving a French port. At this I got very firm, quietly and Coldly FIRM, which I can do if the case be urgent. He quailed a little, but being a Belgian he too remained quiet. Since I have had the reservations since January and have upped Matt's half-fare to Monique's full one, I feel that I can afford to throw my weight a bit, and am simply sitting back until June 14, when Norah and I will have to sign a few papers.... It's marvelous to be almost 147: things are so much easier to be philosophical about: Or something to that effect.... Are you *with* me?

It rained and rained yesterday, and all the peasants are glad. I am gnawing away fast at a book I seem suddenly to be writing for the children(!). I don't know what Covici will think... he expects something delicately spicy about Madame Récamier and I turn up with a quite funny bit of fluff about an Aixois dog![2] I hope to get it off the machine before the Boys arrive... and revise it on the ship.

I've also ripped off some stuff I like... a couple of stories and some very casual chit-chat about things like flies... les mouches de Provence, who are HERE.

Today (Sunday) is always fun... lots of the Château children out from Marseille, and usually a couple of admirers on their bikes from Aix for my girls, plus a few casuals. (We seem to have met some VERY nice people, damn it.)

....

Off the coast of Mexico   *22.viii.55*
To: Henry Volkening

Dear Henry:

We should arrive in San Francisco in about nine days. Then I'll get us moved into an apartment a friend has found, and get the children into schools and so on. And THEN I'll start the work I planned to do on board, which was an absolute and completely unexpected impossibility. At first I was really dismayed, but futilely. This is a Liberty ship sold to Italy after the war, which means that it is a functional and economical little freighter with no concessions made to anything but the cargo... an occasional steep narrow iron stairway from one rusty deck to another, four tiny airless crowded cabins for twelve passengers, almost non-existent plumbing, no place to stay except on our bunks if the one small passenger deck is awash, which it often is during this the rainy season. I finally devised a way to do a rare bit of typing such as this note: I sit on one of our four bunks, with the Hermes on a suitcase on a folding stool in front of me and to one side of the wardrobe trunk. This makes it impossible to reach two of the bunks *or* the washbowl, which is an unfair thing to do to my girls and Monique for long

2. *Boss Dog*, not published until 1990

at a time, not to mention my sacroiliac. Ah well. To quote one of the pilots who have steered us in and out of countless filthy little tropical ports, "The banana's a guest, and the passenger's a pest...." It's been a rugged but basically wonderful experience, and thank God we made it with Norah and the boys....

To get back to the untyped stuff: I THINK I will like what I wrote in Le Tholonet enough to send it to you. I'll get it out of the way as soon as possible after we land, but there will be another delay of about a month. I feel fine about getting to work again, and hope I can send you something you'll like, sooner or later.

Madeleine Mauriac didn't get her translation done and it will probably be in Berkeley when I get there.[1] I hope so, I think the book is a natural. But there is not much I can do about it now....

Thanks for letting me see the letter from *Collier's*, which was of course interesting. I assume you don't want it back.

Yes, it does seem silly to enlarge a story so that it can be cut. But I believe some dressmakers follow this theory, that the more there is to discard, the better the cloth will hang? Ah well again.

It's quite all right about having the thing (anything) come fast-back from *Atlantic*. I mean, it's quite all right with *me*. I always feel uncomfortable about wasting *your* time, as you know.... Needless to say, I'm quite excited and scared about whatever this next step will be, in San Francisco. I hated to leave Aix. I hope I was right to do so. We'll see, sooner or later!

You'd have hated a lot of things about the past two months on this little ship, but even so I often thought of you and bumped amicably into you now and then, standing against the rail watching the dolphins, sipping a lukewarm brandy-and-water, theoretically unsippable but quite acceptable going through the Canal in a hot black rain....

Best, dear Henry...

....

San Francisco, California   *11.x.55*
To: Peter and Madeleine Grattan

Dear Grattans, tous deux...

I've done a good day's work, the first since Le Tholonet, and now it's time to give myself a little present, some time off before supper, to write to you both.

Thank you for your letters. Peter said in his last one that a letter from me helps to unite you, because you both know me. But I'll probably write to Madeleine and then to Peter, because it is easier for me, and you can share what you like of whatever I say. D'ac?[1] This one is simply because I feel like chatting with you. . . .

1. Madeleine Mauriac Grattan wrote *Jexium Island*, a children's book that MF and her daughters wanted to see published in English.
1. Abbreviation for *d'accord* ("agreed")

The trip was very strange and hellish and yet I regret nothing about it. I am going to write about it, but nobody could possibly print what I'll say. I'll do it for your eyes alone! It was very good for us. The children are much wiser. Some of it was a bad way to grow wise, too. Ho hum.

We have a prim pearl-grey apartment with a heavenly view, climbing up Nob Hill with Coit Tower just showing... the sky is beautiful at night, amethystine on foggy ones with the reflected neon signs. The place is old and inconvenient but clean and very quiet. By now... have I told you all this?... I often write to you in my thoughts, so all this sounds repetitive to me... by now we are what might be called "settled," and a carpenter is making temporary shelves to hold about 48 more feet of books (My current literary measurement is in feet, not content!), and it is good to be at work again, even in the face of neglected and probably extinct insurance-notices and so on which piled up while Norah was away and couldn't attend to my local affairs. I'm horribly behind on work... couldn't do anything but EXIST on the ship, I'll get a couple of mag things out of the way, strictly from hunger, and then type the dog-story about Aix, which I think you will find pleasant.

Madeleine, I think, in fact I am afraid, that you are taking the translation of *Jexium Island* too seriously. I feel that you should in effect *dash it off*, to keep your wonderful easy style. Please do it, any way you want, and let me know. My agent mentions it, and we all know, you and the children and I, that it is good. PLEASE. . . .

Madeleine, are you working at Hobart?

Both girls were impressed mostly by how horrible the smog was in Los Angeles... how it had increased. Anne says she also was impressed by how nice her former enemy was (the daughter of a good friend of mine, whom Anne simply loathed for years...). Both girls thought the bread was nasty at first but are growing used to it, especially since I'm seeking out the best possible. Monique was impressed by how rough and brutal a high school football game is, and how horrid jello salad is. (She has been exposed to both at Lowell High, where she is, I fear temporarily, a Senior. Putting her into Première[2] will at least confirm the general low opinion of the American system of education!)

Anne and Mary go to the nearest grammar school, to the stern disapproval of various relatives and self-appointed advisors who expected me to put them right into one of the two snob day-schools. Their school is a kind of psychotherapy ward for racial problems from all over the City, and Anne is now in love with a tall fat Chinese boy and Mary's three "friends" are Mexican, Chinese, and South Carolina Negro. Anne starts tomorrow with an audition at the San Francisco Opera Ballet school. Mary is learning to play the flute, apparently for two reasons: so far she needs only one hand, and it may stretch her upper lip which she considers at least an inch too short for perfect beauty.

Thank you for the pictures of Bibémus,[3] Peter. They are for something permanent.

2. The French equivalent of senior year in high school
3. The stone quarry painted by Cézanne

At least Bibémus is strongly clear in Anne's strange roving dreamy mind... I wish Mary and I could have been there too.

You are right that cities are cages. At first I felt some moments of panic, to be caught in one. But I know why I'm here, so most of the time I can reassure myself and it helped to go up for one night to St. Helena, where I feel fairly sure, now, that I'll buy a small place, to prepare for my later years alone. Even there, some of the old vineyards are being ripped out for subdivisions. Hell.

I know a little of what happened to you when you wrote in Aix... I mean, that it will be impossible for you ever to be the kind of "dedicated" teacher you were before. You broke the easy safe placid stream, the flow. I did the same thing when I stopped writing for about five years. I can never write as casually, easily, nonchalantly again. I know too much now. I am too severe, having, like you, gone through my own heaven-hell. But is that bad? You will quite possibly write even better. And I in turn may become a teacher (!...JOKE...).

Next day: On reading back... did you really come up from the depths empty-handed? Perhaps you are the only one who knows. But the few pages I read, in Le Tholonet, are still clear in my mind... partly because *you* wrote them and my mind was very fresh then, but partly too because they were good. There was a feeling of going straight ahead in them. Direction, I suppose I mean.

However it is, you should not go on feeling "uneasy"... or thinking that what you feel is "uneasiness." I feel sure of this.

Oh, of course I had an idea for the mag stuff, or rather I am trying conscientiously to write what the editors think is *their* idea. Ho hum. Money.

No, California really isn't god-awful. We had to spend about 48 hours in San Pedro, and one day took a cab up to Los Angeles, and I became quite morbid and quaky inside. It was really dreadful in every way: the first of a ten-day smog wave, and so on, and so abysmally UGLY and vulgar and wrong. But coming up the Coast the long stretches of barren beautiful hills and mountains, really from Santa Monica to the Golden Gate, were reassuring and wild. And San Francisco hasn't changed... some handsome new stores on Union Square, the same smart women, the same feeling of excitement and gaiety. As I think I told you, I felt a core of dismay at living in a city again, even this one, but after I'd taken the children up to St. Helena everything was all right. I know I'll go back there. I'll try to sell Bareacres, which I have stubbornly hung onto since Dillwyn died, and I'll get a very small place near the village... in a vineyard. It will be good for the children too, to go back there on vacations and soon. They really love it there. Then when they are out of the nest I'll live there: everything is fairly easy for single and elderly people... climate and so on... and the people themselves are wonderful. Well, I'll start negotiating about Bareacres, and slowly looking for a ratty small old ranch-house with a few trees and grapes around it. Sounds fine!

Yes, Bolinas is marvelous. But it is changing too... people. I said half-jokingly to some friends in St. H (He's a fine printer) that what I really wanted was an abandoned lighthouse. And by George they found one. And it was odd to realize that I would not really want to live all by myself in one, miles from food supplies and wrapped always in fog and sound. A few years ago I couldn't have believed it of myself. Age age age.

Today is Columbus day, and after I buy Anne a pair of soft ballet-chaussons for her audition tomorrow, we drive across the Bay Bridge to see Norah and her boys and go up Strawberry Canyon for a pique-nique. It's a beautiful glowing day with a little blue in the air, the way Paris is pink around the Louvre sometimes... autumn I suppose. Norah has started part-time work again, mainly to keep up her professional standing... it's very demanding emotionally and she looks tired and bored. It's too bad she falls in love with impossibilities: she should marry and even have one more child. Ho hum.

My other sister I see quite often... she stops by for a sherry on her way home from work to Sausalito. She's an odd character... beautiful swank car, beautiful enormous wardrobe, beautiful small house... complete vacuum emotionally, except a faint flicker for my two children. It's too bad.

I must rouse the covey of nubile virgins one by one. Anne and Mary send much much love to you both, and a stern question about WHERE the book is.[4] (By the way, the title is perfect....) Please write. Tell me everything at all that is related to either of you!! Love—

....

San Francisco, California   *1.i.56*
To: Norah Kennedy Barr

Dearest N... we left your place about two hours ago, and I've gone right on talking to you, at you, around you. As usual. So here is a letter, a surprise, eh?

Monique was ironing to Beethoven, and so we went on through the 6th and then the 3rd, and then I moved in, for the recordings we have are impossible for me to get the squeal out of on this quasi-HiFi box, and we are (I am?) listening now to the Bruno Walter recording of the Linz of Mozart (36th I think...). I know that we agree that neither of us has much of a desire for an encyclopedic mind (not to mention our realization, mutual, that we should and indeed might write novels of great social significance), but still I feel that sometime we should immolate ourselves to the point of being able to listen uninterrupted to the rehearsal that old man did. It is really exciting and at times makes being an artist, not to mention a musician, a highly detestable state. That is not why I listen to it. Walking up from the garage, one of the girls asked me why people (I, you...) read murder stories, and I tried to say that it is a kind of game to see how the murderer will be found out and caught. And in the same way, listening to the Walter rehearsal, it is a real game, very thrilling... will Mozart win, will the culprit be surrounded and caught, will our side win? (We do.)

I wonder if you'll get this in January, what with the holiday tomorrow and strikes

4. *Jexium Island*

and stuff. Ah well. I hope we can drive swiftly through the drying mud up-Valley. By now it is blazing bright here. We were promised gale winds up to 50 miles p.h. Pooh.

You always manage to resolve a few questions in my general bewilderment. At least I get them into a more ordered confusion, always desirable.

At this point it seems to me that I would be wise to find (after renting perhaps) a small-ish easy place in St. Helena, which I love for several reasons and where I feel a kind of serenity. Monique will be gone before I know it. Anne will be only partly at home, rather soon and maybe next Fall. Mary should go away within a few years. Me, I doubt that I stay put, but I'm of a nature to like to keep some things that belong to me, and return to them. In Cartagena[1] I said something about turning into a stringy old woman in a sun-bonnet, going up rivers in canoes, and you know that's possible if I should live so long. It's not that I am trying to cram a facsimile of "life" into my living. It's that I need the fixatif (I don't know the right word, but that stuff you spray on a charcoal drawing...) of other ways of thinking and talking and eating and so on. Or so I assume....

Anyway, I hope I can find a place in St. H for us. BOTH children talk peacefully together, for the first time in too long, of having the bike back and a cat and a dog and and and. I haven't mentioned it concretely to Monique, but I honestly think it would do her good to go to a co-ed school of some 350 people and cope with some of the lusty boys and some of the teachers like Mr. Ten Broeck (and Marietta!).[2] The idea tempts me. I feel the Giugnis, Baldi, Vasconi judge and druggist, Brignoli, Martini (FA-THER)[3]... calling me... like Steinbeck on the sand in Laguna feeling that dame in Fresno?????????

Later. That was a joke. I never met people I liked better, nor felt more real with. They ask nothing of me except that I be me, in an equally trusting fashion.

I am now grinding out Lu Watters on the box in the kitchen. It's strictly San Francisco and I find it very good jazz, but do not know if anybody else but Chuck Newton[4] thinks so, since I do not move in them circles. (My girls like it, but Monique turns Aix-pale and gently closes her door, if she is awake and upright. Right now she is resting after doing her ironing and did not even sense my low-down switch of Mozart for Beethoven. Just as well. It's one easy step to Watters... or so I feel.)

Maybe I should [buy] An Ignoramus's Guide to Good Manners Dictionary: why it seems all right to listen to Chinese opera if you HEAR what you are looking for, which I do without wondering just what that may be... and so on. It is impossible for me to say why I can listen to something like the 24 LP sides of Jelly Roll Morton, and feel peaceful, and blue, and even cry, and shag all by myself at times. But I do. Do we need to explain why?

I wonder what other women I have known earlier used for these things? Did

1. Colombia, on the boat trip home from France
2. Anthony Ten Broeck and Marietta Voorhees, teachers and MF's good friends in St. Helena
3. Italian inhabitants of St. Helena and the Napa Valley
4. Charles Newton was MF's cousin's husband.

Mother eat too many chocolates? How much was cruel impatient Rex to blame for that drama of Woman-Against-Herself, with liver finally bowing out to heart? Five pounds of glacéed cherries and a pile of Ethel M. Dell and Galsworthy, and to hell with Whittier... and with Rex...

Later... I'd better get this out of the way. I hesitate to send it, except that you know what I'm saying and it may amuse you to see how a good lunch with you sets me off!

I do hope we go North for a quick look around. I think now is the time for me to fabricate (and I use the word with thought) a kind of perch, nest, burrow, what you will. From it I will go out like that cat in Colette's story, except not to the call of a Tom but because of the fern-seed in my invisible shoes. And it will be the perch-nest-burrow, insofar as books and pictures and beat-up old couches and chairs go, for any children around.

Just a dreamer, eh?

Thanks for insisting we come over today. I hated everything about it, as you can see, and we got home in 47 minutes, with two weaving drivers ahead of us on the bridge and a few thin old drunks on the sidewalks around Mission, solemnly counting their fingers. I drove on the rail-side and we could look at the City. It was worth it. Very beautiful and clearcut. (Like Lu Watters, as a matter of fact.)

Shall we start saying "See you Christmas" THIS soon? Love.

....

St. Helena, California   17.v.56
To: Lawrence Clark Powell

Dearest Ghuce... thank you for writing. I was going to write today. Forgive me as always for typing... I'm working hard and if I get away from the machine I won't come back to it. You understand, condone, and all that.

Me too, I'm in a real spate of creative thinking and writing. This time last year I was sitting under a chestnut tree, high in its branches really, listening to the children in the pine woods and the pigeons. It was a fine enduring dream. I ache almost physically to be back in it again. Never. Nevermore.

But I'm all right here too. The pace is too interrupted a one and at times I give up and go to sleep heavily or read a mystery... a kind of escape or perhaps protection.

When I get my own house again I'll have a desk where I'll *write* to people I love... no typewriter within reach... I'll do it with pens and pencils or even paint-brushes. . . .

Will you give me a copy of the essays? I'll trade you. The book I wrote about the children in Aix seems to be pleasing publishers and so on. I don't know details yet. I may have to rewrite two of the six or seven stories. Meanwhile I am working for mags, for money, but of course with a plan in mind to make another book.

I need some money. I want to buy a little house, and then in 1958 go to Molokai for about a year. Did I tell you this? But right now I want to stay here. It's beautiful... wild

M.F.K. Fisher: A Life in Letters

and serene, rather like Le Tholonet, oddly enough. The house I hope to buy is down in the village, old and solid with a wonderful high cellar made by the Chinese of hewn stone, and a good first floor, and then a beautiful attic, floored but otherwise unfinished. There is a giant persimmon tree, planted by the Chinese too... and there is another 19th C planting. It is shabby and haunted, which is my cup of tea.

My girls sound like a trained-seal act, and Monique and Anneli are still home from school. Some local bug. Me, I'm immune. Hal said it was because I was alcoholized and killed any bug within sight. Which reminds me: a very Catholic friend of mine who is given to muttering little prayers and incantations, the other night when I came into the room with brandy after a two-wine supper muttered, "Hail, Mary, full of grapes." I thought it was funny. But I wonder what the priest said next day at confession? Heresy?

Ghuce, I miss you. Write when you can. It doesn't matter whether we *see* one another, this far along in our relationship, which I must say *is* rather impressively long and also wonderfully good. I'm glad you can fly through the air with such ease, and fly off in NM. Happy landings.

Love

....

St. Helena, California   *17.vii.56*
To: Barbara Marschutz

Dear Barbara: It is very hard for me to realize that I have not written to you since we got home, nor even thanked you for your welcome letter written at the dear old pub.... Please forgive me. I'd like to continue to be in touch with you, and I shall be better about it....

I'll re-read your letter, which will be easier to comment on than if I tried to tell you without any cues, about our life since we last met....

The trip home was fantastic and I am probably going to write a completely unprintable book about it. I knew things were "odd," to put it mildly, when we were forced to go to Genoa instead of embarking at Marseille as promised. Then we had to stay 8 days in Genoa, and you can understand what a ghastly blow that was to my very carefully planned budget... 7 of us to feed and lodge... a real catastrophe. (I wrote to my banker asking for money to be sent to Cristobal Colon. By the time we arrived there we had exactly $3.20, somewhat less than a thousand francs. And the agent refused to bring my money on board, saying the banks were closed. We went through the Canal to Panama City, arriving before the banks were *open*. I grew very firm and announced that if the money was not in the Captain's hands before we left Panama I would jump ship and have the Italian Line fly the seven of us to California. The money appeared magically. But for the first time in many years Cristobal had been filled with beautiful cottons and weavings and so on, which I'd have liked to buy discreetly... it is perhaps just as well that I was broke!)

The reason we could not embark or even touch soil in Marseille was scandalously political: Tito was just beginning to play the "pretty boy" with France, and so many refugees were fleeing from Trieste that he had begged France not to let anyone land!

The ship was allowed by international law to carry 12 passengers as super-cargo . . . but we soon found that below decks, in two stinking dortoirs, were almost fifty refugees, living like beasts. . . .

The ship was plainly unscheduled, so that we'd suddenly find ourselves heading up the Spanish Coast for Cádiz, or sitting for a week out in the blistering sea, waiting for portage in a little one-dock harbor in Central America.

I had made several crossings by carg-freighters, some better than others but all interesting and decent. But by the time we got to Barcelona I knew we had made a mistake. I would have jumped ship there, if I'd not had Monique with us and if my sister Norah and her two older boys had not come clear from San Francisco to make the voyage home with us. I appraised our general state of health as carefully as I could, and decided we'd stay aboard. I honestly think that if I'd known of the rest of the trip I'd have simply walked ashore and banged on the door of the nearest consulate!

A lot of the poor devils below decks left in Venezuela, where there is a great oil-boom in progress, with need for cheap labor and no trouble about passports or false papers.

Then we began to take on the coast-wise prostitutes, who went from one small port to another, working their way on such little ships as ours by entertaining the officers and then the crew. They were a sorry lot, for the most part... quite kindly and nice to the children. There were so many of them at one point that two slept on ironing-boards set up in the junior officers' toilet.

The Captain and First were sickly broken men, both of them POWs for almost six years in England. The ship was quite literally steered and managed by two very young harassed juniors. The crew were for the most part criminals who in Italy are now given their choice of serving part of their sentence at sea, rather like the old galley-slaves: our combination steward-cook-cabinboy-deck-hand, for instance, was a wild-eyed bitter fellow who had been sentenced to twenty years at hard labor or ten at sea for evading the draft by fleeing to New York. The crew worked like *forcenés*, which indeed they were.

We had two boat drills during the entire voyage (which lasted almost three weeks longer than it was scheduled to), and on the first drill the winches were so clogged with dried paint that the boats could not be lowered, and on the second one the auxiliary motors refused to turn over... fantastic.

The water turned dark yellow and smelly in mid-Atlantic, but I found the commissary had some medicinal brandy in stock, and I made the four children drink a glass a day with a teaspoonful of bad Italian *grappa* in it. We all lost a lot of weight, of course, but were never ill. The only sign of trouble we had was very strange skin conditions: blotches, itching, and so on. This last was much worse below decks, and the Captain was very worried about the medical inspections due at the first American port (Los Angeles). Three men were taken off, which was serious, since the ship was so undermanned. It was some sort of virus, apparently, which my daughter Anne, and my little nephew David, and I still carry around, so that we have to be very careful about not being bitten by fleas or mosquitoes....

The food was almost inedible except for decent pasta every day. You can imagine that it is rather hard to eat spaghetti in a broiling oily sea, with the ship covered with millions of stinking jungle birds. But we did.

Norah and I rationed ourselves on reading, when we found we would be overdue. We knitted a lot and everybody played chess and so on. The worst problems were sexual: the men were half-mad, since they were never allowed ashore, even in Italy and Spain, unless they were legally married. Half their wages were kept by the Italian Line as a guarantee and half were sent directly to their families, so they did not even have money for cigarettes unless they stole it. They got a half-litre of almost undrinkable beer a day, except for the oilers, who got 1 litre. (The ship was in such bad shape that they could not even carry bananas on it... no ventilation or refrigeration... so you can imagine what it was like below decks.... Norah's two boys had to be watched constantly: the men were even crazier for them than they were for my girls. At the poor Captain's request we never let the children even go to the toilets alone, and we had to sleep with our cabins locked at night, which was dreadful in the tropics. One of the most surprising things, for me, was that there was literally no place to use my Hermes, even for an hour or so. I tried it on a suitcase in our cabin. It was too painful, because I had to sit on the edge of one of the four bunks with my neck bent. There was a kind of diningsaloon which seated fourteen people, but it was locked between meals because some of the crew slept on the benches between meals.

I went aboard with a good little manuscript to type and get ready for my publisher. Tant pis. I did it almost exactly a year later!

Let me see... I think that more or less gives you an idea of our strange voyage. But by now the children refer nostalgically to "the dear old *Vesuvio*" and Norah and I agree that we do not regret it at all. We survived. We lived in extraordinary intimacy with an assortment of human beings we'd never have met otherwise....

And you can see why it is too touchy to write about: I couldn't name countries and names and so on.

Now you ask, in your letter, how things are for us. (I am apparently in a talkative mood, and hope I'm not boring you.) We went directly to San Francisco, where I had always wanted to live for at least a year, and where my sister Anne had found us a delightful apartment. I put Monique and the girls in good public schools. But it was not right at all: instead of being a wonderful town for parties and fun, which it has always been for me, I was cooking and working all day long, and the children were bored because they could not have bicycles and run and shout....

So we moved up here in February, to the little wine-valley where we spent a year after my father died, and where I'd wanted to stay, *some day.* It was perfect for us, and just this month we have bought an old house (Old for this country: 1891), and in the next two months I will finally settle all my books and pictures, which have suffered from several years of storage and moving and so on.

It will be fine for all of us. The children have good friends here and will go to public school for one more year (Mary perhaps two). I'll miss the open vineyards and oak-groves we now live in, but in the village I'll have much less driving to do, and I'll get some hard work done on two books. As it is now, we are far enough from schools and shops so that I spend a lot of time running back and forth in the car... plus Girl Scouts, piano lessons, swimming, and all that... about three and a half hours a day, and I get home to attend to the typewriter just in time to have 23 minutes left before the next trip. Next winter, *ah!*

We talk often and with a strong poignancy about le Châteaunoir and Le Tholonet. It was a very intense experience for us, and for me it was the most receptive and happy since my husband Dillwyn died. I knew it then, but I know it more now.

Even chasing your damned chickens was a fine part of it!

Now I think that takes care of this side, except that the children are writing a book about Whiskey, who looms as one of their all-time heroes. I'll send you whatever turns out. . . .

Barbara, I can never tell you how important it was in at least three lives to live in your petit mas provençal for those days last year. The signs of it emerge gradually like moss to the top of a pond. And all the time we think of you with clearness and grati-tude and, if you do not mind, with affection.

There are many things I wish I'd done in Aix, like dare ask the price of a couple of pictures and things like that. But one thing I know was good, and that was meeting you. I think I'll come back. The children want to live in Verona for a year and learn some Italian. I might leave them and retreat once more to the sound of the fountains and the slow rhythm of the Cours Mirabeau.... I'll see you again. Meanwhile I hope you'll forgive my long silence and write.

Next day... Since I seem to have written a small volume to you, I might as well add to it!

Here is our new address (If I reread the letter I'd not dare send it, but I'm sure I didn't give this to you...): 1467 Oak Street, St. Helena. I think it is as permanent as I'll ever be again. . . .

If ever you think of it, would you ask the men at LeBlanc if they still have a rather large flat-toned canvas of a gastronomical fantasy... they showed it in their side win-dow, two winters ago... it was rather dim and uninspired but amusing, of a man made of fishes and brioches and so on, eating at a table. There was a loaf of bread in it some-where... I think it was the man's arm... I would like to know if that canvas is still avail-able, and if I can afford it. I was hopelessly broke at the time I kept passing it every day, and I didn't dare ask about it.

Will you please present my greetings to Madame Poullion? And of course to Madame Tailleux... the children have written a couple of times to SaSa with no luck, and Anne has painted a strange picture of SaSa and Mary and herself beside the little brook at Le T.

(All these things make me wonder about why some parts of life are more intense than others. This picture, the preoccupation with writing a book about Whiskey, my own almost painful remembrances of things in Aix and thereabouts, seem so much more real than the very good life we are leading at this moment, for instance. Perhaps some people need to be uprooted in order to exist? Or is it that the comfortable (if very simple) American life we lead makes us less conscious and sensitive to the basic fact that we are indeed *alive*?)

Barbara, once more forgive this wordy message to you, and write again to me. I count on seeing you "at no certain time in no certain place."... Meanwhile here are our affectionate greetings, and always our thanks to you and Leo (Cézanne's youngest pupil!) for letting us stay at le Châteaunoir....

....

St. Helena, California   *19.ii.57*
To: Lawrence Clark Powell

Ghuce, I'm writing to you in pencil because my ball-point pen won't function if I have touched the paper it must ride on—and thusly because I know you hate typewritten letters.

Thank you for that sheet. I passed it on to Marietta Voorhees, who sat for many years at Porter Garnett's feet, and then she took it to Jim Beard,[1] who did too. You see it floats, spreading its own message. Myself, I admired it, but was not moved.

Thank you too for the batch of things today. You are good to keep me on your mailing-list, the private *important* one(!). I'll read them soon.

Dearest Ghuce, I must tell you, the only person in this world to know besides my lover, that I am in love. I know you will kick up your horny heels for me, and sing a little song. It is a reward for something I am not yet conscious of having worked for. I am amazed, because I was dead for so long in my spirit after Dillwyn had to die. I loved people, things. But you know all about that. You have always taught me more than I could ever teach you— I have loved peaceably and fairly quietly for about four years, and I know now that I went to Aix to contemplate my strength to remain peaceable and quiet (and unsuspected!). I found it. But now I find that it is not necessary. I am loved. Completely. God, Ghuce, only you can know what a state of astonishment I'm in! How we could laugh! Kick up our heels again! Cheer! Weep! Be thankful!

I want to live a long time with my love. I know you do with yours. Let us? Some day—

Meanwhile—meanwhile there are many things like 4-H Club tonight with *cos-*

1. James Beard, printer, friend, and husband of Yolande Beard

tumes for 5 girls to do a damn-fool dance, and a salad for me to take, and *costumes*. But my lover has asked my permission to tell "one or two friends" of our intentions to live-until-we-do-die-together, and I must tell Ghuce. Pray for us. *Be silent, friend.*

Later

Try to save a few hours up or down from Sacramento. I want to talk with you. Meanwhile, be good to my beloved Ghuce—

St. Helena, California   7.iv.57
To: *Lawrence Clark Powell*

Thank you, dearest Ghuce, for your wonderful letter! I showed it to my love.

Yes, it's been a long time since Tim died—17 years or so—I have never kept track of things like that —maybe it was 1941?

Now it's over, and I'm alive again. I pretended I was, and only occasionally felt that it was wrong, mostly to my children. No more need for that!

He wrote lately—"—beauty for ashes, the garment of praise for the spirit of heaviness"—and you wear it too, and that adds to my phoenix-self!

Love

(I've been with him for 5 nights and days now, during the last two months—the gods are with us, eh?)

St. Helena, California   30.v.57
To: *Lawrence Clark Powell*

Dearest Ghuce... thanks for forwarding AYF's letter. He sounds very measured and affected, and impressed by his somewhat tardy philoprogenitiveness... not at all the youth who swore to kill himself if ever I conceived with him. It's a good thing Dillwyn shot into our lives: I'd have killed A from boredom before much longer, possibly, so he owes his life to love! Ah well and ho hum.

All goes well as possible here. Mary almost died with some virus invasion and is well again but easily tired... I watch her as best I can. Anne readies herself to spend the summer in southern California with her godmother. I in turn ready myself to do a rather fat series of articles for a magazine... decided to break my non-contract pattern long enough to earn a little folding-money for a possible year in Italy with the children. I've done a few radio and TV and magazine things lately. The Récamier book is dead again. I've not yet adjusted my domestic and professional demands to my own secret schedule, but am not worried about being able to do so before much longer. I am well and alive, and in a stunned way I am happier than I have ever been in my life. You who have known something of my former happiness will understand how astounding this is....

Thanks, my dear, for your occasional card. Please don't stop.

St. Helena, California   *12.x.57*
To: Hal Durrell[1]

To Hal Durrell... greetings, friend, and my thanks for your letters. They stimulate me and amuse me and titillate my thoughts. I want to answer them immediately. But I don't. I used to be able to keep a healthy eclectic correspondence going... it was fun in every sense. But now I seem to have shrunk my time-sense or perhaps only my own physical energy, so that I barely skid through a day's essentials and keep the bills paid and the table stocked. I think it is partly the stage my children are in. They need a lot of seemingly extraneous attentions: driving them to 4-H meetings, taking them to school on wet days, packing lunches, taking them to San Francisco to the orthodontist. It's a period soon over, and for the most part I enjoy it. But it leaves little of *me* for *myself.*

So you find my letters "scrambled." Ah well and Ho hum. I am not scrambled at all. But like you I write as I talk, depending greatly on the person I talk with, and when I reply (often very hastily) to your letters, I reply as if I were talking to each point you make which seems to me to call for answer. So perhaps the scramblement is mutual? Whatever you think, I shall continue to answer your letters as best I can, for you to struggle with or toss away unread....

You are right that my need to write is cracking the whip and hurting me, right now. There is nothing to do about it. I am also a fairly clear-cut "mother-domestic" type, and there is inevitably a war at this point in my children's development, as I said at the first. But the older girl is already at prep-school, and Mary soon will be. I love to cook for people and have a lot of come-and-go in the house, and have a warm welcoming open attractive house... and all this is at war with my professional need for long hours of uninterrupted work. So all right. I can grouse about it to someone like you, now and then.... Most of the time I don't. But it is significant that where I used to say blandly that I'd write a good book if I could live to be fifty, I have now raised the ante to the fairly imminent goal of SIXTY.

I am 49, and while I plan to finish a book by March,[2] it will certainly not be the one I'd aimed to do before July 3, 1958.

My girls don't need anyone to play Grandpop. They lived with my father for six years and his place is unassailable. That is odd, for after my mother died, six years before, they got permission from Rex, my sire, to "adopt" another grandmother... perhaps because they knew her less well?

Yes, I like what you tell me of yourself. I am not exactly *curious*. It is more like *interest.*

I think you are presumptuous, or perhaps warped a little, to decide that you would disappoint me "in person." But I shan't argue the point. I like this way of being close, too... by mail. I used to read a lot of letters, sometimes ashamed of such obvious Peep-

1. A fan who became one of MF's regular correspondents
2. *A Cordiall Water*

ing Tomism, and some of the best were written with complete intimacy between people, even lovers, who never met otherwise....

So let us continue this affaire... I find it pleasant.

It is good to have someone in the world who is *concerned* about me. It makes a woman like me feel frail and lovely, a sweet weak thing to be helped, protected, sheltered... all very phony and laughable but fun, at least in theory!

Malcontented perhaps... the Why an inner quarrel I suppose. I am not alone, certainly. Perhaps I am simply more voluble about it?

(I hope you will overlook my typing... when I go fast I invert spelling and so on... can type a fairly clean manuscript when I have to, but letters to a very few "intimates" like you are shabby jobs indeed.)

2 pps up: I said I am not alone. I mean I am not alone in being the tattered victim of an inner quarrel.

As for the other way of being alone, I am not, either. You men! You prescribe a clutch, a roll in the hay, as if it would solve every quavering of a woman's soul! What she needs is a lot of loving, a good roll in the hay. And of course I agree with you, largely. But I am fastidious and it is not always easy to find the right man and/or woman to make love with. Me, I have always considered myself blessed amongst women in that respect. I have known more than my share of good love-making. But of course there have been long dry spells, which I have managed to survive. A few years ago I divorced the children's legal father, and except for one good affaire with a man I'd known as a brother for 25 years who suddenly needed me for a few times, and I him, I more or less put myself in the deep freeze, sexually... I was thrown with a lot of middle-class American husbands all too eager to consider me, three times married but still The Boss's Daughter, God's answer to their nasty little prayer for freedom. I could not stand them. Then about four years ago I fell in love, the complete way which I had not known since my second husband died, in 1941. But it seemed impossible for me to do anything about it. So I went away to re-adjust myself to this amazing thing that had happened. I did a pretty good job. I got myself pretty well into the Deep Freeze again, both intellectually and physically, but I knew it was the last time I could do it. I am less elastic, emotionally, as I grow older. And then, about eight months ago, I found that the man was deeply in love with me too, and that we could be together although not often and always with secrecy. It is a mysterious pattern, this far along in my life, but I am savoring it more truly than I ever could have, earlier....

So you can be assured, Hal, that while I do not need but do greatly enjoy the embrace of your letters, I am alive and nourished by an active and very satisfying *actuality* of man-woman love. I'm lucky, eh? It can't last too long, but it will do for the rest of my life....

Now about the word *clandestine:* I don't need it at all. You do not scare me by saying I am "on file." If you wish, you may consider everything I write to you as "clandestine." I pick up your cue, follow your lead, in these replies to your letters to me. Certainly I do not write to you as I write to my lawyer or or or. If I had to, I would soon cease the correspondence, since there is too much of it already. But I suspect that I write to you pretty much as I would talk, if we met, with a *recognition* of you as what you are… a *mutual* recognition.

So go ahead, Durl the S.O.B., if you want to be what you call "risqué." Consider all of this clandestine.

I like your story of the busiest woman and the straw-burner.

Yes, I like to talk about sex, if I like the way the other person talks. I agree with you that it is no problem then.

You ask about deadlines:… (Who said *I* was scrambled???? I'm simply following your letters…): I have finished an article about the way to raise children to an appreciation of decent food, for *House and Garden*, and am doing a short piece for *Gourmet* or *The Atlantic* depending on how my agent feels about it, and have a Thanksgiving deadline on five "pieces" for *Harper's Bazaar*. As soon as I get loaded with such hack-jobs I begin to work on things I would rather do, and am getting along fast on a story of a town (Dijon) which I doubt anyone will want to publish but which is fun for me. It is supposed to be a portrait of the place, but of course it is one of me too. Being in love again has loosened my tight dry muscles, and I am writing easily, although there is always some resentment in me when I agree to do things for money.

I am trying to raise and save enough money to take the children to Northern Italy for a year, in late '58, but only if my love can be somewhere in the picture. This seems impossible. The gods may intervene. It is the right time for the girls to learn decent Italian and scrape the rust off their French. But I will not leave my love. So if I cannot, I'll simply use the damned money and send *both* children to prep schools. I'll hole into the basement and perhaps write deathless prose but certainly busy myself.…

C'est interessant que je t'écris souvent en Français, dans ma pensée, et que je te tutoie toujours. Quelle impertinence! Pardonne-moi, mon cher.

Now to the next letter: I do not agree with you that mind-reading and clairvoyance are the same. I do agree fully that there are magnetic impulses between certain people, usually through touch-contact. There is also the thing loosely called intuition, which when sharply developed can scare people.

About your letter to the professor about what must surely happen to what we call Civilization: I did that once to Morris Fishbein of medical ill-fame, and it almost killed him. I wrote a very good paper about the art of dying. Murder. It was fun, and I believed and still do, every word of it. But it shocked the old boy past telling.…

I agree with you about the inevitable disintegration of the Family as it has been set up by the Church.

I myself have managed, sometimes with difficulty, to combine love with sex, thought with feeling. But it is a vanishing art. I don't know how to lead my own children away from the preconceptions their life with me will have formed, but perhaps I can expose them to enough less archaic characters than I… enough so that they will not copy me in the changed world. In my own case it was not the Church that formed me, but a kind of leftover sentimentalism fostered by much reading of English novels… or so I suspect. Yes, I think a lot about them, and how best I can strengthen them. I fall back on the perhaps futile theory that if I feed them good food and teach them how to tell black from white, they will best fend for themselves. But I'm incapable of giving them any kind of religious foundation, by which I mean Christian, since I am agnostic. And I have absolutely no racial feelings (which you do), so that I'm no good on that. And I don't believe in money, as such. And I do believe in freedoms. I'm a hell of a poor model and at times the girls are quite lost and wobbly and must turn to others for reassurance.

I agree with you that a girl with any promise to her at all, for the future that is, should take good lessons before marriage. Otherwise it is a costly and sometimes sad thing to have to use the first marriage as a preparation for the second better one….

That was true with me.

You say "Talk as you type." I do. I talk instinctively in phrases, sentences, and paragraphs. It is disconcerting to some people. They think I *compose* and that I have everything planned before I open my mouth. Not true at all. You will have to get used to it.

You, the pseudo-Thoreau, can rest on the laurels of your uncountable loscouses. Myself, I would compare your way of writing more to Ezra Pound's than to the old Walden fellow.…

School children are increasingly backward. Some friends of mine blame it all on bad reading-habits. Parents do not read, either to themselves or aloud to little ones. The TV goes. It is easier to watch it, and so kill both reading and talking with one stone. Me, I taught myself to read when I was about five, with Grandmother's copy of *The Imitation of Christ,* and have been reading at a great clip ever since, or rather until about five years ago… read a lot more in France in '53–'54 than here. My girls read well and with enjoyment, partly because we don't have a TV of course… Anne, the older lazier one, will settle for Comic Classics instead of wading happily through *Ben Hur* and *Ivanhoe* and so on as I did… but IN SCHOOL the children sleep sitting up, which is why I have taken my kids out for a year at a time, and why I am now sending Anne to a very demanding prep-school. Mary is deadly bored, which is a crime at her age, the keenest of growth (11)… Ho hum again.

We can talk more about dreams. I dream steadily, and was once guinea-pig for some mind-doctors who were trying to prove that such was impossible. They gave up. My subconscious and my unconscious are very highly developed, perhaps a result or perhaps a cause of my exaggerated "inner conflict"???? I get a lot of work done while asleep… take care of professional problems, work out solutions, rewrite with success, discover truer ways to live with people… all interesting but of course tiring at times.

You were fortunate to have that dream about being a woman. So were the women you knew later, of course, because you knew more about them.

I have known only two women who were really interested in pornography except as it could affect men *for* them, and they were both overt Lesbians. I really think men have a lot more fun from it. Myself, I have always had a kind of clinical interest in erotica… it does not excite me personally, but I enjoy it… I like some Greek medallions I have seen, and the best collection in France... beautiful, marvelous, the way love-making is at its finest. But they did not excite me, except aesthetically. As for what I think of as pornography, I am actively bored by the giggly-sniggly effect it has on people. One of my husbands had a large and good collection of it, mostly pictured, and I was BORED. I have never needed any such stimulus, which I suppose explains it. A woman once told me that she always had to read a few carefully selected paragraphs from *Lady Chatterley's Lover* to her husband before they could do anything, and I know of another man who always had to enter the woman's bedroom through a dangerously high tall window before he could manage an erection. All of this interests me clinically, but as I say, has never been necessary for me or for my partners. . . .

I know a man who feels as you do about the Cockneys and their approach to a lot the rest of us keep hidden. Gypsies are like that, too. I have known a few, but have never been "accepted" except on the outside of them.

. . . It is all right that you fell in love with me when you read a book. I'll tell you about my last husband: he was (is) a famous New York Wolf, and he was dismayed to find himself drawn very fast toward me, when we met casually. So he bought a copy of the *Gastronomical Me*, and told his friends he was going "out of town" for the weekend, which meant in their language that he had a rendezvous with some fabulously beautiful dame (he was noted for that...), and he went to bed for two days and read and thought. He did not want, above all things in the world, to fall in love. He had been legally married five times, and had had the most beautiful mistresses always, and there he was, caught, at last. He proposed a day later, hating every minute of it, and we were married. Poor devil, to have LOVE happen to him. It almost killed him and me too, and now he is married again, a very good interesting un-love marriage and he is happy again. End of story.

Yes, it is partly because of my children that I have bought a place in St. Helena... they have a fine life, although by now you know that I must compromise on their educations and that I go away from America now and then to give them a longer view of life. I also need more than I can get of our culture... it is too cluttered for me by smog and noises from cars and TV and immature people everywhere. I want to remain an American and have my girls be Americans, but I must go away. I am at ease culturally when I can be invisible, as I was for about a year in Aix, and as I plan to be again before long. Here I am visible and there is a strange futility about it, as if I were marking time (of which there is little left...). So I shall head for a small village named Cavigliano,[3] once I get the girls settled in a small town like Padua or Verona... and when I am older and they are really out of the nest I want to live for a year or so, probably alone, in a hill-village in Greece. Or Sardinia.

I can think and feel and write better when I am invisible. I become *clearer* to myself... sounds foolish but you'll understand. Here I play too many parts, often because I enjoy them or find them challenging. When I am in France I am more truly real to myself....

Now about losing your address: when I answered your first letter, I honestly did not

3. Switzerland, hometown of her friend Romilda Peri Gould

expect to have a reply from you... and I was preoccupied and thought that though your letter had been unusually interesting, it was doubtful that I would continue writing to you. Then you replied, but with no sign of where you lived nor even of your name, which by then I'd forgotten. And it was such fun to hear from you again that I regretted very much not having kept the first address. I must tell you without undue modesty that I do get quite a lot of mail from people I have never met, and while your letter was far from ordinary, it was in a way simply part of my fan-mail. Do not be miffed at this. It was largely a question of TIME with me. But you were miraculously persistent, for which I'm thankful to those gods were dancing too!

I love vineyards. I have an affinity for them, or however you say it. There is something about the growing of grapes and the making them into wine that is mysterious and compelling to me. I love the sea too, and I miss it here and once thought I could never live this far from it. But I can.

It doesn't look, from the pages beside me, yours on the left side and mine on the right, that we'll need fear to run out of something to talk about.

I started this morning about 5:30 to write to you. There is a slow sweet rain, ruinous to the late vendange but beautiful to listen to. Mary and the cat and the dog and the bird still sleep. The dog is ill... pneumonia... she shivers by a heater and soon I must give her some pills, poor little thing. The bells just rang for early mass. . . .

I agree with H about the worthlessness of most university training. I tapped my toe with boredom and at great expense to my family, through two good prep-schools and five colleges... until I got married to escape and plunged into a small provincial French university where at last I learned to work and study. That was pure luck for me. I had a good brain, already going to seed. It's what I fear most for my own girls, and why I thrust them into new languages and different cultures....

Don't run out of stamps. Don't dread this winter. Don't worry about my moping alone in the Bloomin' Bysement: I'm a well-kissed woman and am blooming myself.... As for what may be your bellyache, tell me and only me what it is doing to you, when next you write.

....

St. Helena, California   *18.i.58*
To: Lawrence Clark Powell

Dearest Ghuce—

Don't despair—we'll see each other. Something will shift into place before long, for it. Yes, we are indeed "behind," but not hopelessly.

I too am doing a bit of tightrope dancing, but most of the time I feel secure about it—get a little shaky now and then—mother, hausfrau, secret wife—what a dizzy pattern! I am quite rattled at times, about not working. I have an electric Royal and *look* at it. I plan to go through boxes of old papers, the next few weeks—

I liked your thing about music—wished it were longer and larger—

Love, always

Berkeley, California   *7. i. 59*
To: Lawrence Clark Powell

Dearest Ghuce—thank you for writing.

I must tell you at once that I have heard from G.C.[1]—the first happy alive letter from him for many years—and it is because of your work for the possible publication of the Browning thing. I shall always love you for this—as if I didn't anyway. G.C. is a fine human being and he was for a long time alone on a mountain-top of self-pity, self-torture. Now the world is rich again for him.

Yes (re your having to hoard your strengths at times), we do wear out—pay a heavy price for knowing what we manage to know. But I would rather be me *now*, weary, blasé, arthritic, than the young unwitting almost unconscious me of Dijon or or or…

Thanks for the newsletter and for the delightful little book—both put on loan but heading for my Powelliana. And thank you for the World book—they did indeed treat you "very well"—Bill Targ can't resist a good book about books—

I am glad the fire skipped you.

What do you mean, Larry, that "now Hal is near a bad one"? Please tell me. It pains me.

The so-called holidays are over—many fine high moments and of course a few low ones—and now the girls are back at their schools and I am back at the typewriter (electric by now—much easier for me—). I am writing a kind of autobiographical biography of Dijon(!).

Thank you again, about G.C. I doubt that we can ever more than guess at its healing—he has licked his wounds to the point of near-madness—a great waste of human energy.…

Abiding love,

. . . .

Aboard ship off Panama   *9.viii.59—9th day—off Panama*
To: Donald and Eleanor Friede

Dearest Friedes—a hasty and lazy note, to tell you that all goes well, indeed *very well indeed*. I'll write more details after the Canal tomorrow—we are high-tailing it for Hamburg with a cargo of fresh lemons—I am mildly disappointed not to see old Hindu friends at the Flower of India in Cristobal, but will be richer in pocket—

This is the smallest and without *any* qualifications the best ship I have ever sailed on—quite a statement, eh? Thank God—I was in no shape to cope with much less than perfection. I slept 18 or 20 hrs. a day until normally "subhuman." The children seem really happy—read-sleep-eat-swim-splice ropes with crew—play bridge/canasta/chess/bingo/scrabble/monopoly with everyone from captain to pantry-boy—one 10-yr-old "extra" whom our kids handle very well—very pleasant de-

1. Georges Connes

tached passenger—we are ½ of list—Sorry I was so vague on telephone—thank you anyway for calling—as of now (3 hrs. out of Panama) we plan to go up Rhine from Hamburg on series of steamers as far as possible (Basel??)—My dears, I'll write at length (!) before Hamburg—and meanwhile tout va très bien, M. and Mme. le Marquis—

....

Cavigliano, Switzerland   *18.viii.59*
To: Donald and Eleanor Friede

Dearest Friedes—a very quick one, to tell you that all seems *almost* in focus! We all feel fine about everything, and I feel, myself, quite smug about the fact that exactly 2 weeks ago this morning we landed (Hamburg—godforsaken place—)!

I have quite shamelessly used Pull etc, and by now can report that as of Sept. 15 the girls are boarders in the *Instituto Sant'Anna*, Lugano, Switzerland. Mary will have a roommate from Locarno who speaks French and Italian, Anneli one from Bern who speaks German, Italian and French. *If* a girl does not come from Schaffhausen Anne can enter as 24th and final pupil in "il corso linguistico": she will have to eat, sleep and breathe Italian with the other 23. If the girl does appear, Anne will be, like Mary, a "listener" in all courses, with several hours a day on private lessons in Italian—that is, until the two can cope with regular schoolwork.

The school is the top one in this canton—not at all snob—simply The Best (!) run by an order of teaching sisters from German Suisse, but long established here. The school is in the heart of Lugano—and I as a cynical old sniffer through all kinds, classes, religions, and races of girls' schools can swear that it is the only one I would ever consent to be a girl in. It is gracious, airy, in impeccable taste—

I can see the girls every day in the parlor, until I am sure they are all right. Then I am to leave them pretty much alone for a time. This scares me, not so much for them as for myself, for the prospect of being Mary Frances Kennedy Fisher Parrish Friede 24 hours a day without a single emotional howdedo to anyone but MFKFPF is an empty one. Or it *could* be. I shall try to find a decent "pensione de famiglia" near the school where I can and must be socially agreeable in Italian at noon and night. I shall also take daily lessons in Italian—I can't stand to be so uncouth—I have the vocabulary, and I understand everything, but I must reply, not in baby talk—revolting!

I love Lugano, and am very glad we'll be there for at least 3 months. It is very Italian but with good Swiss plumbing(!). And the girls will be able to get a lot of French, too—

The plans to enter 1 or both in l'École d'Humanité fell with a crash. I'll tell you at Christmas. *Thank God*—it was a mess, or rather it would have been if we had not met 2 key-people at a tea in Cavigliano!

This is our last night with the Barrs, who leave tomorrow for Lausanne. Noni has rented an apartment at Lutry, near Lausanne, and the 3 boys will go to Le Lycée Jaccard (3 mos. in Zermatt too!). Tomorrow we'll go up as far as Domodossola with them, for fun, and we plan to go over to Lausanne for the Toussaint (Nov. 1 holiday). Arnold

M.F.K. Fisher: A Life in Letters

Gingrich wrote a glum sad letter about the sale of Le Pâquis by his sons, but I still want to see it and a few other places around there. (I tried to get Anne into Pré Alpina up at Chexbres but it was full until 1961, and now I feel Sant'Anna is much better, in every way.)

We have been here almost 11 days now—long slow walks, picnics in mountain meadows, waterfalls below our windows, good simple food. It has been perfect. We have got to know how and when to hop the little electric trains that go past the inn, and just where the post offices–bars–w.c.–pastry shops are in 3 villages and 4 towns, and how to use the telephones and where to find taxis if we miss the trains and *above all* where to rent the pedali, those little pedal boats, in Ascona, Locarno and Lugano.

I swear you can hear Mary giggle from here to the Matterhorn when she and John bump Anne and David's boat in the wake of a lake-steamer. I sit on the shore and slake my fears with a thimble-full of vermouth-gin—

Please write to the girls, will you?: Istituto Sant'Anna, Lugano. I'll be *poste restante* or c/o Connes, Dijon, or until I can find a good pension.

We'll go over to Lugano on Thursday, and have a 4-day whirl of clothes-buying, etc, before the girls take the veil. Clothes are quite chic and amusing in Lugano, and the school uniform is very informal, just so long as it is "navy blue skirt and jacket with white blouse." (This can cover a multitude of delightful sins!) The shops, restaurants, Casino, etc., are fun and sophisticated. Whee! Them salt-mines.

It seems long since we've heard from you. Please write. Write that you are well, busy, busy, well, having fun, etc etc etc— we have some pictures of the voyage, as soon as they are developed—will send. Ear-wise, I wish the Vespa had never been invented. Even up in this village the night is in tatters from them. But there is always the sound of the waterfalls.

Much love from us.

....

Lugano, Switzerland   *29.ix.59*
To: Eleanor Friede

Dearest E... a hasty note to tell you that we sent off a little present to you today, for Christmas... not to burden your air-luggage... I did all I could to avoid customs-bother, and the package will be sent with a false value of 20 Francs in case you are questioned. It is a Lalique . . . cigarette box which the girls spotted in a window and said with one voice was FOR YOU. With love.

All goes very well indeed here (except for the typewriter!). You will be as pleased as I am to hear that Anne and Mary seem very happy indeed in every way... blooming with health, keen about all their work, and highly amused by things. We had a good day on Sunday... I got them at 1:30 and we went to the parade for the Fête des Vendanges... really simple and colorful, with lots of bands and cantonal costumes. We watched the first half of it down on the quais and then took a little boat out onto the lake for a farther view. Then we came back here and for the first time, really, had a chance to yak a bit. I was thinking vaguely of one trimester here to get into Italian, and then perhaps Italy, but both girls are very keen to stay at Sant'Anna, so it is quite all right with me!!! There is a good ballet-school here, and Anne seems willing to temper her enthusiasm for learning to ski (really not too useful a skill in California, and quickly learned if she should be in a better locality for it) if she can enter here next trimester... which she can if she keeps her present speed. Both girls are simply leaping ahead with both Italian and French (I am taking one lesson a day in It., in a desperate and plainly futile attempt to keep up with them... I am really rust-brained...)... they sing a lot in both Italian and Latin... they are not yet ready to go into their regular classes, but should be in another month or so. They are very keen about the clothes here... it is really quite an elegant little town... and they look very nice in their Sunday uniforms. I'll take some pix soon. Tomorrow I have to dash them out for more smocks etc in the inadequate 2 hours, some of which must be spent stoking the furnace. (Sunday... this is just to amuse you and D... we sat and drank espresso and ate chocolate ice before the parade, and then came back here to eat a box of salted wafers, 8 slices of salami, 3 Petits Suisses, half a large tube of cherry jam, and a lot of grapes... and I sent them behind the Convent Curtain loaded with apples and bananas.... They report that the food at school is EXCELLENT....) I am going to Lausanne for two nights, to be back by noon on Saturday for the girls' first free weekend... we plan to take a boat over to Morcote to spend the night and look at the collection of Russian art and visit the 13 C church etc... the innkeeper is a retired chef which is usually fun too... has an inn-restaurant at St. Moritz in the winter... I'll report!

Much love to you both, and I hope the girls' present isn't trouble at the customs....

....

Lugano, Switzerland   *4.xi.59*
To: Eleanor Friede

Dearest Eleanor... hastily, to catch the mail before I leave for Schaffhausen for three days... I am sending a copy of this to the children, whom I shan't see for four, and one of the notes I am sending to Donald, just to keep them up on things.

Impossible to tell you, dear girl, how truly sad and sorry we are that you have *had* to slow down... it is always such a bore and nuisance and so on and *so* on. But at least you can make your own choice! And I do hope that by now you are dozing mit snoozing mit sleeping yet... and drinking long cool glasses of milk like a Good Girl and reading old copies of very soporific English whodunits... and now and then being strenuous enough to take a nap on the massage-table.

The hint in D's letter to the Kantors that you might stay here in Lugano is almost too exciting to wait on, and I am impatient to see Anne and Mary and MAKE PLANS. It would be simply heavenly for us, Eleanor, and I can't possibly say how much I wish, for a thousand actual as well as intangible reasons, that it will happen.

Already in the hour since I got your letter and Donald's (copy) I have popped the girls in behind the Convent Curtain and dashed down to dear old Thom Cooke's to ask a few new questions... by now we are deathless buddies and I have a girl and a man

Mary Frances, age twenty, 1928.

At the Whittier ranch in 1924 or 1925:
Anne, David, MF, and Norah.

Al Fisher, Mary Frances, Larry Powell on beach at Cros de Cagnes, 1932.

Larry Powell, Al Fisher, Laguna, 1934.

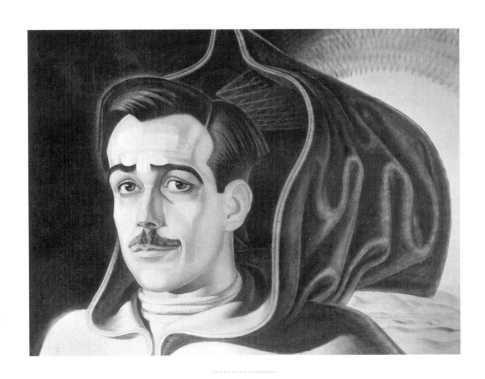

Larry Powell portrait by Szakalski, 1940.

Fay Shoemaker Powell, 1941.

Eda Lord, writer and friend who visited Dijon in 1931.

Dillwyn Parrish in the garden at Le Pâquis, 1937.

Picnic at Le Pâquis: Norah Kennedy, David Kennedy,
Mary Powers, Anne Parrish, Mary Frances, 1938.

Mary Frances with dog Butch.

Dillwyn Parrish painting, 1941.

Dillwyn Parrish and Mary Frances, 1941.

Caricature of Rex Kennedy by David Kennedy, 1942.

David Kennedy and Norah Kennedy at Chapala, Mexico, 1941.

Mary Frances in a publicity shot by George Hurrell for How To Cook A Wolf, *1942.*

Rex Kennedy at the Whittier News, *1945.*

Christening picture: Rex, Mary Frances, Anna, and Edith Kennedy at Ranch, 1943.

Mary Frances, photographed by Man Ray, 1946.

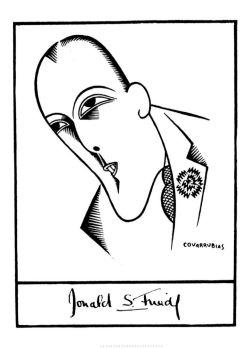

Caricature of Donald Friede by Covarrubias.

The family at Bareacres:
Baby Kennedy, Edith Kennedy, Donald Freide, Anna, 1947.

Donald Friede, Sean Kelly with dog Butch, Anne Kennedy Kelly,
Rex Kennedy, Anna at Bareacres, 1946.

At Bareacres: Donald, Mary Frances, Anna, Kennedy, 1948.

Mary Frances, Kennedy, and Anna, 1948.

Pascal Covici, MF's Viking publisher, on the telephone, 1953.

Henry Volkening and Diarmuid Russell, literary agents.

Sean Kelly, Anna, John Barr, David Barr, and Kennedy with
grandfather Rex Kennedy, Whittier Ranch, 1951.

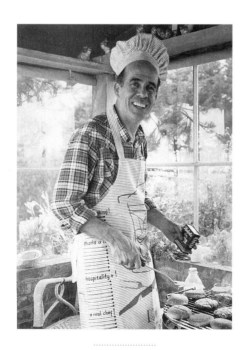

Larry Powell, King of the Maliburgers, 1955.

passionately interested in the Christmas goings-on. They got even more fire in their eyes today! I'll write the details to Donald, who will pass them on to you if they make any sense at all.

And meanwhile sleep like a baby, and dream sweet dreams of all your favorite cats. Much love from us.

....

Lugano, Switzerland   *18.ii.60*
To: Lawrence Clark Powell
(until March 31—then care of Connes again—)

Dearest Ghuce—As I have always said, Los Angeles is *much* nearer Aix than St. Helena—especially by way of Tokyo! ! How wonderful that we'll meet again soon—and *there*.

I don't blame F for being appalled at your schedule. Only you, Powell, only you can live at that speed! . . .

Connes (Le Turel) is not too far from Aix. He wrote of your being there (with F) during the first half of May. I am confident (d.v. of course) that we'll be holed in somewhere before then. (His ancient and honorable father, a wonderful old boy, will be with him—or I'd suggest that you bring him down to Aix—well, whatever happens, I'm sure we will put you up—) . . .

Don't be afraid of your power. Use *all* of it, *now*. You know how—the essential.

Here all is well. I am going to take the girls out of school for the 2nd trimester, and float here and there. They have a very hard year ahead of them, especially Anne, and a *very* serious tough 8 months behind them—school from 8 to 6 and not *1 word* of English.—I want to take them here and there—maybe even to Le Turel, but we don't have a car—surely to Dijon, Beanne, Aigue-Mortes, Vézelay—maybe Paris—they were too young the last time—and the next time they'll be on their own—

I must stop—
Abiding Love

I'm fine but not writing "constructively"—it is irksome—a kind of native apathy except for living with/for the children—Ah well.

Had a good slow week with Norah and her boys—

....

Aix-en-Provence, France   *2.vi.60*
To: Eleanor Friede

Dearest E—. . .

It is very early of a simply beautiful Sunday and the girls have gone off to pick up Jessamyn West and her sister for a day of Arles, Avignon, Les Baux. It seems strange to be alone.

JW[1] etc leave in 3 days (they're at a hotel in Aix—couldn't get them into the dear

1. Jessamyn West, writer

old Roy René—legal convention—) and then as far as we know we are "free" for about 3 weeks. Eda[2] was here for 2 weeks (she and Sybille[3] will be back in October)— the picture was taken after one of the pleasantest meals I can remember, in the open window at Surcouf. Marseille was on a big gay family-spree for Whitsun, with children taking their 1st communion, floating with veils and so on, and surrounded by wine-happy relatives—Bar-Mitzvah Provençal!!—we went up to N-D de la Garde and it looked as if clouds of white moths were fluttering out the great doors and down all the steps. Well: at chez Surcouf we ate cold consommé (it was very hot weather) and lamb grilled with fennel, and *real* wild strawberries! First Anne drank a Dubonnet and the old White Russian who was at E. during Prohibition made me a superb Martini, and then we drank a blanc (not blanc de blanc) from Cassis. Coffee. Wonderful music from fishermen. Ho hum.

And then all the teachers went on strike so the Barrs joined us for 2 days in Cassis— lots of swimming and canoeing, and Maurice Chevalier was making *Fanny* there— one of my long-time loves! Really it was marvelous to watch him—and fun to see how relaxed and gay a big company can be, in Europe—Boyer and Leslie Caron weren't on the set but were strolling around, and half the village was at work doing what comes naturally: fishing, playing boules, sitting—and getting *paid*—a paradise for the producers too for the extras were wearing exactly the same clothes they would have worn in 1924! Well, MC is one of Norah's early passions too, so we turned the 5 kids loose and sat on the quai drinking pastis and smiling gently at him whenever he sat at the next table (drinking coffee). He would bow just as gently now and then, after the 3rd or 4th time with some puzzlement of course. It might have turned into a *thing*. But we had to leave. Ho hum again!

I don't wonder that DF collapsed—nor that the Beach worked its usual miracle.

Your next stint sounds exciting but very tough, and I'm so glad you have the Beach there, always, to give you courage.

Here all goes well. Mary is tutoring for an entrance exam on 23rd. Anne has a week off while the gov't exams are going on for the baccalaureate, and then 10 more days of classes.

I seem to be running a travel-bureau and ticket-office on my 3 days a week in town, and hope that I finally have everything in order for the festival, for us, Norah, the Caroni,[4] and Marietta Voorhees. A new complication is that Anne may get a job as English-speaker in the Festival Office—it is very tough and she'd have to miss 3 chamber-music matinees and the Cathedral concert, but I think the experience would be worth it. I'll know on Tuesday. There are 14 evening things in the 21 days she'd have to work, but they begin at 9—and her hours would be 10–12, 2:30–6. It's a heavy schedule but for 3 weeks—? She's very keen about it.

I think I told you L. Powell had to return to Calif. from London—too bad.

2. Eda Lord
3. Sybille Bedford, British author and Eda's partner
4. Swiss-Italian friends

Don't ever write because we have, dear Squeaky—sit back and breathe when you can, these next weeks!—

Love from us to you both,

....

Aix-en-Provence, France   *18.vi.60*
To: Donald and Eleanor Friede

Dearest Friedls... I must surely owe you a letter or or or... I enclose a few more-and-less horrific things....

It's getting VERY HOT here. We walked to town at 6:30, and marketed and spent as much time as we legally dared at the 2 Garçons (Oh, DF, one of the old-time waiters there gave me a long song the other day, asking me to give you his best greetings... it seems that he can tell a Good 'Un from a Bad 'Un... and he *can*... and you are a Good 'Un.... They are few, he assures me (uselessly, for I already guess as much!)). And by now it is apparently mid-day, although my watch says 4:30, and I am alone with our self-adopted poodle Whiskey and a new red-headed Persian kitten six weeks and six centuries old, named Bazaine in honor of my first Swiss cat and of the famous French general who lost every battle he ever fought. This name seems to be no handicap.... Mary has pedalled over to the Barrs on her Solex... mad dogs and Mary go out in the Provence sun... and Anne has pedalled into a "surprise party" in an old mill... Sur-*preez* part*eez* are The Thing now, and Anne was getting a few bids to them so with her full approval (!) I went straight to the Horse's Mouth, in this case the head of the school, and gave names and dates and places, and she is GOING to them and loves every bit of it, as far as I can see. She wants Mary and John to bust in, too. So far they are shying off like the adolescent colts (dolts?) they are.... Well, at 7 Noni picks me up, and we meet the girls, and all sup on the bosky-green terrace by the big Fountain. And then there is the Corso de Printemps on the Cours Mirabeau, complete with lighted wagons covered with flowers and lighted with candles and drawn by donkeys and preceded and followed by dancers and orchestras from every province in France, in their costumes. Murder. We lead a mad pace... (*MEAN* this...).

Exciting news: Anne got the job as English-Italian-French and possibly Schweitzer-Deutsche interpreter in the Bureau du Festival, and starts on July 1. She is on Cloud 12. It will be a workout, but she will, I am fairly sure, be on deck by 9 at night for the evening operas and concerts. She knows she has all my blessings.

Mary is boning like mad for her entrance exams next week, June 23. She loathes school, but rises to the impossible as usual.

It was marvelous to have Eda here... she has more than fulfilled all I dreamed of her in boardingschool crush of 1923... Donald, Secker and Warburg will do her book in England... I assume this is good.... It was much less fun to have Jessamyn West here, and she made me wonder what DOES happen to good people in this world... ho hum indeed.... (She may well have felt the same about us, but we did *try*....)

Next on the scene are the Caroni, July 14, as far as I know. Etc. Since school ends

June 29 and Anne starts work July 1 and both girls start boning in les Mathémathiques and French at once, I can hardly permit myself to using [*sic*] the word VACATION... but all this adds up to one, really.

How is the beach? How are you both? What are you doing besides publishing books and raising gardens on sand-dunes and and and? Write when you can.

Love—

....

Aix-en-Provence, France   *24.vi.60*
To: Eleanor Friede

Dearest E... and always D of course... I answer your good letter at once. I'm so thankful that Chicago and Cleveland are behind you... now get busy on the Fadiman Therapy! "The essential me" must ALWAYS be the main problem....

Bob Gottlieb is being very tactful and encouraging with Eda... he sounds intelligent too. I agree with him about *Spinster* (have it... thank you anyway...). In some ways it is better than *A Legacy,* but Sybille, I think, will last longer as a writer. She is now in Paris working on both French and Italian translations of that book she wrote about Mexico: *A Sudden View*...? She has enormous energy, and is probably what publishers would think of as a Good Property... or am I thinking of Hollywood producers? Eda Lord is a different cup of tea, and probably a better writer... slow quiet steady small-sales etc etc.... *Memento Mori* is certainly worth a quick look. But I have just read another book about old age which is REALLY good and which makes MM look rather flashy and superficial, which basically it is, *The Big Ward,* by a Dutch woman whose name I forget. *You must read* it for many reasons.

E, I am truly glad you have stopped smoking. I hesitate to say anything like that, for fear of sounding smug and sanctimonious, the way so many reformed people do. But it is painful for me, because I love you, and for the girls too and for the same reason, to hear what is irrevocably happening to you because of one of the strange social habits of the day and of your profession... they are so intertwined, as we all know.... I am perhaps hyper-sensitive to coughs induced by heavy smoking because for several years I lived with Rex Kennedy... his slow end was not a pretty one, and it was the direct result of more than fifty years of chainsmoking. Ho hum indeed. Of course any intelligent person can choose his own poison... and really *must.* I do pray for you, dear Squeaky. . . .

... I feel quite optimistic about the prospects for next year for both girls... and at this point Anne is chewing at the idea (Not my idea) of staying one more year and trying for a Bachot. It is very tough. But it is practically the equivalent of a "Junior College" diploma in the States, and would guarantee her a good job in embassies or travel-bureaus... I'll keep you posted. It would also mean leaving her here for a year, since I think it essential that Mary take her last two years of secondary school in the States, to make it easier if she actually heads into medicine....

Boyer is still A Dream, and I like him much better without the hair-piece! But Maurice is the one for me, even with that competition... my god, such relaxation, such surety, such finesse, such wiseness.

. . . . I must talk with you both, and at length and before long, about a Major Decision about *MFKFisher*. Ah well and ho hum. And meanwhile the schedule is heavy: big party this weekend at Le Tholonet (Noni and I bossing) for various friends leaving for the summer, to play boules on the grounds, have an outdoor supper, and then come back here to watch the bonfires lighted on the top of le Mont Ste. Victoire for the feast of, I think, St. John of Malta....

Anne finishes school on the 29th and starts work at the Bureau du Festival on the 1st of July. Mary finishes school on July 9, exactly three hours before the curtain of *Don Giovanni* opening night. We plan to go in our best store-clothes. Wow. The Caroni arrive with governess on July 14... to stay at Le Tholonet. Marietta Voorhees arrives from St. Helena July 20. The Garfs arrive, from Lugano, July 28. And somewhere between the 9th and the 31st I plan to go to EIGHTEEN concerts and operas. Once in a lifetime, and let the guests fall where they may... local supplies of wine, bread, and cheese will keep them placated if not happy. Mary tutors in the three maths and French through July, and both girls plunge into it in August after Anne's job ends.

As it sounds when I re-read it, I am really piling it onto the girls, but you both know I'm not... they are in wonderful health, and are changing so fast that I am breathless... very keen, prettier all the time, and savoring untellable experiences. I can, though, tell you of some of them when next we meet (Day After Tomorrow...).

Enjoy every minute at the beach, both of you.

Love . . .

....

Aix-en-Provence, France   *24.vii.60*
To: Grace Holmes[1]

Dearest Aunt Grace—I write hastily. This is a fast pace, but there is so much sustenance in the music (*and* the people) that it is not at all dangerous. This afternoon at 4 we all go into Aix to the cathedral. It is all-Handel, which I could do without, but the spectacle is deeply interesting and wonderful of the great church buzzing with people—orchestra and choir from Paris, choir from here, four great soloists, and at the organ the old Maurice Gay. Murder. I plan to stay for his 3rd, then sneak out, to return here and pull together the picnic. Between 5:30 and 6:30 we'll all go up to Bibémus, the deserted Roman quarries Cézanne painted so much—the Barrs, us, our friend Marietta who is here from St. Helena, the Caroni (4) from Locarno. Mary Caroni is a "Cézanne girl" and wants to watch the twilight from Bibémus. We know a man who owns the shepherd's hut where we'll take our picnic, etc— And tomorrow we all go again to *Le Nozze di Figaro*, which grows more celestial each time. So does *Don Giovanni*. One lesson in the festival: the Chamber-Music of Versailles, a bunch of robots of the

1. Grace Holmes was Edith Holbrook's closest friend in boarding school; she became a good friend to all the Kennedy children.

first class in skill, with an automaton conductor. I walked out on the 2nd concert, did not go to the 3rd, but plan to go to the final one, mostly Campra. I do this partly because of the settings—cloisters, courtyards, churches—I'll answer your good letter soon.

....

Aix-en-Provence, France   *31.viii.60*
To: Lawrence Clark Powell

My dearest Ghuce, how sad I am for you and Fay. Wilkie's illness is the hardest kind, for him perhaps but surely for you. In my own way I'll pray for you all. . . .

I've been quite ill for this whole month, but feel well enough now to go over to Lugano for a week—long-promised treat for Anne and Mary—start Course of Sprouts when I get back, to determine whether I'm the victim of an allergy or a virus—damned wasteful and assuringly exhausting—4 illnesses in 16 months. Ho hum.

I am moving from this surprisingly lovely-beautiful-idyllic-heavenly farm, to some dour little rooms in town—the girls don't know yet: I shall spring it on them after a good supper on a lakeside terrace in Lugano—it's impossible for me to be cook-maid-etc etc all alone, with furnace and fireplace, marketing, no car—the doctors say *no,* and part of me is really relieved. I dreaded some of it. And now perhaps I can finish the neglected books? And it will be much more *fun* for the girls to be in town (me, too!)—theatre, etc. Ho hum again. I'll send you an address soon. We'll lodge in a small student-hotel and take half-pension where we used to live.

All my love, dear Ghuce

....

Aix-en-Provence, France   *15.iii.61*
To: Grace Holmes

Dear Aunt Grace:

I write between small trips here and there, getting tickets and so on for our next Jaunt... ten days in Switzerland, for Anne to ski and Mary to see good friends. This finality is rather oppressive, basically: we are fortunate, of course, to have so many friends we regret leaving. One of Dillwyn Parrish's two "quotes": Happy is he who can weep at a departure. It took me years to know what it meant.... Anne and Mary are more mature than I was. . . .

We've had a guest for 2 weeks, a delightful person but very lively. I put her into a hotel across town. Even so, I didn't get much work done, and am glad that she is on her way again. And then the day we get back from Suisse several more people arrive, the first of a flood of Springtime wanderers. Ah well. Fortunately we like most of them very much. Eda Lord will be here for ten days or so, which will be fine... the girls fell for her just about the way I did in 1923.... (I sent you her book, partly because it is about Evanston....)

Oh no... Anne never thought of "languages" as anything but an addition or adjunct or something like that... she is tutoring now with an elderly ex-Comédie Française actor, to polish her French accent a little, and is continuing to do very well in Italian... both girls love the languages, and I feel they know English better too, from having to use the others. As for the school in NY, I of course feel rather trembly about it, as I know A does too. But it is a very fine chance for her to study stage technique, which she has always loved and for which she has a natural flair. She'll get every angle of it at the Playhouse... including acting, which she loves but which she does not have the right "drive" for. She will be 18... very young. But she is tougher than most American girls her age... has had to fight hard to get through her "education," instead of just drifting placidly through it as most of us do at home.... She is not at all interested in going to regular college, except to meet boys, and she doesn't want to fall in love with such young ones as she would be thrown with... she really wants to marry and have several children, and college Freshmen are not exactly indicated there! Well... we'll see.

As for Mary, she chugs right ahead, getting top grades. She really does not like school at all, but is conscientious and studious. She likes the small tough tutoring school she has been in here, and dreads the slower speed of high school teaching at home. But she is firm in wanting to finish at Berkeley High... it is rather egghead, because most of the white children are University offspring... the 57% Negro enrollment, largely from illiterate homes, has a higher IQ and scholastic standing and keeps the whites hopping... also the Barrs will be there and Mary loves to be with them (so do I)....

I feel much better about returning to California, now that it is fairly well decided that we'll stay in St. Helena for the first semester. That will give me a chance to find a decent small flat in Berkeley, and to get used to super-highways, and all that. Mary will go to St. H and tutor to get rid of some American h.s. requirements. It will be good for all of us to dig into the HOME again... re-organize the books, and and and...

I do understand about not wanting to make the effort to go out at night. At home I almost never do, even in Berkeley... all the dull problems of parking and unparking the car and so on. But here in Aix we are about one or two blocks from the constant theatre etc... it is wonderful. . . . And once home, I'll be glad to *stay* there, with all the old records to play again, and a lot of new ones....

The new book will be out in the Fall... proving that even Boston can get a move on now and then.[1] I'm working hard on something else, but have no idea of whether it would please my editor... don't care at all, for it is fun for me.[2]

Yes, my dream life remains very active, but I think it is fading somewhat in my consciousness. On the other hand, the children are developing theirs. It is a question of mental age, I feel fairly sure... although Rex had an active dream-life until he died, unfortunately not a happy one.

Yes, Frank O'Connor is tops... people I know know him very well and say that he is a wonderful person, which doesn't always follow. Ho hum. I know two good writers

1. *A Cordiall Water*
2. *Boss Dog*

who have turned into most unpleasant people in the past few years. I think it takes cold ruthlessness to be a really good writer, and having to be ruthless poisons some natures. (I don't speak of myself here, for I am not what I mean by a good writer....)

I have just re-read what you wrote about my girls. It is true that I could not have helped them, indeed pushed them, into the pattern I have chosen, without Rex's unexpected bonus... and I have had many moments of great doubt, for I have changed them completely from the people they would have become in another pattern. They are not more happy or unhappy than two sensitive intelligent girls would be *anywhere,* I think... and I pray that as older Americans they will be richer in nature than they might have been otherwise. Certainly they are "oriented," if I understand the word. And I do know that they have well-formed and strong tastes for some kinds of literature and music which they could not possibly have developed at home. Well, it is always a puzzlement to me... I know I have made some things harder for them. . . .

I agree with you about good jewelry for older women. I like it, but could live well without it. The only thing I loved was an emerald Dillwyn gave me, and it was stolen and I am sure that by now I wouldn't wear it any more anyway....

Yes, it is possible that I might come back to France permanently when I am much older. It depends on what the children do... when and where they have babies and so on. Personally, I think I would rather be very old in Aix than anywhere. But if I should reach that stage, I might not be able to choose.

Wow... Mary was fifteen last week....... and Anne will be 18 soon after we get home.

I think I told you that we plan to fly from here on June 30: Paris-Glasgow, to stay with friends (The Nuttals, who were very good and dear friends to Edith...), then a week in London to give the girls a first taste of it, and then to Stockholm to stay with Swedish friends... then two days in Copenhagen to see *The Little Mermaid* and drink beer in the Tivoli, and home over the Pole, non-stop.... Murder. But it is the best idea, to do it brutally. If I stay here even a week longer we are lost: the Festival starts, and this year there will be *Dido and Aeneas* again, and *The Magic Flute* and *Cosi Fan Tutti* and and and... and the finest Cézanne exhibit ever assembled... it is really painful....

I send a picture taken by Mary of Eleanor Friede and me... one could say that Donald's fifth and sixth wives look rather like sisters? It is a pleasant surprise that we like each other very much indeed. Donald was suspicious and jealous of that at first, but now he is old enough to think it's a fine thing...!

I must stop this chitchat. I wish you a joyous Easter.... Love—

....

Aix-en-Provence, France   *24.v.61*
To: Donald and Eleanor Friede

And now, dearest Friedls both, some sort of reply to the letters that were here when we got home last night:

Squeakie, I did get the letter of the 7th, but frankly it was fun to read it again! Tut-tut says Old Dr. Fisher about the need for a day FLAT... although that doesn't hurt anyone now and then. The secret is not to NEED it, eh? But you are a big girl now thank God you know when to slow down... or so I hope. And how can I possib you how thrilled Anne is about the fur coat??? I think you are very generous indeed... it seems to me that if you really want to contribute the furs to Operation Warmth, I should pay the furrier for whatever work you and Pupschen decide upon, in the Fall. No? Anne will write soon. She is really happy about it....

Thank you for the special stamps, dear girl. I'm sad to say that the lovely Señora de la Posta has changed jobs, and is cashier in a rather rough noisy bistro by the bus-stop, where upstairs a new and fairly expensive restaurant has opened... not much to recommend it except the snails and the short view of our lady. She looks worn. I'll give her the stamps tonight perhaps, for we plan to have something to eat there and then see Orson Welles and Juliette Greco.

Donald, I can't tell you how much I appreciate your "crash program" for London. And now it all seems settled, and as I wrote in a quick note this morning I am assuming that we do indeed have adequate beds etc at the old St. James House, which sounds absolutely RIGHT.

Tell me: should I write to Mr. Odgen?

And also tell me: what in God's name do I do if he *asks* me about those high-sounding "speeches" I am to make in London? Am I in any danger?

And thank you, my dear old Money-bags Pasha, for picking up still another fat hotel-check. We accept with our usual nimble delight. And everything we eat-drink-dream-see will be with you and E.

Really that was true this last weekend. You would have loathed a lot of it, as a Two-Pillow Man: it was just about as STARK as the girls have yet experienced. But it was marvelous. They were, and still are, in a kind of dream. Me too. Frankly it was god-sent, to be forced, and I mean forced, to cut through this sweet thick coziness in Aix. I can't begin to tell you about it... undoubtedly you'll hear some of it in person: we hired Lov to drive us past Montpellier to Lodève on Friday. I had dreams of staying in a quaint little country auberge. This was one, the Croix Blanche, as far as the front door. Then CRASH. Operation Chapeau Rouge-Dijon, only *WORSE*. Ah well and ho hum. We stood it until the next morning, when Georges trundled into town in his shabby little 2CV... which he continues to drive (some 180,000 km) as if he had never been behind the wheel before. We *crept* (Thank God) then for some 6 hours through the most completely astonishing country I have ever seen... I never thought it could be anywhere, much less France... great gaunt tablelands, gorges, howling winds, flocks of sheep with shepherds from Central Casting... we stopped for lunch at a place about 2500 feet high, and ate like hounds: home-made smoked sausage, veal with Camargue rice, grilled pork chops, fresh peas, sheep-cheese... my god it sounds awful as I write of it, but we were *starved*. We kept on crossing the tablelands and descending at 10 km per hour (Georges's top speed was about 22) into wild canyons and then mounting again... we stopped at a walled village built by the Templars completely empty except for the perfect ramparts... we saw a real dolmen, maybe 25,000 years old, like Stonehenge but all alone... we went up into a village where almost everyone was a relative in some way of G, and saw a most amazing church completely painted inside by a wandering Russian artist in about 1955... he was evidently hungry, for all the motifs were in some way gastronomical, from the Last Supper on to Moses and his manna.... We got to G's before dusk, thank God, up the most fantastic road I have ever seen, straight up a 1200-foot cliff, with 11 hairpin turns in the 4 km stretch. I swore I would walk down when we must leave. But by that time I was so high on mountain air and friendship and the sound of the cuckoos that I rode back down without a quiver. At the top, a beautiful peasant house, and in it a wonderful man 100 years old... one tooth left, one eye slightly dimmed, one mind very bright and even sparkling, one spirit as gay as a new lamb. We came back feeling renewed and full of reassurance, for various tangible and intangible reasons....

And Aix is much brighter too, than when we left it.

And up in the Aveyron and in Aix too we seem more and more to *BE* with you both. It is partly because of the last two Christmases, of course,[1] and partly because Annushka will be in NY next winter. And there are a lot of other reasons.......

To put part of it somewhat bluntly, isn't it wonderful that Nicolas settled things when he did? Most of this renewal and creating of our family ties could not possibly have come about without your delayed bounty from the Czar, I think.......[2]

Back to business: Yes, I have written to the Owens people and to my banker to put the *News*'s boodle into my savings account until return. Meanwhile, please be thinking of suggestions for me, for I have both the innocence and the abysmal ignorance of an unshorn lambkin.

I have not yet heard from St. Helena about what other life policies I have a vague feeling I carry, but will let you know at once. Yes, I shall of course keep up the Accident and Health thing, although I have small belief in it after being so helpless three years ago when I really needed it. Ah well and ho hum... I'm not going to break a leg just to get my money's worth. . . .

The birthday sounds wonderful... what an exciting and fun way to celebrate... the girls love the clipping too, and refuse to believe that DF is actually 60... although the past few weeks have given them a really good indoctrination in how nice really *old* people can be, with Walter Ficklin[3] 80-odd, Georges 71, Pepé[4] 100...! My private prayer is that I can be half as young, at 60, as the pasha is....

Will you please send me a copy of the paperback of *Publishers on Publishing* when it comes out? Or I'll get one on the Coast. No use ordering it now.

Thank you for sending the things to the Studio Club.[5] I do hope Anne gets in.

1. The Friedes joined MF and the girls for Christmas in 1959; Eleanor stayed on in Lugano for a few weeks.
2. Donald's father had been a businessman in Russia; the Friedes received a settlement from Czar Nicolas's estate.
3. Winemaker in the Central Valley and friend of the family
4. George Connes's father
5. New York city rooming house

M. F. K. Fisher: A Life in Letters

And HOW I do thank you for the Bartholomew! Mary already knows her way around London quite well. Me, I must start boning. And we have already decided not to waste time driving for two days. We may get a car for *one* day and go down to Wiltshire to see the Sterns. And we have already been invited to the Royal Ballet and to *Westside Story*... the girls are blissful.

But do please tell me what stand I should take if there were any mention of my speechmaking. I am serious. (Of course, if you have circussed me into a real mess, I can always refer to your calling me your wife, in one letter, and with Squeakie's permission sue you for divorce?????)

Glad you liked Mary's pun. Anne has one for you too, which she *says* she will send soon.

Eleanor, I am so glad to have the recipe for Bitotchki... many thanks. It seems so odd that poor Korniloff was in St. Helena... he gave one rather fabulous dinner up near Calistoga, but it did not work out at all... the idea was to have a top chef at the service of the wineries, for special dinners after tastings etc... so he and his two assistants and some 50,000 dollars' worth of Baccarat glasses and fine china went elsewhere... Korniloff to retirement on the Mexican Riviera, I am told.... Ou sont les verres d'antan?

And where is the afternoon I was going to devote to Business?

Which reminds me, boom boom, that I have DECIDED and have ordered, but straight through San Francisco, a Renault Floride convertible. Wowski. But swank as all hell as it is, it STILL costs less than an overblown Ford tub, even though I am forfeiting a lovely 250 to Ford to get out of their trap. I have asked for a dark green with black leather and top, but may have to settle for a white with black... somewhat bébé-starlette for a staid dowager, but I really couldn't care less....

And now I *must* stop... with much love from us and countless thanks for all the Crash Programming and its heavenly results.

....

St. Helena, California   *10.xi.61*
To: Lawrence Clark Powell

Dearest Ghuce—

I am so sorry that you and Fay had to submit to the fires again. The wind did *not* change, but even so, it is a ravaging thing. I don't yet know how all the Evanses came out, in their little canyon. I fear the news will be bad. Ho hum indeed.

It was better than I can say, to see you again. It gave me a feeling of trust and strength, and of profound gratitude. Not many people manage to make such true friendship survive. I'm lucky, to get this far and still know that you are Ghuce.

Yes, it does seem dreamlike, and at the same time much more real than most of this shadowy routine, that you were actually here. Thank you again for coming.

I'm on the last stretch of the wine book.[1] It is easy to forget it, but I am determined

1. *The Story of Wine in California*

to be shed of it by Thanksgiving. We're going up to Inverness with Norah and her boys—cold, near the waves—I miss the sea. . . .

Abiding love

....

St. Helena, California   *25.i.62*
To: Eleanor Friede

Dearest E....... I should be shot for writing to you, really....... I am in a kind of moral chill about working on the Aix book, and am using you as a hot toddy or shot of adrenaline or something. Please forgive me....... And also the lurid ink....... the electric monster has dried up the black ribbon entirely, and I am scared to change it... really a cowardly-custard today, eh? . . .

Yes, me too, I'd settle for a moitié-moitié with you, this very minute. But you are unique in your ability to drink FOUR cafés au lait... two send me weaving gently, and with three I start shaking. . . .

Thank you for telling me about Anne's Dinner Party. It really warmed my heart. She told me she and Jerry wanted to ask you, but would Donald sit on a bed at a card-table? Yes, I said firmly. Of course. Ah then, what to serve? How could she simmer green beans on a stove that won't simmer? Etc. Now I know it all went off well, and I feel relieved for her... a real hurdle! You are too good to think I had very much to do with her carrying it off well. Probably the only trick she might have learned from me is the air of nonchalance?

I think you should consider Anne's real resentment at having to wear the retainer, before you agree (or rather let Dr. Orzach agree with ANNE!!!) that it is not necessary to swivel the lower tooth into place. Forgive me for this suspiciously mother-attitude!! or do I mean motherly-suspicious?

I think you are very right to keep your stay at the Grosvenor completely temporary. The Cat is yours, whenever you want it for a while. Also anything else you can think of. We bought a good pasty gutty picture of the Ste. Victoire... 18×24, I think. We also bought a strange blue and black thing of a guinea-hen, which I dearly love. Etc. If you want something very gay and busy, DF may remember the big (28×36?) picture of the Café de la Paix, which Dillwyn did. It might be fun for a while?

I re-read the story of how we found Pepé.[1] I think it may be good, but I am afraid it is too long for a magazine. It really is part of a book, or perhaps even a whole one, with various additions. I'll send it along to you MAYBE... thank you for suggesting it, anyway, dear girl.

Oh... I enclose a clipping from a good friend, which may amuse you because of your late questions about HAIR. She is a most eccentric woman about six feet tall, bone thin, with the old-fashioned Colette makeup of black-rimmed eyes, scarlet mouth straight out of Toulouse-Lautrec, and a wild Fizz of bright red hair over her 60-odd-year and thoroughly ravaged face. She was once very beautiful.... DF may have

1. "The Oldest Man," published in *Sister Age*

known her... Elise Cavann... she was married to Merle Armitage for a time, and is now married to Jimmy Welton, the great flautist (he plays everything from the old Benny Goodman trio to first flute under Toscanini...). Well, the news of her wigs is a delight to me. Only she could do it. She just had a one-woman show at the Palace of the Legion of Honor here, and she and Jimmy came to dinner, and I have never seen Mary so completely flabbergasted by anyone... she simply sat and gaped, jaw hanging, and occasionally went off to the bathroom to pull herself together. WEIRD, she kept muttering for a couple of weeks... absolutely WEIRD.

Much love to you both... and to my Wayward Daughter when next you see her.

....

St. Helena, California   *22.iv.62*
To: Eleanor and Donald Friede   *end of Easter Sunday...*

Dearest Friedls... how tonguetied I was, this morning... I know you will forgive me... to my own astonishment I suddenly felt very *émotionnée*....... I had of course been writing one long letter to you in my buzzing ex-brain, and the sound of your voices so near... the next room... simply HIT me. One nevah know, do one?

It has been a good day, but it did not seem at all like Easter, except for that beautiful rooster. Oh what a fine one! He is really the best I have ever seen. Thank you, for years to come....

We were going to take a picture of him, but Mary used all her film at Miss Eleanor's wingding.[1] We'll try again.

That party is behind us, thank God. It was a crashing success, and after all one is seldom if ever ninety, also thank God. The Age of Innocence Cup was a masterpiece, and I think we served about 350 tots of it... to tots of almost a hundred years' range! Oh... one more gastronomical feather in the Friede Hat: the best cooks in the Valley made little cookies, but Mary's Brandy Snaps were by far the *best*. Thank God there too, for she spent HOURS making a good 250 of the pesky little nothings....

I can't tell you now about the trip to Nevada, but it was worth it and I consider it important in a way I do not yet understand. For one thing, it made me feel better than I ever thought I could about my sister Anne. This will interest you, Donald. You know what a consummate MESS things have been for probably that woman's whole life....... now she seems to have attained a kind of serenity which I never dreamed possible. It is almost unbelievable to me that after fifty such destructive years this could happen to ANYONE. I pray it lasts, and I think she does too. For the first time in her life, as far as I know, she is actually TRYING (that's TRYING) to be good to someone besides herself. Mirabile dictu or something like that!!!!!

I found Reno absolutely too ugly to think about. The lobby of the Holiday was indescribable, with all those lonely silent people pulling the slot machines. A surrealist nightmare. Mary was longing to play, but even in Reno she couldn't, so Sis and Bill did it with her money and she got a few mild jackpots and broke a little more than even...

1. "Miss Eleanor" was the mother of Marietta Voorhees.

also swapped silver dollars everywhere and came home with two very old ones....
Blood will tell, etc etc etc.......

I was drawn to the country we saw, once out of the Reno area. It is very austere. I don't know if I am simple enough, or strong enough, to cope with it, but it does make this Valley seem almost painfully cluttered and *pretty*. It is rather the way I feel about living in virgin snow... the color and sound and air of another existence. I might go back, not near Genoa of course but into some cow-village like it. I think I could work well. Here it is very hard for me... everything interrupts me, including the bushes and trees and birds and dogs....

It was good to return, though. Mary got her first taste of REAL bucketing in a little DC-3, and did not approve of it. We fled SF like the black pox, and drove home happily in full moonlight with the top down.

And things have been popping ever since.

Gossip... I have been paid for the wine book, but now the Wine Institute wants me to do a lot of revision to turn the damn thing into a blatant ADVERTISEMENT. I absolutely refuse. I always have and I always will. To hell with stuff like money. So tomorrow morning the president of the Institute and the director of the University Press are bringing me the galleys, and I have the check AND the contract all ready to tear into little tiny dramatic PIECES unless I win my point. Hah. I am breathing genteel fire. (This will amuse you....)

Eleanor, I do hope very much that the contour chair plus rest plus the contour chair plus plus plus have done the trick. You are one of those longboned people who have exactly the same supply of joint-juice as the short-boned ones, and you are pregnable. It is so simple. It is also so damned inconvenient, not to mention pure hell. Please keep me posted. (You did give a few lurking muscles quite a work-out during the moving, admit!)

Tomorrow I start a weird few days with the Wine Dust-up... this week I go to Vallejo to give a talk(!), and to Santa Rosa to have the upholstery of the car repaired and to see a dying friend, and to Napa to adjust some tax stuff with "my little CPA around the corner"... etc. When does Miss Fisher WRITE?

I don't know. But I do know that Dear Old Dote will write very soon, in answer to your letters, which of course are uppermost in my thinkings, especially in the silent hours before dawn. Please let me tell you now, and I know that you know it already: I have full trust in both of you, and basically in Anne too, to weather this foolish but predictable lack of discrimination. Unfortunately it is caused by innocence in its most dangerous form... and that is what frightens people like us, because we know better (or worse?) by now.

Enough, for the moment.

I'm heading for the Last Round-up, complete with Sardo.[2] I would like to eat some caviar and drink champagne, even all by myself. But instead I will make two large

2. Bath lotion

M. F. K. Fisher: A Life in Letters

bowls of cream of tomato soup (Campbells' vintage stuff) with cinnamon on top, and toss Mary into her bed....... Myself into mine.......

Much love, and thank you again for the ROOSTER, and for calling.

E—Mary wore that white embroidered blouse, new pleated skirt—très chic!

....

St. Helena, California   *14.v.62*
To: Eleanor and Donald Friede

Dearest Friedls... I am being much slower than I've meant to, in writing to you.... Thank you for your good letter of the 7th, Squeaker, and for letting me see the EPIS-TLE from Anne. I am glad to see that she can "communicate" if she feels like it. And today... boom boom... I got two short notes from her, the first since some time in March... mostly about what "terrific tension" she is living under and how utterly ex-hausted she is. I tremble slightly at how-when-where the reaction is going to affect her, in this absolutely dead-end.... I trust you to get her to understand, as she never would/could from me, that I will understand COMPLETELY if she feels it best to go back to NY before the end of June... this monotonous pace might easily upset the fine balance she has apparently struck, this past winter... and it would be unfair to all of us if she stuck doggedly by the first tentative dates.... Do help me out on this, you two....

Mary and I had a really fine weekend, and it is hard for me to plunge again into the book.... I am managing to put it off until tomorrow! ! ! We left before dawn, drove to Crockett and parked the car, and hopped the Inland Daylight to Madera, about 5 hours.... We stayed two nights with the Ficklins. It was heavenly. Mary swam twice... the third day was chilly. We slept late, and ate and drank well, and listened to a lot of old jazz, and talked fairly steadily. They are wonderful people, not really exciting but thoroughly pleasurable to be with. I like the way they live, very simply and yet with everything absolutely as it should be: low adobe houses, with cool little patios and ar-cades... everything casual and yet basically elegant. Well, it was a good break from this somewhat oppressive fight I am putting up against the local lotus-eating. (Donald, we ate piles of tiny wild doves, roasted... we thought of you, and somewhere Mary and I've got to do something about that, but what? I can't just take off for Aix whenever I get scared enough! ! ! !) . . . Mary has an almost invisible wishbone....)

(For you, I mean...)

Now to your letter... too bad about the curry, but at least you TRIED it again. I sel-dom eat one, because I have yet to find one I like in restaurants... but so far I have never had any after-effects, thank God. I seldom make them, either, for most people I know do not enjoy them for one reason or another. . . .

Yes, please do write to me of what you both think about Anne's having an apart-ment. Myself, I am opposed to it for a couple of reasons which may not be valid enough. As I know Anne now, minus this last complete re-shifting of her aims-ideals-patterns, etc etc, I still believe that she is the kind of person who in her basic aversion to being *responsible* for anything must depend upon the strength (?) of firmly established schedules and rules. Ever since she was a little girl she has written stern routines and notes to herself: Get up at exactly 6:47 each morning... take shower before dinner EVERY NIGHT... do nails between 4 and 6 each Saturday... and so on. And I am afraid that in this new freedom, she would loosen this grasp on the dull routine side of life... let meals and rest slide too far... get hopelessly disorganized. Another thing: Anne has a very strong nesting instinct, made stronger by her natural need to have her *own* foyer, her *own* taste in everything. I sympathize completely with it. But for a time longer perhaps this need might blind her to the desirability of the people she would share it with.... Well, perhaps these are meaningless reservations, and I want very much to know how you both feel, before Anneli gets home.

The new summer clothes sound great... and you were a darling to get her the extra dress. . . .

I keep sending out feelers about schools for Sweet Marie. Nice people respond nobly, but always with names like Bennington, Sweet Briar.... What they cannot seem to understand is that Mary simply does not have the grades to qualify for entrance in even a second rate college, at this point! She will have to take one and possibly two years of fence-mending before she can hope for entrance in any reputable college. Murder. But thank God she is very young....

Meanwhile she ambles along in a half-desperate inertia... doesn't read anything but comic books and an occasional copy of *Seventeen*, gets barely passing marks, is thoroughly disagreeable most of the time.... Thank God (again!) I have been prepared for this weird phase by having Anne plunge into it first... each time it is still something of a shock, however. There is nothing to do but live through it, and try to remember that it is surely as unpleasant on both sides of the fence!

This apparently necessary period of teenagers is complicated by two main things, I feel: she is basically bored to distraction by the low intellectual level here, and made hopeless by it... and she has to cope with living alone with a much older woman. Women should not live together without men, let's face it. I do all I can to keep "company" moving in and out....... but that is not a fully satisfactory substitute. Ah well and ho hum.

... interruptions... and how did I get off on this tack? Bear with my muddlings....

It is impossible that this school year is almost over, for Anneli! I am PAINFULLY anxious to see her again... it's so exciting, the way people flower....

All my love... I feel as if there is something special to thank you for, and will probably think of it at 3 this morning....

Oh... the picture floated to the top of a box... taken in Baja California in about 1952 or '53, I think... we ate baby lobsters grilled, twice a day, and drank barrels of beer... it was fun, although you'd never know it by Noni's and my hag-faces... she was in the process of escaping from John Barr's clutches, complete with three sons under the age of four... and I too was having troubles. The lobsters were still delicious!

M. F. K. Fisher: A Life in Letters

Berkeley, California   *8.x.62*

To: Lawrence Clark Powell

Dearest Ghuce—I should have written to you, long since. Thank you for your note.

About the wine book—I consider it a good hack job, but I am not excited about it. I think the only reason it was published, after some *11* years of shilly shallying, was that I finally said now-or-never. Ah well and ho hum. I was well paid. I think it is a slick job. (I dislike those heavy vulgar meaningless "gift" books, and am sorry my name is on one.)

Oh—a needle to your blood pressure: a local review (Anon) says that *Maynard Amerine* suggested that I write the text, *last year.* Murder.

Case closed.

Well, I was very ill. I was in 2 big hospitals. Caught in the giant test tubes, since the end of May. Very destructive to the family life, to my finances, to *me.* Once I thought why can't I be flown to Hal? But I was too ill. And he was in the last handwringings of Elizabeth's end.

Now I am at least ambulatory. I have a little apartment in Berkeley (please note address and telephone). I am near Norah, and somewhat nearer (than St. Helena) Menlo Park, where Mary is in the Convent of the Sacred Heart. I was not well enough to handle the St. Helena ménage, but so far am all right here alone in Berkeley.

I am stronger all the time, and hope to drive as far as St. H this next week.

I am anxious to finish the Aix book—before Christmas if possible.

So you return to Europe! I envy you.

It would be wonderful to see you. Please call me if ever you have a few extra minutes in Berkeley—

Give my love to Hal when you see him.

To you, always—

Genoa, Nevada   *31.iii.63*

To: Marian Gore[1]

Dear Marian:

Thanks very much for your letter. I have always liked hearing from you....

Genoa is about fifty miles (I think) south of Reno, and ten miles south of Carson City. It is an almost deserted village which burned to the ground, except for a few brick buildings, in 1907. It was a Mormon fort, and there is still a re-built old log house-and-stockade here, which is a state monument now. There is a big deserted school-house of red brick, and then there are a saloon (The oldest in the state), a general store, and the Masonic Hall, all of brick and stone. And that is all. The houses are for the most part nondescript, made of wood. I am living in the most handsome one, with a widow, an

1. Southern California rare-books seller, specializing in cookbooks

elderly woman of great charm and breeding. She speaks excellent French, which is fun. (She took me in, after the Ranch where I was staying burned down and the proprietors had to use the guest cottage... it is a new experience for both of us, and is working out very well... I have a whole floor to myself, and I enjoy seeing her now and then for meals, although mostly I go up to my sister's....)

Well, the air is indeed like crystal, and I dread breathing the soggy smoggy stuff in Berkeley. In fact, I can't STAND the idea right now, and am planning to go up to St. Helena as soon as I have got Mary back to school and checked with my pill-boys.

I really meant it when I said I was getting a divorce from myself. I think that I was so very ill for such a very long time that unconsciously I gave up life... and it was almost more than I could manage, to find myself alive again and to have to take up where I had left off. I was filled with a dreadful weariness... or listlessness... something like that. And up here I have come into clear focus again, physically but most important mentally. I am much as I was in Aix, except in better physical shape: very keen and curious again.

And that is enough of that! Except that I am interested to see if I can keep up this momentum in St. Helena. I will hold on to the Berkeley apartment until the lease expires in August, so that Mary can go to a good business school this summer... but I want to spend as much time as possible in St. H.

And now about the idea of taking boarders... I am so pleased and amused that you like it. It may not come about. But I do know that I should not spend next year alone in the St. H house, even with Mary home every other weekend or so. . . .

... I think I will try to rent the bedroom and bath that go off the kitchen... they are the only rooms that can be independent, otherwise, of the rest of the very intimate house. It will be good for me to have another human being under the same roof. I'll try to get either a new schoolteacher or a business woman, through the school principal and also the Soroptomists, who are quite active in St. H. It would be simply for lodging, with "kitchen privileges" for breakfast probably, unless that meant stinking up the house with bacon and pancakes and so on....

Then I think I will notify a few people in the valley that as of a certain date I plan to serve dinner, five nights a week, at exactly 6:30, to no more than six people a night. Places can be taken for the day, week, or month, paid in advance. I think $15 a week, to start with... until I see how my bills go.

I would not serve "gourmet" meals, nor meat-potatoes-gravy, but simple dinners of two or three courses, "family style," well balanced, based on American and European regional cooking. I would serve red and white table wines of the bulk class, from Napa Valley, with of course no charge for corkage (!) if people wanted to bring their own.

No diets... fish on Friday of course...

I would encourage people, if there was as much demand as I suspect there might be, to alternate eating there with other places... to have a little variety in conversation and so on....

I would not eat with my guests, nor would I encourage them to linger past 7:30-

M.F.K. Fisher: A Life in Letters

ish… in other words, it would not be at all your idea of chatting with "literate creative people" while whipping up a cioppino! This would be a pleasant congenial change from the ghastly coffee-shoppes in St. Helena. It would not be Dining With Miss Fisher at *all*.…

If it went well, I could serve eight, but never any more.

I would market, cook, serve, and most probably have to wash dishes afterwards… might be able to find help for the latter.…

I figure this would take between four and six hours a day. That would leave me, PERHAPS, time for myself. I would keep a rather detailed log-book, just for fun… reactions to certain dishes, menus used, etc etc.

Well… it might be an interesting experience, and certainly I have to do something about this next year at home.

And my mind is a near-blank about WHAT NEXT. Mary will be started by then on what looks like a round dozen years of medical training. I have no idea about Anne except that I know she does not want to return to St. Helena. The house is much too big and too expensive for me to maintain just for an occasional Christmas vacation. What environment should I next head for? My NY family suggests my living there. My nature asks for someplace like this austere simple country. I can't imagine being in a great city, and yet I know this is not indicated for a single and aging woman. Any suggestions, Doctor?

Work is going very well indeed, but I shan't finish the book[2] before Mary comes up on the 10th and then we fly back to the Bay Area on the 16th. I am not worried. It is taking shape nicely, and I think I can get it well out of the way before summer vacation.…

I really dislike intensely living in Berkeley, except for being near Norah. But I see her perhaps once a week! I think it is subconscious revolt against all the nasty tests and so on with the pill-boys. But I feel that I am well out of their clutches, except for surveillance… and as I said, I am in a twitch to get home and mend a few fences… and yet I dread leaving this completely uncomplicated life. I do nothing but sleep-read-eat-walk-*work*. I am as simple as one of the ewes I see in the nearest meadow beyond my windows. Then there is nothing but land, as far as I can see… finally the Pine-nut Range, blue now with some snow still on the summits… beyond it the Great Desert and Salt Lake City, I think.

How can I leave?

....

St. Helena, California   *11.viii.63*
To: Pascal Covici

Dear Pat… thank you for your note. You know how I feel about hearing from you. And thank you for sending me the Leonard Cohen book. You know how I feel about surprises, too.

I have almost finished reading it. For some reason I have read, lately, several novels

2. *Map of Another Town*

and collections of stories by intelligent sensitive young Jews, of lower to upper middle-class families. I think this the best one, so far. I should like to read more by him... and I seldom say that.

One thing interests and at times annoys me about EVERY SINGLE ONE of these young writers: the comic-book portrayal of their mothers. For the fathers there is impatience, some mockery, and an at times grudging affection. But for the mothers it is the routine caricature: a fussing, doting, stupid, tender female who usually expresses her love by over-feeding the child. Why doesn't one of these bright sensitive boys go behind the silly front and find the woman? And if he does try to do this, why must he continue to strip any possible dignity from what he finds?

Well... this is a general query of mine, and it has nothing to do with the obvious skill and perception of much of the writing, and especially of this boy's. (Not exactly boyish, chronologically!)

Pat, I am sorry there is any confusion and delay about getting that manuscript to you.[1] I have understood from Henry that it would be sent to you at once. It is very good of you to want to read it. I hope you like it. It is of course very personal, in a detached way.

Well, the material for the Old Age book does scare me. But I plan to tackle it. I have a few things to cope with, this next couple of months, in adjusting myself to a new phase in my life. Getting the material into working shape will be part of all this.

Thank you for your encouragement, which I very much need.

I am delighted to see that you say that "it will be good to see Mary." I do hope very much that she can see you and Doro. You are important to her. As I now understand the plans, she and Donald will go directly from the airport to Bridgehampton, to get there in time for Anne's 20th birthday party. Mary will stay at the beach until about time to leave, and I assume that it is then that she can be in NY long enough to see you and D. That will be about August 28....

This has been a good summer, and I feel some relief that it is almost over.

My love, always.

....

St. Helena, California   *4.x.63*
To: Eleanor Friede

Dearest Squeek... I knew when I was writing yesterday that there was another one of your letters. It just floated to the top... I am trying to clean up my desk before the weekend, which promises to be a fairly lively one.

Thanks so much for the very complete little brochure about the Hamptons. I shall keep it. I would love to go there some time. I think I would like to experience the winter, though... people DO, don't they? I mean, the little towns do have year-rounders? Mary thinks I could hole up at the hotel in Sag Harbor where Rocco[1] lived....

1. *Boss Dog;* Covici did not like it.
1. A friend of MF's daughters

M.F.K. Fisher: A Life in Letters

You had just taken your driver's test when you wrote the letter I found. I am sorry you felt depressed about it. Mary says you have absolutely nothing to worry about, in your driving. Did you get the license?

Once in Switzerland Dillwyn thought I ought to have the special test for mountain-work, so I went to Lausanne for it, and have NEVER had such a disagreeable sneering haughty horrible tester. I was literally in a cold sweat when we finally got back to the office. And as he got out of the car (He was very good looking, as I remember), he said quietly to me, "I hope you will forgive my utterly foul manners, today, Madame. The truth is that I am in the throes of the most terrible hang-over I have ever had in my life." He bowed in a gingerly way, and I said, "Well, when you have made your report, why don't you meet my husband and me for a hair of the dog?" Which he did. End of story.

I am glad you still see the good Truman[2] in between all that other nasty-little-boy stuff. I rather hope he never decides to come to see me... I am afraid he would never get past the chitchat, and God knows I have less and less in return, as I grow older... I find myself pretty obviously *bored* by most of it, and indeed by most PEOPLE. (But I do love the ones I do love!)

I too am interested in how and when Anne proposes to stop paying the bills with DF's little lagniappe. Even with the lowered rent, she can't possibly manage it and tele-phone and utilities for less than a hundred, I would guess. And clothes? and food? and and and? Let me know if you happen to hear any hints about this....

I don't take the *NYer* but will try to borrow the Aug 31 number. What you say of the surrealist story reminds me of some very off-beat and earnest and deadly-dull Nou-velle Vague things we saw at the Club des Cinéastes in Aix....

Truman is wrong that two cats are not more trouble. They need two bowls, twice as much food, twice as much pan-emptying and cleaning. They are fun, I admit: by now I am beginning to enjoy The Girls, or rather they have become slightly less disdainful about my continuous and varied attentions to them (! ! ! ! !)... I'll never be exactly chummy with Anak, but she delights my eyes at least... and Niki is a pleasant old dow-ager, very discreet and dainty. But tomorrow when Mary and I go out to the vet's to get some more heart-pills for Yee, my favorite geriatric at this point, I plan to ask about boarding the Girls (I mean now and then). Really, I feel duty-bound to fly down to Riv-erside to see Elsa Mintert,[3] who is very frail... and of course I'll take the curse off that (I dread it) by staying one or perhaps two nights strictly incognita with June Eddy in Los Angeles. And of course I have SAID that I would go up to Genoa for a week or so. I am sure I told you of my rather odd reservations about that. Ho hum. We'll see.

But I agree: you are not ready yet to start a new relationship with a cat.

That is what I am basically grudging about, in this present arrangement with Niki and Anak: they are not MY friends... they tolerate me and I am conscientiously kind and attentive to them... but there is no real interdependence there. Ho hum.

2. Truman Capote, a neighbor of Eleanor Friede
3. Elsa Purdy remarried.

Thanks, both of you, for being so understanding about my feelings on "education." I did write to Anne and tell her that it was my earnest wish that she would grab as much available LEARNING as she could, while she was young and in NY... that is, I would like to feel that she is doing things, even if they cost for tuition, which she can get in NY now and which soon might not be available because of marriage, children, a different milieu. I don't know if I'll ever learn her reaction.

But I have had two letters from her in two weeks! They were well-typed and well phrased... rather "prattling," but even that was balm to my loneliness.

.... Mary just called, to ask if she could bring home one of her new roommates, a very intelligent fat lonely girl from Oklahoma. Fine. Of course she is Catholic so we can't have that enormous steak tonight... it looks like scrambled eggs. Ah well. And quite a lot is cooking for Saturday and Sunday: a meeting tomorrow noon of about twenty foreign students from various American Field Service families in Northern California which Mary should go to (She is quite strong on that, and of course I am on the local "board"...).... a movie tomorrow night... Sunday a big Fiesta with good Mexican music and so on, for the wine harvest.... Wowski . . .

Here the leaves, and the walnuts, and the persimmons, are beginning to fall. The mornings are nippy. I love it. It is very dry, and I keep hoses dripping most of the time, on the junipers and so on. The Michaelmas daisies are done with. I still get a lot of tiny tomatoes, which I love, and now the figs are ripening so fast that I keep all my neighbors supplied. I made some fig jam, just for old times' sake... will try it out on the young ladies tomorrow morning, with English muffins.

Oh... I do like your blue note paper... for me blue is a right color for you, even though you have those brown eyes. I like good old yellow, of course, but get a little bored with it. I found that I did not much like writing on some green paper I got in Carson City... don't know why, for it is a favorite color usually.

I have been very lucky with editors this time, both on the *NYer* and at L.B.[4] Nice sympathetic people. Last time I had the same one at L.B. (Mary Rackliffe) but she had a little trouble with me, because two of her readers were Southerners and could not stomach the chapter I wrote about a cure for bleeding... there were several Negroes in it, all much too familiar with "those darling little white children who got cut," etc etc. I stood pretty firm, which did not simplify life for Rackliffe. But now all is forgiven... except for the word *bezique*, which she insists must stand without an accent because it is played "so much" (?) in America. A minor decision which I am glad to have HER make.

All love—

I am a little disappointed that I won't see much of Mary. But of course I'm glad she wanted to bring anyone home—

4. Little, Brown

M.F.K. Fisher: A Life in Letters

St. Helena, California   *6.xi.63*
To: Henry Volkening

Dear Henry:

Thank you for your letter and the enclosed cover of PW.[1] . . .

I am sure I should feel pleased to have my name on the cover of the PW. But I find myself feeling quite resentful about the little blurb inside. I think the parenthesis "(and not much money)" gives a very false note about the book,[2] and one that is not justified in any way by the prose in it. It sounds like one of those quasi-whimsical diaries written by Fulbright mothers on how to get along on Daddy's puny dollars in a Volkswagen through Yurrup, with all the kiddies getting lost in the Catacombs and throwing up from the top of the Tour Eiffel.

The truth is that we were completely unconcerned about money, most probably for the last times in our lives, and that we lived exactly as we most wanted to, in everything from an apartment at the Merrice overlooking the Tuileries to a 3rd-class waiting-room in Lucerne.

But all that has nothing to do with the book I wrote about Aix, and I do not like that blurb....

Should I tell Mr. Bradford that? It is a ridiculous angle to introduce in a one-line description, to my mind. Misrepresentative.

And while I am sounding off... being tart and/or disagreeable... I will tell you that I was DISMAYED by the drawings for the book. Thank God Mary was there. She did not find them quite as awful as I did, but even so we managed to eliminate several of the worst. The artist, a woman, cannot draw very well (hardly at all), and uses a thick ink line that looks very heavy and Germanic, almost like a linoleum cut. She says that she "knows" Provence, but her way of expressing this is to ring the sun with lines, à la van Gogh, and stick heavy little lumpish "peasant" figures in the foreground. I regret now that I did not simply say NO. But I felt sorry for Mr. Bradford: he seemed like an unsure shy cold timid stiff frightened person.... I wish L.B. could have used the Crespi drawings I sent as models. Ho hum and, I am afraid, ah well. . . .

I got the work done that I took to Nevada... but I am sorry to confess that I did not come back as fired up as I'd hoped, for the next job. Meanwhile I'll be sending off a rather long short thing to you.[3] Miss MacKenzie asked to see more work, and I don't know if you will want to show this to her. It is about a strange trip we took to a wild lonely village in France, to stay with a man who was a hundred years old. It is straight reportage, not a story.

1. *Publishers Weekly*
2. *Map of Another Town*
3. "The Oldest Man"; Rachel MacKenzie was an editor at the *New Yorker* and a great sponsor of MF's work.

Henry, I am sorry to be so stuffy about that ad, and about the illustrations. And I am sorry I really did not find Mr. Bradford an interesting person. But certainly he has been pleasant to correspond with.

Oh... the supper was funny, in a way. First, Mary and I were going to have a little spree, to make up for an absolutely ghastly weekend two weeks before. Then we found that we SHOULD meet an old dear friend in SF to act as one of the judges of the West Coast contestants or whatever they are for the Royal Ballet (London). Then she invited her son along, a real pill, and THEN Mr. Bradford asked if we could meet him that night instead of the next noon!... Murder. So we decided to get it all over with, in relays, and simply moved from one end of the Clift French Room to the other. Perhaps the main trouble was that the food was strictly Steam Table...? Ah well again.

You wouldn't like Nevada. But still I wish you would slide off somewhere as neatly as I did. Now I am being serious, and a Good Citizen and all that: I am doing "Costumes" for a big Christmas pageant, and am getting the Wine Library into really good shape, and am even making speeches for the Associated Chambers of Commerce about the cold fact that this beautiful wine country is right under the noses of the subdivision bulldozers. I am even doing some tapes for the San Francisco Public Library next week... mostly about Fisher, I think. Ah well AGAIN. Come the New Year, I think I will take a nose-dive out of all this... perhaps into that Old Age deal?

Greetings to N,[4] as always.

And love.

....

St. Helena, California   *19.xi.63*
To: Henry Volkening

Dear Henry:

I am sorry if I bothered you with my sounding off so strongly! It is indeed too late to do anything about the so-called art work. As for the blurb... maybe I should write to Ned B... if I do, I'll send you a copy. Ho hum. I still think it has entirely the false connotations....

I hadn't thought about that first meeting with NB![1] But I don't put much stock in such coincidences... I mean, I am not *caught*. I want, in his case, to try again(!).

And thank you for telling me, skilled wily pleaser that you are, of seeing me before we met. I love every word of it, of course. Truth to tell and tit for tat, *I* remember meeting *you*, that same night at Edita Morris's place. I had come down from the Covicis and dinner, with Pat and Donald. I felt very timid, in spite of a new dress which I liked. It was a blur, the party, except for two people, you and a delightful old Swedish lady who was a friend of Edita's. I stayed talking too long with her, and DF relentlessly moved me along, past an ugly smorgasbord. Then DF wangled your coming over, and I took

4. Henry's wife, Natalie
1. Ned Bradford

one look at your eyebrows and said something (fortunately to myself) like "*That's* the one for *me*." I meant it in the *best* sense, of course, and I still do.

Sorry nothing turned up in the magazines. Ah-well and Ho-hum ride again....

I am waiting for the last pages from the "quaint lil ole village typist-of-sorts" (And I do mean QUAINT), and I hope to get the reportage off to you tomorrow. From now on I think I'll try to cope with my own typing... I am slow, when I have to try to do well... but this is frustrating and also very expensive.

I too wish that you could put your feet up here for a few minutes at least. I am concentrating on it. But if ever we do have to meet over a table in SF and no more, let it not be the Wedwood Woom of the Clift on a Sunday night! In other words, it was NOT NB'S FAULT....

No, Anne went through a very tough and at times heartbreaking two years in NY, as I see it. She was trying to adjust what she truly believed an apprenticeship in the theatre with what she chose to accept as the only available one in NY. I wish now that I could have sent her straight to Paris or even Edinburgh or Dublin. Too late now. But she is a fine girl, and I am not unduly worried... just regretful, and very proud of her for being, at 20, "in focus" as much as she is. (She would and could not understand this attitude, right now, I think....)

Best always.

....

St. Helena, California   17.i.64
To: Grace Holmes

Dearest Aunt Grace: I have had a letter to you on the top of my mind for so long that today it was all-insistent. Then your letter came. I shan't even answer it now... you will be interested in the Christmas Caper[1] and so on, but I'll save that report for later.

Suffice it that we are all well, that Mary will be home tonight for the weekend, that Donald's wife Eleanor is here while he is in London, and that I seem hurried but not harried and very eager for this long "holiday season" to end, as it will on January 22.

This is what is on my mind, and has been for several months, and I want your opinion, for you know me pretty well: What do you think of my going to work at Piney Woods, for at least a 2-year hitch?

If I did, I would go back first to talk with Dr. Jones and whomever I'd work under. I would plan to start work next fall, or whenever it was right for the school after about July 1 of this year.

I will be 56 on July 3, and as far as I know I am in pretty solid physical state (although I do not think that the Peace Corps, for instance, would consider me a good risk, because I have lessened endurance for prolonged cold and heat...).

This idea of mine is not at all a new one, and it was strengthened several years ago by learning, inadvertently, that you yourself had once considered something like it.

1. Almost all of the extended family gathered in Genoa, Nevada, where MF's sister Anne lived.

I have reached the point in my life of shifting plateaux. I am no longer needed as a mother in the biological sense, since Mary will graduate on June 4 and will then begin what looks like about 12 years of preparation to be a doctor, none of which she can do here in St. Helena. My older girl Anne has been "out of the nest" for more than two years, and will never return, except to be with me now and then, no matter where I am.

I own a house here which is ridiculous for me to live in alone, and I do not think it wise to try, as I once planned, to take boarders.

I was the oldest child in a fairly big family, and I have by nature and by training a strong sense of responsibility for others, especially those younger or weaker than I. I am perhaps unusually sympathetic with the old (which of course has nothing to do with Piney Woods). I have always been at ease with people of other races... or perhaps I am simply without consciousness. I have always been "accepted," I know... never any feeling of condescension etc on either part.

Well... I wonder if perhaps I should close up this place or sell it, for plainly it has served its purpose and it is no longer sensible for me to stay on here alone, once Mary has left.

Of course I have problems of logistics: what to do with the pictures and books. But they can be solved.

And meanwhile I feel that it is a great waste of human talent and energy for me to remain here. I have many good friends here, and almost surely I can get enough magazine jobs to take care of my needs... and perhaps now and then turn out a book.

BUT...

there *I* am.

And such a pattern is not enough for me, now that I am finished with the maternal phase. I am not married, nor emotionally involved. (My very good attachment of several years ago resolved itself naturally and well, and I am really not interested in anything else of that nature....) I am not qualified to get an American teacher's certificate, so that I must always teach in private schools. I do not particularly want, anyway, to get into a large public school... nor do I want occasional lectureships at colleges. (I have tried that, and it is too hard to blast in and then blast out again... no personal attachment in any way, in any direction....) I can speak well in public, but I loathe giving lectures to yearning "adults" who subscribe to courses.

I think I could teach English literature... basic composition... advanced... and then perhaps work in "Home Economics" as a specialized instructor and lecturer... and also I am a qualified French teacher and instructor in both grammar and literature, and can with very little boning work in Spanish and Italian....

I can't think of any other possible qualifications. On the negative side I am going on 55 [*sic*], have survived one major illness at 53, must use an electric typewriter or dictate, am an agnostic... I could go on about this, of course.

So what do you think? Do you think I should go back to Mississippi and see about it? I think I can accept a token payment... I do not believe in "volunteer" work which

M.F.K. Fisher: A Life in Letters

involves people to that extent, and would want something like board and room and $1 a month, or or or... I would want to know how I was lodged, for I think I would need to be able to sleep alone for a period of one or two years... I would like to know under whom I worked and at what and where and so on.

I would plan to keep some sort of log, and then, if I could, to write about the experience-experiment... if it was good enough. I might even be able to do some of this while it was happening... but only in a positive way... and never for publicity as such, for the school.

A reply to your letter soon, dear Aunt Grace. Please do not worry about this, if it seems the wrong moment for you to think of it. You are older than I, and I feel that you know that I am the last thing in the world from a Do-Gooder, but I feel that there is some use for my experience as a daughter-mother-writer-wife-human.

....

St. Helena, California   *24.i.64*
To: Grace Holmes

Dearest Aunt Grace... what a help you are to me! I wanted very much to get a letter from you today, and I did. Thank you.

My thoughts are increasingly filled with what I can-must-shall-will-should do next in life, and I have discussed them only with you and once briefly with Norah during the Christmas Caper.

She was very much in favor of my going to Piney Woods or doing something *like* that. She knows of my perhaps exaggerated sense of moral responsibility, and so on, and she is also very candid (as I am too) about the fact that I have almost finished the active mother-role and that I am destined to go to waste unless I make some strong move.

Norah is also inclined to idealize ideals, if you know what I mean and you do. She is very easily swayed by the Intellectual Missionaries as I call them privately... the professors who flit between Zen Buddhism and Quakerism, thousands strong, on the Berkeley faculty. She is, in many ways, a real snob about such things, because she has a hunger to feel "liberal... free... unconforming," etc. She also has a strong need for martyrdom of the most complex kinds, and could through me throw herself on the altar of civil liberty or or or.

I don't feel at all malicious in telling you about this... but I must recognize some of the reasons for her very heartwarming enthusiasm when I told her a little of my plans.

(I feel actively rude about talking of myself, instead of answering your really fine letter about the strange meeting with your sister, which is also much on my mind. I'll do it soon... and meanwhile I do hope that I have not plunged you into any kind of distress with this open appeal for your advice....)

I go through your letter of today, very fast, and save the other for later: Thank you for what you said about the *NYer* story. I must take it all with a grain of salt, no matter how much I would like to believe it, for I myself take a pretty dim view of it and have not even opened the magazine. I went through very demanding and often foolish or even presumptuous finaglings, once the story was accepted through my agent... last minute revisions, last *Last* minute consultations with lawyers about things like Libel and Invasion of Privacy, last last LAST minute style-changes demanded by Shawn Himself, who had apparently not bothered to look at the stuff until it was on the presses. I found all this boring. And now the story is out and I am getting the most amazing fan mail... I suppose I should send it to Rachel MacKenzie, who was my editor and who must surely be one of the most intelligent and pleasant and skilled people I have ever had to work with. I liked her best when she sighed (from NY to St. Helena, at their expense thank God), and said very gently, "Well, the *NYer* style does indeed use commas and hyphens in a way quite different from mine when I was an English professor at Radcliffe" (or wherever it was she taught)! I felt that she was giving me a little pat of sympathy and encouragement.

But the fact remains that I do not want to write again for her/them. This sounds very toplofty for me to say. I know it is the best thing of its kind. I also know it pays lovely fat fees which I need actively. But I think I should stick to an occasional book, where the publisher wants to print me because I am *me*, not a projection of himself. There is one more story at the *NYer*, and when the rewrite-act begins I'll simply return the check and withdraw... plead ill health or temporary insanity or something.

Oh... the thing published was an excerpt, highly Bowdlerized, from the book *Map of Another Town* which Little, Brown will publish early in April. I'll send you a copy, natch.

On to Mississippi, which may need me almost as much as I need it! ! ! ! I am glad you think that nothing gets in the way of my being human, for I agree. As for accepting and being accepted, I honestly think that would soon take care of itself, easily and thoroughly... there would be suspicion of my motives at first, which is very understandable... so many white people want to "help," but are conditioned too far back to be anything but self-conscious about it, and I seem to be born without a racial conscience or whatever it is....

Yes, I think there is some demand for languages... the school is now training a lot of students through "Normal School," which I understand in Miss. means teachers' training for the equivalent of the first two years of accredited college.

There are also an increasing number of students from South America and Africa... the latter often speaking nothing but French on arrival. I can use even pigeon-French, and with a quick refresher would be right back in Spanish.

The main thing Dr. Jones is doing now is prepare all possible material for what you so well call that gravitation to a higher intellectual life. He is also training the majority of the students, I think, to be able to earn respectable livings... RESPECTED livings I should say... as farmers, printers, cooks, shoemakers, etc etc. I would most probably not have much contact with these young ones, but would, if I proved adequate, nurse the keener seekers.

At least, this is the way I *see* it.

But I should go there to Miss. and talk with the faculty... present myself. I don't know how to arrange this but am thinking on it.

Plainly I cannot and won't completely shut off my roots anywhere, for I have books and pictures that are in my trust. The thing is to find some decent repository... depository.... No, I would not go to another small town than St. H. I have good friends here, and do not want to use up my vitality in re-establishing some human contacts just to be able to rent a little house(!). And I am not at all satisfied by making myself part of a community, even here in St. H. It is not enough for me... too cozy, too comfortable. It uses only what I wish to give it... no real demands, except upon my own gracious GIVING, which I loathe. No actual human demands...

You ask where else I could find a stimulating spot. No place, I am afraid. I am pretty sure by now that I shan't return to Aix... I hate the idea of being one more slab-sided empty witch-like ex-patriot... the woods are full of them: old English ladies striding about in flapping tweeds. It was a different thing when I had to be alive and protective and and and for two young girls....... I could easily go back there, and before I knew it I would be giving little tea parties and sharing season tickets to the Opera and "helping" a few young foreign students. Nope.

I have long had a rather dim dream of living by myself in a village in Greece, where a dear old shepherdess would bring me a bowl of food once a day and shake out the sheets on my cot... that sort of thing. But I think it is too completely self-centered. And bleak.

About men: that seldom bothers me. I have some good friends here, who are well married to interesting women who are also my true friends, and by now they accept me as an openly affectionate but eminently SAFE woman whom they enjoy. . . . I enjoy men very much, and miss living more intimately with them as such. But I find real enjoyment in what contacts I have with them: I like to talk to the postman and the filling-station boy and waiters and so on. I carry on a lively correspondence with a few males....... In other words, that is no problem, and I know by now that I am past the possibility of marrying again and/or of being a "companion for the golden years" of some nice person who really needs a housekeeper and nurse. I did that for Rex. That was *it*, for me.

(Or so I do firmly believe. Of course I cannot resist real neurotics, and one might be able to talk me into it. But I doubt it!)

About the health angle: I would want to have a room of my own, no matter how small, for I plan to go on with my own work. I assume there are toilet facilities available, for the buildings are mostly new ones. As for heat, I am used to coping with European additions of socks-sweaters-underwear, etc. Diet does not bother me at all... I know what I most need, and can always adapt myself to what is there. I would of course check thoroughly with the doctors about my health, but I think it is pretty solid. I don't think I should be in a jungle climate. I really feel best when I am in a cold thin air like Nevada's which is certainly not the case in Mississippi! ! ! ! The one case I know of the collagen whatever-it-was that nearly finished me two years ago survived as I did, and died about ten years later from a damaged heart, very easily. My own guess is that I will live somewhat longer, and finally be caught by arthritis (rheumatoid). All this is highly problematical, of course, but the fact remains that I feel sturdy and strong, in my own rather cautious pattern.

... And here lengthy interruptions have pretty well dried up this verbose self-exposure, mercifully for you. I feel rather uncomfortable about *using* you so obviously....

I would of course discuss with the people, wherever I went, the chances of my writing a kind of log, at least, of my experience with them. Depending on their reactions I could very probably get some sort of financial advance from a publisher. If not, I would simply go about it privately. I'd make it clear that I *was* writing, of course... that would probably be the best, so that I would be free from any commitments.

About Mary: yes, she graduates on June 4. She will be 18 on March 12. If she had stayed at St. Helena High she would have graduated last June... and she would have had to take at least another year of remedial work... she went into a dreadful slump here, and her being forced to go away because of my illness was one very great reward for it.

She does indeed need a lot of love, but she has that... and as for the "mothering," the shoe is on the other foot and she is inclined to baby me. I think it makes her feel more mature...? She plans to go to school on the East Coast for at least the first two years of college, and more if we can afford it. She loves this house, but I think it will not matter to her where I am, as long as I am well and at work.

She would also be highly amused and excited if I could do something like teach at Piney Woods.

As for Anne, she has landed what looks like a really good job, and will never return to St. Helena willingly, especially if I am not here... she professes, I think as honestly as she can, to despise everything about it and everybody in it except this house and me!!! (This is no sudden anger, but long-standing. I regret it, but do not let it bother me.)

She is being trained to be a receptionist-translator by TWA... a perfect job for her because she must constantly be "on stage"... and she is really wonderful at it because of that and because it is such an out-going job... I hate that word... but she is highly introvert unless she is forced into something where she must *perform*. I think this will be a lifesaver to her. And she will make a nice fat salary, and also get delicious little bonuses like dead-heading it to Calcutta or or or...

In other words, both girls have really left here, as of about mid-June. Mary plans to go to East Hampton as backstage apprentice if the John Drew runs at all... same job Anneli had last summer... it is a breezy interesting vacation for her, in country she loves, near Anne and the Friedes, before she starts a good twelve years of hard study.

And now, dear patient Aunt Grace, a quick look at the letter you wrote. . . .

Oh yes, the play was hard work and an interesting experience. I shan't let myself get into anything more like it, however. It went off well, to a large audience. My costumes were, I am told, quite good. I liked being able to draw and color again, and want to limber up my hands, this coming Spring.

I sent off the "stout but elegant stick" to you. I know you will have to cut YARDS off it, but it is very trustworthy. I am very happy, if you can use it at all. . . .

Red caps with wheel chairs are wonderful... so kind. I know them well, thanks to travelling a lot with Dillwyn and then with Rex... I even used one myself, once. . . .

I love the way the Democrat stigma melted off.... "Some of our best friends... etc"? . . .

I must stop this and release you from my wordiness... be less introspective, and pay a few bills!

I shan't re-read it or it will never get to you, and I do very much want to know whatever you have to say....

Oh... of course I have considered things like the Peace Corps... but I would really be wasted in an office job, which is what I would get, given my age etc. And I have not AT ALL the right missionary spirit... I mean, to try to "convert" people to anything. And I do not want to be available for various lectureships and so on, which is easy enough... by the time these far-out American kids are into college and universities they are far past anything I might possibly pass along to them (except of course for the occasional genius who might hear me...).

On that note... I have agreed to do one more small job, in mid-May, with the faculty of the School of Medicine at Berkeley (Univ. of Calif.). It scares me silly, but I am taking it in cold blood, partly for the money and mostly for some possible weight it may give my future... I am to moderate a panel at a big annual seminar on The Transformations of Appetite, whatever that may mean. Murder. Pray for me. But that might impress somebody, some time when I needed it.

All love, and my thanks, from the heart.

....

Piney Woods, Mississippi   *15.vii.64*
To: James Beard Family

Dearest Beards, One, Two, et Al:

By this stage of my trying to tell you and a very few other people something about why I am glad I am here and no place else in this world, I feel very uncomfortable about being repetitive. Countless times in every day I think that This, or else THAT, is exactly what Elsine would like to know, or Noni, or Yolande[1]... and then it is something else... really an impossible situation. (My rather unwilling plan to write a joint-carbon-thing soon evaporated... obviously!)

I have probably written the most (and also the most repetitively, no doubt) to MV.[2]

1. Elsine Ten Broeck; Yolande Beard
2. Marietta Voorhees

I have also asked her to pass along any tidbits that might possibly interest you, if the moment seemed right and so on. But One nevah know, do one, as Fats Waller and I both say much too often....

Elsine speaks of a one-week seminar on mythology. Where? When? It sounds really interesting... at least to me, for I have been hooked ever since I wallowed through the *Golden Bough,* in 1929–30 et seq. I think the most entertaining book I have read in the past few years is the one by Joseph Woods Krutch called something about "strange beasts"... it is either on the chest in the livingroom at 1467 or it was in the one carton I seem to have lost in transit, the one with my special treasures of course, like my companion of 41 years, the pocket *Oxford.* Damn and blast. But it serves me right for being too "casual" about the US Postal system.

Since ETB wrote to me about that course... or rather, mentioned it in passing... I have thought especially of you, because I have been working with a special English class on FABLES... from Aesop to Thurber. It has been fun... and thanks to living so intimately with wolves in sheep's clothing, and unicorns, and suchlike, I seem more than usually aware of the local beasts and bugs. Now and then, as two days ago when I met an amazing grasshopper on a path, I half-wait for them to speak, like a character from La Fontaine.... (This is also the result of my being fairly isolated, verbally, except in class and at table, and at the first I am definitely the Schoolmarm and at the last I am primarily the Listener. Result: my mind goes on at a wild rate, in fantasies, surmises, and half-flashes of intelligence.)

That grasshopper was the only one I have ever seen like him... plainly a solid respectable prosperous *man,* to all outward appearances... about four inches long, and looking heavy in weight and importance. He was made of deep dull black, like Victorian jet beads, and was so big that I could see the firm articulation of his heavy legs. Toward the end of his body there was a dusting of dark brilliant green-gold, and his short wide wings, held loosely against his body, were of a burning orange-red, like a zinnia. I squatted down and looked respectfully at him, and it was then that I had the fleeting but firm feeling that he might speak to me, the way the animals had in class, when we were reading. Dote, I said firmly, we are all eccentrics here, or else we'd be somewhere else, but let's keep out of the animal kingdom at least! So I stood up and walked off, but told myself to report this encounter to you....

I have seen very few other insects. Now and then there are a few ants crossing the paths, or a stupid little sow-bug. I have seen a few of the pin-thin dragonflies, and one beautiful one about two inches long with gauze wings with one bold smear of silver dust across them, carelessly put on. I am told that there are chiggers in the grass and underbrush, but so far I have not been bitten (and I hope to stay that way...). I got a few mosquito bites the night of the fireworks, July 4, but that was part of the fun, and I was pleased that they only lasted a couple of hours.

And of course there are fireflies, often, in the jungle which is only a few feet from this clearing along the ridge of gentle hills where the school is... it is said to be the highest spot in the Delta, or perhaps in the state, and I would put it at about 50 feet!

Work goes on all the time, in every season, to hold back the almost frightening way this green entity tries to cover us, and I can understand how it, like the creatures in my-thology, becomes an actual *being* in the spirits of the people who must fight it. Perhaps the most untrammeled in it, at least here, is the Kudzu vine, which I think was brought in from Japan to hold down the red clay banks along the countless rivers and ponds in this kind of country. It has become as viciously happy here as the rabbits did in Austra-lia, or the water-hyacinths in the Florida waterway, and I am already used to watching, out of one corner of my somewhat horrified camera-eye, a single strong large tendril of it grow between 15 and 20 feet in a week, up the slope from the jungle and straight for a house or a telephone pole, eager to ENGULF, SEIZE... and eventually to de-stroy, for the weight of these fantastically strong vines can crumple stone walls and whole houses, and topple heavy concrete poles.

Well... in this literally impenetrable mass of violent shaggy swamp-growth, with the Kudzu looped from the top of one giant tree to another like some kind of cobweb in a science-fiction thriller, there is a complete undisturbed world of animals, and of course insects like the fireflies (They are called glowworms here, mistakenly, for they dance in the air and do not simply flash from the bushes the way they do in Provence, this time of year...). I myself have only seen a couple of turtles, the larger about ten inches long I suppose. Anything that comes up here has simply made a mistake... it is too bright and hot for jungle people, and the two-legged ones are unfriendly, as when a really enormous moccasin was killed, the day before I arrived, on the steps of the lit-tle house I am now in (while its owner is on vacation... I feed her cat and water her plants). There are also armadillos (This sounds very romantic to me, to be living side by side with such a strange beast), and raccoons, and several more kinds of poisonous snakes like rattlers and cotton-mouths. I have seen three different kinds of toad, one a dark green and wearing a kind of armor-plating. I tried to touch his head with a grass stalk, and it was so long since I'd done anything like it that I forgot he could not jump any way but straight forward and he almost went into my face in his fright, and I al-most fell back down a fifty-foot flight of steps. Let Well Enough Alone: Aesop.

Oh, birds. I am not a b-watcher... or even a b-lover, as I think you know. I take it for granted that birds should be in trees and other places where they "belong," and I will fight to the finish to let them stay there in good health, BUT. So here I have not actually LOOKED at one damn bird. But I have enjoyed, and very much, hearing a nightin-gale twice, in the night of course, and several times in daylight a bird saying just about exactly as well as I can pronounce it myself, Bob White. Then there are a lot of other bird-sounds... ugly ones from the jays, of course, or perhaps it is mockingbirds? And at night there is the pulsating singing of the frogs in the swamps all around, and an oc-casional wail or haunting cry, surely feline, that makes me wonder if my tough yellow Tom, Scampie, will turn up for his milk the next morning. Why could there not be wilder cats nearby... pumas, or leopards, or tigers? I must ask.... I know we had a lion now and then near Hemet, up from Mexico by mistake....

Now I have to tell you something about the Liberry here... at the risk of making you

slightly sick... with ENVY, that is! First, it is housed in a modern, professionally designed two-story building (three at the back counting the stacks on a big balcony on
the main floor), air-conditioned, beautifully lighted, etc etc etc. I don't know how
many books there are... an amazing number... the librarian is on vacation until September 6. The main room, with catalogs and reference books on one side, and the
wall-space of the other three sides covered by a fascinating collection of photographs
made by Carl Sandburg of Negro writers, artists, singers, dancers, teachers, inventors,
etc etc, is used as a study hall six hours a day (morning, afternoon, evening), and I
would give something quite valuable to me (? ? ? ?... a *lot*, anyway!), to have the St.
H. H.S. students see what that dirty word STUDY HALL means to people who have
fought like stubborn and even desperate dogs-slaves-mules-lions to get into such a
place... and who will go through endless work to *stay* there. I could easily grow almost
hysterical about this, as you know too well! These students, slowly and surely fighting
their way toward being educated decent citizens, almost always from homes where
their parents were not allowed to aspire toward education, even decency, and certainly not citizenship, are required by the rules of the school to work for their full tuition, board, and room. They are not allowed to "graduate" until they have finished
the first 2 years of college: Dr. Jones believes that high school graduates are not yet
qualified to call themselves "educated," nor to cope with marriage, responsible jobs,
and so on. (I agree.) Not all students finish Junior College here, of course... but about
80+% do... and almost 20% go on for MAs and Ph.Ds. (My figures are wrong here:
about 80+% of the students who finish JC here get their BAs... and I forget the percentage of students who finish high school here who also finish JC, but it is very high...
I'll check.) But it is amazingly higher than the U.S. average, in every way... another
proof of course, if one is needed, that people who want something badly enough will
get it!

... later... I am really developing some strange new muscles, climbing down that
soap-box all the time! ! ! !

More on Liberry subject: TEXT BOOKS. I wish you could see these. (Many of the
books in the Library itself are shabby, of course... they are from countless private
shelves, and so on....) I have seen the stacks of the regular academic supplies, some of
the books in steady use for 12 to 15 years, and they are as clean as freshly polished silver,
TRULY... no defacement, no dirty words and moustaches on Queen Elizabeth and
torn-out pages and and and. They don't even look as if they had been DROPPED.

(I don't dare read back in this screed, but I think I forgot to go on about Study Hall,
at least far enough to say that it is exactly that... not a sound is heard, quite something
with up to 150 students... no whispering... people tiptoe... everybody knows how to
use the catalogs and the stacks are open, with permissions required for the second
floor (balcony) for back copies of magazines etc. I have a key to the building, and go
there often... the stacks are fun, and so, in small doses, is the air-conditioning.)

(I can hop up on the soap box again on THAT subject, but shall save it.... In
general I feel just as I always have, about it: if I can choose my own tempo, I would

rather remain at the same temperature as the outside world. But if this tiny cosmos is anything like the rest of Dixie, I would say there are plenty of millionaire air-conditioners around....)

I can always talk about the weather.... This is the first time I have spent more than, say, 8 days in really tropical country. Once we got stuck, on that death-ship coming back from Provence with the Barrs and Monique, in the port serving the town of Caracas, which is about 2 miles straight up from the water. We were there 8 days, I think... or maybe it was 80, or 8 weeks, or or. That was pretty bad. No air stirring. At night we would sit in the dark, on deck, as nearly naked as we dared, and try not to listen to the occasional sound of something unthinkable slipping into the stinking dockside water, and to the coughing from the shacks along the land-side of the one street, where everyone not dying from syphilis seemed to be dying from tuberculosis. Yes, that was bad. And I don't even remember the days. I think we may simply have slept, in our cabins. The one Monique and Anne and I had was luxurious, marked FOR SIX GUN-NERS: we were in a condemned Liberty ship traded to the Italian govt before we started playing footsie with Yugoslavia....

Well, here I do not mind the heat at all, but I suspect that if I did not know I was here for good or bad, I would find myself dreaming of other more desirable ways to carry my body around from one day to the next. (This is really a masterly bit of understatement, I think... and I speak now as an English teacher.)

Yesterday morning, when I piled out at 5, which I do daily except for Sundays when I can sleep until 6:30 if I want to which so far I have not, the little radio in this house where I am cat-sitting announced that it was 69 (with humidity 80). This was the lowest temperature since I arrived on the 22nd or whenever it was. The highest has only been 99... but that day the humidity was 88. In other words, we steam.

I don't mind it, if I can maintain the steady speed of a turtle and NO MORE. I even get out of chairs that way, on the really mean days here... and pick up a pencil from the floor in slow motion....

I think air conditioning is the worst thing in the world here, at least the way we have to go from one to another for classes, meals, our apartments. It means a constant shifting of temperature, and that makes more work for the poor old built-in thermostats we were born with, and in general I say to hell with it. (But I do like it now and then....)

This house is fantastic. It is one of those great big posh "mobile homes" you see being transferred from one race track to another, or one ski-resort to one desert resort... all made of plate glass and aluminum, lined with beautiful wood panelling, with fine Oriental rugs, etc etc etc, and of course AIR CONDITIONING. I swore I would not ever turn the monster on; there is such a rigmarole to go through and everything has to be tightly closed and so on. But I came here from a long class, across the hot campus, and weakened far enough to get all buttoned down and squared away and so on and POW, WHAMMIE, WHOOSH and other Mickey Mousies, a completely unsuspected-by-me thunder storm; wind, lightning, noise, a downpour which would have cooled the air... and here I am, tightly enclosed, with the damn machine whirring and thumping along and all heaven loose outside! Hoist on my own petard or something. Mechanization takes command. But only temporarily. As soon as I finish this I must go to another class. First I have to dash, if possible in a lull in the rain, which now has drops as big as walnuts falling straight down, about 200 feet to the basement apartment where most of my stuff is, to get my umbrella! ! ! !

I don't like this split-living, but could not back out of taking care of the cat and the plants... and to my surprise I am having to be very stern about getting my homework done BEFORE I turn on the excellent TV, for I am hooked on the Republican Caper. It is an extraordinary performance... the first one I have ever watched. I can't help believing, wishfully of course, that my die-hard father would have balked at supporting Goldwater. There again, I'll never know.

There's a lull. I'd better grab it. Please ask me questions, if you have time. I am still working on one you sent me about five years ago: Why do you love L'Harmas. It has, almost literally, turned into a book, which you may see in about a year.[3] (Adv.) Meanwhile, I am a bit quicker, usually... and it will give me an idea of what I have NOT said, so that I won't be repeating myself too boringly.

Please write some juicy gossip, if any... and believe EVERYTHING YOU HEAR about unicorns and other mythical beasts! ! ! ! !

Much love to you all.

....

Piney Woods, Mississippi   *27.vii.64*
To: Norah Kennedy Barr

Dearest None... thanks so much for your letter from Cambria. I suppose that by now you are getting ready to go back to B.[1] I am really surprised (This sounds almost caddish of me! ! !) that you actually plan to send me the Summer's Work of the hanging! ! ! ! I can hardly wait. I think it will probably add some real humanity to what I remember as a grimly ugly hole of a room when I think of the mustard-and-grey colors. I feel sure it can't be that bad, and think what really scares me is adapting myself to a reportedly VERY eccentric old lady... things like sharing a washbowl and toilet at 5:15 in the morning.[2] We'll see!

Yes, all does go well, and no, I am not uncomfortable at *all*, and yes, I sure as hell like what I am doing.

There is a lot I do not like of course. I am at the stage where I know many things are going to be truly depressing to me unless I manage always to remember the good things that are actually much more than their equals. (Awkwardly put, but you know....) Most of the things I do not like are the result of the very reason these people are HERE to begin with. And the reason I am here is to combat them. Ergo.......

3. *Map of Another Town;* L'Harmas is the house MF rented on her second trip to Aix.
1. Berkeley, California
2. From the trailer MF had to herself she was going to have to move back to the teachers' regular quarters.

My only real discomfort is that the honeymoon is over between me and what I assume is chiggers, and I am gradually accumulating bites... about nine as of today. I have not yet seen what is biting me, though! And it is partly because I have been careless: I forget to put on some of the insect repellent, which I used religiously at first and which now I am being careful about (First thing in the morning, up my legs as far as it will go...), and also I am lazy enough to take "one more chance" and shortcut between this trailer and my apartment, some fifty feet by way of the grass and 250 by paths. Ergo, again! ! ! ! ! Or, as we peasants say, *Eh bien!*

But I do indeed like what I am doing, Noni. I know that I cannot and will not become a teacher, the kind who teaches every year, I mean. And yet I cannot imagine stopping this, for a while longer. Surely I will return here, God willing... perhaps next year if I am wanted, or perhaps I might try for some work at Tuskegee or Fisk for one year, just to get a different level... although I now feel very strongly that it is more essential to help the people who have got this far, into the first two years of college, than it is to continue with the ones who have already made that grade. And then as I get older, perhaps I will do straight lectureships, like the suggested one at Davis. But really I cannot imagine working with any but these desperately *eager earnest starved serious students....*

I like your finding a few moments of Provence in those back-hills. I have spotted them from the air, with recognition! That is the kind of country for me... or faute de Provence, Nevada. This too-bright too-juicy jungle repels me... except now and then in moonlight, when it turns hard and silvery.

Your report of hearing from the two girls amuses me. Anne has been digging at me for several years now to suggest that you and David let her "use" the lute, and I have been pretty nasty-firm about saying NO, for she has lost or broken every single thing she has ever taken to NY up to now, and I felt unwilling to involve her further (for I know that she does wallow in guilt, now and then...). Anneli will be at Bridgehampton when I arrive, on her 21st birthday! ! ! ! I suppose DF will be loaded with the usual pound of fresh caviar... and Dom Perignon will flow. That's quite all right with me....

I look forward to eating and drinking exactly what comes along... and SLEEPING as long as I want to.... I really do not get quite enough sleep, because I can't seem to get even decently clean and in order and into bed before 10–11, and then I must get up a little before 5. But I never felt better in my life... have lost about 15 pounds, and plan to shave off a few more before I go East, so that I can gain them back, if you know what I mean! ! ! ! (Hi, Matt! ! ![3] How did you lose weight? Swimming? Me, I simply stopped drinking that nasty delicious old vermouth, and stopped eating what I wanted when I wanted it and instead started eating the minimum of what I didn't want when I *didn't* want it... as for breakfast which I still LOATHE but which I now eat without even remembering that I have done so! ! !). . . .

I can't imagine driving from Cambria to San Diego just to see the zoo, even though that is my favorite one in the world. Once it probably saved my reason... after the fire at Bareacres... DF and I went down there like thirsty cattle to a watering hole....

3. Norah's youngest son

Now you have asked me some questions! I'll see how far I can get in the 15 minutes left before noon dinner (ugh). . . .

I have had a class of about 30, mostly Sophomores but a few Freshmen... only six boys (The ratio in college is about 3 girls to one boy... more boys drop out to marry or go back to farm with their fathers, or support a widowed mother...). I have snooped wthhout shame by getting them to write little papers telling me much more than they suspect about why they are here, what they plan to do next, what kind of music they like, what kinds of autobiographies, and so on. My course has been straight out of my head, and I have worked like a dog at it, and have learned more than I could possibly tell you, about *teaching* and of course myself and and and.... I am very glad that I was tossed into things so brutally: by now I feel quite sturdy on my pins, and I know I can handle ANYTHING... INCLUDING MY Relations WITH Dr. (Sorry about caps after the ...s) Chandler! She is head of the Academic part of the school, and is A CHARACTER. (I mean those caps....) I'll talk more of her, no doubt. I find her a very poignant case, truthfully, and she interests me and although I am not at all scared of her, I am scared of her power. So is she... and dangerously jealous of it, I sense. That is true of one or two others on campus. I recognize them, and heed my wariness.

I can't tell you how thankful I am that I came early. Really, I wonder if I could have managed without danger of depression or over-fatigue, if I had plunged into regular work with a big faculty, ignorant as I was.... This way I have not had to cope with a lot of other teachers (At this point there are only three white teachers and about 2 Negro on the campus... there will be about 30 when school opens...).

Well, my college students are pretty well weeded out by the time they are Freshmen, and all of them plan to go on for BAs and then specialization... several teachers of course, one minister, one girl who wants to be an executive secretary with IBM machines, several medical secretaries and nurses, two doctors, three psychiatric social workers, one Army career man, etc etc. There are outstanding students. There are also several who would be, if they were still not fighting the most shockingly bad speech habits. They are fighting them constantly, but it is heartbreaking to see (hear) them revert, the minute they go through the class-room door. That is the GREAT problem, of course....

Well, I have given a really wild course, pulling every trick to make these kids relax and listen and enjoy... and I think it is working. I don't feel at all cocky about it, but I do feel satisfied, and hungry for more.

This fall I will work directly under Dr. C., probably doing a lot of her dirty work but also getting a lot of the cream too, for I am not trained to do the SRA system[4] which is followed here, and will get a lot of "creative writing" and themes and Chapel Speeches and so on. It will be fun. I have made the students work very hard, but I can see that I am "popular," and my class, which is an elective WITHOUT CREDIT has steadily grown, from about 14 to 29, with only two drop-outs, one because of illness. The best

4. A special reading program

part is that Dr. C. learned through the grapevine that some hard work was going on and is now giving 2 hours of college credit for it, which pleases me.

Then I have two groups of the Spanish speaking girls. They are interesting and amusing, and do not demand as much work, but I still prefer the college work. I make them talk and read and pronounce tongue-twisters and so on. They are here in a rather odd tangle of international wires, and are basically resented by the other students... they are better educated, they seem to be "privileged" because of the language difficulties, some of them are not even faintly Negro, and so on. I'll write more about them, too.... I shan't have these classes this winter, probably, but I would like to meet once or twice a week for conversation: the girls stay closely together and speak Spanish, and have a bad time in classes, and I think I can MAKE them follow the English... I know they have improved very fast, this summer, and I am told that their relations with the Negro girls are much better since I started working with them. (My Spanish is, too! ! !)

I am going to tutor a couple of Negroes in Spanish this fall, and get some of the brighter Mexican girls to help me. I am also going to tutor Saturnin, the boy from Dr. Schweitzer's village... he is fantastically bright, and speaks very good American, much better than most of the students, but he does not *think*... he depends upon volubility and charm. This will interest me, because he is a fascinating and rather frightening character, and he speaks very good French (obviously had upper-class teachers in the school in which he has been since he was five...). He is something of a problem... is here on Passport 18 (!) from French Gabon, as a government ward, and is being financed by a wealthy doctor in St. Louis who read about him in *Stars and Stripes*... too involved to go into, but the reporter who wrote the story, Marty Gershin, was here a couple of weeks ago to see about Saturnin... had the Dr. been right to uproot him from his tribe, was he advancing correctly at Piney Woods, etc etc. My own opinion is that Saturnin has grown past anything more he can get here, and that he should be put into a really good trade school where he can continue his formal education and at the same time develop his really amazing talent for technical design. For instance, the planeload of medicines sent by American soldiers stationed in Germany to Dr. Schweitzer (triggered by an idea of Marty Gerhin's, who was then in the plane etc etc) circled a few times over the hospital and then went off to a landingstrip big enough to hold it, some eight hours away by bus and carriers. When the medicines came into the S. compound Saturnin, then about 12, gave Gershin a perfect charcoal drawing of the plane! This was astounding, because it was the first plane he had ever seen in his life... and it was also a new model and all his details were exact. Gershin did not believe his eyes, and asked that Saturnin bring him another drawing, but instead, in a few more hours, the little boy came back with a model of the plane which he had whittled, TO SCALE. That started the whole thing, of course... and now here is this boy, completely isolated, absolutely unaware of anything but this school. He itches to be out in the world. He is homesick still, but is not ready to return to Africa until he can go as a man. He is very musical, and in a few minutes learned to play, not just strum, a guitar... he had never seen one before. He will draw anything, from a spray of roses to a building, without any flaws of proportion or perspective. Well... you can see what a handful he is, here in this dead-calm in the storm. I wonder what next? ? ? ? ? And meanwhile I am to talk with him in French, and try to get him to THINK! Hah.

As you see. I do go on....

I can't tell you much about the faculty. The white teachers are all elderly, perforce, and eccentric (or they wouldn't be here). There are some who are what I think of as "routine": they teach SRA and the Cleveland Math Program and they correct all the books and cards and they are good women but they are basically dull for me... they love to meet and look at TV and eat "dainty collations" and once a month "treat" the girls to dinner in Mendenhall at The Revolving Table, where you get all the chicken you can eat from a big Lazy Susan and My but it's just de-LISH-us. I am staying in the "mobile home" of one of them. They are good kind women, or they wouldn't be here, and they bore me. I have already met two, fleetingly, before they left, who interest me more: the very ancient librarian, a real "lady" from South Carolina, who perhaps weighs 75 pounds and who was one of the rare-book liberians at the University of California for 1000 years... She is as gentle and remote as an old turtle, and I look forward to her return. . . . Then there is a vigorous woman who teaches chemistry I think... something to do with soil preservation and animal feeding... and also Senior high school English... I like her. She is rather remote too. And of course there will be my new apartment-mate, who, I am gleefully informed from many sources, will HIT THE CEILING to find that she must share her dressing room and bath with anyone (me). We'll see. Oh... right now there is a pudgy elderly fairy, ex-college professor, who comes for three or four months at a time, when he feels like it... he says candidly that he loves working with these beautiful beautiful boys... and he apparently is very good at remedial work. He is not very attractive, but is nice about running errands and so on. We share the icebox while Beatha Baumgarten is in Yurrup, and have gay little chats about whose half of cantaloupe is whose. He is very gossipy, so I turn him off pretty bluntly now and then. He is what Marietta would call an acute case of Logorrhea... can't stop talking....

There are usually about 480 in the school. Dr. Jones used to be proud that nobody was ever turned away, but I hear that now they are having to give quite stiff tests of various kinds, to weed the applicants. It seems too bad, to make an understatement.

No, there is only the school here. The nearest town is Mendenhall, the county seat, ten miles south. I think I wrote to you about it. Fantastic. Just before it there is a crossroads with a grocery store and filling station, pop. 84, called D'LO. Seriously. It is on the maps. It is pronounced Deelou. Then Jackson is about 18 miles to the North. It is where I do not want to go, except for entrances and exits... although I have tempered my first feeling about it. Now I just detest the sound of the name, but I don't have a hot flash....

Here we have a Post Office... a pathetic little store which I like, run by one of the

M.F.K. Fisher: A Life in Letters

first graduates, Miss Myers, who went out as a teacher and started two new schools in the swamp country and then retired here to teach and now bosses the store. That is part of Dr. Jones's technique... when the teachers get too old, he invents all kinds of little jobs for them. For instance, the Chef now, new here, is a man whose family deserted him when he became too crippled and diabetic to support them... Dr. Jones found him a derelict, last year, and put him in a hospital and then brought him here to oversee the kitchens... the poor man was killing himself, so now he sits at a little table at the door of the dininghall, wearing a chef's bonnet, sleeping and occasionally nodding formally when he recognizes someone. He is USELESS, of course, but he has a job made especially for him. He is a gaunt world-weary man, rather like Jelly Roll Morton... beyond evil.

Oh... then we have things like a dairy (Most of the milk is sold outside, but we get good butter and occasionally wonderful buttermilk), and a farm, and a quarry, and a printshop, and and and.

Oh... (I keep looking over your letter), the Negro and White faculty do not see much of each other except during the day, in classes and at meals and "around"... the colored people are mostly younger, married, with families of children and grandchildren, and they have their own homes. Several of the youngest are graduates of the school. I'll tell you more about them.

Now I must go to a class of five of my little pachucas... two are from Colombia, cousins, darling bright amusing girls... two from Mexico are very bright, and one is almost idiotic but very sweet and BEAUTIFUL to look at... etc etc....

All love, Noni,... and do please tell me if you can handle that Operation Bedspread... if not perhaps I can get June Eddy onto it!!!!!!!!?????

....

Piney Woods, Mississippi   *25.x.64*
To: Charles Newton[1]

Somebody in Jackson did admit to the existence of the school, and I got your letter a day or so after I mailed a note to you. ESP rides again, or something....

I would like to cheat and say that I did not get any word from you, so that you would write again. But I did.

You are indeed calling into a pretty dark room. We live on an island, but we know about the wind and the weather... those suspended sentences may well have been the last blow... I don't see how the people here can stand much more of it.[2] Succession is of course the easiest thing to propose. For a time during the first years of WW2 I used to work all night in my subconscious, getting the children away from Hitler. Now I am working on a great exodus from Mississippi. Why not? If Moses could do it without sanitation, locomotion, and so on, and with no sure knowledge of where he could

1. MF's cousin's husband
2. MF was referring to the racial unrest following the murders of civil rights workers Andrew Goodman, Michael Schwerner, and James Chaney.

PUT all those people, why can't we do it with all our "conveniences" and a sure knowledge of just how much space is available and where and so on? ? ? ? This state is a vile sore. Surgery is indicated, immediate and drastic, before the infection spreads ONE CELL FURTHER.

Well.

I do risk losing my few friends, by this trigger-action of mine: I sound off, as Rex would put it. . . .

Yes, I do know what you mean about "the country and the weather." I resent saying ANYTHING good about Mississippi, but let's face it, it is purely beautiful here now, with much changing of color, even along the edges of the damned juicy damned green jungles... and the air clean and full of taste, a good dry healthy clearcut taste. There are beautiful little winding natural dirt roads through the woods, which are a tangle with pines and maples and oaks rising above the undergrowth. I long to walk along them. I even dream of what fun it would have been, forty years ago, to be on horseback. BUT... not here. The other day I drove with one of the teachers down to the county seat, a frightening pretty little town straight from an amateur production of an unpublished Tennessee Williams playlet, and my friend suggested turning off the main road... and I longed to be free again, free in Switzerland, free in California. Here I was ENSLAVED, HUMILIATED, *defiled* really, by a strange horror of being there, of losing myself forever in the filth, not of the swamps, and not fear of being hurt bodily, but a physical sickness about the invisible world I am in here. (I should never have got onto my soapbox again... forgive me, and I swear I'll stay off it to the end of another page....)

So... yes, I know what you mean about the country and the weather.

I feel better, to have you say that the population is deserting all those fine white old wooden houses. Perhaps there will still be room for me, somewhere.... I know that I should work for a wage, but I also know that I cannot and will not ever travel home on the subway. Perhaps I could get one of those f.o.w.o.w. houses and rent a couple of rooms to people like me who don't like to cook... as much as I do, that is.... Keep it in mind. Seriously. Except that you will probably find someone who might like to marry you and do that. I hope you do.

(Just so you keep an eye turned in my direction, I mean.... Make this clear to anyone who may qualify.)

(Seriously) again. . . .

I am sorry. Ho hum. I am glad she is working hard. *To hell* with doctors who have the consummate nerve to be "very hopeful." Why need that be one of their occupational hazards, along with all the others?

Speaking of the boy who defected from Oberlin: John Barr, who is doing a three-month work period here from Antioch, is doing the same, next year, Able seaman. I think it's a fine idea. Life will make more sense(?) after a year at sea. Or so I have always believed. . . .

I approve of ANYONE's bucking the current tendency to keep men babies as long as possible... it is unique to the USA, as far as I can say. One good way to buck this system is to get the hell out of it for a year or two, and then return with a somewhat less nebulous idea of what will be needed for survival. . . .

Yes, if I ever get to Chicago it will be the Drake... room with view. Room with fawning room-service. *Room...*

Your hopes that I "take the time to see a silly movie or read a bad book or drink something deleterious" warm my heart and also make me feel slightly hysterical. I DO see a silly movie, or at least have the chance to, every other Saturday night, when the audio-visual dept. shows an ancient picture (all 16mm) with a cultural message (*Pride and Prejudice, The Barretts of Wimpole Street*), which the sadistic (really) head-of-dept runs out down as low as possible in sound so that he can hear if anyone whispers or titters. (No Enjoyment Allowed...) Last night I went because my old flirt Charles Laughton was being the hunchback of ND, but even Charlie couldn't hide the sound track, and I got out one step ahead of the decibel-boys-in-white-jackets. As for the bad books, I have some 30,000 volumes at my disposal here, and I keep getting more (mostly because of my new job with the *NYer*,[3] which is still only a happy dream as far as actual work goes...). But WHEN TO READ THEM? Hah. I had one free night this week, and I took a bath and got into bed with a truly voluptuous sense of being able to catch up with at least a couple of month-old magazines... maybe even start Nabokov's last thing... finish *Trapp* by Dürrenmatt which I started on the plane from Newark on Sept. 2. Hah again. By 8:12 I was so asleep that I did not even turn over until the bell rang at 5. And now about the deleterious something to drink... man, you're mad! For one thing, Mississippi is dry (with one of the highest alcoholism rates in the world). For another, I don't like white mule, which I'll bet I could get here from some of the surrounding peckerwoods... and wouldn't that be just great, to have them know that a God-damn-Northerner at the nigger-loving Piney Woods School was drinking? And actually, I do not think wistfully of even a glass of cold white wine, here. The thought of enjoying anything like that does not go with the taste and feel of things here. I eat exactly as I breathe, to subsist. But I have removed myself completely from physical enjoyment of such basic functions. That sounds pretty austere. Perhaps it is. But for me it is the only way to survive... which I am doing very well indeed: I have lost a lot of weight, I sleep evenly, my digestion remains unruffled. Now and then I permit myself a moment of deep rage, as a kind of catharsis of the soul. But even that I control. Otherwise I would, quite simply, die. People would think I had gone off my rocker, but it would be only an exaggerated case of what Sartre called "la nausée."

So... no deleterious things to drink. The idea does not even *interest* me. When I leave here, though... HAH. When I flew to Newark on August 15 I got onto the plane in a state of dangerous near-panic: I had to wait over two hours for the plane, I was surrounded by men and women and their frightening children speaking Mississippi dialects, several Civil Rights workers were flying out, the plane was stiff with heavily armed police, and I grew more and more convinced that I could never come back... that I would send for my books and dishes... that I was a coward through and through.

3. "Gastronomy Recalled," a series of essays based on cookbooks

Well, the plane when it finally arrived was hot, crowded, and quite filthy-dirty, smudged and be-slimed as only things in the Deep South can be. But the stewardess was the nicest one I have ever met in America, *really* nice, and the double-martini she brought me was without doubt the second or third best I have ever drunk. I sipped it with pure animal delight. It was worth waiting for… and by the time we got to Birmingham I was solid again and knew I could come back.

Then… I continue, perhaps with a slight nostalgia?… in Bridgehampton I drank almost exactly the way I wanted to, except for a couple of times when "company" was there and I drank too much too heavy red wine after too many Gibsons (I felt absolutely great, but had bad dreams). One morning I got up very early, made myself a small PITCHER of half-and-half (gin and vermouth without ice), went out on the dunes for a fast walk (WITH it, I mean), and then worked happily and boozily for about six hours… came upstairs once for a refill. Nobody cared. Nobody bothered me. That was the morning I turned down a beautiful fat commission from the *Post.* Then in the afternoon I slept like an innocent babe, until it was time to get up and make myself another pitcher of The Stuff and spend a long happy evening, complete with Truman Capote and champagne. So… all is well, you see.

Oh… about being physically fit… hard work and poverty and all that: yes, it's the best way to subsist. I don't know how long I can hold out HERE, but by now I do know that I must have a little more work than I can safely cope with, for the rest of my life. After Rex died I let myself become self-indulgent, too comfortable. Never again. . . .

I shouldn't start another page. The truth is that I have to plan a week's lectures avoiding the subject of William Cullen Bryant. I absolutely REFUSE to teach these poor twisted maltaught Negro kids "To a Waterfowl" or "Thanatopsis." But I remind myself of reading *Heidi* aloud to my helpless little girls and carefully bowdlerizing it of all the sanctimonious Christian Science prayers of Heidi's grandfather, and then later having them reproach me bitterly for having robbed them of all the fun. Perhaps I am wrong again? Well, I think I deserve a little *self-protection* then, which is what it is. But basically I am learning a lot, this year. I decided to make my class of practically retarded college freshman ENJOY *Othello,* and what fun it has been for doc Fisher! I did it without text, from a good recording… then I read a whole lot of critique, from Margaret Webster on up and down… and I would be fairly safe to say that out of a class of 36 people given up as hopeless by the other "advanced English" teacher here, at least half will think of Othello as a blood-brother (if not lover! ! ! !) for the rest of their lives. They "identified," man! And now I am doing the same with my high school juniors: they feel warmth and a kind of jolly affection for BEN FRANKLIN, of all smug old prigs (as taught by everybody but Old Anti-Dote).… We are now sniffing happily around Walden Pond, only slightly schmalzed for local taste with some props like magnolia stumps and the wake of a lazy 'gator. Why not? Thoreau wouldn't mind.……

End of letter. Twerk twerk.

I plan to go to St. H. as soon after May 24 as the law allows. But by then something may have come up… I honestly can't imagine WHAT, but I'm ready for it. And before Christmas I want to do one thing for the *NYer*… that job is too good to let slide away.

Genoa, Nevada *21.i.65*

To: Arnold Gingrich

Dear Arnold:

Thank you for sending me the card at Christmas. It told me that you most probably remembered writing to me in August and wondered if I had got the letter, and it also told me, more importantly for my spirit, either that your wife had emerged from the dreadful dilemma you spoke of in your letter, or that you had found another lovely woman to share your fantastic life with. I hope you will write again, now, and settle that for me. Certainly the picture of the two of you is as romantic as an old Russian engraving: she looks like a tiny princess caught in flight, and you look completely sinister and in control.

I wonder too about your settling (?) in New Jersey? Have you been there long? Do you still stay in a hotel or apartment in NY? Are you still at *Esquire?*

These questions are very naive....

What you say about reading *Map of Another Town* reminds me, pleasurably too, of the telegram you sent me to sign our contract with the little magazine.[1] It was something to remember, even if I did not believe a word of it! And I am very glad that you liked the book about Aix. I enjoyed writing it. I hope to write something else that will please you. You are a critic I value, and have been for a surprisingly long time.

No, I never did get a Christmas card from you, in Whittier. I wish they had been forwarded to me. I left there after my father died, which was perhaps twelve or thirteen years ago, and moved with my children to St. Helena... you probably know of it, a little town in the wine country of Napa Valley. I gravitate to vineyards.

After a year there, I went away for about a year, to make up my mind about settling there... went to Aix-en-Provence. We came back, this time with a French daughter too, and after finding that my dream of living in San Francisco was basically a nightmare we went back to the Vineyards, and I bought a house, and off and on we have been there ever since. My French friend went back to her family. My girls went off to schools. We went back to Aix for somewhat more than two years. And so on. By now Anne has been in theatre schools for two years and worked for one year for TWA as an interpreter and is now living in Berkeley and composing for the lute (!!!), Mary is a freshman at Russell Sage College in Troy, chugging right along toward an M.D. degree (!!!! again), and I am pulling myself into focus after some seven months in Mississippi, teaching (!!! can't resist these) in an all-Negro school.

I don't need to tell *you*, Arnold, that I am quite, and that means totally, unqualified to be a teacher... no degrees, no training. But I find that I love it. Unfortunately, I also find that I can't be Mrs. Friede the schoolma'am and MFK Fisher the writer at the same time. So I pulled out at Christmas... I was getting too involved in futilities, and felt I could do the school more good outside than in... until I return again in June for the summer session. I proved last year I could survive one of those, although I often

1. *Coronet*

wondered *why*. And in the summer there is almost no faculty there, and I can work directly with the people who need me the most... my talents or skills or whatever they may be. So... d.v.... I'll go back in June and meanwhile I must work very hard here, for my return depends on how much money I can make before then. Same old story, eh?

It was a very interesting thing, getting your letter written August 10, after such a long silence, for perhaps a day or two before, I had ruthlessly gone through a box of letters too interesting to throw away, and had been amazed and thrilled by several old ones from you, written from Le Pâquis. They were wonderful, I had kept them because they were simply too fascinating in every way to destroy. My mind was full of you... of what had happened to you in that strange dream... of François[2] and and and...

Then on August 15, one of the worst days of my life I think, I flew out of Jackson with a planeload of mute sick young Freedom School workers, and Donald Friede met me in Newark and we drove right out to his place on Long Island, where I was for a few days with both my girls (Anne was working in NY and Mary was in the back-stage crew at the John Drew in East Hampton)... and there was your letter. It was such a fine full circle that I felt whole again. . . .

By all means do fall in love with Aix. It is worthy of you, believe me. And one of the real rewards to me is that I have opened its door to several really fine people... including two Frenchmen who have known it all their lives and never seen it before now! ! ! ! ! ! (Forgive these things... I seem to feel rather gushy today. Do you remember that word gushy? Strictly 1920s or perhaps before... my mother used it as disapproval....) . . .

Yes, I would have liked that title *A Moveable Feast*. Too late.

Here is a note for your file: my permanent address, as far as anyone can dare call anyplace that, is 1467 Oak Avenue, St. Helena, California. But I hope to be here in Genoa for at least two or three more months, and I do want word from you about a couple of things. (This is certainly "the Direct Approach"!) . . .

And here, once more, Arnold, are all my wishes for you.

....

Genoa, Nevada   *28.i.65*
To: Ted Kennedy

Dear Uncle Ted:

This is not really a decent answer to your very welcome note (letter, I mean) at Christmas. I have you in my thoughts for some reason. I think often of you and of Aunt Etta, but not with such urgency. Perhaps you are sending *me* a message? (Don't laugh... I do think this happens now and then... usually with no contact made. In this case it was....)

I can understand that you do less reading now than ever. It happened to me, differently of course, in Piney Woods: I seemed literally UNABLE to read *or* write. I got up at 5:00 and finished my last class at 9:30 at night, six days a week. The seventh day was

2. François lived near Le Pâquis and took care of it.

the worst, even though I did not get up until 5:30: a constant schedule of chapel, speeches, church, meals at odd hours.... There was never any time for a half-hour of personal retirement... fifteen minutes here and then there. That was probably the reason for my SOLID MONTH, here in Genoa, of sleeping! I take, or happily I now say I *took* little naps at the strangest hours, and would sleep ten hours and then in a couple of hours go into blissful sleep for ten more. It worried me a little, but now I know it was a good thing. I am behind on some deadlines which I absolutely COULD NOT MEET in Mississippi, but I feel myself back into a good healthy routine again. . . .

News is good from both girls, although I think Mary is not too happy at Russell Sage... she says it is not the school she dislikes: she simply does not like *school*. Which is too bad, because she has a long stretch of it ahead of her, to become a doctor. It is too bad that people who know what they are going to become must spend so much time on completely irrelevant undergraduate work, I think.

I don't remember if I wrote to you about leaving Piney Woods? I decided that it was the right time.... So... I left on Dec. 23. I plan to go back for the summer session, mid-June. . . . In the summer. . . . I am at times the only white teacher there... in the regular school session there are about 20 of us, and there is a certain amount of "segregation" which shuts me off from the Negro teachers and staff. In the summer that does not exist. Perhaps it is because we are all suffering the same weather? ? ? ? And in the summer the students who must stay on are mostly the ones who have flunked courses and need help. I'll teach only English, of course... and there too I like the summer session because I can give one elective, so that I get a superior batch of students, making up two of three credits for their degrees.

In a letter you wrote me last July 29, which I don't think I answered (Mea culpa), you asked about "the natural environment" at school. . . . Well, from the school buildings one looks out over the rest of the state, practically. It is mostly swamps, at least south of Jackson to the Gulf, which is about a hundred miles from Piney Woods. . . . I went once to Jackson, and perhaps four times to the little county seat, Mendenhall, with other teachers. I was very uncomfortable always, and dreaded having to leave the campus (for things like tetanus shots and so on). The truth is that I have such a violent disgust and hatred of Mississippi that it was physically painful for me to be a part of it. This sounds very childish and I am not proud of it, but it is the truth and I had to face it, down there.... It is not like that at the school, which exists miraculously as a kind of island, quite removed from the sea around it, *IF* one accepts the fact that the sea is there and must be treated cannily and even respectfully as a constant enemy.

Back to "the natural environment": I am told that the Spring is truly beautiful there, with the land covered with wild flowers of every kind, and even the jungle blazing. Perhaps I'll see it some time. Of course a lot of the land is cleared, and there are corn fields, and sugar cane fields, and orchards of pecan trees. Basically it is poor soil, and badly farmed... typical of the stupid and ignorant state, with a terrible waste of potential in every branch of life. (Believe me, Uncle Ted: Mississippi is a blot on our nation, economically, physically, *every way*. It is a crying shame, to put it foolishly.)

Well... back again to the school (I do get off the track, when I am talking to somebody who can really hear me!): "Is it hot?" you ask. MURDER. I don't mind heat as much as cold, intense degrees of either, that is, but this is like nothing I have ever endured, even in Chicago or New York in a "heat wave." It never lets up. The humidity is often higher than the temperature. The result is that one cannot quite stand to eat properly and it is impossible to sleep normally... one moves slowly through the days and nights, pretending to be more than half-alive. (Personally I find this an active *challenge*, to prove that I can adapt myself to it and still function as a coherent (?) human being, or at least an animal still obeying its more decent instincts. I think this is faintly ridiculous, and I know that in a few more years it will be too difficult for me. Certainly I can understand why the white teachers do not stay there in the summer sessions... they are all of them over retirement age and it is TOO DIFFICULT. The Negro teachers are mostly active in other schools, adapted to the climate, and willing to spend three months without pay at the school to be helpful... in a way it is a kind of vacation for them, especially if they are widowed or otherwise alone. There is one wonderful old teacher named Miss Garrett, who has been working in remedial English at PWS for more than thirty years, just in the summer... she comes up from Louisiana. I hope very much she will be there this summer....)

As for lodging, it is very good. In fact, I feel ashamed of being so nicely housed, when I see the crowded dormitories and the shacks of some of the staff workers (farmers and so on). Every teacher has her own room, often with a small study or sitting room, and mostly with private baths. At first, for instance, I was "suite-mate" in a cottage which had ten apartments in it, and had my own bedroom, sittingroom, toilet and lavatory, and shared a bathroom with the teacher next to me. Then when regular school started I moved to the second floor (The other apartment was on ground level and was very humid) of the original classroom building. One end of the floor had been made into two two-bedroom apartments with connecting baths, and a main sittingroom, where we had a good icebox, comfortable table and chairs for making tea and so on... an electric two-burner... very pleasant indeed, with privacy as one wished it.

Naturally I like to have my own bathroom, but that is something that has almost never happened in my 56+ years, and both times I shared one with a really fascinating person.

That is probably the second most enriching thing about being at the school. (The first, for me at least, is the students.) The teachers are wonderful people. They are all slightly mad, of course, or they wouldn't be there. They are all past 65, and some of them are into their 80s. They are all retired *teachers*, people who have spent their adult lives in classrooms. Most of them show some signs of old age: arthritis, deafness, cataracts. But they either refuse to stop teaching because of the retirement limit or they have tried retirement and can not stand it. They are all "single," of course, and there are spinsters and there are many widows with grown families. Needless to say, there are almost no men. There was one, for part of the time I was there... he came in for a quarter or a semester now and then, over the past several years. He was basically obnoxious and a trouble-maker, more malicious and querulous than any of the poor old

M.F.K. Fisher: A Life in Letters

ladies he despised. And of course there is the inevitable tempest-in-teacup going on all the time, with such a gaggle of old geese. But I could cope with it all, for I *like* old geese. At first some of them were suspicious of me because I was younger, I was obviously not a professional teacher, and so on. But I deliberately won them over, at least enough to be able to have them trust me in all their little feuds and fussings... and I learned a lot! ! ! ! I learned things about courage that I never knew before... when I would feel absolutely unable to go on, I would look at those valiant dauntless old ladies and be ashamed. (I also developed new strengths within myself, of patience mostly.)

No, we did not actually prepare any of our own meals, although there was an ice-box and electric plate available for snacks in every apartment. We ate in the main diningroom, three meals a day except on Sunday when there was only a late breakfast and then a mid-afternoon dinner, very upsetting to one's routine. I found myself eating things I had not touched for thirty years: quite a bit of candy, for instance... and every night when I went to bed, a dish of ice cream! (There is a little campus store... and the ice cream in the South is much better than ours... different....) Several of the teachers had cars, and would market for the rest of us... fruits mostly, and instant coffee and so on. The food at the school is "adequate" I suppose, but typically Mississippi in that it is seemingly without real plan or intelligence, so that the meals are very uneven in size and quality... it's either feast or near famine, literally. I obviously lacked enough sugar, hence my craving for candy... most of the people put enormous quantities of sugar in their coffee. The teachers and staff eat much better meals than the students do, because of the government money the grade school students eat better meals than the college kids... really a vicious system, I think it went over into the faculty, so that teachers who taught grades got government diet, whereas if a teacher had only college students she got less variety and quality in her meals. Ridiculous. Sounds like Soviet Russia, except that Mississippi is not in the same class, on any level... the one time I spent a few hours in Jackson I knew that I would feel much more at home in Moscow.... The main reason I decided to leave the school for six months was that it is on the verge of a complete upheaval and I want to watch it from a distance for a time. Dr. Jones is 80, and is rapidly becoming senile in several areas. (He is a wonderful person, and I thank God I have known him. He trusts me. I can say that I love him.) When he dies, which may not be for quite a time because he is very healthy, the school must change. He has had little to do with it for several years, and it is being run by unskilled untrained and probably very venal henchmen, all of them graduates of Piney Woods *unfortunately*. They are suspicious of the superior education of northern Negroes, and are bungling in a painful fashion... supposedly keeping up the first ideals of Dr. Jones, at least enough to keep him satisfied. I fear he is quite unknowing of the actual administration of the school right now. There is a big trust-fund, which cannot be touched, but there is also an enormous income from contributions, and I think it is being mismanaged shockingly... partly because all men are weak humans, and partly because of the stiff-necked attitude toward better trained people. (The dininghall is a perfect example of this, with stupid extravagances and economies going on... bad planning of meals, terrible waste, no intelligent use of local crops, and so on). The main crime is that the students are being *used* now... they are the excuse for the administration to bring in more and more donations, instead of being the reason *for* the donations. The school is *rich*... in land, money, resources. Yet it lets its land rot, and does not use its natural resources because it has not the trained faculty to teach the students the right methods, and all it does is ask for more money, more money... as if it were still the struggling noble little school it was some fifty years ago. For instance, it has a file of over ONE MILLION names, to whom it mails floods of begging letters and newspapers and so on. Think of the postage! Think of the costs! Think worst of all of the thousands of work-hours put in addressing envelopes by girls who are sacrificing everything to get what the school blandly calls "business training." Think of the effect on those earnest desperate young people, to spend all their work-periods begging for handouts, when what they need and want is a good solid training. It is a dreadful situation, and will soon change, I know... and I want to be a part of the change, for I have been aware of that school for almost 41 years now (!!!)... I first learned of it when I was 16, at Bishop's School. I think that when Dr. Jones dies, it will become either a strictly vocational training school, or an orphanage. The plant itself is superb, thanks to Dr. Jones. There is a terrible need for *anything* like it. But the state is bound to be integrated within the next ten years, and it may be easier to stay segregated at Piney Woods by becoming a public institution like an orphanage. We'll see. One thing I know... it can't exist much longer on the volunteer services of a bunch of idealistic old ladies and the bungling administration of poorly educated graduates.

Well, Uncle Ted... I do hope this has not bored you! I feel very strongly about the school (Obviously!), and am inclined to hop up on the soapbox at the faintest invitation. Forgive me... and for my long silence... and please write to me when you can. (I didn't even start to tell you about my students... I am plainly a case of hereditary compulsion to be a teacher... got it from both sides, of course, but never suspected it until I was 56! Now I am really hooked, and it is a battle to keep on being Fisher with one hand and Miz Freedom with the other... the students call me that because I told them Friede means freedom in German, and they love the coincidence....)

One last thing... can you tell me of a good sturdy ground cover for rocky Nevada soil at altitude 4750 with rugged winters and hot summers? The best thing here, as far as I can see, is violets....

I am living in a little ancient (100+) cottage... will go to St. H. at least briefly before I go back to Mississippi.

Very much love to you and Aunt Etta.

....

Genoa, Nevada   *2.iii.65*
To: Rachel MacKenzie
    Dear Rachel:
    I return herewith the author's proof. It is a beautiful job of editing.

To my surprise I found myself enjoying the story too! This is very rare. I am *amazed* when I like anything I have written.

There are a couple of things I'll send on soon (I hope), for Henry to forward to you.

You ask, "Is life simpler?" I don't know about that. Certainly I have simplified, or at least made more comfortable, the ways of living it. I feel embarrassed about having snoozed almost steadily since I left Mississippi. I realize a lot of it is plain old *escape*. But things are coming into almost painfully clear focus. I have applied for a job for the summer session at Piney Woods, but have an increasingly strong feeling that a way will be found to refuse my services (actually quite limited). We'll see. By now it is quite obvious to the school that I cannot and will not write the kind of sugary guff they would like me to "contribute."And if not, why am I there? They are hysterically afraid of "outside influences," and although I have been discreet to the point of nausea about not identifying myself with anything even faintly active in remedying the general situation down there, in case it might make trouble for the school, the Administration is uneasy about me. I want to go back for two firm reasons: I can take a clearer more detached look at some things that I cannot quite believe are true, and I can encourage a few students in their desperate efforts toward articulacy.

If Piney Woods does not take me, I'll probably volunteer at the Holmes County Community Center north of Jackson... for the summer, that is. In some ways it would make things easier to have a clearcut dismissal from a school I plan to play God with, a little.

(Which I do.)

Yes, I have sent Mr. Shawn one-and-a-half pieces about gastronomical writing. They are quite different, and I don't know which if either of them he likes.

Thank you for letting me go ahead with the thing for *Holiday* and so on. I am letting myself get rather involved with the essay on Maigret and his club-members, while I wait to hear what is decided about the cookery-bookery.

Oh... I plan to leave here in May, be at home in St. Helena to mend a few fences, and then go to Mississippi about the first of June.

My best greetings to you, and my thanks for making me enjoy that story!

....

Genoa, Nevada   *16.iii.65*

To: Lawrence Clark Powell

Dearest Ghuce... much to thank you for... your welcome letter, the pictures, and now the book!

How I wish I had had that book about four months ago! I was teaching History of Am Lit to 11th Graders... some very bright, all trying hard to understand me at least. Can you imagine spending a bare two weeks trying to make almost illiterate young Negroes hear what Whitman was saying, about a country they barely know and are deathly scared about? I at least made his *life* real to them, I think. They did not like

"Manhattan." Some of them began to like "Lilacs," because I tied it so tightly into the Lincoln feeling. They disapproved of Emerson's liking W, for some reason, but also disapproved of Longfellow's disapproval! They loved W's "simmering, simmering, simmering"... they understood it because they are simmering too. Well, if I had only had your book, I could have done a lot more. I'll send a copy to the school... through secret channels so that it will have a chance to be read before it is firmly buried by the maniacal librarian (who can't stand to have books taken off the shelves, especially by Negroes...).

Ghuce, you are too thin. Hold on, or you will blow yourself away, when you get started on "the Mozart and 6 other books."... I love having the pix, though. You look more and more like your ma.

Yes, I knew about Anne Targ's death. Poor woman. She lived in Hell for too long... and so of course did Bill. I am so glad you are his friend. I hope he can come out to Malibu. Did I ever tell you about blandly guiding him to Fisherman's Wharf and proposing all sorts of things his strict orthodox upbringing forbade him, like lobster? He took it like a man... in fact was quite titillated, I think, in a horrified way.

Yes, writing is too slow. We need some good talk together. When? Where?

That reminds me... and I am NOT joking about this: I am beginning to think that I should marry again. Do you know of any nice tired intelligent widowed professor, for instance... children grown, like mine... full past, like mine... mildly creative nature, like mine... preferably not an alcoholic but CERTAINLY not a penny-pincher (I could not stand to live with a miserly person...)... somebody who could accept my being a professional writer and at the same time enjoy my company? Can cook, will travel. (Joke. Laff.) Seriously, I think I could give somebody a few years of real warmth and companionship, and could even be of some use to a bookish person... research, or or or...

This rather odd idea springs from my growing realization that for the first time in my life, really... at least since my sister Anne was born and I came to know responsibility... I am without any *raison d'être* except myself, and I am simply incapable of being an integrated human being all alone. I must have something or somebody to exist for.

Give it thought, for my sweet sake and God's.

Meanwhile... much love from me, and thank you again for everything. . . .

....

St. Helena, California   *24.vii.65*
To: Grace Holmes

Dearest Aunt Grace... your letter is so much in my mind that I am being very self-indulgent and am replying to it instead of to several goading reproofs from magazine editors and so on, which I have kept laid out on the couch in my workroom for almost a week now, feeling every morning that THIS IS THE DAY. It may still be: human patience, even from editors, has its limits. . . .

I don't think I am at all "dreadfully beset," but I do feel quite calm. Now and then

I have a short sinker, with the usual symptoms of guilt, apprehension, and despair. But I am quite used to them by now, and they do not scare me. In fact, I often think that I have formed an inhuman amount of scar tissue, so that perhaps I am somewhat monstrous emotionally. I hope this is not true. But at least it keeps me alive, and I plan to be that way as long as I can manage it.

Yes, it is an ugly thing about Anne.[1] But I did draw the line... on the plan to meet Sean this afternoon at the SF airport and fly up to Reno with him for three days. I felt very selfish about it. Self-protective again! I saw everything very clearly: Sean and Bill[2] are basically very hostile, and I would act as Anti-Dote the Eternal Buffer. I would also be expected to mop up many private tears and smooth many ruffled nerves. I would also have to be an alcoholic blotter, especially for Bill, whose one escape from responsibility is the bottle. I will ALSO find myself doing a month-old cleaning job in the Erskine house. And so, with a dozen footnotes to these main points, I got the canny idea that I should simply bow out. Which I did. I had to call Sean in Washington after office hours, for he is incommunicado in Voice of America–Congo... he was sleepy and FURIOUS. He suddenly had to do this very sad task alone. (I called Bill and he seemed quite pleased, on the other hand!) Then last night I talked for a few minutes with Sis herself. She was on a cloud somewhere, and knew almost nothing about Sean's coming and so on... very vague and mumbly, pinned to the bed with tubes sticking out of her like a Dalí drawing. Horrible. End of story: Barbara[3] takes her state exams in SF on this coming Thursday, and then I think she and I will go up for several days.... I must look over some material I left there in my delightful deserted cottage, and we can help Bill by cleaning and so on.

No, I don't think people are leaning on me. I suspect that when I write to you I manage to imply that, to feel important?

WELL now... how could I possibly have neglected to tell you about Barbara? (It is Ware, not Weare as in Holbrook.) She is my foster-daughter for the next year or more, a "graduate" from Piney Woods Junior College. I was first attracted to her because of a poem she sent me secretly. She was not one of my students. After I left, we corresponded. She had told me she thought of going into nurses' training at a school in Boston which was absolutely free, with all expenses paid. This sounded fishy to me, so I checked with a couple of doctor-friends and found it to be an old peoples' home run by the Christian Science Church... which of course meant that B would be free domestic help, since no disease or pain exists... I investigated, and sure enough she would spend two years changing beds, without any instruction at all in medication and so on... and she would have a piece of paper recommending her to other such discreet institutions as free menial labor.

Well... B could not possibly try for entrance in a Registered Nursing course because she has very low grades in the sciences... they simply are not taught at PW and

1. Anne Kelly asked MF for help during her bout with cancer. MF did respond to her request, in spite of other family problems.
2. Bill Erskine, Anne's second husband
3. Barbara Ware, MF's protégée from Piney Woods

she is not bright enough to pass the College Boards with what she has got at the school. Also it would take two years and quite a bit of money.

End of *this* story is that through more doctor-friends I got involved in a new and very good branch of nursing which evolved after the last war (I mean WW2…!), Registered Vocational Nursing. It is highly thought of by the doctors, and I know that when I was at University of California Hospital three summers ago the VNs did much more actual nursing than the RNs who were usually in charge of the floors and so on.

I passed my dope along to several students and to my fellow-railroader, and by now one other girl I would have loved to come live here has entered the course at the University of Washington (state), and I pray that B will pass her exams and start off in September. She will have to live in SF, and that is our next problem: to find a good family where she can be treated as a student, not a servant (She has classes five days a week, eight hours a day, and two women who have taken the course say there is a great deal of homework)… she could earn part of her keep with a couple of hours of help a day, perhaps. We'll see. Sufficient unto the day, as Wee Edie[4] used to say.

At this point we have five young Negroes out of Mississippi, and more to come in late August. B was brought out on a fast wild ride by one of my teacher-friends… no trouble at all, except some rudeness in eating-places in Texas. Peralee, the little girl who is taking VN in Washington, came alone by Greyhound and had a wonderful trip with kind people all the way. Clarence Jenkins, one of the boys heading for Bremerton and the state university, had a little trouble, I gather… he thumbed his way, foolishly.

Barbara is 20, a tall beautiful girl with a fine-boned face, enormous eyes, beautiful white even teeth which we soon found were a very hollow mockery, so that she is in the midst of extensive dental repairs. She is very sensitive, very dignified, with good basic manners (I mean table and so on), and passionately clean and dainty. She lacks self-confidence and was "the dumb one" of a large family of very handsome and bright children. Tony Ten Broeck, math teacher and dear friend, is tutoring her several times a week and is doing wonders with her feelings of security. I too work toward them all the time. And a few good friends here are fine, too… B works three mornings a week for one of them, to get used to white ways and to add a little to her bank account.

Right this minute her fiancé is here, and they are laughing softly together in the kitchen, over breakfast (That is the diningroom too, in this old house)…. They have had an arrangement for three years, but B could not make up her mind, so I suggested she invite Hollis up here, to take another look. She had not seen him for over a year. He is a sergeant (career) in the Artillery, and an MP… stationed for the last year in San Diego after two in Alaska, and now heading for Officers' Training in Kentucky. About three minutes after he arrived she was wearing a very pretty engagement ring, and they both want her to go on to school this year… they will be married Christmas 1966. I feel fine about it: it gives her an anchor, and he is a quiet thinking dignified young man. (He is also going to get his BA, never finished, while he is in the OT. He wants to go into big-city police work when he gets out, six years from now, B is against it. He

4. MF's mother, Edith Holbrook Kennedy

feels it can do a lot for his race, because of his long training in it in the Army. I think he will do it. She fears for his safety, of course.)

Well... that is the story of Barbara, this far. Oh... she and I are writing a book. It started out as part of my plot to make her use English, but I think it may turn into something. Certainly nobody but us two could do it. She has made a list of things that bother Negroes in Mississippi, and every day we take one of them and go off into our rooms and write everything we can about it, she as black and I as pinky-white. We do not look at all at what we write, nor discuss it beforehand. It may be a slightly fantastic account.... Today's question: How does it feel to go from Piney Woods into Jackson? Yesterday we wrote about how old people are treated in Mississippi county hospitals. And so on. Mad!

Oh... Inez, my cohort, and I do not really support the children. We need more money than we would otherwise of course. But several friends who are richer in their middle years have sent me sums which they assure me would have gone for a case of bourbon or something, and I am using part of this boodle to help with the dental expenses, and have sent part of it to Inez, since at this point she has two kids living with her. Eleanor Friede sent a lot of good summer cottons. A friend here with a tall daughter who just got married gave us a beautiful tweed coat. And so on. The expenses of the VN course are held to about $150, but that of course does not take care of board and room and so on, so I plan to have continuing expense this next year. But Anne (*my* girl) is very stubborn about letting me help her, so I feel that I should spend that money on another person. And so on.

Yes, it's too bad about DF's will.[5] I knew you would get a special wry grin out of it, as an Old Hand at such things.

But in his own way he did do many "nice" things in the last three or four years of his life... madly extravagant flings in Paris, which I would have given my eye teeth to change into school-bills and so on.... He was definitely the sugar-daddy type, but it was very good sugar when it turned up... boxes at the Opera, beautiful gold beads, etc etc etc. Ho hum.

I'll keep you posted about Anneli. I wish I could help her.

I'm so glad the summer has been a good one for you. Here there has been very little real heat... delightful for everyone but the winemen, who expect vinegar unless the sun warms up the grapes a little more. . . .

As for our national "policies," I am not fit to mention them, for I feel actively sick.... How CAN we do what we are doing I yell silently, and silent yelling is very nauseating and probably bad for the blood pressure. And futile. In fact, I don't feel *just fine* at all. But I don't know what to do about it, except try to prepare young people to be strong, for the future. . . .

Yes, I will try to do the *NYer* stuff, at least one, before B and I go to SF for her exams (They are given from 6:30 P.M. to midnight, and we'll stay at a nearby motel... maybe I can show her a little of Fishermen's Wharf and so on... she is as untouched by big cit-

5. DF is Donald Friede.

ies and all that as a person from another planet, or a rare jungle bird. It is very exciting to be with her... I practice what Golden calls gradualism).

... oh... I did a long story about a school-teacher which I think you will like. The *NYer* found it too sentimental (?) and it is now making the rounds. If nobody snaps at it, which would help my bank account at this point, I'll send it along to you anyway for a private chuckle. . . .

Much love. I pray the good weather will continue. You sound as if you were fairly free to hop around town, which means that you move more easily than this time a year ago, thank God. What are your relations with Brother Pain at this point? Is Darvon still all right for you? (I check on this once in a while, because I know three people who are told to take it and who are afraid of dependence.... They confess to NO apparent after-effects... bad ones, I mean.)

....

St. Helena, California   *2.viii... no, ix.65*
To: June Eddy

Dear June... thank you for calling, the other night. I hope I didn't gab too long. I was apparently starved for a conversational outlet, being completely shut off here.

You are an overly conscientious as well as very thoughtful person, as you will admit. Believe me, I had not yet been hooked into expectancy by your pretty checks! They have been delightful surprises each time. The first one, made out to BJW, is the nucleus of her "account" with me, which she is keeping in an old check-book, the way I did with Anne and Mary... she writes checks, keeps up her stubs, and so on. She has saved over one hundred note dollars, even while spending a little on things like greeting cards (She is great for them... Get Well, Congratulations, Happy Father's Day, etc...). The other pennies-from-heaven I am sorry to say I applied hastily to the dental fund, which was dangerously anemic.

Thank you for writing just as you did about Sis.[1] Fifty-five is young for some people. But after my last months there, when I came back from Mississippi, part of me wished strongly that she could leave this world *now*. She was increasingly demanding and irascible with Bill, obviously not well (but that state was chronic), and all the time really frightened of losing this last grasp on reality, her first and only love for anyone but herself. Bill, unaware of it himself, was beginning to chafe. His eye was wandering a little... so far cautiously, to cute waitresses etc, BUT. So for that & many other reasons I am very thankful that their good relationship was spared the ugliness of apathy and antagonism. It would have killed Sis, but because of her nature she would have made sure that it killed Bill too. She is well out of it, and although he is sad and always will be, it is better for a simple nature like his to be able to dwell on the good parts and not know too many of what would have been bad.

As for the suffering, Sis died like a dog, but not because of pain caused by cancer. In fact she told me she was more comfortable after the first operation than she had been

1. Anne Erskine died in the fall of 1965.

for a long time... she was living on Scotch and paregoric for months (but her pattern of self-medication and alcohol was decades old). The last nine weeks of her life were a series of last-ditch interferences of her natural need to die by young surgeons who were undoubtedly doing their "best," Hippocratically and otherwise, but who seemed to have no understanding of what they were doing to her spirit when they kept on operating for what had from the first been diagnosed as a hopelessly inoperable case. Her body tried in every way it could to stop: severe embolisms in both legs, pneumonia twice, abscessed liver and diaphragm, punctured abdomen, on and on. Doggedly they kept chopping into her and then forcing her to keep on breathing (constant oxygen) and "functioning" with five or six tubes in and out. Because of all these medical fireworks she was kept heavily sedated, so as not to risk displacing any of the things sticking into her arms, nose, chest, abdomen, and guts... oh, and legs.... Now, after nine weeks of living hell for her and her husband (and me), and thousands and thousands' worth of surgery and care and medicines, the doctors tell Bill it was no go from the start. He is simple to begin with, and desperate right now, and he pumps their hands and bangs their shoulders and says with tears in his eyes, "You are a couple of wonderful guys. You are great guys. I owe everything to you." (There may be more in this last than can possibly meet his kind good eye!)

Ah well and ho hum indeed.

....

Genoa, Nevada   *4.x.65*
To: Eleanor Friede

Dearest Squeek... here it is very still, with the air clear and cold. Small golden locust leaves drift down, and make a crackling as they touch the ground and the roof. Apples lie everywhere on the grass, under the countless trees the Mormons planted in 1841 or so, and there is a fine smell of cider in the air. All the flowers are gone now except drifts of Michaelmas daisies, which are deep purple here.

I never know which is the most beautiful time of the year in Genoa... perhaps now?

It pains me to know that I must leave, probably for good. I am putting off the main decisions for a few more days. I have never lived in a one-person place which pleases me as does this cottage... there is everything I need for my private "loner" life. Ah well and ho hum.

I think I may go for a month or so to Nevada City. Bill and I stopped there on the fantastic trip from St. Helena (I had never seen most of the country, and was literally floored by it... slept eleven hours as soon as I staggered out of the car...). I enclose a couple of cards which will amuse you perhaps. The place[1] (1854) has been very artfully renovated, and I know I could hole in there and get some hard work done.... I'll report.

One reason I think I'll do this is that I have a wrong feeling about the urgent invitation to go to Jenner, where Norah and a friend have bought an old house and are turning it into a habitable place... it was the hospital for the lumber camp in what is now a

1. Nevada City

ghost-town. The heating is still very inadequate, and of course the weather is wild and foggy on the Northern California coast. And the other day Norah said, "Of course you won't mind our being there most weekends," and suddenly a little bell started to ring again for me. The first time it rang was in about 1932, when Al Fisher and I spent two winters in the family beach-house, rent-free for keeping it open (Depression... no job), and before we knew it the whole damned family was there EVERY WEEK-END... and I would spend the last half of each week cooking goodies and getting the house ready and then spend the first half of the next week cleaning etc etc. "NO, Dote," the little bell said. (It has rung several other times, but never more clearly.) So... I shall risk hurting Norah, and I know Anneli will be disappointed, for she dearly loves Jenner and says that it is the PERFECT place for me, and of course I can't go into details about why I am shying away.... (I should make it clear that this recurring situation is wholly the fault of my own nature, and nobody else's: I really love to engulf myself with hospitality, instead of working at Deathless Prose as I should....)

Usually there is no sound here except occasional slow footsteps of a very old man or woman passing the cottage, the leaves falling, birds, now and then the wild laughing of the coyotes before dawn. But last night the village *rocked* for the annual Candy Dance, which has been held for countless years by the Masonic ladies, for some vague charitable purpose. It used to be essential to the life of these isolated ranchers... saddle horses and wagons would be hitched for riding along the Pony Express Trail, dancing would go on all night in the Masonic Hall, children would sleep in the corners after the big supper served by the ladies. But now it is commercialized, and the Valley people stay home and pull their shades and the town (???? ghost village) is taken over by bristling armed deputies eyeing the gangs of outlanders, middle-aged drunken tourists mostly from California and gangs of white punks and Washoe Indian boys aching for trouble. Last night there was no shooting and no real rumbling, but the Trail is a mess of broken bottles, empty beercans, dirty paper plates....

Bill tended the Store... did not want the two nice old ladies to be there, local widdies who have been helping him since Sis fell ill. At his request I stayed home, doors latched etcetera... I felt that as a world-reporter I should at least take a look at the remnant of the Wild West in action, but I was glad to be out of it... much artificial joviality and singing and Yippeeeeeing until dawn. This morning Bill looks just about as weary and beat-up as the Trail.

He always hires the two biggest Indians in the valley to stand around and look BIG, which is easy, since they are far over 6 feet tall and one weighs about 350. They are old friends of his (and Sis's and mine). But last night they stood him up: Elton arrived stoned, after about a week of slow but steady work at it (Indians go into drunkenness deliberately and slowly, in an almost religious withdrawal from the troubles of life... this was true in Hemet too), and Mike, the bigger one, was making up with his white girlfriend and borrowed Bill's lawn, complete with comfortable chaises lounges, where he and she took care of most of the night, several six-packs of beer, and three tubes of airplane glue.

M.F.K. Fisher: A Life in Letters

All this adds fuel to my current fire of trying to con Bill into flying to Philadelphia, AWAY FROM HERE, for a couple of weeks. It would ease him into the new adjustments of living here alone. At this point everybody in town is a bastard, he feels.... (And there are quite a few, I'll admit... very ingrown, like a remote Kentucky village, with more than the right percentage of people who bay at the full moon etc etc etc.) Bill really loves and understands this kind of country, though, and I think it is right for him to stay here, once geared to it again.

He is puzzled and hurt at my firm decision to leave, and is too simple to understand whatever explanation I might make. But Nevada City is only three hours from here (and four from St. Helena), so he could come down now and then if I did take a little apartment in the National this autumn. I like him very much, but he is too simple for me to fall for in any way. (I like the real neurotics, and am too old to change! Half-joke. Half-laff.)

I am fudging, by rambling on to you: I must go to the other house and plunge deliberately and brutally into the job of going through my sister's somewhat incredible belongings. She was a very elegantly dressed San Franciscan for many years, and since she never gave away a bent hairpin, there are closets jammed with outdated very good dresses, drawers bulging with never-worn handmade gloves, etc etc etc. Murder. I feel like bolting a stiff brandy.... (I am not emotionally involved, at least on the surface. The air is too good here, if you know what I mean and you do....)

How much longer can you stay where *your* air is so good? Hang on until you are FREEZING! Get an electric blanket. Live on hot soup. Sleep with Kitty on your tummy. Anything.

I think with real satisfaction of your deft plans for work, this winter. Very exciting.

....

Genoa, Nevada   *15.x.65*
To: Eda Lord

My dearest Eda... I am writing from Genoa, Nevada, where I am staying for a final couple of weeks. It is very hard to make myself know that I am leaving this wild austere country, in a few days, for the last time. Yesterday there was snow down to about 6000 feet... this little village is at about 5000... and this morning the ground glistens and blazes with hard white frost.

I am sad to tell you that Anne, my sister, died a few weeks ago. That is why I am here now, my sixth flight north this summer: to help her husband take care of personal things like 68 pairs of gloves....

It is good that I could stay here last winter, after I left Mississippi. I could not understand why I seemed to dawdle here. I could not leave. Now I believe it was because I was with Sis in the final and surely the best season of her life: she was serene, happier than ever before in her troubled years, amusing, relaxed. Soon after I left in May she underwent emergency surgery, and the next ten weeks were straight hell. She should have been allowed to die quickly and with dignity, but instead the common routine was followed, of repeated surgery in an inoperable case of general cancer. She finally outwitted the knife-happy medicos, but it was very grim. Ho hum, as Edith would say.

I have not seen Anne's will, which she drew with great care, but I think she left "everything" to Bill and then to her son Sean, with a fairly valuable brooch to each of my girls. Bill is a fine simple man, almost as naif as I about money and such, and I am seeing that he is thoroughly taken care of by lawyers and such. He will continue to live here in Nevada... he is a tree surgeon and a fire warden, and is a true Man of the Forest, so this is the right country for him. He is suffering the classical rebound and now believes he is in love with me, being used to me and also trusting me, a dangerous combination in first grief! Like most newly bereaved men, he is terrified of being "hooked" by one of the hordes of hungry women he imagines waiting to pounce on him, and Dear Old Dote seems a god-sent shield. All this will pass, of course. He is not the man for me... much too simple! But I like him and admire him... and love him for performing a true miracle in managing to give Sis, that complex sad creature, a taste of happiness.

End of story.

I think I am one letter behind... must have left it in St. Helena. (My papers are in an unholy mess, thanks to my many quick flights up here this last summer....) I am rereading one written on August 18. . . . Oh, I see you knew about Anne's illness... yes indeed, she would have "accepted" your love and wishes... she thought of you with a sense of mystery, mixed with some envy because of our own continuing friendship and love, which she could not understand. It was her nature to be jealous of many things which she tried to dismiss, therefore, with disdain... but always puzzlement and regret too.

About Barbara: one avenue after another was closed to her, through extensive tests. I finally got her into deep vocational guidance testing, through bald prestige-pulling with friends... she came out unusually high in personal relations and all that, but abysmally low in academic possibilities. She became increasingly bewildered... and of course restless, for she is extremely alive and attractive sexually, and there is absolutely no social mixing in St. Helena, and I introduced her to the three Negroes there, only one of whom was at all on her cultural level. He is a weak dissatisfied lovable boy I have known for several years... the girls went to high school with him. Like so many young Negroes in this country, he is a drifter, taking and losing inferior jobs, sitting waiting for *something* but too listless to fight toward it. He introduced poor Barbara to several aspects of this attitude, ones he is quite used to as a normal part of his picture, but which frightened her as a strictly raised young Baptist... including high speed driving in a "borrowed" car, and a few sessions with marijuana. There seemed no escape for her. Finally I decided she must return to Mississippi. It was very hard for both of us, but basically she was relieved. What she saw of the life she would weakly choose to lead, rather than the one I would make her lead if she stayed with me, scared her very much. So... I simply blazed into the increasingly sticky situation, feeling abominably tyrannical etc etc etc... and in one wild 17-hour flight from SF I got her safely into her family's arms in Mississippi and returned to my own doorstep, non-stop. Mad. (And the next day I flew up here again....)

I am very anxious to get back to St. H. I plan to try once more my old trick, which never came off too well, of renting a small room somewhere in the little town and keeping regular office hours... do one job at a time and be ruthless about telephones and such. Always before I had the children on my mind. Now there is almost nothing urgent that needs to get to me until meal-times.... Both girls are well-established.

You will be glad to know that Anneli is learning to accept me as a loving friend. Having a child of her own[1] has deepened her, and made her see that she can forget the frustrations of being a daughter and accept me as a person... perhaps even an interesting one. I spent a night in her apartment before I came up here this time. All went well. She is fully alive to the beauties of having Jean Christophe to love and protect... sees the Barrs often... is going to the University, taking a light course so that she can be mostly with Jean Christophe (Advanced English and Introduction to Philosophy...)... now and then she picks up extra money modelling or acting as cocktail-hostess at private parties at the old Claremont, hideously well-bred and stuffy but nice pay.... Edith would roll in her tomb if she had one, but Rex would approve, for Anne is plainly on a good even keel now. I do hope she shakes herself free of the largely invisible Frenchman, but that is not my affair.

As for Mary (called Kennedy too, mostly at Donald's insistence...), she is working very hard at Carnegie... is well into the back-stage angle, and is learning draughting, to her delight. The course is very demanding, and there are only 3 or 4 women with some 300 men. I do hope she can stick it out. I would like her to try one year in Malraux's department of Son-et-Lumière, which she first saw in Bruges many years ago and which fascinates her. We'll see. She is very romantic, and is always deeply involved that way, usually with some sort of emotional cripple: an obese giant, a homosexual actor.... She leads a wild life, and I am glad that she has what is for her the stout staff of the Church to lean upon.

I hope to see her Christmas... I'd like to have her come West, but do not want to spoil her private life. I think Eleanor Friede plans to flee NY this first Christmas without DF, probably to Switzerland with Truman Capote and his friend Jack. So Mary would not have a NY place. . . .

I am very far behind on work, as you can imagine... so much so that I suspect the *New Yorker* is fed up with my lack of material. Tant pis. I have signed to do a long book by next September, for Putnam... really to please my good friend Bill Targ, who is now Senior Editor there. . . .

Dearest Eda, please forgive my long silence, and write to me. Tell me you are well-lodged at last... that you are working... that you are well. Give my love to S. . . . Do you know Castelleras? Is it near you? Friends who have a little house there have offered it

1. Anne's son Jean Christophe was born in March 1965.

---

to me. Perhaps I could come next year? I cannot leave this country for too long, while the children are still in school, but.......

Here is my love to you, always.

....

St. Helena, California   22.i.66
To: Mrs. Hugo Munsterberg
Dear Mrs. Munsterberg:
Your very welcome letter about the cookery of song-birds is not dated, but I know that it came a long time ago. Without attempts at excuse I must tell you I am sorry I have not written before. I was involved in family complications which seemed to stop my tongue for a time. Now all is well. . . .

I know of several references to birds as cookery, but on re-reading your letter I doubt very much that they would be of any interest to you, for you seem extremely knowledgeable.

My girls were raised where poaching was an art, but even they revolted when a neighbor here in the wine-valley snared grape-pickers (winged) and swung them to wring their necks... a cruel Piedmontese! I have eaten fig-peckers too. And in Aix and other parts of Provence a pâté is made of the tiny birds who live on grape-seeds... I forget their names now: one can buy a little tin with one, whole, in a winy sauce and foie-gras, quite pathetic. They are pretty surely snared in the vineyards when too heavy to fly off, the way the migrating robins get, here in the Valley, when they come down from flight for a gorge of the ripe cotoneaster berries... I have seen them topple happily off the twigs and lie for a time, snoozing, until they could take wing.

Well, this is not much help, I am afraid. I do wish you luck on your project. Perhaps I may see it in print?

I can say with Walter de la Mare that I too have seen poulterers' shops "festooned... as if with holly" by strings of little birds, but in Aix, not England... and in Dijon and also, perhaps 30 years ago, in Paris. It is a sad heart-wrenching sight, if one is conditioned that way. But the colors are beautiful too, if one is conditioned *another* way!

In menus of the so-called 90s (1870–1910) there are many recipes for preparing small birds, if one reads the books by people like Ranhofer, or the reminiscences of the self-styled gourmets, from Diamond Jim Brady on up and down. (This is fascinating, and I must not risk boring you....)

My best to you, my thanks for your letter, my hopes that you will forgive my long silence....

....

St. Helena, California   17.v.66
To: Grace Holmes
Dearest Aunt G... thank you for the stamps. I made money on that transaction!
It was fine to have your letter here when I got home from a wild jet-trip to NY. I was

there three days. One was peaceful, spent with Mary up from Pittsburg. She is hurried, over-worked, undernourished, exhausted, and blissful. She'll pay for all of it later, but now is the time! Carpe diem. Then I spent two wild days in small air-conditioned offices crowded with chain-smoking neurotics. The day I came home the taxis went on strike, so I walked and took subways to the fantastic Pan-Am building which straddles Park, and on the 53rd floor stepped into a helicopter to Kennedy Port. It was a beautiful experience, worth the rest of the nonsense.

Result: I have signed to do the text for a book, first of an ambitious series, for Time-Life Books, Inc.[1] This, I hasten to add, has nothing but the name to do with the magazines. I agreed to the essentially fast tough professional operation because of the editor, Michael Field whom I admire, and because I can go to France for a month or so FREE. The deadline is October 1. I got along famously with the various editors and research people who will work with me. Actually, for what I am to do, I need none of them, but have not told them so! They are very serious and dedicated and grim and so on. I hide my inner jaunty detachment....

I get a fat sum, which seemed "wrong" to me, for I have never dealt in such terms. But Henry Volkening, my agent and old friend, said Don't be an idiot. So... by the time I get paid, it may be a handful of pennies if real inflation sets in, and I'll have the main thing, the chance to see a few friends again.

I'll leave, direct polar flight SF-Paris, on June 18, and come back via New York (and I hope Chicago to see you) at the beginning of August, as things now look. Exciting. I am going through a rather lethargic period right now, but will be out of it soon, and bustling about with expired passports and so on.

Thank God you are so right about summer clothes! I am shaking out seersucker dresses I bought six years ago in Aix....

There was a review in the *NYer* of April 30. It was fun to write, and I am getting interesting mail about it. There is a short story in the May 13 issue... no, May 14. It is an odd one, and it seems strange that I wrote it. The two parts I liked in it were cut out, anyway. I think there are about three more reviews in galley. I must try very hard to do a couple more before June 18.

. . . At night now I am re-reading some old novels. Fun. I have all the novels up in the attic, where I sleep. I know most of them aren't worth a nickel, but I have kept them for my own good reasons. . . .

I really do doubt that I ever tackle another lecture course. I am too much of a novice. I don't regret one ghastly minute of this past job,[2] for I know it strengthened a lot of things besides my supply of information... political perception, and so on and so on. But I work too hard at it. I need to catch up with a few other things... get ahead of myself on the *NYer* things, as long as they want me, for they pay well and in spite of the harsh editing are good for my syntax... put order into fantastic piles of notes for the old age book... oh and do the Putnam book[3] I was very graciously released from for the

1. *The Cooking of Provincial France*
2. A lecture series she did for the University of California Extension in Berkeley
3. *With Bold Knife and Fork*

Time-Life job. I'd like to finish that by next Spring. I have no illusions at all about my lasting security in the so-called publishing world, and should ride high on the wave while I can (although I doubt that I have your prognosis of a long age). I feel that security as such is a pipe-dream, but know that money is always useful to young people, so I must try to put some aside. And as of now, I know that whenever I *want* to, I can now get some sort of lectureship again, at least here in California. But I don't want to think of it for a while.

What you tell me about the Admiral always fascinates and occasionally scares or enrages me. . . . I can understand having to serve buffet-style if there are no maids, but the old trick of having less food is very low... luxury-hotels use it too, since people are inclined to serve themselves sparingly to save face. Ho hum indeed. It could be especially vicious in a gathering of elderly people... That new Mrs. Simpson took TWO rolls... etc.

I am drifting for a time, being very neglectful of watering the plants and so on. I keep thinking that I'll start tomorrow... and actually I think that this time I shall. The weather is dry and beautiful, and already dangerous in some areas. Here I stay relatively cool, and the air is sweet with star jasmine and honeysuckle in full flower. A neighbor brought me a great armful of peonies....

This weekend I have a kind of date! I made it before I knew of all the wild goings-on I was slated for, with a man I have known for about 27 years or so. He and his wife bought Le Pâquis from Timmie and me. He is the publisher now of *Esquire* Magazine. There was an entertaining article by him in the May *Atlantic,* a chapter from a book he has written called *Toys of a Lifetime,* out this fall. Oh, his name is Arnold Gingrich. He wrote that he had to spend four days in the City (SF) on business, and would like to save one for me if I would show him "the other side." So I plan to go down in time to give him an exhausting tourist whirl, complete with one-hour Bay tour and so on. He will never be the same again. As I said, it sounded like fun, before I got into this new deal with Time-Life.

Oh... the book will be about provincial French cooking... I mean, of the ten provinces, the real basis of what we think of as French cuisine. I am abysmally ignorant of at least 7 of them....

More soon. Much love.

....

St. Helena, California   *16.vi.66*
To: Julia Child

Dear Mrs. Child:

Yes. I can be in Boston on August 3, d.v. of course. Your suggestion sounds fine, of working and then going up to Kennebunkport on the 5th.

I think I'll forget my silly idea of a private flight to London. It would delay things, and would be an interruption in what should by that time be a fairly well organized pattern of work on the Time-Life project.

I agree with you (and Curnonsky)[1] that there are many ambiguities in the use of the word "provincial"... in fact, we can be in heavy water, semantically. And it is true that sticking to the actual sense of the word will limit the scope of the recipes. That, to me, is a good thing. This book in 200 pages of text and pictures and methods and so on cannot possibly hope to cover French "home cooking" as Mrs. David[2] did, for instance. As for the word "bourgeois," it has several connotations in American, most of them warped, and I think a firm clarification of the word "provincial" and an equal loyalty to it will make the book outstanding, and possibly unique, whereas it can risk being simply another sketchy survey of French cooking-in-general.

Or *French Home Cooking?* I think this might turn away many prospective buyers. I prefer *Cooking of French Provinces* to *French Provincial Cooking* (and I think Mrs. David's publishers will too!).

But there will of course be this and much more to "hassle with Michael about"!

I'll drink to our meeting when I stop for one night in Dijon. I am impatient for both.

Best,

....

St. Helena, California   *16.viii.66*
To: Arnold Gingrich

Darling Arnold, this will fool you! An extra note... I am determined to catch up with you, and I am hoping another letter will come today, and so I want to re-read 10.viii before the mail comes... and anyway I am very restless and unwilling to do the two next jobs: go through all my checking of the past two months (done by a friend), and clean the kitchen which is full of vegetables to wash and vases full of half-dead flowers to be dealt with. I am restless because a crew of men is working in my trees, taking out dead branches and so on... the crashings and choppings have a very bad effect on me, mostly because of having to be on hand when our beautiful orange orchard was uprooted in Whittier I suppose. Today one beautiful tree came out. It died of old age, perhaps a hundred years... a magnificent persimmon tree almost surely planted by the Chinese. It was the largest in California, we all believed, and people used to come to draw and photograph it, and classes of schoolchildren were brought to see the fruit hanging on the bare branches in November. Well, it died while I was in Mississippi, but I waited until now for a possible renascence. Ho hum. Hail and Farewell, and I shall have a thriving "fruitless mulberry" put in AT ONCE, for quick growth and pretty shade. So that's why I'm restless.

Now to the letter: it was odd that I turned blue-eyed for you. Certainly that is the first time anyone has ever seen or remarked it. I don't know why. When I am very disturbed or angry my pupils become very large, I am told, as did my father's, so that my eyes look black. But I was certainly neither disturbed nor angry. I was feeling very

1. A gastronomic critic in France
2. Elizabeth David, British writer of *French Country Cooking*

excited and even a little hilarious, to be there with you and think of how and why a fascinating world-wise man like you would want me to. Oh, the make-up was light green.

Well, as my young friend Monique always said when baffled, Misterio de las pampas.

Oh yes, I wear the ring. It is now part of me. I have seen my three close friends here who have come to supper eyeing it, but no questions have been asked, nor ever will be. My answer would be that it had belonged to a man named Fritz and that I had been given it to wear. Or rather that I was wearing it for a while.... I consider it something you may at any time ask me to return to you, for reasons I would not question.

I keep the medal, which I find pleasant to touch, on the little shelf where I can see it most often, where I also keep lipstick, eye-shadow, pancake makeup, toothbrushes, and two tubes of toothpaste... real glamorous, no? I like it. It amuses me. It makes me feel lighthearted. I think of what you and I put with those letters, and really your words are NICER than mine, and I feel fine.

About the "meaning" of the ring: to me it means that you love me enough to want me to have it. Remember, I am your *simple* girl....

I thought our meeting went beautifully too. I thought you knew that. My god, I was not uncomfortable and I was not restless! If I had felt that something was off-key, wrong, whatever, it would have been obvious *at once* and we would not have met again after lunch at the Richelieu. You must trust me about that. As a matter of fact I thought I was very "overt" indeed to keep calling your office (mostly without luck), and to go to breakfast twice on Wednesday just to see you again, and so on and so on. I felt a well-controlled resentment, not against any of us human beings though, that we could not withdraw into a private Eden and walk hand in hand, sit cheek to cheek, lie mouth to mouth. I'm basically very direct. I think you are too. But we both knew why we must sit across tables, and we both still know that it was the right way for then. And touching the old violins, part of you, and eating smoked trout you like to eat (So do I... delicious!), and drinking from your bottle of Irish Mist were all very real exchanges of love, it seemed to me. I don't know if you go along with this substitution-bit...?

I think it is very funny that you fret about the Collect package! I do hope it comes today. (Went out for the mail... letter from you... refuse to open it until I seal this... DISCIPLINE, man.)

I do love, and I admit it without shame, to get surprises.

Oh, how awful that we *could* have gone to the airport in the Bumpkin! But really I shun farewells in stations of any kind. They are harrowing if they are real, and simply endless and boring if they are not, which is mostly. But it would have chewed me up, I think, to part from you there in public where everyone else was parting. It was better to grin at each other on the sidewalk and then hurry away into lobbies and Officina and all that. Take me somewhere, sometime, but not to a farewell.

Bottom of letter. Counting today's, I have four to go. Lucky me.

The saws and hatchets are still going. Dreadful. But the trees will be the better for it. I want for them to be healthy as long as they live, and it is possible that they will be doomed within the next ten years, if this street is re-zoned again. Then I will go away. But first I will put my own pistol to the heads of the trees, and give them an honorable death.

Grim note... not one to end on. But everything is all right. By now, after a rather lengthy interruption of two friends who had to tell me a few of their troubles, it is the noon hour and the damned saws have stopped and peace it's wonderful. I'll make myself a little drink, pull some tomatoes out of the reefer, and spend a quiet few minutes... first, though, I'll read your letter, which is burning a hole in my apron pocket.

....

St. Helena, California   *19/viii/66*
To: Arnold Gingrich

(I was seeing how that looks... like the ..s better) Good morning, dear sunshine yourself... merry, even. Here the day starts off in the cool grey way that is strictly Northern California and very good for all of us crops. I got up very early, with a rather restless mind, and worked for a time in the patio, taking dead leaves off plants and shifting pots about. Then I puttered in the house, changing a few pictures and so on. When I finish this note I'll trot around to the post office while the streets are still fairly empty... I'm in slacks and am still prim about going onto Main Street in them... sound like my own great-grandmother! In the winter, somehow, it seems different....

Last night I went to a Big Bash. I am really not made for that. Always afterwards I feel very puzzled and "fed up." I cannot figure why. The people are for the most part handsome and highly intelligent, really tops in whatever they are doing or have done. Mostly they are birthright or long-time Valley people, like Dagmar Sullivan, the fourth generation owner of Beaulieu Vineyards, daughter of the Marquise des Pins. Some of them are newcomers, like the Norman Strausses, the Arthur Haileys, who may or may not make it into the "real" group. I am, by choice, a maverick. I like some of the people very much, and they seem to keep on wanting me to come to their places, but by now they know that I never give parties like last night's and that I am often away and that when I am here I almost always say that I am too busy to go to their Little Luncheons and Drinks on the Lawn and and and.

I went to the thing last night because it was the annual Bash of some really dear friends, Paco and Romilda Gould. He is a weird lovable old boy, very Cincinnatus and Racket Club and and and. She is Ticinese, a Swiss "patrician" and still with dual citizenship because she is patricienne of the Peri family in Cavigliano. Remarkable woman. Well... last night I would have begged off, because of course I would not see much of the Goulds anyway at such a rout... but through the grapevine (especially active in this locale, ha ha laff) I heard it was a test run on inviting the two warring Mondavi Brothers. Everybody even faintly interested in the wine industry is on the eager about this: the brothers have split, and Bob is starting his own winery, which completely upsets the balance in the Valley, with Peter keeping on the old winery, control of hundreds of acres of really noble vineyards, etc etc. All this is indeed micro-cosmic... but at least it explains why I did go to the party, even though I knew it would leave me mysteriously disturbed, not because of the Mondavi feud but because such parties always do.

Ah well and ho hum. It was elegant, as all Gould parties are, and most beautiful on the lawns and under the great oaks behind the Krug Winery, and the people were well-bred and important and mostly nice to look at, and the bar was impeccably served by a smart good Negro who knows more about all those people than they do, and his wife Luana and her three girls served a delicious buffet-type thing after count-less masterful "hors d'oeuvres américaines" made by Romilda who is a fine cook, and by now I feel almost depressed, except that it is a heavenly cool grey morning and I am writing to a strange shadow who has abruptly become more real to me than any of these tangibles.

I'm up with you! Hah! 18.viii.66: I think that this is the second of two letters you wrote that day. The first will come along. In it I am almost sure that you are growling over the bone of To Write or Not To Write on buses. It is up to you. If you wrote to me once a week, say, for the rest of my life, I'd be very excited and happy. If you gave me enough warning and then only wrote once a *month,* I'd feel the same way. But while it lasts, I feel it about getting as many letters from you as your life will allow.

As for my little game of catching up, don't worry about it. I did. Now all I must do is catch up with *myself.* I know from experience that quite soon now I'll dive into the work, which is organizing itself in my conscious and subconscious work-shop. When your daemon is in command.......

No, I can't measure *Toys* against this new book. Yet. But I should think you would be vastly pleased that someone finds the new one better. Pleased as a writer. I am... for you, I mean.

I never got to the 46th Floor. I have a suspicion that it is mostly the TL Magazine people who get that far. The Book people seem to have a compulsion to get outside the building. Then there is said to be a very tartly poor cafeteria on the 5th or 6th (?) where plain (but TL) People go. And of course there is a basement restaurant. Oh my. But how reassuring that you ate some good food! And how pleased I am that you liked the Berner Bahnhof. We did too, over many years. As I remember, there was quite a good brasserie-café, and then upstairs a small dark rather elegant restaurant with wonder-ful fresh Swiss wine and, very amazingly, one of the best curries I ever ate, with a great number of condiments....

I am anxious to get the first letter you wrote on the 15, because you complained about not getting mail from me. Ah well. By now you have eaten your cruel words, I bet.

Letting the wives join the banquet for coffee reminds me of Dickens's first banquet in America given by New York City, where his wife and a few ladies were permitted to sit in a screened anteroom and watch the men eat.... They got no food *or* drink!

If you go to Paris for the weekend, will you fly? Or spend 12 days at sea for the two days there? Either way it sounds shocking to me, mostly because I am envious of course....

I did not STOP telling you that I loved you, as you know by now. I simply got the qualmies about being so overt or or or or... I'm sorry if it scared you too. But I do love you, Arnold, and am quite bewildered about it. Now and then I wonder if I am smart enough to cope with it properly. I feel clumsy. I doubt my own abilities to handle what at times seems a hopelessly complicated situation and at other times something simple and natural and fine and and and. Forgive me for being somewhat complicated, myself. And accept as god's truth that I am very glad we met again, in every way. I love U

....

St. Helena, California   *19.viii.66*
To: Arnold Gingrich

My dear fellow-member: First of all, I love you.

How's that for Direct Action, eh?

Next, this is a kind of announcement of A Battle Won. I am not going to write to you any more in the early mornings, for a time: I have let some really rather essential stuff like a report to Henry Volkening and so on go by the boards, because I have felt a strong need to establish a good firm clear contact with you after our parting. Now I think we have. All I want is to know that you know I am here, and attentive, and loving, as well as impatient, frustrated, fretful, cranky, demanding, and a few other things. Let me know when you are sure of this, and we're off on Chapter 6000 of our ritten [*sic*] romance.

Today you cheated: two letters in one envelope. Bonus for me. I reply. It is quite late. Since dusk, I have talked with a friend who was involved in a later meeting with the Planning Commission (among other things). We went down to the Pub and had a glass of very good White Pinot. Then work... phone calls... made myself a drink... got interrupted... work... then a long (2 hours) visit from a very troubled woman whose daughter within the past five months has become an overt paranoid, comade (That's comrade) of my girls... then a quick trot through the cool silent streets to the PO... adjust the faucets for slow night trickles, and change the hoses... inside build new slow drink and take care of some business letters... now to a few minutes with the person who has emerged as perhaps my *raison d'être* in this pattern *sans raison (apparent)*. I am like the old woman in the Provençal Christmas pageant, with my hands frozen upward in a gesture of pure astonishment, that you are in love with me....

Fairly soon, to continue this breakdown of past-present-future, I'll go down to the Bysement, where the Pub is, and make two beds, one for myself and one for my sister Norah, who plans to come over from the North Coast for Monday night. There are three good beds down there, used also for couches, with dark green corduroy covers on them (studio couch). There is also a very good toilet-room with shower.

Then I will come upstairs again and make myself a little fresh tomato omelet, first having put out the list for the milkman for the long weekend. I may or may not drink a glass of milk. I may put some brandy in a glass of milk and take it up to the Attic, where I am sleeping while it is still cool enough. That is my favorite place. Sometimes in summer it is as much as forty degrees hotter than the Bysement, and then I am "down under." In the winter it can become very cold. Then I turn on a little old-fashioned electric pad which I put on my belly. That is enough. Occasionally there is a windstorm, and then the Attic rocks like a bird's nest. I love it up there. Best. One reason is that there is a double-bed. I like to stick my legs into the cool corners.

Tomorrow I plan to get up AND NOT WRITE TO YOU. I must be stern and attend to *rudely* neglected letters to people like my dear Henry Volkening, my colleague Michael Field.

On this subject I had a really warm letter from Julia Child. I think that possibly she and Paul[1] have become good friends. I hope so. I really am drawn to them, for a thousand reasons. You'd approve.

But what I started to tell you was that about 6:30 my friend June Eddy called from Los Angeles. She was discreetly and unblamingly worried about my not having written. Suddenly I faced the cold fact that I had been home ONE WEEK. I had neglected this dear friend. I had been too casual about a hundred other basically important things. I felt abashed by my slothful self-indulgence.

That is when I said I would write to my darling Mr. Rich, silly old droopy lovable elf-basset, famous editor, belles-lettrian (I SAW that word somewhere... don't blame *me*...), authority in Korporation Kultur, angler compleat, #1 houseboy and attendant, man-about-world, collector of fiddlin-stuff, self-named sexual athlete ("in good condition"), dandy, connoisseur of fine cars and fine wimmin. Also damned with sincerity. (That's where I come in, I think?)

So here is the letter, and I have not yet even got to sentence One. I am replying to 16.viii.

The "evocative" card from the Clift was coincidence. Also when I see anything at all, from a postcard to the picture of you leering down the length of your bow, I make it ours. Direct Approach.

This thing of memory is very tricky. All you can do is trust *your own*. I learned this early. I would swear on my own honor or the crucifix of the Holy Child or whatever was most real to me at the moment that what I remembered of a certain moment-in-Time was what actually transpired. But my sister Anne, a very complex and sensitive woman who through no fault of ours grew up in my shadow and hated it, would swear with the same inward sincerity that a completely different thing had happened to the two of us at exactly the same moment in both time and space. At first this frightened me. Then I came to realize that ALL men are islands, no matter what old Donne said. Some bell may toll for all of us, if we are able to hear it, but by god we hear it as no man ever hears it, even the one standing beside us or wrapped in our arms. What you remember is not what anyone else in the world remembers, E X A C T L Y, even if the names are the same....

1. Paul Child, Julia's husband

So stop fretting about your memory. It is yours alone. Somewhere at the beginning of whatever you write, make it clear (for your libel lawyers) that this is *your* version of such-and-such.

And even then you will be sorry, now and then, to have accepted the responsibility, IN PRINT, of baring what might mean one thing to you and quite a different thing to another person involved in the same happening. A good case in point is my rejection by Madame Lanes, this summer. The happenings in the minds and hearts of three people I never knew, her sister-in-law, niece, and aged London friend, could never be foreseen by me, when they apparently mistranslated a book[2] Mme. L had already thoroughly enjoyed, to make her hate me. How can one possibly know about these things? What I remember of her, and was able to put onto paper, even translated into French with malice, is not at all what any other human being would remember of her.

You must write without fear, arrière-pensée. From what I know of you, you are without cruelty. I pray I am right about this.

Oh… back to the letter (double): I'll send you the book by Hal. I'll send you mine… I have some others. It will be a few days. I think it will give you a new slant on some of the problems with Janie. (Or even A. G.?)

That Paris junket shapes into quite a Thing, if you are trying to get your three boys there. Damn. I want to come along. But I am so glad you can turn it into a real caper. GO AHEAD. If they are like my own actual and ex officio offspring, they will come easier if you send tickets and travelling-money. . . .

That Collect thing hasn't turned up yet. I am feeling rather twitchy. But tomorrow is Saturday, one more chance before the black hollow of the Sabbath....

What's this about making girls laugh out loud…? I think that was lil ole small-mouthed MFKFPF??????? I can remember a couple-several times when I have practically guffawed because of something you've said. Who is this other dame you refer to?:::: "one, that I know of, I once made laugh out loud." //////??????? I can't see why you did not tease a lot of them into that very pleasurable euphoric state of open deep-gut laughing....

(When I was a little girl, I would sit with sharp pencils pulling up the corners of my mouth, to stretch it. I would be laughed at and sent out of the classroom. But I had been told that women with little mouths were selfish and "spoiled," except perhaps once by Dillwyn Parrish who treated me as if I were worth the trouble. Significant data volunteered by patient, this would be marked on hospital report of Psychiatric Referral Case.)

Now to 17.viii.66: *Born Free* is STILL running in the SF movie nearest the Clift. I almost went (Again!), but didn't… took a long shower instead. Then I ordered a good supper, as I told you. And idly I switched on the enormous TV and there was a re-run of one of Julia Child's things. I was in the bathroom, and got an eerie déjà-vu feeling, for she is exactly the same, on and off sound. So no *Born Free*. But lucky you, since you like it!

2. *Map of Another Town*

Now my darling Arnold Ging-as-in-Singrich, you say I can send you a kind woid. Have I not? Do you not know that I am out here on the West Coast trying very hard not to sound absolutely daffy? Just because I am typing, and not writing in a trembling hand, that I love you and am fascinated by you and am scared of you and a few things like that, don't think I am turning it out like toothpaste out of the tube. I am SUFFER-ING. I MISS YOU. I want to be with you, together, whatever the way it will be. I think you are a very strange mysterious wonderful person. I can't see what you see in me. That is the truth. But *néanmoins* I am to hell-and-gone out here trying not to sound absolutely mawkish, and you say, "Send me a kind woid." *IDIOT*...

There'll be what I found on proofing a rather dull thing in the Aug 27 *NYer.* THEY say. I never know. Then three or four book reviews, all about books long since remain-dered or OP. I'd better throw something else into the chopper. Tomorrow I start on the TL thing. I mean I *do.*

Dear Insatiable, you need direct contact, and there was a time when it got cut off. I'm sorry. I was in-flight. Reassure me that all is well again. Play me a little tune... a gay one.

....

Berkeley, California   *14.ix.66*
To: Arnold Gingrich

My darling Arnold, my pride and Joy... It is 2:30 and I just this minute sat down at this damned machine... got here twenty minutes ago with letters of 9, 10, and 12, and sat in the filthy but rather comfortable armchair to refresh my soul. You were indeed rather frustrated, this past weekend. I think in a way it is a kind of outlet for you, to get to the wrong movies, have the gas run out, lose half a cuff-link. If these things did not preoccupy you physically, you might well disintegrate, or simply form a small puddle on the sidewalk which nobody but me would ever know about. So be thankful for small favors in the shape of bent fenders etc etc....

For god's sake hold on, in other words. I confess without shame that I too want to eat a crumb or two of the world-generous pie marked A. G. I want to be in on this jug-gling act of yours. I want to be with you if and when you form that small puddle some-where. I am selfish. I am greedy. I want to be with you, sometime, someplace.

I am not angry about this. You don't need to be told... that I am not, I mean. I am not impatient. I realize coolly what I am saying, and all the horrible implications which might be made by anyone but you. I am not afraid of them. Janie, that poor furi-ous witty beautiful spoiled woman, must live her time. But if some of you is left over, I want it. That's all.

Life has been somewhat hit-or-miss here. A few highlights: Norah insisted on cook-ing last night, after a very long demanding day, so I got the things she needed yesterday afternoon, and she turned out an unnecessary but quite good vitello alla parmigiana and I did green beans, and so on, all really to please David,[1] home less than 20 hours...

1. David Barr, Norah's son

and he left to have dinner with friends! Ah well. Oh... I was really booming along, yesterday afternoon, and Anna called with panic in her too-controlled voice, and said casually that she felt quite lonely, and I was up there pronto, very nonchalant too, and this morning she thanked me understanding that she really needed me and I told her that I had faced such moments too. Then... let's see... this morning before I left for work (Norah left at 6:30 for a 7 o'clock breakfast) Marge called that her brakes had failed. Hah. So I could not come to work. At 9:45 I took Anna to the doctor, and sat with Chris in the car for the "50-minutes hour." Frustration here was that if I'd known he would snooze most of the time I'd have brought a book, for I simply cannot read, right now: it takes me two weeks to read a 2-hour book, a snatch now and then at night. Ho hum again. Or did I say Ah well? Last night David got bored with his Antioch friends and brought them back to the house, where they played Beetles and Flamenco quite late... not so thoughtful in a large wooden house with small baby and two elderly ladies who must get up for work the next day (Noni and me). But David is 18. And he really is a darling person. Marge came at 1:30 and I headed down the hill. It is the kind of brilliant day that at Le Pâquis would promise a storm. The bay is slate-blue, with many freighters between the City and Treasure Island.

Did I tell you I had to have a new clutch put in the Caravelle? I am thinking perhaps I should dish it for a damned Ford Compact... second hand. I have put more into this little lovely than I paid for it, and I do not trust it at all on the ghastly hill I am apparently slated to climb indefinitely to Norah's. (I think it is essential for a time longer that I be here where Anna can count on me. Norah cannot be called from her work. Anna is not well enough to be completely alone. So... I pray this will not mean my getting an apartment, for I simply cannot afford it, and it would not be good for Anna to live alone with me. The Barr Boys will soon have their own apartments, and I know Norah likes to have us there... she is not used to living alone, as I more or less am....)

Arnold, I really feel quite sappy and mawkish, babbling along about these family logistics. I must try to remember that you were my flattering but stony editor long before you became, by some fantastic twist, my Beamish Boy. Perhaps some of the details will interest or even amuse you, although I don't think I've been very funny lately.

Yesterday and today I concocted what is quite possibly a master-stew... fine beef in a sauce I kept rather mild because Chris will eat it too, with carrots, little onions, little potatoes. We'll have it for supper tonight, with a cold salad first of marinated green beans... and a bottle of Norah's Bordeaux... she has the remnants of a sporadically good wine cellar. (The one in the Pub is strictly local... I can't afford the imported wines I would buy, and prefer the Californias I know to the mediocre French and German ones.)

If I stop this now, I will have about an hour-plus to work. Murder. But I feel very relaxed and fatalistic about the book. I am coping fairly well with a really sticky family situation, and am working fast when I do work. So... nitchevo.[2] ?Are we downhearted, fellahs? Niet. ?Are we crazy? Da.

2. Russian expression meaning *that's fate.*

The other day Anna and I looked at the existent bills she abandoned in her flight to NY. I thought it was very brave of her. Finally she said, "But Dote, you don't seem to be worried or horrified or or or..." I told her that I was disgusted and that I felt very badly and that I hated the whole mucky affaire, but that I absolutely refused to let it affect my inner balance... words to that effect. What I could not say to her was that I felt that I had developed so much scar-tissue that I was literally a little numb to such gad-fly things as debts, threats, all that. She could not possibly understand. What I did not like about this, though, was that I know that I *have*, willy-nilly, accumulated quite a bit of scar-tissue during the past 58 years, and that I regret it because by the time we are together you may find me too detached, perhaps phlegmatic or or or. I did not like this thought. Of course if a man wanted a fresh unscarred threshold-of-life creature to be his girl, he would not choose a woman my age....

I MUST stop, and hurl myself back into a discussion of provincial French kitchens. (Which reminds me... Achtung Braggies!... I get very nice fan-mail about that thing on Provençal kitchens... it rather surprises me. I have a dreadful thing about Provençal flies. I bet Shawn would find it disgusting, but think I may send it along... ????)

If all goes well, I can leave Chris with Marge on Thursday, and drive to St. H. with Anna, who wants to look at a hideous pile of junk brought from her abandoned house in Berkeley. We'll see. I think it will be hard emotionally for her. Myself, I refuse to make that drive with the baby in the car, in one day. And I simply cannot afford to be away two, until this masterpiece is done. . . .

....

Berkeley, California   *8.ix... no, x.66*
To: Arnold Gingrich

My dearest Ginger... a very fast one... it is later than I think, but I have finally finished the last chapter on the book... now I take the three I have done in the past three days up the Hill (Anna is in a very low period and needs me "around"...), and I THINK I can get them to St. Helena on Monday... I may drive them up.

I am HELLISHLY sorry that you got chopped down a little by the Knopf boys. But you are an editor. You have done it to other people. One good friend of mine told me he brooded for twenty years about some ruthless surgery you did on a story in the early days of *Esquire.* Then he read it in an anthology and he practically kneeled in your direction and bowed to the ground, for you had been right all along. I don't know about this present bit of surgery. There are a couple of anecdotes which I rather suspected would get the knife. As I told you, I did find the chapter on learning to read rather tedious, or perhaps somewhat distasteful because you seemed to enjoy picturing yourself as a brat going "Waaah" all the time, which did not enhance the image of your parents, either. You must remember that I have only one quick reading to rely on. But I do NOT agree about taking out the Budapest thing about language. Perhaps it needs some polishing? After all, few writers turn out impeccable prose, the first time 'round.... In my own case, and in yours too, we know the old newspaper tricks of hot copy. BUT actually there is very little really good prose in modern journalism. Now and then a story comes from deep emotion... but usually it comes from a very experienced old hand at the game. This last you are... as evidenced by *A Thousand Violins*. But there are places where your prose can be tightened, as I feel confident you would be first to admit, if you were still not so close to the book.

I don't know if you dislike my talking this way. I am being detached....

It is fine weather here. We need rain (Not you!). I think there is a football game, which means it will take me a half-hour to get up the hill... the stadium is smack at the bottom of it. Ho hum.

Could you not get off your weekend-kick for once, and go fishing with a friend? It might give you new steam for the winter! I feel that you are a little shack-nasty, and God knows I do not blame you. But this gag about Saint-Angel can wear thin.

Have you ever thought of putting a small heated pool inside? June Eddy is having one built into her new house... tiny, but completely adequate for therapy for a badly damaged spine. Inside, Janie might use it.... Of course it is no good at all for the free-wheeling dolphin-type swimming I am sure you do.... But it is infinitely less expensive, and very good exercise in the cold months. (Lady from Phila. Dept.)

I must dash... market again, damn it, and then home. Tomorrow I must Chris-sit... have encouraged Anna to go with Erika (picnic lunch) to the Greek Bowl to see *Elektra*.... I'll catch up with letters, MAYBE.

Be of good cheer, my darling boy. Sit crosslegged and contemplate your navel. Catch a trout. Think of next May when the soft shell crabs will be in again. Think of me... last May or next May... or even October 8.

....

St. Helena, California   *5.xi.66*
To: Arnold Gingrich

Darling Ginger... here I am again, twice now this morning, waiting for someone, this time an old beau who comes up-Valley for Joe Heidt's dry sherry and likes to stop here too... he is interesting, a very aged buccaneer and mining engineer (Hear hear!).... He always brings sherry, which I perforce drink through the meal, which I hate, and I have some bread and cheese... and today I have found an excellent NY Cheddar (perhaps a little too nippy) and some beautiful crisp apples. Ah well and ho hum. I would like to be with you. . . .

The North side of the house looks terribly spindly. We took out probably fifty poles, some of them very tall. It is basically fun. I like a modicum of order, in order to have everything survive, and I also like change. (When I say these pompous nothings, it is to let you know of what you are in for, perhaps....)

Well... I did compromise with Williams.[1] This idea of having "name" writers instead of anonymous "editors" on the T-L series is his. My book is his first proof of its rightness... I mean, his theory's rightness. So... I spent two harrowing days going over

1. Richard Williams, editor of the Time-Life book

every directive, from him, Julia Child, Irene Saint, Waverley Root, Helen Isaacs, etc etc... wrote ten pages of comments, mostly saying "Omit///cut out... agree///do as you wish..." and mailed them this morning. Williams called and wanted to come out at once and spend no matter how long to "rewrite" with him. I refused flatly. So he is accepting my list, and then *himself* rewriting. Then he is sending me his copy. If I think it still sounds enough like Fisher to carry that proud name (!), I'll go along. Otherwise... I told him flatly and in print too that I think he is taking a real gamble, for I cannot at this moment reconcile my own performance of the original contract with what has lately been demanded. He is willing to gamble. Poor guy... I think he is desperate. So... I am shet of it for a time longer. You may pat my back, darling Ginger.

Aside from that... let's see... Anna called from Berkeley yesterday afternoon, very docile and confused: I had been asked by Norah to go to Berkeley today for two days, but she had changed her mind, etc. Was I or was I not "needed" there? Etc. So I went into a real flip for about two hours of ABYSMAL weltschmertz. Nobody loved me, nobody needed me to bring in kindling, I could not write for beans, I had spent God knows how many years making ghastly mistakes, etc. So I drew a long bath and put in much more than my usual pinchy drab of bath-oil, all this rather early, and I was not hungry, and I thought I would take a long voluptuous BATH and go up to the Attic and read and sip a little milk with rum in it and to hell with life. So I did. I got in the tub. The telephone rang and I felt it was important which it was, and I dripped through four rooms and stood cooling off for several minutes while happy friends called from Mexico City about fairly nice relatively important news. So I got back into the tub, adding more hot water, just in time to get out again for a long talk with Julia and Paul Child. (They were leaving for Plascassier[2]... got bounced off a big Italian liner because of "mechanical difficulties" which Paul said he thought meant No Passengers, so were taking the *Queen Mary*...). They were very sorry but protective, always a nice reaction, about my T-L contretemps. I really do like them.

While I was standing there in the livingroom, thankful that I had not cut the bamboo masking the windows, two friends arrived. I waved them moistly to seats (in another room), went sideways out when I had finally said goodbye to the Childs, and put on something or other. They sat around. So I never got to bed in the state I meant to. As a matter of fact I felt much better than I would have, when I finally got there, if you can figure that out. I got rid of people, and then coddled two fresh eggs in some good broth I keep on hand, making it from day to day with drainings from vegetables and an occasional meat-cube (Gawd!), and ate them somewhat resolutely, and then went to the Attic with a mug of milk and rum. Hah. Fine light delicious sleep. A few minor tangles with the subconscious. Up this morning three minutes after the 7 o'clock matins rang from the

... long lapse here... from the Catholic Church one block away. But what I was going to say after that, who knows? I have spent a wild woolly day, and it is rather late and I have not finished answering your very welcome but basically disturbing letter written on yellow paper on 1.xi.66. Well. I'll continue the report on MFKF... yesterday I

2. Julia and Paul Child's house in Provence

M.F.K. Fisher: A Life in Letters

did make the compromise with T-L, and (no, this was two days ago) did write the stuff… have I said all this? I dare not re-read this letter for fear of tearing it to bits and then not having anything to bother you with when you come in to fiddle at 5-ish A.M.… I ended by feeling 'orrible. Bath episode. Julia and Paul Child called. I felt better. Etc. Yes, I have said this I am sure, but I talk to you all the time for god's sake and can't talk back to MYSELF can I? So today I spent quite nicely, and now I am about to capitulate to my baser instincts and eat something "easy" and go to bed again. Up there I can read, and look at the treetops, and listen to Sat. night Jazz from a few small stations, and sleep in artificial innocence.

Ginger, we are not at all on the same beam about being writers, and you must face this and *now*. You care about publicity, because you and your mind and your habits and your life are geared to it. I do not. I do not care at all if you (or I!) must sign 100 copies of a book. You do. So you go on and care. But don't worry if I do not care, *either* for you or for myself. This is, when one is young and ambitious, a possible block to bliss, whether wedded or not. Neither of us is young but you at least care very much about being a "writer." I do not. Can you stand this attitude in me? Can you stand to leave me alone in it? DF married me partly to be the husband of a fantastically successful female. When he found I wanted only to be successful AS a female, he developed psychogenic stomach pains. I must not let this happen again to anyone I love and admire. (I did not admire him much, in the end, and I detested him for many good reasons, but I gave him all my love.) (I gave it to him while I felt that I had promised to. Now I simply detest him, with an enormous pity.)

Well… I got off the track there. Forgive me, please. I wanted to say that I *understand* your amusement and keenness about signing books and doing FM programs and having interviews and all that, but that I myself am honestly and totally and perhaps completely even-yetski detached from all such shenanigans in re: Fisher. And I don't want you to worry or fret about this.

Catch?

Someday call me in the morning and start out, "Well I'll be a son of a bitch." Really, that's the way I felt too, when I reached toward the west and picked up that telephone, the other pre-day///////

Do you and Janie go to double feature drive-in etc. movies because you don't want to play two-handed bridge? I know many people that way.

And now it's Sunday, a *beautiful* rainy one with some storming promised… snow in the mountains, winds at sea. I love it. The bamboo on the North side is whipping happily, and on the South, very thick and uninhibited, it is lashing about heavily. Great. Nice noises against the sides of the house, the windows. My attic is like a bird's nest, especially in times like this one, and I almost decided to stay in bed today and listen to everything. But I got up. The house is dim. I love it. I prowl about, contentedly, but of course discontented with myself with merely prowling instead of scrubbing the kitchen floor etc etc etc.

I worked for two too-long days on replying to the numberless questions-suggestions-etc fired at me from four or five different directions. I hope it will be all right. I was very flat-footed about telling Williams I feel it quite a gamble. Frankly I don't think it will dim my tiny light too much to sign something I damn well know is not the way I would want it. I don't think the people who buy this subscription come-on are looking for my inimitable style so much as they are for one more status-symbol of quasi-literacy. Well. That sounds pretty god-awful "negative," as Julia would say.

Sorry if I've repeated all this. I don't dare re-read this screed. Did I tell you I finally did get that bath, and by that time felt quite cheerful again, out of the megrims?

Great if you find any duplicates or or or for the Wine Liberry. I hope you are a tiny-winy bit impressed by the list? Myself, I think it very promising. Then we are getting a lot of old and new pamphlets and house organs... labels... artifacts... taped conversations with very old wine people....

Thanks for dates for your next two flittings. Add them to your proposed "cruises" and your yearly stint at the Library and you sound almost *in absentia!* How do you manage it?

. . . Your skillful résumé of the "disaster-cruise" horrifies and disgusts me. I have too many questions in my head, from reading it twice. Why, for instance, take a suicidal alcoholic 180 miles by ambulance from NY when there are both Bellevue and Harkness right there? Sure, "her" doctor was there! But does he not have colleagues? Well, you see I become impatient about such goings-on. And I think one either puts up or shuts up.

You seem to have gone along with every suggestion, followed every whim... from a need to feel noble and forgiving, a mixture of masochism and subconscious revenge, or love of the woman. She has brought you to your knees and kept you there, perhaps in a perverse form of love of *you*. So... if she herself demanded a chance at "reconciliation," with the doctor's backing, and then continued the Mack Sennett act until you were plainly the laughing-stock of everyone on the ship, she must also have hated your guts for consenting to the horrible farce. Her probably psychotic attempt to brain you would indicate drastic need for psychiatric help, probably for both of you, and I am appalled that the doctor would recommend your going on a long cruise together if he knew anything at all about Janie's real reasons for barring you from her room and trying to hurt you with "flying objects." Has anyone tried to find out *why* she pretends to hate you and want to destroy you? Perhaps more important, has anyone asked why you seem to make her want to? And now that something like The Wrath of God has struck her, does anyone question your motives in isolating her in a place she mocks and detests, and in your self-inflicted "duties" like rain-soaked bus rides, ugly onerous trips to drive-ins, etc etc etc?

In other words, I don't dig it, man.

And I think she should have been left to carry out her own wishes, both in NY and in Lisbon. What is wrong with jail? Did she pull the tug of war just to humiliate you further, or to *escape*? Escape from What? You? Why not let her? What are you proving, and to whom?

You see, I don't dig it. I'm with Dr. Baker.

So... having opted once more for "ignominious servitude," what did you do with your victim-victorious while you were having your guts chopped? How did she get along? Was she happy not to have to bar her door against your intolerable advances etc etc?. . .

Well... the reason I asked you why the cruise was a disaster was because you called it that and seemed to indicate to me that you expected me to rise to the bait, which I did because everything you tell me about yourself, for no matter what reason and no matter how inadvertently, interests me profoundly. That's why.

I spent about ten days dockside in La Quayra... think I told you about it. Not pretty... We went up to Caracas for one day... had no more money. At night we could hear the people in the houses coughing... very high TB rate among poor... and poor are about 97% of population. Other 3% kept very fancy fishing-boats, mostly for pleasure, near our dock, and it was fun in a terrible way to listen to the music, usually played and sung by the "cabin-boy"... the captain would be sober enough, but the owners and their beautiful floozies were limber-drunk before they even left port. Then once there was a "Liberian" ship docked next to us, and at night we could see the beautiful black officers in whites, at cocktails with people down from Caracas, very elegant compared to our near-imprisonment. Hah. How the other half lives!

Oh yes, I know I am better off, both economically and for my own pleasure, with the *NYer* than anywhere else. They pretty much let me alone... a few changes here and there... Mr. Shawn loves commas more than I do....

I love your wild eye. I'm glad you don't mind me for that.

My dearest Arnold... I think of you-me-us all the time. ALL THE TIME. It is there in my mind and heart, wondering, pondering, enjoying. Oh... almost forgot to tell you: last night for the first time I know about I dreamed of you! You were the head of a very large delightful family, and I had been invited to your beach house for a weekend. You were married to a rather plain dull woman, polite to me but harried by the large untidy ill-managed house. Once we all sat down for supper and waited and waited, but nobody had remembered to cook anything. I looked down the long table at the wife, sitting there, and saw you, very small and tired, sound asleep, leaning on her shoulder like a child. Before the meal you asked me very politely if I would like a drink, but I remembered what you had said about never having any wine or liquor in the house because of Janie and when I politely said no, you looked very relieved that I had remembered. Once when we were all sitting around in the very cluttered shabby livingroom (the wife kept showing me over the house, apologizing for the mixture of comfortable but bad furniture, and I kept politely assuring her it was a friendly and nice house, which it was), you came very close to me to say something, and touched my arms, and I began to shake, and thought impatiently, "My God, cannot he know that this is torture, to be here at all? How can he dare *touch* me, when he knows how much I love and desire him? Where can I go to tell him this?" There was a darling rather dark-skinned little girl, one of the children, who announced that she was going to be my five-year-old mother. "Lie back now in this chair," she said, while everyone laughed

with pleasure at her serious play-acting, "and I will cover you up and take care of you."
And this is all I remember of the dream, except that it left me with a feeling of real
worry about your obvious exhaustion and harassment... which is of course with me in
my conscious mind too.

Now I MUST stop. Today I must reply to a sheaf of long-neglected letters from
some of my Piney Woods students... some are doing very well, at Tuskegee and in Tou-
galoo.... Did I tell you my young friend from Bastuo—that's *Basuto*-land... has been
made president of the African Students Union at Tuskegee? I am proud of him.

I am proud of you too, Ginger. You know what you are doing, of that I am sure. You
are doing it with grace. That is something I myself pray for... I am far behind you. I
love A.G. M.F.K.F.P.F.

....

St. Helena, California   *11.xi.66*
To: June Eddy

I feel very much like a Veteran today, but in no mood to celebrate the fact! How
about you? . . .

I am trying to growl my way into some *NYer* stuff. It's a fine grey moisty day. Perfect
for reading a couple of Simenons on the couch. Ah well. My super-ego would make
me too guilty.... I think I like the silly old name of Armistice Day, rather than Veterans.
I would *like* to declare some sort of armistice, any old one... with Time, or perhaps
even Space?

I just noticed something consummately silly on my calendar: Godliness with contentment is great gain (Timothy 6:6). What on earth is the man talking about?

Here is something quite funny, in a macabre way, from the Hemet *Star*: the frantic
request of the school board to have an officer help schoolchildren cross Main Street
was turned down by the chief of police on the grounds that placing one of his officers
at the dangerous intersection "would be running considerable risk to his life." Or *is*
that as horribly funny as it sounds to me?

....

St. Helena, California   *24.ii.67*
To: Janet Flanner

I wish almost painfully, dearest Genêt, that I could slip a note under your door, this
minute, and ask if we could meet in the beautiful old bar for a drink. I miss you very
much, which is presumptuous even to say, but which is true.

I regret that I have been bad about writing. I remember you said you like postcards,
and I was going to send many to you, simply as a form of contact. But I have not even
done that!

Perhaps it is a little the fault of your "letters." When I read them I hear you talking,
and see you, and often I reply... but that of course is not putting things on paper, from
my end!

The truth is that I am in a kind of remoteness, or slump. I am very much involved with "family" and constant changings of plans, and all that, and I cannot feel that it is of interest to anyone, and yet I am not skilled enough to rid my thoughts of it, so that I can perhaps be interesting on other planes. This will change, of course.

Anna shows much improvement, both physically and spiritually. But she is still unable to face returning to so-called adult life, and really I cannot much blame her! Meanwhile Jean-Christophe flourishes, and will be two in a few weeks. They have been up here for two or three days each week while Anna had a lot of dental repair work done (I hope it horrified her to see what neglect and bad diet did to her beautiful teeth...), and that of course meant two days each week of driving to and from Berkeley with them. I find it impossible to work while they are here... and that left me two harried days to cope with dull stuff like check-books. A miserable schedule. Now there is a respite in the dentistry... and I find myself rendered absolutely mute by the prospect of two or three uninterrupted weeks. I could not produce a page of Deathless Fisher if a gun were against my skull. Numb, dumb, dry as a crumb... that's me! But I am trying not to kick too much... "when your Daemon is in command, wait, listen, and obey"!

So... after I have written this note to you, I shall go out and stain two new bookcases... since I cannot meet you in the Old Bar.

I think you use exactly the right word when you say that last year was for many people malevolent. It was a striking thing, to me. It strengthens my feeling that we are more than we understand in the power of the planets and stars. I can't quite believe in so-called astrology. But certainly we are swayed, just like the waters and seeds, by the Moon... and why not other less obvious influences? Whatever the causes, too many of my near friends did indeed find last year malevolent.

I had a lot of trouble in it, myself, but there were many good things... the main one, quite probably, was meeting you at the Monhoffs[1] and then having the really freakish luck to be in Paris. No matter how fed up I got with the Time-Life job, I never forgot that.

This morning a nice-sounding man named John McFee [*sic*] called me from the *NYer,* but not on business, or at least so he said... he had turned up a letter I wrote to him a couple of years ago from Mississippi, and wanted to apologize for not having answered it. I felt sympathetic, since part of my present weltschmerz is obviously caused by my knowing that ten or twelve wonderful people are hurt at my long silence. As a matter of fact, I had forgotten all about this young man, but talking with him made me feel more strongly than ever that I MUST write to you, NOW, TODAY.

I keep thinking that the Time-Life thing is over and done with. But last week I spent two days looking at galleys, and *fortunately,* for some fancy re-writing had crept in again, in spite of Dick Williams's sincere wish to avoid it. I feel that since I have been this disagreeable, I must stand fast, and not let them add stuff which I could not possibly have written to what has already been thoroughly chopped and kicked about... at least as long as they insist that I must sign it. I often wish they had capitulated to my first announcement that I would not. But I confess that it was a great help to have that

1. Hildegarde Flanner Monhoff, poet and Janet Flanner's sister, lived with her husband on a ranch near St. Helena, which was threatened by a subdivision.

horrid money: the final payment neatly took care of my income and franchise taxes and the certified public accountant, and then of a slight clothes-spree I went on last week, and now I have only a few dollars in my checking account and I feel much more *normal*.

M. Schneider's "complete tyranny" is the only system, and I send him my discreet blessings. Williams told my agent-and-friend Henry Volkening, after he had flown out here to talk me into signing the book, that he had learned a lot about writers from our grisly experience and that "authors DO know more than editors" at least now and then.

Meanwhile, I hope you resist that awful boodle and do not do Gauguin. Don't do anything for that monster-machine. You will be much freer... and really not much poorer!

The Monhoffs are fighting nobly and well, here. I remain pretty much detached, but sympathetic. I am too cynical. I wish I saw them oftener. This split-life I have led since last September has made such things almost impossible... perhaps it will be calmer soon.

I am reading *Speak, Memory*, and I find myself rather let down by it, but perhaps it is because I am not in a right mood. *Lolita* really bored me, but everything else has in one way or another delighted me. *Pale Fire* I found one of the funniest things I had ever read, partly because the intricacies and puns reminded me to the point of helpless laughter of two of my husbands, Al the sententious pompous professor, and Donald the complex multilingual wit.

Thank you for sending the clipping from the Sunday *Times*... it was strange to see it... I noticed they changed "Mike Romanoff's and 21" to "the Ritz and the Savoy" or something like that... I am put off by the British enjoyment (at least it is very overt!) of what one of them has called my gastronomical pornography. Ho hum indeed.

How wonderful it is that you want to communicate with me, and permit me to reply! I am indeed very fortunate, and should be and *am* ashamed to admit to any weltschmertz in the face of such an unexpected blessing from the gods. I hope Paris is beautiful. I hope you are well and keen.

....

St. Helena, California   *8.iii.67*
To: Arnold Gingrich

Dear Grumps, where is Ginger? Your rainsoaked account of the battery conk-out is D*I*S*M*A*L*, and I could weep or scream for you (if I did either which I seldom the first of which and the second never so far...).

HOW DO YOU SURVIVE?

Would you really like it if you did not have to pit yourself against the elements, these last consisting of everything from the morning bus-driver to God Himself? And at least 18 hours a day...

I think you'd be bored silly.

Well. We'll have to talk about this, for I think you would find me M*A*D-D*E*N*N*I*N*G [*sic*]. And it is too late in life for both of us to be that.

Nous allons voir.

The movies sound fine, since you need them. I hear that *A Man*[1] is playing in SF, and if and when I can verify this I'll try to go twice. But tickets are bought weeks in advance, I also hear. Ho hum. At Least that means it will run for a time. Like *Born Free!* I'll simply go down when the throngs thin. Stay in that elevator shaft at the Clift.

I made a date with Miriam Allen deFord, one of my crushes, for dinner Thursday March 16, and *then* found there was not a free bed at the old pad. Ah well, if nothing turns up when I check in with many bags, I'll go down to the very disreputable hotel where Miriam has lived for some 32 years, since her husband Maynard Shipley's death. I spent three days there once. Fantastic experience. (Miriam is in late 70s... president emeritus of Mystery Writers of America... Poe Awards etc... very sharp geriatric case....) (She thinks I am funny too.)

Like you and this man in New Orleans...

I think while I'm gone you'd better send stuff *here*. Except that I'll be in NY March 21–28 at 45 W 12. Explanations when we meet.

Did big operation on north side of house today and planted many ivy-shoots. Am wearing blue peasant get-up, mostly from Plascassier (or rather, Mouans-Sartous, nearest markets...). Have had good day and think I liked job I got conned into doing for Napa Valley Wine Library Association, which I have been putting off. La vie, hélas,

Est compliquée,

Hé...

las

In 1929–30 I went to a movie every night, in Dijon, with my first husband. It was before sound, but we did it to improve our French in the subtitles. I am so basically naïve that it was long after that I realized we did this because he was incapable of staying too long at a time near me without a diversion. Ah well. Oh dear, oh dear. (I should explain that he did not want to fuck me. He was just afraid that I would want it. Sad. Such walls. I would have liked to be alone now and then. I would have liked to sit across a table under a lamp, turning pages of Rousseau (he Shakespeare) or studying tomorrow's lessons, because we both went to the University. But we were raised to bow patiently to Puritanical lust.) Yrs.

....

St. Helena, California   *7.iv.67*
To: Arnold Gingrich

Dearest Mr. Rich... today while I'm waiting for the PO to open I'll take a quick trip through the letters from you which I haven't answered... PLENTY. (But never enough!)

1. *A Man for All Seasons*

They go back to March 20! I'll just say things now and then, pretty much non sequitur unless you remember. . . .

Re Vivaldi, your news by 'phone yesterday about getting the accompaniment is very good. You tend to play as fast as you can to get it over with (!?), concentrating on fingering rather than phrasing. This will hold you down.

About our being 21 years older, thank you but I doubt very much that I'll be around, then. You may, as an angler. I am fed up with the aging processes,[1] much as I admire the few people I know who cope gracefully with them, and I am sure that if I live much longer I should do it alone. I don't think I'll have any energy left for a partner, especially one acquired late in life.

This reminds me: in Hemet there was a legendary couple of sisters, still completely British after some sixty years there. The bossy one finally died (stipulating that she be buried in black velvet *and* artificial pearls *and* the feather tiara her mother had worn when she was presented at Victoria's Court), and one night when Fredrika took the younger sister Miss May home after bridge, May said, "Oh, how wonderful it is that I can finally *live*, now that Annie is gone!" And that night she died in her sleep, at 86. . . .

The Lost Letter never showed up.

If you still have de Groot's *Feasts for All Seasons* I would like it.

You are wrong to talk of Norah and Eleanor as being "against" you. Neither one is. Norah is "against" my becoming emotionally involved with a hedonist or or or, but has nothing "against" *you*. Eleanor wanted to see if you spoke English, I suppose... a cool professional interest, not concerned with me at all. And neither woman would be at all well impressed if you decided to "*perform*," as you say. I myself would have been taken aback, too. So for God's sake don't try to stand on your head when and if you meet June.... They are all very smart women.

The lunch of non-shad roe was delicious, and I thank you. It was fun to taste the 1872 Madeira... first time for me. Paco is coming tomorrow before he leaves for Cavigliano, and I'll tell him about it. He is the only one who would know the flavor... brown and a little oily and beautiful. I liked the light touch of cognac... would not have liked it drowned, I am sure... in the Beef Tartare. As for breakfast, I am now armed to bring my own soup-powder with me!

Glad you liked the blue soft suit. It is nice. I hated it at first... am not used to being given clothes, and June insisted that I buy it and then she paid for it which was basically very loving of her but which irked me a little for a time. I seem to be in a Blue Period... today is wearing new blue stretch pants of jersey, blue espadrilles, blue and white pullover. And I have the new blue knitted suit. What next?

Tonight the Beards and the Ten Broecks are coming to supper... roast duckling (!), puree de marrons, glazed turnips, and chilled fruits (melon, tangerine, and guava...). I must build a fire and do various hausfrau chores. . . .

Stay in Hemet was dream-like... I worked very hard and often felt too tired to sur-

1. MF had had severe arthritis for many years.

vive, and I learned a lot about human courage and silliness. I hope to make some notes, for the OA book... still not in focus.

Again a reference to how you "failed to pass muster" and so on with E. Ridiculous! You are really very masochistic. I suppose that is all right, if you enjoy it enough. But myself, I don't get any kick out of such self-torture or indulgence or whatever it would be called. In this second insistence upon your "failure" you even decided that you would have failed with Kennedy too! Wow... how sick can we get?????

Arnold, I must make this clearer, I think: I have no qualms or hesitations at all about believing that right now we do indeed make a good team. But I cannot con myself into any pink-silk dreams about 21 years from now. I am too realistic, if anything... to combat your somewhat euphoric dreams, perhaps. I live with Carpe Diem engraved on my heart. That is why I can enjoy to the hilt everything you do and say for me, even the Continent apart. I would like to be a full part in your life, this minute. BUT... this cannot be. And I am too world-wise to believe in anything but *now*. I don't want to live with you 21 years from now. By then, if we should both live, we might meet every Wednesday for tea, or something like that. But that is not enough for me, ever. So... I speak harshly but with complete sincerity. I do not plan to be a 79-year-old lollipop, Mr. Rich. Even for you. If I should live that long, I'll be a bag of bones, probably rather bent and even more probably wracked with arthritic pains, irascible in a barely controlled manner, very impatient of human frailties and quirks, concentrated on my own determination to stay vertical and free. Not an exactly lovable picture!

Fredrika gave me a little sleeve-piece almost as "right" as the hand you have... a very old carved peach-pit from China, where she lived for years... almost as intricate as your ring... lewd monkeys, wise old men, jungle, pagoda, all on a little hollowed seed. Do you want to see it? I'll send it back....

And now it is time to go to the PO and the market.... I love you, Arnold, and miss you... and thank you for calling from Chicago, very exciting and fun and reassuring.

....

St. Helena, California   *8.v.67*
To: Arnold Gingrich

Ginger my boy.... I haven't written for a few days, on the theory of "When in doubt, don't." But I feel badly about it, and want to get back to our pattern of almost a year now, as much as feasible. I owe you several good fat letters, and there are a lot of things I want to talk about. . . .

The truth is that I was really thrown by the Chicago book-section you sent me, with your picture on the front and another inside with your "Selected Letters." It dismayed and hurt me, and I think I should tell you so, instead of keeping up a suddenly hypocritical non-mention of it in our letters.

I was hurt because you were writing to one of your professional admirers and contributors almost the same letters you were writing to me, and at the same time.

I was also embarrassed, *for you*, by what seemed to me the bad taste of including this comparative stranger in your family life: Janie's wheelchair nibbles of that yummy popcorn, the fact that she cannot walk, the implication that because she cannot walk you can no longer go fishing, and so on. I found this in uncomfortably poor taste, made even worse by the apparent permission to *publish* it. Your coy ecstasy over the Christmas popcorn has little to do with the progress of modern editing, not to mention human dignity.

Well... the whole thing was a body-blow to me, and I tried very hard to cool off, and then wrote at least five letters telling you *why*, and then I fell back on the when-in-doubt-don't technique. I don't mind the risk of irritating or even insulting you, but I honestly *cannot stand* the thought of hurting you... you the man... you my Ginger.

So if I have done so, I must pay for it by a new loneliness. But it is as clear to me now as it was when I first read that exposé of your whimsy that I must tell you it cut me low. I feel that the apparent compiler of the "Selected Letters" is a ruthless arriviste, and that you have been "had" to further his own tasteless progress. This is the view I prefer. If you consented to this basically pointless display simply to get yourself into public print, willy-nilly, then I must confess that I have been hoist on the petard I erected last May in San Francisco, and withdraw.

I am interested to see that even you have signed yourself CORDIALLY (21.Feb.66)... and that "nobody, even (your) kids and garbage collectors," has ever Mistered you. You never *begged* me, as you did Mr. Gattis, to call you just plain old Arnold, but I do anyway in my mind and heart, and I also call you *Mister* Rich!

Cordially, then... but with love.

....

St. Helena, California   *26.v.67*

To: Arnold Gingrich

My dear Ginger-boy, I wrote you a long letter this morning, just after two came from you. Once more I shan't send them.[1] The trouble with me is that I am a trained writer, and that when I am feeling angry or disgusted or dismal I can and often do put it into words that are too apt. You asked in one of your letters if perhaps I might be trying NOT to say something to you, and it is true that I have kept letters from the final posting, or not written them, because I have felt angry or hurt or just plain peevish lately. I am very sorry about this, and I hope that it will pass. Perhaps it is Spring? (I am not joking....)

That thing your Whittier *News* sycophant published set me off... that talk about your crippled wife. And from then on I seem to have been goaded by repetitions of it. Today another review came, mentioning that your wife had suffered a "stroke." It all sickens me. I don't think that what happened to Janie should be hidden, but why tell the whole god-damned world on every other page that you are tied to a paralyzed incompetent? Stiff upper lip... flapping.

1. It is not clear whether MF sent this letter or not.

Well, you see why I have not written. I have not wanted to be so blatantly angry. I do not know you at all well, and I am not conditioned to your masochism. And plainly I never shall be.

It is that cold realization that has stopped me, far past the gentle alcoholic glow of the Buena Vista. I cannot possibly let you see through haze any longer, or I would roast in Hell for trickery. I have let you say many sweet somethings, because I have loved to read them. But I simply cannot let you go on with your new toy, Arnold, which is your reconstituted schmerz for MFKFisher the pretty writer. I am a writer all right, but I am not that pretty one you saw two-plus decades ago. And neither are you the Peculiar Fellow of the Lafayette, wearing two-colored shoes and looking forever sinister. You are set in patterns I could never un-puzzle. So am I, I suppose.

You apparently need your own toys, human and otherwise. You push them this way and that... pick them up and put them down... get new ones. I envy you, and I say this with deep sincerity.

But I have other means to keep myself sane, or at least to try to.

One of them has been to write to you, and if you still want me to, I'll keep on.

And meanwhile I can report that I feel very well and am working hard. I seem to be open to all the winds, right now: many different kinds of people call me or come here, and I work on the book(s) and cope unsuccessfully with my correspondence and work in the yard and gradually re-organize the Bysement and the Pub. I am waiting for something. Perhaps it is to go to Jenner on May 29, to see my sister become 50? Perhaps it is to fly to NY to see my daughter married on June 10?[2] Perhaps it is to go to the dentist on June 17? Perhaps it is to die on ooo?

Whatever, I'll always be glad you have been my darling Ginger. Faute de mieux. Et pour toujours.

....

St. Helena, California   *17.vii.67*
To: Arnold Gingrich

Dear Mr. Rich:

For once I have nothing to answer, from you! And perhaps the strikes will slow up any mail that may be on the way. Ah well... ho hum.

I am sure you have been given more than one clipping of this little drawing... naturally I think of you out by your pool in the moonlight.

And it reminds me of a true thing that happened at the Château du Tholonet, which is about four or five miles from Aix and where summer concerts are given during the Festival de Musique in July. (We lived there in the stables for four months, a magical dream of complete simplicity... now it is owned by the State and is an experimental school for agriculture, but the concerts go on....)

There is a long pond, perhaps a quarter of a mile and about sixty (?) feet across, bor-

2. MF's daughter Kennedy married James Wright, a professor in the drama department at Mills College.

dered on either side by straight rows of tall plane trees, with the château at the end. For the first concert of the first season, the London Symphony Orchestra sat on the rather high terrace in front of the building, and the listeners sat in chairs along the two sides of the pond. And as soon as the music started, every frog in Provence started to sing.... Finally the musicians had to stop. All the farm-workers and men from the village (pop. circa 90) came with long bamboo poles to beat the pond and scare the frogs mute. But the minute the music started... It was literally impossible to continue, and people were given their tickets back.

I would like to say that from then on the water was either loaded with liquid tranquilizers or perhaps with good local brandy... I dislike to think what *did* happen to the happy singers, but concerts have resumed at Le Tholonet and from what I am told, the frogs are quiet. Now the musicians are in a shell at the end of the pond but *facing* the château, and the listeners sit on the terrace.

Nice little story, eh? Oh... later that first season *Carmen* was given, and it is said to be one of the most hilarious and delightful shows ever seen, with the singers really belting it out and all the frogs chirping in rhythm.... I wish there were a tape of it.

Nothing new to report here. I am not in very good spirits... no gloomies, but sure-as-hell no braggies. Work goes quite well.

À un de ces jours!!!!!

....

St. Helena, California   *30.vii.67*
To: Grace Holmes

Dearest Aunt Grace... a good fat letter from you... all my thanks!

Don't worry about my being tired. I am in fine shape, and I do rest, actually more than I *need* to right now. I am living a very quiet serene life... very few outside contacts... am neglecting several social commitments... putter in the cool of the morning and evening in my shabby "yard"... chop away at the book.[1]

I was floored (again) for a little while, to have the whole ugly thing begin again with A. But by now I have reached another plateau of what is probably calloused acceptance. She and the baby have disappeared completely. Norah thinks they may have left California. In a really dreadful way this makes me feel relieved, at least for a time: she can be no worse off *anywhere* than she would be in Berkeley. And this time I may never hear from her again. But I think I will. And I look forward to that with real horror, apart from my primeval need to help her. Well... it's a sad thing indeed. The beautiful-and-damned...

I love what you tell me about that summer in the Far West. I always think of you as dainty and fragile, wearing exquisitely made suits and blouses and so on, and it is fascinating to think of you fishing for your breakfast and camping in a forest.... No wonder you looked so relaxed in a couple of pictures Rex took... even dressed to the nines and wearing a large handsome hat, probably to go to lunch at Aunt—? —she

1. *The Cooking of Provincial France*

was the widow of one of my grandfather's brothers, I think, a small generous woman. She and her batty sister used to come every winter to see Grandmother in Whittier. (Once there was a row because the batty one showed me a cobweb with dew on it and said the fairies had made it, and Grandmother denounced that as sacrilegious poison, and there were tears.)

I love Rex for preaching the joys of marriage to you! He often told me you were "a damned attractive woman" and I think he went along with Edith's dream to have you team up somehow (How????) with Uncle Evans, whom he dearly loved. (I too am "amused" when people solemnly urge me to marry again: "… no long list of willing grooms!" The few people I might have grabbed during the past 40 years were not at all my cup o' tea… and it is not something one looks for in the Yellow Pages! Norah says I am always urging even casual friends to write books, just because I write them myself. I suppose it is the same thing if one is happily married?)

About police brutality: yes. I have three friends who "walked" outside the Los Angeles hotel when Johnson spoke there lately, and I believe them when they tell me that the police were unbelievably crude and brutal, and that *they* were plainly and in a well-tutored way "instigating to riot." Ho hum. It is a filthy situation. And now Congress is appropriating millions to train special troops in anti-riot techniques, instead of getting rid of a few of the four-legged rats.…

What Is Spelman Cooking????? Yes, those little chocolate coins! How delicious! They were called Non-pareils, and you can still buy them… Sis and I used to be given one at bedtime, and we would pull off each little bead and eat it separately before we ate the chocolate. I love potato and onion (or leek) soup. But we never seemed to use onion while Grandmother was alive. I make it now, in various forms. I don't think children like caraway tastes.

It is heavenly weather now… hot in the days, with cool nights. I am quietly putting more order into this house, and enjoying it fully… had a professional window-washing, no mean trick with twelve-foot windows, needing a 20-foot ladder outside… about 25 windows on the main floor (and 17 downstairs, 8 in attic—)! Murder. Now I almost have to wear dark glasses inside… after ten years of gradual clouding over, no matter how clean I could keep the inside. And I am doing a slow job of pruning, digging, all that. I really love it, and feel that I should savor every minute… Carpe diem.

The book goes fairly fast now. My typist is getting used to a new baby, and I am pleased to see that I have piled up a fat little backlog for her. I have no confidence in my editor… I really do not respect his taste and judgment. He is of the new breed, a very fine executive and production expert, but not an EDITOR, the way Max Perkins was, or Pat Covici… or even Donald. He is very much in awe of me, which is bad in itself. And he beams happily about everything I do. All this makes me feel uncertain and shaky. Ah well. I am turning out a rather strange book, I think. People may like it, if there is anybody left to read a book by the time it is published.…

Tonight I go to a public meeting of local people trying to reach some positive action about Vietnam. I have firmly stayed away from the two meetings held to organize the group, but I think tonight I should go to *prove* my tacit approval... mainly because most of my friends are involved in it. I take a very dim view of such gatherings... too much talk, no real accomplishment, very murky aims, all earnest and decent but futile... and God knows I don't need to meet with fifty people to raise my blood pressure! I do NOT think that I can do anything, or that they can, right now. This is perhaps defeatist of me. But I am in such a state of contained rage that I cannot and indeed dare not talk in public about the reasons for it. I am too articulate, compared to most people, because of my training. And because I am a writer, people here like to have me get up and say the things that they believe but cannot express or are afraid. And right now I am protecting my equanimity to such a selfish point that I prefer to let them struggle along without me (Joke. Laff.).

This may sound rather odd or smug or something. Forgive me if it does. But it is the case. If we need a new stop-and-go near a school, for instance, some of the parents will ask me to write to the paper to get their own wishes into print. Etc. And right now, if I started to expose what they, *and I,* are feeling and fearing, I would probably be arrested. Or have an apoplectic seizure. (Of course I would infinitely prefer the first....)

So... I'll go tonight, but sit far back and not open my mouth. It will let the committees know that I am "for" them, anyway. I went, and I did.

I think I told you that Mary's husband lost his 12-week job after 6 weeks, and when she called (a very sad-sounding girl) they were heading for his mother's house in Ohio. The silver cord is very tight there. I feel sorry to have their married privacy ended so soon. But it is not my affair.

And so it goes. An Italian friend writes to me, "Little children, little worries. Big children..." etc.

I must stop this gabble. I do hope the weather is decent for you.... Yrs—

....

St. Helena, California   *11.viii.67*
To: Arnold Gingrich

Dear Mr. Rich:

I am PAGES behind you, and don't know whether to try to catch up on your always-so-welcome letters or simply start from here (where here is...).

It is 6:30 of a fine bright day. Marietta has been in for her fiver. I have looked at the plants and decided to water them tomorrow morning instead of tonight. Today I made a good stab at getting back to work... at least took care of some neglected business and organized tomorrow's job and so on. I feel fine. I am sipping now and then at a glass of arf-n-arf. It is wonderful to be alone for a day... no "company." I have had rather a lot lately. Tomorrow I must go to supper and then take my hostess to the first of the three August Moon concerts on the lawn at the Krug Winery... I'm a patron or something and tomorrow will be good, with a small chamber-music group from SF. The moon will be in first quarter. There will be some cool wine to drink, too.

Etc. Trivia.

I wonder if you want to hear about my Spree. It went off well. Norah and I were relaxed and gentle with each other. We talked a lot, mostly about extraneous things. We handle each other deftly. Self-protection, I suppose, for we are very close mentally and verbally. I went down and back on Greyhound and used cabs. The City was beautiful, with cool foggy mornings and bright brisk days. It is always an exciting place to me.

We met at the old Stewart, where Walter Ficklin always stays and where I spent my first SF hotel-days, because Rex had a due-bill there. It was and still is a dismal DUMP, in spite of all and any attempts to brighten it. But it is very well located for shopping and theatres and all that. Except that it is always filled with happy tourists from everywhere, of all colors and languages, I would like to drop a bomb on it. Well... N and I are conditioned to many contretemps there, and I always have a panic-button ready, in most cases an extra pad at the Clift up the street. We stayed correctly at the Stewart for the one night as Walter's guests and then FLED to one of my usual rooms on the elevator shaft at what I always think of now as "our" hotel....... which reminds me that the bus was re-routed on Monday as we came in to the City and we went past that ship that burned while we watched, still rusting and sad at its dock.

Well, I am glad to report to anyone who wants to hear, and you are my captive audience, that Sky Blue Walter[1] is incredibly improved over last year: better attention span, clearer speech, brighter in every way. Of course Lovely Louie[2] looks years better too. We went to La Bourgogne... I have spent good evenings there, but really it is the upper-class chichi that could be in Rome or London or Buenos Aires or or or... too many impeccably costumed waiters, solid silver Georgian service and butter plates, Baccarat glass. (I love quality... you know that... but this oppressive loading-on!!!!) We ate simply and quite well, and then trotted up the street to *Man of la Mancha,* which I enjoyed very much. It is certainly not great, but it is good theatre, expertly paced and produced and with two really good people... maybe three. Then we had a brandy in the sepulchral Redwood Room . . .

Oh... Noni and I went out for a bit of shopping that afternoon and I got some green stockings, which I have not worn since 1942. I have nothing now to wear with them. But *Tondu vaincra.*[3]

So... the next morning N and I dashed up to the Clift, left bags and so on, and went on a slight spree of gallery-looking on Sutter... saw one very good show of modern Japanese oils and that famous "box" show, which I really do like... went to the Maxfield Parrish show because there might be some of Dillwyn and Anne in it because they posed a lot when they were kids and I can always spot them, but there were none this time... mostly third-rate left-over landscapes and a few beautiful sketches for *The Knave of Hearts.* We also went into Williams-Sonoma, really a dreamy place, like the Bazar

1. Walter Ficklin
2. Ficklin's wife, Lucille
3. François Tondu was the manservant at Le Pâquis whose eccentricities amused both MF and Arnold Gingrich.

Français in NY if two real queens were running it. I got out without buying anything, but put a hold on two tart-pans when they arrive in October, too late to make the fruit tarts I now long to do.

Then we dashed back to the hotel and met Norah's close friend Madeleine, an astonishing woman . . . and we grabbed a cab out to the Planetarium to see the highly touted *Mystery of Stonehenge* which I found rather a let-down, because I am so hooked on the place, and have been since 1930, that I expect miracles to happen every time it is mentioned. But the show was good, very slick and "pop." Then we went back to the City and spent hours over a long good lunch at Jack's (THE BEST PLACE AND WE MUST GO THERE...). Oh... we drank two bottles of a really good Montrachet at La Bourgogne, but it was served too cold for my palate. At Jack's we drank a Krug Gewürztraminer at perfect temperature... all the wine men go there and the wine is always correct. I was very gourmande and ate A*L*L of a large plate of boned fresh Rex sole meunière, and then a demi-tasse of good coffee. Nothing before. Marvelous.

Then we started rambling, and usually I loathe this style of feminine behavior, but I was feeling so easy, and was so interested in the two women, that I enjoyed it. We must have looked in a hundred windows, and discussed them. . . . finally Madeleine left to return to Berkeley and N and I simply collapsed on our two wonderful extra-length percale sheets sanitized for your protection TV in every room extra-soft towels pad at the Clift.

We had the poor Yugoslav who has been there for decades bring us up a carafe of house wine, which is Louis Martini's Folle Blanche. We lay very flat and sipped and talked. Very nice.

About 9 we went out, and to a *really* Greek place, where the men get up with serious faces and pull out their white linen handkerchiefs and a woman or another man will join them... I mean him... and they will dance slow or fast, twirling and in unison with many age-old gestures, on the small floor in front of four musicians and sing and play various metal drums and accordions and such-like, including sax. Now and then a man will come from far back in the low long room and take off his coat and go into a dance which only a real man could dance without looking like a homosexual, as graceful as a flower and completely virile. It was fascinating. They all looked very released and clean and strong and serene. I was glad I was there, for one sees so many frightened empty eyes lately, I sometimes think. We drank a bottle of a very dry white wine with almost no resin in it. The food was lamentable, but it did not matter at all. The noise was in the modern decibel-limit, and too bad, for if the loudspeaker system and all that had been cut, the music would have been much better and more inviting, once the people had accustomed themselves to it. Well...

The next day we had a little breakfast in the room, and watched some freighters head down the Bay, and parted. I to the bus. Once here, bustle took over. Beanbag arrived early of course... he is rather heavy going but we got a lot out of the way about the situation in Genoa... the next day two of his friends and their small baby arrived for lunch... stayed much longer than they should have... then I had people in for supper in the Pub, partly business about a couple of local things and partly pleasure, but we were all tired.

Etc etc etc.......

Arnold, thank you for sending me the clippings of this and that. I kept the rather nonsensical one about corkscrews... grist for a possible mill. I sent that quite funny one about the Texas passenger and the chilled wine to Beard (local). And it is true about Hermann's column: I recognized several wrong dates, but I loved his phrase about your looking up "with an expression of lively understanding" before you made your retort courteous about libel.

So much goes on with you. I am so glad you could go to those recording sessions. What an experience! Too bad about having the tape-recorder conk out, but I am so proud for you about the progress with Shub. . . .

Oh... I was stupid not to realize that OF COURSE you must be somewhat discreet about your Lost Weekend. We'll get you a nice little pad at El Bonita, and you can check in there whenever it seems best. And Mrs. Jackson and her bevy of Peruvian birds will watch over you/us and relay any and all messages, I am sure. Here perhaps I should add that I have never gone to these cautionary limits before, but am completely amenable to them. No guilt. Etc. And I am the first to admit that this is a very *intimate* house and that you may well want to go a mile down the road and take a shower and nap in peace and purity. You'll see when you get here.

I see more and more that Janie is returning to life. Like Sky Blue, but slower. She may turn into a wise tolerant human being. Apparently she wants to return to you. She is reading more. She is *listening* to you fiddle. This must give you pause. And me too. I have never been a poacher. . . .

You are mistaken to identify me with the Jenny of that pseudo-novel... really several *novelle*.[4] Not same cup o' tea.

I'll dig up some pictures of Rex and Edith... a couple of stunners really. Interesting, your reason for wanting to look at their images.... It makes me wonder if perhaps I should not be so stuffy about all the glamour-pix and so on that are all I have for my children's lovers to diagnose. . . .

About Riting no Rong, the House[5] has bought another chapter and a kind of allegory I wrote, and I am anxious to get Janet[6] here next week and see if she will let drop in her eminently discreet way what in hell is going on about buying and buying and never publishing.

Meanwhile I continue to turn out the stuff. The book takes shape. I am going as fast as I can, for I am living on a volcano, past experience tells me.... Last word through the double grapevine tells me that Anna and the baby are living in a hippie encampment about fifty miles from here... macrobiotic Zen food, no plumbing, etc. Nous allons voir....

4. *Not Now but* Now
5. *The New Yorker*
6. Janet Flanner

It is interesting that you remember that thing about the mouse. I begin to think that the plainly bookish pieces in the *NYer* should make a separate book, if they ever get around to publishing about five more they have and at least five more I want to write. This cookery deal for Targ is not bookish at all. Just quite me-ish. . . .

Yes, at 169 you do top my weight. . . . Right now I am trying to get back into my private regime, after several wild days in SF and with company. (I don't think I have told you about the visit of the Connes. . . .) But I find delicious little left-overs, which I "eat to save," loving every mouthful... and the next day I have NOT lost that extra ten ounces on each cheek. . . . Ah well.

At Piney Woods the tables, which seated 8, for the teachers, were packed solid for about two by three feet in the middle with bottles of all kinds of remedies. It was revolting. Those people would sell their souls to buy a rotten palliative, and die of malnutrition with a pint of cure-all sugar-water in one hand. Ho hum . . .

This has turned into a screed. It may amuse you. I wanted to mumble on to you, and answer parts of your last letters, instead of being sober and earnest and righteous and stuff like that.

Yrs. Trly.

....

St. Helena, California   *19.viii.67*
To : Arnold Gingrich

Dear Mr. Rich, secret Gypsy Fiddler to people like yr ladyfren...

It is later than I think, and I should be upstairs getting into somewhat more proper dress and shoes to go to the August Moon thing. I really don't want to go. I would rather stay here, and take a shower and put on a muumuu and putter down here and (when it cools off a bit more) upstairs. Yolande[1] was going up to Krug's with me, but went to Drake's Bay instead. And so on. All the people I know have tickets, anyway. Ah well.

I feel lonesome tonight. Not lonely, in the "soul" sense. Just lonesome. I am surrounded by people, even good friends. I just said *auf wiedersehen* to Alice Low, a really dear one... from SF... we talked mostly of our mutual friend June Eddy... she has helped June a lot with the new house, and we are making vague but hopeful plans to go down there for Thanksgiving. I would like to get away from this area for such "family" festivities. They have changed too much, in the past few years, for me to be able to stomach them as such. They are for young people with little children, I suppose?

I wonder if I can or should be back in California from NY by Thanksgiving. I have an idea in my head that it would be a good test of my nerve to stay for at least a month, alone, in a rented room-kitchenette deal near 25 W. 43rd. But I wonder. . . .

I do not fret about this. Time will decide many of the problems... I found a new typist, and am trying her out on a couple of short things. Ora pro nobis.

I got a letter from Hal, ending "keep well and forget your kids."!!!!!!

1. Yolande Beard

Don't know if I told you Anna called on her birthday. I found this almost heart-breaking, that she is so rebellious about such ties and still cannot but obey them now and then. She says she is married, to an unknown guitar player in rock-n-roll... that he is adopting Chris, that they are heading for Montreal for a year, then London, then Brasilia. She sounded like a very sick girl, with a bad cough, and I doubt that she lasts another three months. I tried to keep my cool, as she would say, but was flattened for 24 hours or so. As I grow older I react in a more obviously visceral way to emotional knocks. Boring. I, the Tearless Wonder, drip tears at very unexpected moments. Is a puzzlement.

I still can't re-read your last good letters and answer a few of the many tantalizing things. But I do remember what you said about your speaking appointments. All I can say is My God! Whom do you think you is? Moses? Do you *LIKE* this one-night-stand routine? Whom are you doing it *FOR? AG?* The Firm? Amour propre? Boredom?

... I have just decided: I am not going up to Krug's. Why should I? I'll strip off these dull clothes, shower, put on a crisp clean beautiful cotton Kimono and go-aheads, come down here with a drink... later do some fancy-work in the kitchen, for a few people are coming for supper after the Tasting tomorrow and I must have everything done beforehand. Wow. I feel years younger.

... Tomorrow I am going to have blanched chilled vegetables (green beans, cauli-flower, zucchini, and peeled tomatoes) with both thick or thin dressings... thin freshly baked bread with anchovy butter... compote of mangoes and raspberries... Gringolino... coffee. Hah! The bread is nice, and I'll have it for you if you like anchovy taste, although I know you almost never *(Never!)* eat bread. Neither do I. But people like this. It is made once a week by the local bakery, Italian, and I think it is called fazzola, and it is about an inch thick, pierced all over and clear through with a fork before baking, and then painted with good olive oil while it is hot from the oven. I buy it according to the capacity of the freezer, to keep on hand. I defrost it, spread it well with anchovy butter, and warm it. People like it, with salads.

Well... I feel so carefree about not going up to Krug's that I am sitting here feeling almost cool again, still in my store clothes! Oh... is wearing good old two-piece blue and white striped seersucker, white linen shoes, blue bead earrings ($1 at local Tiffany's...).

Arnold, I am very glad that you are having good fishy fiddly weekends. You did sound rather ragged for a time. Now you seem easier in your skin. I hope I am right. I myself think that Shub[2] is the *deus ex your machina*... and not too indirectly I think he has had a good effect on Janie, who now recognizes that you know what you are doing, with something she has considered a ridiculous affectation and now sees as an important part of your life. Well... forgive me for being this personal. But I do think it is perhaps right ....

Your heading like a homing pigeon to Jake's in SF, and to Perino's in LA, reminds me that the first place I ever sat down in, in Aix, with my two little thirsty girls, was

2. Shub was Gingrich's violin instructor.

LES DEUX GARÇONS? ?????!!!!!! How could we ever have known that it was the place to go, the place to sit down, the place to love? But it was. (By now I have shifted my allegiance to a beautiful new small place down the Cours, in a newly discovered convent... a small frontage, but most fabulous rooms going back through renovated cloisters and ending in the best toilets in Provence AND a very successful bookie-joint run by our old friend Ange, who is now director of the new café!!!!!! Parimutuel. Even the ladies' johns have ticker-tape on the floors.... Then, since I don't bet (on horses), I tidy myself, step through the tape and past the parimutuel room, out through the cloisters, and past the "zinc" and back onto the Cours. Very amusing.) The 2G has become very shabby, coasting on its 150 years of repute, with only 2 of the good waiters left. The toilets, essential in that town of many fountains (!), are dreadful. The owner has grown fat and *je-m'en-foutiste.* Tout passe, tout lasse, tout casse... and meanwhile Ange is doing a beautiful job a few doors down, at the (Guess what!!!) Longchamps.

What happens to Janie when you come to California?

In a way I think it is a good thing that I have joined the Terrible Club.

I don't think there is much connection about the way I feel about Timmie and the way you feel about Janie. Perhaps Helen Mary, but not J. We may or we may not talk about this, sometime.

Dillwyn was a cousin, much younger, of Maxfield. M has one son who is a really GOOD artist. M was a near genius of an illustrator, I would say. Norah and I went to a small show of his in SF, and the best things were two caricatures and some sketches for *The Knave of Hearts.* The landscapes were ghastly. As for Anne, she married Corliss (Charles)... brother of Florence Lamont... piles of dough... almost good satirical portrait in one of her forgotten novels called *Golden Wedding...* her first and really important book was before my time, called *Perennial Bachelor....* It was the first of the modern "best sellers," to everyone's surprise, and Travellers' Aid asked to have it suppressed because of all the runaway girls to cope with. I liked it because it was really about Uncle Boney Lodge, whom I was forced to know rather well, much later. All of Anne's books are autobiographical, and I studied them almost too carefully during my immediate life with the Parrishes. A very interesting and sad bunch of end-of-the-roaders. Anne finally turned overtly agin me, and during her last years I was allowed NO communication with her... doctors' orders. This upset me because I had grown very fond of her, and because she had twelve of Dillwyn's very best canvases, all of which she agreed to return to his trust but which she gave here and there, without a trace. Ah well and ho hum . . .

I don't know about Stonehenge. If we ever get started on it, and we might even make it a project with Jim Beard and his adored tape recorder, for he is hep on S too, but in a very mathematical and knowing way, you could tell more about that man who draws little charts. Wonderful. My own approach is indeed atavistic and unthinking.

Serious, now... please remember this, and perhaps we can tape a good evening of varying talk about Stonehenge... you, through the Brittany experience... Jim and Yolande through the books and distant approach (planetarium etc etc)... I through personal experience. The last time I was talking about it (up there) a Russian friend claimed to have spent a whole night there with Gov't. permission with an artist who was sketching. He said it was filled with "supernatural reactions." Let's go! . . .

Your rather vague plans to go to Paris sound like fun. As a Westerner I think of such a jaunt in terms of weeks or months instead of days, and it seems criminal to go to the Ritz for a *weekend*. But you are half the way over there, when you are in NY. If I lived on the East Coast, I'd do it too....

... Big pause here, while I had long entretien, complete with check for several hours of chopping from slave-labor sons, with Señor Luis Ochoa-Gonzales, a very hardworking man and also a potential power. He is very sharp, man! In another ten years one of his slave-labor boys will be out of Stanford and mayor, and two more will have bought a vineyard, and Ochoa will be thinner and more like a small falcon. (I wear gloves, with him....)

How wonderful it is not to be at that concert! I know too many people. A lot of them I like very much indeed. But I quickly become weary of being gracious and courteous and smile-smile nod speak remember name introduce smile smile. With you I think it is part of your nature, at least long since acquired. With me, I have always had to practice it but I am increasingly freeing myself from it. I think that if it were possible for you to marry me you would find me an absolutely useless thing as a social and professional asset, Arnold. The trouble is that I honestly DO NOT CARE. Some people do, and when they are lucky like me and have good preparation or when they are hep enough to make their own molds, they are probably very happy at it. But I am not. I can do it all. I mean this. But why? Perhaps if I were with a man who mattered enough to me to make it matter too, it would seem time well spent. When I was trying to be a Young Faculty Wife with Al Fisher I was all right, and I could have gone on to being Emeritus Head-of-English Dept. Wife if it had seemed worth it to our human development. But it did not. Timmie was far past all that. As for DF, I was a real disappointment to him, because he wanted me to throw great parties, which I did, to be available at all hours of the day and night for mad dashes in the 1920s-manner to Harlem and Paris and Moscow, which I was not because I had children and no money. Ah well and ho hum. But I continue to think that for a man of your almost hysterical movement I would be a very bad mate. Is there a Golden Mean?

Dear Mr. Pogo-Stick of 1967, I love you anyway.

....

St. Helena, California   *17.ix.67*
To : William Targ[1]

Dear Bill :

I think your letter of September 13 is a masterpiece of delicate evasion of a really

1. William Targ was an editor of Putnam.

ghastly problem: Where do we put this little short story about tears in a book about tripe and turnips?[2]

It was an error! It was not supposed to be sent to you at all! Be at rest, poor Editor! It was supposed to go to the *NYer*, and it got in the wrong envelope. Even a book on Hemingway could not be *that* square....

Thank you for that nice phrase about being a felicitous phenomenon. I am sure I'll forget it, but not the fact that you said it.

Apparently the *NYer* has bought two more chapters of our book. I think this may pose some problems about publication, but that is why you and Henry Volkening are in New York and I am here, I suppose. I'll keep sending material. There was too much for a time, in terms at least of your reading it, but now there will be a slight pause... very soon I'll have a couple more chapters ready for whatever local talent I can unearth... what with the opening of high school and the fertility of the Italian citizens, I am once more caught between class books and the crib....

Yes, I do plan to talk of our own version of a Lokshen Kugel... which actually I have described in its Turkish version before. . . . The "Basic Recipe" from *Jewish Cookery* by Leah W. Leonard stipulates noodles, but I agree with you that the very thin kind (in fact the capellini d'angelo or angel-hairs) make a much more delicate pudding. The Turkish version I have eaten was made with vermicelli, pretty thin.

Things are fairly hectic here, but may improve... at least as far as my work is concerned. I am sorry to have to be so vague about the deadline, but that too may resolve itself soon, and of course I'll let you know at once... and Henry.

Best to you both...

....

St. Helena, California   *[undated]*
To : Hal Bieler

Dearest Hal :

Thank you for letting me come down, at such short notice. It did me great good to be with you again. . . . I hope very much that I can come for longer, perhaps to help you with papers... typing, all that... perhaps in the Autumn? I'll ask you. You will have much to do after your Busman's Holiday... perhaps I can help you with correspondence.

I am very glad you are going to see all those patients on your so-called vacation.

I had something to ask you, which I did not feel was right to discuss during the few hours I could be with you. I'll try to state it briefly (those letters you let me see really scared me away from ten-page descriptions of my day-to-day "symptoms"!!!):

It is possible and even probable that I'll outlive you, chronologically. The thought appalls me but I must face it. In other words, when I must die, you will not be able to help me if I need you. (This sounds completely self-centered. But I am trying to be factual and brief....)

2. *With Bold Knife and Fork*

I would like to die neatly, without too much ugly fuss. I don't like pain, but can accept it. Mostly I hope to avoid lengthy expense and strain for people like Norah or Mary or anyone who must care for me if I were helpless.

I have fairly strong suicidal impulses but by now they are not compulsive. I want to see this thing out... try the whole caper.

So... I want to plan on two things: What my probable death will be... that is, the immediate cause, and then how to put it off for a time with increased physical strength.

On my mother's side (Holbrooks), the family was sedentary, and almost always died of "heart disease." The people were corpulent.

On my father's side, which I am said to resemble, they tended to grow a little heavy in the middle years and then become very thin. They were taller than the Holbrooks. Predominantly they died of diseases of the throat and lungs... no "tuberculosis" that I know of (one case in the Holbrooks but not of the lungs), but fibrosis and chronic bronchitis and so on.

In my own case, I am overweight, but not with fatty tissue: I am definitely *water-logged*. This is less from abuse of diet than from drinking wine and alcohol. I am self-indulgent, and I find real pleasure in drinking. I have never done so with the idea of intoxication, but only for pleasure... and I can stop for a year at a time (as when I was in Mississippi or when I do not like the people I am with, i.e., the Hollywood jobs). I can stop forever, but until now I have not done so. I think I rationalize this complete break with a continuing pleasure by telling myself that I have given up many other real joys in my life and think I deserve at least one left to me?

Well, you have seen me again with your all-knowing eyes, and have told me to shun starches and milk. (I have been careless about these lately.) I assume I should avoid sugar. All this is very easy for me. I shall try to live for a few months on plenty of "mish-mash" and broth and fruits.

The main thing in my mind is to *stay out of the pill-boys' clutches* if I should fall seriously ill. It is not always possible to call on you for help, and if you have time, I want you to tell me how to pull off this plot.

I know very well that my presence is not essential to anyone. But I would like to see what happens, a little longer, with my children and their families. I enjoy working, most of the time. I think Mary is self-sufficient. Anna never has been, but in her case I might be better for her dead than alive: she may have to face remorse and regret (?), but physically it will be a relief to her. I am sorry that I will inevitably leave a mess of pictures-books-papers-furniture for my sister Norah to cope with, if she should outlive me.

Hal, I have no intention of dying soon. But I do want to do it neatly. And I'll be glad if you can give me a few tips.

You have been telling me things for some forty years now, and with one or two real defaults I have got by quite well, thanks to your help. On this last stretch, I'd like to know as much as any human being *can* know (And you are the only person in the world who could perhaps help me here) if I can reasonably prepare for disintegration through the heart, the throat, etc.

Meanwhile I shall simply stick to the vegetables and fruits, and cut out the wine and alcohol. As you know, I don't smoke, nor drink tea or coffee, nor use salt in my home cooking. Professionally I am exposed to a lot of abuses, but I have learned to fake my enjoyment in many ways.

I feel really ashamed of inflicting this on you, Hal. Answer when you can... *or* do not answer at all, in the last-minute rush before you leave. But please know that I wish to end my days nobly, flying *your* colors... for you have added immeasurably to everything good in my life.

Abiding Love —

St. Helena, California   *16.i.68*
To : Henry Volkening

Dear Henry... another enclosure, hopefully self-explanatory. . . .

While I am here, I want to tell you about something that is making me slightly sick. I try not to let it really *bother* me. It may interest you as a past master at binding writers' wounds: The most surprising people, *nice* people, even dear good friends, are saying and writing to me the damnedest stuff about the glossy publicity in the Time-Life throwaway. I feel as if they actually had no conception of what I have been trying to do since I was nine or so: be a good writer. They call me long distance and scream happily at me "MF, you're *in*! You've *made* it!!"... just because of a hazy toothy shot in a subscription gimmick. They write me notes like this one: "Last week you came smiling triumphantly into the house by way of Time-Life Books' notice of *The Cooking of Provincial France*. So this is just to tell you how proud we are for you, and that we take off our hats to you for having reached the top of the tree... joyous congratulations, etc etc."

GAWD. Actually it hurts me. You can add this to your file on the Sensitive Soul Syndrome. Or am I simply being peevish? Or snobbish, perhaps?

Well... that's my grouse for the month, I hope.

(I suppose if some obscure reviewer had linked my name, referring to one of my books pre-doomed to complete nonentity, with someone like Colette or V. Woolf or or or, I'd feel happy as a fat cricket....)

Yur Fren...

St. Helena, California   *5.ii.68*
To: William Targ

Dear Bill :

I am really bad about writing, and hope you will forgive me *again*. I am being a Very Good Girl, and you'll have another fat chapter by the end of this week... it's being typed now. And I am well into the next one. (Life is considerably wilder with Anna and Chris here,[1] but I think it is making me do some quite solid stuff, whenever I can grab a few minutes at the tripe-writer....)

Thank you for your red-letter note of the 24th. I am glad you agree about my going East, much as I'd like a chance to see you again. Perhaps I can come back later this Spring, although right now it seems doubtful. (I am happy to report real progress with my two patients, though....) . . .

Now about the title, and again with my apologies, I haven't meant to be cagey about it, and am sorry if it seemed so. I have known FROM THE START what I would like to call the book, but this of course, and I do mean *of course* means if you like it. Now it embarrasses me to tell you that although I have made and kept at least three copies of the excerpt from Boswell's *London Journal* which tempts me, I simply cannot find one of them! So now I am combing the book again (and having fun...). He was feeling very poor, angry at his father for not sending him money for his gentlemanly tastes, and in a lull socially, so that he could not cadge as many free meals as usual. He had been living on cold chops and bread for several days. Then he was casually invited to a gathering of literary men... "geniuses," he called them... people like Coleridge, but Sam Johnson was out of town... and he ate with enormous enjoyment and *"with very bold knife and fork."* How do you like that? Or more simply, *With Bold Knife and Fork...* it has a good sound, to me. Of course the little excerpt should be at the first of the book... but I assume it is in public domain by now? I think the title Mr. Shawn likes for what he plans to run is rather pompous... or something: "Gastronomy Recalled." It rings very faint bells of everything from *Remembrance of Things Past* to *Brideshead Revisited.* (But probably I would not tell *him* this... unless he asked me.) Well... I want very much to learn your candid reaction, and Henry V's too.

And thank you for the copy of your letter to him. I am glad the last chapter pleased you. The up-coming one is about Bread. It is rather long, and I am going to try to hold down the next, on Fish.

I recall that you asked me, long ago, to note portions in the recipes, and I'll do this when I send the final copy to be typed... also put oven time at beginning of recipe.

And that reminds me that I would like to run a cut version of an article for the *NYer* called "Anatomy of a Recipe," and perhaps the one about cooking for modern children. Miss MacKenzie has assured me that this will be all right, but I'll make very sure, through Henry I suppose(?).

I have been careful about dangers of plagiarism, really no trouble since the recipes and allusions are so obviously MFKF that nobody could be anything but amused. And this reminds me of something I just remembered, which you'll like (I hope... maybe it will scare you?????): in a very nice review from Chicago, perhaps of the revised *How to Cook a Wolf,* the man said that it was without doubt the *wackiest* cookbook he had ever read or dreamed about.... well... at least I have fun!

And seriously I think every recipe I have used, unless I have stated flatly that it was the nadir of all such formulae, or printed solely for amazement, is workable, useful,

1. Anna and Chris moved in with MF in St. Helena for several months before returning to Berkeley.

and delicious. Wow. And also I have *made* every one, and changed it over the years, which is a rare thing, I state as a jaded viewer of the current crop of shameless cheating books being published for kitchen-buffs.

Well... back to my fish.

What a mad social whirl you keep up! I wonder how Eleanor's bash went off... she was like a very pregnant mother of predicted triplets about it, and called me twice, Before and After. It sounds like a lovely deal. But I still hate parties even that big.

I'll send a copy of this to Henry. Please know that if my private title simply does not sound right, it won't hurt me... I'll just use it some other way. But I do think that the casual way I like to cook and write and eat and so on is fairly "bold"... ??????

Best to you both. Why don't you need a quick trip to Fisherman's Wharf or thereabouts?

....

St. Helena, California   *20.v.68*
To : Grace Holmes

Dearest Aunt Grace... I feel very badly about not having written much oftener lately. I hope your silence is to chide me gently, and not indicate that you have been unwell. Please set my heart at rest... for a minute anyway!

I agree with you that King was like Lincoln in having "reached his limit of endurance"... especially when I look at a picture in *Newsweek* printed two days before he died, in which he was marching like a tortured zombie, held up by Abernathy and another aide, at the head of a mob of arrogant hecklers. I am surprised that this picture has never been referred to. Certainly it was never again printed.

I dared listen to very little during that national ordeal of shame. (No TV here.) I listened, but mostly in private. And now I think the first wave of regret has swept past us, and for most citizens there is the heady if dubious plunge into the political campaigns, and baseball again, and Emmy awards and on and on.

Ah well, also ho hum.

My sister Anne used to knit through crises. I never knit any more. I like to, but peacefully... and by now there are several other things I want to do *more*... go to bed and listen to music, or read, and sleep. I found that when I got needles and wool ready for a long tranquil winter's job, I would be through in less than a week, and completely gnarled with stiff muscles and general exhaustion. Silly.

Don't worry about my saving money. Right now, for the first time in my life, I am earning more than I should... Affluent Society indeed... and I think it is fun to spend some of it. I'm damned if I'll invest in govt bonds for napalm and other obscenities, and that's right where it would go if I socked it into a supposedly reputable savings arrangement....

A pashka is a kind of cheese, made of dry cottage cheese and sometimes cream and cream cheese, and eggs either raw or hard boiled, and sugar and currants and spices. It is put in a mold (in our case made of graduated new flower pots) lined with a clean napkin, and allowed to drain overnight. The next day it is made into a cone or pyramid and decorated with candied fruits and so on according to the family habits, with flowers around the base. It is very fresh and not rich, and is eaten after church. In Russian families there is much more food, and of course wine and vodka. We had little dry cookies, and champagne. It is fun to make... a kind of ritual. . . .

Too bad that Alie's Eleanor[1] seems to be slovenly in her way of living. Perhaps she will change. She has a good background. As for Ken's Eleanor... she sounds solid and promising. But right now I am taking a somewhat dim view of what a man can do to all that... I am not happy about the little I can glean of my own Kennedy's progress since her marriage. It sounds like a character change in the most unconnected directions. Ah well again. On the other hand I see Anna fighting hard to hold to a general pattern of behavior which was intolerable to her for a few years. She is shaping into a somewhat wearied but fine young woman....

Oh... you would be pleased about a renewed use of her really deep talent for being with very young people. She is going to an intensive training course for mothers who plan to send their children to the Co-op Nursery school about five miles from here... a growth from Head Start. She is also helping one of our dear friends twice a week in Second Grade, with reading. Plus that, she goes once a week to a psychiatrist in Napa who is actually giving her courage (for the first time in too many years of seeking such help... he is making her learn about *herself*... INSIGHT...), and she has just finished a weekly Adult Education course in refresher typing (12 weeks, and she only missed two...). She is handling all these things, plus the *extremely* demanding job of Chris, without too much apprehension and fatigue.

Chris is on my nerves, now and then... he is a wonderful sensitive strong intelligent little boy, eager to be friends... he loves *people*. His mother has a strong guilt-feeling about the badly checkered past she gave him, and now feels that she must make up to him by almost complete permissiveness. This is not right. But she must work it out with her doctor, and I stay pretty much out of it. Chris is cruel and bullying with her, and he will scream and whine and spit. NEVER WITH ME.

Ah well again.

I am limping through the last chapter. Thank God. Then I must perform major surgery on the whole lagging confused mess... then write a new introduction.... Really, the past two or three years have not been easy on the Deathless Prose Dept!

On the 13th I am giving myself a little pre-birthday present, in Rex's best tradition... chartering a Cessna and flying down to Fresno to spend exactly 14 hours with some very dear friends! I was going alone, but could take Anna and Chris along for the same price (!!!) and thought it might be a good adventure. The people have vineyards and make the best port in America, the Ficklins, and we have known them for a long time. Walter is 83 and has had a series of small strokes... and I want to sit with him once more. He is a wonderful old man. The whole family is good. They live simply but in an almost lost graciousness... adobe house in the vineyards, tiled floors, quiet, good food and wine. Walter stayed with us for a couple of weeks in Aix, and Anna is anxious to see him again too. It will be good for all of us to have Chris

1. Alie was Aunt Grace's niece.

along... the two sons (ages of my girls) are in Vietnam, one just shipped back there after bad wounds....

I hate to end on that note... I sometimes think, lately, that I should never open my mouth, for such grim crumbs fall from it!... Perhaps that is why letters are neglected? I myself am very well.

....

St. Helena, California   *28.viii.68*
To : David Pleydell Bouverie[1]

Dear David Bouverie... I arrived home feeling so pleased with life, so revived, or at least and perhaps so rejuvenated, that I took a shower (It was a very hot ride...), poured the heel-tap of last night's bottle of champagne (tired but delicious...), and hung the Red Credo IN THE KITCHEN. It is right, there... between the lithograph of the truite meunière and the door to Chris's room, where it will stop people in their tracks.

Two or three hours later I still feel very much more alive than I did, say, twelve hours ago. It was good in every way to see your beautiful place, and to eat and drink so pleasurably, and to listen to your deft use of your own wordings about things, but probably the real charge came from seeing, even fleetingly, some of the pictures. I am like a controlled alcoholic about paintings and drawings, and have to be very careful in galleries and museums and such. It has taken years to reach my present level, and I was proud of myself two summers ago in Paris, for there were several amazing shows and I handled them beautifully... chose the rooms to head for, looked neither to right nor left until I reached them, and so on. But it was another thing to stagger past such a mysterious collection as yours, on the dry hillside above the old highway.

Of course within minutes it takes clear form as your self-portrait, which is a risk you must be aware of running. I am sure you are not afraid of it. Who could be, with such witnesses?

I would like to tell you sometime about the true reason I came to lunch today. (This sounds like a teaser in a three-part thriller....)

It will be amusing and interesting to see you again on the 8th, and the only reason I'll call saying I cannot come is that the people who want to show me all of San Diego Bay are having a stabilizer put in their yacht in San Pedro, and will want me to join them there if they can leave on the 6 or 7, to go clear down the Coast. It is something I must do if I have to....

Please accept my thanks, no matter how misanthropically.

....

St. Helena, California   *11.ix.68*
To : Henry Volkening

Dear Henry:

Yes, I did find the thing in the *NYer*, which had been lying unopened on the table

1. MF met David Pleydell Bouverie after he wrote her a fan letter. When they later became friends, he offered to build her a home, Last House, on his ranch in Sonoma Valley.

for three days, until I got a very nice wire from Bill Targ, who sounded pleased. I am detached enough by now to be able to read it with some amusement, and I am interested that I have already had some flattering and intelligent fan-mail about it.

I doubt that the sudden use of two of the pieces is coincidental. I am relieved, for Targ's sake, and am grateful to you.

Oh, it never occurred to me that either you or Rachel would even look at the extra copy of the typescript! Mercy! Please do whatever you want to, with it.

I am really in limbo about the *Holiday* thing right now, but am not fretting. I am, in the theatrical term, "between engagements," and mostly I enjoy it.

I really can't know, for a time longer, if and how and when I'll be able to come east. Please keep the Maître d'hôtel on our side....

I hope you are serious about helping me with the book on old age. I think I should get to work on it soon. I have enough material, some of it already written in full form, to stoke a hotel furnace. And here I am, 60 years old! I used to think I might write a good book by the time I was fifty. Then I raised it to 55. And *now* look....

Well, perhaps I should shrug about that too. We are together in preferring the shrug to the jog, any time... really a civilized form of exercise, since with practice and loving attention it can involve the cranial activity as well as the muscular system....

And it would be a fine thing indeed if you would want to comment on my comments. I'll try to hurry things a little, before you change your mind. One good friend of mine promised to help me with the project, and after a year or so of occasional exchanges of rather interesting data, she telephoned to say, "I can finally sum up the whole thing about old age: to *hell* with it." She was then almost 80, however, and I don't think either of us should wait that long.

....

St. Helena, California   *20.ix.68*
To : Henry Volkening

Dear Henry:

Gee. I'm sorry I was grumpy... probably I sent that copy of Bill's letter to Bill himself. Ah well and ho hum. I'm not grumpy any more, but have nothing to forward to you in proof of it!

And it is now the 22nd, typical of my fractured time-sequence right now, and the first day of Autumn, which I hope will be a good one for you and all of us. I plan as definitely as I can to come back for three or four days, before the end of October.

About Targ: another letter from him, and definitely our honeymoon is over, now that he actually has the book in hand. He wants me to change the beginning... does not like the reference to a rather poor novel, and so on. I can do this easily. BUT his title suggestions continue to be impossible... he suggests *The Anatomy of Gastronomy*, for instance! Or, he writes, "... how about taking off from an old classic, the well-tempered clavier *(sic)* by Bach, and calling your book *The Well Tempered Cook*? I rather like that." I would guess that there are at least a dozen such titles available, right now... the last one I can think of is Arnold Gingrich's *The W. T. Angler.*

St. Helena, California, and Aix-en-Provence, France: 1954–1970   271

Obviously it is too easy for me to be a little bitchy about poor Bill, and I am ashamed of it, when he has been so all-forgiving this far. But he simply does not get the point of my book. He writes, "I'll be reading the manuscript shortly... I'll report to you when I do." So you may get a flabbergasted withdrawal of withdrawal, one more proof that ignorance *was* bliss.

Meanwhile I have a title I think might be fine: *The Kitchen Innocents*. In the book I talk often of a recipe as an innocent, meaning one simple enough for children, grand-daddies, and even the constitutionally naive (like me). There is not a recipe in the book that would ever get past the door of a really classical kitchen... and people like Craig Claiborne, Jim Beard, Mike Field, and even my loyal and dear friend Julia Child are going to be really embarrassed by my whole approach to "family cooking." So it seems to me that with a slight re-writing of the already worn-down Introduction I could make the title clear enough.... And really it has a nice sound to it. What do you think? . . . .

I'm still dead on the *Holiday* thing, but am not worrying. But I do want to meet the deadline, or thereabouts... as I recall, it was rather vague: "in the late Autumn," something like that. I'll send a little ice-breaker off, fairly soon, and this time get a copy to you(!).

I'm afraid I think you are right that even though you should go away, you'd be better off not to. When I was dashing around France two summers ago I thanked God that I had done it before, so that I knew a lot of artful dodges, and that I was not a day older, for the waits, and inconveniences, and disappointments, and frustrations were something I'd hate to have to cope with if I felt fragile in any way.

Well, Henry, the Something Else is a lot of things I am remembering about being a child and young girl in Whittier, and I am almost embarrassed to tell you so. There are simply TOO MANY books about childhoods. I NEVER read them, or almost never. But I did not want to start the *Holiday* thing, nor get into the Old Age thing and then have to stop it for the *Holiday* thing, and I started getting some really strange facts off my mind. I suppose the nostalgia in the pieces for Rachel did the trick... and my gunnis do people like that! I am getting quite a lot of fan mail after the first article, all very happy and usually very lengthy letters telling me what *they* remember about Hershey bars and mashed potatoes and such. Well, here I am, pounding away with real enjoyment about being little in a Quaker village in what is now Disneyland-cum-smog.[1] I am not writing with any idea of trying to publish it. I am taking a little vacation, and clearing out a few more mental drawers.

Yes, right now money is not a worry, thanks to your Machiavellian methods. I take a very dim view of the future and the value of almost anything at all, but I have socked some away, in case a dollar is still worth at least $25\frac{1}{4}$-cents in a few years. I would like to buy a fat letter of credit and head for Provence again, but right now it is impossible. So I sit tight, and now and then invest in a mad case of champagne or a dozen fruit-knives... or write my unpublishable memoirs. All this will change.

1. These pieces became *Among Friends*.

About politics, me too ("totally discouraged"). I can't quite face it. Yes, I'll gladly run with you in 1972 (if we still can and if, as you say, there will be a 1972). Anything but Ministers of Finance...

As for sparrows being cheerful all the time, I suspect they have some low moments. BUT HOW ABOUT THE DOLPHINS? NEVER FORGET THEIR SMILING FACES....

Yrs. non-politically,

....

St. Helena, California   *4.x.68*

To : Julia Child

Dear F*R*I*E*N*D... Thank you for writing to me on September 26. Your letter came the same day I mailed one to you and Paul....

The story by that bright girl Nora Ephron is *delicious*... very funny indeed, with of course a lot of it especially good if one has met a few of the main contestants or whatever they/you may be called. I have not met C.C.[1] but for years he has sent me books and I have exchanged little notes with him and he has invited me to Long Island and so on. The caricature, which is quite funny but not really good, makes him look like Vice-Pres. Humphrey????

Eleanor Friede sends me clippings when she finds them, but she missed this one and I'll ask her if she saw it, and if not send it to her, for she is really fond of both Jim B and Michael,[2] in different ways of course... and she has met you, I believe.

Why would anyone think Paul is a Republican? Does he look like one? That reminds me that when I was asked to serve on a Civilian Defense committee for mass-feeding in case of disaster (! in this little Valley... but a few years ago we managed to house and feed almost double our population after a terrible forest fire...), I agreed very willingly to help, but refused to sign the "Oath"... and the head of the Committee said with real shock and horror, "She *looks* like a lady!!! How *can* she be a Communist?"

I'm sorry about the Bavarian Cream. In the editorial it says that Miss Ephron planned to take a cooking course but gave it up... too bad!

I agree with you about the over-use of "one"... especially in such a book as yours. The introduction must be J. Child, eye to eye with the millions of adoring readers. (The mail still comes in, mostly about you... and you are mostly called "Julia," tout court. Several women have discovered, through you, that their husbands can't keep their eyes off you for one thing and that they love to think about good cooking for another!!!! There seems to be no overt jealousy... just a general amazement. That sounds tactless. I mean that they are amazed that they do not mind losing their husbands to you, because they are already in your thrall, themselves....)

Well... I feel strongly about lifting countless recipes from both bad and good cookbooks and fobbing them off as original. There is really no such thing as an original

1. Craig Claiborne
2. James Beard and Michael Field

dish, I think. Even the greatest are adaptations: there is what the good cook already knows, what he has observed of local tastes, what his best supplies are in different seasons, what somebody suggests to him... and suddenly he is famous for having "invented" Pêches Melba, or Vichyssoise, or *la tapinade.* A true cook always knows this, I think. But cooks must feed their egos as well as their customers....

My early and final experience in so-called plagiarism was when the lawyers of Irma Goodrich Mazza wrote to my agent about suing me for using "her" method of cooking spaghetti (I had already written candidly of my admiration for her *Herbs in the Kitchen,* which I still use and admire). I think we both said something completely classic and time-worn like "Into a gallon of boiling water put one pound of spaghetti..." —something like that. She probably added salt to the water, but I don't, because I think it can toughen packaged spaghetti and we are rather salt-less by habit. Well... it was too funny to be believed, so with a straight face Henry Volkening offered to settle out of court for $15.00, and to our complete astonishment and delight Mrs. Mazza seriously agreed to this, and for years I kept the receipted check pinned above my desk, to remind me that I must be very careful about where I learned how to boil an egg, cut a pound of butter into quarters, or even boil *water.*

Personally, still on the subject, I don't see any reason in cribbing, the way so many second-rate "idea" books do... except that the staff writers who grind them out have neither the time nor the energy to test and adjust. (Nor the skill, most often. I take a dim view of the floods of books I am supposed to look at....) Why buy some mediocre panaché,[3] especially of regional recipes, when they are easily available in any standard manual? At best, they have a few real gems in them which one has to dig out and then copy and file, since the books themselves are shoddy and they take up room. Rarely, like a great planet, comes A BOOK: Mrs. Beeton's, Mrs. Rombauer's, Montagne's, yours. Willynilly, they are enough. But I'll tell you, because I know I can, that even in yours I have "adapted" a couple of things because of local tastes... the mustard sauce for roasting lamb, for instance, which I prepared a couple of times for enthusiastic budding gastronomers all under 18 who could not quite wrap themselves around the correct (your) quantity of the spice. Well... *you* don't care. I learned a lot from your method and from the whole thing, *y inclus* the adolescent potentialities. But I sure-as-Hell would not fob that off as *my* recipe! Nor, on the other hand, would I write for permissions from your publisher and then go on and tell what I did with it. I would straddle the problem, if it ever came up, by saying, "This is the way I learned it from Child, with a couple of minor changes." Do you think that is all right? I do it with (Do I mean *to*???) Escoffier quite a bit... I love some of his things, but am barren of truffles, to put it nicely. I can cheat with good mushrooms and local olives, now and then. And I do it all the time with Rombauer... I read what she has to say about something, and then go on and cope with the piece of meat or or or that's on hand. (Escoffier also helps me with Method a lot... so does Larousse. So, and greatly, do you.)

Well... it's still a knotty question, I suppose. But it seems to me that any IDIOT

3. Mixture, often used for culinary assortments such as seafoods

would be grateful to you for simplifying-rectifying-clarifying an outdated and even obsolete recipe. It will not be *yours*. It will be the way *you* have found it best to prepare.

I wasn't invited to the Wine bash… put too firm a NO on such things with the opening one. (By now would gladly accept the free ride… ho hum.)

I too like the T-L books… very pretty, and some of the recipes are divine-heavenly. Which reminds me that several people have told me that the ones you attended to in the French book have suddenly opened new doors for them.…

Good luck on the wild rush with the book… at its *worst* it must still be fun, to go from notes to stove to files to pantry… I await the end eagerly, and meanwhile I consult Vol. 1 probably once or twice a week, and push it upon brides, friends, and even people. And inside I purr, for you and Paul and I are F*****S.

………………………………………………

St. Helena, California   *18.x.68*
To: Estelle Nemkov

Dear Mrs. Nemkov:

Your letter was fascinating, for many reasons, and I am sorry to be this late in thanking you for it. (Digression: I would love to hear the fantastic story of Mr. G.![1] Yes, he did live in my house in Switzerland, but he owned it outright. It has now been sold by his sons to a rich German lady.)

I am truly pleased that the *New Yorker* articles bring back good memories to you. And I am thrilled to meet a sister of Oscar Mendelssohn, whom I admire very much. I don't consider his dedication effusive! Please convey my respectful greetings to him.

I admire you for your wise and jaunty acceptance of losing one sense. I know two really endowed cooks who are blind, but you are the first I have met who cannot smell. As for old Saintsbury's *physical* recall, I myself am inclined to assume that it was more mental… just as I suspect that I do not remember lying in the bottom of a rowboat in Puget Sound when I was less than three, but that I recall clearly being told about it when I was still very young.

Editors are indeed foolish, and at the risk of libel I think the *Gourmet* editors have often led the pack. I wish you would try again with your article. There is an increasing interest, especially among doctors, in the physiological facets of gastronomy.…

I don't blame O. M. for screaming about macadamias. They are worth their weight in gold, but what does he care, really? He can write with the ease denied to millionaires.

When I was a child in Southern California, there were wonderful guava bushes, and my family made jellies and preserves with what we had not already eaten. Now it is difficult to buy one in a specialized nursery. As for papaya, we can now buy them from Mexico, although they are less good than from Hawaii. We can also get mangoes now and then, but I have yet to buy a good one. . . .

I am much interested in the increasing number of good programs being included

1. Arnold Gingrich

in public school education... I mean musical programs. When my girls and I lived in France, they were active members of La Jeunesse Musicale, which is still the best such program I know about, and here in California I am involved in a thin but promising program in our country, for the lower grades. A small start...

Your letter was very reassuring: I have boiled dressing in my past, and you have dampers! But you have a violinist husband, and O. M. for a brother... and I'm pretty lucky too.

Sincerely,

....

St. Helena   *27.ix.68*
To: Mrs. Haupt

Dear Mrs. Haupt:

I am ashamed to be this late in thanking you for your very interesting letter. I have been away, and it followed me about, and then I'll confess that it got slightly buried under neglected bills and such. I do hope that you will forgive me, although I'm afraid I can be of no help at all about getting a copy of *Map of Another Town*.

Perhaps it would help things to write directly to the publishers, Little, Brown, in Boston. A lot of people want the book, but it went out of print almost immediately. Vroman's may help... of course Pickwick does no second-hand stuff any more. Or go to a good small place like Marian Gore's in San Gabriel and get her to advertise. She used to have a lot of my books, I know.

Meanwhile, how nice it is to know that somebody still wants a copy! I wish I could send you one, but I am in the same boat... got *one* last year through a 2nd-hand dealer, to give to my family.... Publishers are strange critters. (Probably all frustrated authors feel that way...?)

Your life sounds like a very full and exciting one, in every way. I would like to be in your shoes, although mostly I am well pleased with my own. I wish that I had had more children, and I wish that I were not a widow. Otherwise I have nothing to ask for.

About travelling alone: it is very true that there is nothing better than learning new things, new words, new vistas, with a man you love. But two summers ago I was given the chance to go *alone* to Paris and then Southern France (to work on the first Time-Life book about provincial French cooking, which has beautiful pictures in it, in case you do not know it...), and I felt strangely curious... not panicky at all... about being there by myself for the first time in my whole life. Always before I had been with parents, husbands, children. AND IT WAS WONDERFUL. I kept marvelling at what a fortunate person I was, to have been there so often before, so that now it seemed like a kind of distillation of everything good, almost like a reward of some kind. I had to do a lot of things with people, of course, but often I arranged to be alone, and in Paris I walked at least once a day the whole length of the Tuileries, and usually back again, and I ate alone as much as I could. I admit that I did not go out to good restaurants alone at night: that is basically dismal, for most head-waiters wonder if one is either a potential lush or an elderly pick-up, at my time of life! When I could, I ate a big tureen of fresh soup and a pile of good strawberries and drank a bottle of wine on my own attic balcony... and even that had a mysterious satisfaction about it which I could never have understood if I had not done the same thing on the same balcony many times before, with my husband. Well... you see how good things can be! It is true that when my two girls and I lived in Provence, their real charm and their good manners and their delighted curiosity opened doors for me which would have stayed pretty firmly shut if I had been by myself.

I agree with you that San Francisco is a dream-spot for the quick World Tour! I think it would be very nice if we could meet, sometime when you have come that far... I am only 70 miles further to the North, and would be pleased to see any or all of you if you wanted to pretend to visit a couple of wineries and then see me instead! I am not quite as old as some of them... but I do have a basement built by the Chinese!

I am in full agreement with your decision to live fully *now*. On the last trip I took with my husband,[1] we were in Venice and he wanted to go on around the Adriatic on a slow but elegant little ship, and I felt that he was too ill... and soon after that he died. I shall always regret my practicality or whatever it was....

I don't know if you know of a book of mine called *The Art of Eating*. It is still in print, by World, and it is a bargain because there are five (or is it six?) books in it. You might like parts of it.

There is stuff running now in the *New Yorker* in a section called "Gastronomy Re-called"... chapters from a book which will be published in Oct. '69. I suspect that my small world of readers will be completely fed up with it and me, by then....

Thank you for writing... please forgive me for being late... and accept my good wishes for all your family in whatever they may be doing.

And BON VOYAGE.......

....

St. Helena, California   *28.ix.68*
To: Paul and Julia Child

    Chers A*M*I*S:

It makes me feel happy or something like that, to think that our abrupt meeting[1] continues into what I myself accept as a warm and hopefully lasting friendship. My father used to propose a small toast now and then: "Here's to myself, for good men are scarce and few." That is how I feel about you both.

    Here's to you.

I have several things to ask and tell you, but first, thank you for your jolly little card. I am glad you find the things in the *NYer* all right. I often wonder how they will strike you, Julia, once you asked me if I really laughed at la cuisine classique, and I tried to tell you that I never had, that I revered and respected it, and that in general *au-contraire-*

1. In 1940 MF and Dillwyn went to Europe in search of his medication.
1. Julia Child met MF at the airport in Boston on her return from the Time-Life trip to Provence.

Madame-au-contraire. And I have been thinking about that, and wondering how my completely naive small-town Mid-and-Western approach to everyday cooking would strike both of you. And then when the magazine dictated a title for the new section, "Gastronomy Recalled" or whatever it is, I at once wondered what on earth you'd think, for it is not gastronomical at all, but instead very limited, like something a Jewish Arab would write if she had been brought up in Tunis... or an English girl in Addis Ababa perhaps. Well, I feel relieved, and much more, that you like the stuff. I hope it will continue to amuse you now and then. Some of it will of course be shudderful.

I am getting a surprising, and often amusing lot of mail about the pieces, and about four out of five tell me about Julia Child..., "Now THERE is a girl who knows what a decent meal means...." (Really, no mean ones so far... besides reminding me that I have a lot to learn, mostly from JC, they tell me about how much better *their* grandmothers' boiled dressing was....) . . .

Also, have you heard a spoof of JC by Fanny Flagg? I think it is quite funny, and hope you do too. Of course, I must remind you that I have only listened to ten minutes in my whole life of the programs, because I don't have a TV.

I am very glad you went to Mt. Desert Island. Sometimes in my attic, about from midnight to before dawn, I can hear a lot of good noises. One year there were almost no birds, but now they have come back stronger, and I think a little shriller, than ever... nourished on pesticides and insecticides and and and????? I have never seen a moose in his chosen state, nor a bear. Either would raise the hair on my head with plain awe. But I have lived intimately with hummingbirds... probably not the kind on your Island... desert....

I've been wretched about writing to Eda, not to mention a few other people very dear to me. I am glad she sat out les jours de mai... they must have reminded her of a lot of other days rather the same.[2] She has endured so much that I think she is almost indestructible. Perhaps that is why I delay so shamefully in writing to her? I assume she will "still" be there....

Janet Flanner wrote to me that the worst thing for her, in Paris, was the lack of buses and taxis and such. Different from what happened in the South, the restaurants and hotels seemed well supplied with food... if one could only walk to them. And they did a fat business.

I wish I could fly straight to Boston, even if it interrupted The Job. But it seems very doubtful. (I refer to your job, not mine... I am "between engagements," for a time....) I rather wish you were in Plascassier, but I have a good feeling about that solid warm friendly house on Irving Street, and I hope I'll be there again.

Any time you can use me as a sugar lump following no matter what kind of medicine, I am available! It sounds to me as if you lead a mad life in California, with big bashes here and there. I'd probably see more of you in Cambridge. But *IN CASE...* I can recommend this Valley (it is at its peak now, with the crushing in full swing and

2. Student protests in France had shut down Paris streets in May 1968.

the vineyards begging to turn all colors and gondolas rushing along the main road dripping ripe juice...).

I send love, and I hope you are well and excited about the work....

Is La Pitchoune[3] Empty? Who is there? It must be somebody Nice. Right now I remember best the painting of the olive trees, quite cold, and the kitchen table so solid like them but warm.

....

St. Helena, California   12.ii.69
To: Sam Davis

Dear Sam... I liked your letter, and am sorry to be this late in saying so. I was waylaid by Brother Bronchitis, a friend of St. Francis as you may remember... boring rendezvous which I keep occasionally.

To get straight business out of the way, I can report that the two boxes of books arrived in good shape, that I have paid for the second one, and I thank you and F&W[1] very much for the unexpected lagniappe of the first one. There are few left. I hope the general public likes the book as much as my friends seem to. Of course there is some prejudice at work there, but most of them are really interested in the dictionary itself... as I am too. (It makes a very good "bed-side book," and I have tested it on a few fussy visitors....) . . .

I hope you kept on avoiding the HK thing.[2] Here people still seem a little hooked on it, or really on its mysterious after-effects. It is SO complicated to survive in this brave new world....

I am glad you have no need to fret about meshing the daily life and the sitting. . . .

I don't see what difference gin would make, really. Sooner or later you would not want it... or perhaps want it even more? I don't like gin, you know. But I like the way it makes me feel. It dulls the razor's edge. It softens the harshness, now and then, of having to cope with my innate shyness (giving a speech, and that sort of thing...). I don't want very much of it, fortunately for my liver and/or my local reputation. But a little, now and then, is a very fine thing.

I too have heard sorry reports about being a Yank or even an Anglo in places like Egypt. I don't think I could stand the silence, the averted eyes.

I got a little of this when I was in France two summers ago... but NOT from taxi-drivers and waiters and so on! From my closest and oldest friends! There were two things they could not bring themselves to mention, because they loved me and suffered for my being an American, the murder of John Kennedy, and the war in Vietnam. It was actually painful to me, because *they* were *protecting* me. As for the countless unknowns who took care of me, they were courteous, kind, amusing, as French people

3. Julia and Paul Child's house in Plascassier
1. Funk and Wagnall's
2. Hong Kong flu (?)

have always been. (I get a little upset when I am told long stories about how surly and sly they are... NEVER. Ah well and Ho hum...)

It will be fun to break bread together... here, there. Which reminds me that for more than thirty years I have had a firm date with a man I have never met except by letter, for a double Gibson! Here, there...

This surely proves something about the nature of the beast, but I am not sure what.

By the time he and I meet for that drink, we may choose a glass of barley water... and you and I may settle for two little Jars of pureed baby-food. But it will still be fun.

Best... and thank you again for agreeing to mix business with pleasure!

....

St. Helena, California   *18.iii.69*
To: Henry Volkening

Dear Henry: What a wretched business! Bursitis is said to be much more painful in men than in women, which makes it ghastly indeed. And this morning D. Russell called and said you were at home "with the flu perhaps"... Ho hum, verily. Perhaps you should get the hell out of that manic-megalopolis NOW instead of in a couple of weeks? (Now that Mr. Nixon has opted for San Diego instead of Palm Springs, you'd be perfectly safe in the latter Shangri-la....)

I read every word you write to me. And even some of the ones in magic ink that needs a candle-flame in the full of the moon. . . .

Now to your ever-thoughtful remarks: (1) I am comforted that other people have mature children who never write but make long affectionate collect calls.

(2) I do *too* like to have some money when I need it, and whenever Putnam's wants to pay me, now that the book is obviously accepted, is all right.

(3) I realize that it is a publishing impossibility to do what I first thought would be necessary: check the *NYer* stuff with the galleys. So... I would like to stipulate, if it is ethical and all that, that I check ONE MORE TIME on the recipes etc. I'll promise to do it fast, d.v. But even the *NYer* (!) has managed to drop one line from a recipe... and God knows what Putnam's might do. I have made this clear in my last note to Bill T, which had a copy I sent to you (I think).

(4) As you now know, title is heartily approved... and today a most polite and jolly note from T, approving as well my request that the pompous list of references be dropped, and that the chapters carry their explanatory subtitles on the list of chapters but not the chapter pages. Wow. . . .

The *House Beautiful* stuff interests me not. Not one whit, one bit. I thought you wanted me to suggest where Mr. Segal could turn if he had any real interest in turning. As for me, pooh (Unless for some strange reason you asked me to reconsider. Then I would try to drag up some old references or or or or. The prospect dismays me, even on paper...). . . .

(7) I imagine you will not make it to the hushed snack-bar of MacMillan. If you do,

you may not be as amused as I was, because you have been subjected to the Treatment so much oftener than I. But do report, anyway!

(8) As long as we both shall live, I'll enjoy cackling with you over our unwritten masterpieces, and I think the worm-book is the best yet. Please keep on.

A friend wrote to me lately, about something I'd suggested which touched her usually hardened (or numbed) spirit, that when we sat together in a rest home, snarling and shaking our canes at each other, she would remember my suggestion and not hit me. I thought that was a nice promise.

As for our movie-rights, you keep the whole thing. Thanks. (Which reminds me: what movie-man is brave enough to do the consummate who-dun-it, Muriel Sparks's *Memento Mori*? That is a perfect chiller, and I think there are enough wonderful trained but ELDERLY actors and actresses who could do a fine job....)

Which reminds me of Fitzgerald's short story about Benjamin Button. That would make a very good film... or perhaps play? Or has it been milked already? I don't go much out....

I love what you say about Anna. Me too. I agree. I am a woman, and by coincidence her mother, but I understand what you say. Now things are very grim. But each time, and always, I am human idiot enough to think that perhaps it is the *last* time, and that things will smile. The little boy is much in my thoughts, but his die has been cast too... By what? Why? How? That is the puzzlement.

Etc.

I hope you don't think me rash to turn down the *Family Circle* job DR mentioned. Impossible. There is nothing more to say about Fanny Farmer. And I am just about ready, as soon as the soggy ground dries a bit more, to spend a few creaking aching sweaty wonderful days in The Yard, pulling up stuff and cutting out stuff and in general sniffing the *sacre du printemps*.

Once you feel almost fine again, treat yourself with *especial* tender care. Take naps. Do stuff like that.

Yur fren...

....

St. Helena, California   9.iv.69
To: Sam Davis
Dear Sam:

Thank you for writing when you got back. Your feeling for Egypt reminds me a little of my last caper of insisting on taking the Zephyr train to Denver and back: such wretched fipsal assaults, and yet such unbelievable beauty outside. The life we were trapped in. And I am interested by your advice to take tours. Actually, I think this is true almost everywhere. It seems the best way to make travel reservations, hotel too... all that frantic boring detail. Myself, I would always choose to be alone if I were on familiar ground... but otherwise, I might find myself succumbing to the mob-need.

I'm so glad you went back to Greece, and then *stayed* there. For about 30 years, I planned to become an old woman there. I would learn modern Greek; I would live very simply. I would be at home. That dream is gone. But I feel happy that my younger sister still holds to it. She went back two years ago, and I think she'll return.

I am not at all "unhappy" with the dictionary. Of course it is very open to criticism... I'm sure that many of us know this and certainly you and I did. It was fun to do... I mean my very small part in it... and look what happened. Here we are friends....!

With Bold Knife and Fork will be published by Putnam's in October, and meanwhile... the *New Yorker* has to print several more chapters of it. I have already proofed two, and hope for my poor publisher's sake that our capricious magazine pals keep to their gentleman's agreement.

. . . No, I don't fly... I piled up some fourteen hours solo in the days when planes belonging to rich crazy friends were made of matchsticks and linen. Yes, I prefer hedgehoppers, twoseaters, and helicopters to jets. No, I have never made a balloon flight, and by now the prospect would horrify me: I'd want to jump. No, I am not lecturing now, except for a few times a year for a wine-appreciation course we give here in the valley. Yes, I think my life is indeed very full and rich. I am lucky that I continue to want it to be even more so.

I don't know when I'll be in New York. Perhaps in May? I'll let you know.

Has it been difficult for you to get back to the job, whatever that may be?

Best,

....

St. Helena, California   *10.v.69*

To: Rachel MacKenzie, New Yorker *editor*

Dear Rachel...

Here are the galleys for the egg story.

I did not stretch out on my couch, but thanks to your example I sat right down at the kitchen table, with a little glass of dry vermouth (This you did not suggest!), and went right through them. Fine. As always I have benefited, and I thank you and Mr. Shawn. . . .

Here the air is still unpolluted, and of a rare sweetness... right now the honeysuckle, a few weeks ago the wild mustard in the vineyards, before long the smells of ripening grapes and then the crushing.... I have a friend who lost two senses in a bad auto-crash: smell and taste. I often think of this... might it not be better to be blind, or even deaf?

Oh yes, I do think all the time of coming to the East. But I am pinned here... pot-bound like an old geranium... sticky complications about Anna and her child. I feel fine, if somewhat restless now and then, and want to finish the things about my childhood in the Quaker ghetto (Aunt Gwen?),[1] and then quite possibly go right into the

1. This became *Among Friends*.

Old Age file, if I can dig up enough courage and plain guts to do it... some thirty years of shillyshally!

I got a very fat and surprising check from Mr. Greenstein... some sort of payment for something... I do thank all of you very much, and accept it with pleasure. I think I may succumb to my friends' urgings and buy a small portable dish-washer... not *portable* but the kind one can push around. In this past week I have had three gatherings of really wonderful wine people, two inadvertently, and in all have washed and polished perhaps 165 wine glasses, really a tedious if hypnotically agreeable task.... This wild extravagance (The truth is that I hate machinery and gadgets) would cost me perhaps a tenth of the *lagniappe*... I think I owe it to posterity or something?

No, I have not bought a hat.

....

St. Helena, California   *17.v.69*
To: Eleanor Friede

Squeek... dere fren... a few things in my head to tell you, and I never get them onto the paper....

About fingernails: I now follow religiously the Kask Method, and my nails are MUCH STRONGER. I think this is partly because I do give them more care when they are innocent of "polish"????? Also I know that my mother, who was very fussy about such things, always said that liquid nail polish was not only vulgar but harmful. She was raised to use a buffer or buff... I forget which it was called, but of course the back was of sterling silver to match the Dresser Set (brush, comb, mirror, powder box, etc etc...)... and as we daughters began to show signs of possible blossoming, we were initiated into the rites of buffing our nails, to make them shiny and glowing a healthy or tortured pink. I wonder about that now? Well... carry on oh ye Kask Girls!

This will amuse you... yesterday David Bouverie called and asked me if I were brave, and I said sure I was, and he said will you help me out and come to lunch tomorrow with Her Royal Highness the wife of Hussein of Jordan, his sister, and a lady in waiting, with the chef de Protocol and one Jordanian chief from the Dept. of State, plus Matthew Kelly who is the Porfirio Rubirosa[1] of Sonoma County, and I said sure. So I went over there... bad Saturday traffic... got there about noon... wore black canvas flats, black pants, tired old white silk overblouse with faded green designs. Drank gently at champagne and listened to some gossip from David and Kelly... perfectly beautiful weather, with dreadful music piped in not too subtly... some more or less Jordanian jazz from Paris, etc. David had seen Truman lately in SF . . . Pia Lindstrom is a nympho. Etc. David looked as if he had just scrubbed for Surgery, in skin-tight whites by Yves St. Laurent... and Matthew was wearing flaming red cotton pants he had had run up for $2.19 in Puerto Vallarta, held up with an old neck-tie, blue espradrilles, a very pink Brooksy shirt, and a red bandanna, around his neck, I mean. No

1. Notorious ladies' man in the 1960s

earring. Well… the Jordanians arrived in two cars. Her R.H. looked tired: an English girl too common-born ever to be accepted as Queen, it appears, but no dope… seemingly rather colorless, at least today, but I would say very strong-willed. She has dignity, and was simple in her manners… sat nicely, and all that, and when she spoke she said something. She is called Princess Mona, since she cannot be queen, but is always addressed as Your R.H. and referred to as Her R.H. I had never eaten with a queen before, even uncrowned, but soon got used to the protocol. I found the King's Sister, also Her Highness of course, very interesting… a dynamic young woman who is as handsome as I find him, except that his features are a little too big for a woman and she has a heaviness about her face which disappears as one grows accustomed to it. The lady-in-waiting is American born, probably Irish, but Jordanian through her husband for several years. I liked her very much, after I got used to her very small snubbed-nose face. The Chef de Protocol was a typical VIP bureaucrat, and I got stuck with him, more or less… very polished, cautious, worried. The SD man was like an overweight champ, feinting and shadow-boxing. Both men, one fat and one thin, looked as if they had just pranced off the chorus line at Finocchio's… their faces were in drag, and their beautiful eyelashes made them look like Mistinguette on a bad night. They were very cool customers, dressed correctly in impeccable dark silk suits, white shirts, and black ties. The SD man was second to the Chef de Protocol, and attended to various accommodations for about four servants who came along, to drive the cars and open doors and things. (David also had Phyllis at the stove, plus the taller of those two Blacks who were there, plus a new white boy being trained, plus Phyllis's oldest daughter, for servers… all this for eight people. Wow. Very smooth and neat, too.) Oh… The Queen, the Princess, and the little Lady wore scarves tied in the latest correct mode around their drab-blonde and in the last two cases very black hair. Very nice scarves. The Queen and the Lady wore very high minis. The Princess wore a navy-blue linen suit, like your Wragge but without sleeves. . . . Well… you may remember that David is a voracious eater, so we were served a long rich hot luncheon on a slightly stiff hot day, with nice local wines, and I could hardly wait to leave. None of the men interested me. Actually, I would like to be able to spend some time with Hussein's sister… a very interesting girl. The Lady was fun… she plays the naive-but-sharp-as-a-tack foil for the Queen, who is quiet and plodding and as hard as steel.

I feel sorry for Hussein, when they go creeping back royally to Jordan. . . .

I have one other thing to tell you but I can't remember it now. I've got to get down to brass tacks or whatever is most uncomfortable… have my galleys to do for Targ (idée vomiteuse!!!!!), and two mss. to read for desperate and loved friends… the geraniums are still unpotted… Chas Newton and I went to *Anything Goes* tonight, put on by the St. Helena Players which he unwittingly helped start when he was about 12… he loves his summer job but frankly admits that he hates W*O*R*K… news is hopelessly dismal about Anna but I am absolutely tied legally, until and unless Chris is once more picked up for Juvenile Hall… work is at a standstill, to put it neatly AGAIN… I feel quite well, thank you, and hope you do too. Am in a cooking phase, so that I can ignore the galleys, and have turned out a few really very commendable meals lately. Made a superb… yes, I said it, superb… strudel yesterday… used the store-dough which I can get in Berkeley at Co-op… invented a filling… my god but it was delicious, a tour de force which I shall most probably never make again. (Which is all right with me.)

Ask the president of the Kask Nail Saving Security Council about old-fashioned buffing. She probably never heard of it. I think it is reserved for people born before 1920. (That lets you out too!) But I can state that my mother's fingernails were like glowing shells… and *sturdy*. As for the report on El Rancho Beaver, it is strictly for your amusement. Only you would be able to read between lines in this case….

··

St. Helena, California   *24.vi.69*
To: Weare Holbrook[1]

Dear Weare:

Thank you for writing. It is a very occasional excitement for me to find a note from you… perhaps three in some thirty years? But always the excitement… After all, who else would have given me a year's subscription to *Dial?* Who else would have brought me copies of *The Masses*, not yet *New?* Who else… etc etc????

I don't know that it was the Jews who made the *NYer* "so fat and slippery" but I myself find very little time for it, and am thankful Shawn finally bowed to decades of pressure and put in that handy Index. If I'm in it, I put the copy on a pile of possible libel suits. Otherwise I check for "The Paris Letter" and a few things, and undoubtedly miss plenty of titbits….

I am very glad you and Catherine like what I've written lately. It will be in a book in late October… in fact it was already a book and then the *NYer* bought it by chapters, which was fine for my exchequer but hard on the publishers… and I'll send it to you if you'd like it.

It may interest you that I am gradually hewing out some remarks about being a minority-group child in a Quaker ghetto. It is tough to stick to my actual recall and not embroider. Good exercise. Probably unpublishable. Interesting aspect of religious and racial prejudices… also ethnic, with Grandmother so adamantly North-of-Ireland-Iowan in that land of Thees and Thous and daily Snubs.

About my Kennedy grandparents: your letter came while my sister Norah was here for a couple of days. She is now 52, and my sole remaining sibling. Her views and mine about this situation of the grandparents are completely at odds… we are almost ten years apart, and she lived in quite a different family from mine. For instance, I was almost nine when she was born, up in Whittier, and had lived a long life there, and a very good happy one in the main. She was less than three when we moved to the Ranch, and then in a few years Anne and I went away to schools and she and David knew Grandfather and Grandmother Kennedy quite differently from the ways I had been permitted… and had permitted myself, secretly.

1. MF's cousin

At the risk of sounding like an amateur Jeudina or Frungiaa I think that Mother was *conditioned* to believe that all women must hate their mothers-in-law, and that this was because she really hated her own mother and had to transfer the emotion. Well... Edith Oliver Holbrook Kennedy could never understand why I found my three legal mothers-in-law extremely interesting and indeed fascinating human beings, and she was DETERMINED not to trust-like-respect-honor Mary Lucinda Kennedy.

The plain facts are that the Kennedys were as well educated and "cultured," if not more so, than the Holbrooks, and that they had the courage to live chosen ways and not be dictated to. (Rex lost this quality and followed the paths laid out by his wife's family....) Grandfather was a rebel, a hot-head, a bigot, and a scholarly man. I remember the book of cross-word puzzles he hand-lettered for me when I started on "Gallia divisa est...." He read and could even pun in Latin, had some Greek, and could read the Old Testament in Hebrew. He also could whittle like an angel, raise chickens, write clear pungent editorials, set type, drive a topless Model-T like a devil... and when younger beat his four sons mercilessly.

Grandmother (I am getting long-winded, but your letter was the trigger, and I have been thinking much about it lately... and you can always skip and read the signature if you wonder who in hell is writing...)... Grandmother, called Lu by her husband (Mistake... her name was Mary *Luella*, not Lucinda), was a remarkable woman, I think. Only lately people have told me how pretty, how handsome, how beautiful she was. I was raised to think of her as an awkward loutish clod to be seen on the side porch if at all. Edith would go out there when they came with eggs, and usually some flowers, and Grandmother would go out to the side porch and rock back and forth and twitch quietly at a corner of her cheek. When she left, Mother would sigh with exaggerated relief and ask if we had noticed the dreadful old tennis shoes cut out beside the big toes because of the bunions.... All the time Grandmother looked beautiful and never tried to snatch at us emotionally to tell us she loved us too. It was very sad, and gradually I began to hate Mother for this.

Well, I am sounding very hostile to Edith by now. I regret a great deal. But I think that you and I too have made equally dreadful blunders, somewhere along the shifting lines of social realization or whatever it is. I know that my parents did the best they could to raise me to exist in worlds they could not envisage. I am sure Uncle Park and Aunt Virginia tried to with you and John. By now I have one girl, almost 26, who is classified as a manic-depressive, in and out of hospitals and with a consuming hatred and fear of me when she is manic... and I love her dearly and since her conception have done everything in my power to ready her for something better than what she has chosen. So how can I judge my own mother? How can I regret the beatings my father got? And and and...

About that 99% Holbrook ambience: rarely but rather strongly Rex would revolt against it! Usually he simply took off: Duck Lake in Michigan with Walter Kennedy, two weeks in Mexico. He had his own strengths. In general, though, we had a steady flow of "relatives" through our houses in Whittier and then at the Ranch, and nothing was too good for anyone even vaguely Holbrook... but the increasingly rare visits of the comparatively sparse Kennedy Klan were GRUDGINGLY attended to.

Here again my wonder was aroused, and I began to form my own sad opinions....

At this point in my life it seems incredible that never once were you taken to nor invited to the Puente Ranch.[2] But I can understand it in retrospect. Ho hum.

Oh... after G&G Kennedy[3] moved to Puente, we were allowed a couple of nights there over the next few years... we loved them too much, and Mother put an end to them. I was aware of this when it happened, but accepted her explanation that we had to sleep on feather beds and that they were not good for us. I in turn loved them, and was hoist on my own petard (or mattress) by telling Mother how wonderful they were. Anne and I shared an enormous one, and sank into it like two raisins in a soufflé. Well, the days were great things there... we ran around barefoot in Grandmother's violet beds, which she said was good for them: we helped Grandfather gather eggs and watched the chicks being born; the table for meals was always covered with little dishes of delicious things and we'd run out five minutes before supper to pluck off the asparagus tips; several times a day there was a Game, like Acrostics or Jack Straws, with Grandfather very stern and just (and fun). Well, where are the snows? Why did that have to be that way, so stolen?

My mother, after the two old people died lonely deaths, felt great regret. She would have changed it, but it was too late. She recognized Lu as a fine headstrong passionate well-educated person, not the disdained clod she had tried to tell herself and us that she was. Rex died fearing his father and loving his mother, but he had loved Edith more....

Oh... about meals... occasionally there would be great groanings and sneers from Edith, that it was time to invite the Grandparents for Thanksgiving. They were old-fashioned, and believed in meeting once a year to thank God. . . . We always got very cynical about this, instead of enjoying it to the hilt. Perhaps you were in on a couple? Murder. Edith simply could not relax and enjoy (to say an eminently ribald thing about a preeminently upright woman (in spite of herself))... she had to put us on guard against the old American customs as practiced by two people who had chosen their own paths.

Well...

Very complicated.

Perhaps some of this explains why you wondered why "their visits were brief" and you don't "recall either of them staying for a meal or even a sociable sit-down." *Edith was incapable of that.*

To get further back, I think she was brought up to fear and disdain small-town

2. Kennedy grandparents' ranch
3. MF's grandparents

Iowa life. She was the last of a large Victorian batch, as you may remember... Uncle Park was sixteen years older than she, and her mother candidly admitted that she wished Mother had never been born.... She was sent away to boarding school... did not even come home for six years... was then sent to a "finishing school"... and all the time was influenced by the RICH cousins and relatives who were making millions in Pittsburgh, which to her was the epicenter of sophistication and luxury and so on. In other words, she was taught to fear and despise the life her parents and many of her kin were leading, far from the Pittsburgh affluence. And later, when Edith married the penniless newspaper man and in an unaccustomed mood went with him to California, she tried to cling to her Pittsburgh security: once a year we got clothes from De Pinna and once a year a man came clear from England to take orders for mustard pickles and barley sugar, as if we lived in Injah. This poor woman needed a good spanking. And later she felt truly sorry that she had not permitted herself to accept Grandmother Kennedy as a really fine person, and Grandfather as an occasionally scary near-maniac. Too late.

End. I think. You did turn me on, dear Cousin!

Things go fairly well for me, and I hope they do for you both. I am comfortable, as you say you are, and often I am quite irresponsible too.

Love...

<hr>

St. Helena, California   *13.vii.69*
To: Paul and Julia Child

Dear Julia and Dear Paul:

It is Christmas to get a letter from you!

I'm sorry you had to leave La Pitchoune... six months of hard and even harder work, I suppose. I'll pray that you can finish by Dec. 20. What a ghastly job, to double-check for typos in the recipes! Here I've finished with everything but a look at the Index, but my stuff is literally Child's Play compared with what you have done and are doing. Courage, chers amis!

Thank you for being so hospitable, as always. I love to think that if I could go to Plascassier, I *could*... if you know what I mean and you do... stay there in that delightful peaceful house again. Really, I would like to lay a ghost or two, for I was in a state of deliberately suspended animation when I stayed there before. As I've told you, I was half-starved... I used to sneak titbits from Grasse and Mouanes-Sartoux into the cupboard, but I knew it displeased MF.[1] Frances lived on tea, and he on salami and vodka, and then we went every night to a * or ** or *** restaurant where almost always the food was DREADFUL, thanks to the summer hordes. I fared with comparative decency at the little pension, and the last night in Plascassier took the Fields there, where we ate very simply but Frances was pleased because I had asked for fresh pasta, and we

1. Michael Field; he, his wife Frances, and MF stayed at the Childs' home in Plascassier during their research trip for *The Cooking of Provincial France*, summer of 1966.

ended with a really excellent tarte à l'orange which the bonne à tout faire is rightly proud of. The whole summer was a strange gastronomical caper...

... and what a one you danced for Eda and Sybille. S must have purred like a cat with cream on its whiskers... and so of course did E in her silent way, when she sees S is happy. It is too bad she could not drink any of the wines. But she does eat with heartiness which always surprises me... I feel as if she is nourished on cobwebs. (Yes, her cough is distressing... she was here for a few days, and I could not but shudder at it. But she says she feels well. It was fun to have her and S separately, like married people who are occasionally more sparkly when they are seen one at a time....) I love every wine I have ever drunk in magnum... I do honestly think it improves it, although some people doubt me and I seldom have any way of proving my point! I like the idea of putting the slices of beef in the thin crust... and did I tell you that the best (in fact, one of the few *good* tries in this fashionable syndrome) Boeuf W. I ate was prepared meticulously according to your directions in *The French Chef*? The crust was perfect, the best the amateur (but good) chef had ever made. I love the idea of the Pèlerin with the Ch. d'Yquem... so elegant! . . .

Poor Dick W[2] (A good man has lately written to me "How can that poor devil survive pimping so long for that whorehouse?") asked me to do a couple of big jobs... of course to help him out of a pickle... and for what in my scale were enormous fees. I was sorry for him, but very pleased to be able to say no. I do like *him*. He has daughters out here, and I am pleased when he includes me in his visits to them, which he manages to do without seeming *too* paternal. . . .

I can't let myself think about another food magazine. All we need is a GOURMET CORNER in *The Atlantic*! (And as I remember, Charley Morton used to publish timid little essays of mine about eating and drinking!!!!) (Horror.)

Yes, back to T-L, why fool around with amateurs? All they want is names... as I proved conclusively when I said Take the 40,000 words, and here is your check, but just never use my name in any way. A few days later Mr. Luce died, a coincidence which has always bemused me a little....

Here things go well. I am dormant, temporarily... or lying fallow, or something like that. A lot of people come through the Valley, and this is the best restaurant and pub north of San Francisco, and instead of sitting cross-legged and chanting Om Ram Om Ram or like that, I cook while I meditate. I make a lot of cold things based on Provençal cooking, and am glad to know about the Oeufs en Pistouille. Could I use an oeuf mollet? I think so. I wonder if the tomato could be peeled? If it were firm enough... yes. (I find Americans are quite put off by being served tomatoes unskinned (... like serving fish with its spine still in it... I have to F*I*G*H*T to bone my own sole or sand-dab...) in a restaurant I mean. Once at Mme Lanes's in Aix, two American girls there from Smith complained to the Paris Bureau because they had been served some delicious small Mediterranean fish which had not been boned... they had never tasted anything but frozen filet....)

2. Richard Williams, Time-Life editor

My dear Julia and Paul, you are perhaps the busiest people I know, and I am chattering and taking your time. It is nice for me, though. Thank you for leaving latches on doors. And please give my warm greetings to Mrs. de Voto.[3]

<hr />

St. Helena, California   *7.x.69*
To: The entire family

Dear Family:

I have decided upon something which I know promises me times of regret and loneliness, but after long thought I feel that it is wise.

I shan't be at home this Christmas, to welcome you to the real warmth and love that is always yours, when you want to accept it.

For more than fifty years I have been "the oldest in the family," and, because of my nature, have enjoyed almost every aspect of planning for some sort of celebration at the end of the year. By now I think that I should hand over that role to younger people, if there are any who want to play it.

There are now three generations of us who could meet, each one forming or adapting to its own patterns of family life. There are many things about our past few Christmas fiestas that have been forced, or artificially nostalgic and acquiescent. I think it is dishonest, to pretend once a year or so to hang on to the Past.

It is also more of a physical strain on me than it used to be, to try to keep halls decked with holly and the larder full… and the pace a generally pleasant one.

Therefore I plan to absent myself. I don't yet know where I'll go, but most probably it will be alone. That is not an unfamiliar condition to me, and it holds no apprehensions.

I'll hope that all of you, after your own fashions, can spend the holidays in ways that will bring you, and your children of all ages, real enjoyment and serenity.

Thank you having made me believe, through so many years, that you will accept and understand this seemingly inhospitable and self-centered decision.

<hr />

St. Helena, California   *26.x.69*
To: Estelle Nemkov

Dear Estelle: I loved your letter. . . . Thank you for the recipes. I'll try and probably keep the one for Mandel Brot. I like to keep good cookies on hand, although I don't eat them myself. I sent for the Knox booklet (yes, I do love "house organs" and have some beauties and want to write a thing about them), and will look for the Jellied Gaspacho rule. I like it plain, but often use enough rich broth to make it jell by itself. Delicious. The recipe for Coffee Rum Cream is completely zany, and that Mrs. Graham needs a good spanking for her toplofty reply. What got me first was the direction to put the

3. Avis de Voto, widow of writer and historian Bernard de Voto, became a mutual friend of MF and the Childs.

cream, in ripples etc. from a pasty tube, "onto the top of apples." WHAT apples? Nobody had mentioned them before. How fixed: raw, baked, whole, pureed? I read the thing again, for it fell out of your letter first, and then decided the whole thing was a put-on.... (On the back of that was a pretty good recipe for a Biscuit Tortoni!)

I have added "maracial act" to my private vocabulary. Thanks for that too!

I enclose the final word about the cilantro. Sorry. I did everything but hire a tiny oxygen tent. I think this air is simply too hot and dry.... But I can buy dried coriander, and will play with it.

Correction: sour salt, a standby in kosher cooking and in places where there are no lemons, is not made from alum but is crystallized citric acid, from several fruits but mostly lemon, and lime. It can be made synthetically. I use it, but always somewhat timidly. I figure that one teaspoonful equals the juice of a large lemon or two limes. This sometimes is too much... I like it.

That is a good recipe for Avocado Soup. I like that too, but it is pretty rich. So are avocadoes, and I LOVE them. They are very fattening for me. Too bad. The fate of Sol's supper is sad... especially the *boiling* it got! It reminds me of when we first came to California... perhaps it was in 1913... my mother packed in cotton, in a metal box, about a dozen avocadoes and sent them to relatives near Dublin. We heard nothing for months. Finally the word came: complete confusion, because the flesh had all been discarded as too soft and strange, and the stones had been boiled "for hours and hours" without growing tender enough to serve! Ho hum.

(Interesting ethnic note: Puerto Ricans do not like cold soups, and gazpacho is eaten there only by people of Spanish descent. Ho hum indeed.)

I find a reminder here to tell you that I read the book El Gringo Gingricho has written about his affaire with the fiddles, and really it is quite nice. Crown will publish it next summer, and it will get full treatment with plenty of pretty shots of great violins, and charts (at my request) of the 57 (?) essential parts of a violin, and chronologies, and so on. Arnold's text is sloppy and vigorous, as always, and you and Sol will like it, I think, because it has real humility in it, and is often funny and very likable. He overdoes his self-derogation, in order to protect his obvious amateur status, but I think the book will interest a lot of other frustrated fiddlers, and will even be of some value to musicians, for its pictures and chronologies. Well, I feel relieved for him that he has got it off his chest. Mr. Shub is on tour in Europe, and Charles Panell is immersed in family dramas, and AG is now studying with a young woman who is lousing up his hard-learned fingering etc etc, but he goes scraping along happily.

And I must tend my muttons... house full of hungry people. Best...

....

Bridgehampton, New York   *8.xii.69*
To: Elsine and Tony Ten Broeck

Dear Elsine and Tony... this is too late to be a proper thank-you for all you did to get me on that plane! Please forgive me. You are just about the only people in the world

I would ask something like that from, and it is a proof of my loving trust which I know you accept. (Next case, as Nin would say...)

And thank you for your note, Elsine. I did feel as if I were "walking off in the night"... I did not dare turn around, as you no doubt knew. The flight was not very pleasant... two hours late because of so-called turbulence... I really do not like to defy so many laws of Nature at once! . . .

I am glad you like the Swiss prints. Dillwyn gave them to me. Once I took my girls and two of the Barr boys to a village, by tram and bus, and it was COMPLETELY DESERTED, except for one very old woman, toothless and stone deaf... every soul was up into the mountain pastures to bring down the livestock for the winter. It was odd indeed. The doors were all open and some of the stoves were hot and birds caged in the windows were singing. But there were no dogs, nor any cats visible, and NOT A SOUL except the silent old woman. (We were really very hungry, and had to walk for almost two hours to find anything to eat, for two other villages were just as deserted.)

Oh... it is very beautiful to hear the cowbells as the herds go up or come down, or even roam in the high meadows. The tones are wonderful, especially at night. In the winter all the bells are hung up for the next Spring. . . .

I have yet to walk on the beach! There is a real storm blowing. I am being "blooded." Sleet dashes in handsful against the windows, really rattling. The wind is wild, and as far as the horizon there are waves racing sideways in the east wind. It is wonderful. The house is strong and fine and the electricity is on, and I keep watching all the thermostats. There is also a good fireplace in case of a power failure. Very exciting.

I have a good tight little office. The rented electric machine is still too tight, but I am getting used to it.

NY was hectic. Mostly I saw people I really like, and they were discreet enough to stay off business and just take care of the Little Old Lady from St. Helena. I was pampered of course. It was fun, and I was impatient to get out here, as you'll understand.

No, I don't think it is folly to get out of teaching. But I feel that it is something you will return to, in another phase probably. (How about Vista for you both, for 1 year????)

....

Bridgehampton, New York   *9.xii.69*
To: Ted Kennedy

Dear Uncle Ted: I love to get a letter from you, because it makes me think, or at least remember. Thank you for writing. . . .

We agree about store tomatoes. Canned ones are much better, in flavor and texture, and are not expensive. Even store-bought, they are good, I think. But nothing can equal the ones my neighbors grow in St. H. in the summer....

Weather on northern Long Island: bright and icy last weekend when I came, then a one-day but wild storm with wind from the north-east, and now increasing rain-clouds and some wind. Too cold to make beach-walking any fun. I get my exercise by watching the ocean. Then I sleep as if I had trudged a good five miles! I don't know this latitude... there is a map, but it is in the part of the house that is closed off. My part is snug and as warm as I want it, with electric heat which will probably stagger me at the first of the month but is very nice indeed until I get the first bill (and even after...).

I feel a basic detachment and some antagonism about the moon-racing. I keep my mouth shut... most of the time. I think what I hate the most is the complete dehumanization of most of the people involved in the game. They are not *men* as I know men. So lately I have reread *1984* and *Brave New World*, and felt even more out of the picture.... (Interesting family note here... Huxley's book was almost a fetish with Edith K, who bought dozens of copies and made people read them... she often told me that I must reread it, for it would help me prepare myself... perhaps she was right???)

About a dialogue between thee and me on aging: YES, I have carried on one for several years now with Grace Holmes, Edith's one close and long-time friend. She is now 88 or so, and lives in a cooperative place for old people, a former apartment house. I have been there several times. Interesting... I have her very full reports on trying to find a decent place for her last years, and her several decisions....

Heredity and the state of the glands will decide natural life-spans, of course. I wish more people knew this. Behavior has much to do with it, especially the diet. Both your parents had strong unabused endocrinological systems, as witnessed by their earlobes, for instance. Rex was in some ways the puny one of the litter, with long thin bones etc. However, I think he would have lived to 85 or so if he had not smoked so heavily and had been out of the increasing smog of Southern California. His son David was the end of Rex's strain, in males anyway... very thin-boned, and prone to fatigue and with an over-speeded brain. (He had one sturdy child, thanks to his wife....)

Well... Do you think that some such indication of senility as occasional confusion can be averted chemically, by a dosage of various salts etc? I knew a woman, a statistician in Switzerland, who crunched large grains of something like potassium everyday with lunch, for her brain. She bought it at a feed-store. I asked my mentor about this and he said blandly that it could not *harm* her. (He is an endocrinologist... Hal Bieler, who has taken care of me and most of my dearest people for some 40 years now. He is in his 80s, but still delivering a few babies and taking care of patients who come from everywhere, even Alaska and New Zealand... all his teeth, most of his ungreying hair, a slight slowing of his springy step. He honestly believes that "food is the best medicine."...)

Hal admits that there has to be a gradual wearing out of the functioning parts of the body, but that the process can be made relatively painless. He worked with old George Bernard Shaw, for instance, and although he himself never eats meat he seriously urged that fanatical vegetarian to eat two ounces a week of raw beef. Shaw did *not* throw him out!

Which of your five senses do you wish to keep the longest? What would you most regret losing? Hearing? Sight? Taste?

Old André Simon, who has had a very fine palate and sense of smell, is now almost totally blind at 92, and he says it is very boring and sad for him not to be able to enjoy food and wine anymore. A friend who fell on ice and killed the taste smell nerves in her brain has told me of the difficulty she has had to adjust herself to that, and to cooking decently for her very gourmand family. Thomas Edison, on the other hand, often said that his deafness had done him a great deal of good... he was spared many nuisances of noise, interruptions, all that. I have two blind friends, and they are almost extra-sensory in their appreciation of sound... and also of flavors. Well...

I myself, at 61, find that I am lazier in *using* my senses... but so far they are good. I need glasses for reading and typing, a real bore. I eat much less and much more simply, but my palate is probably keener than it was a few years ago. Etc.

Has your taste for reading changed greatly? Do you still read fiction (if you ever did)? Do you feel involved in any way in politics, or are you detached? After your father died, I cleared out the desk at Puente, and the drawers were *stuffed* with editorial clippings. I tried to make some pattern of them, but could not. They were not dated or identified, but were of every persuasion, and I wondered if Grandfather was trying to prove something to himself, or if it was simply a conditioned reflex of a man who had once had to write such stuff himself and might need a little help....

Yes, I would love it if you felt like talking to me. I do plan to write about Old Age. (And before I am too old to hit the keys myself!!!) My file is now so impressive that I'll probably turn my back on it and sit down and write it straight.

The six days in NY were hectic, but I survived them with some of the serenity which I have worked so long for. . . . The most boring part was transportation from lower Manhattan uptown. Costly, too. If I lived there, which God forbid, I would learn to use the subway, much as I loathe being underground. . . .

I am working on a series of things about the first days in Whittier. It is difficult to keep it straight, and not embroider it a little. Nobody else is now around to recall Rex and Edith, for instance, as they were before WWI... I can see and feel them vividly... just as I can see and feel the little cardboard village you and Aunt Etta sent to Anne and me. We sat in the sun on a nubbly green "hash" rug and talked about where the main streets should go and where the trees would be. It was a wonderful present. I wonder if children today, with TV and so on, know such intense enjoyment...

I hope this letter has not bored you. It is fun to have T*I*M*E for things I want to do.

Love to you both, as always.

....

Bridgehampton, New York   *14.xii.69*
To: June Eddy

Dearest June... I'm sorry to be this late in telling you what even my lazy silence must have implied, that I am in very fine shape!!!!

The week in NY was pretty wild, in a carefully controlled way, three breakfasts, five lunches, and four dinners in five days! Wow. I planned everything so that I would see mostly people I really like or find interesting, and I ate very little and drank very cautiously but well... did almost no business except with dear Henry... spoke when spoken to and flashed an occasional smile... in other words, Lady Hard-to-Get. Then E[1] and I came out here, and she left the next day, and I have in this past week gone through a real sou'easter and a southerly rainstorm... all very exciting. . . .

My problem, I think, is (and please don't laugh sardonically for I admit right now that I shall probably forever be hoist on my own petard(s)) P*E*O*P*L*E. I came here to be by myself, uninterrupted, Genius At Work. In the eight days here, Eleanor has been here most of four (weekends). She invited two mutual friends to dinner last Saturday night. The next day she took me to see some more. The next day a really great old woman stopped by for tea (there were only tea bags and she turned pale and settled for vermouth). Then Truman came by and conned me into lunch in Southhampton... he had just got back from his jaunt with the Shah of Iran and wanted to complain, and I do like him very much. Then E came back, bringing two unexpected guests who are going to stay here while I am gone for the next week, so I have had to put away gear I expected to leave layin' aroun'. Then we went to Sag Harbor to an exhibit and then to a long noisy drunken PARTY and then to a tiny-winy little spaghetti joint and baby, I've had it. Except that the people will be here for lunch and then we all fly uproariously down to la Guardia in the Bamboo Bomber, E's plane.

Well... I am letting off a full head of steam to you, and I hope it amuses you, because by the time you read it all will be resolved. Nitchevo. I hate to leave here, for I fell at once into a good work pattern. But I am firmly committed to a couple of days in NY and then three days to and from Washington to see Sean Kelly and his first and new house, complete with wife and two young boys. Have a couple of dates down there. Will travel on the new Metro-Liner, to see if American railroads are perhaps timidly getting hep to the new ways of ground-transit (I HOPE). Then, back here... but to face the ambiguous details of E's whims about Christmas and the New Year, which I had understood I would spend either completely alone or with only her. Ah well.

I say Ah well so smugly because I suspect that I'll take up the *NYer*'s offer of an empty no-strings office and dive into the complete anonymity of existing (I don't call it living) in Manhattan, for a time... after the "holidays."

Here I am neither a renter (although I am paying all the utilities, which are formidable in a winterized house as it is called here), nor am I a guest, nor nor nor.

Well, I'll have to buy a few more clothes in NY, which will set me back a little. And a room in a nice shabby old hotel across from the office will be adequate. When I think of some of the real dumps I have lived in... and worked in...

And that is my Problem of the day, and not much of a one at that! I should be very pleased to meet and/or know the people out here. But the clearcut agreement to come here and be alone has become increasingly amorphous, and right now I must act in a decisive way and not drift too cozily... which is what I have been doing for a long time in California.

Aside from this chitchat, let me report that I have done a lot of good work this

1. Eleanor Friede, in whose house MF was staying

week... got off four sections of the Quaker book to my editor,[2] paid all the new bills, finished and edited the story for *Esquire*, started the elderly Vauxhall a few times to go to the village (4 m.), brought in wood when the wind would let me open the door... made a good pot of soup... in other words, it has been a good five days, and I should be very grateful for it/them and I AM.

And on that almost Christ-like I'll close, chère girl...

Oh, speaking of chère girls, I have agreed to translate the short work-in-progress of Chevalier, of course with *NYer* permission. I have turned down the translations of the two long books. I'll probably do an introduction... that last in quotes, for it will be very informal. I hope I get paid enough to get to Paris. I want to meet the charming old boy... and I want an excuse to see a couple of other oldsters who are more familiar to me and much dearer, like Georges Connes.

....

Bridgehampton, New York   *29.xii.69*
To: Hal Bieler, M.D.

My dearest Hal, how sorry I am that you had that wretched experience with the Novocaine! You of all people, to be poisoned in such a way... and for such a bothersome reason! I feel really distressed about it, and wish that I could do something magical to make it vanish forever from your life. (You understand this... a part of loving you.)

Thank you for writing. As always, your letter gave me more courage, and a warmth I needed.

I do want very much to be with you, for even a few days. Perhaps on my way home? I could fly from France to Los Angeles instead of San Francisco.... It would be in April or May, probably. I'll be in touch with you, of course.[1]

Actually I am not thinking beyond the next day or so, in my present life. It is a good feeling. When I am hungry, I make something to eat (Not bad, although the procurable vegetables are very limited here... celery, cabbage, frozen zucchini, no lettuces but Belgian endive which I like... good butter and eggs... I make soups with herbs in them and frozen greens like kale and mustard...). When I feel like working, I work very hard and fast. When I feel like reading (mostly silly light stuff from the big collection here), or sleeping, that is what I do! Of course this can't go on forever, but I love it for a time.

I am not happy about what Chevalier is sending... it lacks his energy, vitality, passion. I think perhaps I should send my attractive hostess (in absentia) Eleanor Friede over there to speed up his glands a little????

Since I came, I have weathered one two-day nor'easter blow, very beautiful to watch, and now a five-day blizzard with fantastic gale-winds from 30 to 60 mph! I'll

2. *Among Friends*
1. This trip was not taken.

confess to you that on the last night I went through a period of pure funk, for about three hours. I was frightened in the real sense... or at least not of anything as positive as having the roof blow off... I was simply in an instinctive state of *dread,* and I think it was because of the apparently endless *noise...* the terrible strength. Well... I survived it, but it was a most terrible experience, all inward. I forced myself to walk about the house, and I brushed my hair, and sipped at some hot milk with some whiskey in it, and read a lot, and talked in a cold-blooded way, with the functioning part of my mind, to the terrified creature who was so helpless in me. Well... this might interest you. *You* might even call it a purely physical crisis... I myself think it was too much sub-conscious pressure from the outside, which I was really not aware of... I felt quite calm until it hit. That wind never stopped howling, for more than five days and nights.... The surf roared with waves perhaps twenty feet high, and tossed spume magnificently at least fifty feet more into the air. It was wonderful. But... suddenly my body, so puny in the face of such pure natural fury, started to shake. I went into a kind of chill, very violent and with bad pain in the lower back and thighs... breathing was heavy and fast, and heart beat heavily... feeling of nausea... etc etc... all very diagnosable to thee, but to me, completely alone and isolated by miles from the nearest human help, it was simply something to see if I could survive. Rather, I was almost sure I could, but I had to work very hard. I know it will not happen again. It was a "once in a lifetime" thing.

Well, this may interest you. I have read about similar things. My father told me about how in North Dakota women in isolated cabins often went crazy for the simple reason that the wind howled for weeks at a time and when they could look out, the snow was always blowing *horizontally* past the window. If it had fallen straight down they would not have minded.... I have heard the same thing about men on the great deserts like the Sahara: the force of the steady strong wind and the sand forever blow-ing... they get what French soldiers call "le cafard," which is something like panic. (Of course the Dakota women were probably living on pancakes, and the desert men on dates and camel-cheese... but I have been eating lightly and fairly sensibly, mostly of vegetables....)

Whatever the reason, it was an interesting experience. And last night the wind died, and the surf quieted, and I slept lightly and with pleasant dreaming for about ten hours.

End of story.

Hal, little Anna asked for your address, and I gave it to her. She is trying very hard to avoid, or at least put off and keep controllable, another period of what is diagnosed as "manic depression." By now she sees how terrible they are for her child and for people who love her... as well as for her own tortured body and mind. I doubt that she is strong enough to remake herself by now. She is of a very quiescent nature, and must be led and in fact directed and forced to behave in one way or another, I think she is about 7 or 8, and perhaps less, in her sense of responsibility. The last time she and Chris lived with me, for about 11 months, I slowly built them into really healthy people again. But that was destroyed in less than a month, when she ran away, compelled by the terrible shift in her glandular balance. Well... I am glad she at least remembers your name!

Here is my abiding love....

·······································

Sag Harbor, New York[1]   28(IMPOSSIBLE).i.70
To: Yolande Beard and Elsine Ten Broeck

Dear Yolande:

Dear Elsine:

Please forgive me once more for doing this. I want very much to talk with you both, and say practically the same things, and I am happily racing the clock on revisions and so on.... Pretend that we are sitting in front of one of our fires, or around one of our tables....

Let's talk about the weather, since we never have anything to say.... Here we are in the classical January Thaw. Most of the snow is gone, and there are puddles which freeze at night but melt by noon. Today when I go to the PO (at the other end of the two blocks of Main Street from my place), I'll go a little further and see what is happening on the harbor. Three days ago it was frozen solid. I wonder about the fish. I think they go out to sea, for from the Beach House I could watch gulls, the Wild Canadian geese, and occasionally a fishing-boat, catching something about a half mile off shore.

Sag Harbor does not have a fish store, even in summer! People have to go to East Hampton.... Once here I ate the most delicious clams I have ever tasted, but it was in a very touristy place open only on Sundays in winter, and the locals don't go there and wouldn't touch the clams with a riot-stick. Pollution, they say... and send them all to NY restaurants.

There is one good little place here, doing an enormous business, since more and more people who have summer places are "winterizing" them (Another dreadful word!) and retiring to them. It is a hole-in-the-wall, run by four young people from Greenwich Village, and it serves nothing but fresh home-made spaghetti or fettuccini with about four sauces, salad, and excellent little pastries sent up once a week from NY. They have red California Burgundy in carafes. The prices are fair. Why can't somebody do something *simple* like that in our valley?

The accent here is very strange. I really do not like it, and I am not attracted to the people... the natives, I mean. They are very in-bred, so that after more than 350 years here they are small and pinched looking. The girls are at their best at about 14 or so. They marry young. The men are short and tough, with an exaggerated rough way of talking, very loud and jolly with other men and curt and surly to their women. I have not seen any happy-looking children, but then they are so bundled in thick parkas and such against the cruel weather that it would be hard to. The ten-and-twelve-year-olds look strong and handsome, of both sexes. The people in the P.O. and most of the stores (grocery, etc) are almost openly unfriendly... the opposite of Bridgehampton just five miles from here, where getting the mail or buying some bread is Old Home Week.

1. MF moved into Sag Harbor because winter living on the ocean was hazardous.

There is nothing personal about the near-rudeness. I think it is a kind of protective coloring... life is rough here and has been for so long, and now the main income is from the tourists, and what the hell is some foolish old dame doing here in the dead of winter? But I am sure they are just as surly all summer. There are lots of antique-shops, closed now of course, and down on the harbor two big motels, also closed. Many of the people who live in the big old whalers' houses, really good austere architecture, rent rooms in the season. (I am in one now.)

Well, it is a part of our country I did not know about, and a real adventure. I would like to stay in Vermont, which seems to me about as deep early American as one can be (although whites landed here in Sag Harbor before they did at Plymouth Rock!). But it has now become so stylish for ski and all that.... I do like the feeling that I am not a newcomer... that other people have lived and died there. California cannot give that, for almost within our own memories we broke into it and killed the few helpless Indians... and actually they had not been there very long, themselves.... Well, I wish somebody would take a nice leisurely drive through New England for me! The architecture is pleasing, and there are lots of secondary roads. (There are lots of tourists too....) . . .

New York is a very exciting place to be, for a tourist which I have mostly been. I'd like to be there this very minute (except that I'd rather be here!). There are several wonderful exhibits going on... a retrospective of all of Brancusi, a same of Atget... etc etc. And the UN! The NY edition of *Time* is the best guide for that sort of thing. The *NYer* is good for movies and so on and shows and concerts. There is a good guide for restaurants and so on called something like the *Underground Super Market* . . . lots of good ethnic tips about inexpensive *good* places to eat, in every area. If I could, I would stay in a decent mid-town hotel, and force myself to learn the subway system. But taxis when you can get them are much cheaper than at home and the buses when you can get on one are fun too. Oh my... what an adventure!

About mice: as soon as Eleanor Friede had her house "winterized" the dune-mice got the word, and moved in. They are a little bigger than field mice, and of course sand-colored, and they ate the curtains, the blankets, the upholstery, to make cozy nests for literally hundreds of babies. It was a really dramatic invasion. EF did not know about it, and went out with two friends about a month after the house had been warmed, and it was nightmare for a few minutes... the little things squeaked everywhere and ran up the people clear to their shoulders and jumped off shrieking... up the trousers, everywhere. The humans ran away.

It was beyond trapping, and who would do it? So EF very unwillingly hired an exterminator. I have met him, a quiet well-read man who uses something made in England which is *said* to be completely harmless to other animals than rodents. While I was there, EF's cat brought us the only cadaver we ever found, and it was like a dry twig, and apparently without interest to Kinlay.

Well, it is a problem. Do you remember Carlos, our mouse? The girls liked him too. But he did tell all his friends about our tolerant ways, and finally it got beyond me... they took things over. I finally told Bill Erskine about it, and one weekend he came down and I went to Berkeley, and he killed them with the old-fashioned snap-trap.

Ugh. Then once in the Basement I was visited by large rats who never stopped there but simply used it as a nice warm passageway from the North side of the house to the East, where they lived under the old front steps (no more). Please do not laugh at my way of getting rid of them, for *it worked:* I bought a package of something like Rat-B-Gone, and put it unopened on their pathway, which began exactly at the head of my bed. Then I said aloud, slowly and firmly, facing in the direction where they always came from, an ancient curse against them. It is still used in remote parts of the British Isles. I will give it to you if you really need it. (It used to be part of the religious ceremony of exorcising devils, in the Church of England.) Result: perfect, at least for over a year and when I left. . . .

Interesting about the architectural lapses in the new Mondavi palazzo. Maybe that guy from Southern California (Chris May, something like that...?) is trying to prove that he is a second Frank Lloyd Wright, with no staircases to the second floor and so on? . . .

Yolande, did the Forsythia bloom this year? It is hard to believe that almonds are out. Here everything is still very dormant, as you would guess.

Oh... slight business, I honestly don't know about pictures.[2] The one that is still the best, not at all glamour-shot, is the Man Ray thing on the jacket of *The Art of Eating.* I am supposed to have it... I loaned it to World, and if I do it is in the Bysement in the cartons by my bed, in about the one marked 1950, and you can go in there and dig for it if you want to, or wait for me to come back. Or have somebody blow up the one on the jacket? The picture belongs to me, not World.

Oh, murder... Please tell me what to do later about our Centennial[3]... it had not occurred to me that it would be anything but us chickens... but of course if we really have a fiesta (My idea is to have one week of Open House from 5 to 7 and some music and wine and nibbles) I should of course let the Wilson Clan know.[4] Oh dear. Ho hum. It is as bad as a Bar Mitzvah.

Well, this almost *decides* me to come home before long. I do not feel "ready," whatever that is, for France right now. My ticket is good until next November. I told the Smiths I probably wouldn't be home until about May, when Tahoe thaws out and they can go back there. But if I came earlier I could happily hole into the Bysement... cadge a good hot meal from you once in a while, and get along with a hot-plate (about what I do here, actually...). I feel twitchy to be home again. And my God, we must get a few things like Mrs. Wilson's Granddaughter taken care of!!!!

How is this for a letter? Gab gab gab, as my father would say quietly.

I send much love to those two dear men, your husbands, and to you too.

PS... Yes, as soon as I think this ghastly book is finished, I'll come home.

2. For the dustjacket of *Among Friends*
3. MF celebrated the centennial of "The Dear Old Lady" (the St. Helena house) with a series of farewell parties.
4. The Wilsons owned the house before MF.

Sag Harbor, New York   *20.ii.70*
To: Eleanor Friede

Dearest Squeek... I don't know why I have not thought of this before, except that in many areas I am slow and D*U*M*B*:

Do you have any more to pay on the coat you have let me wear, the dashing fur one? If so, will you let me settle the account for you? I feel really indebted to you, and know that although it is not a "city" thing exactly, you would not have invested in it if you had not hoped to wear it. It would make me feel better about having kept it away from you, if I could perhaps clear up any possible debt on it... or at least be sent the storage bills or or or.

Please take me seriously about this.

All goes well here. I sent off a batch of clean typescripts to HV today, with more to ready for him. Then I go into my final stretch of new work. I'd like to get it off my back in a month....

I suspect that I'll not go either to Cambridge or Washington. This is a form of emotional and physical laziness, and I know I'll regret at least the first stop.... We'll see.

That story about the storm... Henry thought it was good, and sent it to the *NYer* on the 13th and they bought it on the 16th, which he considers his own private record. It is odd that I was on the verge, the real verge, of telephoning him to pull it back. Well, too late now... and it will please my CPA to have me *selling* something again! (I'm wondering what he'll do with my income tax next month... I earned only a little over $6,000 last year!)

(But the year before was different... thanks to the *NYer*... mostly into the pockets of my staff of lawyers-gynecologists-psychiatrists et al... Ho hum.)

This may interest you, last night I was invited to dinner at the Liccardis'! There also were that little woman who reminded you of a potential mother-in-law of Anna's, Jerry Somebody's Mom, and her attractive Danish husband, Sven, a former sailor and present antique dealer and cabinet-worker. Rosa Liccardi, her husband Domenick, and of course Rocco, who was almost in drag in a white silk turtle-neck, with a scarlet velvet pullover shirt and an enormous opal ring. We all drank from tiny stemmed glasses, from a pitcher of red wine mixed with ginger ale, before and during the meal. There was a big tureen of a rich excellent chicken soup with rice, and then a big platter of home-made fettuccini with fresh tomato sauce. Next came three platters, one of fried chicken, another of sausages and meat-balls, and a third of eggplant baked with ricotta. Then there was a salad of lettuce and red onion and tomato. There was home-baked bread with garlic butter on it. There was a pause while we drank little glasses of creme de menthe or plum brandy or a homemade and excellent anisette. Then came a really beautiful cheesecake, and coffee. A large plate of butter-cookies appeared from somewhere, and more coffee and diluted wine went on.

WELL... the astonishing thing was that this was, aside from being almost impossible for me to fake my way through, *very poor*. It destroyed forever the popular myth that there is nothing like good home cooking, especially in an Italian family. It was clumsily constructed, and every one of the several lengthy hard-breathing courses contained starch... even the salad was eaten with the so-called garlic bread. The soup was good, or at least had a good honest base, but the rice in it was overdone and it was all too heavy and rich. The pasta, which had been made with great effort on the dining-room table (I was kept alerted to every nuance of this "real Italian meal" for three days before...), was badly cooked in too little water, with lumps and sticky places, and once on the correct platter it was watery and unattractive. The piles of murky turd-like sausages and meat-balls I forewent or whatever the past tense is of the verb *to forego*. I tried to eat some of the flat baked dish of eggplant, but it was so overdone, and so overladen with tough cheese, that I could hardly make a dent in it. The bread was roughly cut from an American-type loaf, and dabbed awkwardly with a "garlic dip" and then dried out to an impossible point. The chicken too I forewent, as did almost everyone, but by then we were in a pleasant gluttonous semi-coma, with plenty of laughing and gabbling, and nobody was offended by the fact that I have, let's be frank, a small Gut. Well... the salad was dreadful, with lumps of raw onion and a meaningless vinaigrette, but it was refreshing. Then the liqueurs came, and they helped a little. I drank some slivovitz, which cut through the vapors nicely, and tasted Rosa's anisette, which was a really fine old homebrew, much better than commercial stuff... about 15 years old, with perhaps 3 pints left in the gallon jug. Then there was the cheesecake, and it was beautiful to behold, but not as good as my own occasional effort in the same field... the cottage cheese and ricotta were not put through a sieve, and tut tut there. But handsome. The cookies which appeared were delicious, and in a daze I ate one.

I think that the family loves Rosa, and has flattered her into thinking she is The Typical Bronx Italian Mama because she is really a very clumsy and ungifted cook. She is an ox-like, i.e, docile and stupid, person. She is *simple*. She loves to shuffle around pleasing Domenick and Rocco and their friends because they tell her in many ways how happy they are to have her doing just that, *pleasing* them in her blind tempestuous indigestible way.

Well... end for now of my local exposé of a Wish-Dream of the American Culture, that there is nothing like simple peasant fare.

It is time to trot northward to the PO....

....

St. Helena   *14.viii.70*
To: Peter Vogel
Dear Peter Vogel:
In reply to your letter of July 20 and your peremptory request of 12 August that I return your manuscript, I do so, herewith, and regretfully unread.
Thank you for entrusting it to me.

I think you are unrealistic to expect a professional worker in any field to be able to read, appraise, and further assist with any creative work. I work. I am also beset, as is almost any mature human being, with many domestic and personal problems. I cannot, when a manuscript is sent to me for no matter what reason, stop all other activities and devote myself to an honest scrutiny of it. There are eager and even reputable persons who do this for a living, and if an artist is in need of such help, he should seek out such advice.

I regret very much that because of your need for action you cannot leave your story longer with me. I also regret that for the moment it is impossible for me to look at it. If I had more time, and you did too, I would be glad to read what you have sent and give you my completely un- and non-professional opinion.

This apparently being impossible for your schedule, please accept my apologies and my sincere wish for your better successes.

PS... readers and publishers are slow. A book I wrote in 1969 will... perhaps, perhaps... be published in 1971. But be of good cheer. (And try to be patient.)

....

St. Helena, California   *27.viii.70*
To: Paul and Julia Child
Dere F*R*E*N*S*:
Thank you for your inner and outer messages. I don't know when the snow will fly, but I do know that I'll be in November at
La Maison des Grenouilles
Les Bastides
06 La Roquette-sur-Siagne, France
Phone: 93 90-23-23
It is a little basement flat across the road from Eda and Sybille, and I have taken it for that month and on as wished, so that my sister Norah and I can have someplace where we do not have to bow to the other boarders over our tea.

Your life sounds absolutely mad and exciting, and it is almost worth my investing in a color TV set... you and Sir Kenneth Clark starting in November... Wow... But I'll be slipping along a Burgundian canal. We will do sixty-two miles in seventeen days.

Then we will go to Porquerolles, and after we have survived the local form of the curse of Montezuma, we will be happy and probably loath to get up to Les Bastides.

I am sorry to agree with you that most of the "great" restaurants are almost the same in New York as in Paris, and and and. In December and March I was served some excellent food and surprisingly enough, some excellent bread, better than anywhere except at the Gare de Lyons, but the best bread I have yet found in America is in Sonoma, fifty minutes over the mountains to the West, in the Valley of the Moon.

That may be one reason why I've decided to move there, and (?!). I have sold this house, which I am sorry you have not seen, to people who understand it, and who will do a better job than I have been able to at clothing it in its proper style. I am building a two-room palazzo on the ranch of an old friend. It will be almost ready to move into when I come back, and of course I am slightly preoccupied with the logistics of condensing three floors into one, and a small one at that.

One reason we are friends is that we both understand the acceptance of NOW. There is all the imprisonment of nostalgia, but with so many wide windows. When I went back to Paris, never before alone, I had never been so happy, because my sisters, my brother, all their lovers and all my own, and our fathers and mothers had taught me to be there.

It would be wonderful if you were at La Pitchoune when I was there... just around a corner or two....

Abiding love,

....

St. Helena, California   *Sunday... about mid-September*
To: Barbara Winiarski   *1970...*

Dear Barbara Winiarski: This is a good little piece, and it would do very well without any change at all. But by this time in my life I am like an old fire-nag, conditioned to respond to bells etc... and I have a compulsive need to tinker with syntax, which I've done occasionally on your typescript. Pay no heed, unless you want to!

I don't respond at all to the title. Can you not get Bobbity in there?

I like what you say about how children watch and learn through their pores. This could be a whole new story for you to do....

I'm sorry about the stains on pp. 2 and 3... was eating lunch of cold ratatouille....

I keep chewing on the title... "The Best of Bobbity"... "Some of Bobbity's Best".... The name is lovable, as you have made the woman be, and it should attract attention to what you've written... (chew chew...).

About the recipes: I think that if the story is published, you will have to revise them to the pattern now generally demanded, that is, to give the title, then the ingredients in their correct amounts and in the sequence of their use, and then the method. No longer can we say "a handful" or "a little"... and I am for this seeming regimentation, because I know from long sad experience how absolutely dumb a lot of readers are about measurements. Then when something goes wrong in their fumblings, you are to blame....

Well, please let me know What Next. I'll leave on October 2, to be back in about 3 months. I don't know people at *Gourmet* any more... staffs change like the weather... but would be glad to do whatever I could to get your nice piece, and the wonderful recipes, into public view. Meanwhile, when you re-type the stuff, will you please let me have a duplicate? I would like to hang on to the recipes for the chicken, the crouton dumplings, the hoska... (I bet I never tackle the last!).

All best, and good harvesting right now!

1970–1992

....

Last House, Glen Ellen, California

David Pleydell-Bouverie, who built Last House for MF on his ranch, 1980

In 1970 her friend the architect David Pleydell-Bouverie built a two-room cottage for Mary Frances on his ranch in the Sonoma Valley. This was Last House, set amid oaks, vineyards, mountain waterfalls, and wildflowers. During the twenty-two years that Fisher returned there from months in Marseille and Aix and a sojourn to Japan, her correspondence grew to embrace fellow writers, fellow searchers, and many who knew her only from her books.

A Considerable Town was published in 1978, and was combined with *Map of Another Town*, reissued in 1983 as *Two Towns in Provence. As They Were*, published in 1983, gathered many of MF's short stories and brought her unexpected fame. *Sister Age* (1983) was the culmination of her years of concern about old age, and is essential Fisher in its combination of humor, wisdom, and deeply heartfelt empathy.

By the mid-1980s, Mary Frances was fighting a losing battle against arthritis and Parkinson's disease, with the added catastrophes of diminished vision and, above all, the impairment of her voice. She was sustained by work: *Dubious Honors* was published in 1988, *Boss Dog* in 1990, and *Long Ago in France* in 1992. Three volumes of memoirs, *To Begin Again; Stay Me, Oh Comfort Me;* and *Last House,* were edited by her and published after her death. Her correspondence was a constant spur for her to continue to write, and she never lost her passionate desire to communicate her heart's greetings.

To: Eleanor Friede

Dearest Squeek... it is an absolutely perfect day, and I am at the Ranch, typing in the Guest House Kitchen while Charlie McCabe pounds out a weekly column in the sittingroom... Think Tank à la Bouverie? I smell quite fishy: a friend gave David a whole sturgeon roe last night, and I have been stripping black eggs off innumerable tendons and muscles for more than two hours. The caviar seems completely tasteless, although very pretty... but there must be some connection there, between fishdom and me, because I am beginning to send out a strong smell! Of course this is strictly a blind flight, and not only my first but my LAST such caper... but I am letting the eggs drip in a sieve, lightly salted. We'll see. I suspect the only thing even faintly flavored will be ME...

... and that brings me to the subject of Pornography Among the Pots and Pans, which I've been thinking about ever since I got your note last night. I'll tackle it, "once and for all," in a minute.

First a report: things are going very fast now at the house, and I may be able to make the big move in a few weeks. The painter is very slow but good. As soon as he finishes one of the two big rooms, the tiles can be laid, and then I can start putting books on shelves. I make two or three trips a week between here and St. H., and the cartons of books pile up alarmingly in the Guest House. People want to help me, but it is pretty much a personal job of putting them where they *have* to be. (Of course I plan to spend at least a year jiggling into place, in general....)

Squeek, is there any chance of your coming out? It is very important to me that you see Last House. I won't really feel *there* until you've been there too. (This is one of those tenuous mysticalities that need no explanation.) If you had a sudden reason to come to SF, and if I were not yet "in residence," we are very welcome to stay here in the Guest House, which as you may remember has four bedrooms. But as things now look, I really feel I'll be sleeping in Last House before too many more weeks. Either way, it would be fine indeed to see you. (No wildflowers yet, but this promises to be a beautiful Spring... and meanwhile the mustard in Napa Valley is breathtaking....)

I'll see the Wrights[1] on Thursday... they are driving up from Oakland early, to St. Helena, and I've arranged for a truck to take some stuff back to their place... a couple of beds, etc etc. K sounds basically weary... she does a big job... but happy. Alex is well. (To my surprise, but it may be a natural protest against my non-pillish approach, K and Jim seem to load him with every injection and capsule known to modern science... he survives, although he has had a chancy infancy....)....

As for Anna, I do not know anything except that she and Steve call now and then and report that all is well. Anna writes, too. I think they are working very hard to stay straight and real together. They dramatize what is actually a really tight financial situation, but I think they will be all right. After much thought I asked them if they would/could accept a monthly sum from me while Steve was in school, and I felt rather proud of them when they gave me a gentle but firm No Thanks.... (Once I get out of the St.

1. Kennedy, Jim Wright, and their son Alex

H. place I may fly up to Portland for one night and then on to NY for a very few days....
I'll keep you posted, of course....)

My hands began to smell stronger of fish, so I went over to the kitchen and tasted the caviar. It is odd... very light, almost fluffy, but with an increasing yet still very delicate taste. I added some more salt, and will try again in an hour or so. *It is not worth the trouble!* (But it may be, by tonight...????)

Business: David thinks the people who have worked on Last House would be pleased to get a copy of *TAOE*[2] with their names etc etc. And I suppose I should grab a few for psoetrity (That really means *posterity*... I just get bored with conformity!!!!) so will you please ask your shipping dept. to send fifty copies here to Glen Ellen, and bill me? (Five of these are ordered by David.) Thank you!

And now to the thing about Sexy Fisher, which I might as well discuss *once*. . . .

As I think you know, I have always been prim, stiff-necked, and basically affronted by invitations to write "off color" texts... How to Cook in Bed, a primer for hungry lovers, that sort of thing. The idea was that I could write the off-color stuff and still sound like a lady... or something silly like that. It always made me huffy, and Henry Volkening knew about it.

Then a few times Fisher stuff has been taken out of context and reprinted, and I have got really foul letters from readings. The worst example of this was done by Little, Brown, who sold something from *A Cordiall Water* to a stud magazine.... I was quite upset by the mail I got, and made a real fuss to HV about getting permission from publishers before excerpts are sold.

Sometimes I am deeply flattered and humble when the word Colette is mentioned in connection with my way of writing, for I know that I could never hope to be as good as she, nor would I try to. But more often I am distressed, for most of the people who read Colette consider her sexy, pornographic, lascivious, etc etc, and they link me to her solely for that. Ho hum, *indeed.* They have not really understood Colette, and all they have recognized in both of us is a native candor, and a straightforward way about talking of sensuous things: the wing of a butterfly, the smell of sweet butter, the light on a cheek. So... I have two reasons for not liking to hear that I remind someone of Colette: one is modest and both are protective of our common purity. (And I honestly believe in that!)

Well... a few years ago a popular writer about food and cookbooks and such, in England... and I forget his name... on the Manchester *Guardian* I think... wrote that I am the past-mistress of gastronomical pornography. His review was sent to me, and I felt outraged. I was going to write to him, to tell him so. I did not, of course. I did tell HV of my dislike of this sort of glib reference. But there is nothing to do about it, of course, except acknowledge that if people can read Colette and fail to understand her, I am an even easier prey because I am not as good a writer as she.

Perhaps Kip Fadiman[3] started the Sexy Saucepan Syndrome with his often-quoted remark. But that English critic helped, with his often *mis*-quoted one. As you

2. *The Art of Eating*
3. Clifton Fadiman, editor of the Book-of-the-Month Club

well know, our mores have changed since 1937! A renewed interest in Fisher as a pornographer, if it happens, can only be a symptom of our avid interest in overt sex right now. It is old hat! We just like to read and talk about it more hungrily than we did twenty or forty years ago. I shall continue to be as straightforward in my voluptuous approach to the pleasures of life as I have been in the past. I shall never write about it, to order.

I suppose it all comes down to the fact that I don't think there is anything I discuss to hide or titter about...?? This applies to eating, love-making, even to the basic need to stay *breathing*. Perhaps I was writing a little ahead of my time... but that is hard to believe! The Greeks beat me to it!!!! . . .

I just wish my fellow-countrymen were more relaxed. They have been conditioned to believe that there is something basically EVIL about physical and moral sensuality. I cannot possibly agree with them. Therefore their titillation from some of what I have written over the past forty years is their problem, not mine! California girl raised in a Quaker town has managed to imply, and for many years into an almost void, that eating and love can both be fun?

Intermission here for sampling and adding salt to caviar... all very Freudian and suggestive, eh, that as I try to tell you about this situation of MFKF vs. Peeping Toms I am occupied in coping with 100,000 eggs from a virgin sturgeon. Twenty-three ski-doo, boys...

Well... dear Squeek it does make me feel rather disappointed, or something like that... perhaps I still manage to expect more than I get from my fellow men?

I haven't dared look at what I wrote in about 1934–36. I know my way of writing has gained some firmness since then. But I feel sure that what I said then I would say now.

So in answer to your question about my being as sexy to an "audience" in 1937–etc as I am now, I think that I was, but that the audience has changed and is looking for more physical learning than it was aware of then. The few people who liked what I was really saying then still like me. People who might have found me a little too blunt, perhaps a little shocking or decadent, now think in overtly sexual terms and words, and they are in the main just as blind and misguided as the ones who linked me with Colette because we both liked the taste of a frozen tangerine, for instance, as much as we did other even more intimate but curtained enjoyments.

It is time to go taste the caviar again... and I have little hopes that I have said much that would explain the term of "gastronomical pornographer." I can state firmly, however, that I am not one. I have never been one. The same people who got a charge from Fisher in 1937 are still around in 1971. There are simply more of them. And their needs for their own peculiar excitations are more open now than they were then. So... certainly I am not going to re-write to eliminate whatever it is that excites them, any more than I am going to cater to their needs with what I am now doing.

Well...

The caviar gets a little better. I am adding astonishing amounts of salt. All this is dripping through... sieve over bowl. If anyone gives you a whole sturgeon roe, perhaps several pounds of it, simply say Thanks-no-Thanks....

I am going to think about this letter. It is a kind of manifesto, really! I feel that I should explain it to you, even though you already know it!!!

The day continues to be idyllic. By now Charlie McCabe is out on the terrace absorbing a little scotch. Paul Cobb and his wife, friends of mine from Oakland, can't come for lunch. Margaret Fabrizio is apparently on her way, since we've not heard to the contrary... she is a friend of mine, a harpsichordist whom David hopes to con into playing at his annual Reading, this year to be in June. (I have been laying these webs for some time, and took him last week to an A.C.T. presentation in SF where she did the harpsichord for a revival of a Restoration comedy. She's very good, and I hope this magical place will sway her. We'll see.) And tonight there are more people for dinner... I think I'll bow out, which I can do very easily here in the Guest House... eat a piece of cheese and some celery! (Re-read this letter!)

Next morning... decided NOT to re-read. All goes well, and I'll head back to St. Helena as soon as I've done my Sunday stint on the checkbooks.

....

Last House, Glen Ellen, California   *29.v.71*
To: Judith and Evan Jones[1]

Dear Judith and Evan: This is an unpardonable time for a b&b[2]... not to mention a few other Common Courtesies like saving my reason if not my life when I could not get across Third and 50th. I know you understand my laxness. Whether you condone it is another matter, and one we can discuss, perhaps, when you can come here.

The cold fact remains that you did take care of me, dear Judith. I doubt that I could have done it without your sure quiet control. That was a lapse due mostly to trying a night-flight from Portland and then a day of work. I know better, now.

(I owe you some money for all this, and I'm sorry I could not repay it in NY... I'll catch up with you, one way or another.)

I think everything is in order with the new book. I was sorry to lose those galleys, but I assume that all is well(?). Please let me know if I can help with anything in my somewhat more ordered life here....

(I am accustoming a new cat to the milieu. He is on my lap. He loves the warm beat of the electric typewriter. He is a smoky beige, part Siamese and apparently part Abyssinian Blue. Wow.)

(So far he has only defecated once in 50 hours, on a rather rare Chinese scroll I got out for a "reading" next week. He is finicky...!)

When I say that I really had fun in New Orleans, people say, "You *DID*??!!" But I did. The weather was merciful... about 90 and of course sticky but with an occasional puff of cool air from off the river. The magazine provided me with exactly the gigolo, a sensitive intelligent delightful boy (26!) from an Iowa farm.[3] I would gladly adopt

1. Judith Jones was MF's editor at Knopf. Evan was her husband; writer of several books.
2. "Bread-and-butter" thank-you letter
3. MF was commissioned by *Playboy* to write an article about a trip to New Orleans. Douglas Bauer was the young man assigned by the magazine to accompany her. The article was never published.

him for life (including his new wife...). We had much the same metabolism and almost without a word we agreed that a tiny-tiny two-hour nap every afternoon was essential. He also liked a dozen oysters at a stand-up bar for breakfast, which added to my general euphoria. We managed, thanks to all this mutual therapy, to go to more than a dozen restaurants, ride the ferry to Algiers, go to Tulane in search of a missing family sloop (of Michael Demarest, who was also with us for three days).... We ate perhaps five superb dishes, and nibbled at 20 or 30 shamelessly bad ones. We walked up or down Bourbon Street at least twice a day, and went to the wax-museum, and and and. Needless to say, I have not yet done anything about *writing* the piece, but am not worried.

Judith, when my sister had to leave for California from France a month before she'd planned to (strikes, etc), I found myself with nobody to talk with except an occasional waiter or chambermaid, and decided to keep a journal for her... silent chatter, much of it cryptic of course to anyone not used to our strong sibling dialect. Norah read it, and said firmly to me that I must send it to Rachel MacKenzie, *not* for use in the *NYer* but simply because she is my editor there. Rachel in turn feels that I should ask you to look at it sometime... perhaps with the idea of a book(?). She also urges me to re-write and re-organize and so on, for her to look at again.[4] At the moment I am not at all interested in this suggestion. I do have a lot of material for a book about how and why my girls and I chose to exist in Provence... the other side of *Map of Another Town*, which was only about Aix. Perhaps I could play the first experiences with this last lonely view? If you feel like seeing the thing now, I can give it to you when next we meet. Or I can wait until the dim day when I've tidied it a bit....

. . . I am gradually accustoming myself to living in a NEW place. There are still boxes to be emptied, but I refuse to let them bother me... and I am encouraging a little dust, a few kindly spiders....

Is there not something VERY URGENT that calls you both to San Francisco? Could you now organize all your writers out here to send you a frantic call for help... Workers of the Knopf World, Unite! . . .

The bakery in Sonoma makes what I have called the best bread in America, but now I know it is only the second-best (and the third best, I think, is at Arnaud's in New Orleans... although I did not eat any *poor* bread there...). I have yet to tackle Julia's method, and wonder if I ever shall... until I remember your results.

Thank you again for all the tangibles and otherwise, and please let me count on seeing you here at Last House, the sooner the better.

....

Last House, Glen Ellen, California   *28.ix.71*
To: Arnold Gingrich

Dear Grumpa... I love it when you get a little peevish... it's almost worth feeling very guilty about having caused it! Your dramatically terse note of the 24th has me

4. This project eventually became part of *As They Were*, "About Looking Alone At a Place: Arles."

grinning with amusement, and also some smug satisfaction, I must admit as "an aging but still lovely woman of 63"... not Fitzgerald's 24.

Don't worry about my having been "turned... into Madame Butterfly"! It is true that I've been on hand for a lot of local capers, largely by choice, but I don't regret it at all. It helped enormously to ease me from one pattern of life into another... I am no longer sitting in a too-big house waiting to have somebody come to stay there with me: children, friends, all that. I am no longer the woman whose children have grown up and whose husbands have died, dusting the corners now and then and trying to write. I have put all that behind me, and am as free as I ever will be from the demands, enjoyable and otherwise, of family life. For them I have deliberately substituted a simpler personal life, more independence in eating-working-sleeping-dressing-etc. I often find it a puzzlement, but I've made my choice, and this is the way I'll live until I'm no longer able to. The past *été mouvementé* has been very good for my spirits: I have proved that I can handle social situations I'd almost forgotten about... and that I need a great deal of solitude. I'll get that now, judiciously spiced with little forays into the world, like my trip today to SF to see the Stein show again and meet Norah and the Stones.[1]

If you think there is any danger of a romantic involvement with "Squire Bouverie," *FORGET IT!* We are as amiably sexless as two bulbs in a flower-bed, two potatoes in a bin. He is an impossible person at times, but I am so detached about him (and he from me) that it does not even annoy me when he is arrogant or loud-mouthed. And he is also such a kind and generous person, and with such unfailing taste in balance and line and color, that I enjoy that side of him to the hilt. Apart from that, we are not even male-female together (and that too may add to my new freedom?).

This morning is wearing first winterish outfit, for the City: new blue panty-stockings of opaque dark blue (very nice... rather *Claudine à L'École*), rather long blue skirt (Marchesa di Grecy, courtesy of June Eddy), dark blue Rodier knit top from last winter in France, that good old green blazer with rather pimpy green shoes to match... let's see... small lapis ear-buttons... green and blue scarf... WOW. Phyllis[2] will take me to the 10:45 bus in Sonoma. I plan to buy an inexpensive (???) dark blue handbag... have always had one until The Move, when Goodwill reaped my hasty harvest. I also hope to get some soft light supple boots, always a problem, though, because of my damned high insteps....

I may duck into a fruit bar or I may go to a late lunch at the Clift and eat sand dabs and drink some white wine. I've decided to take N and the Stones to Le Trianon after the Stein... I'll order dinner beforehand, which I prefer to do, instead of having the table covered with all kinds of dishes. I know it is arbitrary. But in my home I would not ask them what they would choose... that went out with Queen Victoria, thank god.

I now have TWO cats. They like each other, being racial brothers (!!!! but Siamese

1. Humphrey and Solveig Stone, British friends. MF first met Humphrey in Aix in 1954. Later he came to study book design at Stanford.
2. Phyllis Whitman, David Pleydell-Bouverie's housekeeper

are dreadful snobs…), and Ben has already learned the trick of the new "Pet-Dor"… he's smarter than Charlie. They are amusing.

Have I cheered you any, dear Grumpa? I do hope so.

Yes… you are right that the weekend calls have left me feeling that we were au courant, and have therefore pandered to my laziness. Oh dear.

....

Last House, Glen Ellen, California   *30.ix.71*
To: Arnold Gingrich

Dearest Ginger… I wanted to write to you from the Clifto, and just as I sat down for my half-hour before time to leave for Greyhound, the telephone rang and it was Kennedy and she talked for… guess what? So: no letter.

(I think I am in the dog-house with you? No letter since your last very grumpy note of the 24th. Probably something will come tomorrow, saying that I am forgiven?)

The little bash in the City was fun and went off well, I think. The Stein show stands up nobly, and is worth several viewings. We all met in my room and got there in time to see the 15-min. "multi-media" thing, really rather a bore but they run it to try to attract the so-called YOUNG. Then we roamed around. Then we went right to Le Trianon and had a long delicious dinner, with two bottles of a 1947 (?… not labelled, but obviously young and fresh, compared with a labelled '64 I drank lately…) Meursault.

Humphrey ate onion soup (he is trying desperately to gain weight), and Noni and Solveig and I small portions of pheasant pâté. Then the Stones ate sole Dièppoise, with side orders for Humphrey of some kind of potatoes and then spinach (!), and Noni and I Dover sole meunière, really delicious. It's flown to SF every day! It is definitely genuine. Then we had little soufflés au citron. Coffee. Oh, first N and I drank a good martini, being elderly and museum-groggy, and the Stones drank Lala Halls, which are dry champagne with a lichee nut, named after Mrs. Hall who is the widow of the Hall of Nordhoff and Hall and who lives in Tahiti (of course).

(…I have met her, and I like her, and the combination is surprisingly good, but I never order it… would rather have plain *champagne*…)

Well, it was long and pleasant, and afterwards we took a longish walk on the street around Union Square. . . .

We had one astonishing experience: everything is decked and staidly dazzling for (Buy) Britain Week, with Princess Alexandra here and great goings on, and the shop windows are monotonously loyal in their decor… EXCEPT for the one bookseller (Howell), who has a really interesting display. We were, as the Stones would say, riveted by it (in comparison with the general feeling of mockery we had…). We looked at everything in the long shallow windows that lead back to the shop: maps, prints, letters, and so on. We turned to go out. And trudging past us on the sidewalk with a polished great bell slung over his shoulder, all dressed in scarlet and black and gold, was The Town Crier of London. It was so astonishing that it seemed quite natural. I said, "Hello," in my warmest voice, without even thinking, and he stopped, and said that he was on his way to the Sir Francis Drake Hotel and that he had been off the non-stop from London for less than an hour and that he felt very odd. "Of course," I said. "Jet lag," I said. Humphrey said, "I know you. You are the Town Crier of London. Your pictures are in all the papers." "Where are you from?" The poor little man asked. He had very bowed legs, in long black stockings, and he kept shifting the big bell over his shoulder. "Dorset," Humphrey said. "And of course you're from London." "London yes," the man said, "but Lambeth, *Lambeth* London." He asked how to get to the hotel, and then he went trudging off, and his legs were indeed very bowed and tired. We got down to the corner and saw him enter the hotel door, with four or five hippie-kids following him. And I thought with a pang of how stupid I was, not to say, "We'll take you to the door!" Here he was, such a tired little man, with nobody to welcome him or help him!, and ay de más, qué estúpida!

Well, later Noni and the Stones said, Dote will tell this and nobody will believe her. But she has three witnesses. And it did seem absolutely right, to turn away from the one exciting display for Britain Week and see the Town Crier there, so gaudily dressed and so tired. I hate to think I miffed an even better story. It is nice to surmise about, though.

And what stupid planning, not to have the poor little guy met and helped! Socially, in SF, all the accent is on the Princess. (Thus spake ex-subscriber to subversive periodicals like the original *Masses*.)

End of story... except that we kept on walking and sneering and mocking the crass commercialism rampant... walked through Union Square and found all the bench-bums and hippies cleared away for papier-mâché replicas of a "typical pub" and so on... lots of banners flying. Vive l'argent, wherever it is!

I bought slightly madly, as always on a spree in SF; emerged poorer but shod, at least... a fairly nice pair of knee-high boots (last winter's were mid-calf and I used them to the bone...) which will take me a half-hour to lace... some essential gloves and stockings... a couple of French fantasies for Anna and Kennedy. (Have you seen any women wearing the one-hand glove? I suppose it is already too cold there. It is very "young," of course.)

The Clift is increasingly huff-chuff, but it also has the most comfortable beds in the world, and the best linens, and the nicest room service. Ho hum. I'm hooked... until they turn me away because I'm not with the Right People. (They did look crossways at Solveig, who was dressed in high London style, really ravishing but not at all SF....)

I am dawdling about getting to work. The weather is Autumnal Perfection... bright, cold, leaves turning, silence except for quail now and then, full of ripe grapes from the vineyard. Picking starts next week, here... it is in full swing in Napa Valley.

I'm going over there for one night, Oct. 3, a memorial concert for a good friend of mine who was a fine musician, and then supper at the Ten Broecks' and the night in Marietta's empty guest house. Back the next morning . . .

I do hope you are well. I worry about you, but in a resigned way.... I feel that your body is protesting a little too obviously about some of the strains you put on it: the

Shub-bulb, the recurring eye, etc etc. But what might be major surgery for X or Y is like a hiccup to you... and you go whirling on. *Power,* man!

Until soon. I hope that tomorrow will find me off the frown-list....

<hr />

Last House, Glen Ellen, California   *17.xii.71*
To: Paul and Julia Child

D*E*R*E F*R*E*N*S... Thank you for writing to me. . . .

I do feel so grateful to you both for coming here... two people much in demand, constantly sought out. But here it seemed simple and "indiquée!" the way it does in Plascassier... and also the way it did in Cambridge, when you were so kind to me after my strange experience in Provence. (I'll never forget seeing you, Julia, for the first time in my life, in the Boston airport, after being rather involved with a small French child, and knowing that you and Paul would be kind to various wounds....)

I am thinking strongly of finding a place to live in, perhaps near St. Rémy or Salon, beginning next September. I'd like to do without a car. What do you think of something like that house Jim Beard[1] and Elizabeth David once had? I'm quite ignorant about all this, and will thank you for whatever you might be able to tell me.

I'm simply too comfortable here! I *love* it, and could sink into a cozy snooze. I need to be goosed-goaded-gone. What I want is to take off, ONE MORE TIME.... Then I'll come back here and be a Nice Old Lady. If I could find a house, or even part of a *pension,* or a flat in a run-down hotel would you come and see me/us?

(*Of course,* I hope I hear you say...)

Meanwhile, I wonder about Jim B. Please let me know what you know, for although I am a comparative newcomer on his list of lovers, I know we share hopes and prayers and all that....

Things go well here, in VERY cold bright weather. Genie and Ranieri will come up tomorrow for the weekend[2]... he was laid low with a congestion last weekend... It: *congestione;* Eng: *Common Cold* (No matter how you pronounce it, it is a *humiliation...*).

I hope you have happy holidays, whatever and wherever they may be... and of course the richest warmest best of all new years.

<hr />

Last House, Glen Ellen, California   *17.xii.71*
To: Norah Kennedy Barr

Dearest N... yes, it was pretty reckless of you to break the Embarrassed Family Hush![1] Thank you, though... what you think and do not think matters very much to me... perhaps even more than it *should*... or is that possible?

1. "Fat Jim" Beard, culinary writer and friend
2. The di San Faustinos lived in San Francisco but spent many weekends in their house on the Bouverie Ranch.
1. MF complained that no member of the Kennedy family ever openly acknowledged that she was a writer.

What you say about "emotional climates" is interesting. Certainly I was not warm physically when I wrote that book,[2] but I wasn't aware of being out in the cold emotionally, at all… except of course that I had chosen, for reasons still unknown to me, to isolate myself for a time. (I'm doing that more and more. Tell me, Doc… should I wonder????)

I'm doing a completely unimportant book review about Dickens and his wife, and as usual find myself quite absorbed by *them*, not it… and certainly *he* wrote at his best when he was living a tumultuous and demanding life in every direction….

It does seem strange to me that you are getting out of a "career" you have devoted yourself to, at a really young age… I keep thinking "She's too young…." But too young for *what?* Only you can know that, and I feel absolutely sure that you do know.

I like to think of you as a vigorous and eminently *sane* (Mens sano etc) woman well into the 70s and still stamping around life…. But doing what? You are a splendid mother and grandmother, and I envy you that gift, with all my heart. (I feel that I could have been… but my increasing awareness of Sis's resentment of me as the older, and then Anna's fear and hatred of me, left me with a *dread* of hurting anybody any more, ever. I suppose that is why I am withdrawing… to make it plainer that it is HANDS OFF?)

You are right that alternatives to our well-cushioned lives seem goody-goody and/or sanctimonious… I know people thought I was being one or both when I went to Mississippi, and it is impossible to explain that I simply had to *find out for myself*, and could find no other way to do it. On the other hand, Miz Bah, I really don't see you behind the counter in a little jam-and-jelly shop… within two years you would be running a small factory (hiring only Chicanas of course…) working over the books in an executive position instead of stirring the pots….

Well… do you think that a few months in Provence may clear your thoughts? What do you say to next September? I like your idea of being in or yet near someplace… I hate the thought of having a car… maybe we could be pensionnaires for a time, to sniff around…. I'd like either to have a roomy flat or house, or be near a good hotel or inn, so that we could have *people*… for instance, Humphrey wants to take Solveig to Provence late next year… they'd have a car and be everywhere, but it would be fun to have them in and out, I think… etc etc…. Who knows? You might even find yourself with several grandchildren tumbling about in the mud…. Well, I think we should muble alonga bout this.

Actually, I so enjoy waking and sleeping and smelling and eating, right here, that I know it will be an effort to shift. But I long to be less somnolent, less cozy… at least once more in my life! And there's nobody on this green earth I'd rather try it with than you.

On that subject, I can't forget, nor really believe, your saying that you find me a "good traveller" or however you phrased it! I am *bouleversée*. I beam. I qvell. (But I promise never to remind you of it, if I suddenly find the halo a little bent or rusty….)

2. *Among Friends*

It is silly to write at this length, because I'm hoping to see you before you'll even get this. But I feel like mulling over a few things… and we always have to get through the "How's Lukas[3]?" "He's fine. How's Anna?" "She's fine. How's…?"

How are you? I'm fine. My eyes are all right. It was an infection, and not the result of fruit-flies, as I suspected. Elsine Ten Broeck had it too, but at the same time, so we didn't give it to each other or however that works. There was a lot of it in Richmond, I am told. How do these things get about? It was NOT Pink Eye or iritis, and was always accompanied by various symptoms of the Common Cold. Ah well and ho hum. Enough is Enough.

My ten "author's copies" of the translation[4] came today. I haven't yet brought myself to look at the book. The dust-jacket is very blah. I've ordered fifty more… don't know quite how to spread them around… have sent off over sixty copies of the Whittier book.[5] As Arnold Gingrich says, it costs too damned much to write a book… really, it is surprising how brash people are about simply *asking* for copies. . . . Some people I like can buy copies for what I pay for them… $6 in this case, instead of 10… and you certainly qualify there, needless to say. But it is rather sticky when somebody like Mary Caroni writes from Locarno that she would like me to send three more copies at once, inscribed to Lady So and So and two other charming American ex-patriates in Ascona… and what do I do… send the bill? ask for money and then mail the stuff? tell her think again?

Yes.

Oh… somewhat to my surprise (I was pleased, though) the *NYer* asked me to sign another First Reading Agreement. I was quite prepared to have them let it lapse… I haven't sent them anything for over a year, and they have a big backlog of unpublished and by now unpublishable stuff… reviews of cookerybookery etc. I am doing ONE MORE review, really very funny and "current"… and if that is shelved, I'm through.

So we'd better head for Provence while I'm still solvent….

End of ramble, but it was fun. Thank you again for commenting, in a succinct but basically gentle way, about the Whittier Book. It must have been odd to read about the family before you were much into it. . . .

Oh… about eyes… Dickie[6] prescribed no miracle-pills, agreed with my self-medication, and said it was tough. (I continue to like that approach.) He also found my blood pressure a little surprising (I did not, after the past two weeks!), and observed that one ear-drum looked different from the other, perhaps a result of blowing my nose too hard… no damage, no sweat. His moustache and hair are longer by the minute, and a lot of St. Helenans look sideways and are glad he is off the school board… he might be a… well, ugh… a HIPPIE. . . .

---

3. Norah's grandchild
4. *The Physiology of Taste*
5. *Among Friends*
6. MF's doctor in St. Helena, Richard Neil

Bouverie Ranch, Glen Ellen, California   *4.ii.72*
To: Paul and Julia Child

D*E*R*E F*R*E*N*S: How typically generous of you to suggest that I might stay at La Pitchoune! I do thank you, from the heart, and hope that sometime it will come about. It was really like a stifled yawn or sneeze, when I was there (physically at least) with Michael and Frances F[1]... but when I went back for not much more than a few minutes, it was like going home again. I'm sure I could draft the house to scale, and know exactly where things were/are. That is a nice feeling, and a rare one.

I think that *if* I can bring off this proposed stay in Provence, I should try to settle in or near the center of a village or small town, so that I could walk to market and so on. Then I'd rent a car and driver for sorties. I have never had my own car in France, in all the years of living there, and I'd like to keep the slate clean (perhaps foisly... but I shun all the details of insurance, garaging, etc.... /this is a new basic spelling of *foolishly*...). Norah seems to be wavering a little... about both resigning her job and going to France. I'd love to have her aboard, for we travel well together. But I want to come anyway... all kinds of delightful people have promised to come to whatever I may find, and I think I need one more super-colossal SPREE....

It must seem very strange to be 70, chronologically at least. I am 63, and when (rarely) I look straight at the fact, I feel a real *disbelief.* Somewhere something has slipped up... raced the Time-clock without warning me. In other words, I simply don't believe it. I suppose, being a woman, that I am more fatalistic than you.... I never went through a bad time psychologically. I did witness one, though, when my first husband, Al Fisher, turned 30. He had been told by a Gypsy, while he was at Princeton, that he would either be a world-acclaimed poet by 30, or be dead... and, astonishingly enough, he *believed* it. And then suddenly he *was* thirty, and he was *not* a famous poet... and he went through a real spiritual crisis, actually a cosmic fit of the peeves, as if he'd been cheated. Well... I used to say blandly that I wanted to write a good book by the time I reached 50. Then, almost without realizing it, I upped the age to 55... then to 60! Now I simply hold my tongue, for I'm heading fast for 65 and still hope to write That Book....

Dear Jim[2] *must* be much better, to have survived a trip to Richard Olney's eyrie![3] I still feel shaken by that experience, now and then.... I'm sure the sheep-trail must have been repaired a little, enough for a car, because I believe firmly that Jim *could not* have climbed up.... Once there, the beauty, and the good wines, help to dull the awful prospect of climbing back down....

Thank you again, dear people, for offering me the key to La Peetch! I like to know that someday I may be there again....

1. Michael and Frances Field
2. James Beard ("Fat Jim")
3. Richard Olney, writer of cookbooks

Oh... I was so disappointed in the *menudo* that I served to you that I made another this week, and it is truly a triumph... even though I left out both garlic and chili-powder, planning to present some to Bouverie (now home). But he is one of the unfortunate people conditioned to gag at the *mention* of tripe, so I've frozen some. And I missed the broadcast... was all set to view it on Phyllis's TV when a houseful of unexpected company arrived for her. It may be re-broadcast. If you think of it, when next you write (I assume presumptuously that you will!), please tell me what dish was presented... I've never tried to make one à la mode de Caen, although I've eaten enough of it to feed a regiment.

I think I told you about one of the editors at Time-Life who suggested *quite seriously,* when I said that a book on provincial French cooking must of necessity deal with "offal," that the pages concerning it be bound into the book in such a way that they could easily be torn out by people who felt as disgusted as he at the very *names*... liver, kidneys, and so on, and above all, *tripe....*

Even Phyllis said flatly that she would turn on the program for me, but would have to leave the room! (She feels that way about liver, but can cook it to perfection....) So I wonder if you got any such reaction in the fan mail....

I must stop this chitchat... and go through three long bibliographies on wine before the meeting on the 6th of the Wine Library, in St. Helena.

Ho hum.

Love to you both, and always my thanks about La Pitchoune...

....

Last House, Glen Ellen, California   *19.ii.72*
To: Arnold Gingrich

Dearest Mr. Rich: I am as always cordially yours, but have been remiss, as always too, about writing. I find the presence of another person rather demanding. MV[1] is very independent and firm and courageous, as I need not say. But she is definitely just learning how to adjust to the fact that not long ago she was thoroughly *carved*... there too she is patient, and does not overdo. However... as I also need not say, it is a fairly demanding thing for me to watch over her and prepare three decent meals a day. I also give her a little "tea" in the afternoon (So that I don't have to serve dinner promptly at six, which I really loathe both doing and eating...).

I've been thinking about my rather leisurely re-reading of *Cast Down*, and I'm increasingly impressed with what really reveals itself as a near-obsession about performing artists... that's a bad term... creative musicians may be better. You were chewing on this, worrying it, sweating over it. VERY INTERESTING. I feel happy that unlike most of us people you have plunged deeper, no matter how long the wait, into what and where you obviously should be. (This is badly expressed... sorry.)

... And here I am writing some poor excuse for a note, at 9:40 of a gentle mizzly morning.

1. Marietta Voorhees

M.F.K. Fisher: A Life in Letters

MV has set up her desk at the Swiss [desk] in the Big Room. I still keep my very untidy North end of the bedroom (where she sleeps etc. I sleep in your bed...). Today I M*U*S*T work on an introduction I've promised for Paco Gould's nice little memoirs. Then I organize a thing for *Prose*, which I think I told you about... an odd-ball publication, beautifully printed by a zany young billionaire...). . . .

I suspect that you will go down in piscatorial history, if not otherwise, as a man who tickled the trout through sleet and snow, like the postman, on his appointed round... except that he gets money for it!

By now I am really bored with the Hughes[2] thing, in spite of my thanks to you for the clippings. I hope that some "positive" good may come of it, in pointing out to the American Public that it is in a period based on its own colossal gullibility... one of SHAM, from the depths to the heights of financial power and political scheming.

I agree with you that a month from now it will be forgotten stuff. . . .

Your remark about the wood you'd have to carry to the cellar reminds me of a bitter memory my father Rex had about that: his father, the editor of the weekly newspaper, was most often paid "in kind," and Rex was haunted by the knowledge that some farmer who had run an ad would show up with a load of logs to be cut and stacked....

They also got sacks of grain, lengths of cloth, jugs of molasses... never very much coin of the realm....

What is the "very funny Valentine" you think I have/had? (I'm dumb....) (I'm the Goldie Hawn of modern letters...) . . .

About rating a Valentine from you when I'm kicking 100, I can hardly wait! In fact, I doubt that I do wait. I would like to be old but independent, and that is apparently something that is rare. I was talking the other day with an old friend who is in her mid-80s and who has been in a wheelchair for the past decade or so. She said without any pathos or bathos that every night she prayed that she would not wake up in the morning. How sad that seems to me. But I can understand it. She is completely DEPENDENT. (She told me once that the most humiliating thing she had to learn to ignore was being helped onto the toilet....) On the other hand there is Miss Eleanor, MV's mother, who is staying in a so-called rest-home and blooming like a rose. She will be 100 in April. She becomes very doddery when at home, but once she's in that sex-pit her glands rev at 99 miles a minute, and she practically speeds about the place, in her little walker, gloating over her strength and prowess while youngsters in their sixties lie prone on their beds....

I love the clipping about the old lady of 55! Do you remember that deathless description from (I think) Fitzgerald's first novel... *The Beautiful and Damned*?... : "she was a faded but still lovely woman of twenty-seven..."?????

Did you ever get a book I tried to send you for Christmas... something like *How to Fish Good...*? It was probably too ghastly to look at, but I thought it would be a good spoof for you.

2. A fraudulent memoir of Howard Hughes had been sold for book and magazine publication; a media scandal followed.

I suspect that one reason your weight fluctuates is that *you* do. That is, one day you'll skip lunch, and the next you won't, and some days you tear around and use up energies, and other days you have lunch with a couple of beauteous dames and drink some good wine and and and. In other words your metabolism is panting to keep up with you.... To stabilize the actual weight, you'd have to be firm about a set (boring) routine, and that is almost impossible, professionally.

Well... you're a very conscientious man, and also a very nice one, and I thank you for calling me and I hope you can make it tomorrow too... I'm greedy!!!

I must go work on the Paco thing. Ho hum.

....

Last House, Glen Ellen, California   *Easter... 2.iv.72... a beautiful fresh*
To: Mary Kennedy Wright   *day full of meadowlarks*

Dearest Kennedy:

This is a message in reply to your card-file letter of March 23. I have given it much thought.

First I want to tell you how pleased I am that you and Jim hatched the Easter Egg so rightly! That is one nice thing about being older, I find: I can simply *trust* that a few good people will know what to do with the seemingly cold blunt presentation of a little cash... not be rebuffed by its seeming impersonality... not be burdened with a well-meant but useless gadget or white elephant;;;;;;;!!!@@@###$$&&&*()__+++++ +++

On this subject, when next you come up, which I hope won't be too far from now, look at the records if you wish to. I play the boxes quite often, but there are a lot of records that should be in use, because they are so beautiful.... (Some of my treasures seem to have been "lifted"... probably my own fault, in urging people to take them... but I did have some very good spoken stuff that seems gone forever: Colette in her last years, T. S. Eliot, Dylan Thomas... that sort of thing. Ah well.)

Now about your feeling that Norah is "cold and uncaring" and your questions to me about what to do about this sad situation:

I think that I must leave the whole problem, if it is in truth a problem, up to you to try to solve. You are a maturing and intelligent and loving person. With Jim's help, you will decide for yourself whether to write to N, to meet her for talk, to try the telephone, to make your own friendly affectionate essays, to forget the whole thing and decide to resume your childhood *rapport* later... there are countless alternatives.

I am sorry if I seem to withdraw too flatly from involving myself in what is basically your problem.

My relationship with Norah is at this point a good one, although delicately balanced and deliberately planned, perhaps by her too but certainly by me. I am almost a decade older, and I feel that I must and can be the one to decide its course. That is to say, it is up to me to express irritation or insult if I feel either (which of course I sometimes do). So I choose, now toward the end of my relationship, to forget the possible causes for negative reactions with her, and remember her unquestioning help to me in several crises, her quick and tender attentions to me when I have needed exactly that. I prefer to forget much that I regret. There have been periods of great hostility between us, which have cut into me deeply and which I prefer now to avoid ever repeating, if I can help it. At this stage in our lives as sisters we enjoy many of the same things. We can put aside the contentious ones... not ignore them, but not talk of them.

Among these subjects, perhaps unfortunately but perhaps not, are our children. When the five of you were being born and were growing up, it helped Norah and me to raise you as much as possible together. We had left your fathers, for varying reasons, and found a great deal of reassurance in seeing how happy you little ones could be, together.

Now you have all grown into your own patterns, with differing racial and cultural life-styles, and I feel (and probably Norah does too, although we never talk of such things) that you may have absorbed a lot of love and help for your present and future lives. I hope so.

In other words, I hope that the open affection and sharing of your young years will pay off, one good way or another, in unsuspected ways in the future. It is perhaps like feeding a puppy good food so that he will be a healthy big dog....??? (Silly-simile syndrome...)

So... I feel, darling girl, that I should not try to mend any of your fences at this stage in my life-game.

Perhaps you have not known me long enough to know (as two adults, I mean) that I have a great gift for friendship... the long slow deep kind that must be nurtured and planned for and weighed. I am gradually building that with my younger (once *youngest*) sister. I have the advantage of age and experience.

There are many things we do not touch upon. Norah is, as June Eddy wrote me about *Sis* after her death, "a complex and fascinating personality." We do not get onto Women's Lib, politics, liberalism, 1,000 other things, but *especially our children*. We find real enjoyment in ambling through Provençal restaurants and staying in noisy railroad stations and all that. It is *enjoyable*, and at my age one can say that about few things and few people. One becomes more cautious and sparing...

... and that is why, dear girl, I am not going to speak of your notes, nor send them, to Norah. I think you must do it when and if you decide to, yourself. I am too old, and I am too selfish of my serenity, to interfere in a situation that hinges upon the emotions of people who are actually strangers to me in relation to each other: you, Norah.

PS really... I understand the conditioned reflex, for such I consider it to be, of "Family." Try to forget all those pulls. Take what is good. Today, for instance, I am sustained and amused and deeply strengthened by the Easters before you were born, even after... the pashka we made in Carson Valley... the knowledge that you *are*, and that Jim and Alex are with you.

Last House, Glen Ellen, California 4.viii.72
To: Paul and Julia Child

How nice it was of you, D*E*R*E Julia and Paul, to send me the winy delicious cards! I felt "included in"... especially with you and Jim.[1] (I got a good fat letter from him yesterday, to my astonishment: I don't see how he can possibly have any energy left, after he has followed his fantastic schedules. His glands should be invaluable to any scientists qualified to cope with them.... As for the two Jacks, Shelton and Juhasz (or is it Juhazs?), I haven't seen them for about a year, although we write now and then. I wonder what they will do, once they give up the newsletter, which of course I read with some glee....). . .

Are you in Cambridge again? I'll send this note there. I like to think that you may be picking blueberries or something, on the island... which reminds me that I woke with a start this morning, asking myself if Rachel Field and Paul Child could have been cousins and then realizing that I was thinking of Michael Field[2] and that no it would be impossible because she was a born-and-bred New Englander and he was a New Yorker and probably second-generation. I think this odd half-dream was because I am often correcting people as unobtrusively as possible about putting an "s" on your name, and Rachel did not have one and neither did Michael. Well... it is the nearest I've come to thinking even subconsciously about that briefly flaming candle of a man, for some time... not to mention poor Rachel!

I'm going to NY for two or three days in September, to see Henry Volkening, who is leaving his firm. He has been a dear and very loyal friend for a long time, and I want to remind him of that, I suppose. Otherwise I dread the trip. But at least I'll go out to Bridgehampton and walk on the dunes again, before I head West.

My sister Norah and I still hope very much to go to Provence at the first of the year, to stay in a small town and *work*. We don't want a car, and we do want a little kitchen, and otherwise we are pleasantly amenable. Jim has mentioned two places, but neither is in the Guide Michelin, as far as I can tell! I'll think we'll simply head for St. Rémy and see what turns up....

Here, life on the ole rancho is very lively. David's part is fully booked, and mine seems to have a lot of traffic too. We often combine forces, although I can't handle more than eight for meals. I'm pulling up the drawbridge during part of August... simply have to catch my breath with papers and so on, and have crossed off several "important" things like the visit from my #1 Nephew from Bangkok with his family, etc etc. The weather, except for one bad heat-wave, is superb. The voracious cattle surround me, and have managed to defoliate my four grapevines, four walnut trees, and one pampas grass, all of which sends David frantically to his drawingboard to design new foils for next year. (Nothing has worked, so far....)

1. James Beard, mutual culinary friend
2. Michael Field died young, as did his wife, Frances. Rachel MacKenzie underwent open-heart surgery at this time.

Julia, this will amuse you: David's cook is absolutely terrified of you (Do you remember Phyllis Whitman here?), and panics when she opens Vols. 1 or 2. So two days ago I *translated* you into Basic English for her, because D wants to serve your Jambon Persillé to some rich old gents from SF who might buy one of his Sargents for the Palace of the Legion of Honor or something.... I hope to God I've done right by you (and them!).... Phyllis is scared of having to read anything longer than a Rombauer recipe. It turns into LITERATURE, which she is convinced she cannot understand.

I suppose this is a conditioned reflex... self-protective, anyway. And it would be cruel of me, when she howls that she doesn't "understand," to remark coolly that several million people seem to have figured you out... (I would add, "Read Rombauer, then," except that there's no such thing as Jambon Persillé à la Bourgogne in *The Joy of Cooking*... and it wouldn't please the Squire if it were!!!!).

This reminds me . . . that I finally saw one of your shows! Imagine living this long with only one glimpse, when I went into a motel and clicked on the Box and heard a dear familiar voice say BON APPETIT and then sign off! It was the thing about zucchini, and I loved it, being hooked on both the vegetable and the lady. The zucchi are prime now, and I made the grated version à la crème, but without the flour, for some terribly finicky Italian friends, and to their own surprise they simply lapped it up.... (I served grated Parmesan on the side, simply in honor of their tastes, and they hardly used it....)

I hope everything good for you both, whatever you are doing. I think you are in a new series of filmings? Is there any chance of your being out here before Christmas or after Easter? Is there any chance of your being in Plascassier after the New Year? I look forward to the next time we can meet, *wherever*, and one nice thing about a friendship like the one I feel for you is that it can withstand absences. (Let us not make them *too* lengthy, though! Time is turtling on....)

Meanwhile, please send an occasional postcard... and when I come upon a good bottle, I'll lift my glass to you. (This happened just lately, and I *did*....)

....

Last House, Glen Ellen, California   *22.xii.72*
To: Paul and Julia Child

Dear Julie and Paul, dere frens indeed!.......

This is too late for Christmas, but it will bring you greetings for the New Year... as if you needed them from me for any special time at all, I think of you much oftener than you could guess, and always with a nice warm feeling of good luck (mine), and now and then a chuckle of pure enjoyment at what we have done and what we may still do together....

It looks as if I'm going to miss seeing you in Plascassier. Damn.

Norah and I are supposed to land in Cannes, very late on Jan. 28, on the *Colombo*. From what I know (too much) about January crossings, we may well be late. Néanmoins we'll stay one night at the shabby old Carlton, to get our land legs, and then (hopefully) Gatti[1] will meet us and take us directly to Salon. That would be on Jan. 29 or 30... and you leave on Feb. 1. Damn again.

We are being this fugitive or whatever it is that we are being, because we both face moral and physical deadlines and are afraid that if we look to either right or left we'll not follow the straight path, etc etc. It sounds childish for two women of our ages, but it's true: we have a dozen temptations along the road from Cannes to Salon, in the form of dear friends etc etc, and we simply DASSN'T falter. Once we get into a good pattern, we keep telling ourselves, we'll go off on sprees... Marseille, Aix, perhaps Cannes again (to see Eda-Sybille and the Bachmans[2] mostly... if you're gone, which you will be...).

I still feel rather vague about the whole thing, but the tickets are in hand and the passports are renewed.... We wanted to go to St. Rémy, but only one small hotel stays open there in the bad season (mistral), so we'll use Salon as a base, and snoop around by bus. . . .

I looked forward almost voluptuously to being alone, this Christmas, for the third consecutive time and at my own request. It sounds very Scroogy, but is *right*, after more than 50 years of holding a big and generally happy family together, on every level and in every situation... I was the Oldest Child(!!!). So now I have freed my two girls from that obligation, and they are making their own families, and so are my nephews, and I must say just what Father Divine used to say. So... this year I went through all the rigmarole of thankyous and nononos, and settled myself for a day of music I like, odd jobs like going through my shoes for Goodwill, and a bottle of cold champagne to nibble at. And suddenly I find myself doing gastronomical nip-ups for seven Displaced Persons... no place to go but dreary restaurants, no friends in a new land or territory.... Well, I'll have a nice fire going, and good wine and food to hand... and I'll do the secret thing *next* day. Mañana!

Abiding love, for the holidays and far past them... BONNE ANNÉE, too.

PS... Do you know Raymond Gatti? He drove for Jim, too. He's in Sunnyside, Plascassier....

....

Marseille, France   *14.ii.73*
To: Eleanor Friede

Dearest Squeek... I'm not even going to ask you to forgive this long silence. Things have gone so fast and furiously, and so well withal, that when we fall into our two large lumpy beds at night we sleep like happy hound-dogs... and then get up the next morning to do a thousand little things that seem to take up the whole day. (YOU know....)

We remain highly amused at our instantaneous shift from "a small tranquil provin-

1. Chauffeur to James Beard as well as to MFK
2. Laurence Bachman, lifelong friend, had been instrumental in getting MF a job at Paramount Studios. He loaned her a European electric typewriter in France.

cial town" to one of the noisiest wildest cities in France, and haven't regretted it one instant.

The flat is called a "studio" because it has a wretched little cupboard in the bathroom, with a 2-burner gas plate and three battered saucepans and a night-population of silent waterbugs. We have four plates, a salad bowl thank god, three knives one of which actually cuts bread... you know what the set-up would be. We have a good-looking chambermaid who comes every weekday morning to mop the bare red tile floors and push dust around. We're on the 8th of 10 floors of a building put up when reinforced concrete seemed the answer to any problems of future bombardments (1930???), as indeed this monster proved to be in 1943 et seq... not a crack in it, although it's really very ugly and shabby. The elevator is one of those cages that go up the middle. It gets the shakes at the 4th floor, and then pulls itself together.... We've had to invest in a few things like wine glasses, cloth for 2 bedspreads, a sharp veg knife, etc, but in the main it is really fun to live without most of our usual cozy trappings. A balcony runs across the two airy plain rooms... too cold yet to use it for anything but hanging out some panty-hose now and then... and each room has a big studio-bed and a good work table. My smaller room has an armoire which we both use, and Noni's bigger one is where she works and we eat, with a kind of buffet for our dishes and so on, and storage. We have three straight chairs, so we are either vertical for work and meals or horizontal for reading and sleeping.

The ONLY drawback to this temporarily idyllic life is that the hot water is never anything but lukewarm. And it is interesting to see how quickly we have gone back to other copings with the same problem... I, for instance, am now taking exactly the same kind of cat-baths I evolved in 1929 in Dijon, almost literally in a teacup. We are scouting around the neighborhood for a decent masseuse who also has a good hot shower "before or after"... that's what I've done several times when faced with obsolete or non-existing plumbing that I've grown used to accept... here I'm interrupted and what I mean to say is that at home I'm very used to things that I can actually live without....

Meals are fun. Very limited, of course. Four or five times a week we eat in town at some of the very good restaurants... oh, delicious! And here N makes her ritual breakfast of coffee, bread, butter, honey, and I eat some fruit. There are countless little shops in the neighborhood, and we make wonderful salads and try all kinds of cheeses and good breads and very pleasant local wines. Once we bought some coquilles St. Jacques, partly for the beautiful shells which we'll bring home, and they were supersuperb. Once we bought cooked small shrimp, but they were a near miss. We next plan to try moules à la marinière, because we have one fairly large pot and moules are in season now and simply delicious. I eat them every time we are in town, one way or another....

The vagaries of the Italian Line were something of a shock to our funds, what with cables, hotels, taxis, airfare from Naples to Nice, etc etc, but I've sent for more money... and Norah, who was stripped of all her travellers' checks when two of our bags were "lost" overnight in Rome (!!!plus most of the trinkets we'd bought for presents in Naples... really beautiful tortoise shell and coral... ho hum...), hopes that eventually Am Ex will condescend to consider her case, as their occasional letters say. Who writes all the publicity about "immediate refund of all lost checks" ???? It's been two weeks since she wired to Paris about the theft.... Meanwhile, don't worry +#& as this borrowed English-face SCM likes to say... we are perfectly all right, for about 2 more weeks. If things get scary, I'll wire you for help... have no fear...!

Salon was impossible, and within a few minutes we knew that crazy dream was over. The town itself is astonishingly provincial, with beautiful trees, terrible monuments, and except for one restaurant HORRIBLE food. We tried a couple of movies... walked out of one, a silly thing based on the Canterbury Tales... it was supposed to be sexy hohoho. The young people of Salon simply wander the streets in their free time... really sad, *trapped*... the blades stand around pinball machines in little bars, and drink Perrier or countless espressos, and the shopgirls go by threes and fours up and down, and they all meet in one or two of the movies, and rub against each other. The older people walk quickly and look harried. There are several excellent catering-shops with stuff to take out, and the food shops are good, which means that everybody eats at home... except the poor tired middle-aged drummers and a few tourists like us. Fortunately we found Boissin, run now by two young chefs obviously scraping along... very inventive cuisine. And there and everywhere we have drunk delightful wines.... At Boissin we ate a salad of tender curly lettuce, Belgian endive, and small sweet halves of this year's crop of walnuts, tossed together... delicious. Salade aux noix.

Norah is plowing into a lot of research... wonderful books all over the flat. I know exactly what I want to do, and *soon,* and have bought the one book I need. We've been to Aix once, and will go as often as possible, ostensibly for N's work!!!!

We want to see Leo and Barbara[1] soon, of course... and we still collect a fine crew of former pals at the Deux Garçons and Longchamps, some of whom are now running their own little bars and have gone either up in the ranks of waiters or have hit the skids.... But of course I can't see Mme. Lanes, and haven't got in touch with Madeleine Aubergy for some indefinable reason, and our friends the Segonds have left (he died and she's in Paris), and the Bulidons are dead...&&&&. We had a jolly drink at the 2G and one at Longchamps to pull the threads together, and finally went to the Vendôme for a delicious lunch... bought some cloth for bedspreads and a few pottery pitchers to use as vases, and so on. I do love that town. And the traffic on the Cours Mirabeau seems somewhat better, thanks to the new autoroute that deflects a lot of cars. There are still too many trucks, because they don't want to pay the toll-fee on the autoroute. I'm interested to know what has happened to the Roy René, which had one-half closed off because of the traffic noise when I was last there. We'd thought we might stay there now and then, but with our own pad only an hour away, why bother (except that it would be fun to take a hot bath again!!!! and I do want to see my pal the concierge...).

We had great ideas of buying a lot of good posters, but these cement and then pa-

1. Marschutz

pered walls will not take them. But the views are so splendid, and we are so completely at ease here, that it doesn't matter.

We went to see Brando's *Last Tango*. He did a very good job, and of course he is handsomer than ever. But the story seemed thin... and all the sex activity was apparently extremely exhausting and painful to both ME and the girl, and here I've always thought it was such FUN.... Then we went to a far-out kind of "revue" that was trying out for Paris but that I doubt made it that far... really fine actors and excellent black (NY) musicians, but a thin script.... And we went to the newly cleaned Opera House, where we-all went for one Christmas pantomime that was a near miss, and saw a delightful *Beggars' Opera*, Benjamin Britten's new version of the old John Gay... fresh, talented, good orchestra. Fun. The Opera has taken on new life, thank God, and we plan to go to three things. Roland Petit is doing the ballet quite often... doubtless mostly a local troupe. The orchestra is *good*. And the theatre is now the jewel it has been before....

The people here are ageless. I have never lived in an atmosphere of such dauntless vitality as in Marseille. To me they are attractive, the way a magnet is: hard, perhaps ruthless but with real scruples and ethics. I have no desire for physical contact or any attempt at intimacy with them, but I love to be near them. I feel that I understand, at least empathetically, why they are made exactly as they are, short, compact, with small graceful hands and feet and faces of stone.

Mme. Fath, our chambermaid, is of this local breed. She is still very pretty, with intelligent careful makeup, and is perhaps under 40, with a lovely daughter about 16 who will soon become exactly like her mother. She is efficient, very hard-working in an acceptive but not resentful way (What a nasty job, to tend to the kitchens and toilets and so on in a big shabby old place like this!), and utterly detached. She is also thoughtful: she saw at once that we were using our one big pot for some flowers we'd bought in Cannes and then brought from Salon, and she brought two hideous cut-glass vases from somewhere... frinstance. When I asked her about a neighborhood cobbler who could mend some heels for me, she simply took the boots... brought them back today. But I know that even after a year or so of this, I still would not think of asking her if she was married, divorced, even well or ill....

Norah is out in the quarter now, buying a fresh loaf of delicious dark moist bread and a wedge of Brie, and I'll slit a few heads of B. endive and we'll have a nice lazy lunch, with some wine. What a life...

... and here it is nearing 2, . . . and I'm finishing a glass of white wine and wondering whether to go out with Norah who wants to walk into town for some tickets for a big James Brown concert, or stay here and cope with a pile of neglected (fan &&&) mail. I should do the latter, since I can't type here after about 5, because of the light....

The flowers are incredible here. There is a Flower Market three days a week, which we go to like hypnotized chickens, strolling up and down and humming uncontrollably and unconsciously. Right now the cheapest are huge heaps and piles of anemones, both long and short stemmed. Carnations, which are strictly "Provence" to me, and more expensive than in Cannes but still only about ten cents apiece. There are wonderful bold tough marigolds now... and lovely little prim posies of pinks and daisies, and "Spring bouquets" of a rose or two, some blue iris, mimosa, ranunculas, daisies, whatever... we also have three little pots of local herbs: rosemary, thyme, tarragon.

I must be serious... twerk. . . .

Until soon... I wish you were having as much fun as I am/we are. But maybe you are. I am simply more AWARE of everything, including myself, here in France, and especially here, where I've always dreamed of staying for more than a couple of weeks or so....

....

Marseille, France   *13.iii.73*
To: Arnold Gingrich

Dearest Ginger... thanks so much for the three "reports" that came yesterday, giving number of fish caught, temperatures, &&&, as well as your usual tantalizing peeps at ARNOLD GINGRICH HISSELF. I'm glad you snapped out of the fish-syndrome... was it a question of the weather, pre-Spring, luck??? As for the weather, I really can't tell: one minute it is the "ceaseless rains" and then it feels like Spring....
Here we are in bright cool days, and now and then on a café table there is a branch of flowering almond, and the little hedges that separate one terrace from another are beginning to make buds... ah, very nice! Nights are cold, and so are early mornings and early evenings and also whenever you walk from East to West, because of the air from the sea. As for my fishing, it is of course "spectator" but I work at it earnestly, from my first survey of how many boats are going in and out of the Vieux Port, to my next investigation of how the supplies are in the street stands and what the marketing looks like from the tables along the Quai des Belges, to what is marked "Aujourd'hui" on the sidewalk menu of Le New York, which is presently the top restaurant in Marseille. (I think it is excellent, especially in the back, but it is monstrously expensive and we know at least two places that are as good....) Then I settle down, at least as often as possible, with a menu... and yesterday for lunch ate a plateau de fruits de mer that included oysters (Belons), mussels, clams, violets, shrimps, and urchins. A good catch... and I was biting well. The night before, I ate two large bowls of moules marinière. And so it goes . . .

It *is* odd about the feeling one gets, that Spring and a new life and easier days are "just around the corner"... it's very exciting. I don't really have it, here, because everything is very exciting anyway... but I love it anyway, if you know what I mean and you do, and I get strange urges to go on a picnic... I really hate to miss this time of year at the Ranch, but of course I'm glad I'm *here*. . . .

When you talk about the painting vs. colored photos for the book, do you mean the jacket? And are you going to be on the *cover*? I thought the book was to be about other great fishermen...???

You ask about Aix. The "old town" is more beautiful than ever, with the snowballing interest in cleaning and uncovering the old facades and interiors. Some absolute beauties are turning up, from behind a couple of centuries of stucco and false wooden fronts... all in the ineffable rosy-gold stone of Provence. But there is no longer a beautiful view of the city on the hills... it is hidden by countless high-rise apartments, all looking like giant dominoes on end. That is a real shame. Once out of the town, though, the countryside is still harsh and beautiful. We taxied out to Leo's studio and took a bus back, the other day, and although I would not dare walk along the Route de Cézanne to market as I used to, because of the mad traffic, the road looked much the same. In town, traffic is perhaps less noisy than it was, thanks to the new autoroute, but it is still a hopeless desecration... and the fuss to ban some of it still tangles regularly with the Power boys, whoever they may be... politics, anyways.... The Mozart Festival has tapered off to nothing, according to the Marschutzes... thank god we were there in its real prime!!!...

You said very kind things indeed about *Map of Another Town,* and they make me more interested in pulling together the thing about the rest of Provence... I can't feel much interest in producing another book, and this has nothing, as far as I'm aware, to do with the fact that my books ALWAYS fall into a deathly silent pit. It's simply that I seem to feel no urgency at all to "express myself" or whatever it is that one does in writing. I've said too much already. Who listens? And most of all, why *should* anyone listen??? I may snap out of this lethargy, creative or whatever it is. I have, before. And again, I may not. I think I have enough money to take care of my main needs, unless I should live much longer than I prefer to... and I'm well housed. It's simply NO DRIVE, Doc!!!

... and here came your letter of the 9th! Great... Well, I do think you are a shocking crybaby to be peeved because Deane[1] has had facial surgery and is scheduled for an operation so you may get cheated of your *purely* non-professional and benevolent session with him! How about your going on a cruise? Do you think he jumps up and down and hollers because he is missing two of his Saturdays with you????? Tut TUT...

I loved what you wrote about the early morning walk, very grey and soft... Corot. Things like that ALMOST make up for what is to me your inexplicable commuting. I do understand your main reasons. It is simply (I suppose) that I could not accept them for myself... I would rather die.

Sunday Morning the Stones were to arrive at 7:30, and I wanted to have fliers and a note and some presents in their room, and see that it was the one I'd asked for, and so on, so I walked down to the Canebière at 6:30. It was just turning light. I went along the Rive Neuve, and there was a lot of almost silent activity among the fishermen, getting ready to go out or tidying after a night at sea... coiling ropes, all that... not much talk. The streetsweepers were at work, and there were the sounds of their long twig brooms scratching, and the water rushing down the gutters. Then, in town, I could hear footfalls, and in the little *Place* behind the hotel the two fountains! I had never heard them before, but only seen them.... As is often the case, I decided I should get up before dawn *every* morning and walk about the town....

1. Arnold Gingrich's violin teacher

I must tend my muttons... in this case, some dull business letters that la Hublitz for-warded[2]... ho hum....

When do you think we'll meet again?????

<hr />

Marseille, France   *27.iii.73*
To: Helen Marshall[1]

Dearest Helen... ma chère et belle Hélène.......

How fine it was to get your letter! Thank you, more than I can say, for writing to me.

I've had it very much on my mind about being too careless and casual in staying in touch with you. I've had your name on my "special" list for a shamefully long time, for a letter telling you how much I love you and how grateful I am for the strange accident that let me meet you... that sort of thing. And then Time has played its usual sneaky tricks, and suddenly I've found myself (as now) involved in another way of life, and I've kept on being careless. Well, your generous note restored at least enough of my dignity (?) to start me on this apology!!!

A couple of years ago... no, a little more than that... I discussed with Mrs. Brown (Berkeley) my flying to see you, and just where I would engage a room, and so on. Then all my plans changed, and I never brought it off. I was going, on her advice, to install myself at the hotel she recommended in Santa Fe (can't remember it), and telephone to you very casually that I was there unexpectedly and wondered if I could see you. There was something that did not quite click, about this plan... and as you can see, I didn't carry it out.

About then I changed my whole pattern of life, hopefully for the rest of my life. I sold the big old house in St. Helena, which was really too big for me to keep alive by myself and which was turning into an excellent bar-hotel-restaurant while I played chief and sole factotum. I built a two-room (really palatial, though...) house on the ranch of an old friend who had long wanted me to... he is a retired architect, and when I finally succumbed to his persuasions, I simply told him what I wanted, and left for France for several months. The result is delightful, and you would approve. I have just what furniture I most like, from my other houses and my families, and about 5,000 books, and all my husband's pictures and a lot more... and once more I am in country that is "unspoiled"... rolling hills on the east slope of the little Valley of the Moon about 8 miles north of Sonoma. Sonoma is the one town I would have wanted to live in, after St. Helena, so really I have eaten my cake and had it too....

Life at the Ranch can be very giddy, when I want it to... David Bouverie entertains a lot, and fortunately we have good mutual friends and he invites a lot of interesting new people. He keeps a small staff there, so that when he is away, for about half the year, I am never alone on the ranch... which as I get older is a wise thing. If I don't want to be with people, I simply say so... a perfect system, but unfortunately I have found it

2. Erika Hublitz forwarded MF's mail from Last House.
1. Owner of house MF rented in Genoa, Nevada

very hard to work there. I mean serious, constructive, hard work... I find that a lot of people come to see me, and of course I love it, and I love most of them, and I love to cook.... It's a trap, and a familiar one to both of us. So... now and then I simply go away from all that pleasant beautiful life, and hide in some ugly motel....

This time, though, it is different. My younger sister Norah, who came with her family to Genoa to stay in your house with me, that legendary far-away Christmas, resigned from her job in Berkeley this year and we decided to take one more good jaunt together, while we both felt well and so on. We travel very well together, as we have been proving since she was 13 and I was 22 and I brought her back to France to live with my first husband and me. Since then we have shared houses (and countries) many times... not to mention children too. Now, we are the first to confess, it is almost pure pleasure to be WITHOUT children, and even without a house....

We are staying in what is really a pretty stark 2-room flat called a "studio" . . . *BUT*... it is in the town we both feel almost mysteriously drawn to, over many decades, and it has a most astonishing view from the long balcony: we look out past Louis IV's Fort St. Nicolas, which we could almost touch with a long broom-handle, to the Mediterranean and the hills behind l'Estaque on the left, and right down onto the Vieux Port and across it to the beautiful (mostly) buildings and the Quai du Port, countless fishing boats and a few yachts, and a constant come-and-go. We are a good half-hour from "town"... that is, the Canebière... but the walk never seems anything but exciting, day or night.

Our cooking is more limited than almost anyone but you would believe, but we thrive on it, and two or three times a week go on a little spree at one of the many good restaurants in town. Our neighborhood is upper-level blue-collar plus old snob, with numberless small shops, and we can buy wonderful salads and cheeses and breads, and the Provençal wines, which I have *always* liked, in the face of critics like Elizabeth David for instance, are better than ever now that there is more competition.

We're about 40 minutes from Aix by bus, and go there at least once a week. It has all its old magic. As usual, I am a split personality on the subject... feel almost compelled to finish my life there (which has been the case for some 20 years!!!), but want to stay American and be nearer a few people I love dearly, like my children and their children, and Norah and hers....

Norah is doing what I think is really a highly amusing work, simply because she is such an unlikely person, being as near a true iconoclast as anyone I have met: she is studying the legends and myths and the general "cults" of Mary Magdalene here in Provence! This entails delightful little two-day trips to places like Aix, of course, for the Bibliothèque Méjane and the strange church dedicated to La Sainte Pénitente, and to St. Maximin to contemplate once more her highly suspect bones and follow the horrible slippery trails up to "her" grotto... etc etc. It's all very amusing to me, and to N too, but she is really serious about it, and has done a heavy lot of research in the several libraries here in Marseille... and of course the churches &&&. A stone's throw from us is the Abbaye de St. Victor, where great diggings have been going on since about 1965, and there are several clear references to a female who was possibly or even probably Magdalene. And so it goes.

As for me, I want to explain on paper why I am always pulled back to Marseille, but I'm finding myself stuttering... can't see the woods for the trees, I suspect. It would be a part of a book I have almost finished about Provence... excluding Aix, of course, which I took care of, after my own fashion(!), in *Map of Another Town*. I've written one long story, much to my surprise, and think you will like it... that is, if the *NYer* does!!!!

And speaking of Work Accomplished, thank you very much for what you said about the last story in the magazine. I wrote it about three years ago. It was a straight factual reportage, as I'm sure you knew at once. I am glad you thought it good. (I hope to write more that will please you, for that is important to me.)

I do hope that you have fully recovered from whatever it was that made you feel "miserable" on Christmas morning and then kept hanging around. Was it perhaps your own version of the London Flu? I am told that the lengthy symptoms of that are dreadful.... Norah and I were very fortunate we left California in what was called an epidemic, and could easily have carried the bug along with us, onto the Italian ship and then into Provence... but we've been blissfully healthy.

We had the firm idea, in the face of much skepticism, especially from our French friends, that we wanted to spend these four months in a small serene provincial town, far from telephone-people-etc. But after a very short time we knew this was an impossible and even undesirable fantasy... and here we are in the second-biggest, noisiest, most "evil" city in France, and loving every minute of it. . . .

Helen, the picture you gave me is one of my familiars. It is hanging in absolutely the right place, and I look at it, as I did in St. Helena, several times a day. My house has black tile floors and roughly stuccoed walls of white over a light terra cotta color that shows through a little, and it is mostly windows, so that I need few pictures and have little space for them. But that good old red depot is a permanent pleasure to me. . . .

Yes, that was a beautiful interlude in my life, going to Genoa and meeting you and some other less important but good people. I wonder how it happened.... Certainly it was some kind of reward, for me.

I hope you find life more good than bad and that you stay more strong than weak, or at least more up than down....... *Really*, it's so hard to say anything sensible to anyone who is fairly elderly and has a bad heart and and and, but you know what I am *trying* to say... it all comes down to the basic fact that I want the salt to keep its savor for you....

....

Marseille, France   *1.iv.73... Poisson d'Avril!!!*
To: Paul and Julia Child

D+E+R+E+ F+R+E+N+S: (I can also make #. 1/8 . . . and a few other things on this English machine, although I still cannot claim to TYPE on it...)... I write very often to you in my head, to tell you about things here, because you are part Marseillais

Anna, Georges Connes, and Kennedy, in Dijon, 1954.

June Eddy ("small corvair, large June"), Los Angeles, 1960.

Eda Lord, Anna, Sybille Bedford, New York, 1964.

Arnold Gingrich in his jacket photo from The Joys of Trout.

"The Oldest Man": Pepe Connes, Kennedy, Georges Connes, and Anna, 1961.

Eleanor Friede, Bridgehampton, 1970s.

Mary Frances, Kennedy, Anna, and Marietta Voorhees, early, 1960s.

Norah Barr and Mary Frances, Last House, 1983.

Mary Frances and Norah Barr, Last House, 1983.

Larry Powell, Gloria Stuart Sheekman, Ward Ritchie —
old friends at U.C.L.A., 1984.

Anne and Sam Lamott, 1989.

Alice Waters and Fanny, 1987.

Marietta Voorhees and companion, 1987.

David Bouverie.

Judith and Evan Jones in the gazebo at Bryn Teg.

....

The Thompsons:
(TOP ROW) *David, Sylvia, Dinah,*
(BOTTOM ROW) *Benjamin, Gene, and Amanda, at home in Malibu, 1977.*

....

Joel Redon, writer, fan and friend, with Joan Taylor, 1993.

T. C. "Bud" Landreth, writer and boyhood companion of David Kennedy;
friend, fan, and correspondent with Mary Frances, 1995.

Mary Frances at Last House, 1985.

and also because, even if you weren't, I like very much to feel that I am in sort of communication with you.

Thank you for writing to us at Salon. It was a bright spot in what might have been a rather bleak interim, except that we were SO GLAD to be in France again. . . .

Salon still has the noble old "mossu" and the good olive oil, not to mention a still-thriving basket industry. But it was impossible to find a decent pied-à-terre there *in town*. There were several rather elegant *mas* for rent in those off-months, but that meant a car, we didn't/don't want a car. The town was almost asleep... only a couple of 3rd-rate hotels open, to take care of the drummers, and very slim pickin' for food. . . .We found one place open, to eat anything but ghastly table-d'hôte for the exhausted traveling salesmen who would sag into town at night from the farmlands: Boissin, run by two excellently trained and rather starry-eyed young men and their wives, with inventive and basically simple cuisine. It has one star, tops for that area, and deserves it, with a rigid standard, even though so simple. One feels that they are surviving on a very short shoe-string, but that they will make it.

(This same take-over of the young *équipes* we saw again in what would be classified as a 2nd-rate restaurant on the Place de l'Horloge in Avignon... really young chef-owner and staff, and good service of basically "plain" dishes. In both places there was a real feeling of what might well pass for Dedication....)

Well... thanks to Boissin in Salon we managed to survive in fine fettle. And here we are living with a gas-plate in a cupboard in the bathroom, which is why the place is called a studio, and we have two saucepans and a sorta-kinda kettle with a lid. But we also have a large salad bowl, and the neighborhood is filled with countless little shops whose peculiar closing hours we are now quite hep to, so that we eat very well indeed, on salades and good breads and excellent cheeses. Then, as often as we feel it is The Moment, we go to a good restaurant in town.

We are about a half-hour trot from the Canebière. It is always fun, and we are determined not to bow to the bus-system, which of course we'd do if we lived here. We can go along the Rue Sainte, but usually go down to the Rive Neuve because it is so exciting. . . .

Of course the new parts of the place, outside, are really an eyesore... except, thank God, for the Route du Tholonet. It has been "classée," thanks to public protest when it was threatened with being straightened, about five years ago. (That gives me some encouragement, and I am about to write a letter of protest to Mayor Defferre of Marseille, about the new habit of letting huge tourist-buses *and* displays of cars... right now the 1974 Citroëns!!!... park along the Quai des Belges, so that the fish-tables are completely hidden and it is almost impossible to walk past them.... Such stupidity!)

It is too bad, here and in Aix of course, to find several pleasant old cafés and restaurants turned into high-speed snack bars, with suspiciously Howard-Johnson meal-planning obvious on the menus: a great dependence on already prepared hors d'oeuvres like terrines and pâtés, for instance... and of course on the universal "entre-cote grillé avec pommes frites" and then packaged icecreams. Ho Hum. Fortunately

for us, some of the familiar old fish places along the Rive Neuve are still functioning…
and we still like Les Deux Soeurs the best, for simple food and a good vin de Cassis. As
for the elegant places, we still like the Cintra, because we have always had fun there…
went to it in 1932 when it still had a grape-arbor out over the sidewalk… and the service is excellent and while the menu is greatly simplified (I think largely because the
new Cintra Brasserie-Grill downstairs has to share its kitchen) it is still excellent for
things like soles… and wonderful tarte à l'orange. Of course the posh place is now the
New York, as you know… it used to be less than third rate. It is excellent, I think, and
perhaps the best-appointed place in Marseille, with very good dishes… but I don't like
the general clientele: very affluent Germans and Americans. We like to walk out to the
Corniche to Michel's now and then… I don't know how one place can serve better
shellfish than another in this place, but Michel seems to. And probably our favorite
restaurant is the Jambon de Parme… it is as nicely appointed as the NY and the Cintra, and the service is the same, but for some reason the dishes taste even better. At
noon there seem to be a lot of rising youngish politicians and potential Godfathers
there. It is amusing to watch them weave their webs. At night the people are worldly
and rather bored Marseillais…. I suppose it *would* be dull here if one had to stay
around because great-grandfather started the soap-and-olive industry…. But everybody seems to enjoy the restaurant very much. It is very much the way the old Surcouf
used to be.

Of course I still think that Hiély in Avignon is one of THE BEST. Norah and I
went there for lunch and dinner, about a month ago when we went up for a couple of
days… still impeccable. I notice in Richard O's brochure that he plans to have his ladies do their "meal" for young M. Hiely, or something like that…??? I hope R can
teach them some of the family's wonderful simplicity….

Friends sent me the *NY Times* clipping about the Hasty Pudding show… great fun!…
but then, you seem always to find everything highly entertaining… which reminds me
that our little Stones were here, the ones who missed meeting you at Last House, and
Humphrey is delighted that he can now watch you in Wiltshire while he breakfasts!
That seems an odd hour to show something on gastronomy, but he insists it fits in very
well, because more often than not he is eating two tiny bantam-eggs with toast from a
"country loaf" a neighbor bakes for him…. Anyway, he's very happy about seeing you.

We had a fine time after they finally got here, through air strikes here and rail
strikes in England… and they never once suspected that we were FLAT BROKE,
thanks to the strange coincidence of having rather large funds arrive for both of us just
before the European stock market closed. We simply put the hotels on tick, and borrowed from French friends in Aix… and also had four picnic-meals here which were
fun and which saved us enormous sums… it was an interesting experience, but it's really delightful to be able to (i) cash a check and then (ii) spend it without a second
thought….

We never did see Eda, who is now living in somebody's empty flat in London while
Sybille lives in somebody else's empty flat there. S. suddenly decided that she must

leave for England IMMEDIATELY, which apparently they did, although Eda sounded really exhausted... of course had to attend to all the packing &&&. . . . And Eda spoke as if they might not return at all. Ho hum. That was a much better life for her than in a city. . . .

At first I thought of splitting here and letting Norah go on home while I went to England, to see Eda and a few other people. But now we plan definitely... (A jaunty word, indeed!) to fly Nice-Paris-SF... probably on May 21. We've reached the point where we pretend we don't know what date it is at all... perhaps February 30th or something like that... rather than admit that Time is turtling on much faster than usual....

Oh... about Vol. II of the *French Chef*... I'm glad there is going to be one... and I understand thoroughly your preferring not to "do the more personal." You are one of the most "personal" people in the world, on TV, but it would not sound right to have you change your written style/manner/approach. Why not Paul??? Several million people know that he is an intrinsic part of the shows and the books... and he can write superbly in any way he chooses... and he could do "footnotes" *about you* that readers would love and that you could not possibly do yourself. After all, you are partners. I speak for myself, of course, but I think readers would really love to have Paul mention that the reason you both love Un Tel et Tel Plat is because... etc etc etc....

And more or less on this subject, I think that tiny insigne or motif or whatever it is that he drew, of Julia prancing along with a huge spoon over her shoulder, is absolutely delightful and should be used as a kind of trademark, on all your shows and articles and pictures etc etc etc. And now That Is Enough of what I think and what I don't think... but at least it will prove to you that I have both of you very much in my thoughts.

Before we leave, we're going to St. Maximin for a couple of nights, for Norah to check on a few more things. I refuse ever to climb up to that grotto again, but have volunteered to do snooping for her around the crypts and so on. I suspect that our lodging will be much as it was in Salon. But it will be interesting. And then we're going for two nights to the family place of our old friend Georges Connes, in the Aveyron. I'm very glad N can see it... quite indescribable, looking straight down about 1000 (more, I think) feet to the wild River Tarn. We plan to sneak in a flask of brandy, since Georges is very austere and there is no such thing as a hot grog and the nights are FREEZING cold (no heat in the house, of course, which is just about as it was some 600 years ago, except for one flush toilet...).

Forgive this babble, D+e+r+ F+r+e+n+s... perhaps some of it will amuse you. Please stay well. . . .

PS... Aix finally has one star again, and we went to the new place, Charvet... it is about 3 years old, in an elegant old house off the top of the Cours, and is another example of l'équipe de jeunesse that has taken over a lot of the top restaurants, apparently (of course I consider Hiély a young man... but I knew his father!!!). Lots of fresh flowers and three crackling little hearths, and meaningless but showy silver tea sets on the center table, and pretty fairies flitting about in enormous white bow-ties and form-fitting jackets, and the chef-patron in high bonnet taking orders and bowing coldly, and all the generously spaced tables filled with absolutely the dullest, most cautious, most correct upper level of rising young Aixois *and*, what is even duller, their proper beautifully dressed completely bored wives, often accompanied by rich influential silent in-laws. Oh, it was dreadful... and apparently there is a lot of money backing it, and we each ate two of the specialties and two of them were superb, although the kind of thing that can be assembled from supplies... well...

....

Last House, Glen Ellen, California   *17.vi.73*
To: Marietta Voorhees

Dearest M... it seems quite impossible, and rather chilling, that so much time has gone so fast, since you were here. I've been carrying on a fairly steady dialogue with you, which you may have sensed, but of course that does little to encourage our postal system.

I seem alarmingly caught again in the familiar pattern of No-Time-To-Work, and as soon as the Kellys leave, I plan to take my basic requirements up to Lyman Casey's empty livingroom, in the Hexagon, and *hole in*.[1] I am really eager to do something about the notes I made in Marseille, although I am not yet sure what direction I'll take. It would be *sensible* of me to do a kind of introduction to the possible book, in a form that the *NYer* would perhaps print... Our Roving Correspondents or whatever they call their occasional reports. Most of them are from American towns, but perhaps they would like to have me lay a few ghosts about that evil old port (quote)....

The air is so fresh and bonny today that I can hardly stand it. I wish you could smell it too. But of course it is good, where you are. I know. Arnold Gingrich just got back from three days in Milwaukee, and he said that he had not smelled such sweet air since Switzerland and the Bouverie Ranch. Is it the Lake? There are many industries there.... I told him to pursue the question: give the answer to Los Angeles, for instance!

Mr. Saur is still buzzing away at dead wood, but I think he must be about finished. By now I look toward the northern hills easily, and indeed it is a beautiful view. (By "easily" I mean that I can do it without feeling brave!!!) Eleven trees are left, and they are responding well to this fine weather. Now and then a little gust of wind shears off a branch, which is as it should be.

Yesterday some people came from SF and brought me fresh lichee nuts, most delicious, and a big bucketful of live crayfish, which I cooked this morning. I don't know if you like them? I plan to fix them this afternoon and try to keep them well chilled until the Kellys get here.

They arrive on the 19th, in time for dinner, and I'm very glad that they can stay up at the guest house, even though they do have one cat with them. (It is very well trained

1. Lyman Casey was Genie di San Faustino's son. The Hexagon House on David Bouverie's ranch was rented to Ranieri and Genie di San Faustino.

to travel and hotels and such, and uses the toilet!) I don't know how long they can stay, but I hope it is through the weekend. I'd love to come over the hill one day, because I know Sean wants to see you... of course I'll call first. It would be around noon... perhaps a pizza?

Marietta, I have been giving much and deep thought to your "proposal," which is of course what most of the dialogue has been about. Now and then I say something very clear and true, and then I've forgotten it to put in writing. I don't think I need tell you how touched and complimented I feel. But I feel inadequate, in every sense of the word, to agree to a pact such as this.

I have given the art and practice of marriage much thought, and have observed many good and bad ones, and have been married three times myself, legally. I think it demands the capacity to endure, surmount, cope with, fight for a shared and continuous *intimacy,* and that is something few people can accept.

Colette wrote of what she called "conjugal courtesy" as one of the prime requirements of this state, and I think that too is something few people consider when they enter into almost any kind of intimate partnership.

And I honestly think that I am too old to try to establish this courtesy, this intimacy. It demands much more than there is left in me of vigor and freshness and physical passion. It also demands great skill and patience, and I am increasingly short on both. What desire (lust?) there is left in me I have deliberately channeled into other levels... plain self-protection! And I have had to live alone for so long that without physical need for another person I am short of patience for the daily routine of eating and bathing and so on with anyone else. This is especially true, I feel sure, in close quarters, where one must be thoughtful and aware of the partner's appointed time for the daily bowel movement, the short walk, the little nap, the desk-work, the afternoon milk-and-cracker....

No, it is too late... for you or anyone else. I regret with some bitterness and *much* regret that I must confess this. (As Georges Connes once said brutally to me, "You're not being philosophical! You are simply *resigned!*")

You are discovering the mixed pleasures of living alone at a fairly late age. Until a short time ago you could count on having a "home," and a place there. Now you have to make that for yourself, and please believe me, dearest Marietta, that I know what effort it takes, even to *pretend* that it is nice to light a little fire and savor some tea at the desk... and not lie down in front of the TV or simply go to bed and pretend again to read no-matter-what with any excitement. (Ho hum.)

But I've been working on this for some time, and quite deliberately, as compared with your delayed arrival on the scene of Aging-In-General. And I think that our main, and perhaps only salvation is to count our blessings.

And of course that is a very private thing. You may not consider, or even know, some things I would list in my long relationship with you, and the same is true of my own ignorance of your list, of course. The main thing between us is trust, I think. (I *KNOW.*) Then we do like a lot of things, like words, and Sam'l Johnson, and books as such and often what is in them. You like to quote, and I like to catch you up on what you say in quotes. We agree politically, at least in the main. In religion, I seem to be an agnostic or perhaps an atheist, whereas you are dichotomous about Christianity as a faith. (Etc.) But there we have struck a good level of mutual respect.

And so on.

In other words, there is a lot to enjoy, together.

It is spoken, written. It is not side by side hour by hour intercourse.

I know that I could not adapt gracefully to that, even if I were forced to work for my bed and board. It would be easier for money, I suppose... but for the *love and mutual respect* we have, no.

So... I hope you want to take what I have to offer you, in love and respect.

It is possible that you may find some more adaptable person to live with you, and give warmth to your hearth, and if that is what you seek, I hope for it with all my heart.

And always you will have what is left of my heart, in all ways. But for both our sakes, and perhaps mainly for yours, I cannot consider the proposal you made lately.

I remain amazed, and also humbled, to think that anyone who knows me as well as you do would ever consider such an idea, for I recognize myself as many things I cannot possibly admire. There are a few good sides to the stalactite or whatever I am, and I try to keep them shiny. But the rest is not good, and you have seen it all more closely than anyone alive.

Ho hum.

And on that somewhat dim note, I close.

I'll like very much to invite myself, as arranged, to stay with you on June 30 (if not before, with the Kellys). Will you have supper with me someplace? Or could I bring something along that we could augment with a cracker or two?

....

Last House, Glen Ellen, California   *25.ix.73*
To: Norah Kennedy Barr

Well, it was the fairest night in a long time that I could spend watching the satellites... I swear there are two, and by now one is down... Charlie[1] and I enjoyed it very much, over a slow arf-n-arf.... Un gin, un vermouth sec, et je vais les mélanger moi-même... which I did.

The sunset was strictly Maxfield Parrish. Thanks to the smatter of rain last week, there is the sound of many frogs... always amazing to me. . . .

I enclose a copy of my version of what I feel fairly certain is in Mrs. Rombauer (too lazy to look). It is really delicious stuff.[2] I like a little dab of it now and then (finger or spoon), just for the after-tastes. And I suppose it is practically like drinking a glass of tomato juice, as far as a lot of the solids are concerned. And I suppose it is cruelly acidic. Ah well again.

1. One of MF's cats
2. Tomato Velvet

The thought of you there on the crags, coping with THREE dogs in the foggy dew, is almost too much for me. It keeps me busy to feed *one cat*. I often simply lie down... except that when I do, the cat does, and I find that too personal or something. With dogs one stays upright more often, probably... walking them and all that. (I talked with Alice Low[3] today, and we told each other that we thought we would never again have dogs, because we could not stand to put them in kennels! I often did that when I was younger. But now I simply can't stand the thought of it. I suppose it indicates a need for interdependency or or or?)

Speaking of Alice, when can you and I sneak down to SF? We don't need to tell a soul... or we can tell her and go to lunch at her really beautiful little house and tell Chet Rhodes[4] and go to dinner at La Petite Ferme, and buy tickets to several things I hear about on the radio and then tear them up as the moon rises. Two good friends tell me that now that poor What's-s-Name shot himself, the food is EXCELLENT at the ole Clifto, but I really think you'd have to rope and tie me to get me in there....

Oh... I wonder if you are doing your Opera-bit this year? Have heard nothing about it. You KNOW, Norah, that you must try to keep up *some* semblance of contact with sophistication and and and wear.... a low-cut gown at least *once*.......

Well, what all this nattering comes down to is that I'm very sorry I shan't see you this weekend. We must work on What Next....

PS... I either have to go back for more Lotion Triomphale or sue the company for the two weeks I used it... my hair is practically diaphanous... it simply floats here and there, all three strands....

....

Last House, Glen Ellen, California   *29.ix.73*
To: Norah Kennedy Barr

Dearest N... I want to telephone to you, but I suspect that you are surrounded by loving hungry people. The Marseille-syndrome still has me in its clutches, and I talk all the time to you... I think of very funny or equally important things to report to you....

Right now I have a few nothings to report... such as the fact that I feel a personal disappointment that Winston [*sic*] Auden died today... I never even met him, although we kept making somewhat coy rendez-vous, but aside from my personal-impersonal involvement I thought and still think that he is a great loss to us as writers, because he maintained through all his shaggy life an impregnable defense of the language. It did not matter whether he was using Early Saxon or low-class German or American or even English: his ear went side by side with his mind. Ho hum. I have a feeling that I have been ROBBED... TRICKED.... (Of course I talk about the loss to our language,

3. Friend in San Francisco
4. Mutual friend of Alice Low

but personally I had made a date with him at the Stones' in the Spring of next year, when he would be back at Oxford....)

All this geriatric business closed in a bit and I reneged shamelessly on a luncheon date with Janet Flanner at the Monhoffs two days ago...JF sounds fine for a few minutes on the telephone but drifts off into a better world quite soon... and walks in a slow tottery way.... I'll hope to see her again, before she is taken back to NY, but her sister Hildegarde says she may stay longer than planned. And a mutual friend of Fredrika van Benschoten[1] calls me rather (too) often to report on F's life in a "convalescent home" in Hemet, after a bad fall in her ghastly little apartment that I visited a year or so ago. . . . . She is apparently serene and resigned. The only problem is that she really enjoys cigarettes and is not allowed to smoke except with a person there... and wisely too, for it was dreadful to watch her manage to light a cigarette and then casually drop the match onto a pile of unread newspapers... rather like watching Rex pour his carton of milk into the wire wastebasket, but of course worse....

Well, Miss Eleanor[2] is finally tucked away, next to the man who once raped her and has long been lying there... the "services" were only for the family with no clergical assistance. I would say MV is in fine shape... in her 80th year she is in better physical shape than for a long time, and while she suffers a lot of identifiable after-shocks she is glad to be an orphan(!).

I was too involved with life-in-general, and began to feel very trembly, and reported this to the pill-boy. Result: doing too much... cut it out... lie down and take a nap, and work when you want to, but don't have 8 for lunch. So... the icebox has a lot of food in it, and I feel better already, I telephoned people and canceled rendez-vous right and left. I hurt Jim (Skinny) Beard because I was supposed to go tonight to a "wine" dinner with him in Santa Rosa. He'll have to realize that he loves all that and I don't. (I do dislike saying I'll do a thing and then not doing it....) So tomorrow I'm not even going to have dinner with Decca and Bob T[3]... I may go up for a drink... really I'm relieved, because I don't want to say anything about her book,[4] which I find too simplistic. I know she worked hard on it, but I still cannot admire much more than that. She... oh well, why talk about it!!!!! So I'm let off the hook tomorrow.

I'm told not to see PEOPLE. You are not PEOPLE. When do we meet again?????????? Oh, Yolande gave me some seed of those fabulous tall red poppies that grow wild in Genoa (Nevada!). Sis and Bill gave me some seeds for her, but were sure they would not grow. Au contraire... they thrive and seed themselves! They are said to have been brought to Genoa by the Mormons, and now grow in the unplowed meadows. And what I'm getting around to is: would you like to sow them in Jenner? They

1. Friend and neighbor at Bareacres
2. Marietta Voorhees's mother, who died at age 101
3. Jessica Mitford and her husband Robert Treuhaft
4. *Kind and Usual Punishment* (1973)

M.F.K. Fisher: A Life in Letters

have survived one complete change of climate, and might another... down in one of your corner-patches????

I am very tempted to call you (it is now Sunday the 30th...), to ask if you still cater to canines... etc etc.

Yesterday Jed Steele and his bride Annie came in, unannounced and uninvited... Ah, cette jeunesse!... They brought me a loaf of bread from Sonoma, and I made them some coffee and pulled out some tired old cookies. They are a good couple, I think. In the housing-thing at Davis they are not allowed to keep Jed's 2½-year-old Golden Labrador, a really beautiful gentle well-trained dog. Oh dear. (I did not propose calling you.) So they were taking him down to the SF Shelter... where Ranieri got Charlie for me.... Of course I felt many pangs....

Now that the first of September (Joke. Laff.) has come, I hope you will be able to get to work on la Sainte Pénitente as scheduled. I plan to take my basket of deathless stuff up to the Hexagon again this afternoon.... Ranieri has a bad cold and they left early.

I have a recipe for the cabbage pie that Phyllis makes very well. I do suspect her of that ancient trick of withholding the "secret ingredient" and even asked her about it, and she assured me the recipe is straight, so I'll try it once. But on whom? I do know that what she turns out is delicious.

I also have a ghastly sounding recipe that Joe Herger[5] gave me from his wife, for a green tomato pie. I think he hopes I'll make one for him. It is an entrée and contains a pound of hamburger(!).

Oh... I cooked some small Brussels sprouts and did NOT make any broth from them, and they were delicious... just the way they could have been in Marseille. You would have liked them (I think...).

It is frustrating to have a lot of good things in the icebox. But I'll chew along on them and perhaps work instead of cook... one nevah know, do one?

Until very soon, I hope. . . .

....

Last House, Glen Ellen, California   *22.x.73*
To: Yolande Beard

Dear Pen Pal... I've got a good letter somewhere around the place, which I want to answer soon... this note is simply to thank you and the O/G/[1] for coming, yesterday. As always, it was really fine to see you. You both look unusually well, and I hope you feel that way too.

I made a good faggot of the rosemary, and hung it under the bell by the front door. According to a friend who considers herself a witch, it will ward off everything from the Common Cold to Cancer, including of course The Evil Eye itself.... Meanwhile it

5. Ranch foreman for David Bouverie
1. "Old Guard," perhaps

is sending out fine little puffs of scent, which I catch as I go from the big old table in the ex-garage to my typewriter and back again… I'm putting something together about Marseille, although it has not yet declared itself, and find myself trotting like a print-er's devil from one place to another in my two-room palazzo.…

I love having the fossil clam. I told Norah about it this morning, and she almost can-celed a little spree to Monterey for three days to come see it. We both have one of the mounted fossils… and I forgot to show you my two amphora-tips, complete with worm castings… but the clam shell outdates them all, by about a cool million years. My fish is believed to be about 30 million… from what are now the Lower Alps in Provence.

I forgot to tell you that good ole W. Elephant-Hide Sharafanovich is self-invited here today, because one of his boyfriends is DYING to meet me. I said firmly that be-cause I'd been ill, I was not "seeing" anyone, and he blandly said, in the face of my re-peating this, that they would stay only a half hour or so. If they don't leave in that specified term, I am going to have to retire to my room! I swear I'll do it. WS called while I was really ill (I feel absolutely fine now, if I can choose one or two good people to feel fine with!!!!!), and I said I was ill and could not see him, and he said "I promise you I'll just knock at the door… I must see you… etc etc." I said, "Perhaps later in the summer, but I have been quite ill and am not seeing anyone…" but he didn't hear me because he did not want to I suppose, and he came right along, and I staggered into some clothes and served him some wine and then as it was plain that he planned to stay some time, I began to put my head back and try to look wan and fainty, and he went right on talking about what he said to Macy's about their Antique Furniture De-partment, and then what he said to W&J Sloan, and finally I simply STOOD UP, so that as a White Russian and arbiter to us crude Americans of what a gentleman is, he stood up too, and I led him to the door and fell back into bed. REALLY… he is too impossible! I feel guilty about feeling this way, because I pity him as a near miss in the human scale. But socially he is IMPOSSIBLE.

How did I get started on this little peeve? Actually I feel tolerant and benign and to-hell-with-it… if he needs to show off a little to his friend, how can it do more than bore me for a half hour or so? But it is fun to growl to a fellow sufferer now and then.…

It warmed my heart to have you and Jim say such a nice thing about Dillwyn's paintings. I'd like to talk more about them… what do you think I should *do* with them, for instance. I hate to have them burned or scraped off for used canvas when I die. Some of them are VERY GOOD.… Damn. Is a puzzlement. Help…!

Love, and until soon…

....

Bouverie Ranch, Glen Ellen, California   *9.xi.73*
To: Sam Davis

Dear Sam… this is a very good example of the way certain bonds exist between people, even if, as with us, they are not longstanding: for about a week I have had you much on my mind, and yesterday I saw your address when I was looking for another

D and said, "If I don't get a letter off to him right this minute..."... just what you said too, except that you did not dally as much as I.

I'm so glad you wrote! Thank you very much.

One reason I've been thinking about you and Ron is because I'm puttering along in my bathroom, changing a wall of pictures and rehanging a few smaller walls, and with never thoughts of moving that beautiful piece of Greek weaving you gave me. It belongs exactly where it is... to be contemplated from the tub (which is 6' long, and set in the middle of the rather large room). I think it is an apron? I tell people that. They are always baffled by it... why is it not Mayan, Moroccan, anything but Greek?

And thinking about the apron reminds me of the one completely orchid-woman evening I spent with you two... oysters, caviar, music, champagne, macadamia nuts, and the delicious company... one of the most generous and elegant sprees of my life! Thank you for that, too.

Sam, I'm absolutely sure that you are right not to go back to NY to live, and not to fear for the future. Intuition and instinct speak here, on both counts. This sounds presumptuous, but I think we have recognized each other for a long time.

Now to a slower look at the so-welcome letter: I'm very sorry that your mother did not make it when she was so near. But all this is very mysterious, and there must be some *reason* for her having to wait for another chance. I've sat helplessly, too often, to deny this... and I don't think it is simply the hope springing eternal etc, for god knows the people who have to wait the longest are most often the ones who have earned a short merciful leavetaking. I like your remark that your mother is "rueful about the whole mess." Rueful is the right word. My own mother spent six years in bed, waiting for attacks of very bad heart pain which, with each one, might and should be the last. She would shrug, even on a stretcher or under an oxygen tent, and say, "I didn't quite bring it off. Ho hum." It was not suicidal at all... just weariness, I suppose. And when she'd be brought back *again* from the hospital she would be, as you say, *rueful....*

To your job: being a hack is a pretty nerve-tiring thing, except perhaps Meadowville is quiet enough to give you some respite from the traffic. I have some taxi-driver friends, and I think the dedicated ones, men in their 60s, have grown a kind of shell of detachment. The young ones get very up-tight, especially in big cities. I met some absolute loves in Marseille (I have a life-long empathy with cabbies), and am writing about them....

How about flipping hamburgers? This might be fun, if you made yourself get into the air enough, and not breathe that greasiness all the time. I feel more interested in hamburgers than I have for many years, because next week a friend of 12 is coming for lunch, and he has requested it/them, and suddenly I felt panicky and have consulted a few friends with young children or grandchildren. Actually I never made many, because when I was growing up there were no stands, and when my girls were growing up we were mostly in France. The best I ever ate were near Eagle Rock when I went to Occidental College one year and we would sneak a class and go up to a "shack" on

Colorado Boulevard and wolf a huge drippy pile of meat and cheese and pickles and relish and so on, and then dash back to Psych. 1.

My friends tell me the best thing, with a 12-year-old, is to put all the makings on a big tray or table, and then flip the patties in good butter according to wish for rare-medium-w.d., and let the machinery be handled by each person. This I shall do. It is like expecting Prince Charles for lunch (except I can't quite be Mrs. Roosevelt with the frankfurters...).

So... why not work in a good hamburger joint for a while? You could always say *a rivederci*.... And apparently... here I was interrupted, but I am thinking strongly about this short-order sort of thing, which must have a real rhythm to it, and about a spare mean-looking woman who worked for years in the window of a little dump in San Francisco that my children and I passed, deliberately, every time they had to be nearby for orthodontia. They were fascinated by her. She worked in the window of the little place, always with a cigarette stuck to her lip. Her right hand had only the little finger and the first on it, but she used it so deftly that it was not at all shocking. She was aware of our need to watch her, and now and then would give us a kind of wink, through her smoke. We never went in. It would have broken some ring of magic, maybe. She scraped up French Fries and Hash-browns from the big griddle, and tossed hamburgers and heaped buns and put on all the trimmings, with a kind of passionate nonchalance that really hypnotized us. Several years after all this, I made myself stop there at the window, and she was still furious and intense, but much scrawnier. She did not see me. Or maybe she did. But I was alone.

Well now, you ask where is I at? Short (I hope) report: Yes, Norah and I did stay the whole time in Marseille... of course with more-than-weekly bus trips to Aix, and here and there, and then a final four-day fling in Nice. (Now there's a wonderful place, which I've lived nearby for years of my life! The Old Town is where I would gladly end my days. The people are everything that is good about French *and* Italian: courteous, remote, very helpful and with a real life to them....) Norah was doing research, which she loves, on the legends of Mary Magdalene, who is still one of the leading citizens of that Communist stronghold Marseille. She went to beautiful private libraries and even more beautiful public ones, and gathered (gleaned) unbelievable facts and fancies about la Sainte Pénitente, and probably will never put them together for the rest of us pagans. I made some notes, and watched the Old Port, and contemplated my navel. We walked miles a day, and ate very simply. . . . We were in a blue-collar-cum-noblesse neighborhood, very old, and there were good little shops, so we ate fine salads and cheese and fair-to-good bread. Then we went out according to the budget, and from top to near-bottom, and ate enough shellfish to build a small jetty and drank enough wine to fill the Vieux Port.

A couple of times we got bilked... Norah reacted badly to two goes at shellfish... I was immune... but overall the provender was supernacular.... I have NEVER enjoyed mussels-clams-etc more, and that is a rather extravagant statement. I'll admit that I really don't like *"violets,"* those rather squishy eggish mollusks, but Norah does, so if we ordered a *panaché* I always traded her mine for a couple of extra clovisses. We did not eat many oysters: they were very expensive, because of the storms and the transportation from up North. We also ate superb fish, cooked delicately. Now and then, in a top-level restaurant, where we (this is turning into a screed...) were soon recognized as two huge Anglo-Saxon but harmless eccentrics, we ordered a dessert. Rarely. In the Vieux Port places we went to, there was a great vogue (tourist but also French) for tall "Parfait" glasses heaped with ersatz whipped cream and scanty frozen fruits. Enuf.

We drank mostly Provençal wines. There has been a peculiar and amazing change in the Camargue, and the rice-paddies have been converted into quick-growing high-production low-quality vineyards. And some of the wines are very pleasant indeed, especially with the shellfish. They are mostly whites and rosés. They have to be drunk fast, which is easy. (I mean by the calendar... they really are pleasant to linger on....)

We had a few good gastronomical excitements... stayed in Avignon and went twice to Hiély, and so on... but mostly it was good-to-tops Marseille places... such fun! And no, I can't remember eating anything but fish, EVER, except for one beautifully grilled sweetbread in a *luxe* restaurant, once.... I could check with Norah, but as I remember she never deviated from her simple path down to the sea....

About the rat story[1] (I am going from line to line through the letter!): You have caught it more than most people, or indeed *any*. I have had interesting (fascinating) letters about it. One woman, the only adverse critic, told me to go back to the kitchen, and not try to be a "political satirist"... obviously the main rat was Nixon, she said, but my portraits of the two henchmen as Erlichmann and Haldeman did not come off at all. Wow. But Sam, I didn't think that story was "sad" *at all*. I thought it was reassuring. After all, at the end, the woman KNEW....

Now about being well: like all human creatures, I am an Interesting Case. I apparently almost died, but did not... a failing but not sick heart. I am simply wearing out, like an old side-wind Victrola running down.... This was in July. Since then I have made a fine return. As long as I do not buzz around too much, especially with *people*, and see only two or three at a time and not for too long, I hold my own very well. Fortunately I am the kind that never is lonely, so what might drive some gregarious people up the wall is manna to me, and I am getting some work done... and not worrying at all about the current need to take snoozes and stay by myself. There are always people on the ranch, and they take me here and there to buy food and so on... and by now I drive occasionally to Sonoma (6 mi.), and once a month go to a board meeting (Napa Valley Wine Library) in St. Helena, where I stay overnight. In other words, a change of pace!

As for the dirt and flowers you hope I'm near: Yes, Indeed...!!! I'm also near cows, and I must confess that although one or two look very pretty in a distant meadow, seventy clumping around my house are distasteful. They are stupid, and too big, so that I am afraid of their big stupidity, and prefer not to get too near them. So I don't walk down to the post-box on the highway if they are in the lower pastures, and I don't go up the canyon if they are in the top meadows. They limit my Green Thumb, which is

1. "A Question Answered" was published in *The New Yorker* and later in *Sister Age*.

a good thing, but it annoys hell out of me when they discover that they can pull out all the tomatoes on my East Balcony and stamp on them. Ah well.

You sound "in focus," and that is fine. I wonder where your friend stays in Aix... we lived there for about five years, and Norah and I went at least weekly by bus, as I'm afraid I've already said in this tome... some of our good friends have dropped off the vine, but there are some good 'uns left.

I know people who really dig New York, but I think I agree with your friends that it is more exciting in San Francisco. Perhaps it is the air? That heavenly fog that blows in-over-out in half an hour? It has always been a place of sparkle for me... we used to escape to it from Whittier (Southern California... Quaker) when we were growing up. It means PARTY. But I tried living there once, a life-long dream, and it did not work: I had three nubile virgins on my hands, one borrowed from a French friend, and I spent 24 hours a day feeding and protecting them. They were not allowed to walk to schools because of satyrs etc, and they all went at different times in different directions.... I'd had dreams of long prowls through art shows, and lots of theatre, and delicious meals, and I went out exactly ONE TIME in eight months, with infinite arrangements, and it was a near miss all 'round. Ho hum. So I moved the whole menage to St. Helena.... Well, SF is still a magical place, and Norah and I plan to spend a night there on Nov. 15. It will be my first sight of the place since we got back from Marseille. (This has been my season to lie very low, but I'm finally emerging!!!)

I'm very amused by your report on the non-climacteric etc.... Me too. People tell me things about the female version, and I listen and sympathize, but with no sense of reality. It's strictly a question of conditioning (mental... old wives' tales, etc etc) and endocrinology, which most straight doctors are scared to explore. Well... I don't mean to sound toplofty, god knows. But I'm probably as peaceful as an old nun, to paraphrase you. (This reminds me that once I wrote my teacher-friend in France that I felt philosophical about something like having to get a divorce or or or, and he wrote back snappily that I was obviously confusing philosophical detachment with plain resignation....)

As for the state of the Union, I resent having to relegate it to the level of a soap opera, and feel basically sick about the whole thing. But right now I see nothing else to do. Hang in there, baby!

Baby reminds me of Bebe (as in Rebozo), and that reminds me that I said something to myself yesterday that I thought was quite funny, in a mean way.... Kissinger is Disraeli to Mr. Nixon's queen... I don't know if I would ever say that in public, mostly because it would mean absolutely nothing....

I do hope things grow clear and right and SOON, dear Sam.... All my greetings to you and Ron...

PS... forgive me for being this presumptuous, but about those dreadful expenses for the care of the aging: do you and your mother not have Social Security? That is an *enormous* help.... I know from current experience with friends....

Bouverie Ranch, Glen Ellen, California   *23.xi.73*
To: Gloria Stuart

Dearest Gloria, my honey-colored friend:

Yesterday I talked at extravagant length with la belle Sylvie and Gene,[1] and I was filled with love and gratitude for all that you have given me, and done for me, and meant to me... you and Arturo both.

I don't know if I've told you of how beautifully I am surrounded by things you have made for me, and given me: the portrait-globe, which continues to seduce people, the two pictures you gave me... on and on. The globe is an intrinsic part of my livingroom, as it has always been... to the left of the fireplace (now a Franklin stove). The pictures are (chess) in my large elegant bathroom on the "Gallery Wall," and (California) in my little file-room, where I look at it at least twice a day.

I like the proud bull and his family better on canvas than in person: I'm outside the cattleguard here at the ranch and get **BORED** with the huge stupid shuffling creatures, who lean against my walls and eat down everything I try to sow or plant and make great plops everywhere. Ah well. I live on a working *ranch*.

And I am glad I do. I like being in the silent pure air. . . .

When things look up a bit, at least as far as the EKGs signify, I'll hop a plane or an Amtrak and come South for a couple of nights with the Thompsons. I hope I can see you. But such meetings are so veiled by immediacy and what Time has done to us all that in many ways they are near misses, I've found. I wish we could simply sit down and look at each other for a time, and *then* start talking. Well.......

The Ts say your new house is a "jewel." I hope you find it satisfying. You have a real gift for polishing the hidden facets of a place....

You'd like this house, I think. I do. It is what I want and need, with room for work and a modicum of play. The architecture is subtle. But I find myself too cozy, too well-housed, too cosseted. I need a more abrasive challenge, I'm afraid, to feel fully alive. Ah well again...

I wonder if you will ever write to me again.... I wouldn't bet on it, but that has nothing to do with our friendship.

My abiding love to you both...

Last House, Glen Ellen, California   *1.i.74*
To: Marietta Voorhees

Dearest M... sometimes my "facilities are more acute" than at other times, to quote your amusing quotation, and tonight I have done quite a bit of work, on this and that, and feel like replying to what I suppose might qualify as your latest Night Thoughts.

1. Sylvia and Gene Thompson, daughter and son-in-law of Gloria Stuart

Thank you, first, for the cards and the reprints of Grace Bird's poem (she is a *poet*), and the quotation from *Hamlet,* which I wish I could believe.

It is impossible for me NOT to feel that the act of death, and its actuality, are not an enigma. I wish I could agree with you. But I consider it (dying) the final *trick.* Some people know what it is. Most are baffled by it, and therefore frightened.

I don't consider this "a question of semantics."

By "trick" I don't mean, necessarily anyway, that the whole act of being alive is a vaudeville turn, a sleight-of-hand thing. But I can't figure any more plausible reason for us to be on stage for such a fleeting time....

It is nice that you have Mrs. Rook in the Back Cottage to set you straight on English usages. Even if you knew better than she, she would set you straighter. In my own vocabulary, Boxing Day does not mean giving *"left-overs"* to mailmen and garbage collectors and so on, but simply a present they can use, like plain old cash. But of course I am a crude Westerner....

You say that you are always *"in* a state...." Why not be? How else exist...? If you were not in a state, whatever that may mean to you, you would not be aware of yourself, and therefore you would be unconscious and no better than a turnip or potato. Stay in a "state"!

I don't know what you mean when you say that it "would be wasteful and ignoble to give in." What do you mean, *"give in"*? Give in to what? Succumb to your "guilt feelings, grief feelings, discontents"? Tell me, Doc: how does one "give in"? By giving in, do you mean killing your physical body (suicide), or do you mean succumbing to inertia and lying on a bed waiting to be turned from right side to left side? What do you *mean*?

You say that your "guilt feelings, griefs, discontents" will "consume" you unless you convert them into something "positive and dynamic." Great! Go right ahead! But you say you do not know "the technique for bringing about such a conversion, nor any alchemy that could cause it to happen."

When you say things like this I feel baffled and helpless, but with a terrible impatience. TERRIBLE IMPATIENCE. "Stop playing with yourself," I want to say. "Stop this quasi-sensual agonizing."

Well... I'm not much good as a comforter! I become impatient when something I love and revere and admire whimpers overlong. You talked about how it is relatively unimportant whether or not you are "consumed" (by what? Guilt? Grief? Discontent?). Unimportant to whom? Why? How is one consumed?

I begin to fear that we speak in different tongues.

But I can still send you my abiding love.

....

Bouverie Ranch, Glen Ellen, California   *26.ii.74*
To: Margo (?)[1]

Dear Margo:

If you are as generous with your friends as you have been with me, you may soon go

1. The last name of this recipient is unknown.

broke... but if and when you do, you can always get a fat salary as a packer, with some-body like Gump's or Parke-Benet. The goodies arrived in perfect shape, and I have al-ready dug into the chokecherry-hawberry jelly: my first and perhaps last sampling of such exotics. I love your trading system, and wish that we could do it here, but not many people seem interested any more. One of my girls, though, goes every year up toward the Oregon border to a fruit ranch owned by friends, and she takes the sugar and jars and works with the womenfolk, and they divide the spoils, exactly as her grandmother did some sixty years ago. So there's still hope! I have a couple of friends who grow beau-tiful summer vegetables, which I cannot do here because of the cattle, so we reciprocate with things from my kitchen like chutneys and so on. It is a nice feeling.

The name Chexbres comes from a town we lived near, and far back it meant goat. It is pronounced Cheb, with just a little touch of the r, but no x and no s. It was an ap-propriate name, because Dillwyn Parrish did look like an especially beautiful goat.

The little boy who was so good at sitting on the railroad sandwiches[2] is now almost thirty, and a bit too hefty... thanks perhaps to having indulged too well in such dain-ties. He is working his way through the wine business from the ground up, and is now at Robert Mondavi in Napa Valley, happily guiding tourists and pushing cartons around and sweating through the crushing seasons. He is still a darling, and I am al-ways glad to see him. . . .

About recording *your* unexpurgated history of the Mormon church, why not? I hope you kept a dupe of your letter outlining the early history, because it's invaluable. I taught once at a writers' thing in Salt Lake City, and enjoyed feeling like a gentile finally, even though I am not anything else racially. Very dear family friends lived for years in Utah while he was an episcopal missionary there, and his wife gave my mother a privately printed diary of one of the early wives. Mother kept it hidden, hav-ing sworn to, and I never did get a look at it, but apparently it was "shocking." (I think this is the only hidden book I never found, but really, there were only a couple of oth-ers—my family believed in OPEN SHELVES, which got us into some local pickles, of course, but this time I was foiled.)

Your stay in the City sounds just right, and should boost you for a couple more years. Just the thought that Turk Murphy is still blowing is encouragement enough! My cousin's name is Charles Newton, but he did not grow up in San Francisco or Los Angeles. As far as jazz goes, he started at about sixteen in Chicago, and you can't do much better!

I can't really tell you anything but the basic recipe for that broth: one part vegetable or tomato juice, one or two parts clam juice, one part beef or chicken broth. I think that the day you were here, I put one can of clams in the blender to add some guts. All this needs seasoning to taste and is fine hot or cold, but should never boil. One-half part of dry red or white wine is good in it, added just before serving. I'm glad you liked it. As for zucchini, I like them in anything except perhaps ice cream... and I like them picked with the blossom still on. I'm fussy! Things like caviar and fresh brown eggs and baby zucchini need passionate concern....

2. Charles Newton, from a description in "Questionable Crumpets" in *With Bold Knife and Fork*

I'm so glad you and the Campbells came. Please give them my greetings. I hope I see them and you soon.

....

Bouverie Ranch, Glen Ellen, California *1.iv.74*

To: James Beard[1]

Dear Jim: Your letter was a "special" one, the kind that must be answered fully and thinkingly (if possible!), and without interruptions. So I have started two replies, and scrapped them, and this time I'll mail whatever turns up, will-he nill-he, as T. S. Eliot insisted upon writing it. (I suppose he was right, but Time has simplified things like that....) . . .

No doubt you know about Julia's woes. The whole thing was wretched, and although I was of course deeply sorry not to see her and Paul, my main worry was about them and then a few thousand other people. I had several conversations with him, and with the Cousins, and then to my amazement JULIA called, sounding less vigorous than usual, but insisting that Sherlie Barron, "the Opera doctor" in SF, had performed a miracle. Genie di San Faustino was going to all eight shows, but could not get up this weekend because of rain, so I have only heard rumors that some of the demonstrations had to be canceled. I do hope not, and I do hope that J&P are resting (RESTING???) in the Islands by now.

Entre nous, dear Jim. I take the lengthy explanations of having eaten an over-spiced canapé as whitewash for the plain fact that vocal cords can be overworked, over-extended. I speak from experience. Several years ago (5? 6??) I agreed to do two lectures a day, one day a week, for nine weeks, for University Extension... afternoons Walnut Creek, nights Berkeley campus. I thought I was being smart, to knock off the whole thing in one day, spend the night in a motel, and head home again. Undoubtedly I was amateurish, and did not know how to "use" my voice. Each lecture was at least three hours long, and I did not use amplifiers. And for at least four years I had to accustom myself to a chronic small cough, occasional hoarseness, and constant danger of bronchial troubles. By now I am past it, I think, but my voice will never be more than light and untrustworthy. And all this is why I sense or feel or suspect that Julia, who started out as an amateur although much younger than I (I assume), may need to cut down on her wildly dramatic tours. It must be a heady thing, to have so many people climbing each other's backs to hear her... but perhaps they should settle for TV, for her sake.

Well, all this is probably presumptuous of me, but it comes from my real affection and concern, as you well know.

For the second Monday in a row I have canceled a potentially jolly adventure with six dear friends: it is pouring rain again, the wettest warmest March in history, and the wine men are trembling (they are always trembling about *some*thing) that there will be late "black frosts" that will nip the buds. We were going to drive up to the top of the

1. James Beard, culinary friend

M. F. K. Fisher: A Life in Letters

Lupine Field, a beautiful sight, and then up the Canyon to see the waterfall in full spate, and drink a glass of white wine and come back here for a hearty soup and Sonoma bread and baked apples. Last week I had already made the soup when we decided NO GO, so I ate it for the next five days. Today I decided to make it *after* the radio weather reports, so I only have to eat seven baked apples (I'll take a few up to the old foreman Joseph)! All of which proves that we are still Nature's children, I suppose....

I'm sad for you, Jim, that you lost your friend Janet W.

... and here Nature took over and there was a lengthy power shortage because of the rains, and I am fairly stymied without an electric typewriter. But I continue to feel saddened for you. It is an inevitable fact that one must lose touch gradually. But how wonderful that it has all been warm before! I really would freeze to death if I did not have the ashes still glowing in my heart. That is why friendships must be nurtured, no matter how deliberately. A lot of them die out naturally but some are forever.

All this sententious speculating (?) can be blamed on my temporary inability to continue to write to you, perhaps!!! And here I go again, machine humming and wind blowing and all that. I do love weather, will-he nill-he.

I think the confusion about your holdings and ownings and so on, after the accident to your other friend, the agent, is simply dreadful. What more to say? I HATE the idea of your being in debt. It is wrong. Debt, especially when not brought on voluntarily, is a kind of social rape.

I'm glad you could go out to the sticks (a word I'm sure would be resented in Akron and Columbus, and no wonder...). And I'm glad you spent some time with a newspaper editor, because from the moment we met (that polka or whatever it was at Eleanor Friede's) I regretted that you and my father had been born too-early-too-late. In many ways he was a *really* good small-town editor... potentially exciting as such... an absolutely charming and sensitive man.

I should add that I have few illusions about him. But he was honest, and he had "principles," which seem lacking lately. And you and he would have had a fine time.

Ah well. Ho hum . . .

Naturally I hope that you'll stop thisaway in June and that I'll have a chance to see you. I know you love parties. But I really don't... eight people or less are something of a crowd, and this has nothing to do with my present well-being but is a basically asocial trait perhaps. So I probably shan't see you in SF because you're always mobbed there. I'll simply be Country Mouse and hope for the best.

About Oregon: you told me I could peel potatoes there, and I'm now willin' and able. I learn quickly, about how to get out of the cooks' way. Why don't you consider it? I'd stay far in the background, and have lived so often with pseudonyms that I'd gladly double for Ole Miz Timpkins.

(I'm serious.)

About health, since you mention it (mine, not yours): Suddenly it was as if a light had been switched on in a dim room, and I feel W*E*L*L... as the Childs would say. I am solid, mentally and physically: no more apprehension, which is apparently common to "heart" people, and much less exhaustion. In other words, I hopped off that plateau onto another one that may last for ten more years or so. I drive as little as possible, since I have a basic dislike for crazy speed on highways (or rather the people behind the wheels), but I am perfectly able now to travel.

Norah and I were going to go to Washington and then right up to Bridgehampton in late May, but I could see that she thought she should do it to "help" me, which is no longer necessary. I love to travel with her, but I called it off, to her real relief. So I may or may not come back during the summer. . . .

Poor Jim, this is not a letter but a *screed*! Forgive my wordiness....

Work goes slowly here... I learned too much about the joys of enforced laziness when I was unwell... but I think I am writing a book you will like, about Marseille.[2] We'll see.

I do hope you stay reasonably well. Your occupational as well as inborn hazards are greater than most people's. And I hope very much that you feel freer from the horrid worries of confused real estate problems and all that.

Tell me when there may be a chance of another polka, and never forget that I know you are one of the best people I ever met.

....

Last House, Glen Ellen, California   *2.iv. no... v.74*

To: Marietta Voorhees

Dearest M... I'll see you before you get this note, probably, but I feel like writing it to you instead of tackling another snarl in the work.

This present job is a bastard... no gratitude and always snarling.

That dream you reported to me is dreary but, if dreams mean anything, which they do to me, it has significance. The long white dress... yes, how did I get into it?... was perhaps a shroud, or a kind of nun's habit, suggesting purdah. Or or or?

I can't agree with you that "dreams don't proceed logically." I know that many or most of them do not. But now and then I have forced a kind of logic in my capricious subconscious, and have been able to follow a thread, and even dictate (?) some of its logical unravellings. A few times I am able to pick up where I had to leave off, either that time or later by a few days or nights.

One thing I want to discuss in my book about aging is the deliberate cultivation of aloneness, of being alone. NOT *LONELY.* I don't think I am qualified except by experience to do this. I am scared to try. But it is terrible that aging people are totally unprepared for the fact that they may outlive most if not all of their peers, and that they may be abandoned or neglected by their children and younger acquaintances and friends. Many of them fall into whining self-pity, and I say this without blame, because they have never even *thought* about such a state. (In the same way they have never known that most old people itch, and have post-nasal drip... and why... and what to do about it. It is no worse than pre-adolescent ache, or morning sickness in pregnancy, or heat

2. *A Considerable Town*, published in 1978

flashes in the menopause... but nobody considers Old Age a *condition*, which it is. It should be prepared for just as any of the others are.)

Well, here I go! There I went!! . . .

"Your True friend," indeed...

....

Last House, Glen Ellen, California 9.*viii*.74
To: Eleanor Friede

Dearest Squeek...

I give up.

Yesterday, before you had even hit the lower cattleguard, I started to write to tell you that Charlie and I miss you and want you to come back at once, immediately, now.

Then the Washington Web got me, and I spent the rest of the day making plum butter beside the kitchen radio, and even coloring one medieval woodcut, and now and then adding to my higgle-piggle note to you.

So this morning I tore it up, although in a way it was an odd and even funny chronicle of The Day That Was.

It ended with my affronting David. Actually *I* was affronted, but he did not realize that. The story may amuse you, fresh as you are from these un-Elysian fields: He called about 8 o'clock to say that Maya and Paul[1] were so up-tight about the resignation speech that they wanted us ("us" meaning Missus Gilman,[2] him, and me) to meet them at Juanita's for a few drinks. I said something absolutely flat like "How completely vulgar and awful." He went off into a thing about how he asked me and asked me and asked me to join him in things that might be valuable to me as a writer and because he loved me and how I always said "No no NO"... and I said something about not wanting to be with people tonight and he said they were coming up to the Ranch instead of Juanita's and it would be a wake, and I said something about not caring to watch other people shed their tears... fun and games.... And he slammed down the receiver. I wonder how mercurial he will prove to be! Today, after I shake Elizabeth Connes and her boyfren, I'm going up for a drink with the Caens. . . .

Squeek... you did leave so many thoughtful generous signs of yourself everywhere for me. Most of them are intangible, invisible. But then there are books, and my loverly "robes," and of course the wee potatoes. I do wish I knew somebody who'd *appreciate* them... perhaps I can save them until Norah brings Chris[3] over on the 19th...? (No caviar, but have you ever served them hot, wrapped in thin slices of smoked salmon? Marvelous! Fresh dill and an over-generous dousing of melted sweet butter. We ate this once in Sweden at Drottningsholm, and I've managed to make it once here... a success crazy....)

A thousand nothings to say to you, as always...

1. Maya Angelou and Paul Du Feu, friends
2. David Bouverie's close friend
3. MF's grandson, who visited at Norah's every summer and then would go to visit MF at Last House

Thanks for reading those two stories. At least it spurred me to send them to Tim S.[4] Now I'll see if I can face the Marseille stuff again. Real bloc there.

Must go to P.O.... it's Friday... tomorrow closed, and I do want to send off this late and hasty love-word to you.

....

Last House, Glen Ellen, California   *9.viii.74*
To: Eleanor Friede

Dearest Squeek... I forgot to quote something to you that is debatable but reasonably appropriate, I think, about writers. Herman Wouk said it in a lecture at the Aspen Institute. James Joyce said it first, of course... that "ambitious work can be accomplished only in silence, exile, and cunning."

I don't know about the cunning, unless it means that the ambitious writer must slyly and cleverly *arrange* for the silence and the exile.

I just thought of a plot, of how to kill a loving and aging woman: over-work her. David likes to tell, with dramatic gestures, what that dubious guru Gurdjieff used to say about the adoring very-rich or very-talented women who flocked to his clinic near Paris... he'd crack a long whip and thunder, "Get down on your knees! *Verrrrk!!!*" And they did. And according to Gurdjieff and DP-B they loved it and paid through the nose. Well: today I called and asked to speak to Mrs. G (about my pursuit of the new electronic phone-call service), and D reported that she was busy in the garden. Then just lately I saw her (two hours later) hobbling gallantly down for the mail at the gate. And now she has hobbled up again, and while we were chatting a minute, she looking absolutely beat, he was clipping a grapevine (unnecessarily!!!) and he shouted something at us. I called up to him, "Don't shout at *me*!" and he said angrily, "No, I'm shouting at the mail-woman!" And Mrs. G went trotting off dutifully, to have an icy meal with him. Ah, murder.......

Don't decide I'm paranoid about this whole caper. I think it is a puzzler. It is probably not "obscene," as poor Ednah Root[1] has decided in her school-girl frustration. But it is potentially dangerous.

And my mind plays with it. . . .

Very much love . . .

....

Bouverie Ranch, Glen Ellen, California   *31.x.74*
To: Julia Child

How kind it was of you, dear Julia, to write to me! I do thank you.

The bulletin about Paul was a good idea... hundreds of people must have been proving their deep concern for him, and for you both. A dreadful ordeal... and I pray that it is over, done with, of the *past*. Paul is such a strong man, looking at least ten years

4. The literary agent Tim Seldes, who continued the Volkening Agency after Henry V's illness
1. An artist friend of David Bouverie's

younger than the calendar says and acting like a man of *forty*... it will take more than intricate miraculous heart surgery to down him.

Thanks for your news, really non-news, of Eda. I'll write soon to her. I hate to think of her drudging in London. But she does have good friends there too....

I haven't seen the Huxley,[1] but only one friend likes it so far, and he was a close friend of Huxley and loves to read all the letters and so on. I agree with you about footnotes, unless they are in a technical research project, which SB may have decided this to be.

Yes, I did read the Steegmuller about Cocteau, and was put off by its malice and snickery... felt protective of Cocteau, who God knows had no need for my loyalty! But I've read a lot more about that whole Bloomsbury-Paris scene, with real interest. I was first in Paris in September 1929, and my husband made a bee-line for Sylvia Beach's shop, but that was really the nearest we ever touched on the Scene. In 1932 we stayed for a few months down in the Cros de Cagnes, and almost every day walked up to Cagnes, and George Antheil had a villa there, right under the Château. I used to listen along the wall, hoping to hear music... he was l'enfant terrible in those days. But I never heard a sound. Decades later I met him, and told him of how I roamed about his hidden palace, waiting, and he almost cried. He said that he was the loneliest little man in the world, that winter, and would have given half his life to meet us and know us. And what I dreamed of as sparkling witty bits of la Dolce Vita were drab wrestles, alone, with compositions he could not finish, and days and nights of complete sterile solitude. Oh my. Oh dear. But really, how can shy polite people, which he was and we were, bang on doors? It is a continuing puzzlement....

I never even saw Colette, although I had a letter of introduction to her. The day I returned to France after WW2 with two small girls, her great catafalque (?) still stood in the square outside the Louvre... or perhaps it was Notre Dame. It gave me a visceral shock, although I was glad she was out of pain... we'd had no news on the Dutch freighter.

I've met Simca[2] twice, since a few encounters at La Pitchoune where I was hiding behind Michael's skirts (Joke. Laff.). Once she came to lunch here, and Ranieri di San Faustino was captivated by her, which made things very easy for everybody. I served a very simple two-course luncheon, without any domestics of course, and as she left, going to the car, she took my arm and whispered to me, with that pronunciation of "extraordinaire" that only a Frenchwoman of her class can manage, that never in her life had she been offered such an "extraordinary" meal. Well, I pondered long on this cryptic statement, and I remember asking you and Paul to try to find out what she *really* meant. And I still wonder: things were light and simple, and plainly *mangeable*... but there was that subtle nuance of her choice of words....

Well, the second time was lately. I wrote you about it. She simply walked out of the class, leaving it to James, and we went into the parlor of the country-house they had

1. Sybille Bedford wrote the official biography of Aldous Huxley.
2. Simone Beck, coauthor with Julia Child of *Mastering the Art of French Cooking*

rented for the courses, and closed the doors, and she became a warm trusting woman for a time, which we all know is very rare with the French. She held my hand. She was deeply distressed about Paul, and about Jim B, and of course about you. She was completely unaffected, it seemed to me. I felt touched by her confidence in me as a friend of all of you. Then we went out to gather up the two men who'd brought me over the mountains to Rutherford, and James came out, and Simca was once more regal and gracious, not the rather tired elderly upset human being of a few minutes before.

So there you have two aspects of our being together! And I still wonder what she meant with her whispered "extraaaaaaordinaire......."

Of course I am sad and worried about Jim.[3] How can any heart have carried that much overload for so long? How can any human legs have supported it? I could tell when he was last here that he was realizing (not for the first time!) that he must soon go into some new regime. But of course he was talking jauntily of another "project."... We had a short chance for private chitchat, while Chet Rhodes and his friend swam... Jim tried to convince me that I should try a cassette-dictation system that he uses day and night. I remain unconvinced.

This letter is to Paul too, of course, if he feels like being slightly entertained. I look forward confidently and eagerly to seeing you "some time this spring," and will be interested to see your definition of "a leisurely visit"!!!!

My love to you both, as always . . .

....

Bouverie Ranch, Glen Ellen, California   *4.xi.74*

To: Eleanor Lowenstein[1]

Dear Eleanor Lowenstein:

I NEVER told your "spies" that Tabitha Tickletooth was Lady Maria Clutterbuck and/or and er-um!!!! What is more, I know the "spy" who told you that, and shall berate him or something like that.

Only Dickens could have given his wife the name for WHAT SHALL WE HAVE FOR DINNER?

I don't know who named Tabitha T. Do you?

I hate to think that our mischievous friend has plunged you, in my name, into "great distress." He should be more than berated... (But I can't hit a man when he is down, which JAB seems to be, for a time anyway...). Has *Miss Leslie* been brought out in a reasonably inexpensive edition (and if so, why not?)? I should have one. I had a good volume once, which has been lifted by a "friend," apparently.

With hindsight, I now wish that I had decided early on to form a proper little library of gastronomy. But I did not. I gave choice things away, and sent the nothings to

3. James Beard, mutual culinary friend
1. Owner of the Corner Bookshop, who wrote to MF admonishing her for misidentifying Tabitha Tickletooth

M. F. K. Fisher: A Life in Letters

libraries and so on. Too late. Quoth the raven... What I have now is strictly for personal use, both in the kitchen and at the typewriter.

I did not go to NY in October, as projected, but perhaps will come in the Spring. One thing I'd like to do is meet you... one of the FEW things.

Forgive this clutterbucked letter... I am helping the very elderly ex-foreman of the Ranch make his annual crush of Concord grapejuice... undrinkable stuff to me, but a tickletooth to him... (and I do mean *forgive*... these accidents will happen...).

Now to write your spy...

Yrs. respectfully

....

Last House, Glen Ellen, California   *12.xi.74*
To: Norah Kennedy Barr

... I wanted to write yesterday, just for the pleasure of doing it on the 11th day of the 11th month, with '74 equally 11... perhaps the lazy postponement is why I just swallowed one of those stinking little fruit flies. . . .

I enclose the recipe I think sounds worth trying... although it does sound a bit FLUFFY. Mrs. Loebel is very good, I think. I suspect that I would try it with 5 oz. of semisweet chocolate and 2 of bitter. But not everybody likes the dark mean stuff as much as I do. . . .

There were a couple of things I wanted to ask and tell you, on Sunday, but it was *contre-indiqué*. . . .

I wanted to ask if you'd heard anything more about Anna.

Then I wanted to tell you that I decided to take the solemn advice of Dr. Lew, the chiropractor (Who as soon as he saw the X-rays turned olive-grey and refused to touch me again), to see my "medical doctor." So I talked lengthily with Dick Neil, who did not like some of what I told him, and suddenly I was having a complete physical checkup, and must go on Friday for the lab jobs (The Girl with the Vanishing Veins...). It was found, early on, that there has been a radical change in my eyes... Neil did that trick with freezing the eyeballs and measuring the pressure and so on... so he has sent me to an ophthalmologist in Sonoma next Monday. Damn. That means new glasses, and it seems to me as if I just paid for the last set, and Medi-Care could care less about eyes. Ah well and Ho hum.

Neil keeps reminding me that I seem to swing in 10–12-year cycles and that I may well swing out of this thing. Meanwhile I am trying to educate myself to *accept* some of it. It is plainly degenerating. So far I'm not very successful. I find that it *preoccupies* me, not with self-pity as far as I can tell, but with the largely physical planning I often must do to cross a room, or answer the telephone before the people hang up.

So... since you are my dear little sister as well as Next of Kin, I am reporting, and shall continue to unless you prefer not to be involved or whatever you are and would be....

Last night Paul du Feu came for me and I had dinner with him and Maya... one of the most god-awful meals I ever ate, which Maya referred to trustingly as a grande choucroute garnie... lots of delicious ham, FOUR kinds of sausages, and a strange dish of tasteless sauerkraut with lots of carrots and mashed potatoes to stick it together. Incroyable, as the seamstress moaned when she saw the fit of my pants.... Thank God there was some mustard.

Oh... about my pants... I sent them to Goodwill... I leaned over one day to pick up a hairpin, and the whole zipper exploded... they were very uncomfortable after I gained back some 12 oz. of the 20 pounds I did not weigh when they were fitted....

....

Bouverie Ranch, Glen Ellen, California   *23.xi.74*
To: Jake Zietlin[1]

Dear Jake... I got the little catalog from Scripps and thought it was a message that you had not *quite* forgotten me, and then in two days came your letter, and I thank you for both.

I'm glad that you've not... forgotten me, that is. I'm very glad that your will turns you toward me. Neither of us has any illusions of "romance rekindled" and all that. There is no need for such fantasy. But you speak truly, I believe, in saying that we can share a "certain strength and understanding about life."

I don't think it is vain of you to assume (I think rightly!) that we "are now old wise people who have a rich board (hoard?) of experiences and that we should be feasting on the past together."

I don't feel very wise. But I do have a lot to feast on.... And it does not scare me that we might be grim and might be jolly.

It will be fine to see you again, *whenever*.... I can come down to SF, or perhaps you, with or without companions, can drive up here. In SF I always stay at the ole Clifto (which I've known for 50 years through thick and thin... it's now on top, but has not always been!!!).

Well... It will be fine when it happens.

I'm glad Powell dragged you in to be *l'éminence grise* for him... he's still an old fox. I haven't heard from him for some time. Like the rest of us, he probably has only a certain amount of energy to use....

I do agree that you have been a "very active invalid"! No "sleep walker"! Please keep on. There is something to your picture of the dead frog activated by electrodes, of course. . . . A while ago I was trying to tell why I had stopped writing (writing as *such*... as a *job*...), and my sister who is my confidante said, "But you are still doing reviews and introductions and and and..." and I said that it was the way a snake moves and writhes until the sun sets after its death. She did not like that, and it was indeed rather brutal, but true.

What it amounts to, with me anyway, is a cosmic disinterest.

But I'll stay "of good heart" as long as you do. That's a promise.

1. Jake Zeitlin, Southern California book man and old friend

Last House, Glen Ellen, California   *25.xi.74*
To: David Pleydell-Bouverie

Dearest David... I hated, yesterday, to lose any chance of continuing your call. But just as the telephone rang, the two Connes were carrying out their bags, and there they met Irene Haynes coming in... she's a lawyer who is an amateur photographer and who has done some remarkable (I think) pictures of old wineries that I want to see printed. So... I had to say Goodbye to you, and then I put her in a corner, and I tucked the Connes into their car... and there was a deathly 'ush! . . .

Wednesday night I am giving a monumental clam chowder to a motley crew. . . . I'll concoct the soup early in the day, and also a compote of several cooked fruits (au Grand Marnier) to eat with a pound cake I'll make today. White wines, the second one a little sweet. I'll drink to you.

It's good to have the question of your reaction to French food settled! It is hard to define why good French cooking is different in France from anywhere else, but you've hit on at least one of the reasons: *NO SHORTCUTS.*

If you order a *consommé double*, that's what it is, made from the bones, good meat, etc etc, with infinite care in clarifying and storing it. And the garnishes, so-called, are given the same care... and are an intrinsic part of the dish, not just trimming. In other words, there is no such thing as quick cookery! I once hoped that the message of that book I loaned you and Phyllis would hit home... *Stockpot and Steamer...* at least about the ease of making and freezing good broth and glaze... but she was horrified by the plain old *BOTHER*, being well trained to lean on Crosse & Blackwell's cans....

Actually, a month's supply (or more) of excellent strong stock can be made in a few hours, thanks to our reefers[1]....

I don't do it myself, any more, and am often annoyed at my laziness (and my lack of freezer-space). Perhaps I'll reform, before you come home, and stock yours with a few jars of fine bouillon of beef and of chicken to welcome you back. Sounds like fun... except that I'd have to borrow some of your big pots and bring them down here and so on....

Another reason French food is especially good in France is that the produce of land-sea-air is very fresh (except of course for some game). Refrigeration is used as little as possible, except of course for cream etc.... Bread is served within a few hours of the baking, butter is served the same day it is churned... vegetables are eaten the day they are pulled from the garden....

Some people think the soil of France is "different"... but that is really nonsense. There are countless different kinds of soil and different conditions, as in any country. But the French eat *seasonally*, and they pick things very young and tender and then they cook everything fast, almost Chinese-style.... none of the overgrown overdone cabbages and vegetable marrows of good old England! But I have eaten as well in England

1. Refrigerators

as ever in France: at fine French restaurants in London, that used only English-caught fish and vegetables and so on, and then in the country, where things came right from the beautiful gardens and were prepared with appreciation and care.

Well... I didn't mean to mount the podium! But there's no doubt about our half-killing almost everything we eat by picking it too young, transporting it for days in refrigerized cars and trucks, storing it in supermarkets until "ripe," and then treating it ignobly with "easy" methods.

Ho hum.

So... thanks to my rudeness in having to stop short your call yesterday, you get a dividend with this letter, and now are Two in my debt! A heady feeling!

Have you been to Washington? I forget your calendar (except that it is dizzying...).

Oh... we had to put off the Oyster Bash at Inverness (Bodega?)... it rained that one day, and was magnificent the ones before and after. So we'll aim for Dec. 4. It sounds like fun.

There is ONE MORE flower on the espaliered thing on the East Balcony! I really do not care, for the plant itself looks healthy. But it puzzles me. I am trying to grow a strange Wandering Jew with deep purple backs to its leaves, in the two olive pots. The Parsley thrives. And one scrubby cheap little impatiens is blooming like a queen, really very pretty! I pulled out everything else. The balcony was really a near miss this year, for some reason. I'll try again. I wish I could grow torrents and billows of nasturtiums... but I know the air is too dry in summer. Ah well.

I do wonder if you'll decide to send me the cotton dress... I hope so! Love, as always...

....

Last House, Glen Ellen, California   *8.i.75*
To: Marietta Voorhees

Dearest M... I seldom dream about you, but here is a new one, which I'll try to grab while I'm still conscious of it. It was very vivid.

I was busy tidying a big old house for a party to be given for either you or somebody like Portia,[1] a kind of celebration among old friends. I was not invited to it, as I remember, but was attending to all the flowers and dainties and so on. The honored guest sat in the corner of a couch, while several of her friends clustered around her.

I started hurriedly upstairs, to change into the proper clothes. You came in, dressed I think in black pants and that turquoise smoke, looking "sleek and handsome" as Yolande wrote about your appearance at Jack L's party. You went directly to where the old woman (Portia?) was sitting huddled politely, and perched on the arm of the sofa and bent over her.

"Here's my ring," you said, and the guests gasped and murmured as you put on her finger a large beautiful stone, perhaps that Cardinal's Ring you used to wear, but not

1. Portia Bell Hume had recently retired from her position as director of the state department of mental health. She was an old friend of Marietta Voorhees.

the onyx-diamond one from your father. Then you said very clearly but gruffly, "Be glad to make it legal, if you want to."

There was a general feeling of astonishment at this blunt proposal, and the guests murmured, and the old woman began to cry. All this time I was hurrying on up the stairs to make myself presentable before others came.

Then the woman's sobbing changed into what was plainly a murmur of lovemaking with you, and the people vanished, and it was plain to me as I kept on up the stairs that the marriage was being well consummated.

End of dream. I awoke from it surprised...!!!! It seemed very *immediate*.

In one of your notes lately you asked if animals ever talk to me in dreams. Yes, often. Sometimes it is in French, but mostly in a language we both know but one that is unknown to me consciously, a murmur but with distinct syllables, verbs, etc. Once when I was dangerously tired mentally I was haunted and indeed almost tortured by dreams of translating Brillat-Savarin into a cat language, but I could never remember anything about it on waking. It was a terribly painful job, and I would get up exhausted, even more so than when I lay down. "Weird and superficial," indeed! . . .

I meant up a few lines that I could remember nothing about the language, not a sound, but I know I was being instructed by several cats, and was reading their books and really sweating. And now and then my subconscious starts spinning me off on another caper like this and I back away with fright, and climb back to the other world, perhaps afraid that once more I have stretched my mind a little too far.

No news. I love this weather. Today I had to have three new burners installed in my cookstove, which seems to need them every 18 months instead of every 8 or 9 years. Well, I'd rather have a lemon in the kitchen than the garage. And I *WON'T* buy a new one....

I'm gradually getting my Christmas (!) letters out of the way, and am involved reading some mss written (hopelessly) by good friends, all same Kaski.......

....

Last House, Glen Ellen, California   *9.ii.75*
To: Norah Kennedy Barr

Dearest N... you're right, that telephoning is really expensive. But otherwise, between you and me, it's pretty much a one-way street: I'm much more communicative, at least with you (Most people find me reticent or plain close-mouthed...). I know that fairly untrammeled typing is part of a long habit, both personal and professional, whereas with you it has been mostly the latter and therefore easily broken, now that you have retired. With me, I'll probably use the typewriter as a form of articulating, as long as I can find my way to the keys and hit them....

In other words, I'll agree with you that the telephone is an extravagance, and keep right on sending off an occasional letter, into the Jenner void. I'll try to stick to subjects that might interest you, and not be too blatantly self-centered. . . .

I managed by some fancy footwork to keep the slate fairly clear this week, and finally finished the thing I started before Thanksgiving for the *NYer*. I don't know if they'll want it. Rachel has had to stop... it is called a sabbatical but I know she is simply unable to work any more... and I think I've lost my one friend in court. Ah well, it was fun while it lasted! And I'll do all I can to avoid getting back on a magazine contract again. I'm simply too spoiled... which may be read as "too old"? Meanwhile the Marseille stuff is beginning to nibble at my conscience or something. . . .

Today Herger's Pit[1] is full and almost brimming, for the first time since about a year ago December. I do like it when it's full, but think it would spoil the natural ecology completely if Bouverie carried out his occasional dreams about lining it and having it full year 'round.

I now have *two* good friends in the last stages of liver cancer... ho hum... Miriam[2] was given the usual 3-to-6-month verdict, but that was about three months ago, and now she is in hospital with a gangrenous hand, which is a dirty trick to play on her of all people, for she has been chugging right along on two more books. Maybe she can sneak out early. And now Dr. Ben[3] has the same verdict. It is interesting that he was offered three choices: leave everything alone and last 3 months; try hormone injections with a 20% chance of deferring the terminal stage; chemotherapy with a 50% chance. He decided to take #2, which has almost no side effects... as a doctor he is too aware of the very ugly side effects that can go with #3. Well, I do hope he'll feel like having a bit more fun... he and Alan really love to travel, and do it very well. . . .

Tonight I'm going with Riette and Albert Kahn to Dr. Stanford's.[4] A German friend of hers is there. The gemütlichkeit gets a little thick around Hannah, who is professionally a kind of intellectual Mitzi-of-Vienna. However... Margaret has enough bite to her to take the curse off the schmalz....

I was really pleased that Sylvia[5] was sweet as pie about my refusal to do the preface... pleased and RELIEVED. She wrote as if she was relieved.... And then Frances Miller[6] asked me for my opinion of her ms., and I gave it to her, after quoting Timmie's stern dictum never to reply to a friend who asks you for your absolutely candid opinion of his verse-statues-painting-novel, and FRANCES wrote me a most grateful and understanding and appreciative thank-you! This luck can't hold, I keep saying. Quit while you're ahead, Dote. . . .

Last weekend I went up to the Hexagon for a birthday dinner for Montino Bourton, Ranieri's young son. He is said to be or to have been an absolute brat and nogoodnik, but I found him very attractive and generally delightful, and his American wife too. She is slightly pregnant. They have been for three years in India, studying music (and he, cooking). They like this house, and find it "right" for music, so I hope they will

---

1. Herger's Pit, named for Joseph, was created in the meadow in front of Last House during WWII. It filled with water only periodically after spring rains.
2. Miriam Allen DeFord, mystery writer and friend
3. Laguna friend of June Eddy and MF
4. Glen Ellen friends
5. Sylvia Thompson
6. Artist in Bridgehampton who'd written a reminiscence

M. F. K. Fisher: A Life in Letters

come up sometime to play, with their instruments on their backs or however.... They looked at all the rugs and chose the one to sit on! I like Hindu music, but don't know enough about it. I don't know anything about Chinese music either, but feel as if I'm hearing more.... If they do come, before the baby does, maybe you could be here? It would have to be a weekend.... Oh, Montino cooked a curry, nothing like any I'd ever even read about. It was from... oh, I can't remember the region now... very subtle, with fresh shrimps. He ground the powder. There was a black apple chutney, rice of course, and a rather boring paste of chick-peas and spices. We drank a good wine... just good enough, I mean.

There's an ungainly book here that you might like to take a look at, called *Bitches and Sad Ladies*. I got it free because there's a reprint by Fisher, but really it is not very good. It's by and about women, and while some of the stuff is really good, most of it is shrill and best suited to the old Black Couch mumblings. Grace Paley's "Long Distance Runner" would win the prize again, from me... she's really very good when she's good. But my thing is completely out of place in the book, and is there only because I seem to be assuming the dubious position of a Dear Old Women's Libber, which amuses but bores me. It's in the same pocket as being looked upon as an intruder by the commune-people at Shone's Store because *I TOO* buy sweet butter and stone-ground flour and even black-strap molasses! It is an infringement on their territory. And now earnest young women from *Ms.* interview me and ask almost resentfully, "How did *you* happen to be so liberated when you were so young?" Was I? Who is? Maybe I was just dumb. But it never occurred to me to want to be a welder, just because women *weren't*.

It did bug me when Al got paid 50 cents an hour and I only 35, when we were cleaning houses in Laguna and I was doing twice as much as he. And at Paramount I knew there were men in high positions I could never reach, who were ridiculously stupid... but there I could not care less, and would have disdained any suggestion that I should resent them, 'cause I knew that I was much better off than they could ever be, not so much as a female but as a human being. Well, this is an interesting thing to experience... to find myself being made a toute petite éminence grise by awe-struck young ladies who look at me as a definite freak-prophet. Little do they know! I have also been thought to be high priestess of the Squares Inc., an arch conservative and social snob and god knows what else....

Well... I didn't mean to get into this. I'll put the book aside, in hopes that someday I'll see you. Maybe you'll have to be in Santa Rosa? . . .

As I feared, Tim Meadows (CPA) is moaning over my decision to let Steve claim the deductions... and I think perhaps April 15 may be a good time for me to announce that I am no longer going to send the monthly sum. It amounts to well over $250, if I count airplane tickets, extra sums here and there, unacknowledged Christmas checks, etc. Ho hum. But I must assume that if Steve wants to have the custody of Chris as well as Matt, he figures he can support them. Is a puzzlement. Also about how to help Anna, no matter how anonymously... perhaps just paying my taxes is the answer there!

Last House, Glen Ellen, California: 1970–1992

I don't think that money NEED be the root of all evil. Its use can be a good gauge of character, though... and some characters are evil already, and some are hopelessly innocent.

Today seems my day to sound off! But I feel as if you'd been gone a long time, and my compulsion to communicate gets the best of me....

....

Bouverie Ranch, Glen Ellen, California   *15.ii.75*
To: Gloria Stuart Sheekman

Dearest G... my "honey-colored actress"... Lately I have had it much on my mind to tell you how grateful I am to you for letting me read, and keep for a time, the two stories.

And then I watched what I recognized then but now see fully as an act of great human courage, when you went down to the incinerator at Bareacres and burned them. That taught me a great deal about strength.

I have often wished that they could still be read. But: you did what you must do.

So... one more lesson from you, dear girl, and I'm sure you have no idea of what awe I felt... nor how shaken I was when you came back up the hill to the kitchen and said you would like a little drink of something. (I don't mean it was that request that shook me!) I remember that there was nothing but some Pernod, and I made two little nips with water and we drank them without a word. It was the last of a bottle of real absinthe somebody had smuggled, and it felt fine.

Later we had some wine for lunch in the patio, and nothing more was ever said about the two stories. But now I am bringing up the subject, simply to remind you (perhaps) that you have been very important in my life since I was about 23 years old.

Now I feel very proud of you, to be having a show, and back in Business again and sharing your house with David,[1] and and and. (I hear about you from la belle S[2]...)....

I wish I could see what you're painting now. Are you past the circus? I remember looking at the elephants, one night when you and S made a bouillabaisse. That was the night you said I could ask for a canvas and I said "Either... or" and typically you gave me both, and now the *Queen's Pawn* is where I see it several times a day, and *California Spring* with the happy bull and his herd and the lupine and poppies are nearby... is nearby... whatever!

And so are you, in many even more intangible ways. I am VERY glad that we have been friends for so long....

....

Last House, Glen Ellen, California   *28.vii.75*
To: Arnold Gingrich

Dearest Ginger . . . I can't remember when I last wrote, and probably you can't either. We've been in what is called locally a Heat Wave, and any violent activity such

1. Gloria Stuart's grandson
2. Sylvia Thompson

as sitting at the typewriter has been impossible! Today things are much better, but the delightful new habit of stripping to the buff and lying all afternoon on a cool sheet got the better of me, and I spent one last delicious afternoon working hard to keep up the bluff. By now the sun has set, the bell has been rung by Cleveland, and I've showered and must face a few cruel entities (like my conscience!)....

Thanks for settling the problem, not a serious one, of your letters. They'll go in a carton to the Schlesinger,[1] where perhaps in a few decades some resolute researcher will wonder why I knew so much about fly-fishing and never said anything....

Or, more likely, some r.r. will suddenly realize that correspondence hides a realistic picture of public transportation between New Jersey and New York in the 20th century, as well as detailed notes on temperature etc.

Oh, dear Arnold, I never did mean to say that le 14 juillet was/is more important than any other date. What I meant was that the only reason I remember that it was my Grandmother Mary Frances's birthday is that I thought it was *odd*. She mistrusted all "foreigners," especially the French. I was named for her. She was named for Lady Mary Frances Tennant who owned your Strad. Etc. Chain of clownish circumstances... I do tease you a little (very gently and with love) about recalling that day after tomorrow your father would be such-and-such an age, because it reminds me with fondness of June Eddy....

I read a long repetitive thing about running the massage parlors by Talese in *NYMag*. Ho hum. He's a pretty good journalist. I think Tom Wolfe is better. I think Truman C could be better yet if he would stop thinking of himself as a writer. What's so stinky about the word *journalist?* I know people who are proud to be called that... in Paris Janet Flanner loved being referred to by the desk-clerk at the Ritz as la journaliste américaine.... I think if I were starting over again (which god fawbbid) I'd ask to be called that, and work for a paper instead of for magazines. But I love it when somebody refers to me as "a reviewer"... as if that were all I ever wrote....

Ah well... professional vanity.

Somewhere I have a few clippings for you... coals to Newcastle! I've been trying to put my mail in order... the kiss of death. I'm pecking along at the Marseille stuff, and Faville is coming next week, so between the two actualities a few things have got lost. Ah well.

Tomorrow I'm going down to SF for dinner and theatre! Wowski. The Bear Boys[2] will take me. We've worked out a nice occasional binge... one time I pick up the ticket chit, and the next, the dinner tab... all of which they pay in order to preserve their masculine (?????) image, and then report to me. It seems quite simple, at my age. All one needs is a little bravado in proposing this scheme in the first place, and then a sense of enjoyment, both of which I still have. (Oh, it helps to like the people... which I do....) They know good food and good theatre, but are terrified of predatory females.... (So am I, really.)

1. MF donated her papers to the Schlesinger Library at Radcliffe College.
2. MF referred to Richard Foorman and Gene Quint as The Bear Boys because they owned The Sign of the Bear, a kitchenware store in Sonoma.

Last House, Glen Ellen, California　　　　　　　　*1.xi.75*　　*clean slate!*
To: Marietta Voorhees

Dearest M... thank you for calling this morning . . .

As you know by the time this reaches you, I'd like to come in about 9:30–10 P.M. from the NVWL Board meeting on Nov. 16, to stay the night and see you fleetingly before I go to see the pill-boys, and then have lunch with you. I've decided not to go up to the San for physio-therapy[1]... it is a real bore to me right now, and I am being dogged about progress in what I've been taught thus far.

I told you when you called this morning about Albert Kahn's weird experience in the B of A in Sonoma. I asked why it was going on, and he said that last year one of the new clerks decided to come on Halloween (How is that spelled, Doc) in costume, and the "customers" like it so much that they all decided to do it this year....

It reminds me of one time when I told Rex that Al Fisher and I were going to Hollywood to a masked party and that we'd invited Anne and her husband Ted Kelly. He was very bitter and resentful, in a taciturn way, and said, "You will hide behind masks and do what you really want to do." As a matter of fact Anne and Ted did go off on their own hidden pursuits, but I had none! At one point we sat on a long flight of curving stairs and poets read down toward us their works. . . . Al Fisher read a "ballade" that hurt a few people who were not mentioned in it. Etc. I thought the whole thing was fun but slightly embarrassing, as you said recently about "wakes."

You're right about wakes. They were meant to keep the body company until the body was properly encased, and meat and drink were provided to sustain the loyalty. When Grandmother Holbrook died, it was still the custom to provide ample refreshment for people who had come from far away, after the rites, and Mother in her harassment and possible sorrow managed at the door with a fine ham, and a Whittier girl (Quaker) brought a pie! In other words... one tried to ease the burden....

A very tottery little bull-calf just went past the balcony. After the last rain the grass is green, a boon to them. Apparently the grapes have been abandoned. . . .

I'm really sorry that "we didn't seem to coincide too well" when you were here... and quite surprised to have you say so, because I thought things went very nicely and wasn't aware of any tension or or or... once we got over your arriving while Phyllis was here unexpectedly, that is. (She bores me, but does not disturb me... much if at all.) And I honestly wasn't conscious of there being "many things" that you were planning to bring up... of course that's *always* the basic case with people like us, who talk together over long years and do not live nearer and closer than we now can. But there's the mail. And there's the telephone...

Speaking of Peri's calling Mr. F[2] Puddingface, I think of what Donald said of Hu-

1. Physiotherapy for arthritis at the St. Helena Sanitarium, a Seventh-Day Adventist Hospital in Angwin
2. Gerald Ford

bert Humphrey, that he looked fetal. And yet I might vote for him, if forced to... in spite of that somewhat more formed face of today, in spite of his gee-whiz-golly-gosh lingo.... Certainly I can't stomach anything else yet proposed!

In your letter of the 24th you seem to be refuting a quotation I made about how belief is a dangerous thing, but it seems to me you are really agreeing. Perhaps I misunderstand. A snake-handler is in danger *because* he does not believe in the snake (the object) but in his power to handle it or not.... To me that is belief, fraught with danger but valid.

Are you putting me on, Miz Vurris, asking the difference between *un, non,* and *dis?* When in doubt consult your dictionary... or Fowler. They can say it better than I. But there are *great* differences, as you jolly well know.

I have a lot to say... (How she does go on!)... I find it interesting that when last we were here you were not satisfied with our rapport but I was. It proves how dangerous human relations can be... each man is an island, no matter what Donne said. I've long known that what I write to a person may be read in quite a different mood from its beginning. But it's less usual to have that happen face-to-face, I think. Well . . .

I really enjoyed the surprise of talking with Grace Bird while you were out supplying your second meal of pancakes with eggs and cream and so on. She missed perhaps half of what I said, but I talked slowly and clearly (That used to annoy hell out of Rex, but at least he *got* it...) and she rattled on if she did miss something. It makes me wonder again about the old bull-session question: would you choose to be blind or deaf? I think probably I'd choose to be deaf, because although I enjoy good talk I don't hear much of it and can read better than I do hear... and now that my eyesight is less than 20-20 I am aware of physical hindrances to being really blind... how to pin up one's hair, put on some lipstick, that sort of thing. And what would I do without reading, which has been my friend since I was very young? By now my fingers are clumsy with arthritis, and perhaps so is my brain, so that it would be hard to learn Braille. No, I think I'd choose deafness. *But who can choose?* . . .

About Puddingface et al... I remain thankful that I never have to look at all those frightening masks in order to hear the news. You're right to turn on your TV and then turn your back to it in the kitchen!

Abiding love...

....

Last House, Glen Ellen, California   *25.xi.75*
To: Eleanor Friede

Dearest Squeek... impossible that this will meet you at the door! I do hope all has gone superbly well for you, in London and in France. . . .

Yes, I did get quite a few copies of the stories about CC's[1] dinner... including Russell Baker's dreadful spoof. I always feel with that sort of vulgar puff that it is to cover up a ghastly journalistic hole somewhere, in what The Public is allowed to read.... Of

1. Craig Claiborne, who gave a highly publicized $1,000 dinner in Paris

course it was very vulgar, all 'round. I think it came at a wrong time for us goons in the hinterlands to love New Yorkers any more than we now seem to, in order to help the city through its present troubles. VERY bad timing. Ah well . . .

I'm fascinated by your telephone conversation with TC.[2] I think he misses the whole point of what he is doing. Like most self-appointed Messiahs, of no matter what bent, he honestly believes (I think) that he is DOING GOOD. In his case, he thinks he is getting people to read books instead of look at movies or or or because the *book is good*. But I simply cannot agree with him, critically. People are reading the excerpts from what he somewhat frantically calls a book because they are Peeping Toms, malicious snobs... because they can get their feelies and funnies that way... and NOT because the prose is worth reading for anything else. (I admit that twice I thought he forgot to be nasty and was almost like a writer... but for a flash, no more.) Perhaps he's right, that this will be a glowing stained glass window someday. So far it's just one more splash of vomit in the gutter, one more chewed cigar-butt....

Do you think he may have gone a little crackers? (I'm serious.)

Maybe we're really missing what he's doing. I hope so. He's too good to paddle about this way....

Oh... I believe that only the *Esquire* people will publish... nothing will be in the *NYer*. This is hearsay. And I also hear that *Esquire* is slightly desperate, but is thoroughly tied up legally.

To better things... talked with Kennedy this morning, completely absorbed in Life At Mills... every meeting Jim goes to, everything they do, what he said and what she said or did not say to this or that member of the Faculty or student or or or. They plan vaguely to come up before Christmas... haven't been here for several months. (I doubt that they come, for some reason. It's all right.)

News seems almost too good from Anna. She has moved again, to Astoria,[3] and has an apartment and Chris and Sylvie and is on Welfare and is getting ADC and plans to go to college in January, to study to be a veterinary technician or something like that. All I can do is pray. She seems to have good advisors (legal and medical), and while she does sound very high or very low, she's hanging in there. I tremble for them all. Chris has been to either three or four schools in the past three months....

Today I gave a great Last Supper of GRO to all the pots, some of which I don't even need to water again for a few months... the ones on the front balcony will get plenty of rain. There are S*I*X*T*Y!!!!!! And that doesn't count the parsley box, which has a lot of new plants in it, all doing well... nor the long tomato box, which from six pl... no, eight plants produced FOUR sour warped little fruits this year. Well, it's fun. . . .

As for my coming back, I must remind you that I cannot drive now. But the people in Bridgehampton were very good about coming out with supplies. I really think I should be away from here for a time... break the pattern I'm in. I could bring every-

2. Truman Capote
3. In Oregon

thing I needed, in a small briefcase, for the Marseille material. I would like to finish that... of course it's impossible to write all one wants to about such a subject, but I know basically my hopes....

No, really I don't want to go to Sag Harbor at all! I've BEEN to Sag Harbor! I know all the door lintels and the churches and the Library and the Grocery stores and the liquor store, and and and. I'm glad I was there, but I don't want to try it again.

But I'd love to stay at the Beach for a time, if it worked out conveniently for you (and Richard[4]?). You'll tell me about this as it evolves.

It's beautiful tempestuous October weather now, a month late. I do rather a lot of slow gentle cooking... can't read or write until after strong daylight (this will probably change), so find myself brewing chutneys and making sauce Duxelles and so on. Since I can't go places, people come here![5] Tomorrow there's to be some, for dinner. Then Sunday Julia and Paul Child and Julie's sister and brother-in-law and Genie and Ranieri are coming for lunch... since both Paul and Ranieri have bad tremor in the hands, I'm making a thick soup and a thin one to drink from *mugs*, and then old-fashioned baked apples with hot cinnamon-milk. I would have liked to see just the Childs, because we have a lot to catch up on, but this will be fun too. Next Big Bash is when Jim Beard and Chet Rhodes come for the night... again I've asked the San Faustini, because Jim will stay in their guestroom and Genie has a crush on him. I'll put Chet in the one room in the Guest House that Phyllis is allowed to keep open during the winter(!).

Speaking of which, nobody but Cleveland has heard from Bouverie since he left three weeks ago! Of course he's furious at Phyllis for giving notice, and I don't think he'll ever forgive me for telling him I did not like to be spoken to as he'd done. (I really hated to do it, but the time had come....)

A chitchat letter, dear girl, but it brings much love. (I have a little present for you, or rather for a wall, but I can give it to you later....)

....

Last House, Glen Ellen, California   *18.xii.75*
To: Arnold Gingrich

Dearest A... the moon is full, and I think of The Attic and wish that I'd been all I wanted to be. But I was never meant to be cast as an Isolde. It would have killed me off *fast*.

So, as a German friend used to assure me, it might possibly turn out for the best (whatever that is)! I have a couple of your letters to answer, but the moon turned me off: I got up to check on things in my office and the rays, so slanting at this time of year on the black tiles, pulled me to the sight... and suddenly I felt like Isolde *manquée*. A passing fancy.

I'm really interested in your two concerts, one a mini but fun, the other very seri-

4. The writer Richard Bach
5. MF had been having various health troubles.

ous... and except to serious students and music-lovers (?) perhaps a little dull. But for you both it will be fun.

Things have been very *mouvementées* here, as you'd put it. I make delicious little meals, which people drive hundreds of miles to eat, etc etc etc. It's really all I do, besides sleep and try to attend to the top of the mail-bag. The reason I cook so much is that I have turned off ABSOLUTELY AND PERHAPS FOREVER, FROM PERSONAL CREATIVE WORK.

This is an odd realization. Of course I've had dead stages before. But this may well be final. It's too bad, because the Marseille book is about 2/3 done, and it's good. But...

I can still turn out an occasional "piece," as I did for *Esquire* and for *Travel & Leisure* and for the *NYer*, but I've simply stopped being Fisher. Perhaps I'll start again.

Meanwhile it is wonderful not to be gnawed too deeply, driven too hard. I sleep well, get up any time between 5 and 8, contemplate the menu(s) of the day, arrange the house, listen to people chew and sigh and moan, take a nap....

It's a far cry from your own dogged and accustomed round, for sure! It makes me feel very ashamed of myself. But you must do it your way, and I mine.

So it's probably heavensent that things went as they did, moon or no moon. And if this is a sentimental message, you can blame it on Christmas or something!

I'll write more, later... probably.

....

Last House, Glen Ellen, California   *30.i.76*
To: *Norah Kennedy Barr*

Dearest N... a letter just came from you without any dates, but I know it's been on the road, because I'd already heard about going to the circus from Lider![1] Well... there's always the postal service to complain about, if we give up on the weather.

Lida said she felt compulsive about washing her hands while the septic tank was on the blink, and a few days ago the power was turned off here for six hours and I found myself longing almost frantically for hot tea (even red clover!), hot soup, anything that needed a burner going.

Second to the deep pleasure of running water, per se, is water running into a flush toilet (and then out again, of course...). I thought, when I was frozen tight here for almost nine days and nights, that I must have *dreamed* about the days when I took such things for granted.

It's like turning over in bed: it's never the same after one has not been able to for a time. I still do it with a little puff of thanksgiving... *every time*, too.

The circus sounds absolutely wonderful. I've been listening to some nice stuff about it on radio... just my cup o' tea, and it's made me try to remember how many "real" circuses I've seen in my life. I never did go to an inside one... in Madison Square Garden et al. The last time I went to Ringling Bros & B&B was in Hollywood, with Sis, in

1. Lida Schneider was called "Lider," first by Chris.

about 1944... SEVEN rings, and one end of the huge tent collapsed and there was an almost-horrible accident... no panic, though. Then I went to several one-ringers (tent) in France and Switzerland with the children. Once in Dijon I went to a one-ringer with Al, but he hated it because he was sure a man across the tent, through all the dust and cigarette-smoke and so on, was making obscene signs at him. I tried to find him where Al pointed, but could not... perhaps naive? Anyway, we never went to another. But it didn't put me off. . . .

I got a packet of letters I wrote to Grace from Liz Holmes, Aunt Grace's niece or something... wouldn't dare look at them, so shall simply stick them in the Radcliffe box-of-the-moment.[2] It always shocks me to think that anything I've written to a *person* would be kept. And yet I can think now of letters I've got from other people that should be in their archives... Auden, people like that who are important. Until lately I haven't kept any correspondence at all. When Powell asked me about my letters to Hal, his to me, etc., it was a dead blank. Poor Larry was horrified and really disbelieving: he's saved every scrap of paper he ever scribbled on. (This may be the blessed demise of scholastic research: too damn much to work with !!!!)

Until soon... here or there... and don't tease me by saying that I "may be willing to come over" to Jenner! I'M WILLING. I'm eager. Barkis is willin', but is he able? That's the hitch, ma'am. Right now I'm very able, and am clearing the decks (except for a slight indulgence like this note...).

....

Last House, Glen Ellen, California   *10.iv.76*
To: Arnold Gingrich

Dearest Ginger... I send you a couple of clippings that may entertain you fleetingly.

I broke all my rules and even precedents, and went down to San Francisco to Herb Caen's Birthday Bash. Who can resist Benny Goodman? (And I'm very fond of Herb too, and of his wife who conned me into it.)

I stayed with the San Faustini... Bouverie was going down too, and we lunched with mutual friends beforehand....

It is God's truth that by some miracle Maria Teresa kept the whole caper secret, although it involved an awful lot of newsies and noisies. The party was in the Great American Music Hall, a beautifully reconstructed and renovated early SF monument. I celebrated my 17th or 18th birthday in one of the loges, eating cracked crab and drinking sacramental wine (Prohibition) while we looked down on very poor vaudeville acts. Well... this time I was down with the mob, and it was a very jolly simple affectionate party indeed. People drank to their tastes but nobody seemed to be more than quietly happy, and the food was nicely done but unimportant, and Benny blew generously.

I felt that he was cautious, and let his men carry him more than he used to. But why not? And he really was GOOD. I agreed with Plimpton that it was wrong to pretend

2. Grace Holmes died in 1975.

to dance. But I did, simply to get down to the little stage to be nearer him... I stood gasping and smiling like a teenager....

I used to see something of Goodman in Hollywood, when I was drifting from one kind undemanding person to another and went to parties with his current girlfriend. I liked her, partly because she was so beautiful. BG was very good to her, and later married her to a rich NY banker. I see her picture now and then. Actually, I seldom saw BG. But the other night he seemed to recognize me, and we exchanged a little smile.

Well, Herb's party was a lot of fun. And that can't be said often enough, which is why I never go to parties-as-such, and know that I'll never see another like this.

... I am waiting for some more people to come to say Bon Voyage. Every time the phone rings I hope it is they, saying they cannot make it through the rain. (I'm really not as inhospitable as I sound. But right now all I want to do is order my thoughts *AND* my house for a departure....)

A fantasy: We should have gone to Herb's bash together!!!!!! Wouldn't that have been a Mad Caper and a Just Reward???????

On that jaunty note, dearest friend...

<hr>

Aix-en-Provence, France   *12.v.76*
To: Eleanor Friede

Dearest Squeek—I was so happy after you called on about April 14(!) that I must write to you *at once,* to thank you and let you know the whats and wheres. And that was four weeks ago tonight! Mea culpa.

All goes superbly well for us, and we're installed in a perfect little flat until the end of July. You'd approve. Newly cleaned and painted—red tile floor, white plaster walls, big black (real!) beams across the ceilings—first floor up, on short street about five min. (2 short blocks) from *every*thing: Cours Mirabeau, Town Hall, Cathedral, Rotonde—in what is now called Le Centre, once la Vieille Ville. It's one block up from the rue Espariat, where we all stayed at the Hôtel de Provence. We have one very big room with a large kitchen alcove, and then a huge dressing room with all the facilities behind a glass partition. We had to invest in blankets and linens, for the nth time, but otherwise have exactly what we need for a heavenly stay. Norah works every day at the Bibliothèque Méjane, and this time 'round may actually get that book into shape! I work here at the apt., and while I feel that I'm creaking with rust, I'm at least *working,* after 2+ dead years—We buzz all day with small delightful jobs: a long drink on the Cours, the wonderful open markets, an occasional concert or movie—walk a lot, eat lightly but very well, drink rosés and dark vermouth with an occasional gin for a spree—sleep well. In other words—

The trip was simply *too long,* about 36 hrs. in transit from portal to portal—Glen Ellen to Marseille. Since I really cannot sleep on planes, it makes for a strange jet-lag! We drifted around blissfully while we caught up with ourselves—good old Beauvau, Marseille sparkling and extra giddy for the long Easter weekend. We ate shellfish twice a day to make up for lost time and revived surprisingly warm relationships with various local eccentrics—went once to the New York, now *the* place, very good and expensive, and worth it—to our favorite place on the Port, the 2 Sisters—etc.

At first the prices shocked us, but by now we're quite calm about them. And of course having our own kitchen is much cheaper than hotel and restaurant living. And there are a lot of excellent new "takeout" shops, where we can get delicious things now and then: quail roasted with grapes, Parma hams, stuffed artichokes. And we've found an old wine-friend who still will deliver cases of Perrier, vermouth, rosé.

Aix is in a fantastic explosion of students, the most in some 500 comparatively quiet years, and of *people*—perhaps 300% in the past 5 years. The landscape is ruined, of course, by high-rise communities. But instead of having the core of the sprawl turn into a deserted neglected ghost-town, as is happening all over America where the suburbs have their own supermarkets and big stores and so on, the Vieille Ville is called Le Centre, and everybody comes *in* to it. The merchants are happy as clams. More and more of the fine old stone facades are being restored, there are lots of new small shops of all kinds, some very smart and all of them interesting. There's a great new interest in regional things like cloth, baskets, food—

All the small cafés and restaurants that were Algerian or "Arab" when we first lived here are now Vietnamese (some excellent, with lots of fresh vegetables and *noodles*) and the general standard is better than it was even three years ago, in spite of inflation. There is one 2-star, even! It is very expensive of course, and rather oppressively elegant—too many flowers, too many exquisite young Italian gays in waiters' disguise. The Roy René is exactly the same, diningroom and all, and M. Bressan is still running it from his concierge-desk, although it has been bought by the huge Mapotel chain and we noticed a few changes like not turning down the beds at night. (!Spoiled fat cats we are!) The Provence has been turned into *tiny* very posh apartments for rich students, and is called Le Louis XIV! Ho Hum. (We spent 5 frustrating days looking at such places and *worse*, and for a while were resigned to hotel living, horrible for 3 months, with 3 meals a day "out." Now we're *beatific*—)

Dearest Squeek—fly to France, fly to the Beach—work as hard as your spirit tells you, but never as its slave. Thus spake Dr. Fisher—

....

Aix-en Provence, France   *20.vi.76*
To: Eleanor Friede

Dearest Squeek—by now you've been in France and are back in the saddle again, and I do hope you'll report that you spent a few fine carefree days and nights—hashish pipe, Breughel, and *all*—

Yes, Provence works its usual magic with me—I'm more the way I *am*, here! I'm trying not to dread the return to California—no use letting it be a bugbear. But basically it scares me, as I grow older, to face this real dichotomy. It's *wearisome*. Ah well and ho hum. So I'm a good American person, by accident! But the few people I still love are in America too, except for Eda and the Stones in England—is a puzzlement, and by now much too late to solve.

Today is the first of 16 days of Musique Dans Les Rues, and we start up to 2 of the *34* concerts we've marked as *essential*! It's impossible, of course—no seats, all free, in courtyards—cloisters—squares—*very* exciting stuff, like a brass quintet that is going to play with the organ at the regular Sunday Mass at the Cathedral—Cage and other moderns with percussion and piano in a courtyard, Iranian and Moroccan and Egyptian chanting in the Cloister, etc. Lots of classical stuff—lots of jazz. And then on July 16 the Festival begins!

The town couldn't possibly be more crowded than usual, even with lots of people for the Festival—it was up to about 50,000 when you were at the Provence with us, but is now more than a half-million! Of course the landscape is hopelessly scarred by high-rise suburbs, but the Old Town, now called Le Centre, is more beautiful than ever. Several of the streets leading off the commercial side of the Cours Mirabeau are now "pedestrian zones," especially paved, really delightful. The Cours *must* be that, and before much longer. Traffic is incredibly heavy, and the noise makes it almost impossible to talk on the terraces—everybody yells, or sits stunned—but everybody goes right on sitting there!

I'm sorry you've had to come to apartheid with Waller—but at least you can still love each other sight unseen—

Oh sure—I've always known Rocco was a homosexual. But like many others I've known, he likes girls and women as a kind of protection from the world, and he's skilled and thoughtful with them. I don't think kids the age of Anne and K when they met him realized that his interest in them was sexless. If they did, they may have found it agreeable, after the clumsy pantings of so-called normal males of their own age— Well, I'm delighted to hear that he's alive and well and busy. I really like him. I'll pass along to K your news about him and the beautiful Sophia Sayre.

No, Squeek—we have the flat until the *end* of July! We plan to leave on the 30th, spend 2 nights in Marseille, then fly directly to Heathrow—Humphrey Stone will meet us, for 2 nights in Wiltshire to meet my new goddaughters. Then we fly London—Chicago (to skip L.A!)—San Francisco on Aug. 3. We'll stay at the Clifto, and go up to Glen Ellen and Jenner the next day (—can't bear to think of it)—

Yr. Glorious 4th sounds too good—exactly right for 1976! Here we'll polish off the M-dans-les-R with a big-band concert on the roped-off Cours, and then a huge Beethoven thing in the Place de l'Hotel de Ville, complete with the Marseille Opera Company and champagne & & &—what wild lives we all lead, now and then!

This week Evan and Judith Jones and her mother and aunt, both in their 90s, will be at the Roy René—and on July 7 Eda comes for a week. We'll put up here at the Le Manoir, a lovely old restored convent near us. She's had a ghastly winter, and we're very happy she can come—(surgery for throat cancer, drastic deep-ray treatments, etc).—

And along in there (?) I want to finish what I brought along to do on the 3-year-old Marseille opus. I have a nasty job of revising etc when I get home—at least a good excuse to miss some of the Ranch parties!

All love—write good news, dear Squeek—

K sounds fine, is busy with Jim on *9* ballets. Anna is reported to be in Portland again. Ho hum.

<hr />

Last House, Glen Ellen, California   *4.xi.76*
To: Norah Kennedy Barr

Dear N . . .

Yes, the days are unbelievably bright and filled with birds. I've begun my winter feeding in the courtyard... dozens of very small wrens, I think... canyon wrens?

It is very dark, six o'clock, and I'm waiting for a couple of friends at 6:30... the house is wide open and I'm wearing that giddy djellaba you gave me. But I have a fire ready to light in a couple of hours. . . .

Yeah. This has been my year to whimper. Now and then I say it is nothing but self-pity, but that is not quite true. I feel very *angry* about the way people have to exit. It was cruel to make Eda submit to an obviously useless surgical interference so late in the game. After that biopsy, why not just keep her warm and as comfortable as possible? DAMN. As for Arnold, I do *not* think he should have had almost three months of kimotherapy [*sic*] for the terminal lung cancer that had progressed to his brain before it was even detected lower down. DAMN. As for Bob Steele, he chose to sweat it out, and while his last months of life were increasingly sad, he died as "naturally" as one can with Parkinson's... at least peacefully and among dear friends.

Now about Ranieri: he is 8 days into 4 to 6 weeks of cobalt treatments and if he survives them will start kimotherapy. He is already in less pain and can sleep on his left side. But the treatments leave him flat with exhaustion. The first tumor has shrunk a little but a new "node" has developed. And so on. DAMN.

I suppose we'll never again be able to die as people did a hundred years ago. We don't even breathe the same air....

Work chugs along. I like to feel that I'm getting something done that I once wanted to do, but the truth is that I'm really not *with* it... it's a conditioned reflex... the dead snake wriggling until the sun goes down. I've been offered a contract for 6 articles a year for a magazine I think is good, but have refused it... mildly tempted, just to see if I *could* do it. But that would not be fair. So... I may finish what I've laid out to do on Marseille, by Christmas. Then what? Judith[1] wants me to dig out all the stories I've written about aging and old age, for a collection. We'll see.

Here come my people....

Next morning, and I think it is rather interesting that I am deliberately developing

1. Judith Jones

a new attitude toward the passage of Time, especially when it is out of my own measures of politeness. I feel a whole morning taken out of my hands, a morning I planned to spend in a certain way because it might be the only morning I would ever have again to spend that way (in this case to re-read a thing I wrote in Aix and get it ready to dictate), and then Joseph came into sight. He carried a bag with four lemon cucumbers in it, and his pockets bulged oddly with wrenches and vises as well as his deformed bones. He was going to mend a broken faucet. It is very painful to watch him move, so I tried not to. Finally he was satisfied with the faucet under the kitchen windows and crawled in, onto the West balcony and got himself into a chair, and I brought him a good nip of Bourbon. He looked at his watch and said he had about an hour, before he had to crawl back up the hill to turn off the water and look at a new TV. So I simply forgot, or almost, the morning I had planned, and sat passively and enjoyably looking at his face and feeding him questions. I felt fatalistic but also aware that perhaps I was learning much more than I might have from pursuing the other goal.

The same was true last night. Phyllis is alone while her husband readies their mobilehome and so on in Gilroy or wherever it is, and she called to ask me to go out to dinner with her and since that would mean her coming here to take me somewhere and then bring me back, not to mention a dreadful restaurant meal, I asked her to come here. Then I thought it would be nice to ask her friend Jennie Lehmann, who is an interesting attractive woman just my age who seems very old to me. So there was nice fire and the food was excellent (plain), and I simply sat there and listened for what seemed a very long time, and asked a few questions, and poured Bourbon and water. Jennie is not at all coarse. She has a dreadful emphysemic cough, but does not smoke constantly, like Phyllis. Jennie (guess that's the spelling) left about midnight. I had put myself into the trance of believing that this was probably worth more in human Spirit (???emotion??? release???) than working on my own little Marseille kick, but I felt a flash of resentment that after Phyllis's friend left she settled back for a good long self-explanation or whatever it is called. She talked steadily until almost 2 A.M., smoking and pouring "just one more tiny" and hopefully hinting tears to come. I simply sat there, clucking now and then and trying not to yawn. I felt very tired, but admitted that bodies adapt to sleep-loss and so on... my real resentment, quite tampered-down but latent, was that I would rather be doing something else (like sleeping, or reading, or listening to after-midnight radio from Fresno or Chico...). So I smiled, frowned, yawned.

Well... I find this significant of something, Doc. Does it mean that I've become quiescent? Perhaps I have spent 68 years learning how to be sympathetic? Am I merely lazy? As I remember, there is some passive revolt in my social behavior... and I think I have my fair share of human sympathy... and yes, I'm lazy.

Well, Time turtles on.

You, like Fredrika van Benschoten, talk of the weather, the butterflies, the pelicans and seagulls… and occasional odd birds like Nini… bycyclers (I think I mean bicyclers)… I suppose it all balances with my ego-centricity, or at least I hope so.

I wonder if you are docenting? I wonder about aches-and-pains, if and when, although I know you dislike people who tell about such things. And here I am talking about my basic resentment at having to train myself to welcome people who must T*A*L*K*… to you who are trained to do it! It really isn't fair.

PS… Phyllis will soon be gone, and Joseph cannot hack this life (ranch life) much longer, and I hope to be able to talk sensibly with Bouverie about hiring or arranging for competent "help" here on the Ranch. He is supposed to be out here within a few days.

....

Bouverie Ranch, Glen Ellen, California   *1.xii.76*
To: Rachel MacKenzie

Dearest Rachel—I really cannot tell you or *anyone* what joy it gave me to hear your voice today. I have been wondering more than usual, lately, about how to go about learning news of you. Of course I wondered if you had died. Where should I ask? Who would have told me? Of course I could write directly to you: "Dear Rachel, are you alive?" But if you were, should I bother you, even to answer "Yes!"? (All this sounds silly, now that you've called.)

Things go well here, comparatively speaking ("comparatively" is used when I think of a lot of other people, I suppose. I'm *well*, and the roof is being put back again, and the house is beginning to feel warm again—).

My younger sister Norah and I decided very suddenly to go back to Aix and were there for several months. The old magic worked, and after a 3-year puzzlement I worked hard again, and now that I'm home I'm somewhat deliberately hanging on to that impetus. The book about Marseille is a series of explanations of what I've seen and sensed there. I suppose it's rather like *Map of Another Town*, but of course I'm not the person who wrote that. Whether it's good or bad, I need to finish it, and soon. (I am slowed by a boring arrangement of writing in longhand, dictating onto a cassette, sending it to Napa to be typed, revising that draft, returning it to Napa, etc etc. But *nothing* can stop this, by now!)[1]

Aix was perfect. Lots of music, most of it very high quality. We went to Marseille a lot (bus).

The re-entry to Earth-orbit was chancy, but by now Norah and I know its risks, and seem to have handled it quite well. I suppose it's a little like your return to New York and the magazine—

Please do not use *one milligram* of energy on any kind of letter to me. Just know that I feel very happy, since your call. Now I can see where you *are*, again!

Abiding love—

1. Arthritis kept MF from typing.

PS—all this sounds completely egocentric—I, me, I. But I feel shy about asking you things like "Are you serene, are you pleased, are you glad that you are in New York, did you write another beautiful book—?" For one thing, you might think, with your innate courtesy, that you must reply.

....

Last House, Glen Ellen, California   *4.xii.76*
To: Frances Steele[1]

Dear Frances... how good it was to hear your voice on Thanksgiving Day! I do thank all of you for calling.

Yesterday I read some excerpts from a book by an American Indian about ills and medicine and so on... I suppose he would be called a "witch doctor" by the early missionaries, or simply a healer.

And he said something that I have tried to express from the first minute I met you and Bob and then assorted offspring:

When you come to people who are happy and who laugh, join with them, that's the only medicine.

I've said, to special people like my sister Norah, that when I was with you, mostly at the table of course(!), we spent hours eating and drinking and *laughing*. Once somebody said, "But that must be tiresome in the end," or something like that, and I couldn't explain that it wasn't a case of listening to really quick bright conversation so much as it was that *everything* seemed so delightful... enjoyable... happy.

Well... plainly I still can't explain it. But the Indian doctor did!

So I'm very grateful to all of you for the years of "the only medicine."

I know that they can never have the *same* sparkle for any of us, but they will still be very good ones.

Please tell me if and when you feel like coming up for a picnic or some soup by the fire... Theo and John... children... no children... any or all....

And meanwhile here is much love to you and the family.

....

Last House, Glen Ellen, California   *21.xii.76.*
To: Norah Kennedy Barr

Dear N... I do wish, in many ways, that you could have stayed on. But I like to think of you at the Tylers'. After you left I took a short but sleepless rest with Charlie, gently pushing him off the Japanese puff perhaps one hundred times. The reason I am so cruel (?) about this is that he likes to nurse it with his front paws, which tears little holes in it to let out the peculiar stuffing in it, and then he makes a little nipple of the equally strange decoration of phony tie-dye and sucks it until it makes a larger hole. This is fun

1. Widow of Robert Steele (whose pseudonym was Lately Thomas). Both Frances and Robert were longtime friends.

for him, but a basic bore for me. When can I buy another pouf? And why does he not admit that his mother loved him but she died?

Well... I opened the rather large mail. Do you remember Bert Greene, who with his companion Denis took us to Mouans-Sartoux for a long strange very amusing lunch ending with Pernods? (He's not with Denis any more. He's sad, and I hope Denis is too, but Bert has another friend by now. He also got fired at *Esquire* and is free-lancing.) Burt sent five jars of rather odd-looking conserves and chutneys, and asked that I share them with Norah. So I shall. He said that when he felt dubious about things, he headed for the kitchen. And of course that is easy lingo to me, who do the same.

So you have some jars here.

Then I got two records from Chuck Newton, and I just played three sides and am almost ready to throw up... it's all that squealy liturgical Renaissance whuddering stuff, with ancient (???) instruments tweeting along, and a lot of ecclesiastical... well, *ecclesiastical* brays and bellows, and then a high overtone of *castrati* trying to sound like the Virgin Mary and Mother Anne and so on. Oh dear. *OH* dear.

And I got your letter about the banquet. Yes, a lot of aged people find real solace and enjoyment in e8a8t8i8n8g... that's E*A*T*I*N*G.... I don't know about cooking the stuffing seperately (separately?)... except that it certainly wouldn't need as much time to cook as the bird. I have given up all such fripperies, and let kindly onlookers do things like make colossal pâtés for me.

I thanked Bouverie for you, for the cow-pats. I got a letter from him today, all sweetness and vague light. His general message is that everything will turn out all right.

I think Roy de Groot's[1] recipes are the best of that lot, and he doesn't pretend to be "minceur" at all, but simply to be simpler. But I hate his title. I told him so, and he agrees. And speaking of the bourgeois who go to the Vendôme on Sunday and so on, I meant today to show you a book about eating like a king on peasant fare... something like. Absolute nonsense.

That reminds me that I got a new First Reading Agreement from the *NYer* today, and gather from Tim Seldes's[2] cautious noncommittal note that he would suggest I turn it down. But I'm not going to. It only ties me up for another year. And in that year I hope to finish the book and write several reviews which ONLY the *NYer* would publish (those gastronomical reviews). So...

Well, if you have peach and avocado soups and I have both buttermilk and goat's milk (Swiss), and oatmeal, cornmeal, and almondmeal, how can we starve!!

... Then the San Faustini called, and I feel that I'll not talk with Ranieri again. Ho hum . . .

Well, None . . .

I'm about to creep up on those mussels. I do thank you (who *were* you?) for gathering them for me. They will remind me of a thousand other times I have eaten them, very

1. Culinary writer
2. Seldes was briefly MF's agent.

often with you.... One time I ate perhaps the best and simplest in an absolutely *minable*[3] brasserie on that main street in Avignon that had deservedly folded by the time we were last there. It was a ghastly place, with elderly waiters so strung-out on *kif*[4] or something that they were my friends and with drab dank streamers hanging from the ceiling and old confetti on the floor, several days after the pathetic "réveillon"... a bad mistral blowing then, and few customers. I sat for quite a while eating those mussels, and the waiters seemed to enjoy the whole thing too... perhaps a touch of reality, if not a complete jump into fantasy, to see me sitting there like a tabbycat in the shambles...?

Joe Carcioni says that it is very nice now to buy packages of oranges and fruits to give to people you forgot to send a present to. I would be absolutely appalled if I found a carton of oranges on my doorstep.

Cordially...

....

Last House, Glen Ellen, California   *1.i.77*
To: Norah Kennedy Barr

Dear N...

This is the third try at a note to you, because you are much in my mind, such as it is.

The first two, written while PEOPLE were up at the Hexagon, got rather involved, mostly with gerontology.

One nice thing about ageing (sp?) is that while very articulate and qualified people talk of it, they find it almost impossible to "identify" with the subject. They talk of other people.

I suppose this is a form of euthanasia. THEY are coping, while OTHERS seem pitiably to have gone over the hill, down the drain.

Etc.

It has been fascinating, and I wish I had the energy to write about it... people sitting around talking obliquely or at times vociferously about ten-hour surgery for a heart by-pass, the joy of peeing after months of wearing a "purse" after surgery for cancer of the kidney.

I wonder why we cannot wander off into the vineyards, as people do from the "convalescent homes" between St. Helena and Calistoga. Your idea of swimming far west is good, except that sometimes a person finds himself unable to *swim*... or even to lift hand to mouth.

Well... I wish this dialogue could have gone on, but everybody went to other appointments-in-Samarra.

I cooked quite a lot in advance, so as not to spend the whole time bending over the stove, and went into a slight panic when I found that Paul and Julia were planning to stay two nights instead of one, which is complicated for me because of the marketing.

3. Pitiable
4. Hashish

I scrambled things together from the freezer and the icebox, and it was not too good but was "manageable." Then they left this morning. . . .

Next morning, and I'm waiting in icy meadows for Margie Foster to come to help me answer a lot of Christmas mail. She's a tiny girl who is always cold, and first I give her a mug of hot tea (she's Scottish), and then I keep her supplied with either cookies or what the Nuttalls[1] call Suckie-Sweets... (she's a sugar-buff, I'd say.)

....

Last House, Glen Ellen, California   *26.i.77*
To: Norah Kennedy Barr

Dear N... I'm Fine. How are You?

In fact, I feel superfine today, although I went to bed at 2:30, read for two hours, and then stayed awake (pleasantly) until I got up at 8. I may take a nap this afternoon, so far have no wish to.

Reason: I went to SF with the Bear Boys for the first night of the new Prokofieff *Romeo and Juliet,* and it was a beautiful thing in every way. (Tell me what critics may say....) It was done last year, but the ABT ran out of money for sets, and it was played against cloth curtains etc. Now it is fully, if very simply, "set," and to my mind it is a beauty. It will stay in the repertory, along with Bolshoi, London, Denmark and one other house that I forget.

Packed house, very good audience. Big orchestra (62!), *very* well directed. Had never heard full score before and was much impressed. Smuin and Christensen did a masterly job with the choreography. And Bill Pitkin, who sent us the tickets and sat with us and later had supper, designed the most beautiful, perfect costumes I could dream of... very 15th C., but all made of pure thin silk and very fluid and supple, so that they were in constant motion. (The dancers love to work in them... completely unhampered.) The colors are dazzling, and subtle too... the Capulets are all in the palette of scarlets-reds-yellows-browns, and the Montagues are blue and purple and green and so on. It's really exciting when they tangle, which of course is often. The sets are ingenious, spare, and just right for the way I think life was then.

Oh... the dancing was superb. A beautiful company.

(You can see that and why I still feel high....)

The Boys and I stopped in Sausalito at Soupçon... very good. . . . You probably know the little place in Sausalito. It's worth heading for. Then we went to the Opera House. The audience was fine. SRO and that too was gone! Bill Pitkin was blissful. Then we went backstage... they were striking the set for the symphony boys, but will set it again on Saturday... and then we met Pitkin at the Deli out on Union, which if you don't know it is very typical, whatever that means, and with good food and good service and generally pleasant. (In other words, I was and am euphoric.) I ordered a glass of white wine and an "appetizer" of smoked salmon, and really did not feel like eating, and the tall-dark-handsome waiter looked horrified when he came to clear the

1. Family friends from Britain who visited MF in Marseille

table (It was 2 or so...). "I'll fix you a little bag," he said. "You've got at least three dollars' worth of lox right there...." So he did! Charlie and I will eat it for lunch. I like it better than he does... and isn't that fortunate!?

Well... great fun. Today is hollow and blissful, and tomorrow I start a real workout for four days. Then I draw up the moat, as Albert Kahn[1] quotes his mother... except for a small collection of you, perhaps MV, and you.

Ranieri has been given a 4-to-6-week deadline, but of course I hope he'll get out before then. He wants to see me soon, so Phyllis will take me down there for an hour tomorrow afternoon. In the morning I must shop for the next days, if I can get me wits together before then for a list... have to go to the eye-man in Sonoma too. My main problem about the weekend is to get one batch of people out, and the dishes washed, before the next ones come in. I think I'll bake a lot of apples. Etc. Must stock cream, butter, bread, salads. Etc.

Oh... I have finally found a good book about Provençal and Niçois food !!!! I'll get a copy for you. It's really good. . . .

About the clipping from the *Guardian*, which I'll send on to my friend who runs the Euthanasia Educational Council in NY... Mrs. Henry Levinson.

Of course I agree with the letter writer. Absolutely right. I hope she can bring it off for herself, and help a lot of other people in the same trap. I worry, though, about the prescription she purloined over forty years ago from her husband... it may be completely worn out by now, so that she will be cruelly tricked when she turns to it. (Lately the expiration date is marked on a prescription, but I don't think it was then, in England or anywhere.) Horrible thought.

One of her sentences should have been cleaned up, by the editors, because I am sure from the rest of her letter that she did not mean it as it reads. "It is suicide that I contemplate, but it could equally well be called euthanasia. I wish very much to avoid that word. People react against it instinctively. It does not matter whether they are intelligent or stupid, the first do not want to think at all of suffering, dread, pain, misery: the second are not able to think constructively and clearly."

I believe that in her second sentence she was referring to "suicide" and not "euthanasia." But... perhaps in England the latter *is* instinctively reacted against? I don't know. But I doubt it.

Well... it's mostly a clear and poignant statement, and I pray for the best escape, for Meg Murray first, and then the rest of us. (I do worry, though, about those tired old pills that have been such a comfort to her. The one prescription Dr. Frumkes ever gave me I carried for about ten years in my wallet, knowing I could have it filled if I really wanted to. It finally fell to pieces, but for a long time it was a comfort. As for what Hal promised me, I asked him twice in 45 years if I could have it on hand, and both times he said I was "not ready yet" (How could he know?)... and then he broke his word. Ah well. Oh, Frumkes's little white paper was for a very cautious dosage of a tranquillizer... wouldn't calm a baby, probably. Hal's "little black pill"

1. Glen Ellen friend and activist writer

was *it*. And I still feel angry that I don't have it... to cheer me for the next forty years?????)

I don't know why you'd feel "guilty" about our recent Late Hours! I thought they were fine. Let's try again. How about as soon as possible? After your visit, and then last night, I'm all for a bit of gentle carousing, even *à deux* by the fire. Meanwhile, on to this LAST WEEKEND... which I know will be interesting. It ends on Sunday afternoon, with about 19 people here to say a rivederci to Phyllis... all her children and their loves and children, and Joseph. Bread. Cheeses. Wine. Bourbon. 7-Up.

Then there is the clanking of the moat as I throw it up.

....

Last House, Glen Ellen, California   *31.i.77*
To: Norah Kennedy Barr

I arranged to go to SF at 2 this afternoon to see Genie and R, but at about 8:45 R called. His voice, as it has been lately, was high and thin and hoarse. (He said a few weeks ago that he sounded like a *castrato*, but of course it is not that.) He had to go to the hospital for a transfusion and would probably not be at home when I came.

"Don't worry," he said. I said, almost crossly, "I'm not worrying. I'm sad, that's all, I'm sad." He said, "Be sad. That's all right."

Genie came on the phone. She said the transfusion was necessary because the cobalt was destroying so much that R did not have enough blood left and was feeling faint. The transfusion would make him stronger.

Stronger than what? For what?

What a dreadful trap they are in!

But at least they are determined to stay together.

Madeleine Grattan wrote to me that for several days before Peter died in hospital she lived in the same room with him and they lay together and were in constant close communion. I hope that G and R can do this. And I have a strange (Is it?) knowledge that if I got down to SF before he died I would stretch out beside him on the bed, not touching but sending off waves of deep affection....

R would absorb them, Genie would come into the room and see our two long bodies lying there, and she would smile... not jealous or annoyed. Then I would get up, like a disembodied body, and drift out of the room and along to the sittingroom where I might pour a glass of vermouth and put it untouched by the long couch. Then I would go down the stairs to the kitchen and Geraldine would get my coat and I would float on further down to the car and be driven home, still lying quietly beside the almost vanished R.

This dream I may tell him... or her later... or never. But it is very strong and healthy, and perhaps some of it will get to him.

I am probably aware of R's dying because I have been so inadequate in other deaths, like Rex's, Edith's, Timmy's, David's. I stood by. By now I know a little better how to *be* there.

At first I felt that it would be an affront to the person's dignity to intrude. I was very shy. *Intrusion*... it was a private problem. But now I know how not to intrude. Or I think I do. I think I know how to be there without demands, and to offer what I have without demands too.

End of report on R.

....

Last House, Glen Ellen, California   *7.ii.77*
To: Marietta Voorhees

Oh dear... I/we forgot the shortbread! Well, auf wiedersehen, which I hope can be soon....

Dearest M... Charlie and I did take a little nap... very pleasant, as is mostly the case (By now in my "maturing," I sleep better in one hour in the afternoon than in six at night, an interesting change of metabolism or something... but only when I am alone here. If people are in and out, I stay upright and feel none the worse for it... and sleep just as usual at night. Can't win!).

Norah called to say she could come to lunch tomorrow. That's fine. I see her seldom... about like you.

You and she are the two people I would be most *left alone by,* if by some fluke I should outlive you. Of course I'd feel a profound and hopeless sadness if Kennedy should die... somewhat less shock if Anna did, because I'm accustomed to accepting some things about her. I'd grieve deeply for *children* if they were cut off. But basically you and Norah are the two who would leave me bereft and without a rudder, if you escaped before I did.

I have this all figured out, eh?

Well, I've been too much involved lately, I sometimes feel, with the departures of people whom I depended on, whether or not they knew it. I'm bored with death(!). And one revenge upon me is that I almost always love people older than I, so that it is natural for them to beat me to it. Georges... Leo[1]... etc etc.

I have a comforting feeling, though, that you and I may manage to leave at about the same time... like my Kennedy grandparents, who died within three weeks of each other (he in a rage against Jehovah who played him the dirty trick of being left to mourn for his wife, when he'd always assumed she would mourn for *him.* What an ego!).

Oh... one more thing about dying: my friend Alice Low told me that for almost a year she was actively angry and peevish and put out at June Eddy for dying. I was astonished by this, but I can understand it. Alice loved June and we all thought that we'd be nice old ladies together as much as possible (and more often than before). And suddenly June died! She walked out on us! Alice really *resented* this for a while. She was lucky to feel that way, instead of being greatly relieved for all concerned, as I was when my poor sister Anne died. (By now Alice has got out of her angry shock, and is simply regretful and lonely for June's presence.)

1. Georges Connes and Leo Marschutz

Enough of this, at least for now...

I'll keep some shortbread on hand for you. Margie[1] does not protest at making it for me, and it keeps very well in the icebox. Maybe you'd like a Batch, as she calls it???

What do *you* do at Langley-Porter[2]... scan a little Santayana, take a short snooze? I hope all this goes well, as I need not tell you. I remember that bi-weekly trips to Napa were often rather difficult, but perhaps that was because little Chris was with Anna and me. Or perhaps he made things *easier?* The air-conditioned Safeway was my salvation, with him. After her session, Anna was always very hungry....

....

Bouverie Ranch, Glen Ellen, California   *8.vi.77*
To: Alice Low

Dearest Alice:

Were you the person, or really the dear friend, I was talking to last Saturday evening when I simply said "rattlesnake" and hung up?

I know this sounds quite crazy, but the story is that I was talking to somebody I very much wanted to be with, at perhaps 7:00, when my two young English friends ran into the living room and said something like "Listen! Is that a rattlesnake?" I did listen, and of course it was, so I had to hang up right away, and by now I honestly do not remember who was at the other end of the line!

It was indeed a rattlesnake coiled ready to strike by the front door, but held at bay by my fine cat Charlie. The English kids were horrified. I knew Charlie would keep it there... fifteen years on the desert proved to me that cats are impeccable in this strange art... and I called David. He came right down and did the poor thing in with one clean shot. He's a very fine marksman. Later the foreman came down and buried the head and presented the seven or eight button tail to Solveig, who arrived with it in London the next day just in time to rattle it for the Queen's Jubilee.

End of story... except that I do remember you called and cannot for the life of me remember if it was you I hung up on. Ho hum. Age is taking its toll!

Are you behaving yourself? I want to come down soon again and see for myself, and you do not need to bribe me with fresh caviar!

Much love, beautiful Alice.

....

Last House, Glen Ellen, California   *16.vi.77*
To: Marietta Voorhees

Dearest M... Tried a few times to call you, with no answer. You're a gadabout.

Some notes here to answer... and always my thanks for the Clipping Service!

Re Sitwell and Vanguard... that Press has never been "vanity," but rather a small prestigious house. I think there is the other kind in NY in VANTAGE. This in turn

1. Margie Foster, Glen Ellen friend, secretary, and shortbread maker
2. A psychiatric hospital. Marietta accompanied a family member for outpatient treatment.

is not to be confused with VINTAGE, which is the paperback outlet for Knopf and Random House. Ho hum. (Sitwell's "Eccentrics" is a continuing delight, I think....)

Your definition of your inner life ("a tangle of doubts, disappointments, griefs & guilts bound in shadows and in miseries") is almost too dreadful to think about. Basically I'm inclined to refuse to accept it. But you made it! I didn't. If you honestly feel it to be a true one, I don't understand *how* or *why* you have put up with it for so long. For me, it would be intolerable, and I would either change the whole pattern violently and drastically, or end it.

You say "It could not be otherwise & I've come to accept the fact." (Bull shit, as your father might well say....) Then you go tra-la-la with a gallant smile, "laughter & the love of friends & wonderment at life's mysteries," and my delicious little pots of custard and so on. (More b.s.)

I was so relieved to see you looking well again when you came over the hills last week. Indeed, you looked better than before your last bout with "a cold." You may well have needed to rest your body, and since you resent doing it on your own volition your body simply decided for you to lie down for three days. Apparently you begrudged the whole plot! What's wrong with lying down now and then?

You say that "the common cold has in recent years been a very uncommon thing for me." I do not agree at all, and nobody else who knows you would do so... you totter around, spreading it generously, barking and blowing, *at least* once a year.

This time you had a slightly different strain of the virus, I suspect by your convalescence. (I suppose you take all the available "shots" to prevent such invasions, like Flu etc...??? One has not yet been arrived at for the C.C., of course....)

I'm not able to contradict George Abbott's dictum about an unhappy childhood as a prerequisite to being a great actor, but intuitively I disagree.

As for another dictum, a bastardized Biblical utterance, "Blessed is he who can receive," Dillwyn used that as one of his two quotes. The other was "Happy is he who can weep at a departure," and it took me a very long time to understand it.

Now about keeping friendships in constant repair, I didn't remember that good old San[1] said that, but I agree fully. I think you use the word "repair" differently from his usage.... I think he meant in fine state of healthy polish and condition, like a good saddle or a tight house. We think of "repair" as something needed by neglected articles.

And I have long believed that friendship, indeed any relationship that is worth the trouble, needs a lot of care and protection. It needs at times to be fought for, to survive. Strong as it may be, it can wither and die with neglect, overnight.

Sometimes people are unaware of the fragility of what they hold in their hands, and too late they wonder what happened to a good thing. Often they blame it on other people... or Time, or Space. Often they are right! But I myself know that if I want to keep a friendship alive, for my own soul's sake, I must work hard to do it, and never stop.

1. George Santayana

Now and then I've deliberately let a friendship end (die... wither... taper off...). Sometimes I've regretted this, bitterly or with resignation.

But to compensate, or perhaps comfort myself, I know that I have spent a great deal of myself on friendships that to onlookers might have seemed worthless or meaningless.

Well... as you can see, I simply don't agree with you about comparing a friendship to "a car... in constant need of repairs."...

A car is to be used and enjoyed, a means to an end. Friendships are not always enjoyable, but certainly they are not to be *used* and they are not a *means to an end*, at least in my own thinking. They happen, and they are to be savored for as long as they last. But keeping them alive and healthy, while a lot of deliberate work, is not a mechanical job.

You say that you have been "coasting," not "repairing," in our own relationship. I don't quite believe you, perhaps because I do not want to. But that is your problem, eh, Doc?

If you wish to think of all this in terms of cars that need "constant repairs" and so on, I must agree that any fine motor needs attention and tuning and cleaning and nourishing *all the time*. Ask any racing driver.

Or keep on driving small cheap cars that can be turned in every few years.

End of comments on a few notes that I haven't answered... and I'll wager you're glad!

I'm sure I told you that Norah and I hope to fly back to Washington on July 5, then on up to Bridgehampton on July 8, to return July 13. I feel that Norah may renege on this: we are involved in Anna's current manic phase, and Chris is at Jenner, and N is inclined to throw herself on the martyr's wheel, as you know. (I should be ashamed to say this. She is a gallant and generous person, and is taking almost the whole unexpected load of Chris's unexpected arrival etc....)

Well... we'll see. Meanwhile I'll keep trying to catch you in your den....

....

Last House, Glen Ellen, California,   *20.vii.77*
To: Paul and Julia Child

D*E*R*E F*R*E*N*S, the *most* d*e*r*e:

It is of course impossible that you've been in Plascassier and are now back in Cambridge, loins girded for the new show, and that I've not written some sort of message of hail-and-farewell-and-*bon retour*. I wish I had. I'm sorry I didn't. But I hope you know that I *meant* to, because my thoughts were very often with you, in many ways too complicated to go into.

To your good generous letter: Yes, it was very upsetting about Jim. But he came up here one day for lunch, while he was "resting" in SF before the summer courses in Oregon. Then I heard nothing. Then, a day or so ago, I heard that he'd fallen ill again up there. But nobody has *told* me... and there are people in his current entourage who probably would, sooner or later: Ms. Cunningham, Chet Williams, etc. So all I can do is agree with you, as I have for quite some time, that he "will one day go off in his own fashion." He knows exactly what he is doing... and I've rarely met anyone as quietly sure of all that.

Yes, I did finish the Marseille book,[1] and to my real astonishment Knopf wants to print it... in the face of the cold fact that no book of mine has ever sold until it was OP![2] In this day of tomes of everything from parapsychology and demonology to the art of assassination, it seems strange that anyone will want to read about a dirty evil old French town. Ah well. Publishing is no longer anything I recognize, except that there are still a few fools in the game.... (The book will be out in the Spring, d.v., and I'm already correcting pull-out pages... there is some repetition in it, because I wrote it in three batches....)

About the so-called nostalgia: I can't and wouldn't ask poor Mr. Shawn about it... but I was interested to get a "reject" for a story I sent... not fiction, but a reportage... about NOISE. I think noise is a current and increasing problem, and I wrote what I think is a pretty good thing about it... its effects on sleep, nerves, all that. The trouble was that it was Aix-en-Provence 1976 instead of Topeka Kansas of the same period. So the story, which Mr. Shawn wanted to run (he said) was killed.... Nostalgia, *la recherche des temps perdus,* a furrin influence....... I still think the noise-problem is current and universal. Ah well . . .

Julie, I liked the *New York* article very much, and Norah read it on the plane to Washington last week and gave it a full A for Axcellence. I've quoted parts of it a few times since... was on a "wine panel" on the 17th and at least five people talked ignorantly of *la nouvelle cuisine* and *la cuisine minceur* as one and the same, and I *pounced* on them, backed by you-yourself, *l'éminence grise.*

Do you know-think-believe that above the door to his kitchen filled with apprentices Escoffier lettered a sign, *FAIS SIMPLE...*? I do. Compared with what was going on in France when he was young, and then through his life, he *did*. But now he's mentioned as the last of the great "fancy cooks."...

Two friends went lately for a gastronomical adventure (14 days and they emerged fairly unscathed!) in Paris, and they paid up to 300 francs for a lunch, and relieved their palates and livers by eating quite a lot of Japanese food too... and they wrote blissfully that the most subtly beautiful delicious amazing marvelous thing they tasted was a sole poached with mushrooms and shallots and then sprinkled with crumbs of bitter chocolate. How about this? The idea shocks me. But they are very perceptive in their palates and education, and they *loved* it. Is it revolt against tradition? I really wonder and ask. . . .

In your neglected letter, Julie, you asked who Allanah[3] was/is... and by now you know. She's been very rich, on and off, thanks to family and a few "marriages," and

1. *A Considerable Town*
2. Out of print
3. Allanah Harper

M.F.K. Fisher: A Life in Letters

once published a small stylish "literary review" in Paris, as I understand it. She was quite beautiful and dashing, and a few years ago still was. I dislike her because she was very cruel and mean to Eda.... resented her for many reasons too complicated to go into. (*"A nest of women!"* as Janet Flanner once described the scene...) I'd like to know your impression of Allanah if ever you have the time to give it.

About cobalt and all related subjects: I feel so strongly, indeed violently, that it's best I not get into that. I'd write several more pages, all passionately opposed to chemical interference. . . .

And . . . I am also passionately opposed to a great deal of *surgical* interference. Ho hum.

Norah and I flew back to Washington on family business, two nights of temp. around 101 and almost equal humidity... it reminded me of Mississippi in 1964, and then we went up to Bridgehampton for 4–5 days to cool our souls at Eleanor's. It was a mini-jaunt, and I told nobody, in pure shameless self-protection, that we'd be "east of the Rockies.".... Maybe I'll go back in April and be *polite*, for a change. (I find that increasingly wearisome.)

Dear people, how are you? Are you pleased to be in Cambridge again? Was the stay at La Pitchoune revivifying? Are you excited about the new show? Is there any chance of seeing you, here, there, anywhere? Do you remember, now and then, that I love you both?

....

Last House, Glen Ellen, California   *14.i.78*
To: Norah Kennedy Barr

Dear N... you saw this flippant but quite good thing about current lingo in the *Chronicle-Examiner,* but the uncut original from the *NY Times* is better.

It's especially apropos because I "accomplished" another letter to a writer. I find this an increasing chore in deception and ambiguity. First I write what I think. Then I wait 24 hours and tone it down. Then I send off a polite meaningless unhelpful unwounding (?) note of bland good wishes. I hate the whole thing. Once lately I wrote to a rather good friend, telling her this process, and she wrote back to THANK me for not risking our relationship by any "rank candor." In other words, people send me their books to "criticize," but God fabbid that I do. Timmy was right. Ho hum.

Well, I did it again, although the book makes me gag quietly... I think I showed it to you...Joyce Goldstein's world-shaking new theory that since we must eat to live, we should enjoy it. She has put this shocker into current words, with lots of language and intuition and sensuality and meditation (while preparing the love feast) and high intuition while serving it, always with what Sis Kelly would call luvluvluv. Oh my. She finds big cocktail parties very "sensual" because of all the finger-food. She likes *diners à deux,* where one eats in the bedroom, ending with very smooth chocolate mousse in two goblets but with one spoon.

Well... it was a hard fight, Mom. And I too used my own form of Semantic Spinach....

Speaking of that. I was sorry you had to leave the table tonight, but I needed to give you the magic word THOMÉ.[1] ...

In the older days I'd have settled for La Palette, but not now... I mean, if the people at Thomé didn't want us. Not now. I wonder about that strange little village at the end of the bus-line. I don't know it at all... have walked there a few times... in May it might be all right...??? *(Chilly.)* (It *will* be chilly in May....)

Well... I do hope all this happens. And meanwhile I'm glad that I'll see you in a week.

<hr>

Last House, Glen Ellen, California   *12.vi.78*
To: Norah Kennedy Barr

THERE WERE NO MORE TWO PEOPLE THAT DIDN'T RESEMBLE EACH OTHER THAN MY SISTER AND ME....

(verbatim, Gladys G, UCBerkeley *summa cum laude,* 1917)

Dear N... This gem of syntax or whatever it is was inspired by what seems to be a continuing astonishment, that you and I are friends as well as siblings.

You know my own feelings about this situation, apparently so rare. The blood-ties are of course accidental, and the rest of it is a fine combination of circumstances, deliberately shaped for the most part, as must come about in most friendships.

I was lucky. It's that simple....

It was fine to talk with you. (This is now Wednesday, June 14! Yesterday was Sis's birthday, and when she became very mopey because there were firecrackers on July 3rd for mine, Rex and Edith erected a whole scene to comfort her (which it did, for years), that I'd been born one day before the 4th, but that *she* had been born one day before *Flag Day.* So Rex always put up the flag for her, so that she would not have some kind of bilious attack and throw up on the 4th.... That poor girl was gnawed by jealousies for most of her life. At the last they became cancers.) ...

As for today, I feel D*U*L*L, as the Childs would type it. Too many pecky jobs face me. Or do I mean picky? No. But they make me feel a little ploppy. Grudgingly I'm going up to the Ranch for lunch, because a man named Perry Rathbone will be there, and I enjoy him, and because DP-B begged me to help him out (he is not only w.e.a.k. but is very hoarse, so Luke[1] and I must entertain the old boy!). Rathbone is or was curator of the Boston Museum. But he knows a lot about wines and I'll turn him onto young Luke, and pray that D does not feel obliged to croak constantly into the dining-room from his bed.

Anne Lodge's Strawberry Preserves... a very good recipe. DO NOT BRUISE. I

1. The inn at Le Tholonet, a village near Aix-en-Provence, where MF, Norah, and Genie di San Faustino stayed
1. Young English houseguest of David Pleydell-Bouverie

wish I were making some. I haven't been to a so-called market yet... once to Shone's as depressingly nil as ever, but I did come away with scallions-celery-zucchini-romaine. Friday after I go to St. H. I'll hope to pick up some fruits.

No "cultural shock," as people now call the Homecoming Blues... it may be a question of age? We were there. Now we are here. Nothing is the same. Nothing ever can be. Therefore, why expect it to be? Etc.

Physically I find that I would rather snooze on my bed than work or eat or talk. I must control this. I sleep lightly and very pleasantly, any time of day or night. Oh... cough is vestigial. Throat still sore. Arthritic pangs and twinges are much stronger here than in Le Tholonet. End of report.

No news from Anne. Kennedy and family found San Diego hot, crowded, too military, but with good moments at Zoo and Sea World or whatever the local Marineworld is called. They almost starved... abysmally bad food, as I'd hinted to her. They went to Disneyland... one huge commercial thing, with a store between every tiny amusement thing, and all the flowers plastic in the Tropical Jungle that Jack and Bill Evans designed and were so proud of, and plastic elephants spraying colored water. It really sounds dreadful. K. says no child should ever be taken there again.

Rachel MacK writes: "I'm writing you from home about seeing you—my joy, your generosity, the funny supper. Part of the joy was meeting Norah. How I wish that I might be where I could see her often."

I agree. And Julie and Paul do too.

For Rachel I did the Author's Proofs of a short story[2]... the one I think is pretty good, that Mr. Shawn was puzzled by. He finally gave it his nod, when I defined it as a possible allegory. But he still stuck at my having the protagonist think of her son-in-law as a stud (among other things). I doubt that it is printed. We'll see.

Today (It's now about 8, a lovely evening indeed) I went up to the Ranch. It was quite funny, and I left as soon as we stood up from the table. The meal was odd: a kind of pâté (can) in a thick aspic (canned), with peeled poached Italian tomatoes on top; hot boiled beef served with a tray of four kinds of mustard, broccoli with a "Hollandaise" from Guerard's cookbook, made with no butter, no egg; nice little vanilla meringues served with a "*minceau*" custard made without butter-cream-eggs. Sanka. We drank an excellent Beaulieu Reserve Pinot Noir, much too red and heavy to be served at noon on June 14. David croaked at the head of the table. Perry Rathbone and his friend were panting over Luke, who naively devoted himself to me as the elderly and only female at the table. But all is well, and D will shed him tomorrow as he goes for 2–3 days of consulting with his brokers etc., and Perry and Friend have convinced Luke that he should stay in one of their studios instead of going to the YMCA. (With limited time in SF, he plainly prefers the latter, and as an Eton drop-out he shuns the gay world right now, but I think he's trapped.... His problem...)

Well, after that peculiar luncheon I came down the hill and snoozed for perhaps three hours! It was not the food, which I really did not eat. It was a *protest*, I begin to

2. "A Question Answered"

believe. Which will be stronger, my true enjoyment of living here or the protest? And why protest, anyway? Well, I'm going up on Saturday night because Maya and Paul will be there and so will Jane Childs, and I like all of them. But I think the symptoms are interesting: almost helpless sleeping, lack of thirst and appetite, disinterest in a really big pile of urgent mail. Ozma of Oz, wave your wand! (And I *DON'T* mean you, magic sister!)

One of my favorite correspondents told me that she wrote a weekly letter to her son, and that once he replied, "You don't *have* to fill the page each time, Mother!" And I don't either.

One thing stays in my thoughts: how patient and understanding you were/are about my walking slowly. It must have been plain EXASPERATING, and I thank you very much.

....

Last House, Glen Ellen, California   *17.vi.78*
To: Paul and Julia Child

D*E*R*E F*R*E*N*S indeed... dearest Julia and Paul...

When I got home, there was your heart-warming letter of April 28, and on *June 11* came the one written June 2!!!! I'll probably answer them very gabbily, because I'm finally coming out of a delicious and prolonged snooze after the trip, and I want to talk with you both. Just skip. Or put aside. Or reach for the wastebasket . . .

About the Marseille book... please don't worry if you really don't like it. We're bound to have seen and felt it... I mean the place itself... in completely different ways. For instance, I really don't think that Dufy watercolor is "right" at all... although I've seen others that I liked. Murder... I don't mean to compare myself with Dufy! But he had his view, and you have yours and I mine... and I wish we could all meet on the Vieux Port, say for lunch today!!!!

How very kind you are to suggest that we stay, or rather that I stay on in France, or however it was, some of the time in your delicious guest-room! That is F*R*I*E*N*D-*S*H*I*P. And you well know that (1) I'd give anything to stay on, and (2) that I'd give anything to stay again at La Belle Pitchoune. Thank you. I've tucked your invitation into a special compartment where I hide a few real comforters for lowlowlow moments, to give me strength and cheer. . . .

I agree with you that there will always be fishwomen in Marseille. They are a breed apart, as you once said... and in only some fifteen or so years I have seen older ones replaced by their daughters or nieces without a ripple. By now I even imagine that I can spot, on the Canebière for instance, up around Dugonnier, youngish girls (under 25) who are *destined* to grow into exact copies of the relatives they'll replace.

As for the healthy drama and strife and screams, I know of several people here who could use some of it, instead of pills and doctors. It's terribly frustrating to mind one's manners about native needs for hamming... tantrums are nonsense, compared with the daily show put on by every fishwoman worth her salt. I suppose it would be *impossi-*

ble to breed Anglo-Saxons into that mold, although I've read that some of the street-sellers in London have kept to their own rules for a couple of hundred years. Well . . .

Julie, I got a very nice letter from Mrs. Mauny Kaseburg, who told you in Seattle that she liked something I'd written. You suggested that she tell me, and she did, but she did not put any address on letter or envelope, although she asked if she could meet me in the Autumn. Do you by any chance keep an address list of your students? (Don't hesitate to say No to this pesky little request....) This one was leaving for her second summer as a *stagiaire*[1] at La Varenne. She sounds nice.

Oh... that flight... it was too long, but we knew it would be and chose it instead of getting involved in NY. We were exactly 24 hours in transit, from Nice Airport to Glen Ellen, and since neither of us can close an eye on planes, it took a little time to catch up with our local brain-clocks. The Air France Nice-Paris was the only civilized part of the basically non-human and tedious experience... at 10:30 A.M. a handsome steward *begged* us to accept a glass or two of Moët Brut, with four really delicious little sandwiches. From then on it was downhill all the way, and I do mean very down, including the wine served on United: Beringer's Pinot Noir and Chenin Blanc. Execrable, as we found on the flight SF-NY. We tried beer, but it was tasteless. So Norah looked at a movie she'd already seen, and read an old Simenon.

Oh... it was sad that you could not stay on in Nice, because (This is only one of the reasons, of course!) we went to the only really good meal we ate there. We ate quite well... but more for the fun of the people and the streets and so on than for the food, except for this one experience. The place is called Los Caracoles, but the Spanish decor etc is muted. It is called "la maison de la Paella," but the only indication Spaniards were dining there was that a lot of the tables had pitchers of sangria coming and going... constantly renewed. The service is of high quality, very discreet and unobtrusive. The dishes we ate were excellent, really. I especially liked a Moules à l'Estragon, served on a thick piece of toasted brioche bread, to my surprise. The sauce was light, thin, and perhaps too faintly flavored with tarragon, but plainly beautiful. And we growled about how the St. Moritz has one star and two forks and is really *nothing* compared to this Caracoles. Ho hum. What does one do? I suppose it may be a question of location. The basically over-sauced stodgy Swiss place is just off the Promenade, behind the Casino. Los Caracoles is at 5, rue St-François de Paule, on the corner very near the Marché aux Fleurs. Its business was moderately lively, but at the St. Moritz, where the tables are impossibly close together, people were standing in line. Ho hum again.

I've reported "the birth of a new star," in this case the half coffee and half instant, to Norah. I think the secret is that instant DOES contain monosodium glutamate. I have always suspected this. Salt used to be the answer, and I have a 1945 Army Cook's Manual to prove it again... and our very ancient French teacher at Miss Harker's School always tipped a pinch of tablesalt into her demi-tasse (She was really Austrian, however). I've heard that the Instant coffee people deny any additives.

1. Intern

Last House, Glen Ellen, California: 1970–1992

395

I never ate a skate wing… never even saw one! But I do love *raie au beurre noir*, which I suppose is a relative? Haven't tasted it, either, since about 1931 in Dijon… it was a "cheap" dish then, fortunately.

That cigale is tough, and loves any weather but sings best in full sun.

....

Last House, Glen Ellen, California   *14.viii.78*
To: Norah Kennedy Barr

Dear N… this is self-indulgent… I have a day alone, and am using it to be CON-STRUCTIVE and so on… but it was so nice to get your letter this morning that I really say je m'en fiche to some of the schedule.

By "schedule" I mean mostly the old letters. I'm creeping up on them.

I'm glad you liked the thing about the beachers.[1] Would you mind keeping it for me? I have only the one copy, and Frances Ring, the editor, asked me how I liked the illustrations, so I looked at them and thought they were well-intentioned and told her they were very nice, and that was my look at the magazine. So… I plan to write some more stuff for it, because I want to break away a little from the *NYer* set-pieces.

They take good hard work, but I like to do looser stuff too. I have a few things planned, in both patterns.

Yes, isn't it strange about how some tastes diminish, as you say! I've been thinking about that. I still love chocolate, but seldom eat it because it is simply not *good* enough. But wienies, no matter how charred… and squeezy buns… oh dear. Perhaps it is fortunate that I no longer climb down cliffs to the chilly sands! As it is, I feed a few potential Beachers here, and they are a captive crew! Tomorrow the two little Gilmans are coming down (SANS family) and they'll eat the Belorussian hodgepodge (I made a beautiful one this morning), and Zucchini Jalisco and Pan Fiesta and baked nectarines. They will drink Mrs. Fisher's Infamous Fruit-eze. And the next night four young friends will come (they are not vegetarians, like the Gilmans) and they will eat more Belorussian mishmosh and Pan Fiesta and barbecued chicken Mr. Pometta will do for me so that I can pick it up on my way back from St. Helena that morning (I get him to forget the sauce!), and a platter of fruits if I can get them tomorrow morning, if anybody up at the Ranch will take me to market. Etc. I'd still settle for "an oyster or a mussel." . . .

I get better news about the dreadful wildfire near you and Cazadero. And the sunset last night was not ominously beautiful… bright glowing beams all through the house, and a burning globe to the West, with black clouds that they seemed to pierce.

Of course I thought of other times. (Why not?) I thought of Helen W and how she arbitrarily snatched up the two small children and some dinners and took them up the hill, in Hemet… she didn't *ask*… she yelled to me that she was taking them. I knew they were all right. The next day Bill W came down the hill and said they were. I didn't see

1. A piece in *Westways*

them for three days, but I knew everything was all right, and better up there than down where we were, in the burned-out area.

It is interesting that my girls kept a clear memory of this strange happening. About 8 or 7 years later, when we were living in Aix at Mme. Lanes's, her neurotic daughter Henriette, who really hated being connected in any way with her mother's genteel boardinghouse, said to Anne and Mary, "But you two spoiled rich little Americans can never understand what it was like for me to have a grass fire burn to within fifty feet of the lower terraces of our country house... you do not know what reality is..." (etc). And Anne and Mary looked at each other and did not smile or frown. It was really interesting and heartwarming. The poor silly woman did not know what they knew. They did not mock her.

Really, I don't know what they remember(ed) of the fire itself, but they were very aware of its destruction, and when they and Donald and I resumed our lives at Bareacres, things were greatly changed for the children... of course, all of us. The temperature was different, without the underbrush, and the air with its smells was dry and very pungent, from the ashes and the desiccating creatures that had been roasted... snakes-moles-squirrels-toads....

It took about three–five years to recover the sage and yerba santa and cactus and all the little Spring flowers. I don't know about the animal-reptile return.

HOW DID I GET ON THIS??????? . . .

Until whenever (as long as it's soon!).

<hr>

Last House, Glen Ellen, California   *30.xi.78*
To: Norah Kennedy Barr

Dear N... this is the first time I've typed for almost three weeks, and it is not at all the letter I've had halfway into my thoughts to write to you. That was to be about how thankful I am that *you* are my sister and not anybody else in the world... on that line, anyway.

Today Mary Churchill took me down to see Dr. Haddad at 1:15, and he was pleasant, and asked me to come back in two weeks. He was a little disapproving of an area below my poor old navel that is not healing as fast as it should, on the interior... the exterior incision is fine.[1] He thinks it is because he worked too close to the old scar (1941). It's nothing to fret about... and I am unaware of it.

He was not pleased by my lack of voice, and made an immediate appointment with a "new" doctor, Boyajian, whom I saw after I left Haddad. He is young, swarthy and rather fat in a healthy way, very Armenian. I like what I suppose is his aura.

He found me unusually prone to gagging, so anesthetized my throat enough to get one-third of a look at my voice-box. He will have to look more thoroughly two or three more times, but assures me that the ordeal grows simpler for me.

1. MF had had abdominal surgery to repair adhesions from a surgery long before.

He explained with his hands how there are two vocal cords, etc. It's quite complex, really, in a basically simple way. And as far as he can now tell, one of the two cords, most probably my right one, is paralyzed. That explains the small wheezy voice... it is letting half the air go past, and is not joining the other cord to form the "box."

This, he says, is not uncommon in post-operative states, especially in females, whose cords are thinner and less rugged than in males. It is a clear state of trauma, and usually mends itself.

In my case it is not mending, as yet. It may do so fairly soon, or in up to six months, or perhaps never.

In the meantime I am to speak as little as possible, and then only person-to-person, "One to one."

He said he would like to give me a graduated 8-day treatment of a new cortisone derivative called Prednisone (5mg, beginning with 2 daily doses of 4 small white pills and ending with one pill twice a day... 44 in all, I think.)

I told him that I was given cortisone some 19 years ago, during a bout of what was called rheumatism but which I now call arthritis, and that I am strongly against its use except in dire need. He said that the whole structure of cortisone treatment had changed, even in the past two or three years and that he gave himself the same treatment he had suggested to me when he fell prey to poison oak, his private *Chien Noir*. (I always forget if it is oak or ivy....)

I asked him if I could skip it, and he said of course... that it would be a gamble, but that he could promise me there would be no side effects as far as he himself knew.

I decided to take it, and I'll start to use the stuff tomorrow morning. No coffee, tea, or alcohol... I'll miss the latter a little, since I have had two half-glasses of Vermouth and am sipping a third right now (I mean, during the past three days...).

I believe Boyajian that 8 days will not do much harm, and I want to gamble. We will know what good it may have done, in two weeks, and then go on from there.

I told him I had agreed to make a short speech on Dec. 20 to the first graduating class of the California Culinary Academy, and he said to call it off.

I asked him if, in case this seemed an indefinite condition, there would be any remedial work I could do, and he said he knew a very good voice therapist who might help. He also said that sometimes there are ways of bypassing and re-enforcing new muscles in the voice box etc. He said all that could be talked about when necessary.

Well, Mary got the little pills for me at the Dear Old Adobe, and just as we turned off Napa Street onto Route 12 I almost began to cry. I realized at once that I was in a flash of pure anger... rage... probably frustration too. It passed at once.

But for the first time since The Pickle I am having to be a little dogged about depression-apprehension-the blues. That is why I am telling you about it! (I most probably won't mail this to you. But because of my conditioning it is good for me to try to write about it, instead of pretending to listen to the radio and trying to be interested in short stories, and pretending to give a small damn about what to cook for my next meal.)

In a note from Riette a couple of days ago she wrote about how amazingly *resilient* I seem to be, and I have savored the word several times, liking to think that I may well be. I do seem to survive occasional set-backs well. *Tough* is another word for it, perhaps. Or is it simply "that ghastly super-ego" that you once said was always on my shoulders?????

Well, tonight I still feel tough and resilient, but little sneaky wisps of dismay creep past all my barriers, and I wonder how I could stand to speak for the rest of my days in this breathy croak... how I could ever dictate letters or material... what dear little children like Lukie and Oliver and Alex and Chris and Sylvie would think of me... how people I love to talk with could sustain even tolerable chitchat with me....

I feel stricken, alone in a cold wind... cut off....

All this is a passing period of apprehension, of course. We'll see what happens next.... And long before the 8 days of pills are up, I may have back my old light alive voice again....

An interesting thing, that reminded me of the night the roof blew off and I found myself planning exactly how to have my hair cut... by whom... how to "set" it by myself... how I would look: when I got Mary's marketing put away, and rested for half an hour, I went right to the sharp scissors and solemnly cut about five inches off the thin yellowed tail of my hair! In my hand it looked like a wisp of smoke or fog, and in spite of its thinness my head does feel lighter and better.

I'll read this in the morning, and most probably destroy it and then perhaps telephone... except that there's nothing much to report, besides the fact that I'm to go back to Haddad and the throat-man in two weeks. I know you'll kick at the use of cortisone, but I've decided to do it, for *eight days only.* The man assures me that is all that will ever be given... a yes-or-no deal.

End of Poor Me talk...

The night you left, Charlie outdid himself, and brought in a very large rat which he left stiff and almost intact right in front of the bathroom sink. He had eaten one bite out of its neck, so it was obviously poisonous. Then he'd been very sick three times in the livingroom! It was really quite a mess, and I was glad he waited until you got away. (I bend like a willow, thanks to that workout and my native *resiliency*....) . . .

Tomorrow I'll assemble a good chowder for lunch on Saturday, when I also hope to get rid of some of that quince jam and a few muffins. I wish you were going to be here... I think you'd like the Fillins as much as I think I too would... if you get me (I hope they are talkative!).

Suddenly (Here I am back again on the subject I thought I'd settled) I feel like getting out some old tapes I used for the Marseille book, to listen to the way I used to sound! It's childish. Tomorrow I may even do it. Tonight it would compound my lurking dismay, I think.

Instead I'll go in and pour about 2 more ounces of rare old Lejon, and make something faintly tasty from leftover eggplant before I eat a loverly warm baked apple with arf-n-arf. I may listen to see if anybody got murdered or blown to bits this afternoon, or I may finish an old *New York.* The cover of *Newsweek* is covered with peaceful relaxed corpses in Jonestown.

Monday Richard or Mary[2] is coming to take me to town to buy woolly nighties for my two girls... and perhaps something bright for the front door... two little red-pepper trees maybe? Really not even ivy is very happy there... absolutely no sunlight. (Of course that garage is shamefully filled with neglected books... my full fault... I pulled them out for things I may never write for the *NYer* and now they won't fit back on the shelves! Books SWELL, I swear, when they are lying around.)

Let's talk about Christmas. If you suddenly have a delicious invitation to spend it here or there, I *trust* you, dear Noni, to understand that I am not only extraordinarily resilient most of the time, but am eminently adaptable to being alone. The more traditionally crowded the day, the more pleasurably I savor it by myself... putterputter, old records to play, a bottle of champagne to sip over ten or 12 hours.... So... (Naturally I'd rather do it with you, in any way indicated! But you are quite truthfully the only alternative.... Odd thought, really: you *are* the only living person I'd consent to spend Christmas with!!!!!!)

On that high note....... (I no longer feel shocked, either... everything is all right, for the next eight days anyway....)

....

Last House, Glen Ellen, California   *2.i.79*
To: Evan and Judith Jones[1]

PS... Judith... misdirected envelope to office... gabby letter, for leisurely & even bored look later...

Dear Judith and Evan... I meant to write to you on New Year's Eve, as well as several times before. Time and the Unforeseen crept up on me....

There is much to tell you about. The main thing in my mind is that this new year be as you most hope for, in every way, for both of you and for your loved people.

To two good letters, with all my thanks:

I'm glad you opened the Vella Jack. I find that it holds well, kept cool. I like it, grated or, with a strong wrist, slices at the end of a meal with fruit. It is also very reliable for hearty cooking.

Evan, I don't think you went to the small Vella factory when you were in Sonoma. It is very simple, and I hope they keep it that way. But the Sonoma Cheese Factory is so blazingly successful that I tremble... by now they are selling Italian and French things made with processed Brie mixed with currant jelly, etc etc! They continue to turn out very good decent Jack, *but...*

Don't give my recent interruption ("This last sudden siege of illness," as you put it) another thought. It is in the past, except for making me feel a little panicky about

2. Charmoon Richardson, MF's driver, and Mary Churchill Studer, mutual friend
1. Judith Jones, Knopf editor

working to finish the Japanese thing.[2] My voice has improved greatly in the past week, and I'm to see the throat-man tomorrow. I'll confess I felt depressed, now and then, to think of voice-therapy and so on. Now I feel confident that I can escape that. There is still no volume at all, so that I can't yell insults at Charlie (or call across the room), but I can forego all that as long as I don't wheeze and squeek!

In shorter words, I've been very lucky.

And *of course* I knew that you, and a few other very special people, were praying for me!

(Yes, I'm "resilient," too... or at least I now assume so. At the time one is being all that, one's too busy to know about it! A few people have told me that it was plain I was fighting, and that my "will to live" was strong, and so on, but all I was doing was trying to hang on to my human dignity!)

So... by now things are fine again. I'm ignoring piles of mail, and long lists of thank-you notes after Christmas, and all that, and except for this ABSOLUTELY ESSENTIAL LETTER I'm sticking to the Japanese job.

It will be fine to get it off my back. It's really very hard to keep it straight-line gastronomy.... I keep shooting off on "asides and footnotes"... everything from chauvinism both national and male, plumbing, even toothpicks (They might qualify?). I'm trying to write as a naive (dumbdumb) awkward Westerner... it would be presumptuous to pretend to be anything else, after two weeks in Osaka! I have piles of elegant books that have been sent for me to study in depth, about everything from Japanese industrialization to the Zen symbolism of the Tea Ceremony, and I refuse flatly to open even the dust jackets until I've finished this job. I want to stay naive.

Thank you for telling me about Miss Scott-Maxwell![3] I agree with you that it is she who will know when to move on. She is so highly evolved or whatever the word should be that she is in full control of things like her need to breathe, or her will to keep her heart pumping a little longer.

Many people study to learn this art or trick, and some of them do, or at least I have read so. Myself, I've known three, one man and two women, who lived a long time and decided for themselves when the right time had come to get out of the trap... or to withdraw....

Il Maestro's Miss Whiteside reminds me very much of Rachel MacKenzie's talking about her long work with Mr. Singer[4] (And what a reward that Nobel must have been to *her*...!), and his real happiness with a very young secretary who could not even type English, much less Yiddish, but who brought a happy sparkle to the old man's eyes.... He knew how to make her giggle happily, and they were fine together, and Rachel approved.... (I don't know about Mrs. Singer... am sure Mrs. Rubenstein is well conditioned by now... sat next to her and the children several times during the Festi-

2. MF was offered a trip to Japan by her friend Shizuo Tsuji in exchange for her writing a foreword to his *Art of Japanese Cooking*. She invited Norah to accompany her (October 1978).
3. A. Florida Scott-Maxwell wrote a book about old age and dying, *The Measure of My Days*.
4. "Il Maestro" was pianist Artur Rubinstein; "Mr. Singer" was writer Isaac Bashevis Singer.

val d'Aix in about 1963 or '64, and she was a nice poised middle-aged wife-and-mother....)

And yes. SPEAKING OF INDESTRUCTIBLES: I've seen Jim[5] a couple of times and he and Barbara Kafka plan to drive up for lunch while they are working in SF.

First he came (my fault for mentioning he was in town) to the first graduation from the California Culinary Academy, where I was to speak. He made a graceful impromptu speech, and of course the kids were thrilled that he was there. Then he and Genie di San Faustino and Chuck Williams came for a long quiet serene lunch on the 30th. And then he called rather late on New Year's Eve... was with Chuck and Chuck's partner Mike, old friends... the three gentle kind somewhat kinky gentlemen sitting alone with a cat or two after a good dinner... feeling withdrawn but still sentimental. Chuck is the youngster of the three, worn and wan but a very tender person; Mike is a fastidious alcoholic authority on several periods of antiquities, and very important in art circles in SF when he is not in the luxurious clinics Chuck patiently tucks him into... (Only Sylvia Townsend Warner could write about such a banal situation, not for publication...).

Well, I don't think Jim looks at all well. I don't think he *feels* well. But he is indomitable, and continues his customary wild pace in SF as if he were a lusty fifty and not a tired 75-or-so. I noticed that he talked compulsively about what he'd said to the Princesse de Broglie in Harry's Bar in Venice in 1952... that sort of thing, that had nothing to do with what Genie and Chuck and I might be saying... he *gabbled* a lot, but it seemed to keep him feeling good, and all the time he was the same quick-minded and loving friend... it was as if his real self and his exhausted but still worldly self were standing side by side, to keep him from falling into a quiet torpid death... one on either side, propping up his tired old body.

I'm sorry that Evan's piece was cut. I wish it could have gone straight to the *NYer* as a Profile. Probably there is no chance of that now. But could not a new arrangement be made, for a candid and lengthy thing with Jim? I know that a lot has been written about him, often corny. But Evan is the one who could leave us a definitive portrait.... Jim was elated when we met at the Academy, and said he'd send me a copy of what the *Times* did. But later, up here, he was concerned only with Evan's feelings, and he did not mention sending the story. Oh dear. I'd like to see it. But what can be done about a truer version? (I know I shouldn't bother either of you about this, but it does bother me very much....)

Judith, I'm so sorry your sister has been in trouble. I hope things will be better, in every way, and for all of you. Yes, such dreadful things in a family life can work wonders of awakening new love and fanning tired embers....

(Small case-in-point: Norah and my younger girl Kennedy were brought together while I was in the hospital in Sonoma, after years of "estrangement" that had been especially painful to Kennedy. It was all because she married a man who was antago-

5. James Beard

nistic to everyone in her family and to everything in her life that had happened before he entered it. K. is a completely dedicated woman, and gave up most and at times all of her close family ties. She is very happy with her husband, or at least she loves him devotedly, but even so she felt sad about the deliberate estrangement. Norah, older and more philosophical (?) about what can happen in lives, perhaps fretted less. But suddenly I was lying like a drugged animal in a glass box in Sonoma, and there the two women were, drawn together by something much stronger than any other tricks of Time and Circumstance....... Now that I am well and strong again, they may never really meet again. But I know that Kennedy was given new strength and confidence while they were together.)

I do rattle on, with you two! Here I am, just re-reading your letter of November 5....

I didn't mean to be secretive about going to Japan. It happened slowly enough... I think I agreed to do the introduction for my friend Shizuo Tsuji before N and I unexpectedly sailed off for another 6 weeks in Aix. The whole project sounded crazy, really. I did not quite believe it, I expected N to be horrified when I said Shizuo wanted her to come along, but all she said was "When do we leave?"

She was a tower of grace and strength, and I could never have done the strange adventure without her. We were together all the time, and slept in the same luxurious rooms every night, and so on, and never got in each other's way except with mutual amusement. It was really a very exhausting schedule we followed, and neither of us wants to repeat it. But we are more than glad that it happened. We agree that if we could do it in exactly the same almost regal manner, we might possibly consent to a shortened replay. Otherwise neither of us ever wants to go back to Japan... or at least for a long time.

It is not so much because of the great cultural gaps between us, and of course the language barrier (which I would remedy with some superficial ease if I had to be there long... for the polite phrases at least), as because of the latent paranoia everywhere. The country is simply *too crowded*. If the people were not kept in a state of almost military discipline they would go berserk and tear each other to pieces, I feel absolutely sure. And that is not a good feeling to have. We did see moments of easy relaxation, especially one morning at the start of The Week of Health and Strength, when 2200 of the 2600 students of l'École Hôtelière Tsuji gathered for a track-meet and picnic at a public playing-field in Osaka. The students were in organized "clubs" with banner and club-colors and so on, and they competed, and really they seemed to be having a fairly jolly relaxed time, at least compared to when we'd seen them in the demonstration-theatres and halls at the school. But first they sprang into rigid ranks, each man and woman in proper place without confusion, and went through routine setting-up drills, which they do all over Japan every morning... just like the Strength Through Joy things I once watched in Hamburg just after WW2, with bomb-pits all around and the half-starved workers shivering in their blue-white skins. The young Japanese were strong and healthy... schools like Tsuji get the pick of the crop, but even the school-kids, who always march two-by-two, look very strong.... Well, for the track-meet there was a certain relaxation, but even there in the bright October air I sensed that the young people were completely disciplined to obey any command. It was like *Dr. Strangelove.* Who will press the button? If these young students, or the 8-plus millions in Osaka or the 13-plus millions in Tokyo, or the 100-millions everywhere in a space smaller than California, were told to dance-laugh-march-sleep-kill, that is exactly what they would do, without question. They are not robots, like many of the highly disciplined Germans before the last wars. They are simply *overcrowded.* They are latently half-frenzied half-maddened by the weight of all the people around them.

Most of them must commute to work. Most of them work in huge buildings and enormous corporations. And in order to get to work, which they are taught to worship, they must push and shove themselves ruthlessly onto probably the most elaborate transportation system in the world, and then shove their ways back to their incredibly cramped living quarters. They live on the edge of mass murder-rape-genocide, I honestly believe.

Well, I could not stand it, this lurking paranoia. Neither could N.

(Here I am proving that I cannot be trusted to talk about Japan, except by putting on glasses that let me mention only the cooking! I get up on a soap-box all too easily!) . . .

Oh Judith... what a heavy job, the FFarmer![6] I do hope all goes well. . . . When I was growing up, one could always tell an Easterner by what cookbook he relied on (among other things!): An Easterner read Farmer, and a Mid-Westerner swore by Mrs. Simon Kander, and so on. By now I suppose Mrs. Rombauer has brought the country more or less together... and of course Julia C.... Very few people west of the Alleghenies will question any modernizing you've done... and how could you possibly repeat some of the directions? Well, I hope the job hasn't tired you too much. You're the only one who can really know where you must put the most of yourself....

(About the Marseille book, a really tiny whistle in the great orchestra of FFarmer... I'm glad people still want to buy it. I keep getting whines that no bookstores have it in stock, but what can *I* do? Except be glad people do want it...)

I've been thinking about the idea (yours and Lescher's[7] and mine) of putting together some things, printed or not, about Provence.[8] There are quite a few. I still think I could clarify (I mean *edit,* I think) the longish view of Arles, and I have several more things about the area that I have never sent anywhere... and perhaps some things could be reprinted, like "The Oldest Man" and a couple of other things from the *NYer.* Well. First comes Japan. Then I'm going to do a small piece for the University of Calif. about words in gastronomical writing... something like that. Then I owe a couple of articles to magazines. *THEN*... it might be fun to assemble some stuff.

I don't know about making a mishmosh... Switzerland, France, Japan. Right now

6. *The Fanny Farmer Cookbook* was revised by Marian Cunningham and edited by Judith Jones.
7. Robert Lescher of Lescher & Lescher became MF's agent after Henry Volkening's death and a short stint with Tim Seldes.
8. Judith Jones encouraged MF to put together collections of her stories and articles. This was a preliminary discussion, which may have led to *As We Were.*

it sounds rather opportunistic or something.... But I'm really thinking all the time, not just coasting along on Japanese no-nos!

Meanwhile I'm thinking very much about you both. I miss seeing you. You are dear to me. When can we meet again? Please give my love to your mother and Aunt Hilda.

....

Last House, Glen Ellen, California   *2.ii.79*
To: Lawrence Clark Powell

Dearest Ghuce...

You do seem in a moody confusion about whatever it is you are writing. You must and will get out of it.

Of course I'll read whatever you send me. By now you know that you may not like what I tell you about it. (I hope you'll send it anyway.)

I think it a little late to "agonize over the pain it will cause Fay."

If you really do not want to hurt Fay, stop writing.

You say that you can't write any more... so the logical question is to ask you if you finally do not want to hurt her.

I think you will continue to do both, as long as you live.

("Which comes first, the chicken or the egg?")

Why should you consider withdrawing this new book, unless it is that you actually do want to stop hurting Fay?

When in doubt, don't. (Another cliché, but a useful one...)

If you are "upset," it is because you are in doubt.

Fay is a reticent and subtle person. Self-revelation is to her a private thing to live with. Public revelation of "what has moved ((you)) the deepest and most" is distasteful to such a *private* person.

You want to tell the whole world, the movie-goers, anyone who will listen, that you felt this or that, kissed this or that, penetrated this or that piece of flesh or poetry or painting or music or sunset or toasted bread.

By now you should have learned how to eat the cake and have it too. You've practiced the craft into an art, Ghuce.

So go on exactly as you've chosen to go, and live with whatever guilt you can still call up from your fires, and send me the troublesome typescript if you still want my cold-blooded view of it. . . .

Love

....

Last House, Glen Ellen, California   *13.v.79*
To: Genie di San Faustino

Dearest Genie... thank you for calling. I loved to hear your voice, even if it said I wouldn't be seeing you today.

Don't worry about our not meeting as often as we'd both like to. It's partly "circumstance," with things like gas shortages and weather. It's also because I don't drive. And it's *also* because Time is making the life you had here at the Ranch dimmer (and perhaps more merciful and less actively painful about its having stopped)... and I was in a small way part of all that, so that any urgency about keeping me as part of it is dimming too. This is one of the facts of life.

Another fact of your life and mine is that we are almost surely the kind of friends who will always stay that way, no matter how long we have to wait between real meetings. This is all part of what Ranieri left you (and of course me too!), and he acted as a kind of cement for us, and always will.

So, between Ma Bell and my typewriter (you call when you feel like and I'll write in the same way), we'll stay in some sort of unquestioning *rapport* as long as that mysterious cement stays strong.

At least that's how I feel.

If you married again and found yourself in Singapore, or I pulled up stakes and settled into a shabby villa outside Le Tholonet, or or or... we'd still be "in touch," and if we met on the street in London after years apart, it would be timeless between us.

Well, I'm being rather long-winded about what I think we both understand without words!

Today is beautiful indeed. Dr. Stanford decided to come at 5 this afternoon instead of ten this morning, which is fine with me... it means sherry instead of coffee, that's all. And of course it will be really HOT then instead of just plain lovely.

It's wonderful to have the house wide open, and no heat going. And I'm making Charlie's food, which is rather stinky, so I'm glad to have all the windows open. (It's not stinky at all if you like meat, but I'm increasingly a non-meat person... no dietary or religious principles involved... simply don't *like* it....)

I'm going to do quite a bit of re-write on the Japanese thing... don't have to, of course, but think it will be better if I do, since it's been accepted. Ho hum.

So I want to get rid of it before I go out to Norah's on May 22... and should be pondering on it now instead of writing to you.... (I wish you could hear the birds here today... many meadowlarks this year, and quail, and lovely trillings that I don't identify....)

....

Last House, Glen Ellen, California   *21.v.79*
To Paul and Julia Child

D*E*R*E Julie and Paul....

Of course I'm pleased and amused that you liked what I once said about Gaspacho.

Nice coincidence... I was going to tell you, when next I wrote (which is *now!*) about a new thing I did with the basic mishmash... I've tried it a couple of times, and really like it.

Some people were coming from Tokyo (not

... next morning... here I was interrupted (telephone) and turned on the radio and learned (1) that Boston was in an electrical blackout and (2) that 5,000 San Francisco gays were storming the City Hall.[1] Needless to say, I spent the rest of the night listening. In a few hours you and the Harvard University hospital had the lights back on... but things stayed very ticklish indeed in SF, and they still do. The air is filled with pleas for peace/calm/reason and so on. Issues have been confused, to make an understatement. It seems now to be turning into a direct confrontation between the Police Dept. and the homosexual community, using the feeble conviction of a confessed murderer as an excuse. Ho hum. Today was scheduled to be a "celebration" of Harvey Milk's birthday, but it's not at all the way he would have wanted it.

So... the people coming from Tokyo were not connected in any way that I know of with Tsuji's book... the man is chief coordinator of the current show touring this country called *Japan Today*, head of the American Studies Dept at the U. of Tokyo. His wife is a teacher and writer, and they are probably the most "liberated" and supportive Japanese couple I have met.

But I always feel shy about serving a meal to Japanese. And once one of them told me of how he still remembered a gaspacho I'd served on a very hot day some twenty years before. So I had some good beef stock and plenty of herbs and scallions and mushrooms and some Italian tomatoes, and I produced a really nice thing, of a bed of coarsely chopped watercress and a lot of a very stiff aspic loaded with paperthin vegetables. It was pretty, and refreshing, and very stimulating too. I used Knox's gelatin of course, and made the aspic very high in seasoning and very stiff. We ate a huge platter of it, with two kinds of bread and then strawberries and cookies. (I kept wanting to serve some kind of cheese, when I was pondering the menu, but that's simply impossible with the Japanese, no matter how sophisticated they are....)

So... full circle with the gaspacho, and I'm eager to know what Rosie[2] did to turn it into a salad... must have sent me an ESP wave!!!!!

Today I'm going out to Jenner for two nights and a spot of work. I get a lot done there... ignore the telephone and so on. Norah's coming for me on her way home from a stay down on the Peninsula before her grandchildren go to Zurich for the summer with their Swiss mother.

I *hate* to think that you won't get back to La Pitchoune before the end of the year.

....

Last House, Glen Ellen, California   5.*vi*.79
To: Norah Kennedy Barr
    Dear N... I feel like being in touch with you, and don't want to call, for various reasons we both know. So I'll tell you about a very strange little adventure I had, two mornings ago. It is in my thoughts, not distressingly at all but with wonderment.

1. Following the shooting deaths of Harvey Milk and Mayor Moscone
2. Rosemary Manell, friend and culinary assistant of Julia Child

On the outside upper edge of my toilet bowl... no, I mean my washbowl in current lingo... the edge across from the spigots, there is an overflow safety-out. It is about three inches long and $3/4$-inch high, and does not show unless one bends over the bowl at a certain angle, facing the mirror.

So I was bending at that angle, splashing cold water on my face in the early but bright morning, and in the mirror when I raised my head I saw a little black face peering at me from the outlet.

Of course I was amazed, startled, taken aback... not scared. I looked hard at the face, and then verified it by leaning into the bowl and looking outward. It put one little armlike tentacle out beside its cheek, and kept staring at me. It was plainly alive.

I touched it, and it was indeed cold and slimy, but it did not pull away.

I got a toothbrush from the basket on the counter, and put it in beside the little thing. It was stuck there, and I had to push and manoeuvre, but I finally got it almost unstuck and then put a towel over it and pulled it out and took it to the big fern in the garage.

It made a dead heavy sound when it went into the fernstalks. I thought that I had probably killed it, pushing and pulling it through the safety slot, but in about an hour it was out of the green shade and heading for the heat. It moved slowly, and I still think I hurt it.

It was definitely not a newt, nor was it like any frog I have ever seen. It was about $1^{1}/_{2}-2''$ big with four legs and no tail and a somewhat froglike head. It seemed very sluggish, and stayed cold to the touch and as if skinless. It was more black than anything, but I felt that born in the right place it might have a greenish spotted skin.

Well... the rest is sad: an unexpected visitor half-stepped on it as it staggered out toward sure death on the blacktop, and we looked at it and it was still moving, so I let it go on. Then the next morning Margie came to type and said that Charlie had made a little mess in the garage, and he'd dragged it in and perhaps eaten a nibble but left most of it in a small but definitely red-blood smear on the floor, with two little legs sticking up as if in labor.

That is the end of the story of Whatever It Was that came out of an overflow pipe in my bathroom that is almost never used. And of course I wonder about its conception, wherever that was, and its life, and its final desperate escape into a smear on my cement floor. Plainly it had to get out of whatever it was in. How did it feed itself, to manage to grow as much as it did? (Why?)

Well.... in a half-hour or so Portia Hume and Mrs. Crum will come for lunch, which I'll serve to them after Bouverie flits down to salute them with a small dutiful vino. MV came yesterday. She seems completely fed up with PBH (Portia Bell Hume) as an extremely dull woman. She said Portia had ALWAYS been dull, and I asked her why she'd always been such a devoted friend then, and she said she licked their boots (Portia's and Sam's). So I said that perhaps now MV must pay for this fifty years of lip service. She did not like my opinion.

　　　　　　　　　　　　　　M.F.K. Fisher: A Life in Letters

Of course we all do this, and I am acceptive of a lot of people who bore me silly, because they are important to my getting a book done or published or something like that. But I don't make lifelong pals of them. This is what MV seems to have done with Portia, and now she is really trapped. Or so she *feels*. It is an interesting situation.

Meanwhile she accepts all of Portia's invitations to lunch and dine here and there.

I've been rather belligerent lately, first about saying NO to a few proposals (professional, not amorous), and then to my editor at *Westways*. The June issue has a thing by me which does not "read" like me at all, so very unwillingly I checked it with my script and found it rewritten in at least five places, with prose that (as Julie said about the word *margarine*) would never pass my lips... and countless style changes. I don't mind about the latter. Each magazine has its own style sheet, and mostly I go with it. BUT if an editor wants my own way of writing and accepts it, then I want it to be printed that way. Otherwise she can simply hire writers on her staff. So... regretfully I had to write to Frances Ring, whom I like personally too, and tell her I was whimpering. I wonder what will happen. (Meanwhile I'm not going to finish the story for a July 1 deadline that I'm somewhat dully doing for her.) Well... all good for the adrenals, I'm told! But I myself prefer not to bother about such things...

Petunias bust out all over. They smell spicy now and then. I love it.

....

Last House, Glen Ellen, California   *4.ix.79*
To: Judith Jones

Dear Judith:

This will be too long and wandering for an office letter, I suspect, so I'll send it to you at home.

It was really fine to get your call this morning. Thank you. I'm sorry my careless silence worried you... but it's very nice to know someone who does worry. (!!!... egocentric!)

I've been very remiss about letters. I find this current dusty job of going through old material[1] very absorbing. A lot of it is too faded for me to read. This is as well... a lot of it is not worth reading. Yes, it's wonderful that the Schlesinger ladies want us to clutter their shelves! I really can't believe it, but am being good about sending boxes off, now and then. I can understand the value of Julia's work, and certainly Fannie Farmer and all your decisions about her should be there. But I don't understand the possible research value of somebody like Fisher. I do not question, by this time... simply bundle up stuff and notify poor Elizabeth Wector,[2] who comes up and then has it correctly baled in San Francisco and sends it off. (She is a Good Girl... very devoted to her many causes.)

1. To prepare for the Schlesinger Library
2. A friend who persuaded MF to donate her material to the Schlesinger

Well, I meant to get rid of all the Marseille material before I started to dig for buried tidbits about other places, and then decided I'd better jump right in and let the untidiness take care of itself. So... poor Elizabeth can wait to get the next batch of boxes....

And meanwhile I do thank you and your Assistant from the heart, for sending your old material to Cambridge. E. would too, if she knew! It saved us a lot of extra bother, out here. . . .

Yes I'm glad there was some champagne for me. I drank it with you. (I've been sent fruit, and flowers, and wine, but never ALL TOGETHER! *Wow.*)

I appreciate (in *many* ways, I mean), what a job it is to list the published material, and I feel almost apologetic to your poor Assistant.

This reminds me that Eleanor Lowenstein of the Corner B.S. is helping one and perhaps two people to do "official" Fisher bibliographies, and she might be of help in a tight place. Her client is a private collector, but a young university librarian in, I think, Claremont or Pomona in California, is also in some contact with her.

Your report about #4 girl is unforgettable. I send her all my wishes for finding what she wants. Certainly she needs your blessings. She must adapt to such a small new world... an island in every way. But a bigger one would have its own insularities. I know about three young people who have made inter-racial marriages here in the university cultures, and they have been really fine for awhile and then have been dissolved, not because of family differences. But I have one good friend, Frances Miller the artist in Sag Harbor and Bridgehampton, who was married for many years to an upper-class Haitian. Her family froze her out. His family froze, too. And after some two decades, the man and woman parted, because they could no longer run away. It was very sad, to me. And then there is Decca Mitford's girl who married a fine young Black politician... two darling little boys... there developed what Frances has called a racial weariness, and now they are apart. Oh dear.

I want to cut out a lot of such barriers between people. Perhaps these shy attempts will gradually crumble them. I don't think it is as complicated for mixed-blood children now as it was a century ago....

It's a wonderful idea to write about bread, for children! I would like very much to see it (and *read* it!), if that is possible. A friend brought me a round "country loaf" of white bread a while ago, and it tasted odd after the sourdough I now use, but I froze some of it and it is *delicious.* I haven't baked for several years: the kneading is beyond me. But I do make fake-breads with a biscuit-dough base that doesn't need much hard work... poor substitutes but useful. Yes, there are not only spores in the woodwork! There are invisible spirits at work in yeast itself, and when they start playing with heat and cold and lurking bacilli and human megrims, they can become very powerful.

Rosie Manell came up last week. She's painting hard again. She's *good,* when she's good. Now there's a woman who eats like a big healthy frisky young horse... she's trying so hard to keep her weight in control that I devised a rather hefty lunch that *altogether* added to about 350 calories, and she ate 325 of them... I simply sat back and watched her as she galloped through the fields of watercress and alfalfa sprouts and so on. She drank floods of my good tap-water, and a couple of glasses of thin white wine. She drew intensely for about four hours. It was interesting to watch. What energy! What voracity!

You said in one of your letters that the '40s seemed to have been a "prolific time" for me, and I thought about that. Yes, they were. I made a little list in my head about some of the happenings. It may interest you in one way or another:

In 1940 my husband Dillwyn Parrish and I had been evacuated from Switzerland and were living on desert land in So. Calif. He died. I went to work at Paramount in Hollywood for one year... broke contract. Married, had two daughters, divorced. Wrote for three magazines at once. Published *Wolf* and a couple or more books... one so-called novel. Did translation of B-S. Started partial collapse. Etc.

It really was a strange decade, and I don't quite believe it, by now. I learned a lot and went headlong into things like having children and doing anthologies and so on that I would never consider now (if I could!). I coped with three monthly deadlines, right through babies and all that. When I was married to Donald Friede he tried to play Svengali to my short-lived Trilby, and I did a lot of writing at his request, mostly unsuccessful scripts for Hollywood etc.

During this decade my husband and then my only brother committed suicide and then my mother died. At its end, divorced, I moved to the family Ranch to live with my father for the last six years of his life, during which time the children and I caught our breaths, so to speak.

End of report, I think. There is a lot more to it, of course. But yes, I did "write" a lot in the '40s, and I know I would be hard put to it to re-read most of the pieces, but I do believe that I wrote honestly, and did not try to please this audience or that. I needed the money desperately, after Timmy's long illness and then Friede's alimonies[3] and so on, and then being alone with the two little girls. But I like to feel that I did not put up with any nonsense about having *House Beautiful* add a cupful of marshmallows to my salad recipe....

(Once a magazine told me that its average reader was now in the $40,000 bracket and that I should write "toward" that economic level. (This was in about 1948 or '49.) I said I didn't know anybody like that, and suggested a substitute. She took over, and I felt fine. Her readers liked her... she flew in her table flowers from Hawaii for small dinner parties, and did not serve potato soup....)

So... here it is 1979, and I feel fine! I'm aware of how Time hurtles past, of course. What we said today about the new female metabolic rate with its additions of self-confidence and success and their effect on longevity... it's all amusing, and may well come about. (The Black Widow Syndrome?) Meanwhile I keep on being thankful that I know men like Evan! (Timmy. My father. Many more.)

I've always liked being *partners*, with a man or a woman. For instance, I now feel a partnership with Norah. It's my own idea of being *equal*. I was very fortunate to grow

3. Donald Friede was responsible for alimonies to his former wives. MF did not want or receive alimony.

up to think this was the normal and right way for people to live together. It startles and scares me to know how many people think they can live together, and sometimes even manage to do so, without knowing this. Well... I do think I've been *unusually* fortunate... not always *"cozy et confortable"* as I once learned to say from a French chauffeur, but at least free.

This is a patchy letter, perhaps impossible. If you've got this far, you know it brings much love to you and Evan.

Oh... thank you very much for sending the *Nat'l. Geo.* It's especially welcome for its rosy picture of Paco and Romie Gould, because he died last week... 95! Except for the last year or so, he had a basically fine fat life....

....

Last House, Glen Ellen, California   *12.ii.80* et HOMAGES
To: Norah Kennedy Barr   A l'Honnête Abraham!

Dear N... it was good to talk with you tonight. Matt sounded fine, too.

Version #3 sounds arduous, for some reason. I hope it's fun too. How pesky to lose track of characters, I would surmise!

(I've been going through some cutting and editing, myself, and consider it an exercise in creative humility, if nothing else....) . . .

I thought I had two boxes of *Among Friends* and now find they are the Marseille book. But if and when I ever stir my stumps again, I KNOW that I have some copies of the Whittier book, and am delighted that you want them.

That is indeed a "mild and good natured" book, but it was very hard to write, and even in its genteel emasculated form it has riled and/or hurt people. I regret this, of course. But I don't think I am a strong enough writer to try to turn the coin over, and get into the suspects' passions that I often felt boiling around me when I was 5 or 8. I was basically a secure and trusting child, I knew I was loved at home. I could not concern myself that others of my peers were not. ALL THAT CAME LATER.

There is one thing I wish I had the time and the power to write about, and that is the story of Aunt Gwen[1] and Mother. But I don't. And what does it matter? . . .

The new copper stuff for the Russian Kitchen sounds fine. Be sure to spray it thoroughly with an anti-rust/fog/damp solution before you hang it. Or hire a wandering serf to polish it frequently.

Your plans sound vague. All I'm interested in is seeing you again. And NATURALLY I'd love to see Mattieu again, and meet his girl Jodie. So you please call me when you find you can make it thisaway. I have a nice piece of Vermont cheddar for you, which Stephanie Greene sent me from Brattleboro. Right now it is rather creamy but sharp. In a few months, if you want to keep it, it will simply be sharp. (She thinks jack cheese tastes like mud. I don't agree, in some cases.)

When I was about 5–6, I ate quite a lot of mud, and rather liked it. Sis and I "cooked" in the Back Yard, and got to know what was best for mud-pies, and best for

1. Gwen Nettleship Shaw, an honorary aunt who often cared for the Kennedy children

mud-soup, and best for mud-3-layer cakes. We had all kinds available. We often mixed the dough or batter with orange juice, since there were several trees to hand. Not bad. Never lumpy. Mother always liked to see what we would bring in to show her, but she and Grandmother did not do any tasting. We were not discouraged.

There are a lot of herons in this valley, too! And there are many coyotes in the hills. I hear them in the early morning, the first time since Carson Valley in 1962–3. Here they sound more like wild dogs, with barks and yelps instead of what I remember as the real keening wail, but they are *real*, all right. (Charlie does almost no hunting now, but that is partly Old Age....)

....

Last House, Glen Ellen, California   *30.iii.80*

To: Sylvia Thompson

Ma belle cherie. I'm sorry to be this late in thanking *all* of you for letting me see you! It was really heartwarming, in every way. And of course I loved having you as my first and probably only Easter Bunnies! I took a few of the eggs down to Berkeley to my grandson Alex, but of course kept the nice little trivet and Gloria's fish for my own pleasure.

I thought of the fish when I was eating lunch in the Wrights' patio, because they are very keen about carp now, and have built a big pool for them, and there was a lot of Springtime frolicking, with gold and blue and silver fish engaged. One of them reminded me of the one sitting now on my table, with one matter-of-fact side and the other wildly designed and colored... in the Berkeley case, gold and black. I like mine better.

At least the Wrights have given up on raising monitor lizards, except of course for Rudi, who is now almost five feet long and has the run of the house. (One more reason to eat lunch in the patio!!!)

The gas-happy friend who took me back and forth went to dinner with me at Alice Waters' Chez Panisse, for what I am sure is the best restaurant meal I have ever eaten in this country, and one of the best in my life. I do hope you and Gino and Gloria had a chance to go there... or can plan on it, next time 'round. Alice is very excited about opening her upstairs Pub on April 1. She already had the new pizza oven burning. She'll make the classical Genoa-Nice kind, baked about 4 minutes at about 500 degrees, like *socca*. It seems hard to believe that Americans will like that, after the soggy thick pizzas we're used to, but her magic will probably work there as well as downstairs, where I saw people eating a salad of *mezclun* that they would not have touched here or at Norah's... and to add insult to injury, she had put in several *olives niçoises*, and in general Americans will not touch any olive with a pit in it.... Well, good luck, Alice!

Sylvie, did I ever ask you if you'd caught a thing I did for *Westways* about Mrs. Teter's Tomato Jar? I mention it only because it is about a legendary woman out on the desert, perhaps a hundred years ago. (That whole issue was about Western women, as I remember... and I *think* it was February 1980....) Your book sounds really fascinating, and I'm eager to read it. Please work hard and fast... and keep all your research notes etc for a good college library like the Schlesinger at Radcliffe, which is devoted to American females, and which is already quite prestigious. (For instance it has a fantastic collection of Lydia Pinkham letters! And Gertrude Stein. And Mary Cassatt. And so on... including moderns like Julia Child etc. Do please think of contributing....)

I sound as if I have a vested interest in the Schlesinger. I don't... !!! I just think it's a good idea. And the archives are expertly cared for....

Today there are many more lupine showing through the grass, but it's simply too thick and short for most of the wildflowers to push through. The weather is windy. I think you picked the best of all the days! And I hope you all felt 1/1,000,000th as well as you looked.

Much love all 'round, and again my deep thanks for coming...

....

Last House, Glen Ellen, California   *17.iv.80*
To: Norah Kennedy Barr

Thank you for your letter, dear None. I'm not really sorry that I was on your mind, although I am that you were supposed to be thinking of other things at the school.

I am very much interested in what will happen in this Census taking and in your being in it. (I do hope somebody comes around here. It would be the first time in my life.... I'm not much interested in the "personal" stuff, but I'd like to be counted as one more person of voting age, after all these years of voting.)

I am answering your letter as you wrote it, so now I go to the thing about pain, and the fact that I have been in it lately. I can tell you that I am not now. The hip-thing tapered off and is now merely a discomfort, and it is not new to me, because it has teased me since I first lived in your Berkeley House, when on Mondays I would come down the steps after I'd left Mary/Kennedy at Willard. . . .

It was, I think, the beginning of arthritis troubles, and it was like a "catch" or a hiccup, in the joint. I asked doctors about it, over the years, but they were not interested, and I usually gave a kind of kick, as if it were a cramp, and it went away for a time.

By now it is *there*, and two or three times, as during last week, it has been crippling. So?

As for the tremor or palsy or whatever it may be called, it has let off a bit and does not pounce during the night as much as it was doing. I don't know what it is, and most probably never shall. I'm supposed to go to Neil for a "routine check" on May 1, and may be either sprightly or dottery according to whatever forces are in command. I hate the trembling. It makes it impossible for me to hold a book in my right hand, and that sort of thing. So far I am managing pretty well, I think, although it becomes stronger with social stress so that I really do not like to go out to restaurants, because the whole right side is involved more plainly. Ah well.

About ten years ago Grace Bird[1] said blandly to Marietta, as they walked up Channing, "I'm falling apart, falling apart, in bits and pieces." (She's still functioning quite well, although now in a kind of glorified "retirement hotel" on Lake Merritt....)

This leads neatly into something that I really wish I could talk more clearly about. It is about the next years, in my life and then in yours, when physical and perhaps mental changes will take place.

I don't think that I need "gradually" to "come to the realization that the only long-term plan is for us to combine forces somewhere."

I have always known that this would not / (This slash-mark is a Freudian ??? / as well as a clumsy one, because I am trying out a rented typewriter and am also confused about how to say what I want to...)... I feel strongly and sternly and passionately that you should stay as long as you can in Jenner or wherever you may choose to be, to welcome and nourish and sustain the people who come there to be with you.

(I think I said that rather well. It is true.)

You are needed by them, and they keep alive your warm and coolly loving nature.

Here I must tell you that I feel you are mistaken to suggest any change in your present and future life, to plunge in I don't know what direction you would plunge in, if you were footloose, but I do know that you are well installed there in Jenner for several more years, in *every* way... warm family life, many friends, garden, work(s) of your choosing. I plan to do everything in my power to keep you there, where you belong.

Your suggestions about remodelling this place or installing a "mobile home" are good ones, but NOT FOR YOU. I may discuss them later with Bouverie, if the time seems right(???). But it is *NOT* "the only logical long-term plan" that you give up the whole scene in Jenner to take care of an older sister.

The truth will always be there, that you are the only person I would ever want to live with or near. But I refuse to have you leave your full good life as it now is and as it will be for some time yet, and it would be foolish for me to try to install myself nearer you, where I would be even more an immediate burden than I'd be here.

Probably I'll have increasing up and downs, physically, but the last real downer has taught me quite a lot about plain old survival, and, now on an up-grade, I feel that I can hang in here for quite a time longer... in fact, perhaps as long as I need to.

There is much more that my mind is saying about all this, but I'm really trying to keep it short (as well as clear?). The main thing is that I am deeply reassured and warmed and made more confident by your expression of love, and that I'll do everything I can to prevent your shattering parts of your own life by devoting yourself to what is left of mine.

About Dr. Neil: if he suggested my going up to the San "with baths and massage," I would refuse to go. I am sure he would not... the baths and massage are too difficult and exhausting, right now. And the San is not its old ruggedly simple cheerful self. It is now a lab, run for and by people who spend millions on laser-machines and scanners

1. Berkeley friend

and must *use* them, whether or not the patients need such intricate games. As for the plain diet, which I really liked, everything is now strictly Steam Table, delivered in Styrofoam containers fitted onto plastic trays, reeking of Adventist yearnings for the taste of a chicken, a slice of bacon....

Speaking of massage, I turned off Mr. Starrett's weekly visits, as I think I told you, and I feel much better, much as I enjoyed his rubbings at the moment. When I say that I believe he was stirring up potential troubles in me, I sound as if I consider myself a kind of time-bomb, and perhaps that is really true! Odd thought.

As for pulling any punches with Neil, I wouldn't bother. I am loyal and fond... but he cannot possibly do much more, right now, than tell me to put two aspirin by my bedside.

About your school (I think it is time to change the subject), and the personal questions people are supposed to answer... I've been sent THREE questionnaires in the past three days by people like Claussen,[2] asking me about my views on the draft and so on. I throw them away. I resent them. But I would answer the Census. And I think Lida's[3] idea is all right. Why not? Once the Census-taker has the name and occupation, or perhaps not even the latter, why not let the people (when possible) do their own reports?

I'm so glad you are drifting round in a few free days, planting things! I finally found a packet of Scarlet Runners, which I hope will cover the trellis on the East Balcony. I also got more good strong parsley and a lot of white Cascade petunias, so as soon as I've got today over with (interview, photog for *Ms.*) I'll do some puttering too. . . .

I wish that I could write as much as you do, in as little space. I find myself growing very GABBY with you, or at least repetitive. I'm sorry about that. This wandering letter is really very serious, because it tries to say how much I thank you for your absolutely crazy loving devoted loyal proposal about getting me through the next days and/or years. What it proves, I think, is that we are friends and sisters too.

....

Last House, Glen Ellen, California   *16.v.80*
To: Marietta Voorhees

Dearest M... thanks for the letter I have just read, and for the clippings. . . .

No, the common housefly is not mentally telepathic, I think. But he has many more eyes than do we. And he also senses when a weapon may have been lifted through the air and then toward him.

I'm glad you liked the gingercake. I did too, although I do not think there was any "stuffing" in it, beyond the candied fruits I mixed in.

Today was another in a series of visitations from people I knew 10,000 years ago: Dillwyn Parrish's first wife, and her husband, came for lunch. I'd not seen either of them since 1942. I felt quite shy about it, but it went off simply and with real affection

2. Podiatrist
3. Lida Schneider

and enjoyment. They are handsome interesting people. If she had not fallen in love with him, and left Timmy, it would never have occurred to me that I might rope-and-tie him, myself. By that I mean run away with him and divorce Al Fisher and then get married and finally widowed. What fools and idiots we've been, and how interesting it is to emerge like bubbles in a wine-vat at the end!

Spring is fine here. There are many birds... two young mockingbirds practicing day and night, and some meadowlarks, and a pair of mourning doves.

And my balcony-garden thrives, so far. It has never done so well.

You mention your "unconscious mother complex." How could you, as a student of "Philosophy," and apparently a devotee of Jungian teachers, have been unaware of your relationship with your mother? This is something I cannot understand. (But so are plenty of other things... your sudden realization, after some thirty years, that your niece's feelings about you were not wholly pure, for instance....)

(By Pure, I mean sexless, I suppose....)

Next day... all goes well, in beautiful weather. A man is disking the vineyards. The birds are silent, until he stops his tractor. Charlie just brought in another small squeaky tidbit, so I've left him alone, and come back to the typewriter.

I do hope you feel well, at least most of the time. I do too.

....

Last House, Glen Ellen, California   *3.ix.80*
To: Judith Jones

Dearest Judith... every time Norah and I have talked, either by telephone or more rarely face to face, in the past weeks, she has asked me if I've written to you, and I've confessed that I'd put it off again. But yesterday I knew that I must do it, and I addressed the envelope, and then your letter came!

I could never tell you how much I thank you for writing. I've been *miserable* about all kinds of imagined disasters that might have struck you and Evan, of my professional misbehavior, and on and on.

The main thing on my mind has been concern that anything I might write would be ONE MORE BURDEN, if indeed you were in physical troubles. Then I felt fearful that I had hurt you personally, or had damaged some professional plans.

In other words, I was in a real pickle: should I write? Should I not? And everything is very rosy again!

I'll try to keep this short. I am thinking of a thousand things to ask you and to tell you, and most of them should and could/can wait or be forgotten.

I'm very happy that you've had the peaceful restorative time in Vermont. It sounds exactly right, and I plan to lift my glass to Bryn Teg[1] whenever you say the word. And meanwhile I'm so pleased that little Teg[2] has found you both.

I'm truly sorry that Brier had to leave... a grievous blow, after more than your fair

1. The Joneses' Vermont home
2. The Joneses' dog

share of them this year! But it sounds as if Teg will be much easier to accustom to city needs....

(Have you noticed how people can weep openly when an animal dies, in spite of staying dry-eyed at the death of a dear friend? It is as if we wept for the whole world and all our human sorrows, to mourn so unaffectedly a dog or cat.)

I am glad you did not tell me, when last we talked, of Brier's leaving, I would have started to cry... and it would have been for all the doubts and pains of my stopping work on the Places book,[3] and for the various ordeals you and Evan had fought through, and in general it would have been a complete waste of Ma Bell's time....

Well... I called Norah last night and told her you'd written a loving letter to me, and she said "Oh, *good*," very happily. She also sent her love to you both.

She's fine, I think... feeling the financial pinch on a fixed income, but living happily and buying a whole live salmon for Lucullan sums of people who are coming to dinner. She's been taking the Census, partly for the pay and partly because she loves that wild country around the "estero" of the Russian River. She also likes to tackle impossible isolated roads to the ranches up there. (Usually nobody is home, so she has to try again and again....)

I think her main economy is not to travel. (Probably it is mine too, although I think the wandering days are over... the plain logistics of airports and baggage and so on are real hazards for me by now....)

About wild berries, my older girl lives halfway between Mt. St. Helens and Portland, in Oregon, and after the first Big Blow a bear wandered into her woods on the farm. He was a tired refugee, and did no harm... slept all day and ate all night, which disturbed her dogs/cats/goats/geese/ducks but did not worry her... EXCEPT that he ate every single berry in the woods! She was planning, with her children and neighbors, to pick everything and "put it up" for the winter....

After the second blast, the bear headed back for Mt. St. Helens.

The only good thing about that man who abandoned a cat is Carlos Montoya! I hate him, otherwise. This despicable thing happens often in places where people go for a time in the summer... like Napa Valley, where really beautiful animals are simply left behind when rich city people have to put their children back into school after a couple of bucolic months. One of the best cats we ever had was a half-starved kitten up in a tree, near St. Helena. She was plainly very racy, and a "character"... we wooed her down, and convinced her the world could still be bright for her. She moved into town with us, and lived there for several years. Then the girls left, and she was rather bored and resentful of my new dog and of a couple of other cats in our house. And when the man next door hanged himself, she went there and proved a real godsend to the widow. She went between the two houses until I sold mine and came here to Glen Ellen. All I needed to do was parboil shrimps to have her appear at my feet. Meanwhile I was glad the widow had her company. She died about four years ago, a happy old lady. But I still hate people who use animals as occasional toys. . . .

3. *As They Were*

I'm glad you found a good doctor when Evan topped off his escapades with a fractured wrist! There are a few of them... and, out here anyway, there is a growing trend toward "Family Medicine" and old-fashioned GP work. Apparently the chief hazard is the young doctors' wives, who do not want to spend their lives in small towns and country communities. Better air, better schools... but no social excitement!

I was sorry not to see Jim... had a couple of chances, but I no longer dash down to SF for a party(!), and he was too involved to take a day off his fabulous job of being JABeard. I don't think he'll be able to live "quietly" up in Oregon. Of course a lot of people really love him in SF... but what a pity that he can't be in his own home in New York... clear out that menagerie....

I'm sad that Auntie Hilda[4] finds life less exciting as she finishes it off. I wish it could be an increasing enjoyment. But apparently that is not the pattern. I'll always think of her as she was, so giddily delightful, the day we met for lunch at the Jambon de Parme and she flirted with the pretty charming Marseillais next to our table, on her banquette... and the day we all ran from a rainstorm at an afternoon concert, to our one-room flat, and she said, looking out one of the two windows, with a geranium on the sill, "I feel as if I am living in a beautiful painting!" She was pretty wonderful the night she came down (up?) to dinner when Norah and I saw you in NY... she wore a hat, I remember, and seemed a little remote, as if she were about to catch a train to some mysterious country. But she was still delightful.

I have clear but less vivid impressions of Phyllis... all of them are good, really more forthright.

Well, I send them both my affectionate wishes, at your discretion. (They are fine, and I can see how you came from them.)

About how I am faring, here at the Ranch: all goes well, in an unseasonably cool summer. The wine people are worried about sugar-content for the grapes, and are even pruning the vines to get more sun onto them. Farmers are never happy, of course. There have been only two days of real heat, but the sun has been bright and the air is drinkable.

Socially I've retired pretty completely from the whirl up at the Ranch... I don't like a lot of David's new sets of "friends," but when some old favorites are there, I manage to see them, mostly down here.

Very rarely I go out to dinner at a few friends' houses, but it's much easier to have them come here, and a lot of them do... and of course in summer this is convenient for a stop-over in the vacation travels, especially for lunch and/or dinner.

I've developed a whole new way of marketing, because I go only once a week and must be more or less prepared for whatever is marked in my date book PLUS the "unannounced." A young man comes every Thursday morning and we have a fairly routine circuit, Glen Ellen, Sonoma, home. Now and then he takes me over to St. Helena to dentist etc.

Physically I am accustoming myself to some of the unpredictable changes of aging.

4. Judith Jones's Aunt Hilda went to France with the Joneses when she was more than ninety years old.

My eyesight is of course worsening, but I am simply NOT READY for any surgical interference, and choose to cope with things here at home, where I know every tile in the floor. Now and then I wonder if I am being foolishly stubborn, but usually I feel that I am right.

(I see that I'm going to go on to another page, so I'll stay on this subject a bit longer....)

When I went for a first or second check-up with the eye-men (all 7th-Day Adventists because the field for ophthalmology is so rich there, given their good but inadequate religious diet) they seemed quite surprised at my lack of progress. I should have been much worse off. They asked me what I'd been doing... some secret drugs????? I said, "When I can't read, I type. And when I can't type, I cook." They said very solemnly, "An excellent psychological approach." We parted... for an indefinite period.

Now to what you call "the Madison Avenue" side, I've chewed on this bone to its near extinction, about having to tell you that I should not go on with it now anyway, and the main thing that has worried me was so completely unthought of that I still feel really *awful* that you would in any way feel any guilt about neglecting me or whatever it was that you did feel. How ridiculous! How bad! I was really flabbergasted when you told me that. *Nonsense.*

I simply got into something that I too was really unaware of, after many years of ignoring it: the danger of reading my own printed stuff.

The project grew increasingly dangerous for me, to my true amazement. I thought that perhaps it was because I was aging fast, or that I might be losing my wits, or that....... on and on. Neurotic symptoms that I had been taught how to put far behind me appeared again. There's no use going into all this old picture, but the fact remains that I realized that I must get out of it, even if it meant hurting or "deceiving" you, one of the important people in my life.

This back-out, tossing in the towel, reneging, was extremely painful, as you more than anyone but perhaps Norah will understand. But since then, even with the constant worry of what I might have done to you and of what might be happening to you and Evan, I have been much better in every way. I sleep more pleasantly, eat with enjoyment, and have been writing some magazine pieces to patch the bank-book after the months spent on *Places*. All goes well.

I think we can put together that book,[5] when and if the time is right. Meanwhile I am fairly ready to go with the pieces about Old Age. I can't yet face looking for two or three things I'd like to include. They are buried in the mounds of papers I seem to have written on in the past decades. (With *Places*, I grew increasingly morbid about how insipid, phony, worthless it all was... I felt that I'd cheated every reader I ever had, with my basically worthless prose.)

So, dear Judith... today is a good day, because I know that you and Evan are renewed, and that Teg is with you, and that we love each other and one another.

5. *As They Were*

M. F. K. Fisher: A Life in Letters

Last House, Glen Ellen, California   *8.ix.80*
To: Sylvia Thompson

Ma belle Sylvie... thanks so much for your card. How can you say so much with so little? It's wonderful! (I've known two people who could do that. In one short sentence they described the past six months....)

As far as I know, the American edition of E. David's bread book[1] has not yet been published, although there were great plans for it here. Translation was too difficult, and publishers backed out of such a thick and partly incomprehensible (to us Yanks) work. . . .

Rumors are that it will never be re-done for the Yank market. It is a fine book to have, and I hope you can have a copy. It is in many ways too weighty, but it says a lot that one must dig out alone (which is what scares the American publishers).

I sense that the honey-book will be a good one. I hope you have reached or soon will reach the point in your writing life where you recognize that... oh dear... this is complicated... Research is never wasted, because people like you will absorb it through the skin, like *dmso*[2] perhaps. Then what you've filtered into your spirit will be ready, as what happened to *you*, not to the women. Who cares whether Benjamin Ocherstitz came to a mining camp in 1847? The whole thing is to read about why *you* are writing about them *as yourself.*

A case in point is that for almost 40 years I have been collecting everything I could about Old Age. All during this time, when I was doing many other things, I seemed to be absorbing the messages, and almost unconsciously I wrote a lot about the aging process, as the doctors like to call it. I've read every book from Simone de Beauvoir to Jung. The papers piled up. And now I know that I have already written the book[3] I first planned. The research and the clippings and books and so on are far beyond any attempt to look into them.

What I am trying to say is that I think you are wise to drop the planned research on the five women, and write *what you know,* as the current result of their strengths and weaknesses.

Very few readers want to know about how Aunt Agatha baked bread in a California mining camp, in Vermont, or any place. What readers want is to know why *you,* *Sylvia,* are writing this book. And you can tell them. You are [the] distillation of what some fine people have given you.

I seem to be involved, this very minute, in somewhat the same pattern, of watching my next oldest cousin[4] pile up ROOMSFUL of papers, journals, old pictures even in daguerreotype, of the American ancestors in his family. He is obsessed by this new

1. Elizabeth David, *English Bread and Yeast*
2. Dimethyl sulfoxide, an analgesic
3. *Sister Age*
4. Ronald Kennedy

Roots-Kultur. I don't think he'll ever write the book he envisages, because actually he is afraid of writing about himself. But he'll probably do a vanity-press job and send copies to the members of the clan.

You are a different cup o' tea. You are a professional writer, and can do what you want. (He is very literate and articulate, but basically insecure, which you are not, as far as I know. He is not at all sure of what he wants to prove... what he knows and what he accepts. You are age-mile lights beyond him.)

Well, forgive me, dearest Sylvie, for the soap-boxing...???!!! But I find myself hoping *deeply* that you will write *Sylvia*, and not a lot of researched and even historically annotated footnotes to the lives of five (?) women from whom you evolved. They are all in you, and are part of you and it would be good to know, *through you*, what they gave you to make you what you are.

Well... I keep wanting you to go back to the straightforward approach to a subject that you showed in your first book.

I say this baldly, but with love. You write so well... it's wrong to waste any of yourself on tedious research work....

I know the book you'd envisaged about your female ancestors would be very good indeed....

Much later, after many visitations etc etc... mostly neighbors bringing me beautiful extras from their gardens. They feel very sorry for me, because the cattle won't let me garden, and about this time of year they panic about their overflow!!!! Lucky me. I feel like an Old Testament prophet, being fed by the birds....

No... you're right: it can't be September 1980, much less Sept 8! I find myself saying, "as soon as Summer's here. I'll so-and-so."

Love all 'round, as always.

<hr />

Last House, Glen Ellen, California   *12.x.80*
To: Norah Kennedy Barr

Dear N... WELCOME BACK! I feel as if you'd gone to another land, which really you did... POMP AND CIRCUMSTANCE, in the best sense of those words.

A few people still have a sense for panoply. In most of us it is deadened, or plain *gone*. I think the Europeans still remember more about it than we do. And of course Arne is a Scandinavian.

I think the English, and especially the homosexuals, are the ones keeping it alive now. Reynold Stone's funeral and then burial... Eda's... and of course Solveig and Humphrey's wedding: all that is a form of pageantry that we simply do not use, here. And how about Winston Churchill's funeral? He had every costume designer and parade-master in England working on that for *years*. Here, the best show we can offer, in that vein, is John Kennedy's funeral... beautiful panoply complete with tiny son saluting as his father's bier rolls by, and exactly the right music, even the right weather... and the stonefaced widow under her black veil.

And the costume parties, the bals masqués, that are a part of "life" for a lot of our friends... they have a deliberate rhythm that is quite beautiful, even if it may seem forced or unnatural to an onlooker. Once Al Fisher and I were getting ready to go to a masked party Gloria was giving in Hollywood, and Rex, with whom we were staying, got very scornful and stern about the mockery of it. Sis was getting a divorce then, and was coming along, and we all knew a couple of her old boy-friends would be there too... Rex said that we put on masks in order to act out our secret wishes. (We all got rather noisy, as I remember....) I told Rex he hid behind his white plumes and fake sword and tail-coat as a Shriner. We all got pink, probably....

Well, I know that one reason I spent a strange Christmas in Avignon while you bounced around in the Bay of Biscay was that I really could not face staying at Les Bastides with all the "Nest of Women," as Janet called them.[1] There were three or four masked parties planned, and I was invited to them (probably as a subtle joke). For one last year, I was told, Allanah had a coiffeur come from Paris to do her hair, in flat Grecian curls of pure gold, to match her body-make-up of gold, as a prince or something. Etc. Sybille was going to be carried into the ballroom of the hotel the ladies had taken over in Cannes, on a palanquin... she would bring a bottle of 1879 Oporto to the hostess, and under her rented golden robes she would be dressed as a Limey sailor of the same year....

So I got out. It was lonely but better. (And it still is!)

But I've been thinking a lot about this need to indulge now and then in a so-called masquerade, to hide oneself as Rex would say or to hide death or even joy. Perhaps we need more of it.

So... Welcome Home, and I hope you'll tell me about Arne's Bash.

Charlie is a happy cat, after months of bitter neglect and so on. Last night I broke down and turned on the bathroom heater. Of course it's about half for my own pleasure: I hate to take showers in a cold room, and would much rather save energy by cooking some soup over a fire of twigs than be naked and chilly. This is spoiled and selfish. But as long as I can decide for myself, that is what I want, and Charlie goes right along, and has been perhaps 18 mm. away from the heater for 23 hours. He got up for a stretch and a good supper, and is now back. I assume that his bodily enjoyment compensates for other neglected functions.

There have been a lot of people in and out. I am preoccupied by the logistics of the kitchen, and often have a hard time remembering one face and person from another. Yesterday I called a man Jason for three hours, until I realized he had grown a beard and was called James. He did not seem to mind, nor did his girl.

All these people bring extra vegetables and "in" tidbits like balsam-vinegar, which is now the thing to do. I have some for you, simply because of the pure Italian kitsch of the bottle. *Aceto balsamico*, the kind Ranieri and Genie brought me and that can now be got at Williams-Sonoma, is very good, and I use it sparingly on extra-good

1. Eda Lord, Sybille Bedford, and friends. Les Bastides, near Cannes, was where Eda and Sybille shared an apartment in the home of Allanah Parker.

salad greens... $^1/_4$ to $^3/_4$ plain wine vinegar. The stuff I've been brought is diluted already.

It's like being "into" tofu maybe... or one thin slice of kiwi....

I think I am slowing down rather fast, physically. This does not bother me... I like to do slow manual things in the kitchen. But I am finding it a consummate bore to attend to check-books and fan-mail and business letters, and wonder if I should try to put some of this into professional hands. Perhaps we could talk about this?

Until soon, I hope, one way or another. . . .

....

Last House, Glen Ellen, California 3.vi.81
To: David Pleydell-Bouverie

Dearest David... I am thinking all the time of you, and hoping that each hour brings you more relief. What a wretched thing to happen!

A few days ago you said that after your last raffish weekend you planned to pull up the drawbridge for a month of R&R. I laughed a little at the idea... but certainly neither of us knew that you might have to do it earlier than you'd planned!

Thanks for marking the story in *Newsweek* about breast-feeding... hardly new, but interesting. And I must tell you of a very funny conversation I had with IR,[1] of course on condition that she never know I've mentioned it. (Norah was here too... the day you left IR here after your prowl through the lower meadows on Audubon business....)

I said, just to be silly, which is always fun with her and Norah together (or singly) that I'd heard on the radio about a 9-yr-old English girl who won first prize for her essay on breast-feeding. It was three sentences long, and stated that she recommended it for all ladies because there were no bottles to wash, the milk was always at the right temperature, and best of all the cat could not steal it.

IR looked completely blank. I said something about its being one of her pet projects, and she looked even more puzzled. I'm sure she was not putting this on for Norah... she really did not know why on earth I was repeating such a silly little story.

So I reminded her about the night she was leaving, to stay for the Martins' bash before she and Richard flew back to England. She wore a long-sleeved high-necked evening frock of grey, with some pink on it, and she was doing stitchery, and her cheeks were very pink, and she said finally, "The two things that have held England together are the Anglican Church and breast-feeding."

She was *vehement*... "NEVER! NOTHING OF THE KIND!!" she protested. Norah was quietly hysterical, for I'd already told her of this evening, mostly because we could not change the subject and there were people there who felt rather uncomfortable (including you, perhaps???). IR kept on denying that she'd ever said such a thing. Norah said she wished she'd said it herself. I said that IR could not possibly remember it because she was plainly feverish and perhaps distraught.

Well, we slid into an interesting description of how she did feel and what she did say, those last 24-or-so hours... by now she firmly believes that by the time she got back

1. Dowager Countess Radnor, cousin of David Pleydell-Bouverie

to Aventurn[2] she *and* Richard were perfectly well again, so that she could not possibly have given flu-bugs to half the tycoons of California, as you'd reported.

So she left in a good mood, especially because Norah said again that she wished she could claim the summing-up of the salvation of the UK. But she refuses flatly to admit anything but a cursory interest in breast-feeding, and believes amiably and affectionately that both you and I are hopeless fabricators of strange tales.

End of anecdote, but I think it will amuse you as much as it did N and me. . . .

Meanwhile I hope to astonish her by sending off the final work on the *Places* book.[3] Knopf is announcing it for Spring 1982. Ho hum. I did a magazine piece lately because two old editor friends are now running the thing, and was absolutely FURIOUS to find that it was for the house-organ of The Diners' Club! But why be squeamish? By now practically every publication in America is owned by AmEx or Squibbs Drugs or or or. How can we sort out our employers? And once I did a very nice little travel-piece for the slick magazine Ford Motors published for owners of Continentals, and quite inadvertently saved a whole family and its château from bankruptcy. &&&&

Enough chitchat. Please feel more comfortable every minute and hour... and call when the spirit moves you.

························

Last House, Glen Ellen, California   *12.vi.81*
To: David Pleydell-Bouverie

Dearest David... a quick

... but not quick enough! Colestar[1] just came down for the basket, as I was starting this note to put in your private copy of the new little book.[2]

I wanted to explain to you that I found myself involved in a pun. . . . I signed myself in the book as your tenant, and then saw what I'd written and went on to end "from Mary Frances (Tennant)."...

Lady Mary Frances Tennant was the benefactress of my great-great-grandmother in Ireland... she was pro-British and lived mostly in London, but while in residence every year in No. Ireland she took the girl under her wing... helped her go on with her already good education, which was amazing then except that the protegée was daughter of the Anglican minister in Donamore.

So... when the protegée married, she named her first girl Mary Frances. That was my great-grandmother. And the family has been full of them ever since... all because Lady Tennant was kind to a young Irish girl.

In my own life, a couple of nice strange things have turned up because of this connection. Arnold Gingrich, who made a small but amazing collection of rare violins, mostly Strads but I think four Guarneris, bought the Gudgeon Stradivarius that was known (is known) as the Lady Mary Frances Tennant Gudgeon, partly because he

2. The English home of Isobel Radnor
3. *As They Were*
1. David Pleydell-Bouverie's housekeeper
2. *As They Were*

knew a fine fiddle and partly because he stayed mildly enamored of me for some forty years and wanted me around. He had no idea that there was any connection at all! And then Eda Lord rented a flat in London for several years because the owner was an absentee Irishwoman named Mary Frances Tennant, and Eda knew me as Mary Frances, but of course did not have any idea of the connection.

And So On.

And speaking of gudgeons, thanks again for my lunch today, which will consist of four slices of sturgeon with the rest of the caviar sauce (both delicious)!

I think the Strad Gudgeon is called that because it is smaller than most of the Strads, and is considered very supple and darting. (To play, I mean.)

Aside from all that, all goes well. I hope you'll have had a good weekend by the time you get this (!!! Christmas maybe...).... Norah is coming Monday but not for overnight, to check on what I've pulled together since she left. (Not bad... the book is almost *FINITO.*) ...

Last House, Glen Ellen, California 29.vii.81
To: Lawrence Clark Powell

Dear Ghuce... thank you for sending along to me the little pamphlets and booklets, all valuable because of your choice of printers as well as for their contents.

As I told you, I let Humphrey Stone take a few from my Powelliana shelves when he was here in 1977(?). I think I'll send him your complete file, when I no longer need it nearby. I don't know anyone who would understand and respect it better.... (How do you feel about this?)

Of course I've already read *Remembering Henry Miller.* On second look, it is even more revealing of LCP rather than HM. *Two* creative egos!

As for your "keepsake" about Stelter and McIntyre,[1] of course I loved reading it, because I WAS THERE TOO!!!! The design is good, although I don't like those little cookies around the page numbers. I think you dwindled a little, for reasons best known to yourself and the Patrons of the Library, on Ben Stelter. But of course he was less "colorful" than Mac. . . .

And what about you, old Ghuce? Do you find yourself putting things in order? Do you work more slowly? Does it bother you? Are you scared? I myself don't like the possibility of losing physical/mental control, but since there is nothing to do about it, I simply chug along, and enjoy the good moments.

DO THE SAME!!!! All my love...

Last House, Glen Ellen, California 22.ix.81
To: Bud Landreth[1]

Dear Bud... this is no answer to your letters, but a hasty note to enclose in the mss.

1. C. F. MacIntyre was a professor at Occidental and U.C. Berkeley as well as a poet and friend of LCP.
1. T. C. "Bud" Landreth, a friend of David Kennedy's, was encouraged to pursue a career in writing by his friendship with Mary Frances.

I want to get it off when I do my weekly trip to the big city of Glen Ellen and the metropolis of Sonoma tomorrow.

I've read the two stories with full attention. As you know, I don't do this professionally, but now and then I *want* to. I don't believe in unsolicited advice or comment or even counsel, but when a friend sends me some writing I think I owe some comment. Here it is then, and I'll write more when I have time, if there is anything left to say:

"Friend Bo" is not a story, as it now stands, but an incident drawn from the writer's past experience. It is clear to the writer, but its significance is lost or at best puzzling to a reader who knows nothing about POWs or or or. I myself can identify it in your own life-story, because of the novel (which I am not yet ready to return to you). . . .

"Shaft Speed Sara" (That is a very provocative title that would sell well to a hardcore stud magazine, but that is meaningless until the last few lines, to the average reader) IS ALSO VERY DIFFUSED. For instance, the main theme is the narrator's love for and search for his brother. (There is also much hatred in this.) But it starts too late. It should be made the *whole thing*. About two-thirds through the mildly gripping story of "victory evacuation" and so on, the brother-thing grows strong, and by the time the voice says, "Hello, Little Brother" the reader is ready to find the hair rising, the scalp prickling.

But then the narrative trickles off.

This is a strange and good account, but it needs to be stripped down. You simply cannot, *ever*, tell everything about being a POW, whether at the beginning or the ending of the countless years. So you must say one thing at a time.

I wonder if you are writing any poetry now. Several times in both these stories you are writing it, and I wanted to pull out the words and re-line them on a single page. I think that it would be very good to write poetry, right now. It would narrow and pin down your use of words, as well as one thought, one reaction... not a thousand thoughts, all hinted at but never really *said* in the concise perfection that poetry demands.

Please think of this.

A friend who has worked for many years for my agent is now starting her own agency in NY, and I wait for word of what kind of "new" writers she wants. I'll keep you informed.

....

Last House, Glen Ellen, California   *19.x.81*

To: Elsine Ten Broeck

Dear Elsine... here's a catalog that Bouverie brought down for me to pass along, and you are the right person (Right Person) to see some of the stuff in it. (Don't return.) I almost had a couple of the Cézannes framed, to send to my girls, but I decided not to. That one of *A Deserted House* or whatever it's called is where we lived in Châteaunoir for a few weeks, but Cézanne put a chateau on the far hill behind it, for some reason. When we lived there, it was not deserted at all, but very warm. We house-sat while the owners were sketching in Italy. I had to gather the eggs from about thirty very grumpy hens, because my girls were even more scared of them than I was. There were also ten magnificent pigeons to feed on the terrace twice a day. It was a strange beautiful period in our lives... at least mine. (I think I felt shy about reminding Anne and Mary, in their own new lives....) . . .

I hear great reports about how well you both look, and all that... from people like MV and the Beards of course. That's music to my ears....

About 30 years ago I decided that YB[1] is the truest example of a DOUR person I had ever met or would ever. So I find her almost impossibly *amusing*. This sounds silly, and I've tried to explain to her why I often have to laugh or giggle to her face, but I don't seem to make it clear. Ah well and Ho hum. She is one of the nicest kindest most trustworthy friends I have ever had, and I am deeply fond of her... and every time she starts out with her grim tale of utter abysmal woe and dire dealings I go off into somewhat hysterical gales of laughing. She seems quite used to it by now, and puts up with it.

I.E: I called a while ago, and said at once, "I just felt like hearing your voice. How are you both?" And she said grudgingly, "Oh, hello. Excuse me while I turn off the washing machine and the vacuum cleaner. Oh. Is that Mary Frances???? Well, things in their usual state of confusion and dirt here... & & & & & &." And I sat chuckling and trying to sound solemn, here in my workroom.

Well... I know you and T and I agree....

Oh... one thing I might take seriously, if I could... she said that Jim no longer liked to go to parties etc, and she thought it was because she was not attractive. This worries me. I told her she was a beautiful smoothly dressed person, as she grew older, & & &. But do you think she simply pulled this out as one more complaint?

Now on to MV(!): she came over a while ago, and I think she looks quite dapper and well. She seems in a state of remission or something, about her niece's "condition." But she is really obsessed by the prospect of dying, and of death.

I wish she could find some help from a good priest or teacher.

Is there anything we could do about this? It must be very scary for her, and she says she tries very hard to evade ever facing it, which of course is a pathetic evasion.

You and Tony have looked Death straight in the eye more than once, and so have I, but here is MV well into her 80s who has never really done so.

Perhaps there is nothing to be done.

(I know she goes to lectures and so on, but she does not consider them anything but words for *other* people....)

Well... I didn't mean to get off on these subjects! Isn't it strange, what an old Christie's catalog will do???!!!

Very much love to you both. I hope the olives turned out well. We'll meet when the time is right, and meanwhile the postal rates go up on November 1, and I DON'T CARE.

1. Yolande Beard

Last House, Glen Ellen, California   *27.x.81*

To: Norah Kennedy Barr

Dearest N... do you remember the way Mother used to mock Aunt Petie about mentioning the makes of expensive cars? Aunt Petie would say that So-and-So and she would come down in So-and-So's Cadillac or Packard, never just "drive down."

Well, last night I pulled out the last soggy lump of those elegant sandwiches E. Wector had brought the day before, and I was chuckling the whole time....

At lunch I did not eat one because I was so fascinated by the descriptions of what I was supposed to be eating. Later I did not eat my leftover because I can't bite into big lumpy things. Later still, for supper, I was laughing too hard.

I am AMAZED at what people call sandwiches, today. They seem to be stacks of all kinds of bean sprouts and spinach leaves and goat cheese and *miso* and maybe some mustard, between two fragile slices of bread. They shatter easily, and fall or drift downward, irrevocably.

When this new vogue is mixed with the "In" set, it is doubly hilarious, because one is reminded that the bread is from Tassajara, the sliced turkey from Bon Appetit, the cheese from Délices de France, the *cornichons* from Calmart.... (The mustard is NOT plain old Grey-Poupon bottled in New Jersey, but a rare blend from Alsace.)

Well... I know people, and nice people too, that ask me to bring them their Gucci handbags from the hall instead of just their handbags. They can't help it, I think.

End of report, probably... except that I do dislike large piles of *sprouts* in things... bean, mung, cress, no matter. I like all these things, but why not eat them as entities?

Ah well again.

Went to Kwei-lin King[1] today... 4th time. Best so far. I don't expect or want any miracles, but only some substitute and/or relief from the chemical approach to muscular disorders.... Well...

The rain is wonderful. It started slowly, more than 24 hours ago, and by now is gusty and stronger. A real dripper!

I found your list of Missing Persons, and have clipped it to JBJ's[2] letter. I don't like her new suggestion for a title... it sounds like a book by a radio commentator of the Sixties.... I think *As They Were* would be better than *As It Was*. Or is that too oblique?

Meanwhile... l have been wondering if you'd let me pick up some of your gas-bill for coming over here? I hope you will say yes. Gas is no joke, these days. (Truism of 1981.)

1. An acupuncturist MF saw for her arthritis
2. Judith B. Jones

Last House, Glen Ellen, California   *21.iii.82*
To: Lawrence Clark Powell

Dear Ghuce... thank you for reminding me that I didn't send the letter I promised with Spack's[1] books.

First, before I explain that, I must tell you that I NEVER type a note to you without feeling apologetic for doing it on a machine. I agree completely with you about the personal force of writing by hand, to express love or esteem or even anger. But I can't do it any more... and have often used a typewriter for speed, in the past. Now I use one only to communicate, no matter how much my persona seems missing in this cold type.

Well...

I found, in writing to you to thank you for letting me see the two "novels" by WMS, that I was halfway through a letter already on its ninth page! So I tore it up. Only you and perhaps Norah in this whole world would have understood what I was saying, and why I could say it. And it suddenly seemed both silly and destructive... silly for the three or two of us, and possibly destructive of things we all had found in the books.

I am not a novel-reader, by now, unless somebody like you writes one. I'm lucky that I've read a great many of them, for the past sixty-plus years... from left to right through everything... Walter Scott, the Russians, Proust.... But I don't *have* to, any more, unless something like professional curiosity or personal enjoyment tempts me.

Of course it was impossible for me to be removed and impersonal about Spack's two novels. I kept some detachment as a writer reading another writer's work, but otherwise I read avidly, at times anyway, for some interpretation of a familiar incident, some new look at an old story, some bit of intimate gossip to laugh at.

Well... it's simply too complicated to try to explain. But I must tell you that I think you write better, and know more about *everything*, than poor S ever could.

He writes in a strictly slickly Princetonian way, with the cultivated huff-chuff detachment of an upperclass academic. You could imitate this, but you don't need to, because you haven't the time nor energy to waste on proving your manliness nor your erudition. You know what you are talking about, and poor Spack does not know about more than two types of women and even fewer of men, which means himself.

He writes about (1) Smithie sex-pots and (2) middle-aged fribbles. He writes also about an idealized synthesis of himself in several roles... Simon–Hugh–and the other one whose name I forget... really horny aging clubmen toying with their limited range of females but actually merging in a single homosexual prototype who fucks, eats, even dies and is buried.

Well, as you can see, Ghuce, my reactions to the two exercises in suave kiss-and-tell were wordy!

I thought of a thousand facets of Al Fisher's fumbling life, and mine, and even

1. William Spackman, Al Fisher's lifelong friend from Princeton days, wrote *An Armful of Warm Girl* and *A Presence with Secrets*.

yours. I remembered the hundreds of letters from Spack that Al took to Dijon and got me to read, and I wondered what he was trying to tell me then, and what Spack was trying so elegantly to tell me now.

A lot of all this seems simply SILLY by now, of course. But when it is happening, it is real enough... as when the Spackmans and Dorothy Matthews came to Dijon... and when I stopped to see them in Oxford and took them a good *tâte-vin* and an elegant baby-dress for their first child, that Al and I really could not afford to buy....

Ah well and ho hum.

My mind goes on, once it sniffs a lure, and certainly the relationship between AYF and Spack was lifelong, as well as thoroughly camouflaged by such things as these two exercises by Spack and Al's several marriages and their good-old-boy hemming and hawing.

What a *waste*!

Do you think this sort of closet-life still goes on, or are intelligent people more IN-TELLIGENT by now? Is it too late?

Did I ever tell you that I've talked at length with Truman Capote about a summer Al spent flitting around the edges of Truman's set? Interesting. TC felt very scornful, impatient, compassionate, about such ambiguity.

But on the other hand, did I tell you about the time I talked with Al's mother, to tell her that I had left her son?

And so on. You can see why I abandoned the first letter!

It's a fascinating story that will not be written, at least now.

But I still wish, as a tired old professional, that WMS would write straight and not so wittily, huff-chuffily crooked. And I am sorry that such an interesting man kept himself so limited in his range of partners! He knew only two kinds of socially acceptable whores. But at least he went to bury part of himself, in the last third of his second display of utterly adorable tri-lingual wordiness.

End of grouch or regret or whatever it may be. What it comes down to, perhaps, is that I regret very much that there is such sham and evasive trickery in good people.

Well... we're all good, in our own ways, and I am glad you write straight instead of crooked prose!

PS... I think you'll be interested in Norah's reactions to reading both books, which she did eagerly because she knew Al quite well.... She kept saying almost angrily to me, "But that's not Al AT ALL...." And when I'd ask her who ever said it was, she would contradict everything. It was quite funny.

I think Spack did write in an engaging way, and Norah kept reminding me... his style is devious and sometimes witty. But he is also drearily tedious, and is not a novelist in the right sense of that word. Even Norah, who still reads good novels with great relish, admitted this.

Ah well again... and much love, and thanks for sending me the books. I trust you escaped paying any great Library fines!

To: James Beard,[1] *of St. Helena, California*

Dear Jim... here's a rather elderly clipping I got yesterday, that may amuse you. It's from a NY paper, but I forget which one.

A few friends who worry about my being completely out of touch with the world because I don't read newspapers (!!!) send me batches of clippings, when they pile up a few. This one was in a fat packet from my big black friend Jim Pollard, in Harlem.

It's interesting to make a kind of composite picture of myself, from what people think I want to read, or *should*.

Pollard's include articles about food, wine, animals, and women. He's more on the mark than some others, who really clip what *they* are interested in. Arnold Gingrich, for instance, sent a lot of stuff about trout fishing and fiddles. Eleanor Friede's offerings are mostly about NY publishing. Etc . . .

It's heavenly weather over here, and the wild flowers have not been this thick and vivid since the Spring I came here, eleven years ago. The Stones were here then.... (Isn't it strange that they now have four daughters and live at Fonthill???)

We probably wouldn't see each other, and I mean you and your Bride and me, more than I see the Stones, even if I still lived in St. Helena. But that doesn't keep me from missing all of you, and feeling very close to you. (I think I just wrote a colossally bad sentence, but let's leave it lay where I flang it....)

Speaking of bad wording reminds me of a little game I'm playing with the title of the new book (May 24). It's no good: *As They Were*. A cruel friend has suggested that it be called *Whom Were We Anyways?* I feel that my counter-suggestion is better: *Like We Was*. Oh well and ho hum. Knopf seems happy about the Kirkus and PW reactions, so I assume I didn't send Judith Jones another dud. We'll see, fairly soon... (I wanted to call the thing *Other Places*, or something like that).

It's too fine a day to get to work. But I must.

Last House, Glen Ellen, California   *18.iv.82*

To: Lawrence Clark Powell

Dearest Ghuce, I'll send this along, on May 22, just to prove to you that I did try to write, and that Fate or something made the machine a basket-case for about a week. My little Scottish typist brought her bulky old IBM for one morning, but I didn't feel like using it and her for anything but "business." So you got put off....

No, I never got a piece about writing *The River Between*. I'd like very much to see it. Mails are peculiar, out here in these beautiful boondocks (and perhaps elsewhere?).

(Did I tell you that I plan to send my whole list of Powelliana to Humphrey Stone, on my death? He will understand and cherish it. He already has several books, as you

1. "Skinny Jim," printer and friend

know. Your letters will be closed in the vaults at the Schlesinger Library until 25 years after my death... but Der Nuke may settle all that beforehand....) . . .

Your letter about Spack et Cie is wonderful. Yes, I too wish we could talk face to face, hand in hand probably, about a lot of all this strange part of both our lives.

I think the saddest thing about this "exercise in perversity," as you rightly call it, is that there was such lifelong and even fierce and paranoid refusal to get *out* of it.

Damn. I rage when fine people, especially when they are privileged to have education as well as sensitivity, stay hidden and giggling in their tiny cupboards. God! I do rage. What waste!

I suppose there is a fear-filled excitement about all this, a certainty of their superiority.

Well, I become incoherent... obviously!

So... (next day!)... I made myself a little supper and read month-old copies of *Newsweek*! But I am still sad and angry, and of course always will be, about the terrible waste of potentially rounded human beings. They'll simply have to continue their development further, in other forms, I suppose. But Spack is still a tittering schoolboy, and he must be nearing 80... and so were all the characters in his books. I think Al was somewhat more "evolved," in a few ways. But he too seemed to get *stuck*... I don't think he grew, inwardly, very much. And neither man seemed to be able, yet, to *learn*, no matter how much they read and talked and slept with older spirits.

Mary Anne, for instance, Spack's wife when I knew them in Dijon and Oxford, was light-years older than he. So was her sister Dorothea, who was Al's girl, more or less, while he was at Princeton.

I remember questions she asked me about Al, when we were alone for a few minutes now and then in Dijon, and by now I know why she was asking. She said, for instance, "Al seems not to have changed at all! Do you think being in France will help him grow up?" I didn't know what she meant, then, and rather resented it....

I don't agree with you at all, that I was "victimized" by Al. It was the other way around, more possibly. I was truly in love and loving, but the truth is that he gave me a chance to get away from my life as a young American woman and into another culture, which I could not quite figure out how to do by myself. In other words, I grew up very fast, once away from California! But he did not, much as he seemed to become more worldly and so on as he aged.

I don't see how you could make *seven* drafts of anything. But I want very much to see what you finally decided to say. And I believe firmly what I said about your writing. When I said it, I was thinking of course of my recent reading of the Spackman "exercises," and of Al's sad attempts to write straight honest words about anything at all, and the comparisons were almost hilarious. Neither of those two poor souls would have *dared* be simple, the way you do, and the way I do.

Maybe they were always trying to be somebody or something else. Or perhaps they were too scared to *look*. You and I are not. (Well, we may be *scared* now and then! But we go right ahead.)

So I don't agree with you that you too were "victimized" by Al. I honestly don't know what you mean by that, for either of us. How was your friendship with him part of being victimized? Explain if you feel like it. I do feel sorry for what seems his "sterile life," but I don't think Spack's "few glittering *jeux d'esprit*" made him any less sterile... or not much....

There are too many things in your letter that I'd better leave until next we can talk together. I can never agree with you about some of your facts, of course, any more than you might of mine. I don't like some of your *reasons*, might be a better way to put it. But you know all that. But it has nothing to do with our innate love for each other, and of each other.

And how about things as they are now? I sense that you and Fay are better companions by now. I am glad you helped teach S. how to be her own new strong self, and I hope she will be a rich fine person in her new life, with you as her friend/teacher. What she has chosen to do sounds right, and enviable. (I used to think that if I ever met a vintner or a doctor with three children about the ages of my two, I would marry again, thanks to my lives with three such different men as my legal husbands and then a few very valuable affaires. But I made no effort to look for a possible partner... perhaps embarrassed at my cool schemings??? I am very glad that I am alone now, as I have been for many years.)

Work is slower than it used to be, and I know that I do things partly in order to prove that I am still alive enough to finish them (!). I'm working hard, and I think you are too. I honestly believe that there are things that make the long experience worth struggling through, although now and then, on a creaky day, it is rather difficult to accept what are too loosely called "the rewards of old age." I don't mind *looking* old, but at times I resent the infirmities of the Aging Process. I've never been one to do things by halves, and by now I have cataracts on both eyes, osteoarthritis, and Parkinsonism on my whole right side! All of these conditions are advancing at a good pace, too. But I cope quite well with them, so far. I wish Hal were about 65 years old, to my 73+, and could scold me and tell me I've been a fool or a good girl now and then. But what a lot he taught us all!

(I still pass out copies of his book to every possible reader, and this very morning gave one to a young woman who types for me once a week (fan and business mail). She's a psychotherapist at the nearby county mental hospital and much interested in the magic powers of diets to help disturbed people....)

By the way, did you know that Hal's book finally got out of the clutches of some fairly tacky publishers and is in paperback with Vintage Press (Knopf)? I am pleased.

Knopf publishes the collection of old and new stuff about places on May 24, and I'll send you a copy as soon as I get one. It's a very unimportant but pleasant book, I think... dates from my first published piece, in about 1935, in *Westways*! And I'm trying now to condense some 45 years of doing research on Old Age into a short introduction to the collection of stories Knopf will bring out next Spring.[1] I think I told you... took a quick look at all the cartons of clippings and articles and notes and so on I'd gathered for so long, and simply baled them up, for Radcliffe. I'm too old to write what I always

1. *Sister Age*

thought would be my "best" job, and really I am not qualified to tackle it: I'm not a scientist or a sociologist or an economist or or or. And the so-called serious stuff about Old Age is already over-handled by everybody from Simone de Beauvoir to Dr. J. C. Gluckemhimer. So Norah and I took a good look at some old stuff, and I'd been writing about age for at least 45 years! A lot has been published, but a lot hasn't. And the Knopf people are quite excited by what we pulled together. End of report... except that it's odd to be trying to find a few thousand words to cover what I worked on for so long and seriously, and meant to be a *tome*.

Enough... or even too much, in this drawn-out short note to you!

I do like brevity. But this was the time to be wordy.

....

Last House, Glen Ellen, California   *9.vi.82*
To: Marietta Voorhees

Dearest M... the roses you brought me from Mrs. Calkins's garden are still beautiful! I think two have bit the dust, but the rest look lovely.

I was very glad that you felt like driving over the hills, the other day. I hope it was worth it, for you too. I didn't feel at all angry at myself or frustrated, when you left, but only glad to have been with you for a while. That's a great improvement over some of the past experiences. Maybe I'm growing up a little!!!???

I'm glad you took a little time off, and saw the Thorncrofts and all that. (I do hate that term "advantaged children." Why not just say "rich"? Or if it really meant "above average" why not that, or maybe "bright"...? Ah well.) . . .

As for chefs looking like chefs, today they all look like bearded children... a lot of them are really well-trained, but they are given too much responsibility too soon and are often arrogant brats... no time yet to learn the humility of real artists, which great chefs are. I hear that Ron is doing a v.g. job up at the Auberge. But I disapprove of his being sous-chef already.... It's only his second job since he graduated! He should serve some time in at least two great European kitchens before he qualifies....

I'm plainly a stiff-necked old fuddydud on this subject (and several others). . . .

No, seduction is *seldom* subtle, to my mind.

I'm really sorry that I find myself in small rages and storms of annoyance at your using your "joshing" and so on, with *me*. It's very egotistical of me. You can't help it, by now. Why should I think I am different from all the rest of your entourage? (Except that I do!)

Things chug along here... lots of people... yes, Ed Wyle is about right with his estimate of 25 or so... it's purely and plainly a kind of game, with me, to stay alert and try to think of other things than myself. I enjoy planning and cooking meals, and making myself stay nicely neat and tidy and talking and listening and smiling... stuff like that. Now and then I get panicky about my professional commitments, and then I get to work and somehow meet most of the deadlines... publishers' and my own. It's a familiar pattern. Sometime I'll simply not follow it, because I am finished. Meanwhile I stay fairly calm about it.

Right now I am fudging about a re-write of the introduction to the Old Age collection. I'll do it next. Then I have firmly told the UCPress-Sotheby people that I can't make the July 1 deadline for their preface, but that it will come along soon. (I am a complete blank on this... put off by their title, *Wine and Life*. Rubbish. Norman Vincent Peale...) I also have to try to re-write an old lecture for the Wine Library... don't know if I can, but told Gunther[1] I'd try. And I want to do a piece about fad diets... on my mind for a long time. And I am chugging along on a kind of ABC... *Old Doc Fisher's Homely Diatribes* might be a good title....

It sounds like some work ahead. But all I have to do is get to it, instead of having interesting people come to lunch and supper and so on!!!!

I'm getting some very interesting mail about the new book. But the nicest thing anyone has told me is what you said, about getting through a depressed period by reading about my being alone in Arles. Thank you for telling me.

I left out a lot of my personal battles in this piece, and talked mostly of the people and sounds and the Gypsies. I became quite overtly neurotic about heights, and had a very rough few times after I went up to Avignon... walking along the Rhône on the high dikes... getting to my hotel room, which was on a third-floor balcony that went down into the lobby... it was very difficult. But I didn't see any point about discussing such things. Some critics think I am *hiding* parts of my life, but it's simply a matter of taste, I feel. And I've never felt that I was being autobiographical... I wrote about my own reactions to things simply because I was not a good enough writer to ascribe them to people I could not know. I mean that I've had to write about what I *know*. I'm not writing from imagination, because I'm not good enough to.

Ho hum again.

On to some supper... left-over from a nice lunch that two friends brought. One brought a copy of her new novel, in such small print that I don't have to try to read it. She writes very well, in an unimportant way... the novel is in a first printing of 100,000 copies, and will sell in super-markets, and she is happy. The other girl is a commercial photographer, more of a real artist than the writer. But I like them both. They brought good bread and tomatoes and chicken salad and a slice of duck pâté and sweet butter and a pineapple upside-down cake! Tomorrow I'll eat the rest of the pâté with Norah... she loves it. Tonight I'll finish the salad. I made the writer take the other half of the cake back to her husband, who loves it too.

....

Last House, Glen Ellen, California   *24.vii.82*
To: Bud Landreth

Dear Bud:

I'm about a month later than I meant to be in thanking you for your good letter and for letting me see the manuscript of *Brothers Together*. I hope you'll excuse me. I got caught by some neglected deadlines.

1. Gunther Detert, head of the Napa Valley Wine Library at the time

M. F. K. Fisher: A Life in Letters

Thank you too for the tearsheet from the *Alberta Report*. It is a fascinating story, and I've sent it along to a couple of women in Santa Rosa, who brought out a cookbook a couple of years ago to benefit a welfare project. It suddenly took off, and I know that they will be relieved to hear that it happens now and then in other places.

You'll be amused to hear that I got a peppery note from Aunt Petie, very annoyed at a review in the *LA Times* of my last book. I must write to reassure her that a soft answer turneth away wrath. It was the only bad review the book has had. A really sour frustrated exhibit by a sour frustrated woman, who plainly hated to be handed a Fisher book to review when Fisher should be handed her book to review. She used a lot of adjectives like narcissistic, egomaniac, deadly boring, etc. etc. So I wrote her a nice little thank-you note, as I do all reviewers, and told her it was a great relief not to read the old Hallmark greeting card sticky sweetnesses. And I got back a tearful letter, telling me how much I had always meant to her and her friends and and and. End of story, but I must tell Aunt Petie that everything is sweetness and light.

I wish you would go on with the idea of that booklist for a frozen winter! Meanwhile I have an almost full carton of things I have been finding that might interest you in another such season... and now you hint that you may not have one! What shall I do with the books?

I don't think (obviously I am answering your letter line for line...) that you should spend any time on learning how to write a sentence! You are way ahead of most people, already. You and I agree that a sentence not only begins and ends, but that it has a verb in it, and the nouns and pronouns needed, and perhaps adjectives and so on. A lot of people try to ignore this basic fact, but so far without much luck.

I can't take F. M. Ford's report of his dialogues with Conrad very seriously. Ford wants to take a great deal of credit for that, of course... I mean, for the strength and beauty of *Heart of Darkness*. But I don't feel that he has much of a leg to stand on, and I don't agree at all about the triumph of the so-called French influence. . . .

The Whittier-oil story is worth working on, mainly, in my view, because it gets you out of that camp. You are very good about people, and I hope you will absorb yourself in them and everything you can remember as well as suspect and even imagine about them. I would like to see what you write about Mr. Essley... I don't remember him at all but I do remember his old man, through my father. . . .

You say that your days of isolation may be over. Of course I am interested. Does it mean that you will be in Cereal[1] but with a companion, or does it mean that you will move to another place nearer people more like you? Tell me what you feel like, and meanwhile send me your new addresses as you have any, because I hope very much to stay in touch with you.

I don't remember where the barber shop was. I am sure it started that column. I do remember the Poinsettia on Philadelphia, but it seems to me that Bert's place moved onto North Greenleaf, up toward the old Myer's store. I was surprised when I went to the Ranch to live, how many people read that column of Rex's. I never paid

1. Cereal, Canada, where Landreth lived

much attention to it until he started dictating to me. A lot of it seemed real twaddle, of course, but it carried an almost frightening lot of power in local politics. I found it scary.

Answer to specific question, except that I cannot answer it(!), I don't know which stories are best, of either Conrad or Nabokov. I like them all. I have not read them for a long time. I think the last thing I read of Nabokov's was *Pale Fire*.

On this subject, I think that the more you read the more fun it is to write, but I have never read in order to learn something. I don't think Edmund Wilson is a very good writer. The fact that he is considered so, at least from his literary criticism, is a sad comment on our literary poverty.

Well... I've gabbled along much more than I meant to. I hope I haven't bored you.

It's really fine news that there will be a grandchild! I'm happy for all of you. (Where is Sylvan Lake?)

All my best, Bud...

....

Last House, Glen Ellen, California   *29.viii.82*
To: Norah Kennedy Barr

Dear N,

Business: I enclose a check for the loan you mentioned. I am very glad that you told me it would be useful, and that I can agree with you! Please do not fret about repaying it... I am in a fat period, it seems, and am not at all pressed for The Wherewithal or whatever it can be called.

Pleasure: I also enclose a small check with the request that you take all the present Barrs on a little spree somewhere, with my envious blessings. I don't think you can go very far, but at least it will cover some good polkas, a few beers, perhaps a bowl of kartoffelsalat mit kaltschnitzel... or maybe a few goblets of chilled Dézélay while you are in the Vaud?????

Joe Herger came for a birthday (88?) schnapps with me, the other day... he looked really well, and yodelled a bar or two with a good twinkle in his eye. It always surprises me when he says GESUNDHEIT when he clicks glasses... I think of it as a sneeze-wish. His step-daughter Diane is a good girl... she's simply enormous now, which he really loves. David always says that Joe's knees actually buckled when a really fat woman like Juanita would appear at the Ranch. So Diane, quite beautiful in the face, simply waddles around him, and he smiles in rapture. He is almost totally deaf, but seems to understand when he wants to. Often he sits with a remote half-smile, in another world, while we murmur on about cruel wives and so on, and then suddenly he'll contradict us or say, "Ja ja... she vass von bitch."

They stayed more than an hour. I felt tired afterward, but very glad that Diane is such a loving intelligent slob. (When I asked her if she'd like some fruit-juice or or or, she said, "No... this is my last day of vacation, so I spent it all in a singles-bar with my best girl-friends and we played poker and I drank four Bloody Marys." She seemed completely sober, and was not bragging or guilty or anything.)

Today nobody is here, and I am trying to be *reasonable* about the ugly untidy piles of mail. I know that somewhere are some legal papers to sign. Etc etc. I must write a sharp letter to the *WWDaily* man, whose interview in *W* may get both of us into trouble... my old beef about the difference between onto-press printing of a news story but reference to subject with an "interview." This one is out of context and half-cocked. Damn. Etc . . .

This reminds me that last night I "skimmed" *As They Were,* for the first time. I am getting very poignant and even unsettling reactions to it in the fan-mail, and I decided that it is affected and wrong of me to refuse to read it (or anything I've written). So I spent a few hours on it, and I think that (thanks mostly to you and your patience with my distaste for my own stuff) it is all right.

This sounds silly, to anyone but you. But I feel more mature now, and know that I can re-read what I've written without any physical qualms anyway. I am detached, not involved except professionally.

I found some of the stuff in the book quite interesting. The report on la rue Brueys was boring at times. I was interested to see how often I've written about the effect of *sound*... Brueys of course, and Arles, and Long Island... and then far back to the plaza in Chapala and so on.

Well... thank you again for getting out this book of stuff, the current one as well as the *Sister Age* thing. I think I got over a hurdle, last night. But one nevah know, do one?

Speaking of *Sister Age,* I really cannot locate a couple of things I told Judith I'd like in it, in all this mess of papers, and she has to buckle up by Sept 1, so... too bad! I think we may have to put together another collection, called *Son of Sister Age.* Or should it be *Daughter*?????? (I think I wrote a good thing about souls... can't find it, which is probably all to the good....)

I hope you are having a nice little fiesta today for the Birthday Girl... and that the big weekend will be fun in every way. Please give Matt my love. I'm sorry he can't go to Zurich, if he would like to. (Maybe he's afraid that if he got there he'd not come back??? Nous verrons.)

....

Last House, Glen Ellen, California   *7.ix.82*
To: Paul and Julia Child

Dear Julia and Paul, T*R*E*S C*H*E*R*S A*M*I*S:

This is a *special* note! I feel very honored to be invited to add to your book of admiring and respectful and loving messages... and all I can think of is that the first time I met you, I knew I would be your friend for life, even if we seldom met again and you did not care. I was infinitely fortunate, because you liked me too, and we've managed to meet much more often than seldom.

That was about twenty years ago, I think. Julia met my plane in Boston. I'd been staying in La Pitchoune with the Michael Fields, purportedly to work on the try-cake book about provincial French food for Time-Life, and it felt strange to be in the house of people I'd never met, so that I was more than usually shy about seeing you.

And there you were, standing at the bleak airport gate like a familiar warm beacon... old tennis shoes, a soft cotton shirtmaker... tall boarding school teenager from Pasadena: We'd met before, not in this life but *somewhere*. I went happily along with you, and felt home again.

And I still do... Plascassier, Nice, Glen Ellen, Marseille....

That night in Cambridge, in a big cool house that was like ones I'd always known in Southern California, an editor from Time-Life dined with us, and was puzzled at how little the summer's work seemed to matter to anything but his project. We ate a *jambon persillé* you were experimenting with. And the next morning Paul and I walked on the Commons, and watched Watusi visitors throw Frisbees and then float after them in the sun and shadow. We talked about e. e. cummings and Dos Passos and my husband as if they too were there again.

And the next day there was a roadside picnic (cold sliced steak...), as we headed for Kennebunkport where you would leave me on your way to the Island off Maine....

It is all part of my life... the real part, the best.

You welcomed me, at the Boston gate and on the Commons, as if we'd all been there before and would be again, and I am very thankful.

My love to you both, as always...

<hr>

Last House, Glen Ellen, California   *12.x.82*
To: Lawrence Clark Powell

Dearest Ghuce... FINALLY it has all floated to the top! And what a rich haul it is! I have a lot to thank you for, as always. . . .

The May 1979 copy of *Booklover's Bounty* is of course interesting, although I wish it were more about WR[1] and less about other "names" in that world. Of course I read his remarks about Al and me with special interest, just as one always studies hardest his own picture in a group of them. It is fascinating to see what other people remember, too... that my return to Dijon ended Al's writing *The Ghost*... that I was "subservient"... that Al typed his one script of *The Ghost*, and so on. Ah well. And Ho hum. *Tout passe*, eh? . . .

What have you done about the new story? Did you pick it up again? Why didn't Capra like it? Yes, please send it to me if you want to, and I'll promise not to let it get away from me(!).

As you know and understand, it's hard for me to remain professionally detached with your things. Mostly I can, though. I see, for instance, that I read *Behind the River*

1. Ward Ritchie

Between with real care, and that I made copious notes. Some of them, though, are very personal reactions, and have little to do with the general evaluation of the piece. For instance, on pages 8 and 11 I get almost peevishly bored with your recital of honors and incredible amounts of dedicated work and fabulous assignments and so on... "Mr. Big!" I note, and "Big Boy again!" And some of your careless or hasty syntax upsets me.... I hate it when you start a paragraph "Let me go back." (P. 2.) Who you talkin to, man? Me? I'll "let" you. This seems affected to me... rather professorial and droning. And I don't like things like "I layed over." (P. 9.) That's bad grammar, and it is misspelled, I think... an Americanism that is all right, but you don't use it correctly.

All this is piddling. My firm summing-up, then and now, is "Very good. Clean and Spare (mostly)." And what could be better?

I think the description of your work will be of interest to anyone involved either personally or as an observer of the so-called Creative Process. I can't see it as more than an historical document, in its present form. It has strange changes in phraseology, so that one minute you are writing in a stilted pedantic way and the next in a loose colloquial one: (p. 10) "At the idyllic Sagebrush Inn I reworked the story in light of the landscapes I had re-traversed. For the first time I felt in charge of the word."

Ah well again... not much use to you as a keen critic, certainly! But my heart's in the right place!!!

Did it really take you 28 years to write *The Blue Train*? Or do you mean that you wrote it 28 years after it was happening?

Oh... I have Auden's book of Goethe's trip, but I simply groan with boredom, in spite of his magic with that plodding egocentric account... I mean WHA's magic, of course. But I'm very glad you like the book. And it was fun to read a couple of mentions of Kniep, who apparently was the only faithful friend in a big batch Goethe tried to keep with him. Did you see the big Kniep sepia I have here now and then? I forget if it was down here from the Ranch when you last came. It's under glass, and not right at all here, but Bouverie likes to have me keep it when he's away. It's supposed to be a sketch of either Tuscany or the country back of Nice, which of course was Italian then. It is really a rather Anglicized version of a German landscape... billowy oaks(?), romantic vistas of far gentle hills.... But Kniep did indeed know how to use those pencils... its technique is masterly.

Frances Ring[2] wrote to me lately! She was really such fun to work for... let me do what I felt like. I really hate working for the *NYer*... swear I'll stop, but I am really fond of W. Shawn, and I respect him, and now and then he writes me a tiny sad little note and there I am again. The last thing I did I swore would *be* the last... the magazine insisted on cutting out any possible imitation of the way our cook Rose used to talk. And now I'm caught again, because they want a story I wrote some forty years ago, because it will be in the collection Knopf will do next Spring, BUT do I mind their re-writing

2. Editor of *Westways* magazine

some parts that are "a bit too bold"? HO HUM AGAIN. Yes, I do mind. But as long as Shawn is there, I'll let them keep my language pure and sweet, I suppose.

Forgive me, dear Ghuce, for letting your always-welcome notes and offerings and mss. disappear! It won't happen again, I promise.

When do you think we'll meet again? (I thought especially of you, perhaps, while the fires were near Malibu last week....)

....

Last House, Glen Ellen, California   *6.xi.82*
To: Lawrence Clark Powell

Dearest Ghuce... I'm always happy when I hear from you. And thanks for the beautiful card! Yes, old Turner's back! Do you remember a big picture in the Tate called something like *Seamonster at Dawn*? I had a couple of good books of Timmy's with lots of plates in them, about Turner, but gave them to somebody.... Ho hum. Well, even on book-covers he is *my* painter, I think. Once I was sure it was El Greco. Etc. Etc. But by now I think Turner is the one, the pick of the litter.

Thank you, dearest L, for saying I'm "helpfully honest." Sometimes I worry, even with thee, that I am not "helpful" really. And I worry about being honest, which I know I am. Timmy believed thoroughly that one should NEVER be so, when even a dear friend asked for it, for an "honest" opinion about a poem or carving or painting or or or. He said that no friendship, no matter how deep and true, was strong enough for honest criticism. I never could agree with him, and I know that when he asked me, I always gave him my most candid view. Sometimes it hurt him a little, and as he grew worse, and had to take more medicines, I know he sometimes was very angry if I did not like something he had painted, and without a word he would paint over it, or even destroy it. Well... I hope I've never hurt you with anything I've said about your work.

I'm very glad *Southwest Book Trails* has been re-issued. I'll lend my copy to Marietta Voorhees. She saw it when it first came out, but I'm sure has forgotten it... it will please her to see again the dedication to EF... as you may know, she grew up with the Fergusson children in Santa Fe and/or Albuquerque, and was especially fond of Erna.

I hate to bother you about this, but I'd like very much to send a copy with your autograph to Humphrey Stone. I could write directly to Mr. Gannon, but I don't know the price of the book. To avoid letters back and forth, could you get me a copy, sign it, and have it mailed to me? Then I'd send it on to HS with some books I'm mailing to the children for Christmas. I ask this ONLY ON CONDITION that you'll tell me the price of the book etc. (And I wouldn't be so importunate to anyone else in the world....)

Once you sent me a clipping about a relative of yours who killed herself in very old age. I want to see your collection of letters from the "18th Century throwback."

No golden leaves here yet! Everything is about 3–6 weeks off schedule this year, and I still wait, atavistically I suppose, for Summer.

Please keep on smiling for me.

Last House, Glen Ellen, California   *22.xi.82*
To: Theo Steele[1]

Dear Theo... that is really a beautiful little bottle, especially with its clear-glass stopper. Thank you for giving it to me.

I think the color is yours... it is Theo-color. I've always loved it, but never identified it until now with a person. I used to have a short bottle that was almost the same... I think it was a Bromo-Seltzer bottle, although my family never used that, so I wonder where I got it. I was about 7–8–9. I kept it in a lug-box that Father gave me for Christmas, when we were apparently rather hard up, perhaps in about 1913 or so. He gave one to my little sister Anne too. He rubbed them down, and painted our initials on them. They did not have any lids, but it never occurred to us to touch whatever the other kept in hers, at opposite ends of our little clothes-closet. One summer I put some pretty little pebbles in mine, and then a few years later I started collecting some rather rare shells called coffee-beans at Laguna, and kept them in my blue bottle.

Well... years later a friend who has blonde thick hair and blazing dark-blue eyes told me she had a strong love for that color, and I tried to find some old Bromo-Seltzer bottles in junk-stores, with no luck. But I did find her four one-pound jars made for Pond's Cold Cream, of almost that color. They made handsome candle holders with short thick votive-type candles in them... good light.

But your bottle is the best. I think it might possibly have been a pharmacist's bottle, perhaps for something like an early version of Eno's fruit Salts????? Or for some elixir that should be protected from the light???

That was such a nice day, when you and John and Francie were here! Thank you again for coming. (Norah and I finished off the good pieces of pâté etc etc etc, and blessed you too....)

Why didn't I ask you a lot of the questions in my head, about going back to school? Certainly you look as if it agrees with you! Do you feel excited about tackling prescribed books and assignments and all that as a comparative adult instead of an immature person? It was fascinating to me to watch or rather listen (because I seldom see my younger girl but talk now and then by phone...) to Kennedy as she picked up her student work after a 14-year pause. Once she called me, really quite peeved, and said accusingly, "Why didn't you ever *tell* me to read Poe? He's *marvelous....*" I was highly amused....

Please give my love to Francie. Do you think the trip to NY was good? Is she well? (1000 more questions I never asked you, that Sunday!!!) Francie is, increasingly, one of the VIPs in my life, although nobody would really guess it I suppose. Certainly I can't explain it. And I feel quite presumptuous about it... about the mysterious feeling I have with all of you, that we've been together a long time.

1. Daughter of Frances and Robert Steele

I have neither the time nor the skill to tackle this subject, and perhaps it's just as well (or even better!). But if I could, I'd like to try to write about this *family* thing, as it seems to have evolved in my own consciousness at least. I have known many "families," of course, and have experienced all the shallow and deep reactions toward them as entities, units, forces, shapers, all that. But there have been three in my personal experience that were mine... three that I belonged to. (There were almost four... I am *almost* a member of a strange strong German-Jewish family, but only in two+ generations.) There is my own immediate family, to which I belong firmly, although I don't feel any mystique at all about consanguinity. There was the Evans family,[2] a large handsome brood. I met them in about 1933, and although I am still in occasional contact with only two of them by now, I feel as shaped by them as I do by my own parents and siblings... or almost. And then there is the Steele family, as I've known it through your parents and you and Jed and less immediately through your sisters and Jonathan and then your children and Jed's and Jonnie's boy and and and.

I don't know why I got into this thing, Theo, and I hope you'll forgive my wordiness.... How did that color of blue get me into this? I have thought A LOT ABOUT IT LATELY. SORRY ABOUT caps...

I hope you all have a good Thanksgiving, in your chosen ways. I plan to, too. Today there has been quiet steady rain, but the radio predicts bright cold weather for Thursday.

·····

Last House, Glen Ellen, California   *4.i.83*
To: Lawrence Clark Powell

Dear Ghuce,

A quick one, to send you much love and all my high hopes for your work and everything else in this new year... plus a couple of nice silly tidbits to make you smile. Did you get an invitation from the *Occidental* Magazine to contribute to a new column in the Class Notes called "I Remember..."? It includes a wonderful page called "Guidelines," giving some ten suggestions about what to remember, and ending with quote "The entire palate of life during your college years is subject for such reminiscence. LENGTH, 70–200 words."

There is no use making any comments at all about your palate during some four extremely and wildly turbulent years there....

My most cheerful personal news (oh, I bowed out of the Oxy invitation!) is that I have been nominated or rather elected to be an honorary Armenian. I feel fine about it. It is because I wrote an innocent little thing in a recent *New Yorker*, which is now being called erotic etc., and which the Central Committee of the Armenian General Benevolent Union of America thinks qualifies me. The letter of announcement says that this appointment entitles me to talk knowingly of Michael Arlen and Saroyan and to

2. Hugh Evans and his son Bill, who followed his father's career and became chief gardener for Walt Disney's theme parks

be the object of glowering looks if ever I visit Turkey. So now, when I am polled by academic boards and asked to put something in the complete blank of honorary degrees and literary awards, I have something to say.

End of report.

How about you?

....

Last House, Glen Ellen, California   *19.ii.83*
To: Sylvia and Gene Thompson

Dear Thompsons both... la Belle et le Beau...

Thank you YES... I was indeed your Valentine! Thank you too for asking me to be! The message came, and finally went, exactly as it was meant to... USPS and then Little Red Lane....

And thank you for sending me the picture, Gene. I love it. Yes, I wish I could see your house, but I doubt it muchly. I'd like to see a picture of it in the snow. . . .

Betwixt and amongst us we'll keep the presses turning, and I look forward to seeing *Nobody Came* next summer, and of course will send down *Sister Age* when it turns up... perhaps late April. Keep on, both of you, and so will I. . . .

As for flavoring eggs with truffles, the truffles must be fresh and the eggs must be tightly covered. A good compromise, and I mean COMPROMISE, is to break four fresh eggs into a jar, add one fine fresh or canned truffle, and close it for at least two but not three hours. Remove the truffle, mince it with a little sour cream, gently make an omelet of the eggs, and fold in the truffle-mix. Pure heaven.

One good truffle now costs about $12 tinned (urbani are the best... not the white but the black), or around $40 fresh. It's mad. Apparently the French and American govts hope to produce them by 2000 for about $40 a pound. I asked if this would not destroy the exotic rarity etc. Answer, no, because proteins will be comparatively priced... that is, the substitutes we are now being conditioned and prepared for. A beefsteak, when there is one, will have taken the price-place of the truffle as an exotic unprocurable. On our present scale, truffles will be where Maine lobsters now are... about $40-plus a pound, but not $400–$700, as animal meats will be then.

So earth-worm brownies, anyone????? (I've already eaten one....)

All goes well here. I'll write more and soon. Sylvie, you're next on my list, à toi seule mais toujours à vous deux.

....

Last House, Glen Ellen, California   *1.iii.83*
To: Lawrence Clark Powell

Dearest Ghuce:

You write that you are "afraid" you've reached the age of self-scrutiny. Don't be afraid.

I never wondered much about it, but perhaps assumed that you might never attain this level of interest. Of course it can be uncomfortable, but it is also of real and rare interest and even fascination, if indulged in deliberately.

I don't like, though, your apparent negativism. Why are you seeing *"all that's wrong"*?

Probably the main trouble with you is that you are, as you say right off, seeing all this, or at least some of it, "for the first time."

That is an amazing and perhaps unique thing about you, Larry... at least in my own looks at people I love. It is *astounding*, really, that any human being as sensitive and aware and even empathetic could have lived even half as long as you have and never look at himself. (Sorry... getting mixed up in agreement of tenses or something like that. But I'm writing very fast, because I want to tell you about how I've been pondering your note written on the 23 Feb.)

I do hope this negative introspection or whatever it can be called... this somewhat bilious "self-scrutiny"... does not cause you undue pain.

I mean this sincerely, and am not being sarcastic, although you may remember, as I do, that sometimes I have mocked and teased you a little for being so god-damned self-assured and bland about walking rough-shod over people's conditioned nerve-ends... and about always saying so serenely that you had never done one single thing in your life that you were ashamed of, that you regretted. And all the time I myself, and other even better people, were ashamed and embarrassed and even very angry at you for your smugness.

Well, now you ask me a few questions, and I can answer some of them, and I shall. This is partly because you tell me that once I wrote to you, in "the first flush of Diane," and that you loved me in spite of my letters and that you still do.

CAN I CORRECT ANY OF... ALL THAT'S WRONG WITH ME? Why should you, dearest Larry? What is done is done. You are *you*. It would be absolutely maudlin and wasteful and mawkish to try to turn yourself into a kind of "parfit knight" at this stage in your life.

And anyway, Time is taking care of all that. You're no longer the wild stallion charging across no matter what heavenly pastures, and yet you know very well that you are not meant, *ever*, to be a snickering old man re-living his non-existent conquests, like WMS or a hundred other even better writers.

You know, and so do I that any sort of retreat into cozy senility is impossible for you. You will die as you have lived, Ghuce, and I don't want you to waste any more time trying to lick wounds that you suddenly see.

Many of them are wishful, you know.

You ask, ARE THE IMPERFECTIONS TOO DEEP EVEN TO REACH? Probably, I would say, if I knew what ones you were asking about. *Yes,* I say... too deep, even to lick slowly. Leave them alone. Perhaps find out, if it does not cause even more of this itching, why you are worrying them now. Is it because there is no other way to enjoy your misery?

But why are you miserable?

Actually, I don't think that you are. I suspect that you are *enjoying* this so-called Age of Self-scrutiny. You may be a little bored with being 76 and an Éminence Grise in Academia. Your subconscious may have said, Well, Ghuce, how about a little guilt for a change, just to round things off?

You ask, ARE THERE EVEN MORE (IMPERFECTIONS) I'M NOT AWARE OF? Probably there are. (I say this because surely you expected exactly this answer!) But how could there not be? Who do you think you are, for god's sake? Did you honestly assume that you would descend into your teak-and-marble-and-golden tomb a Perfect Being? Hey, man! *Imperfections,* he says. And thus spake Zarathustra....

Now, in your note, I reach the mention of the list of such imperfections that I sent you about Diane et al. Dear Larry, I know that I did not write them to you to whip or taunt you, and indeed I do not remember them at all but am sure that they came from my heart. I've known you longer, and in many ways more closely, than any other man, except my father. (This is odd.... I'd never even thought of it before!)... And I want you to listen to what I am saying now, and stop trying any puritanical efforts to examine old hurts, lick old wounds, open closed doors. OF COURSE your past is not all lily-white, and OF COURSE you can cringe and shudder at some things you have said or done or not said, not done. But you are, in spite of all the kudos and honors, a human being, and therefore you cannot have breathed more than a few breaths without hurt.

So now you have time to look back, and you feel uncomfortable. If that is what you want, go ahead. Much will pain you, if you want to be pained.

But why? How about the other side of it? Since it is really too late to do much anyway, why not think of "all that's *right...*"? Instead of correcting the wrongs, why not add to the rights? Since it is indeed "too late" to reach all the imperfections, why not ignore them and their possible but unsuspected companions?

Ghuce, forgive me for sounding so ghastly-dull pollyannish! But I do think it's an utterly foolish waste of your time to start looking for old guilts and regrets and so on. STOP.

....

Last House, Glen Ellen, California   *30.v.83*
To: Norah Kennedy Barr   *Decoration Day*
                                                                  Memorial Day
                                                              Norah's Birthday
                                       Grandmother Holbrook referred to this
                                        rather scornfully as Civil War Day.
                                          Mother did not like this, so teased
                                          Grandmother about being born on
                                     Bastille Day. Then there was silence.

Dear N... The past sixty-five years probably seem much longer to you than they do to me. I hope that you feel that living through them has been worth it.

From my own viewpoint, I feel very proud of you and of the way you have shaped your life. You have behaved with honesty always, as far as I know, and that is one of the hardest things in this world, to survive. And you have stayed beautiful to look at, which is also a rare thing, and you keep on growing deeper and subtler. You could have stopped this growth almost anywhere and still be ahead of most people, but almost willynilly you seem to unfold... an eternal blossoming.

Well, this may bore you from the first word, and I'm sorry about that, because I hate to risk any such reaction from you. That sounds very silly, given the fact that I am very aware of the cold fact that I bore you more often than not! (It's stronger than I am... and often I know even before I open my mouth that the words I'm going to say will sound utterly dull stupid dead. Ah well.)

One thing is sure, that I cannot imagine my life without you in it.

This has been true since you were born. It always will be. I have always been very *aware* of you, far past the usual and "normal" levels of sibling consciousness or female interest or social exchange. Much oftener than either of us imagine I've deliberately withdrawn from your various lives, for fear of seeming oppressively or even unhealthily needful of being involved with them.

As far as I know, I have never once felt even a twinge of jealousy of you, physical or sexual or mental. This seems odd, maybe. Certainly you have always been much better looking than I, and much more intelligent, and more creative. And certainly every man I have ever known at all intimately has been openly attracted and drawn to you. And most important of all, perhaps, you certainly were/are more "creative" than I. But I've always simply accepted all that as part of my very deep love and admiration and respect and whatever else it must have been, about the long time I have known of your co-existence.

Of course I knew about your creation several months before you were born. I used to watch for Mother to throw herself catta corner across the bed, after Father had gone down for breakfast, and pat her forehead with some Indian Hay cologne on a hankie after she stopped a few wracking dry retches. She would thank me and say that they would not happen much again, and we would go downstairs.

Then when she was very ill, with some sort of growth that was removed up in an old remodelled house, by Dr. Wilson, I knew that she might die and that the baby in her might die. I don't know if Rex was aware that I knew. Probably he was not. The Mc-Clure girls were all helping then, and I realized that there was friction between them and Grandmother, who stayed mostly in her rooms, but it was not until much later that Grandmother felt the fetus should be removed when the tumor was, and that she was angry with Father. The McClure girls sided with him, and made him special dishes that he did not eat... raisin pie, once, I remember. Sis and I thought it was delicious, and we finished it in the kitchen with Margaret and Bertha while Grandmother was in her room and Father was up at the hospital.

When Mother came back, she took Grandmother's little apartment downstairs, and Grandmother walked very slowly upstairs once or twice a day, which she was not supposed to do. Mother kept telling us how kind Grandmother was to do this. And a long time later she told me that she would always hate her mother for not wanting you to be born. (There were many other reasons, of course.)

On about May 28 of that year little Anne was put to bed in the one nice bedroom in the shabby old house Aunt Gwen and her father and brother Raymond lived in, on the corner of Painter and Philadelphia. Mrs. Nettleship had died about a year before, I think, and her room was left exactly as she had wanted it. Windows looked east, up past the College to the hills, and south into lots of old trees along Painter, and the furniture was of white painted wicker. There was a dainty dressing table with three mirrors, the first I ever saw. The curtains were white and thin. It was the most feminine room of my life, like the yellow satin chaise lounge in a tiny unused parlor downstairs, with a ridiculous marble mantelpiece in it and no room for even a chair. The rest of the house was dark, shabby, crude.

Little Anne was already ill, with heavy fever. The pretty room was dark and stuffy, and probably stank already with the horrid smell of measles. Mr. Nettleship and Raymond must have slept and eaten there somewhere, and Aunt Gwen must have gone on cooking and caring for them, but mainly she was readying herself to help with your birth, while she took care of Anne and me.

I slept on a cot next to Anne, since it was foregone that I would soon have the measles too. And by May 30 I was feverish and very "loppy," as Mother would say. I was not allowed to go past the screen door of our house, where the nurse was already in charge. I tried to call up to Mother, who was in labor, but one of the McClure girls came and told me crossly to go back to the Nettleship house and stay there.

I tried to climb up into the old apricot tree between our houses, but felt too strange and sickish. I looked in on Anne, who slept with little moaning sounds, in the dark hot room, and then I went through the empty house to the little room with the yellow satin chair in it and read *Through the Looking Glass*. Alice was talking to her kitten, I remember, as it played with a ball of yarn, and I tried to talk aloud as she did. I said, "I am having a little sister." But it sounded so strange, there in the tiny room, and I felt so foolish to be pretending to talk to an invisible cat, that I knew I would never talk to in that ridiculous way even if Alice did; then I closed the book and went upstairs and undressed, even though it was not yet supper-time.

Later that night Aunt Gwen came slowly up the steep staircase of the old farmhouse. She stood in the doorway and looked at us from the lighted hall, and said in a flat tired voice, "Mary Frances and Anne, you have a beautiful little sister named Norah."

Anne did not even rouse herself, perhaps from deep fever-dreams, but said in a croaky way that surprised me, "Yes. I know." Aunt Gwen said something like "Oh, you're such a smarty!" and went down to take care of Mr. Nettleship.

After the first few days, having measles at Aunt Gwen's was delightful. And Father came at least once every day, always with a crazy present for each of us as we grew better. He never came in, but would talk to us from the doorway, and read us poems he had written to each of us and then toss the new little copy-books in to us and ask us to write more poems back to him for the next day. Once he brought Anne a funny little plaster dog that stuck out its tongue when she pulled its tail, and she named it Teddy Rosy-belt. Father was very pleased, because he admired Roosevelt, and he frowned at me when I laughed at Anne's pronunciation and said it sounded just right to him. Of course he brought me something that day, too, but I was embarrassed to have been mean to Anne and didn't remember what it was.

Finally we were allowed to get dressed and put on the dark goggles that Father had brought for us (as if they were glamorous presents and not the medical necessities thought essential in 1917), and we went to see Mother and you.

And that is all I remember about it... except perhaps that Mother looked very soft and beautiful, with enormous smiling brown eyes, sitting in a low chair with you in her arms.

And the next day Aunt Gwen took Anne and Margie Thayer and me to the Selig Zoo in Pasadena. We all wore black glasses, because we'd caught measles the same day at school, from Grace Keller I think.

That is as good an end as any, to this odd crumb from so many calendar years ago.

It is by now quite early in your birthday, and later I'll call you. There are several small nothings to say, besides HappyHappy, and as I try to think now about how I began this letter to you, I have a feeling that I may have sounded rather mawkish. But I know that I don't need to add to whatever I may have said that my enduring love for you is not blindfold. I've never felt in any way that you were a flawless and impeccable human being.

But I do know that I have never once faltered in my respect and my unquestioning devotion.

End of Birthday Greeting Card.

It seems improbable, or perhaps even impossible, that I've never thanked you for the eight days I spent at Jenner... eight days you presented me on a silver salver! Dolce far niente, indeed... what lazy bliss, with no telephone, no marketing, no cooking, no mail, no responsibilities....

It was strange and in a way dismaying to find everything exactly the same, when I got back, except of course for new piles of mail. I dawdled for a few days, and then slipped right into a period of frustrated indolence, with the damned foot.[1] Ho hum. Thank you for making it seem almost humanic....

....

Last House, Glen Ellen, California   *16.ix.83*
To: Lawrence Clark Powell

Dearest Ghuce:

This is not a real answer to your nice card, but a quick note to tell you that all goes very well indeed, and that I am a medical miracle, with not a single hitch in my amaz-

1. MF had an infection in her foot that would not heal.

ingly fast recovery, and that of course I blame the whole extraordinary success of both the implant and the hip replacement on Hal Bieler's diet of zucchini and "calcium broth." (My otherwise evil living may have had something to do with it too....) Suffice it to say that although I am currently bored silly by hours of physiotherapy, I am childishly thrilled to graduate from a clunky walker to a comparatively elegant chromium cane, as of yesterday and almost one month ahead of schedule. End of report.

I'm truly sorry not to have thanked you before for the remembrance of Duncan Brent. It is a beautiful little book, solemn and serious but not oppressive. I am proud to have it, and proud of you for creating it. Of course it makes me wish that I had known them. The other day I said to Norah that you seemed to have a special gift for making other people express themselves to you with a clarity and poignancy that they probably are not much aware of. I remember reading a letter, in that English bookseller's memoir of Jake, a letter he wrote to you that actually gave me a sharp pang of envy. I thought, God damn, I wish Jake or *somebody* would ever say anything like that to me.

I know this sounds very puny of me and I hope you will excuse it. Today I am "on my own," for the first time in more than two months and I must tell you that it is wonderful. I've been unusually fortunate that both Norah and Kennedy have been able to take turns being here when I've not been in hospitals, and since they are two of my most favorite people I've enjoyed every minute of it. In Kennedy's case, her misfortune was my good luck since she is not moon-lighting at Woodminster this summer (only white female stage-manager west of Mississippi!), and has not signed her contract with Berkeley Rep... she's trying to make up her mind about being married, after 16 years. Ho hum. I managed to keep my mouth shut most of the time, and often remind myself that just because I would do this or that does not make it advisable that anyone else behave the same way.

I'll write again soon, and meanwhile can report that the Richman and Gloria did come for lunch one day.[1] They seemed relaxed and are just about as I have always known and loved them for the past 52 years or so! I can't see how this late blooming discovery of physical and mental companionship can be anything but wonderful for them both. I doubt that they marry, but why should they? . . .

I'm so happy that you are working, and letting your mind go back to rememberings of your father. Isn't it odd that I knew about him before I knew you!? My father knew him because of the citrus business, so important then. I wonder if you will be able to separate him from your mother, in your writing. I myself know how very hard it is to try to tell the truth stripped of what other people in their own lives have made it since it actually happened. I think that writing a book about my first ten years was the toughest job I ever gave myself. I learned a lot, but will never try such a deliberate trick again.

Much love,

1. Ward Ritchie was called "The Richman" by L. C. Powell. Ritchie and Gloria Stuart fell in love after they were both widowed.

Last House, Glen Ellen, California   *3.xii.83*
To: David Pleydell-Bouverie

Dearest David... it was very nice indeed to hear your voice this morning, even though you sounded farther away than the 6 astronauts or whatever they are now cruising Outer Space.... Thank you for calling. . . .

The "Gourmet Dinner" at your club sounds completely and correctly gourmet-dinnerish, and I hope it was fun, too. How did the Sonoma Cutrer Chardonnay sneak in there? I think the wine-jury felt supremely broad-minded, anyway, with Western upstarts like Bouverie keeping an eye on things.

That reminds me that today I'm supposed to go to a tiny little intimate luncheon for 16, chez Sammy Seb.[1] I had to bow out, thank God because I can't stand a few of the guests... people are coming from London for pix etc. And Julia the honoree will be here for three days next week... Paul of course, and Rosie Manell. Noni is coming over, but only for one lunch because she now has a 9-weeks-old dog and is too fond of Lida to leave her in charge for overnight(!).

The literary outpourings of your staff leave me humbled, and I hesitate to write more than "having fine time... wish you were here"!!!! I haven't checked on how Chinese herbologists smell, lately anyway, but certainly the air is very sweet here now. When people walk out to their cars their feet crush the falling eucalyptus buds, and they look almost dazed for a minute. I put some buds in their hands.

Later.... Elaine,[2] to continue my Life Among the Literates, was rather put off by two of the Limey team who came up to get Catherine Stott from the London *Observer.* It seems that they drove up to "the courtyard" and got out and were about to wander into the Inner Court (All this is in Elaine's phraseology) when she went down to ask them who in hell they were. They said they were looking for me, but since she had seen them leave la Stott three hours before at my door, she knew they were snooping journalists. (They were, and I am somewhat affronted by this report, since I had no idea they'd been up at the Ranch when they came and I made tea for them....) They asked silly questions about how the Ranch was called Bouverie, after the street the London *Times* was on, etc. Ho hum. Elaine then repeated verbatim your very well researched spiel about journalists-in-general, and I agreed solemnly with her that we are a pack of rats. She is definitely a defender of your faith!

I'm glad you could go to Atlanta. I think that if I were to choose a good place, I'd choose that, except that it is in Georgia.

I'm glad too that you could see your 21 letters collected, in the Rosenbach! (You do write good ones, even if now and then you don't mail them. I remember one to the current pope.......)

And I'm so pleased that you like Frankenthaler. Did you go to her new show? I

1. Samuel Sebastiani, local vintner
2. Elaine and Paul Ingle were ranch caretakers for David Pleydell-Bouverie.

think it's the best yet. I do wish she'd pinch herself down, though. Who has all that space? Once she painted about 8 small canvases for a man I know in NY, whom she loved for a time, and I wonder what happened to them.... (Maybe you can ask her....?) Meanwhile I content myself with posters and catalogs.

And I couldn't afford to buy anything, anyway. NO MORE ACQUISITIONS, I keep saying. (Not even a Polynesian fly-whisk...)

The stay at the New Osaka, as Norah calls it, was very strange. In Japan we knew we were guests and we knew we were bugged 24 hours a day, so we said nothing except an occasional groan of exhaustion. But in Los Angeles, there we were in Osaka and Tokyo again, piss-elegance in true Hiltonesque, and everything that had angered and annoyed and ruffled and insulted and amused us was suddenly alive again, and OVERT, so that we literally revelled in mocking everything and everybody. God, it was wonderful, in a nasty way! But there was ONE GOOD MOMENT, when we went into a small Japanese restaurant near the hotel, in reclaimed slum-lands back of the old City Hall, and ate tiny maple-leaves dipped in transparent batter and deep-fried to a crisp delicacy as if they had been frozen. They were incredible. They were like the scene in *Dr. Zhivago* photographed in a beautiful country-house that has been left wide open by the invaders, so that everything is covered with crystal ice but still passionately alive.

The dessert at the "banquet" after the Awards,[3] for only 56 of the Chosen Few, was, a summing up: A tall "sherbet glass" filled with layers of fruit sorbets and heavy mousses, topped with raspberry syrup and bits of walnut, and with a leaf of Belgian endive stuck in each.

Nobody will ever believe this. But there were 55 other people there. At my table, where I sat to the right of the "Executive Vice President," a female bird-brain who must surely know where several Chandler bodies are buried, she had once been head of the FOOD DEPT., like Mimi Sheraton at the *NY Times,* so we did not dare even look at each other or or or. It was astonishing. (Should we try it sometime?)

I liked the three other prize-winners... two did not show up, because one was dying and the other was in Paris. Old Fernand Braudel gave a neat little thank-you via satel-lite, which was flashed into the auditorium where the awards were given. Somebody read an endless dull poem by James Merrill, while we had to look at a huge picture of him behind the podium. (His caricature was the only recognizable one. Who cannot draw a living corpse?) I sat with old Walter Percy, a very nice fellow, and I liked Thomas Keneally, who with his wife had flown in from Australia, and Seymour Hersh, whose book about Kissinger you may have looked at (It's good).

Well, a big fuss was made about a "leather-bound volume" of my favorite book, and since I have never liked anything I ever wrote I settled on *Sister Age* because I thought it would be nice to send it to old Alfred Knopf, who will be about 94 this year. So it was PRESENTED... trumpets off-stage to left, of course. I tottered on-stage, took it with a quavering thank-you, and then left it in our sittingroom.... It was really hideous, and

3. MF was given an award by the *Los Angeles Times.*

I don't think I'd have dared send it to AAK... puffy cinnamon-brown leather, lots of gold leaf... very terrible. Some important Japanese executive no doubt found it amongst the Naugahyde volumes of hotel directories and Gideon Bibles and Book of Buddhas in the sittingroom and said Ah So and threw it into the wastebasket for me.

End of report, I think. Oh... Carey man came for us on very stormy day and the Golden Gate was closed because of wind so we went to the Bay Bridge and there was a one-hour delay so we finally took the Dumbarton and went through Palo Alto to the SF airport. It did not matter at all. The car was a mile long, and like floating in cream. The driver's knuckles were a little white at times, but we did not care. We missed four flights, but had nothing to do that night in the New Otani but meet Matthew. We went down to the bar for a dreadful drink. It was unbelievably shoddy, a nightmare of Oxy-Ory, as it is now called: Occidental-Oriental vulgarity pulsating with supercilious mockery and detestation. It was filled with really beautiful secretaries waiting for their Japanese bosses to join them from all the council-chambers in the hotel. They wore really exquisite clothes, in the latest style from Givenchy and the Tokyo Paris crowd. We got out soon, and took a cab to a middle-class Chinese place, very bright and ugly after all this phony darkness.

It was interesting that all the important diplomats and executives seemed to be travelling with their wives, children, and very ancient nannies or grandmothers. It took them a long time to get in and out of the hundreds of silent elevators in the New Otani. The man came first, never with his lovely secretary, but with his beautifully dressed smiling silent wife three or five steps behind him. Then came a small son and a smaller daughter, five steps behind the mother, dressed by Pierre Chardin or some-body and silently smiling. After them, head down and smiling silently, came the nanny or perhaps grandmother, very very small indeed.

(I seem to be feeling wordy... I know you don't mind. I suddenly want to tell you some things about our being in Osaka again in Los Angeles.)

It is true that since the American Occupation the Japanese have added a few inches to their height. It is a question of diet, apparently. People born at the turn of the century are about three inches shorter than their children. And the third and fourth generations back from Now are really tiny... tiny little old bent-over gnarled things. We saw them getting in and out of elevators, for those three days or weeks or centuries we were there.

And I did not realize until a few days after we came home, and Norah went out to Jenner and her new dog, and I got back into my patterns here, that all the time we were in Japan Norah was ACUTELY uncomfortable. She was aware of being a big pink-skinned female as she had never known it before. She was constantly uncomfortable. I, on the other hand, have always, no matter where, accepted the fact that I was a freak, different. I've always, no matter where, turned myself into a ghost, invisible. And since Norah and I have often travelled into foreign lands together, I've stupidly assumed that she felt as I felt. But the truth was that when we were in Japan in 1978, she was deeply and constantly *uneasy* about being freakish, an enormous unwelcome uncouth grotesque *female,* unwelcome always, accepted perforce.

My god! I too was unwelcome, and I was female and uncouth and gigantesque to my hosts. But it did not bother me at all, because I've *always* been a ghost, invisible.

So when I finally knew how ugly this whole thing had been for Norah, five years ago in Japan, I felt shocked and sorry. I felt selfish and unthinking.

Well, David, you'll understand all this. But how can I ever make it up to my little sister? She is a beautiful person, and a finely wrought object in every way, and she never once whimpered, in those long days in Osaka....

Well. Don't worry. What can it *possibly* matter to Guess What?

All really goes very well, with Norah and me too. She'll be over to see Rosemary and the Childs, as I said. And I've thrown away the cane and every day forget more and more that I am now worth $3000 of pure titanium. The other day when my dentist put in two new gold crowns I asked her who got all that precious metal when a person died, and she said, "The undertaker." So I asked my lawyer about how to get precious metals into the hands of the inheritors rather than the body-burners, and I'd forgotten that he is a devout Catholic so may have to find new counsel. Do you have any suggestions?

David, I'll probably not send this, but IN CASE, it brings my love always, and my heart's wishes for your happy holidays and a fine exciting healthy rich new year.

....

Last House, Glen Ellen, California   *9.ii.84*

To: Norah Kennedy Barr, Anna Parrish, and Mary Kennedy Wright...

I want to tell you what some of you may have to think about, since chronologically I'll not outlive any of you....

I wish and want and hope to die in my own home. Some of you may want to help me do this.

Rex Kennedy told us that he wanted to die in his own house, "at home." It was difficult at times, and even painful and unpleasant, but we brought it off. And I must tell you that I myself feel that it was worth any physical and perhaps spiritual inconveniences I had to put up with for a time... quarreling nurses, sad and sometimes very scary character-changes in my father. A few hours before Rex died, in a cosmic rage at finding himself only mortal... and I know he was frightened too... Dr. Bruff said, "You must keep in your mind that this is not your father, the man you have known." This helped me accept the raging roaring old lion in his next-to-last hours, and the suspicious wily fox of perhaps five days before that. It was *not* Rex, really, or at least it was not the man I knew as my father and friend.

And this may happen with me, although I, and all of you, devoutly hope that it will not, and that I can leave the scene easily.

BUT...

I want to leave it either by myself or with a few friends, HERE, or with you.

I know that nurses, either RN or "practical," are hard to find and hard to live with. But they exist. And the situation by the time they are needed is a temporary one. As for the expense, they cost no more than the kind of rest-home or nursing-home you might find, that you would want me to end my life in. There are a few, perhaps, but we all know that most of them are simply living graveyards... and that living corpses are not often treated as decently as dead ones.

I hope to leave enough available cash to take care of such possible expenses. If there is not enough, you will simply have to borrow for more. It will be worth the doing, believe me, a few years along....

As for the personal physical side, I feel sad if you must try to carry out this wish of mine. I apologize to you now, for whatever trials it may put you through, and I thank you with all my heart. Between and among you, there will be enough energy and love to see the thing through. It may mean a temporary displacement, and it may even change the lives of your children or your friends, but I believe that it will not be bad, eventually. And meanwhile, I'll send this little manifesto to you, and then leave it lay where Jesus flang it.

What it comes down to is that I hope somebody will enable me to die in my own bed, if I do indeed need help then.

With love and thanks...

....

Last House, Glen Ellen, California   4.v.84
To: Lawrence Clark Powell

Dearest Ghuce:

I'm sorry to be so long in writing to you.

Yes, your postcard was indeed a little grumpy, and by now you know that I have indeed read the book and thought a lot about it. I still believe that it is more about the country than about the effect of that country on people. They are less real to me than they are to you, of course. I am glad though that you keep right on writing exactly as you need to and want to. In the same way, I can only read you as I myself am. I find your people, especially in *El Morro* less important than you do. I want you to write as only you can about where they were, and not about what where they were did to them. Obviously I can't express myself about this with any satisfaction, so I'll stop. The main thing to say to you is that you have done a very good piece of work, and that I am proud of you and of it. . . .

I don't remember why or what made me say "why don't you?" but certainly apologize if I did so in any way that was offensive... and meanwhile I look forward to seeing your "Portrait" and do not understand at all why you say that you are prepared for my not liking it. I think you are still being rather grumpy, or perhaps you are simply turning into a testy old professor, and I am turning into an equally testy old bitch. I hope not, in both cases! Try to remind yourself that just because I am a woman I am not necessarily destined to act as the cold water for any "ardent nature" such as yours may be. . . .

....

Last House, Glen Ellen, California   *14.vi.84*
To: Elaine Leotti

Dear Mrs. Leotti:

I'm sorry to be so long in thanking you for your letter. It was very exciting to read again about Ovide Yencesse. Yes, of course we speak of the same man, and I envy you for having one of his medals. The only tangible I own is a copy of a charcoal drawing by one of his sons, Pierre.

You probably know that Ovide Yencesse became one of the best medalists in the world because he was so small. He told me that he simply could not handle the big mallets and chisels that he would have needed to use. He discussed this at length with Rodin, and agreed with the older man's advice that he become a medalist. I think O.Y. was basically bitter and frustrated, but he seemed to send out waves of true gentleness and very subtle power. He was married to a large woman, and they had a huge family... something like 12 children as I remember, all of them tall, strong, handsome people. They were very generous, and what I think could truly be called ebullient. They lived in a shabby old villa a little outside of Dijon, and held open house every Sunday, and ate and drank and danced to records and occasionally to live music provided by friends.

I went to Dijon in 1929, and the first year there I went to night classes at Beaux Arts with M. Yencesse. The second year I was more serious about it, and went every day in the mornings, three times a week to him and two to the other famous teacher there whose name I forget... a very second rate, socially prominent water colorist. He was much less of an artist than Y. but everybody said he was head of Beaux Arts because he was a Count in Burgundy. He was said to be extremely jealous of Y. artistically I suppose. Y. was completely without social pretensions, and with his family lived a rich, noisy, full life. As I remember, the two men were never seen together in public, although Yencesse was not at all self-conscious of his tiny size.

He was not even 5 feet tall, and everything about him was in perfect scale. He moved rather like Charlie Chaplin, very gracefully but never effeminately or even daintily. He had a thick head of rather short hair, and a rather full but pointed beard, and dark eyes. He was always extremely courteous with me, and when we met in public he bowed and kissed my hand. In the Ateliers he was businesslike and often rather brutal, mostly to the men students when they did something clumsy or really poor in the large Statues and things that they worked on. They were a mixture of young Italian apprentices to the people who provided elaborate tombs and headpieces in the cemeteries, plus a few very serious young artists studying for Paris and heading bravely for the Prix de Rome. There were a few dilettantes, of both sexes, and of the upper classes in Burgundy. The girls and women headed mostly for their peer, the water colorist, and for a long time I was the only woman working with Yencesse.

For a long time I was in the same Atelier with the boys, and paid little attention to them. (I was newly married and deeply in love, for one thing....) Then one morning I found my stuff moved out into a long gallery where we kept the tubs of clay, and M. Yencesse apologized to me for this apparent isolation and said that he had a real row before his classes started that day, because when he went into the big atelier he found that one of the boys had stuck a banana in each of the life-size clay statues that several of the students were working on. (I can't even write about this without chuckling, because we both started off with such complete and bland politeness.) He managed to imply that I was far too innocent and naive and generally well bred to have understood the crude and suggestive trick that some rude fellow had pulled off in hopes of embarrassing me. I, in turn played to the hilt the role he had cast me in, and did not even blush or lower my eyes or titter, all of which he fully expected me to do. That's the end of the story of course, except that I remember very vividly how really pained and embarrassed he was as he tried to explain to me why I had to continue to work all alone in that long gallery.... In fact, I suspect that he discussed the whole thing with the water colorist and that between the two they managed to get me more interested in going to the silly classes with all the other young ladies, where we sat unsmilingly drawing a handsome Italian, stark naked, for several hours each morning. Now and then I would hear a great roar of laughing and talking from M. Yencesse's rooms, and I wished I could be there instead of in such comparatively discreet company.

End of report, I think... except that I notice that Yencesse died in 1947, which I did not know. That means he was 80! I know that three of his boys died early in World War II. I am sorry that he could not have died in '37 instead. I wonder if he grew even tinier as he aged....

Please excuse me for this rambling answer to your letter. I hope you don't regret suggesting that I share something of what I remember.

Very sincerely,

....

Last House, Glen Ellen, California   *17.ix.84*
To: Judith Jones
Dear Judith:

It was very good to hear your voice again. Thank you for calling. I can still hear the Vermont part... relaxed and unworried about work, at least for a few hours. And Norah was here, soon after, and I told her about Aunt Hilda's tossing her cane across the airport waiting room... nothing more there, except that we both send you our sympathy and love and congratulations and everything connected with the plain fact that you are doing a beautiful job helping a terrified old lady do her best. (My friend, Jayne, is typing this as I talk, and she is now coping with what might be called Life with Father, who is an autocratic old rascal of 89, whose dog has just died after 16 years, and she suggested that after terrified I put miserable. I do not agree, because physically neither Aunt Hilda nor Grandpa is physically any more miserable than a lot of us. But we do not yet know except vicariously what a doctor would call the death anxiety that comes at night....)

About the *Reader*: Of course I don't agree at all with Mr. Gottlieb that it is a cinch to put it together.[1] It depends entirely on who does it, and what he or she wants to prove that somebody said. In the case of Fisher, it could be about food or traveling or old age or sex or children or or or. Or it could be a beginning-to-end collection about short stories. Or of essays. Again, or or or. In other words, God help us all.

But you do know, Judith, that if there is anything I can do I want to. I have absolutely no interest in any such project, myself. Neither, I think, does Norah, but I know she would want to help you if she could... you and me.

And I wonder what about diaries or journals...? When Norah was going through stuff for *As They Were*, she turned up a lot of journals, although I was firmly convinced that as I wrote them I had destroyed them all. This was because I once read that people keep records of their own inner and outer doings solely in hopes of having them read some day, and I did not and do not believe this. I was really amazed to find that I had not thrown them all away. I picked up one, and read about a page, and was literally shocked to find that less than two weeks after I married my first husband or rather was married to him, I was wondering why on earth I had done it. Until I read that page, I'd been thinking since at least October 1929 that I was a blissful, dewy eyed, ignorant and completely fulfilled young female! So who was that woman who wrote that page?

So here's a whole new can of worms, maybe. Or should I do what I thought I had done, and burn it? Why do I hang on to it?

Change of subject: I love what you said about the *Journal of Gastronomy*. That whole subject still distresses me. The editor gave me a rather peremptory notice about having my next story done by November 2, and I told him I was taking no more work indefinitely... I never told him that I would write ever again, but it was quite toplofty of him to assume that I would. He had asked me for names of possible writers, so I gave him Jeannette Ferrary's and also Angelo Pellegrini's, and they both leaped at the chance, and all I can hope is that they get paid (which of course I did, much to my surprise).

I'm sorry that I seem to have been rather vague about Bob's[2] attentions to me, and I told him so. Lately, I did tell him very firmly what he has known for many years, in fact since he "took me over" from Henry Volkening, that I do not want to work for the Conde Nast people. Suddenly I found that I was doing not only a reprint of the Pellegrini afterword from North Point Press, for *House & Garden*, but a rewrite of the Toklas introduction for *Vanity Fair*. The first was rather easy, but I must have spent a good

1. Judith Jones wanted MF to put together an *M. F. K. Fisher Reader*. Robert Gottlieb, then a Knopf editor, was encouraging her to do it.
2. Robert Lescher, MF's agent

twelve hours on the telephone with two editors and a copy editor from *VF*, going over every single paragraph, word, and grammatical structure of that silly Toklas thing, which I had loved writing and which I now will barely recognize as very British rather than completely American prose. I told Bob that from now on I must flatly refuse any possible connections with Conde Nast. I told him I was truly sorry if this would cause him any embarrassment, but *too bad*.

I really do hate to be unpleasant with Bob, because he always comes through as a poor wounded butterfly type, completely the "gentleman" and making me feel like a clumsy oaf, and I know that neither of us is that. So don't give it any more thought. . . .

This is obviously in reply to an old letter, but I did want to tell you that I appreciate very much whatever you're doing with the *Reader*, and I do want to help if possible.

Please give my love to Evan, Aunt Hilda, your Mother, Teg, and especially JBJ.

....

Last House, Glen Ellen, California   *24.x.84*
To: Lawrence Clark Powell

Dear Goose,

No, your letter didn't get here before I left for Jenner, and I got back a couple of days ago. I loved getting your note with the Salisbury Cathedral Constable. Do you know that once I was stuck in Salisbury with Mother and my sister Anne for five days? Something about a badly wrenched knee for poor Edith... and Sis and I spent twelve hours a day in and around the Cathedral. I feel as if I know every stone in it, which of course I don't. And now Janet Stone (no pun meant) lives in the Close, and Isobel Radnor goes at least once a month to the Sunday morning services, partly to please the parishioners as she sits in the iron cage that was built for her family so long ago. She's now Dowager Countess, and is very good about her job, and she is a much nicer person than Janet Stone. . . .

I'm glad you finished the book about your father. I hope I can read it, but I wish I did not have to wait until '86. Is there any chance of seeing your script? And what are you publishing in '85? Here I am chipping away at my Project,[1] and am somewhat abashed but not scared to realize that Christmas is day after tomorrow!

I've been saying blandly that I would finish it by then, as if it were eight months away. Ho hum. I've been very good about not taking on any deadlines until I finish it.

I seem to have gone through the classical period of any older writer's life doing prefaces and introductions for my friends, and right now I have four new books to look at, because my name's on the cover along with the real writers! The only one I really care about is a foreword to the new edition of the *Alice B. Toklas Cookbook*. It was fun to write, and in the book it is just the way I did it. A completely anglicized version will be in *Vanity Fair* next month I hear. The new editor of that ridiculous attempt to whip a dead horse is an Englishwoman, and she must have spent ten hours on the telephone from

1. During the last ten years of her life MF worked on a "secret project" that consisted of short essays, some of which were published in *Last House*.

New York, going over every word of the completely unimportant material as if it were Holy Scripture. Ho hum again.

It was fun to be out at Norah's, away from telephones and so on, and I chugged along happily in her little back bedroom, which used to be the delivery room for the pregnant camp followers when her house was the hospital for the loggers on the Russian River. I call it my Think Tank. So far I carry on very well its reproductive aura.

Love,

....

Last House, Glen Ellen, California *11.xii.84*

To: Weare Holbrook

Dear Weare:

It seems impossible that I haven't really answered two letters from you in the past year or so. I must have sent you a note sometime along the way, because you replied that you hoped my proposed "profile" about Grandmother Holbrook would do justice to her. You won't be surprised that I have not even thought of it for some time. I'd really like to write why I remember what I do, if not exactly what I do remember, but I rather doubt that I'll ever get to it.

As I think back, I probably wrote to you while I was out at Norah's. When I am there, I have absolutely nothing to do except work... no telephones, no friends, very little cooking, no people at all except for meals with Norah and occasionally her housemate.... I get a hell of a lot done, and I feel really happy and in a way *clean*. So I stayed a week that time in July. Then in October I went back for two weeks, and almost finished a book I would like to do. I have not touched it since, and I am now laying plans to con her into asking me to come back for a couple more weeks in January. And perhaps then I will go on a bit about Grandmother Holbrook...?

I don't think that Grandmother was much "mellower" when I knew her than when you were a boy. She was a very stern person, but I never heard her say a disagreeable word, and this sometimes astonishes me because she and Edith lived in close quarters for many years and Edith was an emotional impetuous woman, as well as a spoiled willful daughter. Now and then Mother would retire to her room, and probably weep, but Grandmother never even flicked a stony frown or smile. She and Rex were friendly always, but never affectionate.

The first time and the only one that I ever saw a picture of Grandmother looking almost happy and relaxed was when John's wife sent me an old clipping that ran in your column in the Onawa paper. A lot of the family stood on the front porch of the house there and Grandmother looked sweet and smiling. I was astonished and almost shocked.

When I was small, I must have trusted her completely. I remember sitting for hours at a time on a little stool with my head resting on her knee, while she taught me to read and to knit. I read the Bible to her, and later some rather stupid stories she bought from itinerant peddlers. But when I read things like the *Wizard of Oz* I always did it upstairs in the empty guest room with the door shut. I knew that it would be impossible to propose anything so trivial to her. She was, as I think I once wrote, something as important as a tree or a warm fire, but I never loved or liked her as a human being, and when she died, soon after we moved to the Ranch when I was 11, I don't think I even blinked. This is astonishing to me. I can remember a lot about her dying in her bedroom, and the nurse who slept on a kind of couch in the livingroom, and then the pleasant whoop-ti-do of lots of relatives and the baked meats after the funeral (which I did not go to), but there was absolutely no sense of missing her or of regret or even of interest.

Well, she never told me not to be a smart-aleck, but perhaps there was not time enough, and I'm very glad you contradicted her! I wish I could write one tenth as well as you do.

This is a good place to stop, and I don't dare look at the other letter, except that I must tell you that I too find my own deterioration fascinating.

I hope that yours has not progressed far enough to ignore this little squeak from me....

....

Last House, Glen Ellen, California   *8.i.85*
To: Judith Jones

Dearest Judith:

I'm really embarrassed about never having mentioned to you the book by Jeanne Lemlin about *Vegetarian Pleasures*. I do so now no matter how sketchily.

I took a quick look at it when it came, and knew that I wanted to see more of it, and then there were the holidays and then my eyes went all funny-like. They still are, but are plainly much better every day, so this afternoon I looked at the menus and the general plan of the book, and I like the whole thing.

I think it may be a little redundant. However, the variety seems almost endless, and I especially like the desserts and the use of fruits. Some of the recipes are too simple. (Cantaloupe with Strawberries and Lime, for instance! Why not?) They make me feel rather peevish, probably because they remind me that I am still childish too. And what is so world-shaking about a breakfast of orange and grapefruit sections with kiwi, maple pancakes, and coffee or tea? Ho hum. It doesn't make me want to get out of bed. And how about granola with milk or yogurt, blueberry muffins, and Coffee or tea? Wowski.

And of course some of the recipes in any vegetarian cookbook are bound to sound ghastly, in an almost subtle way... curried chickpeas and ginger stew, for instance! The idea makes my sensitive palate quiver.

I still like the book very much indeed. It has not a hint of the saintlike patience and nobility of most such born-againish collections, and it's written well and clearly.

And I hope I have not been too forthright or however you put it, and I do thank you very much indeed for letting me see the galleys. I'll pass them along to a good cook who is an excellent vegetarian as well... I think the correct term for her is lacto-vege as we cognoscenti would say....

Much love to you both, and my compliments to Miss Lemlin.

....

Last House, Glen Ellen, California   *13.iv.85*
To: Norah Kennedy Barr

Dear None:

What you last wrote to me (damn! After all my nagging you never put a date on! I think you wrote last week some time...) has been much on my mind. I'm dictating this to Marsha,[1] obviously, and I still feel somewhat shy or reticent or something about very personal words, although I know that she understands completely all this. So what I will try to say may sound rather stiff.

It was really funny that you wrote about the word "failing" that it was a strange Victorian one, so Marsha and I looked it up and indeed it does exist. See *Webster's International.* Of course I hated to talk about anything Victorian or otherwise about "failing" but I am not at all scared of how I meant the word. I meant that my bodily capacities were gradually becoming less strong and/or usable. That is inevitable and not at all to be frightened by or even dreaded. I myself, inwardly, am not "failing."

I must tell you that I have absolutely no feeling at all, as you say you do, that "we are slowly inexorably sailing away from one another." I sure as hell hate to think that *you* feel that way, though. I don't know why you do, unless subconsciously you want to. I would hate to have to accept that reality, and I might protest a bit, but I know that it is possible, especially in your relationship with me: younger sister with older. It is impossible for me (older to younger), except by empathy. I myself have not had to fight the real dichotomy or whatever it is between what you know now of me and what you still have to carry with you about being a little girl when I was a big girl... about having to stand by when you were five, say, and I was 14, while I bought tickets to the zoo and led you toward the hamburger stand and so on. You know what I am trying to say. I no more wanted to be boss sister than you wanted to be the dependent child. But we've gone over that before....

Of course I do feel angry now and then about being nearer my own natural end than you are, or than Kennedy is, or or or. I'm glad that you approve of that. I am not always "resigned," as you say. But really, chronologically and by the calendar, at least if we were Christians, I have outlived my three score years and ten by now and it seems logical and even likely that you and Kennedy and even a few other people may have to mourn for me instead of my mourning for you. This in itself is unfair, but...

As for the "quiet slipping away," it can happen, although I doubt that it ever will be quite that simple with any of us. I do feel quite sure, though, that I will not slip into a cosmic rage as did Rex and his own father. The main thing, with me and I imagine with most of us, is that I would prefer not to be too helpless... incontinent physically,

1. Marsha Moran, MF's friend and assistant for twelve years

mute and completely dependent. But who can tell? I do think that women are more acceptive and aware than are most men. However. That remains to be seen, in my case and yours and so on.

Now about my real reluctance to hint around about when do I see you? and all that. I know you understand that I don't want you to disrupt anything at all in your own life in Jenner to drive over here and then turn around almost at once and drive back. I know that you have things to do in Santa Rosa, and that you can pick up little dainties and plants and so on along the way, but even so...!!! Meanwhile, I'll call you today, when I'm sure you're home from the PO, and see when next you can make it. The sooner the better, always... for me anyway.

I want this to get in the mail. I've tried to be clear. I have a horror of sounding cold and too abrupt, in dictating. I'm still having an awful time doing anything personal, even on tapes, although I'm practicing, and so far I am absolutely at an impasse about doing any *Fisher*... that is, real prose the way it is in my head. I honestly don't think it matters too much about that, although I have a lot more I would like to finish. But staying in touch with you and even your and my children and a few dear friends is, this far anyway, really a haunting problem. I suppose the thing is not to let it be either haunting or a problem. Ho ho ho, and to hell with the whole thing. I'll send this off this morning, and meanwhile call you about WHEN NEXT. . . .

....

Last House, Glen Ellen, California   *31.v.85*
To: Lawrence Clark Powell

Dearest Ghuce:

Yes, I did read *Across the River*, but not Chandler's[1] letters. Thank you for sending the page about the book. I agree with it too.

I thought when I read it that it was very sad, and was much more important, or perhaps I mean significant, in Hemingway's life, than the critics said. To me, it was unforgettable. There was a terrible wisdom and weariness in it, all mixed in a sad way. Probably, if I were to write about either him or his works, I would rank it very high on the autobiographical ladder.

I am struck by Chandler's overt sentimentality. Hemingway was sentimental too, but he never seemed to be coarse or banal about it, as Chandler and people like Gene Fowler and even Steinbeck occasionally are (at least in my eyes).

Gloria, as you probably know, has a show opening and is also giving a big bash for Sylvia's 50th birthday! She has sent me two printed invitations! She says that Ward sets them up, which I assume means that she runs them off the press??? I do think this is all very nice and touching and so on, and I keep on hoping that they will be young lovers forever....

All goes well here. Of course I'm furious at you for managing to avoid Glen Ellen, because please never fool yourself into thinking that I don't know when you are out here on the coast!

1. Raymond Chandler

Jake Zeitlin wrote lately. His handwriting is firmer than before his last geriatric adventure in the hospital!

Love always, in spite of myself!

....

Last House, Glen Ellen, California   *22.x.85*
To: Jim Fobel[1]

Dear Jim Fobel:

This is a late reply to your good letter and too hasty, but I do want to thank you for writing, and for the kind words you say about any books I have written that have given you pleasure.

It is also to thank you for sending me the copy of *Beautiful Food*. It's a handsome book, and I like many things in it. They are clear, and fun to read. Some of them seem a little fussy to me, but I've never been very strong on decorating ices and so on. Most of it is very practical as well as tempting. And of course the design of the book and the general makeup is pleasing.

I love your report on oysters. It makes me very hungry for them... or perhaps I should say that it arouses my latent appetite, the one that is always lurking there. And imagine finding a real pearl! You are the only person I ever knew who really did that. A few people have had my own peculiar luck in turning up some scruffy little misshapen tooth-breaking crumb... Of course, I did meet some professional Japanese pearl divers once... they were third or fourth generation, and they looked like beautiful little black seals in their wet suits. Their mothers used to dive in thick bathing suits with long-sleeved underwear underneath against the occasional biting fish and the rocks and so on. And their grandmothers etc. used to wear full kimonos, which I do hope they got off decorously enough under water, although I wonder about surfacing again and putting them on before the bosses saw them. And imagine holding their breaths and doing all this stripping underwater as well as pulling up the oysters.

What are you doing next, and where? Do you live so that you can see the Park in New York? I hope you'll feel like writing again and telling me a few details.

Oh, I wanted to ask you why you were prejudiced against pan roasts (oysters). I assume that's a thing of the past, though.

My best to you.

....

Last House, Glen Ellen, California   *23.vi.86*
To: Lawrence Clark Powell

Dearest Ghuce:

I loved hearing from you. I think you did not feel very well, though, as you were writing. I'm sorry about that, and I wish you did feel better or whatever....

I think I've told you already that I have a strong feeling about the book about your

1. Fan, cookbook writer, artist

father. It may be the best yet. No, I did not much care for the first go at your autobiography. It did not tell what I see as the truth, about much at all that I honestly did and do believe was the truth about you. I wonder if you will be any more honest this time... but really, the question of what honesty may be is very moot or whatever it is called. I wondered whom you were writing this book toward, or for, or even at. But enough of all that. You've heard it before at least from me, and I suppose I should feel proud or grateful that you still remember any of my candid words.

I am sorry Fay doesn't like the heat. I assume your house is air-conditioned? People always assume that mine is, and even with the curtains blowing in a hot wind off the pastures they compliment me on how wonderful this air-conditioning is. I don't explain that I'm of the school of behavior that chooses hot moving air to cold dead air.

My cousin Ron is out here along the coast. He's the one who lives in Rio Verde. The other night at dinner he groused quite loudly about how nearly untenable the desert around Tucson becomes in the Summer, and I felt quite impatient with him (which I have been doing for some 74 years!) and said something about how White men are intruders onto those sands, etc etc. Ho hum. (I suppose what I was really saying was "Shut up and go home to Minnesota!") But I do feel bored with all this griping about or rather by the intruders. I think of the Indians at Palm Springs, and how they've almost died out since their tiny oasis became a fashionable part of Sun-Belt life, with full cooperation of the Metropolitan water system, so that the ecology has completely changed and the air is almost impossibly hot, just as it should be, but with a very high humidity because of the countless swimming pools and green green lawns and golf courses... and the Indian lungs have simply mildewed unto the third and fourth generations. Ho hum again.

I like very much your new book-plate.

You say, "What next?" about books to write, and go on about coasting for a while. I don't think you should. I think that people like you and me have reached a certain point in our lives of real creativity, unfortunately with dwindling energies but with a strong need to continue to live. Probably you are tired and you deserve to be. But if you live you must write more. If you stop writing, you may well be finished, as you have already said when you suggest that these two could be your last books. Of course we'll both finish pretty soon, and we both have almost hourly reminders of that. But I don't think that it is at all wise for you to stop now. Why don't you write a book about potatoes, or alcoholism, or me? (Joke. Laff.)

Much love anyway,

....

Last House, Glen Ellen, California   *31.x.86*
To: Lawrence Clark Powell

Dearest Ghuce:

You hope I'll have time to read your last two books, and I assure you that I have read them both already! Of course, the bibliography is hardly the sort of thing I would devour from cover to cover! It's well done and extremely impressive, and I'm proud of

M.F.K. Fisher: A Life in Letters

you for having produced so many good things in your life. I read every word of your book about your father or a reasonable facsimile of him as presented in your romanticized version. I was really disappointed when I saw that you called it a novel. I felt that you took the easy way. Damn, I said… it's an evasion, and Ghuce is scared to tell it as it was or is. But I read it anyway, and I think that you did a very pretty job. I wish you had done it as a non-fiction memoir or portrait. I wondered how I would say this to you, because you know that I care much more than I should about you and your integrity as a writer and as a human being and, in this case anyway, as an honest son. I still think that you evaded something and it worries me, and I don't know why you did.

By now, you are probably even crankier than you were when you wrote! I'm sorry if I've offended you, dearest Ghuce. My evasions did not fool you at all, of course. I did hope that maybe I could sneak past your severe eye, and not say anything about my first reaction to your novel. Actually, I don't see why you bothered to write it at all. I do think, though, that what you produced would please your mother.

Ho hum. I'm really sorry about this. Meanwhile, I must tell you that it's a good story, as you have chosen to tell it, and I hope very honestly and sincerely that you yourself are pleased with what you've done. I don't think I know much about your father that you don't know too, and certainly you've done a neat little job of placating the gods. He was much more dynamic and alive than you allowed him to be in your story, of course, but as a novel he is expertly contrived, and of course it's smoothly and pleasingly written.

I didn't know about your going out to Oxy… I wonder if you ever plan to come this far again in California? I know that friends saw you in Santa Barbara lately, too. And poor Jake… he sounds pretty low. He wrote very lovingly about hearing from you almost every week. I love you too for calling him.

Please don't be cross at me for doing what you asked me to, about the book…. I'm proud of you for everything you do to keep on using our language, as you surely know by now. My disappointment was completely personal… and not important at all.

··

Last House, Glen Ellen, California   *18.xi.86*
To: Joel Redon[1]

Dear Joel Redon:

I wonder if you are French? I hope I have spelled your name right.

Yes, I did get your last letter, and thank you for it. I don't know about Jean Rhys, but I doubt that she drank for 25 years. I do agree with you that she was a writer, though.

I don't think that Carl Van Vechten stopped writing because he had best sellers. He was a good writer, and a real one, but that does not mean that he would always be one. Perhaps best sellers did him in. He would not be the first good writer to be wounded or killed by success… that is, if being a best seller means that one is successful. In fact, I honestly do not think that there is any connection. There is, of course, a great deal of connection between being an author and success. A best selling author is a man who

1. Fan, author, and later friend who died of AIDS

usually works very hard and does a good job and more often than not is successful. But he may never be a writer, and seldom is.

You seem to wonder, at least twice in one paragraph, what writers do when they're not writing. Why do you think they should be "doing" anything at all?

You ask in your first letter if I am afraid of death. No, I am not. I am curious about it, that is, the actual act of dying, and I hope to be fully conscious and aware. Perhaps that is because I am a writer, although I feel fairly certain that there is no danger of my living to describe it.

In other words, dear friend, don't worry about being a writer, because if you are one you probably won't know it anyway.

All best, and I will write something more, if you will.

....

Last House, Glen Ellen, California   *25.xi.86*
To: Joel Redon

Dear Joel Redon:

I like the paper. Are you an actor? I like your writing too, and wonder what kind of pen you've used.

I hope your doctor is right that the KS syndrome is the least painful and that it will go very quickly for you. There is no use prolonging anything like this. I also feel as you do about publishing. Do what you want to do and what you can and keep it all as easy and simple as possible.

I'm sorry you had to shout at your father, but I don't think you should be angry because he seemed "cool and regular." He probably did not know how else to behave. He was plainly very disturbed indeed since he asked for copies of the doctors' letters. Don't worry about hating him now. There is no time for that. I do think that many German people are "austere and forced" but I don't think I would dare call them inhuman or unhuman.

Why do you worry about anybody? I can see why you want to apologize to your friends... that's not at all silly. It reminds me of how angry I was, really angry, when a dear friend died before I thought she would. It was ridiculous, and it was certainly not her fault that she had to die. And I suppose that some of your friends will seem to drink too much or to talk too much, but you must forgive them as best you can, because many people have different ways of showing things that they are not used to showing.

I don't know why you think that writers are less afraid of death than most people. I mean that their being writers does not make them less so, if they are afraid of other things too. When I told you I was not, I did not speak as a writer but as a person. I am not afraid at all, simply because I'm not afraid of anything. And of course, I do not mean to boast at all about this. Perhaps I should apologize. Perhaps it is like being born with no ears or something. It's simply a fact. Once I felt a little scared and frightened, for about three hours, and it was pure plain hell, and I knew that I could not stand it any longer. I did not know what I was afraid of, which probably made it worse.

I wonder if you will change your mind about mailing out some stories. Perhaps this is the time for you to write very hard and fast. I don't know, but I hope you'll write to me.

....

Last House, Glen Ellen, California   *25.xi.86*
To: Joan Holt

Dear Joan Holt:

I have a lot of things to thank you for… clippings and the pictures of your delightful grandchildren, and especially your letters and cards! They've all interested me enormously, and I think you are a very generous and thoughtful person to spend any time on them and me.

I'm very glad indeed that you like any of my books. It amuses me to have you speak of being old at 64! I do remember, though, that there are times when one looks in the mirror or feels annoyed at a sudden clumsiness or twinge, and there is at least a presentiment of what may lie ahead. By now, I'm almost 79, and I must admit that there are many physical things that I did not expect would happen to me… some difficulty in walking straight and so on. It's fascinating how they can be observed and accepted with no thought at all of their ever being a personal problem. And of course when anyone asks if there can indeed be *good* things about growing older, it is often difficult to remember any. The fact remains, and I am very sure of it, that I do like many things about being old. For instance, I am much less involved with what are called the so-called amenities: if I want to excuse myself from almost any company I feel quite free to do so. And sometimes I feel impatient with the hedging and the hum-hawing that can so often go on about unimportant problems, and it is really a pleasure to simply cut them short! This does not need to be done rudely, but many people are affronted by it, no matter how discreetly and nicely it is done. Too bad.

About Zurich, I'm sure you know almost exactly where I got the old painting of Ursula Von Ott. And of course, you know the covered bridge where I went by myself to throw my wedding ring into the Rhine. And you surely know the area where there were several below-street pubs… there were two or three in the late '30s, where I sat in the corner and pretended not to listen to the Spanish dialects that were so full of passion and hatred and connivings.

I don't need to tell you how much I hope that these coming holidays will be fine and fair in every way for you and your families and all their children. It's a good time of the year.…

....

Last House, Glen Ellen, California   *1.xii.86*
To: Anne Lamott

Dear Annie:

I think you're absolutely right about having children. I think one of the most amazing and also one of the happiest days of my life was when I found that I was going to have Anna. And as far as I can remember, I never once had a qualm about the whole business, except perhaps for a few minutes when I realized that Donald Friede really hated children and was deeply frightened by them. Of course, there was no doubt at all that I must leave him, since neither of my kids had asked to be born and I certainly did not/could not stay with him instead of with them. That was really not difficult at all.

Yes, you're a good tough girl, and it seems funny to be saying that just a few minutes after I agreed with a woman whom I greatly admire that I too am very tough! She said it was a compliment, whether or not I took it as one. I wrote at once to her, to say that I did and to thank her... and now here I am agreeing with you that you are tough too.

Imagine knowing Old Stone Face for so long! I do envy you.

Your suggestion that maybe Evan[1] doesn't find you physically attractive is really funny.

I love your phrase, thanks to your Grandmother, "bimbos and blowsy women." The only other person I have known who used blowsy was my mother. It is one of those words that never need defining.... If you ask what writers make me laugh out loud, the first one is you. The book did not really, although I found the first part somewhat hilarious.[2] And no, I've never read *The Confessions of Zeno*. And no, I don't care much for Barbara Pym. Once I was trying to read her, and I said, "Why don't I read the real stuff about the vicar's tea?" And I reached for Jane Austen and found that I'd given away my beautiful old set. Damn. Yes, I do like Thurber, and I think he does make me laugh, although I have not read him for a long time and I really have a rather sad feeling by now.

I had a good conversation once with my mother about why Thurber called a lot of his drawings "the war between the sexes." I honestly did not know there was one. Of course by now, I think I know more of what he meant, and I feel rather astonished that in my own home I was really unaware of it. Of course, I knew right away that men and women are very different, but war between them was unheard of and unthinkable.

Yes, you're very right about the turd or the nerd... it's much too exciting to be anything but horrible, and I am partly scared silly and partly almost joyful about the whole mess. Last week I found myself so involved that I was actually looking forward to other midnight-to-5:00-A.M. talk shows. I paid for it on Saturday, and had to take an anti-spasmodic, which to my doctor's amazement acted as a complete knock-out, so that I slept for 40 of the next 44 hours. By now, I feel full of beans again and can hardly wait for midnight. Today, I heard all this business referred to several times as Contra-gate. Disgusting. I really do think that it is going to make Watergate look like a teaparty.

I wonder if you are going to that bash at Square One tonight. Mary Hall called me today and said she would give me a low-down tomorrow.

Yes, I have a very special friendly interested sisterly etc. feeling for you too.

I like it very much.

1. Evan Connell
2. *Hard Laughter*

Last House, Glen Ellen, California   *8.xii.86*
To: Loverne Morris

Dear Loverne:

I knew that I said something the wrong way about Pio Pico![1] Thank goodness you
were the one who caught it. Mother told me about the reaction of the older Quaker
ladies to Old Pico, who spent his last years, before he was taken off to his daughter's
place, sitting contemptuously on the steps of the Greenleaf Hotel. From what she said,
they were pitiless. He did indeed die a penniless and very bitter old man. That I knew,
although of course, by 1911, when we first got to Whittier, he'd been dead for more than
a decade. About his "mansion" (hohoho…), I did know that very well, before it was
taken in hand by the historians. There was a part of it with a second floor, where he
used to give fine dances in his heyday, but by about 1915, when we started prowling
around it with Uncle Evans, we were not even allowed to climb up there because it was
so shaky, and of course, most of the adobe walls were crumbling down fast. I think that
in 1912 or '13 the Rio Hondo jumped its banks and took away part of the rambling old
house and some of the outbuildings. And as you say, enough about Pio Pico!

Yes, I do like frogs, and toads too. Once in Southern France, Norah and I rented a
little house called The House of Many Toads, where they were as big as dinner plates,
big quiet heavy things. Mine here are tiny and black… they have large loud croaks, really startling to come from such tiny mouths.

From what you tell me, the costs for living at your place sound ridiculously low. It
also sounds like a very nice place, and is the only one I've ever heard of that I thought I
could stand. You told me once that you do have an occasional "hell fire and damna-
tion" sermon to stomach… but you also have champagne at your birthday parties! And
the best thing, from what I gather, is that you can be as much left alone as you wish.…

Please don't worry about writing anything more unless you *have to*… and you know
what I mean by that. I find that at my relatively youthful age of 78+, I often choose to
read or even crawl underneath my coverlet rather than work. I don't feel at all embarrassed about this, although now and then I'm a little peevish about having spent so
much time learning how to say what I no longer care about saying.…

You know how much I hope, dear friend, that this holiday season will be everything that is what you all want… thee and thine.

I send you much love.

Last House, Glen Ellen, California   *2.ii.87*
To: Joel Redon

Dear Joel:

When you wrote to me Saturdays were fun because you got a card or note from me,

1. Governor of California under Mexico

I promised myself that I would see that you had one every Saturday from that minute on. And now I am quite sure for at least two Saturdays there's been nothing at all from me, and I feel really ashamed of myself. Ho hum.

There's no excuse for this. I think very often of you, and have a great many questions I want to ask you. Meanwhile, I'm reading the Crevel book,[1] and find it interesting... even more than I planned to when I remembered that I had already read it in French. This was in about 1929. Of course my reasons are quite different. Now I am interested in it because you sent it to me and want to know what I think of it. Then I read it because it was being talked about a lot, and I was trying to read both the new ways of using French and the old ones. Some people then thought that Crevel wrote in very surrealistic fashion, and I remember talking about this with several very traditional people who were really quite shocked that I found it almost old-fashioned in style. (I still feel that way about many of the very "ultra" French writers of the early twentieth century. Lately I've been listening to Cocteau reading some of his early stuff, and I find it almost ridiculously affected and old-hat. So do I Salvador Dali's foreword!) René Crevel's book is good. I'll write more when I finish it. Of course, I am much interested in the subject of suicide, and have been for many years, and he says many valuable and thoughtful things about it.

Oh... I'm sorry that you paid any money for the book. It was printed this year by my publishers, and I could have got it for free, and as many copies as you wanted. Please look at the listings of North Point Press, and tell me if you want or need anything from them.

It's a far cry to Pagnol, but would you like to read the really very fresh nice memoirs he wrote about being a young boy and about his mother and father?

I'll write more very soon... and this is a promise to myself as much as it is to you.

....

Last House, Glen Ellen, California   *25.ii.87*
To: Joel Redon
Dear Joel:
Several things to reply to and to ask you and thank you for and so on!

Number 1: Thank you for sending me the black thong. It must be filled with oil, but it looks like licorice. It stained not only the envelope but your note and I am keeping it apart from the rest of the mail until you tell me more about it.

The truth is, and please do believe me, that I have never read your story about the leather string. You never sent it to me. You have sent me two manuscripts. One was "The Moon of Cherwal" (very good, clear writing) and the other was "Friends and Enemies." I know that *Christopher Street* is publishing the one about the string, and I am very glad, although I wish that you had waited a little longer because I do feel that you

1. René Crevel's *Babylon*

might have been paid more money than they can afford right now. *However...* water under the bridge etc.

As for "Friends and Enemies" I've already told you about my reaction to it. It is extremely hard for me to separate or position myself, or whatever you'd say, to read a story about living and dying by anyone I feel I know. In this case, I tried very hard to stay detached, and in that deliberate mood I can say that I think the story is not firmly defined and is in a way rather scrawny... not properly filled out in the right places. On the other side, I was deeply moved by it, and I remember it vividly and with real pain. On the detached side again, it is not trite but it is something that any human being must know about and accept as part of his own living and dying. Therefore, I doubt that it is as shattering to Mr. and Mrs. John Doe as it is to Mary Frances and Joel. Needless to say, I don't like to write this way about something this close to you, especially to a person who has actually written it about his own self. Ho hum.

About pictures: I think that of the three men you have sent me, I prefer Picasso. I like the sad little guy in the first picture. The macho fellow in black leather complete with shades and muffler did not much interest me. Do you know that I knew Man Ray very well? I like absolutely everything he ever did and I think his picture of Picasso is beautiful and wish he could do a real one of you. Once he did a true picture of me, not the glamour shot for *Vogue* or *Vanity Fair,* and I cried, because there I was, the real me, no make-up, very tired indeed, streaky dull hair.... It was very good for me to see my bones beneath the skin for the first time, and suddenly I knew what I still know, that it was the first time anyone had ever seen me.

And speaking of pictures and so on, did you know that when Liberace died and there was some discussion of what would be announced, the Riverside County Coroner finally said that death was caused by "an opportunistic disease caused by AIDS?" My goodness.

This reminds me that once the Los Angeles County Coroner told me that when in doubt or under any personal pressure, he could always safely say that a person died of uremic complications or even pernicious uremia, or simply kidney failure. This could even be said of people just hanged in prison or electrocuted or or or, because kidneys *always* fail. End of report.

Thank you for the two Xeroxes. I found them both very interesting, especially the one about Naltrexone.

Why have you cut out Oregon? I wanted to ask you that a long time ago... I mean, why you went at all and if it was a compulsive need to see your parents once more or whether there was some vengeance in it... getting even with Dad and all that. But you say that your friend is ill. I wonder if you mean Paulo in San Francisco. I do hope not. I think San Francisco would be a good place for you to come if you felt able to.

And this leads me to another suggestion or question or or or: if you still plan to come to Paulo, do you want to give him my name and telephone number and suggest that we get in touch with each other? This is, of course, up to you. Since you wrote the story of "Friends and Enemies" for the two of us, I feel as if we had more in common than you yourself may suspect, so that even if you did not plan to come out here yourself, I think that I would still ask you for his address in SF....

I hope this comes to you on a Saturday, but any day will do, because it brings you my loving greetings.

<hr />

Last House, Glen Ellen, California   *22.iii.87*
To: Paul and Julia Child

D*E*R*E* F*R*E*N*S:

Here comes a letter maybe... no more cards right now. I continue to use the spoon, Julie, and love it. Thank you again, and often. And that reminds me: do you ever use that Whacker? It was meant for beating abalone, as I remember, but who has abalone these days... unless, of course, you have a secret source down near Seaview? I use my Whacker a surprising lot, and I do love the smooth balance. It has the same feeling as the bowl of this spoon. Should they be called Gastronomical Discoveries?

If you are almost at the end of *Fish* on March 14 you have only 20 more letters to go by August 31. Pooh. Not to worry...

About those TV shows... you know I don't have the necessary mechanics so I've never seen one. The only adverse criticism I have heard is that you change your clothes too often in a half-hour show!!! Otherwise, you are the usual phenomenon. I have no idea about things like why you work so hard, but what you tell me about prime time and all that makes me shudder. Go ahead, and always with my most loving blessings (and of course that includes the Pope *and* me!). It'll be fun to have Rosie there too. She called the other night and I hope very much to see her "between engagements."

I agree with you that "bookery is damned solitary" and I'm being completely lazy after getting off to Judith my last minor masterpiece.[1] I do feel rather sorry for her with you working on your end and me on mine and God knows how many other wordy souls in between. But, as Rex Kennedy used to say, "She *asked* for it!"

I have a wonderful picture of you and Paul with the new Moulton-Adler work of art,[2] speaking of masterpieces. You both look somewhat awed but you make a handsome trio and I'm proud of the picture.

I don't need to say Dear Julie that I am sorry that PC is withdrawing from us all. I'm very happy indeed to have known him for a long time now. I salute him with deep respect and real love.

As for you, I know you will come through all this. I still send you all my love and my prayers too.

Avanti

1. *Dubious Honors*
2. This picture is reproduced in the insert.

M.F.K. Fisher: A Life in Letters

Last House, Glen Ellen, California   *6.iv.87*
To: Amanda Thompson[1]

Dear Amanda:

It was good of you to write to me, and please tell your young man that I admire him and you both for doing your first run-on work on your new computer. I too would be nervous, but it doesn't show at all in your exceedingly neat typing.

And you certainly do not need to remind me of where you came from! I think I knew you before you were born, and then I was at the house in Malibu for a few days when all four of you decided that you were my unofficial god-children. This made me very happy, because I felt the same way, although I made it clear that we must always recognize Dinah[2] as Numera Una or whatever. And I do remember that afternoon when you came up with Sylvia. The pool is lined with purple tile and is up at David's. It's my floors that are black. And I still don't have a television, and there are still a lot of things that Sylvia does not understand about me. I now have a box in the kitchen, but only for VCR... and I am happy to say that Sylvia still loves me very much, and I do her.

About television, though: there is one now in the room I have made out of the garage for a friend[3] who is staying with me, and this week we plan to put up an aerial for it, and I'll probably condescend to go in now and then to watch something.

A couple of weeks ago she invited me to her room to look at a re-run of something about Edith Piaf, and it was so terrible that I said something very crude about serials and now I think I am morally committed to at least one more look at the little box. It had better be good!

I'm very glad that you finished shunning Fisher! The story about the woman in the storm[4] is of course straight reporting, and I remember forcing myself to make a few notes during the whole business, and then writing it as soon as I woke up from the deep sleep I went into after the storm. I did not re-read it, but gave it to Eleanor Friede in a couple of days, after she came up to see the damage the storm had done to her house where I was staying, and she sent it from her office to the *New Yorker* when she got back to work. It was written so "straight" that it really tipped up the magazine a bit, and has been in several anthologies since then, variously described as contrived and artificial and psychologically incorrect and so on. All of this perhaps says pooh to the use of truth, which is one we both strive for, but that does not discourage me at all, and I feel sure it never will you either.

As for writing a novel, I am glad you almost finished your third one. I admire you

1. Granddaughter of Gloria Stuart, daughter of Sylvia and Gene Thompson
2. Amanda Thompson's older sister
3. Mary Jane Jones, MF's companion and friend for a few years
4. "The Windchill Factor" in *As They Were*

very much for even one. I wrote something that was called a novel,[1] simply because my publisher insisted that every writer must get rid of at least one, during his lifetime, but it was really a collection of several short stories tied together by a too obvious and time-worn trick. I am not proud of it, *except* that I worked hard with all my honesty intact.

Perhaps incidentally, I know a man who is now on about his seventh novel, and apparently he has no desire at all to publish them or even to have anyone read them. I admire this too, very much.

I too would like to meet you as a friend. We've both grown a bit, and know more than we did the last time. And about what of my own work I like best, there are some stories that I know are good, like the one about the storm, but I don't remember them. I think the best and most pleasing book I've written is *A Cordiall Water*. It is short and rather cheerful... and very honest. It is a rather comforting little book, the kind to be read on an air-trip or during childbirth maybe. Probably the best thing I've done, technically anyway, is my translation of Brillat-Savarin's *The Physiology of Taste*. It is by far the best translation yet done of this minor classic, and I can say this so blandly because I did not write it myself and I know that it will be outmoded before much longer and most probably outdone in quality. It's a literal job, and is good partly because I know good English-American and partly because when I did it I recognized how unusually clear and honest and straightforward the old prose was. It was written in a period of French letters when the language was extremely ornate and full blown and what one would call gushy. I do hope you will take a look at it. Please do not buy it. I'll send you a copy of anything I have, at the drop of a word....

Don't let any discouragement creep into your use of electronics. I'd say you are in control... and don't ever worry about your mother's flying into a rage at anything you and I ever do. Tiny memories or occasional information or even the lack of either poses no problem for either Sylvia or me. Please tell her anything you wish to about our starting this new correspondence, which will end as quickly or as indefinitely as you yourself wish. I send much love, with great expectations, and of course I send much love also to Gene and Sylvia, which they will know whether or not you ever mention it or me to them.

....

Last House, Glen Ellen, California   *29.iv.87*
To: Paul and Julia Child

  D*E*R*E* F*R*E*N*S:

And thank you, chère amie, for your last good letter... from Santa Barbara. I know you got this awful invitation from our mutual friend Margaret, but I want to send you a chance, since I cannot accept it myself, of having another free (gift) cocktail of rhubarb-champagne. (Do not report.)

Which reminds me... do you remember when people in France were trying to push apéritifs and even champagnes based on artichokes? It's all the same, I must say.

1. *Not Now but* Now

M.F.K. Fisher: A Life in Letters

You asked me about Mary McCarthy's book, more-or-less questionably about herself, and I wonder if you have seen the April 20, 1987, copy of *New York* magazine? Rhoda Koenig reviews her memoirs and Gloria Vanderbilt's, and I do recommend your taking a look, and can send it to you if you don't have it. It's pretty awful, and exactly the way I feel about such stuff. It says, for instance, that one thing these two girls have in common "is a lordly vagueness about many aspects of their lives...." If you don't read it, of course it does not matter one way or the other. I must tell you, though, I never did like M McC, and I think that anyone who wrote the *second* autobiography was suspect. *However,* I do wish you'd get to it right now and write about yourself if possible. If you can't write about that, write about Julia Child. But never-ever-never write what you think anybody in the world wishes to know about you as Julia Child. That's all.

Obviously, there's much more to say about this, but not for now. I do wish you had taken my first suggestion, when you called and said that you had written 382 pages on cabbage, or something like that, that you would simply do a complete Julia Child dictionary or encyclopedia. Why not a whole book about cabbage? Why not two volumes on meats from Agneau to at least Veau? Why should you send off all these really good words to *New York* and have them cut you and cut you? I do mean this. *Why not* your own dictionary? If I were at least ten years older and perhaps 50 years younger I'd really love to be able to look up anything from asparagus to zucchini (and as a matter of fact, in your column the thing on zucchini is a tiny-winy Bible to me!), and it simply kills me to think that Judith and all those other people back there, much as they love you, are simply shredding you down into the corporate wastebaskets.

Perhaps I should stop this little sermon right here. What I really want to say is that you must write your own stuff, about you, and right now. Do it for Paul. (I am sure you've talked about this with him, but please talk more... to Paul and me. Paul and I are a big crowd of two, and we really are a big crowd.)

Of course, you are right that a book is final. But if you say the truth as you see it, and that goes for the plural as well as the singular, that is all you need, and it will be a very good book indeed. Please do get to work right this minute.

About books: I don't know about that thing I sent to Judith.[1] I think I hurt her feelings deeply by saying on the telephone that she should not come out for "a week," to work on it with me... to do any changes she suggested in two hours. I said this because I not only like her but I love her and I feel the same about Evan. But she read it differently. Ho hum. I don't think she liked the book much, but even less than two hours will fix it up out here, and I've told her so and I hope that she and Evan will come out soon... and *not for work.*

You ask me about how I liked Matt Kramer. I honestly do not remember him or it, and of course by it I mean his story in the *Wine Spectator* which I have not seen. I get rather odd comments about it and him, which make me think he himself was not too keen about me. If and when I know more, I'll report.

1. *Dubious Honors*

Please give my love to Paul. I think very often of you both, as I'm sure you have sensed by now, even in this awful jumble of a note to you. . . .

Much love,

....

Last House, Glen Ellen, California   *7.v.87*
To: Lawrence Clark Powell

Dearest Ghuce:

Here is a very quick answer to your letter of May 5, the good old Cinco de Mayo....

I'm glad that Pierre stopped on his way back, and also that you told me about him, because I was going to write to him at the JPL in Pasadena. As you know, he and Janine[1] were here for a too short visit, and they brought me a picture or rather about twenty pictures that he took from the roof of the Pénarderies.... Pierre spent hours zigzagging them together, and then Janine, wrote "Les Pénarderies 1986" at the top and like a damn fool I completely forgot to ask either of them to do anything else... even to *sign* it. It's pretty big and clumsy to mail back but I think I'll try to do it anyway. Meanwhile, Pierre swears that he's going to do a much better job, which he'll send me. This one covers only 150 miles!

I agree with you that he is not bad as a person. I really found him most disagreeable and in fact a definitely unpleasant fellow for the first 40 years of his life. In fact, I thought he was an arrogant bastard. But every time I've seen him since about 1968 or '69, he's improved. This last time he was actually likable! And of course, I've always liked Janine, and it was reassuring to me that the two of them seem happy together by now. The last times he was here he was alone, and made it very plain that he hated her being more "important" than he in their common field. I don't think he was jealous at all, but rather resentful. She does not care one way or the other, I feel sure, and they were really very pleasant to have as a team. (The last time they were together in about 1967 or so, when Henriette spent a year with them in Pasadena after Georges died, they were plainly bored as a couple. In other words, *tout passe*....)

Please do send me your memoir of meeting Georges, if you have an extra copy.

I don't know about yours and Normie's plan for the ultimate retreat. If F does outlive you, perhaps it might be fine for her to find some solace in being near the ocean again. But I think you are meant to be near those mesas and mountains.

I have no doubts at all that your reservoir will soon be full again. The trouble with me is that mine is too full right now, with no available outlets. Rather painful.

What about this balderdash you write about "last payment on your filial dues?" I refuse to believe that any son owes his mother anything at all, just as the mother herself owes nothing to her son. At least, I think that is true for me, although as I say it I begin to wonder. Anyway, I do look forward to reading anything you say about your mother. I am sure it will come as a real surprise to me. I wonder if you'll tell the truth, even as you see it.... I know that it will be impossible for me to write anything about my mother

1. Pierre and Janine Connes, son and daughter-in-law of Georges Connes, both eminent scientists

M. F. K. Fisher: A Life in Letters

because I thought I owed it to her, but of course you and I are not the same children of the same parents, thank God.

Norah's youngest son Matthew is going to be married on the 23rd, and she already looks worn to the bone and really frazzled. She thought she was going to have about 20 people down in the garden, but by now the number is at least 85, and every day or so Matt adds a few more from Malibu, and it's too late to engage a decent place near Jenner. At least she has finally consented to get a caterer. Ho hum. In other words, I do wish I could see you again, dear Ghuce. I start a thousand sentences with every one that gets on this page, and the few that do get printed would probably be better left unsaid. Ho hum indeed. Why don't you just come up here sometime?

Meanwhile, here's my love always,

....

Last House, Glen Ellen, California   *11.v.87*

To: Pat Brown

Dear Pat:

I can't tell you how good it was to hear from you. And *Honey from a Weed* came today, and although I write in great haste, really just an earnest for a future letter, I must tell you that Alan D[1] did send me a copy, and that i was truly impressed by the handsome presentation and so on, but was not at all caught up in the contents. Patience Gray writes very well and her erudition and research are most impressive, but in general I have to give a big ho hum and "put it aside," which really means forget it in my own simple vocabulary. However...

HOWEVER...

... This time 'round I'll really take a more serious look at it, and I may even find it a fascinating and delightful and enriching proof of something I already know, that it's your book and you should bring it out.... I promise you I'll tell you. I think that perhaps I was turned off a bit by Alan's wild enthusiasm. He even sent me the galleys! I began to wonder if he himself had written it. I've been rather antagonized, I fear, by impressively researched books that are worth absolutely every bit of time, trouble, and money that has been spent on them. I think immediately of the one by a delightful woman, whose name I forget now, called *The Oysters of Lourmaquier*. It was indeed worth everything, perhaps even including its winning of the National Award and so on. I did try to read it, since it was written about oysters and everybody I most admired told me I should. But it was so self-assured and pompous and plain *dull*....

Well, dear Pat, I do hope I am mistaken about this one. I really want to be.

I agree with you and Mr. Broyard[2] about books. I don't toss a single book away. I do send at least fifty a month out, some on loan, but mostly because people want them or need them more than I do, but still I have more than 5,000 here. Just about all the wall space that is not already windows... no seashore, but every prospect pleases. What do

1. Alan Davidson, culinary author
2. *New York Times* book critic Anatole Broyard

you think about *Les Misérables* and *The Hunchback of Notre Dame* as London's smashes? Several people have told me about the first, and had me almost convinced that I could be wrong and that the whole endless story could indeed make a musical tragi-comedy. Then I was sent a complete performance cassette of the second, and I found it almost incredibly boring and not even very musical. But I'll take your word for it, and with complete trust and encouragement, that the Royal Shakespeare *Liaisons Dangereuses* is really good. I've never seen it but read it with great enjoyment.

And this reminds me that I'm listening to a lot of cassettes now, and that I have heard but once too often (my own silly fault... who else plays the cassettes but me?) the collected poems of Cocteau, read by JC himself. The first few times I was horrified and fascinated by his very old-fashioned diction, strictly old-time Comédie Française, straight out of fourth-year French in any American college or even 6th Grade in Aix. Then I forgot all that and I've been really almost scared by how truly cruel and S&M the old boy was. It's very sad.

And that reminds me.... Have you seen that little chapel a few miles outside of Paris that Cocteau and his friends painted on the inside? It's really worth the trip out there to Milly-Les-Forêts, I think, or perhaps just plain Milly. It was damned by the Catholics during the Crusades and only the lepers went there to be cared for by a few mad priests and then to die. So the walls are covered with all the herbs that were used in those days to help pain and so on. And there are parsley stalks forty feet high and the roots of the Autumn crocus on one side of the little chapel and then the stalks going clear across the central ceiling with the blossoms hanging down on the opposite side, dripping their pollen toward the litters that crowded the floors, with all the condemned dying people on them. It's really very beautiful and peaceful, and when I listened to some of Cocteau's tortured words speaking such prim French syllables, I think again of the beautiful job he and some of his poor gay friends did. I'm sure that those colors and the serenity everywhere have helped many more than just the lepers.

I think it was quite the vogue for a while to take on those old abandoned chapels and use them for personal showpieces.... Picasso has one in Vallouris, and I know of two that in England were turned into studios. There they are called redundant churches by the government, and there are no longer any more for rent or sale. And then the British government took over a whole lot of redundant farms, and they too are no longer available. Some friends of mine bought an old barn and the foreman's townhouse at Fonthill when it was declared redundant and Humphrey Stone moved his presses into the barn after the very small publishing house that was at first housed in a beautiful old "redundant" brewery was taken back by Her Majesty. And the latest word from Humphrey's distraught wife is that the government has changed its mind *again*, and now four tract houses for low income people are to be built between the house and the barn. It's plain murder of one of the most beautiful countrysides I've ever seen, in Wiltshire between Stonehenge and Bath, near the Cathedral at Salisbury. And I don't know why I'm prattling on about this, except that very indirectly it

M. F. K. Fisher: A Life in Letters

leads me back to my solemn promise to take a much deeper look at P Gray's book, now that it is also P Brown's....

Forgive this wordy note when I meant to write a hasty one! Perhaps my report will be somewhat shorter.... Meanwhile, much love indeed.

....

Last House, Glen Ellen, California   *1.vi.87*
To: Lawrence Clark Powell

Dear Ghuce:

Thanks for the proof that you have made your final payment to your filial dues. I hope you feel fine about it. I wonder if your mother did as much white-washing in her memoirs as you did in your payments to both parents. I'll add this last labor of love to your handsome collection for Humphrey Stone, and I know it will be of more value to him than I can imagine. And if I sound severe, it is simply because I am very stern with you, as always, and as always with real love and admiration.

More very soon,

....

Last House, Glen Ellen, California   *3.vi.87*
To: Deborah Daw[1]

Dear Deborah:

I'm sorry to be this late in thanking you for your good letter of April 25.

I wonder how your diet has worked by now. I can't see anything wrong with what you tell me about it. I know that forbidden fruits and vegetables are unbelievable always. Alcohol I can take or leave, and I think I could easily live without any wheat or even dairy stuff, but I do hope vegetables and fruits are never on the wrong side of my list. Vinegar could easily be a no-no, but if you can have lemon juice and hot water, you need not worry about starting the day right. I think it's impossible to spend a year reading any book at all, even *Two Towns in Provence*! I hope that you find more time on your hands for all the good stuff, by now.

You ask about having to learn to fit the style of a magazine. I suppose one does that more or less intuitively, but I never had much trouble with editors. Once, I remember, I had to have a school teacher drink a glass of milk instead of sherry in a mid-western publication! This was no doubt because in most of the states like Kansas alcoholic beverages are strictly forbidden to any public servants. Ho ho ho. And of course, the checkers at the *New Yorker* put any writer through a hard time for the first few years.... I had to be very sure of chapter and verse and any possible references if I mentioned any name at all from Plato on down to John Doe, Jr. It was very good for me, and I do agree with you that if you like to work with somebody it's much better to be published than not, as long as you respect and admire that person.

1. A fan

I'm not even going to answer your thing about having one of the *New Yorker* authors print your piece as his, but I will tell you that I think *Geo* is probably the nicest magazine I ever worked for. I really loved it, and felt very badly when the whole thing folded. And I don't believe that you are making excuses, at all. Perhaps you are a little chicken, as you say... too scared to write about things in your own way. You are afraid of being rejected perhaps. And all I can say is that you should not be afraid. You should keep right on writing, and writing the way you want to, and sooner or later you will find somebody who agrees with you. And do please remember that most editors are writers *manqués*, and feel obliged to take out their own frustrations with their constant niggles on writing that they really envy and even resent, because they didn't write it themselves.

I'm truly sorry that you and Steven have lost a friend. It's all very shocking, this new immediacy that AIDS has forced us to look at. Of course, I'm glad that your friend died so quickly, if he had to. I am sorry to believe that we must grow more accustomed to it instead of less. I find this so in my own experience, lately.

Of course, I'm especially sorry for poor Steven. He seems to have had more than his share of sorrow. But there too, it's hard to know how such things are apportioned. Who or what decides how much a given person can stand?

Back to ridiculous nonsense: I'm sorry that your nice stinky vinegar is going to waste, if indeed it is. By now, of course, you may be off that particular dietary hook, and able to bathe yourself inwardly as well as in the tub. Do you have my recipe for pickled grapes, speaking of vinegar? Please tell me and I'll send it to you if you want it... although I have not used cider vinegar for them (the grapes). . . .

I hope you'll write soon again, Deborah, and tell me about the state of several important things, including your own insides. Please give Steven my love. This goes for you too.

....

Last House, Glen Ellen, California   *19.viii.87*
To: Holly Parker[1]

Dear Holly:

I wish you'd write to me oftener. My reasons are many, but they're all good ones. If you ask me for any I'll give them to you....

Maybe you are lucky that your zucchini blossom and then fade, and never have any babies. So many people start saying to me, almost as soon as they've got the seed in the ground, "What on earth will I do with this enormous crop? Who eats zucchini? My kids don't, my husband doesn't, and I hate it!" Etc. etc. etc. Myself, I love zucchini, and I eat them year-round even when they are very expensive, but the only answer to people is to say, "Then don't plant them!" I do believe that the more you dislike the zucchini the quicker and better they grow... and of course if you turn your back for more than 12 hours on a lovely tender thing about 4 inches long with the blossom still on one end, it will turn into a 2-foot monster, thick-skinned, and with a watery taste-

1. Holly and Tom Parker were Napa Valley friends.

less inside. Even chickens do not like them. Once I had a Swiss gardener-friend in Whittier, who grew what he called bikini, and he would bring in a monster about every 50 days, of course along with some tinies which killed him to pick so small, and when I would ask him what on earth to do with it, he would say, "Schtoooph it!" I did this once, and gave him half of it, and even not counting my precious time, I figured it cost almost $6.00 in meat and cheese and so on and so on. End of report, except that I do love zucchini.

About drought… We're just about to face the worst one in some 100 years here. We don't mention it, though. It would be bad publicity for the Bouverie Audubon Preserve! And over 2000 schoolchildren a month come here for eight months of the year, and David has just installed beautiful new toilets, which at least 1000 will use, of course… and this is plus the regular visitors, etc., and our waterfall, which of course subsides to a good trickle in the Summer, is bone dry for the first time in over 87 years. Murder.

No, the pinkish-yellow haze in my old eye does not make me at all sick to my stomach. In fact, I enjoy it. The new eye is cold and clear like ice,[2] and the two together make everything exactly right for me, and for some reason I've improved so greatly in the past three years that now I do not even wear glasses until about 4:00 to nightfall depending on wear and tear.

I am exactly 12 days older than you, chronologically. My Chinese midwife told Mother that I was 100 when I was born, so that does give me more than a slight edge over you. And like you, I remain as always strikingly beautiful, even though nobody knows it but me.

And Tommy worries me a bit too. In fact I have no idea of what he really looks like now, and when he calls he says he feels great, but his voice is often shaky and old (and why not?). And of course now and then he does ramble a little bit… and there too I suppose I could say why not…. Ho hum.

And much love to you both, and especially to that strikingly beautiful Holly.

....

Last House, Glen Ellen, California   *25.ix.87*
To: David Pleydell-Bouverie

Dearest David:

First I must tell you that I'm truly sorry to have turned off the little rendezvous last night, to meet the new person up here. I do want to, as you know. And then I think I asked Marsha to say that I'd call you today, and I have not. People came! Etc.!!

These all seem quite legitimate excuses, but probably the real one is that, although I'm going through a small arthritic tempest and am very stiff and even somewhat uncomfortable physically, I'm disgustingly cheerful and even healthy inside. And I think that can be very boring to someone who feels rather poorly or badly, both inwardly and out, which may or may not describe you. So, I'll go on with my fan letter, which I

2. MF had had a cataract operation.

promised to write to you after we both talked about them, and you said that they were mostly phonies and I said that mine were not. I truly do have great respect for people who write to me and tell me how and why they have found something I have written good. They are not the kind of so-called fans who send 25 cents for an autographed picture....

So...

Dear Mr. Bouverie:

This is to tell you that for almost 30 years I have loved you. I remember our first meeting, when you came over the hill, after an introductory postcard, and had lunch in the kitchen, with my older girl and her little boy Chris. Chris hated you because you were another man and he behaved very badly. Anna and I, on the other hand, liked you immediately, if for probably different reasons. And now, somewhat later in our lives, I feel quite free and happy to tell you that I still love you, and very dearly too. Perhaps I know you better, but that has nothing to do with my first impression, of trust and confidence in a very strong man.

I sign myself, with complete sincerity, which by now I know you trust, your ever-loving friend—

··

Last House, Glen Ellen, California   *29.x.87*
To: Joel Redon

Dear Joel:

I got your good note of the 26th today, and I'm returning your several manuscripts and/or printed stories, with my sincerest thanks for letting me see them and my equally abject and sincere apologies for having scratched into them as I did. I'm sure that most of my comments and corrections will be as unintelligible to me as they are to you! They are messy, though, and I'm very sorry for that. And from now on, I'll not mark on them, but on other scraps of paper.

About the '85 Diary, I'm not yet through with it but will send it off soon. I'll also send you the script of "Friends and Enemies." Thank you again for letting me share its honors with Paulo.

I'm returning, with the other things which I'll note in this letter, your script of "Michel." I thought last night that it would make a very good murder story, and I see now that at the end I wrote a one-sentence finale that seemed blood-curdling to me. Unfortunately, by today it too is illegible, and I'll try to figure it out again before I enclose it with the package.

I did find the other in the series, "Sitting in the Back Room of a Bar," and will return it with the first manuscripts along with your addition on page 2 of the October section.

Please don't think the Diary is at all burdensome! Far from it! I'm reading it with full attention and some real excitement. I hope to return it and the one to me and Paulo very soon, as I've said.

And I think from now on I'll not put any comments at all on any of the stuff you send me, and then I'll return it as soon as I've read it. I consider this an agreement as well as a promise.

And now to your cryptic note of October 22 about eating. I remember very well that little conversation in the oddly nondescript little breakfast room we sat in. I think you believe exactly what you said, that eating is something you do because you have to. I also wish to tell you that I am struck in almost everything I've read of yours, but especially in your personal diaries and journals, by your real preoccupation with the whole subject of food. Of course, some of this is dictated by the fact that you often wrote of being hungry, and not being able to eat and then wolfing down some stale crackers and having cramps and so on and so on... and I could add ad nauseam, except that would be a nasty joke. In other words, Joel, I think you care one hell of a lot about food. You resent it because you do. But perhaps you're that way about sex, and drugs, and booze, and breathing. There's a real disgust there, of course, but you cannot deny that you are preoccupied by the fact that you have to eat to live. And that, of course, is what I'm talking about when I say that "at least you must try to enjoy it a bit when you're around me." And in that sentence "enjoy" and "me" are both underlined, in my own vocabulary. This is because I honestly believe that since you do have to eat, even a stale cracker now and then which you know will make you hurt, you might as well "enjoy" not only the eating but even the pain that you anticipate. And I would underline "me" because that is *my* belief, and *I* said it.

And I say it again: since we must eat to live, we might as well enjoy doing it.

Of course, this presupposes that since we must breathe we must also choose to do so... that is, we either live or we die, and it's purely a matter of choice. If you choose to die, stop eating and, of course, first of all, stop breathing. But if you have chosen to live, it presupposes the cold nasty horrible fact that you have chosen to breathe and that in order to breathe you must eat, and of course perform a few other functions, which are basically just as ugly and simple, but which can and should be acts of grace and pleasure.

Thus spake everybody including Zarathustra and Nietzsche and even old Lady Fisher Herself.

End of sermon, and onto the next case, with much love as always.

....

Last House, Glen Ellen, California 14.i.88
To: Angelo Pellegrini[1]

Angelo Mio:

Thank you for letting me read those ruminations. Of course I thought they were very funny and witty, and I do agree with you that those horrible treatments must have been successful, for you sound as charmingly and homily wonderful as ever. (I love

1. Angelo Pellegrini and MF were wine judges at the LA County Fair in the early 1940s. Pellegrini wrote *The Unprejudiced Palate*, and MF encouraged its republication in the 1980s.

what you say about your Beatrice, and I hope you notice that I am not addressing this note to your house, as you have instructed!)

I don't know what to say about *Father and Son*. I wonder if you'd let me look at it. The title makes me wonder if ever you saw a book that has always stayed in my mind, written by a young Chinese-American in San Francisco in about 1942, called *Father and Glorious Descendant*. This has nothing to do, of course, with the fact that I do want to see your own *Father and Son*!

Now, what to do? In a way, I can understand why North Point is "not interested." I seldom hear from them, and they are increasingly busy people and I miss the old more interdependent days. As for the letter which you let me see from the U of W Press, it was a good one, and a couple of years ago I would have agreed with them that the book would interest the *New Yorker*. By now, I do not know.... This year I did not sign the First Reading Agreement, for the first time in almost twenty years, and I assume that indicates a kind of disinterest on my part, or plain senility(?). Anyway, I don't see any point in bothering them now with what is almost surely the return of your script, probably unread. I've submitted several things in the past months, but nobody bothers to read them at all... and I say this without any boo-hoo-hoo, and in fact, with some relief because I do think it is mean to whip a dead horse (and neither you nor I is dead or even horsey...).

Now about an agent: have you ever used one? (And I refrain from asking you the usual Why Not??!!!) I do know a man out here on the Coast, who acts as a kind of super-agent for the Eastern people. As I understand it, he is increasingly interested in becoming known as a specialist of homosexual novels, and from what I recall of my past many lives with you, I doubt that you would qualify. My own agent, Bob Lescher, in New York, has refused even to consider taking on a new client for the past ten years or so, so he's out. I still think you should send the script to me... *if you want to*. Plainly, I'm a bit at sea about all this.

Meanwhile, I love tripe in any form and this minute am full of a big bowl of home-made menudo. So don't worry about that. Very much love,

....

Last House, Glen Ellen, California   *29.i.88*
To: Lil Bernstein[1]

Dear Lil:

It's always a good day when your letter comes, and I start answering it at once and then am always surprised to find how much time has gone by before I really get to it. I feel flattered, of course, that anything I've written has slowed down your cleaning fervor on a weekend in January. I find, though, that even cleaning out a drawer is a slow process for me... I pick up this or that and then it's worse than any quotation or good passage from a book. Perhaps it's rather like looking up a word in the dictionary... ten minutes later you're ten pages ahead or behind, and having too good a time to stop.

I don't know anybody this year who's going down to the ABA. The last time it was

1. Lillian Bernstein, friend and bookseller

in San Francisco I meant to hole in at a good hotel, and run a kind of watering hole... not set foot in Moscone Center myself, but simply see a few good old friends in my rooms. It is perhaps fortunate that fate and a germ or two prevented my going down, because I found that I had hurt the feelings of several good people by not including them in my very casual invitations to stop by after work or whatever.... And as for having a booth there, I think you're very wise indeed to avoid that. You most certainly do not need it with the store there alongside the buildings, or at least in the same city. . . .

I'd love to see a picture of the store... please send me a card or whatever and I'll return it to you with great care. . . .

You ask me if I'm working, and I can say that I am, and there will be a book out by North Point Press in the early Spring, a collection of the forewords and introductions and so on I've written from 1962 through 1987. It's called *Dubious Honors,* and was fun to do, especially because I could write what I really thought about most of the stuff that had been printed earlier. Of course, I had to pull a few punches.... The ghosts I was going to lay in Whittier were either non-existent or easily placated. I went down[2] feeling a certain amount of anger or pique about the attitudes that hurt my father's image when I wrote a book called *Among Friends.* I was determined to be sweet and gracious and smiling and never show my basic annoyances. But when I got there I was so impressed by the fine reactions of all the people during the recent impact of the earthquakes, that I forgot my own petty thoughts, and was filled with admiration and a certain sense of humility. And everybody was very nice to me, of course, and I met a few people who remembered my father with great admiration and so on, and we stayed eight days instead of four-plus because of terrible weather, and I left absolutely drenched with heavy rainfall after sitting for forty minutes on a forklift at Ontario airport. It was a fitting end to a very happy and amusing trip, and funny too. I was caught out there on the airfield because the stairs up to the airplane were felt to be too slippery for the wheelchair to be carried up. It was a long time in the rain, and all the time the driver of the forklift was sitting snugly in the cab in front of my open perch, dressed in complete Sou'wester hat, gauntlets, overcoat, and boots. I saw Mary Jane waving frantically from the door of the airplane, and the stairs were wheeled away, and we trundled across the muddy field and I rose majestically some forty feet in the air in my wheelchair, and when I reached the top of my solo flight, I looked back and saw the airport windows filled with people from Whittier waving their handkerchiefs at me and I gave them my best Queen Mary bows to right and left and then was sucked into the plane and we took off. It was a fitting finale to a very pleasant and funny experience.

You mention taking some of the books off my hands... I can't face empty shelves right now, although it's a problem to keep them available for any new stuff that comes along. I suppose we should talk about it sometime but not now. Why don't we do it next time you're up here? I hope that will not be too long. Please remember I've never seen you since you've had your hair cut!! What will you shed the next time you come up North? Is a puzzlement and something we should discuss at length, and soon.

2. MF was invited to attend the one hundredth anniversary of Whittier, California, celebrated following a devastating earthquake. She was accompanied by Mary Jane Jones.

Last House, Glen Ellen, California   *12.ii.88*
To: Gloria Stuart Sheekman
   Dear Gloria:
   Dear Mrs. Sheekman: (Which means, dearest Honey-Colored-Actress Herself:)
   I just found a note that you wrote to me in about 1933 or '34, from Sunset Boulevard. It started out in French… not too good but not bad, and then went on in such a relaxed and happy way that for a minute I wished that we were all that innocent and proud again and not the staid and cautious crickets we've turned into. (I have anyway, I often suspect, and perhaps you have too. *Anyway,* we are not those relaxed carefree critters.…) In the letter, among other things, you talked of playing in *Mr. and Mrs. North* on weekends (…"wonderful. I adore it…"). Ho hum. You were living there then,[1] or R Benchley was ("he's a nice guy and will be fascinated by you"). Brackett was there and Grouch et al. You also sent me a wonderful recipe for Peasant Caviar, and I still eat it often and with gusto.

Last House, Glen Ellen, California   *25.iii.88*
To: Norah Kennedy Barr
   Dear N…
   I was much happier to get your two notes than you will ever know. Thank you.
   Sixty jars of Seville Orange Marmalade! Maybe you *should* stop.…
   I wish I felt happier about the beautiful wildflowers, which have never been more spectacular, because they are not hidden this year by any grass at all. The lupines are already almost over, but the poppies are good for another week or two. So far this Spring, I haven't heard one bird.
   About Lida:[1] I simply cannot stand the idea of her being so loaded with antibiotics and other medical miracles. If she does drive, she'll be so loaded with things to keep her from having an attack while she drives that… etc. etc. etc. Ho hum. And it is hard to give up driving, I really think that was the toughest thing of my many minor capitulations in the past years. It was by far the nastiest blow to my ego, not to mention the superego and the alterego and all those other little bastards, to have to admit that I was dependent finally on other people's skills. Anyway, please give her my love.
   There's too much to say about Barbara Tritel.[2] I hope she is not a pest to you. No, I don't think I like her. No, she has not interviewed me over any period of time and I know very little about her, and I hope she is not a bore to you in any way. I think that I've made it clear to her as I have to several other people that I'd be very glad to give her whatever help I can and that if she does publish anything I wish to see it before it

1. The Sheekman family lived at the Garden of Allah, a cottage community of Hollywood writers, with Robert Benchley, Charles Brackett, and Groucho Marx.
1. Lida Schneider shares the Jenner house with Norah Kennedy Barr.
2. Barbara Tritel Quick hoped to write a biography of MF.

goes to press, and that there is no such thing as an official biography. I think she is the least interesting of the several people who are involved in such ephemera. . . .

I don't have many anxiety dreams anymore. I almost wish I did. My worst one was checking on passports and tickets and so on before and even while I was rushing with the children to catch a train or a bus or even a ship. I'm sorry you dreamed about our being captives of Matt and a friend.

And of course, I hope the strawberry social is a successful and beautiful bash.... And that reminds me that Mary Jane and I are going to New York on April 4 and will be back on April 7. The whole thing sounds crazy, but once again my superego rose to an occasion of some sort. It seems that about 3½ million dollars are scheduled to be raised on April 5 in the Rainbow Room of Rockefeller Center, for AIDS and Meals on Wheels, and it was something in my honor, for want of a better name to lend it, and I spent three days making a film that will be shown, since I refused to go in person. Then it was told to me that if by chance I would go there, they'd raise double the sum *easily*. So off we go, and Mr. Rockefeller will get $71,000 for new curtains instead of $35,000+, and it seems that he's flat broke after restoring the whole top floor of the Center in Art Deco under which I myself tea-danced in 1935, as I remember to the lilting music of Paul Whiteman. Murder. Of course, we're going to stay at the Plaza in a suite, and I plan to see absolutely nobody, that is besides some 2,000 people in the Wainbow Woom, except Squeek and Bob Lescher for lunch on Wednesday, and Bert Greene[3] for supper that night *in our rooms*. And nobody except these few people and Maggie Waldron[4] know that I am not staying with Squeek, but am actually at the Plaza... with Mary Jane of course. She plans to jog through Central Park every morning, and see *Phantom of the Opera*. She is also planning various changes of costume, and I suspect that she will end as belle of the ball somewhere or other. . . .

Noni, is there any chance that you could come over here in between strawberry socials and Rainbow Rooms and stuff like that? Or should we leave it as it now stands? I cannot guarantee my voice at all.... It's very hard for me not to talk when I want to and even when I don't particularly care. But I do care very much about saying something to you no matter how dumb it may sound at the time! Dr. Parson says that this is obviously Parkinsonian and that if I went to a voice specialist to ask about some sort of amplifier that could be put on my throat, I would be told what I already know... that it would be a complete waste of time and money. So... sometimes I squeak and sometimes I sound almost like me, but in a very faint way. Ho hum again. The fact remains that I'm not very interesting any more, and that is too bad. Perhaps we'd better leave it up to the mails??? (Of course, I hope you will disagree with this and want to come right over.)

Meanwhile, chère Madame, I beg you to be the recipient of my heartfelt wishes for Easter and the Christian season and also happy Passover to y'all, with hearts and flowers everywhere.

3. Friend and culinary writer
4. Friend and culinary writer, promoter responsible for the trip to New York

Last House, Glen Ellen, California   *2.v.88*
To: Joan Reardon[1]

Dear Joan:

It seems strange that I've not written to you as soon as I got your good letter. I hope you'll forgive me, I've thought often of things I want to say to you, and have re-read parts of your long note, and then decided to wait until a better time.... Tut tut, I know better.

I wonder how things go now about the work you did at the Cambridge. Of course, I'm anxious to see what you've written about Julia. When I first heard on the radio last Sunday about her accident, I thought more of Paul than I did of her, because by now he is completely dependent upon her. But she called on Monday and said that Rosemary Manell had come down at once, as of course I was sure she would. So Paul and Rosie, who get along very well together, were holding the fort up while Julia would stay at least ten days in the hospital. She sounded rather wheezy, but very well and determined to get a decent rest. But then on this past Sunday, I saw two friends of hers who had checked on her in Santa Barbara and on Friday, four days after she broke the hip, she was at home again and refusing any canes or walkers or suchlike, and hopping around painfully without a cane. Ho hum.

I don't think there's ever any danger at all of your producing a hagiography of either Julia or Alice W... or even of me. None of us is saintlike in any way!

I can understand your determination to steer clear of doing a rounded portrait of anyone. I feel sorry for you. It is hard to know what to put in a biography. I'm willing to talk in any way you want with you about this or any other problems that may arise from your reactions to anything you may have read in my papers. I know that I need not repeat this to you. I appreciate more than I can say your instinctive need to walk in a gingerly way. Please understand that and know that I trust your taste always. I don't know that there is any need for me to try to read between the lines, but of course I will do that if and when you want me to.

You ask if I think that it's true that a talk never loses in the telling. I don't think it does, if it is well told.

And of course, I think here of the old story about putting ten famous artists in a room with one model and having ten different models emerge.

I'm glad that your Christmas was in Wisconsin. And I'm sorry about not sending my recipe for Ginger Snaps: just triple or quadruple the amount of ginger in the Rombauer recipe... and they should be very small. They are wonderful for parties at the end of any long meal or drinking bout... better than anything else for traveling whether one is queasy or not... in general, a good remedy for motion sickness, as well as a delicious cookie any time at all.

1. Joan Reardon was at work on a book, *M. F. K. Fisher, Julia Child, and Alice Waters: Celebrating the Pleasures of the Table.*

I'm sorry that I haven't urged you to write any questions at all to me. Between us, we should be able to talk easily on paper or even face-to-face or by telephone. So do fire ahead on any questions that come up.

Marsha and Mary Jane both send their best to you. And I send much love, along with my heartfelt apologies for this silence. Please write soon to me and tell me that all goes well with you. It does here. I seem to be slower than I meant to be, but I feel well and full of ideas....

....

Last House, Glen Ellen, California   *8.viii.88*
To: Judith and Evan Jones

Dear Judith and Evan: . . .

Things go well here, although they do not taper off as I wanted them to after too many people decided that I really should celebrate my 80th birthday. Few of them knew, of course, that it was the first time that anyone has ever paid any attention, mainly because I was born just a few minutes before the Fourth of July, which was a day of general whoopdido for all of us, especially since it was one of the three days each year when Father did not get out a paper. It was in every way a real fiesta, but I don't think it ever occurred to any of us to celebrate my birthday as such... especially with the Statue of Liberty beaming down especially brightly that day, *of course*....

So on about July 15, after we'd all celebrated like mad at Domaine Chandon, a festival that started with my going over there on Bastille Day in honor of my grandmother Mary Frances, who was born on July 14 as a passionate and violent loather of everything French, whom we teased all day long on that one time, but yearly... We'd start out by congratulating her for sharing honors with the French Revolution etc. etc., and by noon she'd be furious and red as a turkey-hen, but still laughing. Of course, this went on all Bastille Day, and it was the only time of the year when we ever dared be anything but extremely quiet and respectful and loving and generally ladylike with this real lady. So when I found that Domaine Chandon went slightly crazy on Bastille Day, with all the waiters in outrageous drag and, of course, imitators of Chevalier and Piaf singing their hearts out in the courtyard and champagne flowing like water everywhere, that was the place to celebrate Grandmother's birthday.

And by now, it's really a tradition there, which is fine for me since they always pick up the chit! But it's by far the nicest day for outdoor carousing in a genteel but rowdy way. So... on July 15 I decided that I would never again celebrate a birthday, and especially my 80th. In fact, I felt rather pale... not at all hung over or surfeited in any way, but simply tired, so I went to stay in an enchanted forest for a few days, only two miles away but really a thousand, with Pat and Marsha Moran. And now everything is fine again, and perhaps even better... and this is not meant in any way to explain my long silence! Of course, I wrote about 580 notes to at least 570 well-wishers, thanks to a few very generous but unthinking remarks from people like Sokolov and Mimi Sheraton and so on. That may explain why I feel so bland about saying to hell with them today, so that Marsha and I can write to you and a couple of other important people in my life!??!

Judith, I'm having some interesting sessions with a good friend and mostly myself, reading with some astonishment some old things that I never thought of sending to any editors or or or. I can't remember if I told Bob Lescher about this discovery or whatever it may be of several cartons of stuff. I'll probably send some of it on to him so that he can sift it a bit before he may send it to you... that is, if he thinks it's of any interest. Myself, I'm surprised to find that I can read it very easily, solely because nobody but me has ever seen it before. Once a thing is in print, I never dare look at it, as you know. This is a quite different and new experience, though, and I'm really enjoying most of it. (I find some of the journals too painful, still....)[1]

Please let me know when you're going to leave for New York again. Time passes so quickly that you may already be planning to head for the city again, but I hope not.

Much love to you both,

....

Last House, Glen Ellen, California   *11.i.89*
To: Elgy Gillespie[1]

Dear Elgy:

I do thank you for suddenly(?) being such a faithful friend. You're one of the few I hoped would be, so all is doubly well. I'm home now, and better every minute,[2] but I'm flat as a pancake, and I'm eager to feel less fatigued. Enough of that.

I feel very strongly that an "authorized" biography is impossible and I have good reason for this firm belief, which I'll be glad to expand on anytime you ask.

I'd be delighted if you did a biography of me for any of a million reasons, except the shoddy one, which some people will, of course, set on, about my reasons or non-reasons for talking and not talking. Pooh, as far as I myself go. But of course, I know it means a livelihood no matter how poor in soul, or how rotten or noble. So somewhat to my agent's horror, I refuse categorically to give my "official permission" to *any*one for *any*thing. I cannot think of anyone, except a girl who knows me better than you do, whom I would even consider handing this really ghastly burden to. And this is because you both have a quirky, even funny, way of ascribing things to me exactly as I would do them myself, even when I haven't. In other words, both you women write so much the way I always want to that I'm very happy indeed that you want to do a biography, and if anyone ever wants proof of that, you have my full permission to keep this letter and quote from it.

I don't think I want to see *anybody* for another couple of weeks or so. When I do you're one of the top three on the list. I'll keep you posted or you can call me whenever.

1. Some parts of these journals and other unpublished pieces were later published in *To Begin Again, Stay Me, Oh Comfort Me,* and *Last House.*
1. A journalist
2. MF had a second hip replacement operation in late 1988.

Love, and I hope that life in the slums is what you need this minute. And what do you think of the Master of Glide?[3] I really do love him, in spite of all his flaws and mistakes and stuff. Fortunately he does not remember me.

Best always,

⋯⋯⋯⋯⋯⋯⋯⋯⋯⋯⋯⋯

Last House, Glen Ellen, California   *20.ii.89*
To: Sylvia and Gene Thompson

Dearest People; and especially ma belle and her beau:

I'm truly sorry to be this late in thanking you for sending me the jolly Christmas gifts. As you probably know by now, although really I don't know how you could or would or should, I missed the so-called holidays completely, and have been home only a couple of weeks from an unexpected stint at SF and Sonoma hospitals... a damn nuisance and a waste of time, but I managed to escape in one piece, and although I'm still a bag of bones, I feel better every minute. End of grim story, except that the hip replacement, which I went in for on December 8 with plans to spend a good ten days, mostly in physical therapy, is a modern miracle in every way, even better the second time around. The first time, some six years ago, it was almost equally a good job, of course, although my local orthopod did not have the reputation of Dr. Welch. After all, what can be better than to have assisted Joe Montana in his last burst of football glory? The truth is that a colleague of the great Welch got me into favor by saying that M. F. K. Fisher needed his help. He did my hip gladly, feeling sure that I was at least a gold-star Olympics champion, either a Fischer playing tennis for Sweden, or a frau Fisser swimming for Switzerland. When he found that I was only a writer, the deed was dutifully done, of course, and he left grandly for the outer regions of Tahiti for some scuba diving.... It was then that twelve other ambitious younger specialists, who longed openly to take the old boy's place someday as King of their own fields, moved in on me... ruthless people they were, too! I did escape, thanks to Norah and Kennedy and another dear friend... they literally moved me out on a stretcher and I was sent by ambulance to Sonoma Hospital... apparently the only way one can transfer from one hospital is to go into another, in this state anyway. Of course, the three women knew in advance that I would have to be smuggled to my own home until room was found for me in the Hospital, so I had round-the-clock trained nurses at a ghastly sum, of course, for about ten days, and I stopped hallucinating after about the fourth day here, and was formally back in my own skin by 7:00 of the morning the Bush people took over with Washington's bible in hand. And I've felt fine ever since. By now, the real nightmare has fallen into place and has been dealt with, and I can think with complete bland composure about the long steady progression of people who flitted across from left to right, every night and almost every day, while I was down at St. Mary's. You both were there almost every day or night at least once, and I was always pleased that you came together. Arthur came once or twice, too, once with Gloria, but she was

3. Cecil Williams, minister of Glide Memorial Church in San Francisco

oftener with you both. Ward was there too, sometimes, but I don't remember anything he said to me. He left a warm feeling at the foot of my bed once. You two were much warmer always. And so, oddly enough, was my poor old Rex. He never spoke to me after the first time he was one of the revenants, when I chided him for wanting to come to the hospital at all. His hatred of them was known to everybody in California at one time, when he was made official hospital-goer for the 32nd Degree Masons of Orange County. This was to punish him for being so hateful of anyone who was sick in any way, so when he turned up grumpy and surly as always in the face of my obvious illness, I told him that he need never come again. And he sighed and looked away from me. And from then on he came always with Mother and whenever I saw them together I felt a great wave of warmth from him, although he never looked directly at me. Well, I do thank you for being part of this parade. I don't know whether you were aware of it or not, but it did help to keep me alive. End of all this chit-chat, which Norah first decided was purely paranoidal, until she realized that I was deadly earnest and must escape, and *soon*.

My excuse for writing to you today, through Marsha, of course, is to forward the clipping to you, and incidentally to tell you what I'm sure you know, that I am very proud of the book, and also proud that this very nice old lady Mona Moffat[1] has seen some connection in it between thee and me, ma belle. I consider it a great compliment, as I need not tell you, although I will tell you right now that I think there is very little connection between your style and mine. You can and will write rings around me, as we both know without any quibbling. But enough of all this.

I send much love as always to you, and to the four children... which reminds me that I got a Valentine from Amanda...!

P S. Those crazy little presents did not turn up until about a week ago, and they acted exactly as they were meant to, so that I'm still laughing about them. They gave us all great pleasure. The "all" here includes Chris, my grandson and Anna's oldest boy who is here for a time. He now has a part-time job as an apprentice busboy at Chez Matisse, in Santa Rosa... it's a perfect avocation for anyone who is interested in choreography as passionately as he is.

....

Last House, Glen Ellen, California   *27.ii.89*
To: Joel Redon
    Dear Joel:
    Your letter was especially welcome, although I feel almost hesitant about telling you that I have not yet written a word about *My Name in Soft Cement*. I want to write something for it for sure and I feel equally sure that I will do it in time for publication. Meanwhile, I'm glad that you're changing publishers. Please keep me posted about all

1. A reviewer

this. Here, too, I feel I have little right to ask anything at all about what happens to you and your books and everything else. But the fact remains that I do. It's one of those mysterious things. A quick bond is formed or not, and willy-nilly, between people who are often unaware of it. In my own case, I am very aware of it with you. "Ours is not to reason why…"?

About Harry: I agree with you about the name, but it is of no real matter at all. I hope with all my heart that it is what you need and want, for now or for forever. It's amusing to me that H finds you make him feel younger, because you are one of the oldest people I have ever met.

You asked about my health and how I feel. My health is very good I think. I'm not frail but I'm fragile, much as steel is fragile. And silver or gold is frail… it snaps when it's bent or very cold. Steel never breaks, and it can be bent double. I'm emerging from a bad experience in two hospitals, where I was trapped in a senseless battle with a group of doctors whom I never really met, and for whom I was nothing but a piece of meat. I have emerged feeling rather tired at times, but basically unbroken… which is to say I'm spent but I survived. One result of this recent battle is that my voice is disappearing. This is combined with an inability to write with my hands. It's frustrating for me, because my mind is still very full with words and how best to use them. This is an age-old preoccupation with me. So far, I find that cassettes are an inadequate excuse for my sometimes wandering thoughts. I manage to keep up with some deadlines, though. This is good for my morale, and also keeps the checks from bouncing too loudly. In other words, I'm well, if somewhat slower socially than before. I'll probably never gain back the weight I lost, though. I'm a bag of bones. And that, I think, is my current picture except that I must tell you that I feel stronger every day. Old Time is playing its usual mess of tricks.

Please write when you can. I feel very happy to hear that you are better. . . .

Love as always,

....

Last House, Glen Ellen, California   *19.vii.89*
To: Paul and Julia Child
   D*E*R*E* F*R*E*N*S*

How I wish I could come to the party for Paul. I think often of those pictures… the ones he painted, and especially the photographs I saw when I was first in Cambridge with you both. I thought then that perhaps we might collaborate on a book about his years in Provence, and I have thought often with real regret that it did not come about. They are indelibly in my mind… by far the best Provençal pictures I've ever seen of that country. They had all of Paul's real vision, but the cruelty that showed itself in his paintings was absent there, or perhaps I mean that the country itself is so cruel and clear that there was no need to add anything of his own. I'll write more very soon. Much love to you both,

Last House, Glen Ellen, California   *20.vii.89*
To: *Joel Redon*

Dear Joel:

This is some sort of reply to your last good letter.

I never thought one way or another about glamour as being a part of any job. I don't think of writing as anything but hard work, but it's always been very rewarding to me. And by "rewarding" I do not mean anything connected with payment in money or by anyone in the world. It's a lonely job always. It is also infinitely preferable to anything I've ever done except love and being a mother. But it has nothing to do with what you mention: empty paper cups, sweaty rooms, unplugged phones. It has a lot to do, of course, with boredom and frustration. And I can see that there's no use talking any more about it, *except* I would rather write a good sentence to you than live even one minute longer or one day or one year.

You certainly plunged your parents into the thick of one part of New York life... Stonewall, National Gay Parade Day, etc. etc. I wonder why you did this. I also wonder how they reacted. . . .

And now to your dream, which I feel very pleased about your having. I hope you hang on to it. Before I read your own reasons about it, I must tell you that I like it and it makes me feel good. And now to what you think of it and the real reasons you give for it.... I'm truly sorry that you lost the manuscript. It's a hell of a thing. And no wonder you cried; and now you'll hate me, nasty old muse or whatever I am, for telling you that I don't think it matters one bit except perhaps physically. As your dream told you, the burdens grew lighter. I'm sure that carrying around the extra weight and then having it turn into a kind of lightness and then to have it leave you singing a song told you much better than I can what I'm now trying to say. What's the use of all those silly clippings anyway. You don't need them, and you never did really.

And now I'm beginning to sound very sententious, which is embarrassing. Please forgive this, Joel, and pay no attention to my firm belief that you're much better off now than you were before the script was lost etc. etc. I doubt that you believe this but it doesn't matter one bit.

I'll write more soon.

All my love,

....

Last House, Glen Ellen, California   *11.viii.89*
To: *Lawrence Clark Powell*

Dearest Ghuce, or do I mean Sly Fox?:

Yes, thank God we can read between the lines. You keep right on writing to me and I will to you, I promise... as long as I live.

I think I prefer "sombre" and "noire" to "douce," but you're right! It depends purely upon one's age plus one's companions, I think.

I honestly forgot that it was *Finnegan's Wake* that AYF tried so hard to understand... or was he trying to help other people? Do you know about the time he wrote to me, "demanding" that I "return" a dictionary of Estonian and Latvian and French and English that he was convinced I had stolen from him at least 20 years before when we were still legally married? Of course, no such dictionary existed ever except in AYF's imagination.

Do you still love baseball?

I still don't but I listen now and then to the Giants....

Much love,

....

Last House, Glen Ellen, California   *18.xii.90*
To: Lawrence Clark Powell

Dearest Ghuce:

Dawson did a nice job on *Islands of Books*. Of course, I'll send it on to Humphrey Stone later, but I'll take a good look at it first. I'll have Marsha read parts of it to me.

I seem rather decrepit lately but I continue to feel well. Sister Age is close by me always and I know she's with you too, but I'm sure that we are both coping. Have you figured out just why? It's a question of dignity. I don't know the answer, but it adds enough spice to the dish to make it edible, whether or not I want to eat it. The only answer for that is to say *bon appetit* to myself and to you too.

Love,

....

Last House, Glen Ellen, California   *23.i.91*
To: Lawrence Clark Powell

Dearest Ghuce:

Transcendental is the word. I don't believe in all this stuff about grief because I think we grieve forever, but that goes for love too, fortunately for us all.

Love,

Index of Correspondents

....